White, Donald
Medieval history; a
source book

Medieval History

THE DORSEY SERIES IN EUROPEAN HISTORY

EDITOR THEODORE S. HAMEROW *University of Wisconsin*

STROMBERG *A History of Western Civilization*

BLACK *Posture of Europe, 1815–1940: Readings in European Intellectual History*

WHITE *Medieval History: A Source Book*

SENN *Readings in Russian Political and Diplomatic History,* Volumes I and II

GOOCH *Interpreting European History,* Volumes I and II

Medieval History

A SOURCE BOOK

by

DONALD A. WHITE

Hollins College

1965 · Homewood, Illinois

THE DORSEY PRESS

First Printing, August, 1965
Second Printing, April, 1968

PRINTED IN THE UNITED STATES OF AMERICA

Preface

This book was born out of the conviction that students of medieval history, perhaps more than any other period, need to have some acquaintance with primary sources. At the time this book was conceived, almost four years ago, there was nothing adequate in print to serve this purpose for medieval history as a whole. I have seen nothing since to make me change my mind.

In compiling this book I have attempted to follow one cardinal editorial principle: include as many complete works as possible or at least large sections of works. Little snippets of things chosen from here and there have value only for the person who selected them and for the students he is teaching. Unfortunately, considerations of space and copyright have forced me to violate my principle more than once, so that what follows represents a compromise between what I would like to have done and what I in fact did.

This editorial principle I followed enforced its own restrictions on my choice of material. The reader of this book may be surprised to discover nothing in it bearing directly on Islam or Byzantium, the rise of the national monarchies, or the development of towns and commerce. Their omission was deliberate either because they were not suitable to the type of treatment I chose or, as in the case of the national monarchies, because they would have taken much more space that I had at my disposal.

The reader may also be surprised by the fact that I close this book at the end of the thirteenth century. This was not entirely a matter of space. I am among the many scholars who now feel that the half-century between 1275 and 1325 inaugurated a new period in European history intermediate between medieval and early modern. No doubt a concluding chapter on the nature of this change, which would include the episode of Boniface VIII and a selection from William of Occam among other things, would have been useful. But here again the tyranny of space intervened.

Finally I must acknowledge the unfailing efficiency of Miss Dorothy Doerr of the Hollins College Library, Miss Claire White who helped prepare the manuscript, Professor Gaines Post, who read the book in manuscript form to my great profit, and to my students who suffered through the ordeal of its composition.

DONALD A. WHITE

Hollins, Virginia
August, 1965

Table of Contents

Chapter One

The Reorganization of the Roman Empire in the Fourth Century

THE problem of the transition from the ancient to the medieval world has vexed and fascinated historians at least since the time of the Renaissance. Yet if we deal with this transition primarily in terms of "how" rather than "why" its principal features stand out quite clearly, the first of them being the reorganization of the Roman Empire in the fourth century.

Roman development in the fourth century was a response to the crisis of the third: the penetration of imperial frontiers by barbarians, governmental instability, and a general economic and social debilitation. In each of the areas of crisis the fourth century emperors took drastic steps to prop up the sagging fabric of the Roman Empire. The first of these steps, in time and importance, was the simultaneous reorganization of the imperial defenses and administrative system.

The antiquated political and military machinery of the Principate broke down in the third century. It was not that the Empire had become too big; it was in fact smaller. It was simply that the job it had to do was greater. Above all else, the third century Empire faced a greater barbarian pressure than its predecessor. Consequently, the army increased in importance and slowly in size, from three hundred thousand to at least four hundred thousand. Further, the army had a venerable tradition of meddling in politics which the defensive needs of the third century naturally reinforced. Successful generals became emperors and fought other successful generals to remain so. Here, due to the lack of any workable system of imperial succession, is the explanation for the incessant civil wars which were the principal feature of the governmental instability of the third century. As barbarian invasions continued and the army continued to increase in size and importance, the fiscal machinery of the Empire also broke down in an attempt to shoulder the crushing financial burden of defense. In short, one intelligible explanation of the crisis of the third century is to see it in terms of a vicious cycle beginning with the frontier threat and ending with an oppressive system of taxation and a debased coinage which in turn led to the decline of the municipalities, the simplification and fixation of social classes, and a lively separatist tendency in many of the provinces of the Roman Empire.

The fourth century reorganization did not solve anything; at best, although it was no mean achievement, it kept the Roman Empire in the West in a state of suspended animation until well into the fifth century. But in doing so it fundamentally changed the character of the Empire in a way which pointed toward the Middle Ages.

◆ ◆ ◆

For our purposes, the process of Roman reorganization began with the emperor Diocletian at the end of the third century and continued, in the hands of the Constantinian and Theodosian dynasties, down to the promulgation of the Theodosian Code in the second quarter of the fifth. There were two general, though interrelated, lines of development, the military-governmental and the socio-economic. Under the first category fall the reorganization of the army and the imperial administrative system as well as the attempt to solve the problem of imperial succession. Under the second come the reform of coinage and the taxation system as well as the imperial attempt to control most aspects of economic, and hence social life.

The defensive concept of the early Empire was based upon a relatively small number of legions, only twenty-eight as late as the beginning of the third century, assigned to fixed garrisons on the perimeter of the Empire. The interior was undefended either by men or fortifications. The increasing barbarian ability to penetrate Roman frontiers demanded a change in defensive philosophy, a change which most historians now associate primarily with Diocletian, although he drew extensively on the experiments of his predecessors. Diocletian abandoned the fixed garrison concept and created mobile field armies (*comitatenses*), located not on the frontier but at strategic points in the interior where they could swiftly move to crush any barbarian invasion (or imperial rival). The *comitatenses* were naturally the best troops and since one of their aims was mobility they contained a high proportion of cavalry.

Diocletian and his successors by no means neglected the frontiers themselves. Although the troops there (*limitanei*) were often inferior to the field force (one suspects that in some areas they were little better than militia), they had the advantage of elaborate frontier fortifications. Nowhere is the contrast between the early and late Empire so apparent than in the field of military architecture. The frontier defenses of Rome in its palmy days were made of men and earth, not stone. Now, every threatened frontier received an elaborate series of stone forts and walls, often, towards the end of the fourth century, tied together with signal stations.

The legion itself also changed its character to suit the new conditions. Once self-sufficient units of over six thousand infantry plus auxiliary wings and cohorts of infantry, archers, and cavalry, the legion by the time of Constantine had been broken up into its component parts. The legion was now much smaller, roughly a thousand men, composed exclusively of infantry (*pedites*) or cavalry (*equites*), the latter now having equal or even superior prestige than the infantry. And, as mentioned before, the proportion of cavalry to infantry increased until by the early fifth century they were equal. In composition, the *pedites* were largely Roman at the beginning of the fourth century and always remained so, in the sense that the infantry legions continued to be recruited from the peasantry of the Empire. The *equites* were predominantly non-Roman from the beginning and as they increased in number the army became progressively Germanized.

The reorganization of the imperial administrative system was closely connected with the reform of the army. For one thing, the separation of the civil and military machinery of the Empire which was one of its essential features, had a purely political motive. Diocletian had had bitter experience with the combination of military and civil power in the hands of one man. One also suspects that the breaking up of the army into smaller units served something of the same purpose. On the other hand, the work that the civil administration had to do was largely military as Rome became more and more of a garrison state in the fourth century. The recruitment of men for the army, feeding and clothing it, and above all paying it, was the constant preoccupation of the civil branch.

It was also true that the administrative system produced by the Republic and early Empire, which had never worked very well, could not cope with the vastly increased governmental task undertaken in the fourth century Empire. As reorganized by Diocletian, the Roman Empire was composed of four great prefectures, two in each half of the Empire, which were in turn subdivided into twelve dioceses, each headed by a vicar. Thus two new administrative units intervened between the emperor and the province, the old basis of imperial administration. And the province itself was reorganized, the general rule being to divide each of the old provinces into two. Although at first glance the effect of this reorganization might seem to be decentralization, quite the reverse was true since not only the prefects, vicars, and governors (correctors, presidents, etc.) but each official on their staffs were made appointive by the emperor. Finally, it should be apparent that the number of administrative personnel must have at least doubled by virtue of this physical reorganization alone.

Diocletian also attempted to regulate the system of succession. In the very first year of his reign Diocletian appointed his friend and fellow-officer Maximian co-Augustus, giving him authority over the western portion of the Empire. Subsequently, both Diocletian and Maximian chose junior colleagues called Caesars. Once established, it was hoped that the system of Augusti and Caesars would prove efficient enough to prevent the outbreak of civil war and provide for an orderly transference of power when the senior Augustus died. This it did not do completely, breaking down for the first time after the abdication of Diocletian himself. If the fourth century suffered from fewer civil wars than the third it was due more to the establishment of relatively stable dynasties than to Diocletian's innovation. Yet, despite occasional lapses, the system remained in use at least insofar as there continued to be two administratively distinct halves of the Empire.

At the pinnacle of this new administrative structure was a new type of emperor. Diocletian abolished the constitutional fiction of the Principate, substituting an emperor who was in theory as well as in fact absolute. His edicts carried the force of law without registration by the Senate, which from this time on was merely the governing body of the city of Rome. Rome even ceased to be the capital of the Empire since throughout the fourth century the emperors, surrounded by their Household troops and officers, sought more strategic locations: Trier and Milan in the west, Adrianople and ultimately Constantinople in the east. In keeping with the new absolutism were the new practices—the wearing of the diadem, an elaborate court ceremonial, and new titles of address—*autocrator, basileus.* These "trappings of oriental monarchy," which would have been so hateful to the Roman Republican tradition (and to some extent they were hateful to the fourth century), were accompanied by the creation of an Imperial Household with its Provosts of the Sacred Bedchamber and Castellans of the Sacred Palace, and by the creation of new central bureaus.

◆ ◆ ◆

The effect of the crisis of the third century upon Roman social and economic life had been disastrous. The decline of interprovincial commerce, depopulation in town and countryside, inflation (via debasement of the coinage), the flight from municipal burdens which was only a symptom of a more general breakdown of political morale; here is a partial list of the economic and social ills that the fourth century emperors had to cope with. Their response, as before, was a radical reformation.

The state had to maintain certain essential services. The land had to be cultivated because taxes had to be paid. Taxes had to be paid because the army and the civil service had to be paid, and both were larger, more expensive, and more important than they had been before. The imperial post system and the roads it traveled on had to be maintained for the use of the army and imperial officials. The army had to be supplied with men, food, clothing, and weapons. The populace of Rome and Constantinople had to be fed, bathed, and entertained. Consequently, the Roman government had to insure that these services were performed. It was for this reason, and for no other, that late Roman economic and social life became so regimented.

To see how the process of social and economic regimentation began one must look first at the reform of the tax structure undertaken by Diocletian and Constantine. Economically, the Roman Empire had always been and would always remain predominately agrarian. Hence the most productive source of revenue had to be a tax on land and agricultural labor. It is not surprising then to discover Diocletian inaugurating just such a tax, the *capitatio-iugatio*. Although the details of its operation are still somewhat vague, it is reasonably clear that for the majority of the peasant class the *capitatio-iugatio* was a single tax, computed not only on the basis of the amount and type of land under cultivation but also on the number of persons cultivating it.

Now the institution of the *capitatio-iugatio* gives us the key to another development. It was obviously in the interest of the Roman government to keep the land under cultivation, an interest it shared with the large landowners. But the trend of the third and fourth centuries was in the opposite direction as the population contracted. One regular remedy for this situation was the importation of German colonists (in the West). Another was simply to bind the existing peasantry to the soil. So again with no surprise we begin to hear of a new institution in the fourth century, the *colonate*. Like the *capitatio-iugatio*, the colonate is still something of a puzzle; nevertheless, its essentials are clear. The *colonus* was a free man who had been bound to the soil, by imperial decree on imperial estates at first, by imitation by the large landowners and official collusion later. And initially the *colonus* was bound to the soil so he could pay taxes. With the colonate we find another key, this time to the social philosophy of the later Roman Empire: the way to maintain essential services is to bind people to their stations.

The fate of the curial class (*decuriones*) gives us another well-known example of the principle of social coercion. The municipality (*civitas*) had been the unit of local government in most parts of the Empire. Free and self-governing in its best days, it too became caught up in the web of governmental regulation. The *curiales* were once a natural aristocracy of families whose men had been freely elected to the municipal senate, or *curia*, from which they took their name. Their burdens had always been heavy and their services unpaid. As magistrates they had charge of public buildings, roads, police, and the management of the public finances, for which they were held accountable. They had other duties in connection with the relief of the poor. As the *curialis* rose to the highest magistracies in his municipality the cost of public office could become ruinous since custom prescribed that he furnish buildings and elaborate spectacles for the amusement of the populace.

The economic troubles of the third century hit the curial class hard. With the productivity of the soil declining, many *curiales* were unable or unwilling to shoulder the heavy but honorable burdens of their class. Some of the fortunate ones could rise into the senatorial class; some, as the Theodosian Code so eloquently testifies, sought refuge in the church, the guilds, the army, and the civil service. In the face of the flight of the *curiales* the imperial government saw no other solution than to apply its specific remedy to insure that essential services were performed; it bound the *curialis* to his station.

All individuals who possessed more than twenty-five *iugera* of land were now required to become *curiales* and to share the burdens of the magistracies. Moreover, these burdens were added to. The *curiales* acquired responsibilities connected with the maintenance of the roads and the imperial post, with the military commissariat and, most onerous of all, in connection with the collection of taxes. The collection of the *capitatio-iugatio* devolved upon the members of the *curia;* further, they were held personally liable for the whole amount of the assessment.

The same principle was applied to provisioning the cities of Rome and Constantinople, another essential service that the imperial government could neglect only at its peril. The dole at Rome and Constantinople was a system of massive outdoor relief which by the fourth century included the free distribution of bread, oil, and pork as well as free public baths and other entertainments. Voluntary guilds had been organized (*collegiati*) of shipowners, pig-herders, bakers, bath-stokers, and so on, to perform these functions under contract to the government. In the fourth century, predictably, the voluntary element disappeared as guild membership was made hereditary.

Although other examples could be given of the social regimentation in the later Roman Empire, we might turn to the least regulated and most fortunate class of the later Empire, the senators. After the establishment of imperial absolutism under Diocletian, the senatorial class, as a class, temporarily lost their connection with government service. But soon, as early as the time of Constantine, they were readmitted to imperial service and in greater numbers than before. Indeed, by the middle of the fourth century the senatorial class had practically absorbed the old equestrian order and had become the backbone of the greatly expanded imperial civil service. Consequently, a new social aristocracy developed under the late Empire, composed of the old equestrian and senatorial orders and firmly tied to the imperial service. This new order of nobility has been called by later observers the *clarissimate* because entrance to it and station within it depended upon one's rank in the civil service, which was now graded in terms of *viri clarissimi, viri spectabiles* and *viri illustres.* Furthermore, a distinction arose between those who held the social and imperial rank of *vir clarissimus* and those who were entitled to participate in the proceedings of the Senate, which was confined in practice at first and by law later, to those who had reached the highest rungs on the ladder of imperial service. In other words, except for the comparatively few people who remained senators in the old sense, the rank of senator designated an empire-wide class of families who enjoyed the possession of considerable landed wealth, members of which at one time or another had arrived at a certain rank in the civil service. Like other classes in the late Empire, they had compulsory public duties peculiar to their order and certain immunities, notably, exemption from municipal burdens. With their considerable, often fantastic, landed wealth and their control of the administrative machinery of the Empire, the senatorial class was in a position to frustrate any attempt by the central government to control them. Eventually, as their tradition of public service began to wane, they began to do so, in the process absorbing members of the curial class, either as clients or full-fledged members of their order, and large numbers of the peasantry who became *coloni* on their estates.

◆ ◆ ◆

The principle upon which the late imperial government operated should be apparent by now. The fourth century emperors, beginning with Diocletian, were faced with one overwhelming task, that of preserving their state from external threats. In order to accomplish this they were forced into a far-reaching program of administrative, social, and economic restoration based upon a system of compulsion and regulation. Although that program has been much criticized in modern times, because it was one of state control rather than free enterprise, it is difficult to see what else could have been done short of a fundamental, and impossible, reformation of the social and economic structure. Indeed, perhaps it is misleading to think of the compulsion and regulation which pervaded late Roman economic and social life in terms of principle at all. Certainly the issue was not one of state regulation vs. free enterprise. The issue was what to do with a society which had already broken down. Here, as a useful reminder of the spirit in which the fourth century emperors approached their work, are the words of Diocletian: ". . . We, who are the protectors of the human race, are agreed, as we view the situation, that decisive legislation is necessary, so that the long-hoped-for solutions which mankind itself could not provide may, by the remedies provided by our foresight, be vouchsafed for the general betterment of all. . . ."

1. *The Theodosian Code*

This is the most important source for the social and economic history of the later Roman Empire. Promulgated by Theodosius II in 438, it contained all imperial legislation from Constantine (312) through Theodosius himself (437). Later, the post-Theodosian legislation was added down to 468. Unfortunately, no complete manuscript of the code exists and much of it has been lost, especially in its earlier sections.

The extracts from it presented below are in some cases highly excerpted. For this section I have selected titles which illustrate the themes outlined in the introduction, although no attempt has been made to group them by topic. An exception is the few titles pertaining to the Christian church which will appear in later sections.

I have used the translation of Clyde Pharr, *The Theodosian Code and Novels and the Sirmondian Constitutions* (Princeton: Princeton University Press, 1952).

I, 5, 11 (398). All persons who govern provinces shall exact payment of the delinquent taxes for their term of office when they have laid aside their administration. Those landholders whom no sense of shame can move to fulfill their public obligations shall be notified three times within a year, and if they do not complete all such public obligations, they shall pay double the amount of the debt. . . .

V, 14, 30 (382, 389). If any person should cultivate and equip waste land which belongs to the imperial patrimonial domain and should make it fertile and useful, he may defend his right to hold it by perpetual and private ownership, but subject to the patrimonial fixed land tax thereon, he may hold it for himself, and he may leave it to his descendants, just as though it were a family estate, acquired by succession from his ancestors.

V, 17, 1 (332). Any person in whose possession a colonus that belongs to another is found not only shall restore the aforesaid colonus to his birth status but also shall assume the capitation tax for this man for the time that he was with him.

1. Coloni also who meditate flight must be bound with chains and reduced to a servile condition, so that by virtue of their condemnation to slavery, they shall be compelled to fulfill the duties that befit freemen.

V, 19, 1 (365). There is no doubt that coloni do not have the right to alienate the fields that they cultivate, to the extent that even if they have any belongings of their own, they may not transfer them to others without the advice and knowledge of their patrons.

VII, 2, 2 (385). If any man should desire to take the oaths of imperial service, first of all, in that city in which he was born or in which he has established residence he shall execute formal records and shall thus prove that neither his father nor his grandfather was a decurion and that he is completely free from obligations to the compulsory services of the municipal senate.

VII, 20, 2 (320, 326). When he had entered the imperial headquarters of the army and had been saluted by the military prefects and tribunes and by the Most Eminent men, the acclamation arose: "Augustus Constantine! The gods preserve you for us! Your salvation is our salvation. In truth we speak, on our oath we speak."

1. The assembled veterans cried out: "Constantine Augustus! To what purpose have we been made veterans if we have no special grant of imperial privileges?"

Constantine Augustus replied: "It is My duty the more and more to increase the happiness of My fellow veterans rather than to diminish it."

2. Victorinus, a veteran, then said: "We pray that you do not allow us to be compelled by law to perform compulsory public services and to bear grievous burdens in all places."

Constantine Augustus replied: "Indicate more plainly. What are the compulsory public services especially that most persistently oppress you?"

All the veterans said: "Surely, you yourself fully understand."

Constantine Augustus then proclaimed: "Be it known that it has just now been conceded to all veterans by My munificence that no one of them shall be compelled by law to the performance of a compulsory municipal service nor to service on public works, nor to any tax payment, nor by the magistrates, nor to any imposts."

XI, 2, 4 (384). Whenever, in accordance with custom, payment is demanded in the case of regular taxes or of taxes due, not the prices of natural products demanded shall be paid, but the natural products themselves. . . .

XI, 16, 15 (382). Men of the highest ranks or of the greatest honors, also the counts of the imperial consistory, Our imperial secretaries and all chamberlains and ex-chamberlains shall be exempted from all compulsory public services of a menial nature. All other persons, moreover, who are protected by the prerogative of service within the palace, either as palatines or as members of the imperial service, shall obtain a similar privilege only if they can prove that an exemption of this kind belongs to them by the provisions of previous statutes and that such benefits were not granted to them as individuals but were conferred upon some high rank or some organized group as a common privilege. With reference to the churches, rhetoricians, and grammarians of both branches of learning . . . , the ancient custom shall remain in force.

Of course, . . . the extraordinary public services shall be demanded absolutely from all persons, and you shall remember that hereafter neither a petition nor any usurpation shall profit any person. The exemption from compulsory public services of a menial nature shall be as follows: the patrimonies of the dignitaries listed above shall not be charged with making flour, baking bread, or service in the breadmaking establishments, and such men shall not be charged with furnishing supplementary post horses . . . or wagons, except for furnishing those supplies which are customarily used in guarding the Raetian border or those supplies by which the interests of the Illyrian expeditionary force are served. . . . From such persons the performance of personal services, the furnishing of artisans of any sort, or the burning of lime, shall not be demanded as a contribution. The patrimonies of the persons thus exempted shall not supply lumber or wood and boards. Such men shall cease making the payment of charcoal also, except what is regularly required for the minting of money or the manufacture of arms, according to ancient custom. They shall not be subject to the duty of constructing or repairing public and sacred buildings, or of providing quarters in their homes for State guests. They shall not be burdened by the care of the roads and bridges. No duty of supplying recruits shall be enjoined upon them.

XI, 23, 1 (361). The compulsory public service of the chief tax collectorship for recruit taxes shall be sustained by Senators, and the necessity shall be imposed upon them to the extent that with them shall be associated only the tax liabilities of other Senators for the purpose of fulfilling this compulsory public service. The land tax units or the capitation tax units of no other person shall be joined to the tax liabilities of Senators, since the Senators must so sustain the compulsory public service of chief collectorship for recruit taxes only to that amount which they themselves sustain by the tax allotment. . . .

XI, 23, 2 (363). There is no doubt that the office of recruit tax collection and collections of plebeian capitation taxes are the compulsory duties of decurions and are services of a lower grade. Therefore such compulsory services must be removed from the Senatorial houses.

XI, 24, 1 (360). You have reported that a multitude of coloni located throughout Egypt have betaken themselves to the protection of those persons who are supported by their high rank of various degrees and even to dukes. Therefore, if it should become clear that any person has assumed unto himself such great lawlessness that he should harbor such persons and by the promise of protection he should block the possibility of their fulfillment of their loyal services, We command that such persons shall be compelled to pay any tax dues that shall be proved to have been delivered to the account of the fisc from their own resources by the other villagers from whose community such coloni have withdrawn.

XI, 24, 3 (395). If any person from your office or from any order of men should be discovered to have received villages into his protection, he shall suffer the established penalties. Moreover, landholders shall be duly coerced to obey the imperial statutes, even against their will, and they shall be forced to satisfy the compulsory public services. But if it should appear that any villages, depending on the power of their protectors or on their own numbers, have resisted the performance of their compulsory public services, they must be subjected to the retribution that is dictated by reason itself.

XI, 28, 2 (395). For the provincials of Campania We remit the taxes of five hundred twenty eight thousand and forty two jugera which appear to be located in deserted and unkempt districts of the said province, according to the report to Us of the inspectors and the records of the ancient documents, ...

XII, 1, 13 (326). Since we have learned that the municipal councils are being left desolate by those persons who are obligated to them through birth status and who are requesting imperial service for themselves through supplications to the Emperor and are running away to the legions and various governmental offices, We order all municipal councils to be admonished that if they should apprehend any persons with less than twenty terms of service in governmental offices . . . they shall drag such persons back to the municipal councils. They shall know that henceforth the regulation shall be observed that if any person should desert his municipal council and enter the imperial service, he shall be recalled to the municipal council, not only if he was born to that status, but also if he should possess an adequate amount of property to perform his compulsory municipal public services. . . .

XII, 1, 18 (329, 353, 326). It is our will, indeed, that the sons of military men, according to the former regulation, either shall pursue the aforesaid service of their fathers, or, if they refuse to perform military service and had reached the age of thirty-five years, they shall be assigned to the municipal councils.

XII, 1, 33 (342). Since Your Sublimity [the Count of the Orient] has reported that many persons evade their due compulsory duties and thus contrive to pursue privileges of Our privy purse and, by the rights of coloni, they evade nominations to the decurionate, We sanction that if any man should possess in private ownership more than twenty-five jugera and should control a larger measure of land from Our privy purse by his own cultivation and oversight, every frustrative action based on privilege or birth status or any other defense shall be barred, and he shall be vindicated to the municipal council. Also, if a man should have property of even less than twenty-five jugera of his own and should work a small or smaller amount of land from Our estates with the purpose of cultivation, he shall likewise be assigned to the municipal council.

XII, 1, 47 (362). Decurions who evade their compulsory public services on the ground that they are Christians [i.e., clerics] shall be recalled.

1. The municipal councils shall be exempt from the tax payable in gold and silver which is levied upon tradesmen, unless perchance it should appear that a decurion is engaged in merchandising to any extent.

2. Since it has been reported also that certain decurions have fled for protection to the homes of powerful men, to prevent such shameful refuge We have decreed a fine, so that if any persons should flee for protection to the home of a powerful man, they shall pay one solidus for each head and those who receive them shall pay the same amount as a fine.

XII, 1, 55 (363). If any man should be the father of thirteen children, not only shall he not be called to the service of the municipal council, but also, if he should be a decurion he shall be presented with a most honorable leisure.

XII, 1, 58 (364). If any person born of a family of decurions should be made a Senator before the completion of his compulsory public services to his municipality, he shall forfeit the enjoyment of such rank until he is absolved from the compulsory public services. When he has fulfilled these services, if he should wish to avoid the expensive Senatorial Order, he may renounce that dignity. If he should remain a Senator, his children who were born after such rank was obtained shall now be held as Senators, praetors, and quaestors, but they shall not be obligated to the compulsory public services of decurions.

1. But no rank and no length of employment in the imperial service shall protect any person if he is demanded back by the municipal council on the ground that he derived his birth status from decurions.

XII, 1, 62 (364). If a decurion should steal into a guild of artisans for the purpose of evading other duties, he shall be restored to his pristine status, and in the future no person who derives his birth status from decurions shall dare to aspire to the duties of such a guild.

XII, 1, 72 (370). If any tradesman should purchase farms and should be called to the municipal council as the holder of any landed estates, he shall not be assisted by the protection of his compulsory duty, namely, that with the money which he has invested in business he assumes the gold and silver tax which is levied upon tradesmen. But if he should be nominated to a municipal council, he shall be subject to the compulsory duties of that municipal council to which he gave himself of his own accord by converting the use of his money into the profit of farm land.

XII, 1, 75 (371). If any person should attain to the office of civil priest of a province and to the rank of chief decurion by discharging his compulsory public services step by step and in order, not by favoritism and patronage that he has solicited, but by labor, after the record of his administrative acts has been approved, if the opinion of his fellow citizens is consonant and he is publicly approved by the whole senate, he shall be held exempt from compulsory services, he shall enjoy the leisure which he earned by the testimony of continuous labor, and his body shall be free from such outrages as is not fitting that dignitaries should sustain. We also decree that the honor of ex-count (honorary) shall be added to him, an honor which is customarily obtained by those persons who have proved their loyalty and diligence by the administration of the municipalities.

XII, 1, 77 (372). No person, oblivious of his birth status and of his municipality to which he is bound by the right of residence, shall strive to ascend to the governorship of a province until he has been promoted by completing, step by step, the compulsory public services of his municipal council. He shall not begin at the office of duumvir or of civil priest, but he shall observe the regular order and shall sustain the responsibility of all the offices, because We do not permit these offices to be conferred either through favoritism or through the connivance of the judge upon those who rely on the prerogative of the office of advocate. They shall not steal into the first ranks as chief decurions or as civil priests when they have not assumed the performance of any of the duties of decurions. But after they have fully discharged the compulsory public services and the duties of the magistracies of their municipalities, step by step, each shall be given access to public administrative offices, with Our assistance also.

XII, 1, 99 (383). The order with which men of the Jewish faith flatter themselves and by which they are granted immunity from the compulsory public services of decurions shall be rescinded, since not even clerics are free to deliver themselves to divine service until they have discharged all the service due to their municipalities.

XII, 1, 109 (385). It is our will that no persons shall be compelled to perform the office of superintendent of the public games if they are unwilling and that all things must be referred to that status in which they are now found. Therefore, if any decurions have fully discharged all the compulsory services and have left no honorable duty which they appear to owe to their municipality, to the extent only of that kind of compulsory service and similar services that were consonant with the status of their lineage, after they have paid to their municipality all the services that the public welfare demands, even though they should perhaps be unwilling to present games, nevertheless they shall be compelled to present them on account of their legal status, and they shall enjoy the rank of ex-count which has been granted to them generally and in perpetuity. The right of osculation also and the right to sit in council with the judges of the provinces shall be granted to them.

XII, 1, 133 (393). If anyone from the number of plebeians, in the presence of the senate of any municipality, should be proved to be suitable because of the ownership of farms and money, he shall be added to those persons that are obligated to the performance of the compulsory public services of decurions.

XII, 1, 146 (395). We observe that many men are hiding under the shadow of powerful men, in order that they may defraud their municipalities of the services which they owe. Therefore, a fine must be established to the effect that if any man should violate the general rule of the prescribed law, he shall be forced to pay to Our fisc five pounds of gold for each decurion and one pound each for each member of a guild.

XII, 1, 149 (395). To the ruin of the municipal councils, the decurions are seeking to divest themselves of their obligations, and by all sorts of pretexts of patrimony, however acquired, they wish to change their own birth status by assuming the burdens of shipmasters. In this situation, since We are not able to restrain such actions entirely, We make a reasonable distinction. Therefore, a municipality shall not lose the citizen whom it bore, but the patrimony which comes from the order of shipmasters shall deliver the man whom it enriches, in proportion to the measure of such enrichment, because no man is compelled to purchase anything or to accept a gift or to enter upon a disadvantageous inheritance, since in deliberations with respect to future unions, provision is made also for the interests of heirs. Therefore, Your Sublimity in expediting the performance of compulsory public services shall permit no man to withdraw from his parent, the municipal council. You shall also provide both that the order of Our municipal councils shall be rendered safe from damage and that the patrimonies of shipmasters shall not be lost, but both statuses of public service shall be kept safe.

XII, 1, 171 (409, 412). It is Our pleasure that the chief decurions of the municipal councils in Gaul shall not withdraw until they have completed fifteen years in the administration of the duties of their senate, and throughout this regular number of years they shall fully express their gratitude to their municipalities. Although all such men ought to be recalled who appear to have escaped in a short time, nevertheless, We decree that moderation must be employed, and thus We order only those now to return to the compulsory functions which they evaded who are detected to have withdrawn within the past six years. No man shall refuse to accept the periods of time for service which are so beneficially established, since upon the completion of all their duties they obtain the adornments of splendor and honor.

XII, 1, 173 (410, 409). For the relief of the fortunes of lower grade decurions and for the restraint of oppression by the powerful, it is Our pleasure that from the approaching eighth year of the indiction [September 1, 410], the tax assessments which are administered by each municipal senate under the stress of various contingencies shall not begin until they are made known to the governors in the records of the provinces and confirmed by their authority.

1. But also the gold which is brought together as a consequence of such a tax payment must be delivered to the gold tax receiver in such a way that the tax receipts shall bear the name of the taxpayer, the day of payment, and year of the consulship, the month, the account, and the amount paid, in order that the equity of the tax assessment may thereby be made clear, and the assessed taxpayer may be supported by manifest documents.

XII, 6, 11 (366, 365). No man shall be permitted to serve for a continuous period of two years in the office of taxation, and no man after the completion of this compulsory public service shall be constrained to the performance of the same service, unless he should free himself from the bond of the former duty. For it is not the part of the just man to burden persons who have rendered acceptable service, nor is it the part of a prudent man to retain persons who have proved to be unacceptable. Therefore, when an entire year has elapsed, each such tax receiver shall be compelled to set forth on what accounts he has disbursed the taxes that he has received, so that if any person should be apprehended in theft, he may be able the more easily to make good the loss, since it is recent.

XII, 6, 4 (365). We command that a letter shall be given to the Most Noble Proconsul of Africa that if a receiver of taxes payable in clothing should be selected, either from the number of the chief decurions or of the dignitaries, in accordance with the merit of his devotion and industry, he shall be instructed to sustain the burden of this compulsory public service for one year only. However, those persons shall be excepted who are protected by the privileges of palatine imperial service, and those who have performed offices and ministries and prove that they have obtained their honor by the merit of the terms of service and by the merit of their rank. . . .

XII, 6, 7 (365, 364). To the duties of receiver of tax payments in kind shall come those men who know before all else that they are not decurions. Therefore, if any persons from the body of the various office staffs should be found suitable in character and in property, they shall enroll their names as though on an official register in each province, and arranged in accordance with this order, they shall complete the duties of tax receivers for a year. In this way they shall fear no other obligation to any other compulsory service.

XII, 6, 31 (412). We do not allow decurions to be occupied with lowly duties or extraordinary burdens, lest the public welfare should be impaired. Therefore, it is more equitable that the receipt of taxes payable in clothing should be customarily administered by the proconsular office or by those persons who have served their terms in office. For it is to their interest to investigate the account of such tax payments and to examine their quality, since it is more suitable that they should have the responsibility for the protection of such goods. For it is not equitable that the aforesaid office should obtain the benefits and that the losses connected with such tax receipts should belong only to the decurions. Therefore, We remove such an unjustice from the decurions, with the exception of those decurions who are detected as having been employed or as being at present employed in the aforesaid office.

XIII, 3, 1 (321, 324). We command that physicians, grammarians and other professors of literature, together with the property which they possess in their own municipalities, shall be exempt from public obligations and that they shall perform the duties of honorable offices. We forbid also that they be summoned into court or suffer any indignity, and if any person should molest them, he shall pay to Our treasury one hundred thousand coins nummi [each worth about ½ of a cent, USA].

XIII, 3, 1 (333). In confirmation of the special grants of imperial favor by previous sainted Emperors, We command that physicians and professors of literature and also their wives and children shall be free from the performance of every obligatory and compulsory public service. They shall not be held to the duties of military service nor receive quartered persons nor perform any compulsory public service, so that they may more easily train many persons in the liberal studies and the aforesaid arts.

XIII, 4, 2 (337). We command that artisans who dwell in each city and who practice the skills included in the appended list shall be free from all compulsory public services, since indeed their leisure should be spent in learning these skills whereby they may desire the more to become more proficient themselves and to instruct their children.

(Appended list.) Architects, makers of paneled ceilings, plasterers, carpenters, physicians, stonecutters, silversmiths, builders, veterinarians, stonemasons, gilders of arms, step-makers, painters, sculptors, engravers, joiners, statuaries, workers in mosaics, coppersmiths, blacksmiths, marblemasons, gilders, founders, dyers in purple, layers of tessellated stones, goldsmiths, mirror-makers, carriage-makers, directors of the distribution of the water supply, glass workers, workers in ivory, fullers, potters, plumbers, furriers.

XIII, 5, 3 (319, 315). If any shipmaster should impetrate an exemption, either surreptitiously or in any other manner, it is Our will that he shall in no manner be admitted to such exemption.

1. But also, if any person should acquire a patrimony obligated to the compulsory public service of shipmasters, although he may be of very high rank, the privileges of his honor shall not assist him in the least, at any rate in this respect, but he shall be held to this compulsory public service either for the whole of his estate or proportionally. For it is not just that a patrimony obligated to this compulsory public service should be exempted and that all persons should not bear the common burden in equal shares.

XIII, 5, 16 (380). We confirm the rank of the equestrian order that was conferred upon you by the sainted Constantine and Julian, eternal Emperors. Since this is so, if any persons should dare to assail you with bodily injury, in violation of the interdicts of innumerable sanctions, he shall atone for the daring of this monstrous crime by a fitting expiation. . . .

1. To the foregoing regulation the following provision is added, namely, that you who hold a certain rank in accordance with Our decree shall not fear that you will be joined to another class of men, nor shall you be afraid of becoming bound as decurions in your own municipalities. Thus, from no bond, from no cause, from no person shall the duties of decurions touch you especially since according to ancient constitutions, . . . you assert that it has been more commonly established as law that in many cases the compulsory service of shipmasters also vindicates for itself decurions ordinary.

XIV, 3, 8 (365). The office of Your Sincerity shall be on guard that if any man should once and for all be assigned to the guild of breadmakers, he shall not be granted the opportunity and power in any way to withdraw, even if the assent of all the breadmakers should strive to obtain his release. . . . Not even this privilege shall be granted to any breadmaker, namely, that he may pass from one breadmaking establishment to another.

XIV, 4, 1 (334). Since the guild of swine collectors has dwindled to a few persons, We command that in the presence of the Roman people as they stand by in public assembly, the collectors shall tell upon whom exemption has been conferred and upon whom the burden has come, so that when these facts are adduced in the midst of the public reckoning, the usage governing the property of shipmasters shall be set forth as a precedent. Therefore, they shall recognize that their own property is obligated to the compulsory public service of swine collectors, and they shall choose one of two courses: either they shall retain their goods which are obligated to the compulsory public service of swine collection . . . , or they shall nominate responsible persons, . . . , who will satisfy the requirements. . . .

XV, 3, 6 (423). Far be it from Us that We should denominate as compulsory public services of a menial nature the construction of public roads and bridges and the work on pavements dedicated by the titles of great Emperors. Therefore, no class of men, by merit of any high rank or veneration, shall be exempt from the construction and repair of roads and bridges. We also gladly ascribe the property of the divine imperial household and the venerable churches to such a laudable list. The judges of all the provinces shall be notified of this law, so that they may know that what antiquity decreed should be assigned to the public roads must be furnished without the exception of any person on the grounds of either reverence or high rank.

The Novels of the Sainted Theodosius Augustus, Title 22, 1 (442)

1. Your present report declares that Your Excellency has been disturbed by the harshness of such a very unjust situation and that you have requested a remedy from Us. For often many persons who do not derive the birth status of the decurionate from the lot of their ancestors, of their own will and by the generous purpose of devotion have considered it a distinguished thing to endow their municipalities with magnificent gifts and benefits. Others, even when no necessity for constructing a public work was incumbent upon them, have exalted their municipality with the various adornments of buildings. This desire to improve their municipalities should be extolled with the highest praises and commendations, but it has involved some persons in the burdens of decurions, others in the toils of investigations. Thus, a thing which is beyond all indignation, a person is compelled to render an account of his own generosity, even though he would not have rendered an account of his luxury.

The Novels of the Sainted Valentinian Augustus, Title 10 (441)

Justice must be preserved both publicly and privately in all matters and transactions, and We must adhere to it especially in those measures that sustain the sinews of the public revenues, since such measures come to the aid of the attenuated resources of Our loyal taxpayers with useful equity. Very many persons reject this idea, since they serve only their domestic profits and deprive the common good wherein is contained their true and substantial welfare, when it profits all persons, especially since this necessity for tribute so demands, and without such tribute nothing can be provided in peace or in war. Nor can the continuity of such tax payments remain any further if there would be imposed upon a few exhausted persons the burden which the more powerful man declines, which the richer man refuses, and which, since the stronger reject it, only the weaker man assumes.

1. Therefore We correct this injustice, and under the first heading of this sanction We decree that if any persons should obtain landed estates that are acquired from the ownership of the imperial household, either from My Piety or from any of My sacred imperial kinsmen, . . . they shall undergo the same condition of performing compulsory public services as all the other landholders.

3. We now include in this edictal law a provision not unlike the former ones, or rather a remedy whose usefulness extends almost more widely, and without any distinction of honors, persons, or privileges, We issue the general sanction that the repair of the roads and other compulsory public services of this kind . . . (lacuna) by the emulous zeal of all men, whereby such services may be fulfilled both more easily and more durably. For the Emperors of a former age and the generosity of Our sainted Fathers bestowed such privileges on the Illustrious titles in the opulence of an abundant era, with less disaster to the other landholders. Although even then this practice appeared unjust, still in the beginning it seemed more mild. However, in the difficulty of the present time this practice is obviously not only inequitable because of the very nature of the circumstances, but it is also impossible for a few and very poor persons, who are oppressed with the multiple burden of their own compulsory public services and those of others and who will be entirely prostrated unless they are revived at some time by the association of suitable persons. Must it perhaps be considered contumelious that, contrary to reason, the name of "sordid" compulsory public services has been invented, whereby there are designated by a vicious appellation the building and repair of military roads, the manufacture of arms, the restoration of walls, the provision of the annona, and the rest of the public works through which we achieve the splendor of public defense, without which no success for the greatest affairs results, by whose aid We guard alike the safety and the glory of the Empire, and not to proceed with details, without which services no necessary work can be accomplished?

2. *Diocletian's Edict on Maximum Prices*

Promulgated in 301, this famous edict has survived almost in its entirety from numerous fragmentary inscriptions. One reason for this state of affairs is that the edict failed to achieve its purpose—to set maximum prices for certain commodities and wages. Diocletian was attempting to reduce the high cost of living produced by the inflationary economic situation at the end of the third century. But if the Edict of Prices failed, Diocletian did successfully pursue a deflationary policy with regard to coinage by bringing coins of full weight back into circulation. He issued a true silver denarius of 3.41 grammes (the weight it had under Nero) to replace the badly debased antoninus; a gold solidus weighing 5.45 grammes; and, in the same year as the Edict of Prices, he issued a "common" denarius of silvered copper. Under Constantine the solidus was reduced to 4.55 grammes of gold.

The preamble to the edict is given below in its entirety except for the first paragraph; the schedule of prices has been omitted. The translation is taken from Naphtali Lewis and Meyer Reinhold, *Roman Civilization,* II, The Empire (New York: Columbia University Press, 1955), pp. 464–72).

AS WE recall the wars which we have successfully fought, we must be grateful to the fortune of our state, second only to the immortal gods, for a tranquil world that reclines in the embrace of the most profound calm, and for the blessings of a peace that was won with great effort. That this fortune of our state be stabilized and suitably adorned is demanded by the law-abiding public and by the dignity and majesty of Rome. Therefore we, who by the gracious favor of the gods previously stemmed the tide of the ravages of barbarian nations by destroying them, must surround the peace which we established for eternity with the necessary defenses of justice.

If the excesses perpetrated by persons of unlimited and frenzied avarice could be checked by some self-restraint—this avarice which rushes for gain and profit with no thought for mankind . . . ; or if the general welfare could endure without harm this riotous license by which, in its unfortunate state, it is being very seriously injured every day, the situation could perhaps be faced with dissembling and silence, with the hope that human forbearance might alleviate the cruel and pitiable situation. But the only desire of these uncontrolled madmen is to have no thought for the common need. Among the unscrupulous, the immoderate, and the avaricious it is considered almost a creed . . . to desist from plundering the wealth of all only when necessity compels them. Through their extreme need, moreover, some persons have become acutely aware of their most unfortunate situation, and can no longer close their eyes to it. Therefore, we, who are the protectors of the human race, are agreed, as we view the situation, that decisive legislation is necessary, so that the long-hoped-for solutions which mankind itself could not provide may, by the remedies provided by our foresight, be vouchsafed for the general betterment of all. . . .

We hasten, therefore, to apply the remedies long demanded by the situation, satisfied that no one can complain that our intervention with regulations is untimely or unnecessary, trivial or unimportant. These measures are directed against the unscrupulous, who have perceived in our silence of so many years a lesson in restraint but have been unwilling to imitate it. For who is so insensitive and so devoid of human feeling that he can be unaware or has not perceived that uncontrolled prices are widespread in the sales taking place in the markets and in the daily life of the cities? Nor is the uncurbed passion for profiteering lessened either by abundant supplies or by fruitful years. . . .

But now we must set forth in detail the causes which have pressed and driven us to cease our long-enduring forbearance and to take steps. . . . Who does not know that wherever the common safety requires our armies to be sent, the profiteers insolently and covertly attack the public welfare, not only in villages and towns, but on every road? They charge extortionate prices for merchandise, not just fourfold or eightfold, but on such a scale that human speech cannot find words to characterize their profit and their practices. Indeed, sometimes in a single retail sale a soldier is stripped of his donative and pay. Moreover, the contributions of the whole world for the support of the armies fall as profits into the hands of these plunderers, and our soldiers appear to bestow with their own hands the rewards of their military service and their veterans' bonuses upon the profiteers. The result is that the pillagers of the state itself seize day by day more than they know how to hold.

Aroused justly and rightfully by all the facts set forth above, and in response to the needs of mankind itself, which appears to be praying for release, we have decided that maximum prices of articles for sale must be established. We have not set down fixed prices, for we do not deem it just to do this, since many provinces occasionally enjoy the good fortune of welcome low prices and the privilege, as it were, of prosperity. Thus, when the pressure of high prices appears anywhere—may the gods avert such a calamity!—avarice . . . will be checked by the limits fixed in our statute and by the restraining curbs of the law.

It is our pleasure, therefore, that the prices listed in the subjoined schedule be held in observance in the whole of our Empire. And every person shall take note that the liberty to exceed them at will has been ended, but that the blessing of low prices has in no way been impaired in those places where supplies actually abound. . . . Moreover, this universal edict will serve as a necessary check upon buyers and sellers whose practice it is to visit ports and other provinces. For when they too know that in the pinch of scarcity there is no possibility of exceeding the prices fixed for commodities, they will take into account in their calculations at the time of sale in the localities, the transportation costs, and all other factors. In this way they will make apparent the justice of our decision that those who transport merchandise may not sell at higher prices anywhere.

It is agreed that even in the time of our ancestors it was the practice in passing laws to restrain offenses by prescribing a penalty. For rarely is a situation beneficial to humanity accepted spontaneously; experience teaches that fear is the most effective regulator and guide for the performance of duty. Therefore it is our pleasure that anyone who resists the measures of this statute shall be subject to a capital penalty for daring to do so. And let no one consider the statute harsh, since there is at hand a ready protection from danger in the observance of moderation. . . . We therefore exhort the loyalty of all, so that a regulation instituted for the public good may be observed with willing obedience and due scruple, especially as it is seen that by a statute of this kind provision has been made, nor for single municipalities and peoples and provinces but for the whole world. . . .

3. *Ammianus Marcellinus*

Unquestionably the finest Roman historian of the late Empire, many scholars think Ammianus second not even to his model Tacitus. The excerpts that follow illustrate some of the qualities which have called forth this praise; the depth of detail, the unparalleled ability to depict character, and the fearless criticism. Rather oddly, the *Res gestae* of Ammianus was little known, or at least seldom cited in antiquity, Priscian being the only citation I am aware of. The work has come to us in a truncated form. Originally, it began with the reign of Nerva (where Tacitus left off) and continued, in thirty-one books, down to the death of Valens in 378. Of these, only the last eighteen survive beginning with the year 353.

Almost nothing is known definitely about the life of Ammianus. He was born about 330 in Antioch. He came from a good family; such is the usual inference from the fact that as a young man he was enrolled in the *protectores domestici,* part of the imperial bodyguard. In 353 he was attached to the staff of Ursicinus, commander in chief of the army in the East, to whom he became closely attached and whose fortunes he shared in both halves of the Empire. After the deposition of Ursicinus in 360, he served under the Emperor Julian, taking part in the Persian campaign of 363 in which Julian lost his life. Sometime subsequent to this, Ammianus left the army and settled in Antioch where he apparently devoted his time to study and writing. In 378 he went to Rome where he remained until his death sometime after 391. It was there he wrote the bulk of his history. The translation is from J. C. Wolfe, *Ammianus Marcellinus,* Vols. I and III (The Loeb Classical Library; Cambridge, Mass.: Harvard University Press, 1956). Reprinted by permission of the publishers.

XIV, 6. The Faults of the Roman Senate and People

1. Meanwhile Orfitus was governing the eternal city with the rank of Prefect, and with an arrogance beyond the limits of the power that had been conferred upon him. He was a man of wisdom, it is true, and highly skilled in legal practice, but less equipped with the adornment of the

liberal arts than became a man of noble rank. During his term of office serious riots broke out because of the scarcity of wine; for the people, eager for an unrestrained use of this commodity, are roused to frequent and violent disturbances.

2. Now I think that some foreigners who will perhaps read this work (if I shall be so fortunate) may wonder why it is that when the narrative turns to the description of what goes on at Rome, I tell of nothing save dissensions, taverns, and other similar vulgarities. Accordingly, I shall briefly touch upon the reasons, intending nowhere to depart intentionally from the truth.

3. At the time when Rome first began to rise into a position of world-wide splendour, destined to live so long as men shall exist, in order that she might grow into a towering stature, Virtue and Fortune, ordinarily at variance, formed a pact of eternal peace; for if either one of them had failed her, Rome had not come to complete supremacy. 4. Her people, from the very cradle to the end of their childhood, a period of about three hundred years, carried on wars about her walls. Then, entering upon adult life, after many toilsome wars, they crossed the Alps and the sea. Grown to youth and manhood, from every region which the vast globe includes, they brought back laurels and triumphs. And now, declining into old age, and often owing victory to its name alone, it has come to a quieter period of life. 5. Thus the venerable city, after humbling the proud necks of savage nations, and making laws, the everlasting foundations and moorings of liberty, like a thrifty parent, wise and wealthy, has entrusted the management of her inheritance to the Caesars, as to her children. 6. And although for some time the tribes have been inactive and the centuries at peace, and there are no contests for votes but the tranquillity of Numa's time has returned, yet throughout all regions and parts of the earth she is accepted as mistress and queen; everywhere the white hair of the senators and their authority is respected and honoured.

7. But this magnificence and splendour of the assemblies is marred by the rude worthlessness of a few, who do not consider where they were born, but, as if licence were granted to vice, descend to sin and wantonness. For as the lyric poet Simonides tells us, one who is going to live happy and in accord with perfect reason ought above all else to have a glorious fatherland. 8. Some of these men eagerly strive for statues, thinking that by them they can be made immortal, as if they would gain a greater reward from senseless brazen images than from the consciousness of honourable and virtuous conduct. And they take pains to have them overlaid with gold, a fashion first introduced by Acilius Glabrio, after his skill and his arms had overcome King Antiochus. But how noble it is, scorning these slight and trivial honours, to aim to tread the long and steep ascent to true glory, as the bard of Ascra expresses it [Hesiod] is made clear by Cato the Censor. For when he was asked why he alone

among many did not have a statue, he replied: "I would rather that good men should wonder why I did not deserve one than (which is much worse) should mutter 'Why was he given one?'"

9. Other men, taking great pride in coaches higher than common and in ostentatious finery of apparel, sweat under heavy cloaks, which they fasten about their necks and bind around their very throats, while the air blows through them because of the excessive lightness of the material; and they lift them up with both hands and wave them with many gestures, especially with their left hands, in order that the over-long fringes and the tunics embroidered with party-coloured threads in multiform figures of animals may be conspicuous. 10. Others, though no one questions them, assume a grave expression and greatly exaggerate their wealth, doubling the annual yields of their fields, well cultivated (as they think), of which they assert that they possess a great number from the rising to the setting sun; they are clearly unaware that their forefathers, through whom the greatness of Rome was so far flung, gained renown, not by riches, but by fierce wars, and not differing from the common soldiers in wealth, mode of life, or simplicity of attire, overcame all obstacles by valour. 11. For that reason the eminent Valerius Publicola was buried by a contribution of money, and through the aid of her husband's friends the needy wife of Regulus and her children were supported. And the daughter of Scipio received her dowry from the public treasury, since the nobles blushed to look upon the beauty of this marriageable maiden long unsought because of the absence of a father of modest means.

12. But now-adays, if as a stranger of good position you enter for the first time to pay your respects to some man who is well-to-do and therefore puffed up, at first you will be greeted as if you were an eagerly expected friend, and after being asked many questions and forced to lie, you will wonder, since the man never saw you before, that a great personage should pay such marked attention to your humble self as to make you regret, because of such special kindness, that you did not see Rome ten years earlier. 13. When, encouraged by this affability, you make the same call on the following day, you will hang about unknown and unexpected, while the man who the day before urged you to call again counts up his clients, wondering who you are or whence you came. But when you are at last recognized and admitted to his friendship, if you devote yourself to calling upon him for three years without interruption, then are away for the same number of days, and return to go through with a similar course, you will not be asked where you were, and unless you abandon the quest in sorrow, you will waste your whole life in paying court to the blockhead.

14. And when, after a sufficient interval of time, the preparation of those tedious and unwholesome banquets begins, or the distribution of

the customary doles, it is debated with anxious deliberation whether it will be suitable to invite a stranger, with the exception of those to whom a return of hospitality is due; and if, after full and mature deliberation, the decision is in the affirmative, the man who is invited is one who watches all night before the house of the charioteers [i.e., a plebeian], or who is a professional dicer, or who pretends to the knowledge of certain secrets. 15. For they avoid learned and serious people as unlucky and useless, in addition to which the announcers of names, who are wont to traffic in these and similar favours, on receiving a bribe, admit to the doles and the dinners obscure and low-born intruders.

16. But I pass over the gluttonous banquets and the various allurements of pleasures, lest I should go too far, and I shall pass to the fact that certain persons hasten without fear of danger through the broad streets of the city and over the upturned stones of the pavements as if they were driving post-horses with hoofs of fire (as the saying is), dragging after them armies of slaves like bands of brigands and not leaving even Sannio at home, as the comic writer says [Terrence; i.e., not leaving a single servant at home]. And many matrons, imitating them, rush about through all quarters of the city with covered heads and in closed litters. 17. And as skilful directors of battles place in the van dense throngs of brave soldiers, then light-armed troops, after them the javelin-throwers, and last of all the reserve forces, to enter the action in case chance makes it needful, just so those who have charge of a city household, made conspicuous by wands grasped in their right hands, carefully and diligently draw up the array; then, as if the signal had been given in camp, close to the front of the carriage all the weavers march; next to these the blackened service of the kitchen, then all the rest of the slaves without distinction, accompanied by the idle plebeians of the neighbourhood; finally, the throng of eunuchs, beginning with the old men and ending with the boys, sallow and disfigured by the distorted form of their members; so that, wherever anyone goes, beholding the troops of mutilated men, he would curse the memory of that Queen Semiramis of old, who was the first of all to castrate young males, thus doing violence, as it were, to Nature and wresting her from her intended course, since she at the very beginning of life, through the primitive founts of the seed, by a kind of secret law, shows the ways to propagate posterity.

18. In consequence of this state of things, the few houses that were formerly famed for devotion to serious pursuits now teem with the sports of sluggish indolence, re-echoing to the sound of singing and the tinkling of flutes and lyres. In short, in place of the philosopher the singer is called in, and in place of the orator the teacher of stagecraft, and while the libraries are shut up forever like tombs, water-organs are manufactured and lyres as large as carriages, and flutes and instruments heavy for gesticulating actors.

19. At last we have reached such a state of baseness, that whereas not so very long ago, when there was fear of a scarcity of food, foreigners were driven neck and crop from the city, and those who practised the liberal arts (very few in number) were thrust out without a breathing space, yet the genuine attendants upon actresses of the mimes, and those who for the time pretended to be such, were kept with us, while three thousand dancing girls, without even being questioned, remained here with their choruses, and an equal number of dancing masters. 20. And, wherever you turn your eyes, you see a throng of women with curled hair, who might, if they had married, by this time, so far as age goes, have already produced three children, sweeping the pavements with their feet to the point of weariness and whirling in rapid gyrations, while they represent the innumerable figures that the stage-plays have devised.

21. Furthermore, there is no doubt that when once upon a time Rome was the abode of all the virtues, many of the nobles detained here foreigners of free birth by various kindly attentions, as the Lotus-eaters of Homer did by the sweetness of their fruits. 22. But now the vain arrogance of some men regards everything born outside the pomerium of our city as worthless, except the childless and unwedded; and it is beyond belief with what various kinds of obsequiousness men without children are courted at Rome. 23. And since among them, as is natural in the capital of the world, cruel disorders gain such heights that all the healing art is powerless even to mitigate them, it has been provided, as a means of safety, that no one shall visit a friend suffering from such a disease, and by a few who are more cautious another sufficiently effective remedy has been added, namely, that servants are sent to inquire after the condition of a man's acquaintances who have been attacked by that disorder should not be readmitted to their masters' house until they have purified their persons by a bath. So fearful are they of a contagion seen only by the eyes of others. 24. But yet, although these precautions are so strictly observed, some men, when invited to a wedding, where gold is put into their cupped right hands, although the strength of their limbs is impaired, will run even all the way to Spoletium. Such are the habits of the nobles.

25. But of the multitude of lowest condition and greatest poverty some spend the entire night in the wineshops, some lurk in the shade of the awnings of the theatres, which Catulus in his aedileship, imitating Campanian wantonness, was the first to spread, or they quarrel with one another in their games at dice, making a disgusting sound by drawing back the breath into their resounding nostrils; or, which is the favourite among all amusements, from sunrise until evening, in sunshine and in rain, they stand open-mouthed, examining minutely the good points or the defects of charioteers and their horses. 26. And it is most remarkable to see an innumerable crowd of plebeians, their minds filled with a

kind of eagerness, hanging on the outcome of the chariot races. These and similar things prevent anything memorable or serious from being done in Rome. Accordingly, I must return to my subject.

XXX, 7. Valentinian's Parentage and His Deeds as Ruler

1. It is now in place to go back and (as we have often done) in a brief epilogue run through the deeds of this emperor, from the very birth of his father to his own decease, without omitting to distinguish his faults or his good qualities, brought to light as they were by greatness of power, which is always wont to lay bare a man's inmost character.

2. His father, the elder Gratianus, was born at Cibalae, a town of Pannonia, of a humble family, and from his early boyhood was surnamed Funarius, because when he was not yet grown up and was carrying round a rope for sale, and five soldiers tried with all their might to tear it from him, he gave way not an inch; he thus rivalled Milo of Croton, from whom no possible exercise of strength could ever take an apple, when he held it tightly in his left or right hand, as he often did. 3. Hence, because of his mighty strength of body and his skill in wrestling in the soldiers' fashion he became widely known and after holding the position of one of the bodyguard and of a tribune, he commanded the army in Africa with the title of count. There he incurred the suspicion of theft, but he departed long afterwards and commanded the army in Britain with the same rank; and at last, after being honourably discharged, he returned to his home. While he was living there far from the noise and bustle, his property was confiscated by Constantius, on the ground that when civil discord was raging he was said to have shown hospitality to Magnentius when the usurper was hastening through Gratianus's land to carry out his designs.

4. Because of his father's services Valentinian was favoured from early youth, and being commended also by the addition of his own merits, he was clad in the insignia of imperial majesty at Nicaea. He took as his imperial colleague his brother Valens, to whom he was greatly attached both by the tie of fraternity and by a sympathy, a man with an equal amount of excellent and bad qualities, as we shall point out in the proper place. 5. Valentinian, then, after suffering many annoyances and dangers while he was a private citizen, had no sooner begun to reign than he went to Gaul, to fortify the strongholds and cities lying near the rivers; for these were exposed to the raids of the Alamanni, who were raising their heads higher after learning of the death of the emperor Julian, who was absolutely the only one whom they feared after the death of Constans. 6. But Valentinian also was rightly dreaded by them, both

because he increased the armies with a strong reinforcement and because he so fortified both banks of the Rhine with lofty castles and strongholds, that nowhere should an enemy be able to hurl himself at our territories unobserved.

7. And to pass over many things which he did with the authority of an established ruler, and the reforms that he affected either personally or through energetic generals, after admitting his son Gratianus to a share in his power, he secretly, since he could not do so openly, caused Vithicabius, king of the Alamanni, son of Vadomarius, a young man in the first bloom of manhood, to be stabbed, because he was rousing his people to rebellion and war. And joining battle with the Alamanni near a place called Solicinium, where, after falling into an ambuscade and all but losing his life, he could have utterly destroyed their entire army, had not swift flight saved a few of them under cover of darkness.

8. While he was accomplishing these exploits with due caution, the Saxons, who had already broken out into formidable madness and were always rushing wherever they pleased without reconnaisances, had then invaded the maritime districts, and had almost returned enriched with the spoils which they took; but by a device which was treacherous but expedient he overwhelmed and stripped of their booty the robbers thus forcibly crushed.

9. Again, when the Britons could not resist the hordes of enemies that were overrunning their country, he restored them to freedom and quiet peace with the hope of better conditions, and allowing almost none of the plunderers to return to his home.

10. With like effectiveness he also crushed Valentinus, the exile from Pannonia, who was trying to disturb the public peace in that province, before his design came to a head.

Next, he saved Africa from great dangers, when that country was in the throes of an unexpected disaster; for Firmus was unable to endure the greed and arrogance of the military officials and had aroused the Moorish tribes, whose ardour can always easily be fanned to any plan of dissension.

With equal courage he would have avenged the lamentable catastrophes in Illyricum, had he not been overtaken by death and left that important matter unfinished.

11. And although these successes which I have mentioned were brought about by his admirable generals, yet it is also well known that he himself, being a man of nimble mind and hardened by long experience in military life, performed very many exploits; and among these it would have been a most glorious feat if he had been able to take King Macrianus alive, who was at that time formidable. He had made great efforts to do so after he learned with grief and sorrow that the king had escaped from the Burgundians, whom Valentinian himself had aroused against the Alamanni.

XXX, 8. His Cruelty, Greed, Jealousy, and Cowardice

1. This is a brief account of the emperor's deeds. Now, in the belief that posterity, being bound neither by base fear nor by base flattery, is usually an uncorrupted judge of the past, I shall give a summary of his defects, to be followed by an account of his excellent qualities. 2. He sometimes assumed an appearance of mildness, although his hot temper made him more inclined to severity; for he evidently forgot that a ruler should avoid all excess, as he would a precipice. 3. For he was never found to be content with a mild punishment, but he continually ordered blood-thirsty investigations one after the other; and in his cruel inquisitions some were tortured even to the danger of their lives; in fact, he was so prone to cruelty that he never rescued from death any of those who had been capitally condemned, by merciful terms in a warrant which was presented for his subscription, although sometimes this has been done even by the most savage of princes. 4. And yet he could have contemplated many examples of the men of old, and might have imitated native and foreign instances of humanity and righteous mercy, which the philosophers call the kind sisters of the virtues.

8. The greed for greater possessions without distinguishing right from wrong, and of seeking advantages of various kinds through the shipwreck of others' lives, grew ever greater and became excessive in this emperor. This fault some tried to excuse by offering the example of the emperor Aurelian, declaring that as, when the treasury was exhausted after Gallienus and the lamentable disasters to the state, he fell upon the rich like a torrent, so Valentinian, after the losses of the Parthian campaign, feeling the need of a vast quantity of expenditure in order to provide reinforcements and pay for his troops, mingled with cruelty the desire to amass excessive wealth, affecting not to know that there are some things which ought not to be done, even if one has the power to do them.

10. Besides this there was a fire of envy in the very marrow of this same emperor, and knowing that most vices are wont to assume the appearance of virtues, he had ever upon his lips the saying, that malice of severity is the inseparable associate of rightful power. And as men of the highest position always think that everything is allowed them, and they are strongly inclined to suspect those who oppose them and to overthrow better men than themselves, so he hated the well dressed, the learned, and rich, and the high-born; and he depreciated brave men, in order to give the appearance of surpassing all men in good qualities, a fault, as we read, by which the emperor Hadrian was inflamed.

11. This same prince often denounced cowards, calling such men sullied, unclean, and deserving to be thrust down below the humblest estate; and yet he himself, in the presence of empty terrors, sometimes turned abjectly pale and dreaded in his inmost soul something that did not exist at all. 12. It was the knowledge of this that led Remigius, marshal of the court, when he perceived that the emperor was boiling with anger at something which had occurred, to hint among other things that some outbreaks of the barbarians threatened; and when Valentinian heard this, immediately he was so overcome with fear that he became calm and mild as Antoninus the Good himself. 13. He never intentionally chose cruel judges, but if he had learned that those whom he had once advanced were acting cruelly, he maintained that he had found men like Lycurgus and Cassius, those ancient pillars of justice; and he often urged them in writing to punish even light offences with all severity. 14. Those in trouble, whom a reverse of fortune had befallen, found no refuge in the kindness of their prince, which had always been a longed-for haven, as it were, for those tossed on a stormy sea. For the purpose of a just rule (as the philosophers teach) is supposed to be the advantage and safety of its subjects.

XXX, 9. His Virtues

1. It is fitting after this to pass to those acts of his which were praiseworthy and to be imitated by right-thinking men; and if he had regulated the rest of his conduct in accordance with these, his career would have been that of a Trajan or a Marcus. He was very indulgent towards the provincials and everywhere lightened the burden of their tributes; he was always timely in founding towns and establishing frontier defences. He was an excellent critic of military discipline, failing only in this, that while he punished even slight offences of the common soldiers, he suffered the serious offences of his higher commanders to go to excess, often turning a deaf ear to the complaints made against them. The result of this was turmoil in Britain, disaster in Africa, and the devastation of Illyricum.

2. In every observance of chastity he was pure at home and abroad; he was stained by the foul touch of no obscene feelings or lewdness; and for that reason he controlled the wantonness of the imperial court as if by a curb; and this course he could easily keep; he showed no indulgence to his own kindred, whom he either restrained in retirement or honoured with unimportant posts, with the exception of his brother, whom, compelled by press of circumstances, he admitted to a share in his own eminence.

3. He was most cautious in bestowing high official positions: under his rule no money-changer governed a province, no office was ever sold, except at the beginning of his reign, a time when it is usual for some

crimes to be committed with impunity through reliance on the distractions of a new ruler.

4. In war, whether offensive or defensive, he was most skilful and careful, a veteran in the heat and dust of the battlefield. In council he was a foresighted persuader of what was right and a dissuader of wrong, most strict in examining all ranks of the military service. He wrote a neat hand, was an elegant painter and modeller, and an inventor of new kinds of arms. His memory was lively; so was his speech (although he spoke seldom), and he was vigorous therein, almost to the point of eloquence. He loved neatness, and enjoyed banquets that were choice but not extravagant.

5. Finally, his reign was distinguished by toleration, in that he remained neutral in religious differences neither troubling anyone on that ground nor ordering him to reverence this or that. He did not bend the necks of his subjects to his own belief by threatening edicts, but left such matters undisturbed as he found them.

6. His strong and muscular body, the gleam of his hair, his brilliant complexion, his grey eyes, with a gaze that was always sidelong and stern, his fine stature, and his regular features completed a figure of regal charm and majesty.

Chapter Two

The Germans and the Decline of Rome

THE second major step in the formation of the Middle Ages was the penetration of the Roman Empire by the Germans and the subsequent eclipse of the western Empire in favor of a series of barbarian successor states. It was a complex step overlapping at many points the other stages in the development of the Middle Ages. In its first phases the barbarization of the Empire was synchronous with the crisis of the third century and the reorganization of the fourth. In its later phases, corresponding to the establishment of Germanic kingdoms within the frontiers of the Roman Empire, it was simultaneous with a radical transformation of the conditions of Roman life and thought, a process already begun in the fourth century.

◆ ◆ ◆

The historian, as opposed to the anthropologist, can be content with the statement of Jordanes who said that the Germans came from the "Isle of Scanzia" (i.e., Scandinavia, which all classical antiquity thought to be an island). From there, where they were at least by the first millennium before Christ, they began a prolonged phase of emigration southward in about the second century of the same era. Henceforward, for more than a thousand years, the Scandinavian regions would send forth wave after wave of her sons to complicate and sometimes to govern the history of Europe. Here is one of the prime facts of early medieval history. The reason for it can hardly have been different from that which has prompted Scandinavian emigration in modern times: the pressure of population on meager natural resources aided by an adventurous spirit.

The migration from the Scandinavian homeland took place in two major phases. The first filtered through the Jutland peninsula into the Elbe-Oder region and from there further south and west until the Germans appear in the pages of Caesar in the first century before Christ. By the time of Tacitus, a century and a half later, those Germans had occupied much of what became modern Germany, being contained on the west and south by the Rhine-Danube frontier of the Roman Empire. These are the West Germans whose principal groups were known in the fourth century (although not to Caesar and Tacitus) as Franks, Saxons, Alamanni, and Thuringians.

The second phase of Germanic migration, somewhat later than the first, originated in Sweden and its adjacent islands. Beginning with the Vandals, they crossed over to the mouth of the Vistula, followed by the Rugii, Burgundians and finally the Goths, Gepids, and Alans. These East Germans, as they are called, were on the Baltic coast by the beginning of the Christian era. From the Vistula region they developed a mostly southeastward migratory pattern which brought the Goths and Alans onto the fringes of the Roman Empire early in the third century. Like their western brethren, they, especially the Goths, were a terror to the Empire during the troubles of the third century, forcing it to abandon the Roman province of Dacia in the 270's.

As the two Germanic groups diverged geographically, cultural distinctions appeared which help the student sort out the messy details of the Germanic migrations. The eastern group, some more than others, came in contact with peoples like the Sarmatians and took on some of their steppe nomadic characteristics. Others, like the Ostrogoths, now distinct from their kinsmen the Visigoths, acquired a settled form of agricultural life but began to imitate the nomadic use of cavalry in warfare. Another distinction is that the East German people as a whole and especially the preeminent portion of them, the Visigoths and Ostrogoths, had closer contact with Roman civilization at an earlier period than their western counterparts, with the exception of the Alamanni. The Visigoths, living in an area with a sub-Roman population, developed a lively trade with the Roman provinces across the Danube, exporting slaves to pay for their imports of Roman goods. Above all, it was the East Germans who first received Christianity through the intermediary of the Visigoths who became Arian Christians between 382 and 395 when they were settled in the Roman province of Moesia. Finally, although this is not a cultural distinction, it was the East Germans who first penetrated the Empire in force and established kingdoms within it. It is for this reason that the material in this chapter deals mostly with the East Germans.

The political and social institutions of the Germans prior to their entry into the Roman Empire has frequently been a matter for controversy. One certain fact is that the basic social and political unit was the tribe, not to be confused with the much larger unit which sometimes goes under that name. (The Visigoths, for example, were not a tribe but a confederation of tribes, as were the Franks, Alamanni, and so on.) The tribe had its elective chief, a council, and an assembly of warriors. Within it were social gradations based upon wealth at least by the fourth century, whether or not there had ever been a period of primitive equality. The noble class, described by the Romans as *optimates* (the "best men"), were distinguished from the others by their dress, indicative of their wealth and social prestige, and the possession of a *comitatus* or "following" (see Tacitus below). There was also a class of "slaves" who corresponded more to the Roman *colonus* than the Roman slave in his dependency; the Germans did not recognize a class of rightless men. Above them were the freemen, distinguished by the possession of property and their ability to bear arms, always the badge of freedom and political competence in Germanic society.

Economically, the early Germans ranged from a semi-pastoral state among the more primitive groups in the interior to the highly settled agricultural life of the Goths and Alamanni. In this respect, as in others, the economic level of the Germans varied in direct proportion with their distance from the Roman Empire. If the early German shunned towns, as Tacitus tells, he did not shun the material amenities of Roman life, nor was he totally devoid of the means of getting them. Roman traders were active among the Germans from a very early period, accepting furs, amber, and slaves in return for their wares.

Through the medium of trade, and through service in the Roman army, an impressive list of Latin words came into the various Germanic dialects prior to their entry into the Roman Empire. But aside from this and the use of certain Roman material objects, including money, there was surprisingly little cultural interchange between Roman and barbarian. Apparently, the Germans had little to learn from the Romans in the way of agricultural technique. Classical art and architecture had no appeal for the German; if anything, the cultural interchange went the other way. Christianity did come from Roman sources but the essential point is that it did not do so while the Germans were beyond the Roman frontiers. Little is known about early Germanic religion due to the fact that Roman writers understood very little about it. Nevertheless, it was impervious to Christianity, and even capable of persecuting it in the case of the Visigoths, until German entry into the Roman Empire broke down the tribal structure on which it was based.

The constitutional structure of primitive German society hinges on the rather puzzling concept of "peace." In principle, every free man was considered to have his own sphere of peace within which he was absolutely unfettered from the point of view of law (if not from the claims of family and custom). However, the individual's sphere of peace impinged upon those of others, hence the individual had to be prepared to defend his peace against the encroachment of others; he was his own law. It was this threat of retaliation rather than any public authority which produced the rule of law in Germanic society. Among the Germans of historical times the existence of courts of law no doubt pointed toward the concept of public authority. Still, these courts had no original jurisdiction, that is, cases had to be voluntarily brought to them (to which extent the litigants temporarily abandoned their peace) and had no power to enforce their decision other than the consensus of the community.

It follows from the above that the primitive political structure of the Germans will be similarly distinct from Roman or modern ideas on the subject. As we said above, most tribes had elective chiefs whose authority was sharply limited by the general assembly of warriors, itself controlled by the *optimates*. Actually, the Romans were in a better position to understand this than we are since they understood the distinction between authority, a personal charisma due to character, family, position, etc., and *potestas*, the legal power to compel. It was the concept of *potestas* which Germanic society lacked on every level.

Now we do read of kings in early Germanic society. It is partly a matter of terminology; Roman writers often use the word to describe chiefs, the careful ones using diminutives, like *regalis* and *regulus*. But as we get towards the end of the migration period we observe a well-developed tendency among the Germans to put themselves together in larger groups, confederacies, which in time of war had leaders to whom Romans did give the title *rex*. Furthermore, among the Ostrogoths and Visigoths at least, royal clans existed by the end of the fourth century. Yet the constitutional situation described above did not change with the development of the confederacy. As we shall see later, the origins of Germanic monarchy lie in the period after the entry of the Germans into the Roman Empire.

◆ ◆ ◆

We have already discussed the nature and significance of the reorganization of the Roman Empire in the fourth century. One part of it needs reemphasis and elaboration here because it was not basically altered by the advent of the Germans and thus forms one of the essential elements of continuity between the Roman and the early medieval periods.

It was in the sphere of rural life that the most lasting innovations of the later Roman Empire occurred. The Empire in the West had always been predominately agrarian. With some few exceptions where a genuine urban life existed, the Roman municipal system formed a thin veneer over the network of villages and farms which sustained the fundamental economic activity of the West. In this area three things happened. As we have seen, one was the rise of the colonate, a type of dependent tenure called forth by the twin phenomena of the fiscal needs of the state and the manpower shortage. The other two are closely related; the growth of the *villa* system and the emergence of the *potentes*.

The large, landed estate was not an innovation of the late Empire. What was new was primarily a matter of degree; the increasing tendency of the large estate to absorb all other forms of economic activity and an ever larger proportion of the population, and partly of organization of the *villa* (or *latifundia*) itself. The *villa* was composed of two parts: the *villa* proper, the dwelling and outbuildings of the owner or his representative along with the land immediately surrounding it (demesne), and the outlying land of the peasants attached to the *villa* by various sorts of tenure. Originally, the demesne was tilled by slaves, a practice which generally went out of use in the late Empire as the landowners began to see the advantage of converting their slaves to *coloni*, who did not have to be fed and from whom they could demand rents.

The colonate was one means by which the population of the late Roman *villa* grew; another was the *precaria* about which we read much in the Theodosian Code. The *precarium* was a type of land tenure well known to classical law. Although it had subsequently gone out of use, it revived and flourished in the late Empire, in a slightly different form and with a slightly different spelling (*precaria* instead of *precarium*). The arrangement was this: A lesser landowner, if in economic difficulties and/or in need of a powerful patron, would make over his land to such a man, receiving in return the use of it for a term of years, from five (usually renewable) up to one or two lifetimes. Since the *precaria* offered not only security but the use of a larger plot of land than the original owner contributed, we begin to see why in the troubled times of the late Empire the arrangement became so widespread. Through either arrangement or its variants, the *villa* began to swallow up not only individuals, into the *precaria* for those who owned land or the colonate for those who did not, but also whole villages.

We first begin to hear of *potentes* in the second half of the fourth century. They were men of great wealth, drawn from the senatorial class, whose position in the civil service of the Empire made them virtually immune from governmental regulation. The threat they represented to the Empire was clearly recognized by emperors from Valentinian I on. It was they who were the owners of villas, not one but many; it was they who received into patronage the depressed farmers of the countryside along with the fugitive *curialis* and guildsman from the town; it was they, in short, who were undermining the system of social regulation and the maintenance of essential services which that regulation was meant to serve. In the process they were defrauding the treasury, for they offered a haven from the imperial tax-collector. The government was powerless against the combination of wealth and position which made them what they were; all it could do was make use of them. Sooner or later they became responsible for the collection of recruits for the army (from among their *coloni*), for the administration of justice on their estates and, ironically, for the collection of taxes. Later we read of their private armies. Mostly undisturbed by the Germanic invasions, they, their way of life, and their source of wealth form an element of perfect continuity between the late Roman and the early medieval period.

To the Roman of the fifth century, or for that matter of any of the previous five centuries, Germans were no novelty. At the beginning of the Empire he would have been aware of Germans as agricultural slaves. Later he would have been familiar with them as colonists on depopulated lands. Even Italy received her share in the fourth century. In some of the frontier areas, particularly in northern Gaul, Germanic *laeti* (military colonists) existed from the late third century on. By the fifth century Romans would have known whole peoples established within the frontiers of the Empire as allies (*foederati*); what was probably the most crucial settlement of all, that of the Visigoths in Moesia, occurred at the end of the fourth century.

Germans were no strangers to the army from a very early period. From about the end of the fourth century they came to dominate it. After the death of Theodosius in 395, the wielders of actual power in the western Empire were all Germans of some sort—Stilicho, Merobaudes, Ricimer, Aetius, Odoacer—and these men served as consuls, intermarried with the imperial family and had members of the cultured Roman aristocracy as their close friends.

The Roman was also familiar with the German as an enemy. Germanic pressure had been severe on the frontiers since the third century. Romans of the vintage of Paulinus of Pella would have witnessed the disaster of Adrianople and the sack of Rome. Some of them would have suffered from the ravages of the Alans and Vandals and have been forced to give up part of their lands to the Visigoths in Aquitaine and Spain. But they would also have been aware of a long series of Roman military victories over the Germans after 378. At mid-fifth century they would have seen Visigoth, Frank and Saxon fighting under the banner of Aetius against the Hun.

As we read Sidonius, we must conclude that the advent of Vandal, Visigoth, Burgundian and Ostrogoth made surprising little impact on the Roman Empire in the West. The pace of change was so slow that the "fall of the Roman Empire" went unnoticed. There was consciousness of decline—Sidonius, for example, remarks that Roman arms were "palsied with age"; there was consciousness of literary decadence and, a persistent theme, moral decline. There was also hope for the future through a combination of German vigour and Roman culture.

It is no longer necessary to combat the humanist interpretation of the Germanic invasions which created the concept of the Middle Ages, the miserable period intervening between the glories of classical antiquity and the rebirth of civilization. The Empire did not succumb "to an overpowering advance of whole tribes and peoples, animated by hatred of Rome, sweeping away the remains of an effete civilization, and replacing it, in a sudden and cataclysmal change, by a spirit and by institutions of a perfectly different order." The essential fabric of Roman life remained in those barbarian kingdoms established on the fringes of the Mediterranean.

This is not to say that nothing happened; the life of the sixth century was not the life of the first or second or even of the fourth century. The Germans entered a world already displaying many symptoms of decline. The decay of urban life and of long distance commerce cannot be laid to their door although they no doubt reinforced it. The replacement of a native merchant class by Syrians and Levantines began in the third, not the sixth century. Again, since the Germans were still at the stage of a purely agrarian economy when they entered the Empire, they only fortified a rural predominance which was already characteristic of it. They did not cause the decline of Latin or create the ignorance of Greek. They are a symptom, not a cause, of the decay of ancient civilization.

But the future did not lie, as Jordanes hoped, in the combination of Germanic vigour and Roman culture. At least it did not lie there immediately. Nor did the future lie with the Mediterranean world. In subsequent centuries the focus of power will shift northward and in this shift we shall find the creative process which produced a new civilization.

1. *The Germania of Tacitus*

Publius Cornelius Tacitus (c.55–c.120), member of a distinguished Roman family, was a lawyer with a long legal and political career before he became an historian. As a literary and historical artist he is the leading figure in Roman historiography. His major historical works include a biography of his father-in-law, Agricola, the *Germania*, the *Annales*, which covered the history of the years A.D. 14–68 in eighteen books, and the *Historiae*, dealing with the events of the years 68–98 in twelve books.

Tacitus's ethnographical work on Germany, written at the very end of the first century, is the most extensive and valuable work of its kind. Except for a few lines elsewhere, notably in Caesar, it is the fundamental literary source for the early Germans, although the precise extent of his knowledge of the German tribes is still a moot question. Modern scholarship, utilizing mostly archaeological evidence, has both confirmed and denied Tacitus's observations, with the balance tending toward the latter. Nevertheless, the *Germania* contains a solid core of truth based upon the best information, even if second-hand, at his disposal. Another problem with the *Germania* is, since it was written in the first century, to what extent its picture of the Germans is conformable to the conditions of later times. Again, scholarly consensus confirms the essential validity of Tacitus, while recognizing that certain political developments, like the growth of the monarchical principle, and social changes, particularly a more settled form of life, had taken place.

The translation has been excerpted from the *Translations and Reprints from the Original Sources of European History*, VI, No. 3 (Philadelphia: Department of History of the University of Pennsylvania, 1899).

I SHOULD say that the Germans themselves were an indigenous people, without any subsequent mixture of blood through immigration or friendly intercourse; for in ancient times it was by sea and not by land that those who wished to change their homes wandered, and the ocean, hostile, as it were, and of boundless extent on the further side, is rarely traversed by ships from our part of the world. And not to mention the danger of the terrible and unknown sea, who indeed would leave Asia or Africa or Italy to seek Germany with its wild scenery, its harsh climate, its sullen manners and aspect, unless, indeed, it were his native country? They tell in their ancient songs, the only kind of tradition and history that they have, how Tuisto, a god sprung from the earth, and his son Mannus were the originators and founders of their race. Mannus is supposed to have had three sons from whose names those nearest the ocean are called *Ingaevones,* those in the middle country, *Herminiones,* and the others, *Istaevones.* Certain people assert with the freedom permitted in discussing ancient times that there were many descendants of the god, and many tribal names, such as Marsi, Gambrivii, Suebi, Vandilii, and that these were their true and ancient names. But the name Germany, they say, is modern and of recent application, since those who first crossed the Rhine and expelled the Gauls, and who are now called *Tungri,* were then named Germans; thus what had been a tribal, not a national name, spread little by little, so that later they all adopted the newly-coined appellation that was first employed by the conquerors to inspire fear and called themselves Germans.

◆ ◆ ◆

I myself subscribe to the opinion of those who hold that the German tribes have never been contaminated by intermarriage with other nations, but have remained peculiar and unmixed and wholly unlike other people. Hence the bodily type is the same among them all, notwithstanding the extent of their population. They all have fierce blue eyes, reddish hair and large bodies fit only for sudden exertion; they do not submit patiently to work and effort and cannot endure thirst and heat at all, though cold and hunger they are accustomed to because of their climate.

In general the country, though varying here and there in appearance, is covered over with wild forests or filthy swamps, being more humid on the side of Gaul but bleaker toward Noricum and Pannonia. It is suitable enough for grain but does not permit the cultivation of fruit trees; and though rich in flocks and herds these are for the most part small, the cattle not even possessing their natural beauty nor spreading horns. The people take pride in possessing a large number of animals, these being their sole and most cherished wealth. Whether it was in mercy or wrath that the gods denied them silver and gold, I know not. Yet I would not affirm that no vein of German soil produces silver or gold; for who had examined? They do not care for their possession and use as much as might be expected. There are to be seen among them vessels of silver that have been presented as gifts to their ambassadors and chiefs, but they are held in no more esteem than vessels of earthenware; however those nearest to us prize gold and silver because of its use in trade, and they recognize certain of our coins, those with milled edges bearing the stamp of a two-horse chariot. They are more anxious also for silver coins than for gold, not because of any special liking, but because a number of silver coins is more convenient in purchasing cheap and common articles.

Not even iron is abundant, as is shown by the character of their weapons. Some few use swords or long spears, but usually they carry javelins, called in their language *framea,* tipped with a short narrow piece of iron but so sharp and so easy to handle that as occasion demands they employ the same weapon for fighting at close range or at a distance. A horseman is content with a shield and a javelin, but the footmen, either nude or lightly clad in a small cloak, rain missiles, each man having many and hurling them to a great distance. There is no particular adornment to their weapons except that their shields are distinguished by the most carefully chosen colors. A few wear cuirasses, but hardly any have helmets of metal or leather. Their horses are noted neither for their beauty nor their speed, nor are they trained to perform evolutions as with us. They move straight ahead or make a single turn to the right, the wheel being executed with such perfect alignment that no man drops behind the one next to him. One would say that on the whole their chief strength lies in their infantry. A picked body of these are chosen from among all the youth and placed in advance of the line where they fight mixed with the horsemen, since their swiftness makes them fully equal to engaging in a cavalry contest. Their number is fixed; there are a hundred from each canton, and from this circumstance they take their name among their own people, so that what was at first a number is now become an appellation of honor. The main body of troops is drawn up in wedge-shaped formation. To yield ground, provided you press forward subsequently, is considered a mark of prudence rather than a sign of cowardice. They carry off the bodies of the fallen even where they are not victorious. It is the greatest ignominy to have left one's shield on the field, and it is unlawful for a man so disgraced to be present at the sacred rites or to enter the assembly; so that many after escaping from battle have ended their shame with the halter.

They choose their kings on account of their ancestry, their generals for their valor. The kings do not have free and unlimited power and the generals lead by example rather than command, winning great admiration if they are energetic and fight in plain sight in front of the line. But no one is allowed to put a culprit to death or to imprison him or even to beat him with stripes except the priests, and then not by way of a punishment or at the command of the general but as though ordered by the god who they believe aids them in their fighting. Certain figures and images taken from their sacred groves they carry into battle, but their greatest incitement to courage is that a division of horse or foot is not made up by chance or by accidental association but is formed of families and clans; and their dear ones are close at hand so that the wailings of the women and the crying of the children can be heard during the battle. These are for each warrior the most sacred witnesses of his bravery, these his dearest applauders. They carry their wounds to their mothers and their wives, nor do the latter fear to count their number and examine them while they bring them food and urge them to deeds of valor.

It is related how on certain occasions their forces already turned to flight and retreating have been rallied by the women who implored them by their prayers and bared their breasts to their weapons, signifying thus the captivity close awaiting them, which is feared far more intensely on account of their women than for themselves; to such an extent indeed that those states are more firmly bound in treaty among those whose hostages maidens of noble family are also required. Further, they believe that the sex has a certain sanctity and prophetic gift, and they neither despise their counsels nor disregard their answers. We ourselves in the reign of the divine Vespasian saw Valaeda, who was considered for a long time by many as a sort of divinity; and formerly also Albruna and many others were venerated, though not out of servility nor as though they were deified mortals.

Concerning minor matters the chiefs deliberate, but in important affairs all the people are consulted, although the subjects referred to the common people for judgment are discussed beforehand by the chiefs. Unless some sudden and unexpected event calls them together they assemble on fixed days either at the new moon or the full moon, for they think these the most auspicious times to begin their undertakings. They do not reckon time by the number of days, as we do, but by the number of nights. So run their appointments, their contracts; the night introduces the day, so to speak. A disadvantage arises from their regard for liberty in that they do not come together at once as if commanded to attend, but two or three days are wasted by their delay in assembling. When the crowd is sufficient they take their places fully armed. Silence is proclaimed by the priests, who have on these occasions the right to keep order. Then the king or a chief addresses them, each being heard according to his age, noble blood, reputation in warfare and eloquence, though more because he has the power to persuade than the right to command. If an opinion is displeasing they reject it by shouting; if they agree to it they clash with their spears. The most complimentary form of assent is that which is expressed by means of their weapons.

It is also allowable in the assembly to bring up accusations, and to prosecute capital offenses. Penalties are distinguished according to crime. Traitors and deserters are hung to trees. Weaklings and cowards and those guilty of infamous crimes are cast into the mire of swamps with a hurdle placed over their heads. This difference of penalty looks to the distinction that crime should be punished publicly while infamy should be hidden out of sight. Lighter offenses also are punished according to their degree, the guilty parties being fined a certain number of horses or cattle. A part of the fine goes to the king or the tribe, part to the injured party or his relatives. In these same assemblies are chosen the magistrates who decide suits in the cantons and villages. Each one has the assistance of a hundred associates as advisers and with power to decide.

They undertake no business whatever either of a public or a private character save they be armed. But it is not customary for anyone to assume arms until the tribe has recognized his competence to use them. Then in a full assembly some one of the chiefs or the father or relatives of the youth invest him with the shield and spear. This is the sign that the lad has reached the age of manhood; this his first honor. Before this he was only a member of a household, hereafter he is a member of the tribe. Distinguished rank or the great services of their parents secure even for striplings the claim to be ranked as chiefs. They attach themselves to certain more experienced chiefs of approved merit; nor are they ashamed to be looked upon as belonging to their followings. There are grades even within the train of followers assigned by the judgment of its leader. There is great rivalry among these companions as to who shall rank first with the chief, and among the chiefs as to who shall have the most and the bravest followers. It is an honor and a source of strength always to be surrounded by a great band of chosen youths, for they are an ornament in peace, a defense in war. It brings reputation and glory to a leader not only in his own tribe but also among the neighboring peoples if his following is superior in numbers and courage; for he is courted by embassies and honored by gifts, and often his very fame decides the issue of wars.

When they go into battle it is a disgrace for the chief to be outdone in deeds of valor and for the following not to match the courage of their chief; furthermore for any one of the followers to have survived his chief and come unharmed out of a battle is life-long infamy and reproach. It is in accordance with their most sacred oath of allegiance to defend and protect him and to ascribe their bravest deeds to his renown. The chief fights for victory; the men of his following, for their chief. If the tribe to which they belong sinks into the lethargy of long peace and quiet many of the noble youths voluntarily seek other tribes that are still carrying on war, because a quiet life is irksome to the Germans and they gain renown more readily in the midst of perils, while a large following is not to be provided for except by violence and war. For they look to the liberality of their chief for their war-horse and their deadly and victorious spear; the feasts and entertainments, however, furnished them on a homely but liberal basis, fall to their lot as mere pay. The means for this bounty are acquired through war and plunder. Nor could you persuade them to till the soil and await the yearly produce so easily as you could induce them to stir up an enemy and earn glorious wounds. Nay even they think it tame and stupid to acquire by their sweat what they can purchase by their blood.

In the intervals of peace they spend little time in hunting but much in idleness, given over to sleep and eating; all the bravest and most warlike doing nothing, while the hearth and home and the care of the fields is given over to the women, the old men and the various infirm members of the family. The masters lie buried in sloth by that strange contradiction of nature that causes the same men to love indolence and hate peace. It is customary for the several tribesmen to present voluntary offerings of cattle and grain to the chiefs which, though accepted as gifts of honor, also supply their wants. They are particularly delighted in the gifts of neighboring tribes, not only those sent by individuals, but those presented by states as such—choice horses, massive arms, embossed plates and armlets. We have now taught them to accept money also.

It is well known that none of the German tribes live in cities, nor even permit their dwellings to be closely joined to each other. They live separated and in various places, as a spring or a meadow or a grove strikes their fancy. They lay out their villages not as with us in connected or closely-joined houses, but each one surrounds his dwelling with an open space, either as a protection against conflagration or because of their ignorance of the art of building. They do not even make use of rough stones or tiles. They use for all purposes undressed timber, giving no beauty or comfort. Some parts they plaster carefully with earth of such purity and brilliancy as to form a substitute for painting and designs in color. They are accustomed also to dig out subterranean caves which they cover over with great heaps of manure as a refuge against the cold and a place for storing grain, for retreats of this sort render the extreme cold of their winters bearable and, whenever an enemy has come upon them, though he lays waste the open country he is either ignorant of what is hidden underground or else it escapes him for the very reason that it has to be searched for.

Generally their only clothing is a cloak fastened with a clasp, or if they haven't that, with a thorn; this being their only garment, they pass whole days about the hearth or near a fire. The richest of them are distinguished by wearing a tunic, not flowing as is the case among the Sarmatians and Parthians, but close-fitting and showing the shape of their limbs. There are those, also, who wear the skins of wild beasts, those nearest the Roman border in a careless manner, but those further back more elegantly, as those do who have no better clothing obtained by commerce. They select certain animals, and stripping off their hides sew on them patches of spotted skins taken from those strange beasts that the distant ocean and the unknown sea bring forth. The women wear the same sort of dress as the men except that they wrap themselves in linen garments which they adorn with purple stripes and do not lengthen out the upper part of the tunic into sleeves, but leave the arms bare the whole length. The upper part of their breasts is also exposed. However, their marriage code is strict, and in no other part of their manners are they to be praised more than in this. For almost alone among barbarian people they are content with one wife each, excepting those few who because of their high position rather than out of lust enter into more than one marriage engagement.

The wife does not bring a dowry to the husband, but the husband to the wife. The parents and relatives are at the ceremony and examine and accept the presents,—gifts not suited to female luxury nor such as a young bride would deck herself with, but oxen, a horse and bridle and a shield together with a spear and sword. In consideration of these offerings the wife is accepted, and she in her turn brings her husband a gift of weapons. This they consider as the strongest bond, these as their mystic rites, their gods of marriage. Lest the woman should think herself excluded from aspiring to share in heroic deeds and in the dangers of war, she is admonished by the very initiatory ceremonies of matrimony that she is becoming the partner of her husband's labors and dangers, destined to suffer and to dare with him alike in peace and in war. The yoke of oxen, the caparisoned horse, the gift of arms, give this warning. So must she live, so must she die. What things she receives she must hand down to her children worthy and untarnished and such that future daughters-in-law may receive them and pass them on to her grandchildren.

Thus they live in well-protected virtue, uncorrupted by the allurements of shows or the enticement of banquets. Men and women alike know not the secrecy of correspondence. Though the race is so numerous, adultery is very rare, its punishment being immediate and inflicted by the injured husband. He cuts off the woman's hair in the presence of her kinsfolk, drives her naked from his house and flogs her through the whole village. Indeed, the loss of chastity meets with no indulgence; neither beauty, youth nor wealth can procure the guilty woman a husband, for no one there laughs at vice, nor is corrupting and being corrupted spoken of as the way of the world. Those tribes do better still where only the virgins marry and where the hope and aspiration of married life is done with once for all. They accept one husband, just as they have one body and one life, that they may have no thought beyond this, no further desire; that their love may be as it were not for the married state, but for the husband. To limit the number of children or to put any of the later children to death is considered a crime, and with them good customs are of more avail than good laws elsewhere.

In every household the children grow up naked and unkempt into that lusty frame and those sturdy limbs that we admire. Each mother nurses her own children; they are not handed over to servants and paid nurses. The lord and the slave are in no way to be distinguished by the delicacy of their bringing up. They live among the same flocks, they lie on the same ground, until age separates them and valor distinguishes the free born. The young men marry late and their vigor is thereby unimpaired. Nor is the marriage of girls hastened. They have the same youthful vigor, the same stature as the young men. Thus well-matched and strong when they marry, the children reproduce the robustness of their parents. An uncle shows the same regard for his sister's children as does their own father. Some tribes consider this relationship more sacred and binding than any other, and in taking hostages lay special stress upon it on the ground that they secure thus a stronger hold on the mind and a wider pledge for the family. A man's heirs and successors, however, are his own children, and no wills are made. If there are no children the next heirs are the brothers, then come the paternal and maternal uncles. The more relatives a man has and the greater the number of his connections, the more honored is his old age. Childlessness has no advantages.

A German is required to adopt not only the feuds of his father or of a relative, but also their friendships, though the enmities are not irreconcilable. For even homicide is expiated by the payment of a certain number of cattle, and the whole family accept the satisfaction, a useful practice as regards the state because feuds are more dangerous where there is no strong legal control.

No other race indulges more freely in entertainments and hospitality. It is considered a crime to turn any mortal man away from one's door. According to his means each one receives those who come with a well furnished table. When his food has been all eaten up, he who had lately been the host becomes the guide and companion of his guest to the next house, which they enter uninvited. There is no distinction between guests; they are all received with like consideration. No one makes any difference between friend and stranger so far as concerns the rights of hospitality. If the guest on going away asks for any gift, it is customary to grant it to him, and the host on his side feels the same freedom from constraint in making a request. They take great pleasure in presents, but they do not reckon them as favors nor do they put themselves under obligations in accepting them.

As soon as they awake from sleep, which they prolong till late in the day, they bathe, usually in warm water as their winter lasts a great part of the year. After the bath they take food, each sitting in a separate seat and having a table to himself. Then they proceed to their business or not less often to feasts, fully armed. It is no disgrace to spend the whole day and night in drinking. Quarreling is frequent enough as is natural enough among drunken men, though their disputes are rarely settled by mere wrangling but oftener by bloodshed and wounds. Yet it is at their feasts that they consult about reconciling enemies, forming family alliances, electing chiefs, and even regarding war and peace, as they think that at no other time is the mind more open to fair judgment or more inflamed to mighty deeds. A race without natural or acquired cunning still continues to disclose the secret thoughts of the heart in the freedom of festivity. Therefore at such a time the minds of all are free and unconstrained. On the next day the matter is reconsidered and a particular advantage is secured on each occasion. They take counsel when they are unable to practice deception; they decide when they cannot be misled.

But they do not employ slaves as we do with distinct functions prescribed throughout the establishment. Each has his own domicile and rules his own house. The lord exacts a certain amount of grain or cloth or a certain number of cattle as in the case of a tenant and this is the extent of his servitude. Other duties, those of the household, are performed by the lord's wife and children. To beat a slave or to punish him with chains and task work is rare. They occasionally kill one, not in the severity of discipline but impetuously and in sudden wrath as they would kill an enemy, except that the deed goes without punishment. Freedmen do not rank much above slaves; they are not of much account in the household and never in the state, except only in those tribes that are ruled by kings. For there they are elevated above the free born and the nobles. The inferior position of the freedman elsewhere is the mark of the free state.

To trade with capital and to let it out at interest is unknown, and so it is ignorance rather than legal prohibition that protects them. Land is held by the villages as communities according to the number of the cultivators, and is then divided among the freemen according to their rank. The extent of their territories renders this partition easy. They cultivate fresh fields every year and there is still land to spare. They do not plant orchards nor lay off meadow-lands nor irrigate gardens so as to require of the soil more than it would naturally bring forth of its own richness and extent. Grain is the only tribute exacted from their land, whence they do not divide the year into as many seasons as we do. The terms winter, spring and summer have a meaning with them, but the name and blessings of autumn are unknown.

There is no pomp in the celebration of their funerals. The only custom they observe is that the bodies of illustrious men should be burned with certain kinds of wood. They do not heap garments and perfumes upon the funeral pile. In every case a man's arms are burned with him, and sometimes his horse also. They believe that stately monuments and sculptured columns oppress the dead with their weight; the green sod alone covers their graves. Their tears and lamentations are quickly laid aside; sadness and grief linger long. It is fitting for women to mourn, for men to remember.

2. *The Gothic History of Jordanes*

Jordanes, or Jornandes, was a Goth, presumably an Ostrogoth, who was originally *notarius* or secretary with a noble Gothic family settled in Italy with Theodoric. He was obviously Christian and by the time he wrote the *Getica* possibly a monk or an ecclesiastic. If the latter, he may be identified with a certain Bishop Jordanes of Crotona who was with Pope Vigilius in Constantinople in the year 551. In any case, the latter year was the date by which both of his historical works were completed, the *Romana*, a compendium of universal history, and the *Getica*.

Although it has no claim to literary merit, Jordanes' *Getica* is important because it is the earliest surviving work by a Gothic historian and because it contains information found nowhere else. Jordanes was a conscious compiler, drawing in this work on a wide range of classical—and post-classical sources. What merit the work has is due mostly to the fact that his principal source of information was the lost Gothic history of Cassiodorus.

Jordanes' purpose in writing was the same as Cassiodorus, to reconcile the Romans to the fact of Gothic domination both by glorifying the Gothic race and by attempting to give them a classical ancestry. This last was facilitated by the confusion, complete by the sixth century, between the ancient *Getae* and the comparatively modern Goths. Thus Jordanes (or Cassiodorus) was able to graft episodes involving Scythians, Parthians and such famous individuals as Xerxes, Alexander, Sulla and Marius onto the Gothic past.

The translation has been taken from C. C. Mierow, *The Gothic History of Jordanes* (Princeton: Princeton University Press, 1915), pp. 88–92, 93–98, 100–115, 120–24, 128–37.

The Divided Goths: Visigoths

THE Visigoths were terrified as their kinsmen had been, and knew not how to plan for safety against the race of the Huns. After long deliberation by common consent they finally sent ambassadors into Romania to the Emperor Valens, brother of Valentinian, the elder Emperor, to say that if he would give them part of Thrace or Moesia to keep, they would submit themselves to his laws and commands. That he might have greater confidence in them, they promised to become Christians, if he would give them teachers who spoke their language. When Valens learned this, he gladly and promptly granted what he had himself intended to ask. He received the Getae into the region of Moesia and placed them there as a wall of defense for his kingdom against other tribes. And since at that time the Emperor Valens, who was infected with the Arian perfidy, had closed all the churches of our party, he sent as preachers to them those who favored his sect. They came and straightway filled a rude and ignorant people with the poison of their heresy. Thus the Emperor Valens made the Visigoths Arians rather than Christians. Moreover, from the love they bore them, they preached the gospel both to the Ostrogoths and to their kinsmen the Gepidae, teaching them to reverence this heresy, and they invited all people of their speech everywhere to attach themselves to this sect. They themselves, as we have said, crossed the Danube and settled Dacia Ripensis, Noesia and Thrace by permission of the Emperor.

Soon famine and want came upon them, as often happens to a people not yet well settled in a country. Their princes and the leaders who ruled them in place of kings, that is Fritigern, Alatheus and Safrac, began to lament the plight of their army and begged Lupicinus and Maximus, the Roman commanders, to open a market. But to what will not the "cursed lust for gold" compel men to assent? The generals, swayed by avarice, sold them at a high price not only the flesh of sheep and oxen, but even the carcasses of dogs and unclean animals, so that a slave would be bartered for a loaf of bread or ten pounds of meat. When their goods and chattels failed, the greedy trader demanded their sons in return for the necessities of life. And the parents consented even to this, in order to provide for the safety of their children, arguing that it was better to lose liberty than life; and indeed it is better that one be sold, if he will be mercifully fed, than that he should be kept free only to die.

Now it came to pass in that troublous time that Lupicinus, the Roman general, invited Fritigern, a chieftain of the Goths, to a feast and, as the event revealed, devised a plot against him. But Fritigern, thinking no evil, came to the feast with a few followers. While he was dining in the praetorium he heard the dying cries of his ill-fated men, for, by the order of the general, the soldiers were slaying his companions who were shut up in another part of the house. The loud cries of the dying fell upon ears already suspicious, and Fritigern at once perceived the treacherous trick. He drew his sword and with great courage dashed quickly from the banqueting-hall, rescued his men from their threatening doom and incited them to slay the Romans. Thus these valiant men gained the chance they had longed for—to be free to die in battle rather than to perish of hunger—and immediately took arms to kill the generals Lupicinus and Maximus. Thus that day put an end to the famine of the Goths and the safety of the Romans, for the Goths no longer as strangers and pilgrims, but as citizens and lords, began to rule the inhabitants and to hold in their own right all the northern country as far as the Danube.

When the Emperor Valens heard of this at Antioch, he made ready an army at once and set out for the country of Thrace. Here a grievous battle took place and the Goths prevailed. The Emperor himself was wounded and fled to a farm near Hadrianople. The Goths, not knowing an emperor lay hidden in so poor a hut, set fire to it (as is customary in dealing with a cruel foe), and thus he was cremated in royal splendor. Plainly it was a direct judgment of God that he should be burned with fire by the very men whom he had perfidiously led astray when they sought the true faith, turning them aside from the flame of love into the fire of hell. From this time the Visigoths, in consequence of their glorious victory, possessed Thrace and Dacia Ripensis as if it were their native land.

Now in the place of Valens, his uncle, the Emperor Gratian established Theodosius the Spaniard in the Eastern Empire. Military discipline was soon restored to a high level, and the Goth, perceiving that the cowardice and sloth of former princes was ended, became afraid. For the Emperor was famed alike for his acuteness and discretion. By stern commands and by generosity and kindness he encouraged a demoralized army to deeds of daring. But when the soldiers, who had obtained a better leader by the change, gained new confidence, they sought to attack the Goths and drive them from the borders of Thrace. But as Emperor Theodosius fell so sick at this time that his life was almost despaired of, the Goths were again inspired with courage. Dividing the Gothic army, Fritigern set out to plunder Thessaly, Epirus and Achaia, while Alatheus and Safrac with the rest of the troops made for Pannonia. Now the Emperor Gratian had at this time retreated from Rome to Gaul because of the invasions of the Vandals. When he learned that the Goths were acting with greater boldness because Theodosius was in despair of this life, he quickly gathered an army and came against them. Yet he put no trust in arms, but sought to conquer them by kindness and gifts. So he entered on a truce with them and made peace, giving them provisions.

When the Emperor Theodosius afterwards recovered and learned that the Emperor Gratian had made a compact between the Goths and the Romans, as he had himself desired, he was very well pleased and gave his assent. He gave gifts to King Athanaric, who had succeeded Fritigern, made an alliance with him and in the most gracious manner invited him to visit him in Constantinople. Athanaric very gladly consented and as he entered the royal city exclaimed in wonder, "Lo, now I see what I have often heard of with unbelieving ears," meaning the great and famous city. Turning his eyes hither and thither, he marvelled as he beheld the situation of the city, the coming and going of the ships, the splendid walls, and the people of divers nations gathered like a flood of waters streaming from different regions into one basin. So, too, when he saw the army in array, he said "Truly the Emperor is a god on earth, and whoso raises a hand against him is guilty of his own blood." In the midst of his admiration and the enjoyment of even greater honors at the hand of the Emperor, he departed this life after the space of a few months. The Emperor had such affection for him that he honored Athanaric even more when he was dead than during his lifetime, for he not only gave him a worthy burial, but himself walked before the bier at the funeral. Now when Athanaric was dead, his whole army continued in the service of the Emperor Theodosius and submitted to the Roman rule, forming as it were one body with the imperial soldiery. The former service of the Allies under the Emperor Constantine was now renewed and they were again called Allies. And since the Emperor knew that they were faithful to him and his friends, he took from their number more than twenty thousand warriors to serve against the tyrant Eugenius who had slain Gratian and seized Gaul. After winning the victory over this usurper, he wreaked his vengeance upon him.

But after Theodosius, the lover of peace and of the Gothic race, had passed from human cares, his sons began to ruin both empires by their luxurious living and to deprive their Allies, that is to say the Goths, of the customary gifts. The contempt of the Goths for the Romans soon increased, and for fear their valor would be destroyed by long peace, they appointed Alaric king over them. He was of famous stock, and his nobility was second only to that of the Amali, for he came from the family of the Balthi, who because of their daring valor had long ago received among their race the name *Baltha,* that is, The Bold. Now when this Alaric was made king, he took counsel with his men and persuaded them to seek a kingdom by their own exertions rather than serve others in idleness. In the consulship of Stilicho and Aurelian he raised an army and entered Italy, which seemed to be bare of defenders, and came through Pannonia and Sirmium along the right side. Without meeting any resistance, he reached the bridge of the river Candidianus at the third milestone from the royal city of Ravenna.

◆ ◆ ◆

But as I was saying, when the army of the Visigoths had come into the neighborhood of this city, they sent an embassy to the Emperor Honorius, who dwelt within. They said that if he would permit the Goths to settle peaceably in Italy, they would so live with the Roman people that men might believe them both to be of one race; but if not, whoever prevailed in war should drive out the other, and the victor should henceforth rule unmolested. But the Emperor Honorius feared to make either promise. So he took counsel with his senate and considered how he might drive them from the Italian borders. He finally decided that Alaric and his race, if they were able to do so, should be allowed to seize for their own home the provinces farthest away, namely Gaul and Spain. For at this time he had almost lost them, and moreover they had been devastated by the invasion of Gaiseric, king of the Vandals. The grant was confirmed by an imperial rescript, and the Goths, consenting to the arrangement, set out for the country given them.

When they had gone away without doing any harm in Italy, Stilicho, the Patrician and father-in-law of the Emperor Honorius—for the Emperor had married both his daughters, Maria and Thermantia, in succession, but God called both from this world in their virgin purity—this Stilicho, I say, treacherously hurried to Pollentia, a city in the Cottian Alps. There he fell upon the unsuspecting Goths in battle, to the ruin of all Italy and his own disgrace. When the Goths suddenly beheld him, at first they were terrified. Soon regaining their courage and arousing each other by brave shouting, as is their custom, they turned to flight the entire army of Stilicho and almost exterminated it. Then forsaking the journey they had undertaken, the Goths with hearts full of rage returned again to Liguria whence they had set out. When they had plundered and spoiled it, they also laid waste Aemilia, and then hastened toward the city of Rome along the Flaminian Way, which runs between Picenum and Tuscia, taking as booty whatever they found on either hand. When they finally entered Rome, by Alaric's express command they merely sacked it and did not set the city on fire, as wild peoples usually do, nor did they permit serious damage to be done to the holy places. Thence they departed to bring like ruin upon Campania and Lucania, and then came to Bruttii. Here they remained a long time and planned to go to Sicily and thence to the countries of Africa.

Now the land of the Bruttii is at the extreme southern bound of Italy, and a corner of it marks the beginning of the Apennine mountains. It stretches out like a tongue into the Adriatic Sea and separates it from the Tyrrhenian waters. It chanced to receive its name in ancient times from a Queen Bruttia. To this place came Alaric, king of the Visigoths, with the wealth of all Italy which he had taken as spoil, and from there, as we have said, he intended to cross over by way of Sicily to the quiet land of Africa. But since man is not free to do anything he wishes without the will of God, that dread strait sunk several of his ships and threw all into confusion. Alaric was cast down by his reverse and, while deliberating what he should do, was suddenly overtaken by an untimely death and departed from human cares. His people mourned for him with the utmost affection. Then turning from its course the river Busentus near the city of Consentia—for this stream flows with its wholesome waters from the foot of a mountain near that city—they led a band of captives into the midst of its bed to dig out a place for his grave. In the depths of this pit they buried Alaric, together with many treasures, and then turned the waters back into their channel. And that none might ever know the place, they put to death all the diggers. They bestowed the kingdom of the Visigoths on Athavulf his kinsman, a man of imposing beauty and great spirit; for though not tall of stature, he was distinguished for beauty of face and form.

When Athavulf became king, he returned again to Rome, and whatever had escaped the first sack his Goths stripped bare like locusts, not merely despoiling Italy of its private wealth, but even of its public resources. The Emperor Honorius was powerless to resist even when his sister Placidia, the daughter of the Emperor Theodosius by his second wife, was led away captive from the city. But Athavulf was attracted by her nobility, beauty and chaste purity, and so he took her to wife in lawful marriage at Forum Julii, a city of Aemilia. When the barbarians learned of this alliance, they were the more effectually terrified, since the Empire and the Goths now seemed to be made one. Then Athavulf set out for Gaul, leaving Honorius Augustus stripped of his wealth, to be sure, yet pleased at heart because he was now a sort of kinsman of his. Upon his arrival the neighboring tribes who had long made cruel raids into Gaul—Franks and Burgundians alike—were terrified and began to keep within their own borders. Now the Vandals and the Alani, as we have said before, had been dwelling in both Pannonias by permission of the Roman Emperors. Yet fearing they would not be safe even here if the Goths should return, they crossed over into Gaul. But no long time after they had taken possession of Gaul they fled thence and shut themselves up in Spain, for they still remembered from the tales of their forefathers what ruin Geberich, king of the Goths, had long ago brought on their race, and how by his valor he had driven them from their native land. And thus it happened that Gaul lay open to Athavulf when he came. Now when the Goth had established his kingdom in Gaul, he began to grieve for the plight of the Spaniards and planned to save them from the attacks of the Vandals. So Athavulf left with a few faithful men at Barcelona his treasures and those who were unfit for war, and entered the interior of Spain. Here he fought frequently with the Vandals, and, in the third year after he had subdued Gaul and Spain, fell pierced through the groin by the sword of Euervulf, a man whose short stature he had been wont to mock. After his death Segeric was appointed king, but he too was slain by the treachery of his own men and lost both his kingdom and his life even more quickly than Athavulf.

Then Valia, the fourth from Alaric, was made king, and he was an exceeding stern and prudent man. The Emperor Honorius sent an army against him under Constantius, who was famed for his achievements in war and distinguished in many battles, for he feared that Valia would break the treaty long ago made with Athavulf and that, after driving out the neighboring tribes, he would again plot evil against the Empire. Moreover Honorius was eager to free his sister Placidia from the disgrace of servitude, and made an agreement with Constantius that if by peace or war or any means soever he could bring her back to the kingdom, he should have her in marriage. Pleased with this promise, Constantius set out for Spain with an armed force and in almost royal splendor. Valia, king of the Goths, met him at a pass in the Pyrenees with as great a force. Hereupon embassies were sent by both sides and it was decided to make peace on the following terms, namely that Valia should give up Placidia, the Emperor's sister, and should not refuse to aid the Roman Empire when occasion demanded.

Now at that time a certain Constantine usurped imperial power in Gaul and appointed as Caesar his son Constans, who was formerly a monk. But when he had held for a short time the Empire he had seized, he was himself slain at Arelate and his son at Vienne. Jovinus and Sebastian succeeded them with equal presumption and thought they might seize the imperial power; but they perished by a like fate.

Now in the twelfth year of Valia's reign the Huns were driven out of Pannonia by the Romans and Goths, almost fifty years after they had taken possession of it. Then Valia found that the Vandals had come forth with bold audacity from the interior of Galicia, whither Athavulf had long ago driven them, and were devastating and plundering everywhere in his own territories, namely in the land of Spain. So he made no delay but moved his army against them at once, at about the time when Hierius and Ardabures had become consuls.

But Gaiseric, king of the Vandals, had already been invited into Africa by Boniface, who had fallen into a dispute with the Emperor Valentinian and was able to obtain revenge only by injuring the Empire. So he invited them urgently and brought them across the narrow strait known as the Strait of Gades, scarcely seven miles wide, which divides Africa and Spain and unites the mouth of the Tyrrhenian Sea with the waters of the Ocean. Gaiseric, still famous in the City for the disaster of the Romans, was a man of moderate height and lame in consequence of a fall from his horse. He was a man of deep thought and few words, holding luxury in disdain, furious in his anger, greedy for gain, shrewd in winning over the barbarians and skilled in sowing the seeds of dissension to arouse enmity. Such was he who, as we have said, came at the solicitous invitation of Boniface to the country of Africa. There he reigned for a long time, receiving authority, as they say, from God Himself. Before his death he summoned the band of his sons and ordained that there should be no strife among them because of desire for the kingdom, but that each should reign in his own rank and order and he survived the others; that is, the next younger should succeed his elder brother, and he in turn should be followed by his junior. By giving heed to this command they ruled their kingdom in happiness for the space of many years and were not disgraced by civil war, as is usual among other nations; one after the other receiving the kingdom and ruling the people in peace.

◆ ◆ ◆

And what more? Valia (to repeat what we have said) had but little success against the Gauls, but when he died the more fortunate and prosperous Theodorid succeeded to the throne. He was a man of the greatest moderation and notable for vigor of mind and body. In the consulship of Theodosius and Festus the Romans broke the truce and took up arms against him in Gaul, with the Huns as their auxiliaries. For a band of the Gallic Allies, led by Count Gaina, had aroused the Romans by throwing Constantinople into a panic. Now at that time the Patrician Aetius was in command of the army. He was of the bravest Moesian stock, the son of Gaudentius and born in the city of Durostorum. He was a man fitted to endure the toils of war, born expressly to serve the Roman state; and by inflicting crushing defeats he had compelled the proud Suavi and barbarous Franks to submit to Roman sway. So then, with the Huns as allies under their leader Litorius, the Roman army moved in array against the Goths. When the battle lines of both sides had been standing for a long time opposite each other, both being brave and neither side the weaker, they struck a truce and returned to their ancient alliance. And after the treaty had been confirmed by both and an honest peace was established, they both withdrew.

During this peace Attila was lord over all the Huns and almost the sole earthly ruler of all the tribes of Scythia; a man marvellous for his glorious fame among all nations. The historian Priscus, who was sent to him on an embassy by the younger Theodosius, says this among other things: "Crossing mighty rivers—namely, the Tisia and Tibisia and Dricca—we came to the place where long ago Vidigoia, bravest of the Goths, perished by the guile of the Sarmatians. At no great distance from that place we arrived at the village where King Attila was dwelling, a village, I say, like a great city, in which we found wooden walls made of smooth-shining boards, whose joints so counterfeited solidity that the union of the boards could scarcely be distinguished by close scrutiny. There you might see dining halls of large extent and porticoes planned with great beauty, while the courtyard was bounded by so vast a circuit that its very size showed it was the royal palace." This was the abode of Attila, the king of all the barbarian world; and he preferred this as a dwelling to the cities he captured.

Now this Attila was the son of Mundiuch, and his brothers were Octar and Ruas who are said to have ruled before Attila, though not over quite so many tribes as he. After their death he succeeded to the throne of the Huns, together with his brother Bleda. In order that he might first be equal to the expedition he was preparing, he sought to increase his strength by murder. Thus he proceeded from the destruction of his own kindred to the menace of all others. But though he increased his power by this shameful means, yet by the balance of justice he received the hideous consequences of his own cruelty. Now when his brother Bleda, who ruled over a great part of the Huns, had been slain by his treachery, Attila united all the people under his own rule. Gathering also a host of the other tribes which he then held under his sway, he sought to subdue the foremost nations of the world—the Romans and the Visigoths. His army is said to have numbered five hundred thousand men. He was a man born into the world to shake the nations, the scourge of all lands, who in some way terrified all mankind by the dreadful rumors noised abroad concerning him. He was haughty in his walk, rolling his eyes hither and thither, so that the power of his proud spirit appeared in the movement of his body. He was indeed a lover of war, yet restrained in action, mighty in counsel, gracious to suppliants and lenient to those who were once received into his protection. He was short of stature, with a broad chest and a large head; his eyes were small, his beard thin and sprinkled with gray; and he had a flat nose and a swarthy complexion, showing the evidences of his origin. And though his temper was such that he always had great self-confidence, yet his assurance was increased by finding the sword of Mars, always esteemed sacred among the kings of the Scythians. The historian Priscus says it was discovered under the following circumstances: "When a certain shepherd beheld one heifer of his flock limping and could find no cause for this wound, he anxiously followed this trail of blood and at length came to a sword it had unwittingly trampled while nibbling the grass. He dug it up and took it straight to Attila. He rejoiced at the gift and, being ambitious, thought he had been appointed ruler of the whole world, and that through the sword of Mars supremacy in all wars was assured to him."

Now when Gaiseric, king of the Vandals, whom we mentioned shortly before, learned that his mind was bent on the devastation of the world, he incited Attila by many gifts to make war on the Visigoths, for he was afraid that Theodorid, king of the Visigoths, would avenge the injury done to his daughter. She had been joined in wedlock with Huneric, the son of Gaiseric, and at first was happy in this union. But afterwards he was cruel even to his own children, and because of the mere suspicion that she was attempting to poison him, he cut off her nose and mutilated her ears. He sent her back to her father in Gaul thus despoiled of her natural charms. So the wretched girl presented a pitiable aspect ever after, and the cruelty which would stir even strangers still more surely incited her father to vengeance. Attila, therefore, in his efforts to bring about the wars long ago instigated by the bribe of Gaiseric, sent ambassadors into Italy to the Emperor Valentinian to sow strife between the Goths and the Romans, thinking to shatter by civil discord those whom he could not crush in battle. He declared that he was in no way violating his friendly relations with the Empire, but that he had a quarrel with Theodorid, king of the Visigoths. As he wished to be kindly received, he filled the rest of the letter with the usual flattering salutations, striving to win credence for his falsehood. In like manner he despatched a message to Theodorid, king of the Visigoths, urging him to break his alliance with the Romans and reminding him of the battles to which they had recently provoked him. Beneath his ferocity he was a subtle man, and fought with craft before he made war.

Then the Emperor Valentinian sent an embassy to the Visigoths and their king Theodorid, with this message: "Bravest of nations, it is the part of prudence for us to unite against the lord of the earth who wishes to enslave the whole world; who requires no just cause for battle, but supposes whatever does is right. He measures his ambition by his might. License satisfies his pride. Despising law and right, he shows himself an enemy to Nature herself. And thus he, who clearly is the common foe of each, deserves the hatred of all. Pray remember—what you surely cannot forget—that the Huns do not overthrow nations by means of war, where there is an equal chance, but assail them by treachery, which is a greater cause for anxiety. To say nothing about ourselves, can you suffer such insolence to go unpunished? Since you are mighty in arms, give heed to your own danger and join hands with us in common. Bear aid also to the Empire, of which you hold a part. If you would learn how such an alliance should be sought and welcomed by us, look into the plans of the foe."

By these and like arguments the ambassadors of Valentinian prevailed upon King Theodorid. He answered them, saying: "Romans, you have attained your desire; you have made Attila our foe also. We will pursue him wherever he summons us, and though he is puffed up by his victories over divers races, yet the Goths know how to fight this haughty foe. I call no war dangerous save one whose cause is weak; for he fears no ill on whom Majesty has smiled." The nobles shouted assent to the reply and the multitude gladly followed. All were fierce for battle and longed to meet the Huns, their foe. And so a countless host was led forth by Theodorid, king of the Visigoths, who sent home four of his sons, namely Friderich and Eurich, Retemer and Himnerith, taking with him only the two elder sons, Thorismud and Theodorid, as partners of his toil. O brave array, sure defense and sweet comradeship, having the aid of those who delight to share in the same dangers!

On the side of the Romans stood the Patrician Aetius, on whom at that time the whole Empire of the West depended; a man of such wisdom that he had assembled warriors from everywhere to meet them on equal terms. Now these were his auxiliaries: Franks, Sarmatians, Armoricians, Liticians, Burgundians, Saxons, Riparians, Olibriones (once Roman soldiers and now the flower of the allied forces), and some other Celtic or German tribes. And so they met in the Catalaunian plains, which are also called Mauriacian, extending in length one hundred *leuva,* as the Gauls express it, and seventy in width. Now a Gallic *leuva* measures a distance of fifteen hundred paces. That portion of the earth accordingly became the threshing-floor of countless races. The two hosts bravely joined battle. Nothing was done under cover, but they contended in open fight. What just cause can be found for the encounter of so many nations, or what hatred inspired them all to take arms against each other? It is proof that the human race lives for its kings, for it is at the mad impulse of one mind a slaughter of nations takes place, and at the whim of a haughty ruler that which nature has taken ages to produce perishes in a moment.

But before we set forth the order of the battle itself, it seems needful to relate what had already happened in the course of the campaign, for it was not only a famous struggle but one that was complicated and confused. Well then, Sangiban, king of the Alani, smitten with fear of what might come to pass, had promised to surrender to Attila, and to give into his keeping Aureliani, a city of Gaul wherein he then dwelt. When Theodorid and Aetius learned of this, they cast up great earthworks around that city before Attila's arrival and kept watch over the suspected Sangiban, placing him with his tribe in the midst of their auxiliaries. Then Attila, king of the Huns, was taken aback by this event and lost confidence in his own troops, so that he feared to begin the conflict. While he was meditating flight—a greater calamity than death itself—he decided to inquire into the future through soothsayers. So, as was their custom, they examined the entrails of cattle and certain streaks in the bones that had been scraped, and foretold disaster to the Huns. Yet as a slight consolation they prophesied that the chief commander of the foe they were to meet should fall and mar by death the rest of the victory and the triumph. Now Attila deemed the death of Aetius a thing to be desired even at the cost of his own life, for Aetius stood in the way of his plans. So although he was disturbed by this prophecy, yet inasmuch as he was a man who sought counsel of omens in all warfare, he began the battle with anxious heart at about the ninth hour of the day, in order that the impending darkness might come to his aid if the outcome should be disastrous.

The armies met, as we have said, in the Catalaunian Plains. The battle field was a plain rising by a sharp slope to a ridge, which both armies sought to gain; for advantage of position is a great help. The Huns with their forces seized the right side, the Romans, the Visigoths and their allies the left, and then began a struggle for the yet untaken crest. Now Theodorid with the Visigoths held the right wing and Aetius with the

Romans the left. They placed in the centre Sangiban (who, as said before, was in command of the Alani), thus contriving with military caution to surround by a host of faithful troops the man in whose loyalty they had little confidence. For one who has difficulties placed in the way of his flight readily submits to the necessity of fighting. On the other side, however, Attila and his bravest followers were stationed in the centre. In arranging them thus the king had chiefly his own safety in view, since by his position in the very midst of his race he would be kept out of the way of threatening danger. The innumerable peoples of divers tribes, which he had subjected to his sway, formed the wings. Amid them was conspicuous the army of the Ostrogoths under the leadership of the brothers Valamir, Thiudimer and Vidimer, nobler even than the king they served, for the might of the family of the Amali rendered them glorious. The renowned king of the Gepidae, Ardaric, was there also with a countless host, and because of his great loyalty to Attila, he shared his plans. For Attila, comparing them in his wisdom, prized him and Valamir, king of the Ostrogoths, above all the other chieftains. Valamir was a good keeper of secrets, bland of speech and skilled in wiles, and Ardaric, as we have said, was famed for his loyalty and wisdom. Attila might well feel sure that they would fight against the Visigoths, their kinsmen. Now the rest of the crowd of kings (if we may call them so) and the leaders of various nations hung upon Attila's nod like slaves, and when he gave a sign even by a glance, without a murmur each stood forth in fear and trembling, or at all events did as he was bid. Attila alone was king of all kings over all and concerned for all.

So then the struggle began for the advantage of position we have mentioned. Attila sent his men to take the summit of the mountain, but was outstripped by Thorismud and Aetius, who in their effort to gain the top of the hill reached higher ground and through this advantage of position easily routed the Huns as they came up.

Now when Attila saw his army was thrown into confusion by this event, he thought it best to encourage them by an extemporaneous address on this wise: "Here you stand, after conquering mighty nations and subduing the world. I therefore think it foolish for me to goad you with words, as though you were men who had not been proved in action. Let a new leader or an untried army resort to that. It is not right for me to say anything common, nor ought you to listen. For what is war but your usual custom? Or what is sweeter for a brave man than to seek revenge with his own hand? It is a right of nature to glut the soul with vengeance. Let us then attack the foe eagerly; for they are ever the bolder who make the attack. Despise this union of discordant races! To defend oneself by alliance is proof of cowardice. See, even before our attack they are smitten with terror. They seek the heights, they seize the hills and, repenting too late, clamor for protection against battle in the open fields.

You know how slight a matter the Roman attack is. While they are still gathering in order and forming in one line with locked shields, they are checked, I will not say by the first wound, but even by the dust of battle. Then on to the fray with stout hearts, as is your wont. Despise their battle line. Attack the Alani, smite the Visigoths! Seek swift victory in that spot where the battle rages. For when the sinews are cut the limbs soon relax, nor can a body stand when you have taken away the bones. Let your courage rise and your own fury burst forth! Now show your cunning, Huns, now your deeds of arms! Let the wounded exact in return the death of his foe; let the unwounded revel in slaughter of the enemy. No spear shall harm those who are sure to live; and those who are sure to die Fate overtakes even in peace. And finally, why should Fortune have made the Huns victorious over so many nations, unless it were to prepare them for the joy of this conflict. Who was it revealed to our sires the path through the Maeotian swamp, for so many ages a closed secret? Who, moreover, made armed men yield to you, when you were as yet unarmed? Even a mass of federated nations could not endure the sight of the Huns. I am not deceived in the issue; here is the field so many victories have promised us. I shall hurl the first spear at the foe. If any can stand at rest while Attila fights, he is a dead man." Inflamed by these words, they all dashed into battle.

And although the situation was itself fearful, yet the presence of their king dispelled anxiety and hesitation. Hand to hand they clashed in battle, and the fight grew fierce, confused, monstrous, unrelenting—a fight whose like no ancient time has ever recorded. There such deeds were done that a brave man who missed this marvellous spectacle could not hope to see anything so wonderful all his life long. For, if we may believe our elders, a brook flowing between low banks through the plain was greatly increased by blood from the wounds of the slain. It was not flooded by showers, as brooks usually rise, but was swollen by a strange stream and turned into a torrent by the increase of blood. Those whose wounds drove them to slake their parching thirst drank water mingled with gore. In their wretched plight they were forced to drink what they thought was the blood they had poured from their own wounds.

Here King Theodorid, while riding by to encourage his army, was thrown from his horse and trampled under foot by his own man, thus ending his days at a ripe old age. But others say he was slain by the spear of Andag of the host of the Ostrogoths, who were then under the sway of Attila. This was what the soothsayers had told to Attila in prophecy, though he understood it of Aetius. Then the Visigoths, separating from the Alani, fell upon the horde of the Huns and nearly slew Attila. But he prudently took flight and straightway shut himself and his companions within the barriers of the camp, which he had fortified with wagons. A frail defense indeed; yet there they sought refuge for their lives, whom but a little while before no walls of earth could withstand. But Thorismud, the son of King Theodorid, who with Aetius had seized the hill and repulsed the enemy from the higher ground, came unwittingly to the wagons of the enemy in the darkness of night, thinking he had reached his own lines. As he was fighting bravely, someone wounded him in the head and dragged him from his horse. Then he was rescued by the watchful care of his followers and withdrew from the fierce conflict. Aetius also became separated from his men in the confusion of night and wandered about in the midst of the enemy. Fearing disaster had happened, he went about in search of the Goths. At last he reached the camp of his allies and passed the remainder of the night in the protection of their shields.

At dawn on the following day, when the Romans saw the fields were piled high with bodies and that the Huns did not venture forth, they thought the victory was theirs, but knew that Attila would not flee from the battle unless overwhelmed by a great disaster. Yet he did nothing cowardly, like one that is overcome, but with clash of arms sounded the trumpets and threatened an attack. He was like a lion pierced by hunting spears, who paces to and fro before the mouth of his den and dares not spring, but ceases not to terrify the neighborhood by his roaring. Even so this warlike king at bay terrified his conquerors. Therefore the Goths and Romans assembled and considered what to do with the vanquished Attila. They determined to wear him out by a siege, because he had no supply of provisions and was hindered from approaching by a shower of arrows from the bowmen placed within the confines of the Roman camp. But it was said that the king remained supremely brave even in this extremity and had heaped up a funeral pyre of horse saddles, so that if the enemy should attack him, he was determined to cast himself into the flames, that none might have the joy of wounding him and that the lord of so many races might not fall into the hands of his foes.

Now during these delays in the siege, the Visigoths sought their king and the king's sons their father, wondering at his absence, when success had been attained. When after a long search, they found him where the dead lay thickest, as happens with brave men, they honored him with songs and bore him away in the sight of the enemy. You might have seen bands of Goths shouting with dissonant cries and paying honor to the dead while the battle still raged. Tears were shed, but such as they were accustomed to devote to brave men. It was death indeed, but the Huns are witness that it was a glorious one. It was a death whereby one might well suppose the pride of the enemy would be lowered, when they beheld the body of so great a king borne forth with fitting honors. And so the Goths, still continuing the rites due to Theodorid, bore forth the royal majesty with sounding arms, and valiant Thorismud, as befitted a son, honored the glorious spirit of his dear father by following his remains.

When this was done, Thorismud was eager to take vengeance for his father's death on the remaining Huns, being moved to this both by the pain of bereavement and the impulse of that valor for which he was noted. Yet he consulted with the Patrician Aetius (for he was an older man and of more mature wisdom) with regard to what he ought to do next. But Aetius feared that if the Huns were totally destroyed by the Goths, the Roman Empire would be overwhelmed, and urgently advised him to return to his own dominions to take up the rule which his father had left. Otherwise his brothers might seize their father's possessions and obtain the power over the Visigoths. In this case Thorismud would have to fight fiercely and, what is worse, disastrously with his own countrymen. Thorismud accepted the advice without perceiving its double meaning, but followed it with an eye towards his own advantage. So he left the Huns and returned to Gaul. Thus while human frailty rushes into suspicion, it often loses an opportunity of doing great things.

But Attila took occasion from the withdrawal of the Visigoths, observing what he had often desired—that his enemies were divided. At length feeling secure, he moved forward his array to attack the Romans. As his first move he besieged the city of Aquileia, the metropolis of Venetia, which is situated on a point or tongue of the land by the Adriatic Sea. On the eastern side its walls are washed by the river Natissa, flowing from Mount Piccis. The siege was long and fierce, but of no avail, since the bravest soldiers of the Romans withstood him from within. At last his army was discontented and eager to withdraw. Attila chanced to be walking around the walls, considering whether to break camp or delay longer, and noticed that the white birds, namely, the storks, who build their nests in the gables of houses, were bearing their young from the city and, contrary to their custom, were carrying them out into the country. Being a shrewd observer of events, he understood this and said to his soldiers: "You see the birds foresee the future. They are leaving the city sure to perish and are forsaking strongholds doomed to fall by reason of imminent peril. Do not think this a meaningless or uncertain sign; fear, arising from the things they foresee, has changed their custom." Why say more? He inflamed the hearts of his soldiers to attack Aquileia again. Constructing battering rams and bringing to bear all manner of engines of war, they quickly forced their way into the city, laid it waste, divided the spoil and so cruelly devastated it as scarcely to leave a trace to be seen. Then growing bolder and still thirsting for Roman blood, the Huns raged madly through the remaining cities of the Veneti. They also laid waste Mediolanum, the metropolis of Liguria, once an imperial city, and gave over Ticinum to a like fate. Then they destroyed the neighboring country in their frenzy and demolished almost the whole of Italy.

Attila's mind had been bent on going to Rome. But his followers, as the historian Priscus relates, took him away, not out of regard for the city to which they were hostile, but because they remembered the case of Alaric, the former king of the Visigoths. They distrusted the good fortune of their own king, inasmuch as Alaric did not live long after the sack of Rome, but straightway departed this life. Therefore while Attila's spirit was wavering in doubt between going and not going, and he still lingered to ponder the matter, an embassy came to him from Rome to seek peace. Pope Leo himself came to meet him in the Ambuleian district of the Veneti at the well-travelled ford of the river Mincius. Then Attila quickly put aside his usual fury, turned back on the way he had advanced from beyond the Danube and departed with the promise of peace. But above all he declared and avowed with threats that he would bring worse things upon Italy, unless they sent him Honoria, the sister of the Emperor Valentinian and daughter of Augusta Placidia, with her due share of the royal wealth. For it was said that Honoria, although bound to chastity for the honor of the imperial court and kept in constraint by command of her brother, had secretly despatched a eunuch to summon Attila that she might have his protection against her brother's power; a shameful thing, indeed, to get license for her passion at the cost of the public weal.

So Attila returned to his own country, seeming to regret the peace and to be vexed at the cessation of war. For he sent ambassadors to Marcian, Emperor of the East, threatening to devastate the provinces, because that which had been promised him by Theodosius, a former emperor, was in no wise performed, and saying that he would show himself more cruel to his foes than ever. But as he was shrewd and crafty, he threatened in one direction and moved his army in another; for in the midst of these preparations he turned his face towards the Visigoths who had yet to feel his vengeance. But here he had not the same success as against the Romans. Hastening back by a different way than before, he decided to reduce to his sway that part of the Alani which was settled across the river Loire, in order that by attacking them, and thus changing the aspect of the war, he might become a more terrible menace to the Visigoths. Accordingly he started from the provinces of Dacia and Pannonia, where the Huns were then dwelling with various subject peoples, and moved his array against the Alani. But Thorismud, king of the Visigoths, with like quickness of thought perceived Attila's trick. By forced marches he came to the Alani before him, and was well prepared to check the advance of Attila when he came after him. They joined battle in almost the same way as before at the Catalaunian Plains, and Thorismud dashed his hopes of victory, for he routed him and drove him from the land without a triumph, compelling him to flee to his own country. Thus while Attila, the famous leader and lord of many victories, sought to blot out the fame of his destroyer and in this way to annul what he had suffered at the hands of the Visigoths, he met a second defeat and retreated ingloriously. Now after the bands of the Huns had been repulsed by the Alani, without any hurt to his own men, Thorismud departed for Tolosa. There he established a settled peace for his people and in the third year of his reign fell sick. While letting blood from a vein, he was betrayed to his death by Ascalc, a client, who told his foes that his weapons were out of reach. Yet grasping a foot-stool in the one hand he had free, he became the avenger of his own blood by slaying several of those that were lying in wait for him.

◆ ◆ ◆

Since I have followed the stories of my ancestors and retold to the best of my ability the tale of the period when both tribes, Ostrogoths and Visigoths, were united, and then clearly treated of the Visigoths apart from the Ostrogoths, I must now return to those ancient Scythian abodes and set forth in like manner the ancestry and deeds of the Ostrogoths. It appears that at the death of their king, Hermanaric, they were made a separate people by the departure of the Visigoths, and remained in their country subject to the sway of the Huns, yet Vinitharius of the Amali retained the insignia of his rule. He rivalled the valor of his grandfather Vultuulf, although he had not the good fortune of Hermanaric. But disliking to remain under the rule of the Huns, he withdrew a little from them and strove to show his courage by moving his forces against the country of the Antes. When he attacked them, he was beaten in the first encounter. Thereafter he did valiantly and, as a terrible example, crucified their king, named Boz, together with his sons and seventy nobles, and left their bodies hanging there to double the fear of those who had surrendered. When he had ruled with such license for barely a year, Balamber, king of the Huns, would no longer endure it, but sent for Gesimund, son of Hunimund the Great. Now Gesimund, together with a great part of the Goths, remained under the rule of the Huns, being mindful of his oath of fidelity. Balamber renewed his alliance with him and let his army up against Vinitharius. After a long contest, Vinitharius prevailed in the first and second conflict, nor can any say how great slaughter he made of the army of the Huns. But in the third battle when they met each other unexpectedly at the river named Erac, Balamber shot an arrow and wounded Vinitharius in the head, so that he died. Then Balamber took to himself in marriage Vadamerca, the granddaughter of Vinitharius, and finally ruled all the people of the Goths as his peaceful subjects, but in such a way that one ruler of their own number always held the power over the Gothic race, though subject to the Huns.

And later, after the death of Vinitharius, Hunimund ruled them, the son of Hermanaric, a mighty king of yore; a man fierce in war and of famous personal beauty, who afterwards fought successfully against the race of the Suavi. And when he died, his son Thorismud succeeded him, in the very bloom of youth. In the second year of his rule he moved an army against the Gepidae and won a great victory over them, but is said to have been killed by falling from his horse. When he was dead, the Ostrogoths mourned for him so deeply that for forty years no other king succeeded in his place, and during all this time they had ever on their lips the tale of his memory. Now as time went on, Valamir grew to man's estate. He was the son of Thorismud's cousin Vandalarius. For his son Beremud, as we have said before, at last grew to despise the race of the Ostrogoths because of the overlordship of the Huns, and so had followed the tribe of the Visigoths to the western country, and it was from him Veteric was descended. Veteric also had a son Eutharic, who married Amalasuentha, the daughter of Theodoric, thus uniting again the stock of the Amali which had divided long ago. Eutharic begat Athalaric and Mathesuentha. But since Athalaric died in the years of his boyhood, Mathesuentha was taken to Constantinople by her second husband, namely Germanus, a nephew of the Emperor Justinian, and bore a posthumous son, whom she named Germanus.

But that the order we have taken for our history may run its due course, we must return to the stock of Vandalarius, which put forth three branches. This Vandalarius, the great grandnephew of Hermanaric and cousin of the aforesaid Thorismud, vaunted himself among the race of the Amali because he had begotten three sons, Valamir, Thiudimer and Vidimer. Of these Valamir ascended the throne after his parents, though the Huns as yet held the power over the Goths in general as among other nations. It was pleasant to behold the concord of these three brothers; for the admirable Thiudimer serves as a soldier for the empire of his brother Valamir, and Valamir bade honors be given him, while Vidimer was eager to serve them both. Thus regarding one another with common affection, not one was wholly deprived of the kingdom which two of them held in mutual peace. Yet, as has often been said, they ruled in such a way that they respected the dominion of Attila, king of the Huns. Indeed they could not have refused to fight against their kinsmen the Visigoths, and they must even have committed parricide at their lord's command. There was no way whereby any Scythian tribe could have been wrested from the power of the Huns, save by the death of Attila—an event the Romans and all other nations desired. Now his death was as base as his life was marvellous.

Shortly before he died, as the historian Priscus relates, he took in marriage a very beautiful girl named Ildico, after countless other wives, as was the custom of his race. He had given himself up to excessive joy at his wedding, and as he lay on his back, heavy with wine and sleep, a rush of superfluous blood, which would ordinarily have flowed from his nose, streamed in deadly course down his throat and killed him, since it was hindered in the usual passages. Thus did drunkenness put a disgraceful end to a king renowned in war. On the following day, when a great part of the morning was spent, the royal attendants suspected some ill and, after a great uproar, broke in the doors. There they found the death of Attila accomplished by an effusion of blood, without any wound, and the girl with downcast face weeping beneath her veil. Then, as is the custom of that race, they plucked out the hair of their heads and made their faces hideous with deep wounds, that the renowned warrior might be mourned, not by effeminate wailings and tears, but by the blood of men. Moreover a wondrous thing took place in connection with Attila's death. For in a dream some god stood at the side of Marcian, Emperor of the East, while he was disquieted about his fierce foe, and showed him the bow of Attila broken in that same night, as if to intimate that the race of Huns owed much to that weapon. This account the historian Priscus says he accepts upon truthful evidence. For so terrible was Attila thought to be to great empires that the gods announced his death to rulers as a special boon.

◆ ◆ ◆

Let us now return to the tribe with which we started, namely the Ostrogoths, who were dwelling in Pannonia under their king Valamir and his brothers Thiudimer and Vidimer. Although their territories were separate, yet their plans were one. For Valamir dwelt between the rivers Scarniunga and Aqua Nigra, Thiudimer near Lake Pelso and Vidimer between them both. Now it happened that the sons of Attila, regarding the Goths as deserters from their rule, came against them as though they were seeking fugitive slaves, and attacked Valamir alone, when his brothers knew nothing of it. He sustained their attack, though he had but few supporters, and after harassing them a long time, so utterly overwhelmed them that scarcely any portion of the enemy remained. The remnant turned in flight and sought the parts of Scythia which border on the stream of the river Danaper, which the Huns call in their own tongue the Var. Thereupon he sent a messenger of good tidings to his brother Thiudimer, and on the very day the messenger arrived he found even greater joy in the house of Thiudimer. For on that day his son Theodoric was born, of a concubine Erelieva indeed, and yet a child of good hope.

Now after no great time King Valamir and his brothers Thiudimer and Vidimer sent an embassy to the Emperor Marcian, because the usual gifts which they received like a New Year's present from the Emperor, to preserve the compact of peace, were slow in arriving. And they found that Theodoric, son of Triarius, a man of Gothic blood also, but born of another stock, not of the Amali, was in great favor, together with his followers. He was allied in friendship with the Romans and obtained an annual bounty, while they themselves were merely held in disdain. Thereat they were aroused to frenzy and took up arms. They roved through almost the whole of Illyricum and laid it waste in their search for spoil. Then the Emperor quickly changed his mind and returned to his former state of friendship. He sent an embassy to give them the past gifts, as well as those now due, and furthermore promised to give these gifts in future without any dispute. From the Goths the Romans received as a hostage of peace Theodoric, the young child of Thiudimer, whom we have mentioned above. He had now attained the age of seven years and was entering upon his eighth. While his father hesitated about giving him up, his uncle Valamir besought him to do it, hoping that peace between the Romans and the Goths might thus be assured. Therefore Theodoric was given as a hostage by the Goths and brought to the city of Constantinople to the Emperor Leo and, being a goodly child, deservedly gained the imperial favor.

Now after firm peace was established between Goths and Romans, the Goths found that the possessions they had received from the Emperor were not sufficient for them. Furthermore, they were eager to display their wonted valor, and so began to plunder the neighboring races round about them, first attacking the Sadagis who held the interior of Pannonia. When Dintzic, king of the Huns, a son of Attila, learned this, he gathered to him the few who still seemed to have remained under his sway, namely, the Ultzinzures, the Angisciri, the Bittugures and the Bardores. Coming to Bassina, a city of Pannonia, he beleaguered it and began to plunder its territory. Then the Goths at once abandoned the expedition they had planned against the Sadagis, turned upon the Huns and drove them so ingloriously from their own land that those who remained have been in dread of the arms of the Goths from that time down to the present day.

When the tribe of the Huns was at last subdued by the Goths, Hunimund, chief of the Suavi, who was crossing over to plunder Dalmatia, carried off some cattle of the Goths which were straying over the plains; for Dalmatia was near Suavia and not far distant from the territory of Pannonia, especially that part where the Goths were then staying. So then, as Hunimund was returning with the Suavi to his own country, after he had devastated Dalmatia, Thiudimer the brother of Valamir, king of the Goths, kept watch on their line of march. Not that he grieved so much over the loss of his cattle, but he feared that if the Suavi obtained this plunder with impunity, they would proceed to greater license. So in the dead of night, while they were asleep, he made an unexpected attack upon them, near Lake Pelso. Here he so completely crushed them that he took captive and sent into slavery under the Goths even Hunimund, their king, and all of his army who had escaped the sword. Yet as he was a great lover of mercy, he granted pardon after taking vengeance and became reconciled to the Suavi. He adopted as his son the same man whom he had taken captive, and sent him back with his followers into Suavia. But Hunimund was unmindful of his adopted father's kindness. After some time he brought forth a plot he had contrived and aroused the tribe of the Sciri, who then dwelt above the Danube and abode peaceably with the

Goths. So the Sciri broke off their alliance with them, took up arms, joined themselves to Hunimund and went out to attack the race of the Goths. Thus war came upon the Goths who were expecting no evil, because they relied upon both of their neighbors as friends. Constrained by necessity they took up arms and avenged themselves and their injuries by recourse to battle. In this battle, as King Valamir rode on his horse before the line to encourage his men, the horse was wounded and fell, overthrowing its rider. Valamir was quickly pierced by his enemies' spears and slain. Thereupon the Goths proceeded to exact vengeance for the death of their king, as well as for the injury done them by the rebels. They fought in such wise that there remained of all the race of the Sciri only a few who bore the name, and they with disgrace. Thus were all destroyed.

The kings [of the Suavi], Hunimund and Alaric, fearing the destruction that had come upon the Sciri, next made war upon the Goths, relying upon the aid of the Sarmatians, who had come to them as auxiliaries with their kings Beuca and Babai. They summoned the last remnants of the Sciri, with Edica and Hunuulf, their chieftains, thinking they would fight the more desperately to avenge themselves. They had on their side the Gepidae also, as well as no small reënforcements from the race of the Rugi and from others gathered here and there. Thus they brought together a great host at the river Bolia in Pannonia and encamped there. Now when Valamir was dead, the Goths fled to Thiudimer, his brother. Although he had long ruled along with his brothers, yet he took the insignia of his increased authority and summoned his younger brother Vidimer and shared with him the cares of war, resorting to arms under compulsion. A battle was fought and the party of the Goths was found to be so much the stronger that the plain was drenched in the blood of their fallen foes and looked like a crimson sea. Weapons and corpses, piled up like hills, covered the plain for more than ten miles. When the Goths saw this, they rejoiced with joy unspeakable, because by this great slaughter of their foes they had avenged the blood of Valamir their king and the injury done themselves. But those of the innumerable and motley throng of the foe who were able to escape, though they got away, nevertheless came to their own land with difficulty and without glory.

After a certain time, when the wintry cold was at hand, the river Danube was frozen over as usual. For a river like this freezes so hard that it will support like a solid rock an army of foot-soldiers and wagons and sledges and whatsoever vehicles there may be—nor is there need of skiffs and boats. So when Thiudimer, king of the Goths, saw that it was frozen, he led his army across the Danube and appeared unexpectedly to the Suavi from the rear. Now this country of the Suavi has on the east the Baiovari, on the west the Franks, on the south the Burgundians and on the north the Thuringians. With the Suavi there were present the Alamanni, then their confederates, who also ruled the Alpine heights, whence several streams flow into the Danube, pouring in with a great rushing sound. Into a place thus fortified King Thiudimer led his army in the winter-time and conquered, plundered and almost subdued the race of the Suavi as well as the Alamanni, who were mutually banded together. Thence he returned as victor to his own home in Pannonia and joyfully received his son Theodoric, once given as hostage to Constantinople and now sent back by the Emperor Leo with great gifts. Now Theodoric had reached man's estate, for he was eighteen years of age and his boyhood was ended. So he summoned certain of his father's adherents and took to himself from the people his friends and retainers —almost six thousand men. With these he crossed the Danube, without his father's knowledge, and marched against Babai, king of the Sarmatians, who had just won a victory over Camundus, a general of the Romans, and was ruling with insolent pride. Theodoric came upon him and slew him, and taking as booty his slaves and treasure, returned victorious to his father. Next he invaded the city of Singidunum, which the Sarmatians themselves had seized, and did not return it to the Romans, but reduced it to his own sway.

Then as the spoil taken from one and another of the neighboring tribes diminished, the Goths began to lack food and clothing, and peace became distasteful to men for whom war had long furnished the necessaries of life. So all the Goths approached their king Thiudimer and, with a great outcry, begged him to lead forth his army in whatsoever direction he might wish. He summoned his brother and, after casting lots, bade him go into the country of Italy, where at this time Glycerius ruled as emperor, saying that he himself as the mightier would go to the east against a mightier empire. And so it happened. Thereupon Vidimer entered the land of Italy, but soon paid the last debt of fate and departed from earthly affairs, leaving his son and namesake Vidimer to succeed him. The Emperor Glycerius bestowed gifts upon Vidimer and persuaded him to go from Italy to Gaul, which was then harassed on all sides by various races, saying that their own kinsmen, the Visigoths, there ruled a neighboring kingdom. And what more? Vidimer accepted the gifts and, obeying the command of the Emperor Glycerius, pressed on to Gaul. Joining with his kinsmen the Visigoths, they again formed one body, as they had been long ago. Thus they held Gaul and Spain by their own right and so defended them that no other race won the mastery there.

But Thiudimer, the elder brother, crossed the river Savus with his men, threatening the Sarmatians and their soldiers with war if any should resist him. From fear of this they kept quiet; moreover they were powerless in the face of so great a host. Thiudimer, seeing prosperity everywhere awaiting him, invaded Naissus, the first city of Illyricum. He was joined by his son Theodoric and the Counts Astat and Invilia, and sent them to Ulpiana by way of Castrum Herculis. Upon their arrival the town surrendered, as did Stobi later; and several places of Illyricum, inaccessible to them at first, were thus made easy of approach. For they first plundered and then ruled by right of war Heraclea and Larissa, cities of Thessaly. But Thiudimer the king, perceiving his own good fortune and that of his son, was not content with this alone, but set forth from the city of Naissus, leaving only a few men behind as a guard. He himself advanced to Thessalonica, where Hilarianus the Patrician, appointed by the Emperor, was stationed with his army. When Hilarianus beheld Thessalonica surrounded by an entrenchment and saw that he could not resist attack, he sent an embassy to Thiudimer the king and by the offer of gifts turned him aside from destroying the city. Then the Roman general entered upon a truce with the Goths and of his own accord handed over to them those places they inhabited, namely Cyrrhus, Pella, Europus, Methone, Pydna, Beroea, and another which is called Dium. So the Goths and their king laid aside their arms, consented to peace and became quiet. Soon after these events, King Thiudimer was seized with a mortal illness in the city of Cyrrhus. He called the Goths to himself, appointed Theodoric his son as heir of his kingdom and presently departed this life.

When the Emperor Zeno heard that Theodoric had been appointed king over his own people, he received the news with pleasure and invited him to come and visit him in the city, sending an escort of honor. Receiving Theodoric with all due respect, he placed him among the princes of his palace. After some time Zeno increased his dignity by adopting him as his son-at-arms and gave him a triumph in the city at his expense. Theodoric was made Consul Ordinary also, which is well known to be the supreme good and highest honor in the world. Nor was this all, for Zeno set up before the royal palace an equestrian statue to the glory of this great man.

Now while Theodoric was in alliance by treaty with the Empire of Zeno and was himself enjoying every comfort in the city, he heard that his tribe, dwelling as we have said in Illyricum, was not altogether satisfied or content. So he chose rather to seek a living by his own exertions, after the manner customary to his race, rather than to enjoy the advantages of the Roman Empire in luxurious ease while his tribe lived apart. After pondering these matters, he said to the Emperor: "Though I lack nothing in serving your Empire, yet if Your Piety deem it worthy, be pleased to hear the desire of my heart." And when as usual he had been granted permission to speak freely, he said: "The western country, long ago governed by the rule of your ancestors and predecessors, and that city which was the head and mistress of the world—wherefore is it now shaken by the tyranny of the Torcilingi and the Rugi? Send me there with my race. Thus if you but say the word, you may be freed from the burden of expense here, and, if by the Lord's help I shall conquer, the fame of

Your Piety shall be glorious there. For it is better that I, your servant and your son, should rule that kingdom, receiving it as a gift from you if I conquer, than that one whom you do not recognize should oppress your Senate with his tyrannical yoke and a part of the republic with slavery. For if I prevail, I shall retain it as your grant and gift; if I am conquered, Your Piety will lose nothing—nay, as I have said, it will save the expense I now entail." Although the Emperor was grieved that he should go, yet when he heard this he granted what Theodoric asked, for he was unwilling to cause him sorrow. He sent him forth enriched by great gifts and commended to his charge the Senate and the Roman People.

Therefore Theodoric departed from the royal city and returned to his own people. In company with the whole tribe of the Goths, who gave him their unanimous consent, he set out for Hesperia. He went in straight march through Sirmium to the places bordering on Pannonia and, advancing into the territory of Venetia as far as the bridge of the Sontius, encamped there. When he had halted there for some time to rest the bodies of his men and pack-animals, Odoacer sent an armed force against him, which he met on the plains of Verona and destroyed with great slaughter. Then he broke camp and advanced through Italy with greater boldness. Crossing the river Po, he pitched camp near the royal city of Ravenna, about the third milestone from the city in the place called Pineta. When Odoacer saw this, he fortified himself within the city. He frequently harassed the army of the Goths at night, sallying forth stealthily with his men, and this not once or twice, but often; and thus he struggled for almost three whole years. But he labored in vain, for all Italy at last called Theodoric its lord and the Empire obeyed his nod. But Odoacer, with his few adherents and the Romans who were present, suffered daily from war and famine in Ravenna. Since he accomplished nothing, he sent an embassy and begged for mercy. Theodoric first granted it and afterwards deprived him of his life.

It was in the third year after his entrance into Italy, as we have said, that Theodoric, by advice of the Emperor Zeno, laid aside the garb of a private citizen and the dress of his race and assumed a costume with a royal mantle, as he had now become the ruler over both Goths and Romans. He sent an embassy to Lodoin, king of the Franks, and asked for his daughter Audefleda in marriage. Lodoin freely and gladly gave her, and also his sons Celdebert and Heldebert and Thiudebert, believing that by this alliance a league would be formed and that they would be associated with the race of the Goths. But that union was of no avail for peace and harmony, for they fought fiercely with each other again and again for the lands of the Goths; but never did the Goths yield to the Franks while Theodoric lived.

3. *Cassiodorus: Variae*

Flavius Magnus Aurelius Cassiodorus Senator (c.485–c.580) belonged to a distinguished Roman family which for four generations had served Roman emperors and their barbarian successors in the highest positions of state. Cassiodorus was no exception, successively serving the Ostrogothic Kings Theodoric, Theodohad, and Witigis in various administrative capacities. In about A.D. 537 Cassiodorus retired from public life to return to his home in southern Italy where he founded the famous monastery of Vivarium. There he collected the finest library of the time, the product of his new role as a conscious transmitter of classical and Christian antiquity to the new age. For Cassiodorus was the first to systematically utilize "the vast leisure of the convent for the preservation of divine and human learning and for its transmission to posterity." From his pen, or those of his disciples, came a great corpus of translations from the Greek—historical works, biblical commentaries, theological tracts—which may have otherwise been lost or at least unintelligible to a west now ignorant of the Greek language. It was at Vivarium that the first complete text of Jerome's Vulgate was compiled and arranged by chapter and verse. Cassiodorus also wrote original works of which the most important was his *Introduction to Divine and Human Readings.* This was designed to be an introductory manual for the study of theology and the liberal arts and was widely used as such in the early Middle Ages.

Equally important are the literary productions of his early years. The lost Gothic History, written between A.D. 518–21 served as the principal source for Jordanes (see above). Above all, there is the collection of official letters written by Cassiodorus as *Quaestor,* Master of Offices and Praetorian Praefect which go under the title of *Variae.* Together they form the best source for the history of Ostrogothic Italy and provide the most detailed knowledge we have of the conditions in any of the barbarian successor states in the west.

The small selection from the *Variae* given below has been taken from the translation of Thomas Hodgkin (London: H. Frowde, 1886).

I, 16. Theodoric to Julianus, *Comes Patrimonii* (508?)

IT IS an excellent investment to do a generous thing to our subjects. The Apulian "Conductores" [farmers of the royal domain] have represented to us with tears that their crops have been burned by hostile invaders. We therefore authorize you to deduct at the next Indiction what shall seem the right proportion for these losses from the amount due to us. See, however, that our revenue sustains no unnecessary loss. We are touched by the losses of the suppliants, but we ought on the other hand to share their profits.

II, 5. Theodoric to Faustus, *Praepositus*

We are always generous, and sometimes out of clemency we bestow our gifts on persons who have no claim upon us. How much more fitting is it then that the servants of the State should receive our gifts promptly! Wherefore, pray let your Magnificence see to it that the sixty soldiers who are keeping guard in the fastnesses of Aosta receive their *annonae* [formerly, and possibly here, a tax levied in kind for the provisioning of the army] without delay. Think what a life of hardship the soldier leads in those frontier forts for the general peace, thus, as at the gate of the Province, shutting out the entry of the barbarous nations. He must be ever on the alert who seeks to keep out the Barbarians. For fear alone checks these men, whom honor will not keep back.

II, 7. Theodoric to Suna, *Vir Illustris* and Count (507/11)

Let nothing lie useless which may redound to the beauty of the City. Let your Illustrious Magnificence therefore cause the blocks of marble which are everywhere lying about in ruins to be wrought up into the walls by the hands of the workmen whom I send herewith. Only take care to use only those stones which have really fallen from public buildings, as we do not wish to appropriate private property, even for the glorification of the City.

II, 16. Theodoric to the Senate 1 (507/11)

[Theodoric has appointed Venantius, *vir illustris,* to be *Comes domesticorum* because of the services of his father. This letter is the notification to the Senate. As was customary the letter recounts the merits of the appointee, in this case of his father, who was apparently involved in the original assessment of the *Tertiae*, the land division between the Ostrogoths and the Romans. The first part is omitted.]

We especially like to remember how in the assignment of the "thirds" he joined both the possessions and the hearts of Goths and Romans alike. For whereas men are wont to come into collision on account of their being neighbours, with these men the common holding of their farms proved in practice a reason for concord. Thus it has happened that while the two nations have been living in common they have concurred in the same desires. Lo! a new fact, and one wholly laudable. The friendship of the lords has been joined with the division of the soil; amity has grown out of the loss of the Provincials, and by the land a defender has been gained whose occupation of part guarantees the quiet enjoyment of the whole. One law includes them: one equal administration rules them: for it is necessary that sweet affection should grow between those who always keep the boundaries which have been allotted them.

II, 24. Theodoric to the Senate (507/11)

We hear with sorrow, by the report of the Provincial Judges, that you, the Fathers of the Senate, who ought to set an example to your sons (the ordinary citizens), have been so remiss in the payment of taxes that on this first collection nothing, or next to nothing, has been brought in from any Senatorial house. Thus a crushing weight has fallen on the lower orders, who have had to make good your deficiencies and have been distraught by the violence of the tax-gatherers.

Now then, O Conscript Fathers, who owe as much duty to the [public weal] as we do, pay the taxes for which each one of you is liable, to the Procurators appointed in each Province, by three installments. Or, if you prefer—and it used to be accounted a privilege—pay all at once into the chest of the Vicarius. And let this following edict be published, that all the Provincials may know that they are not to be imposed upon and that they are invited to state their grievances.

III, 9. Theodoric to the *Possessores, Defensores,* and *Curiales* Dwelling at Aestunae (507/11)

We wish to build new edifices without despoiling the old. But we are informed that in your municipality there are blocks of masonry and columns formerly belonging to some building now lying absolutely useless and unhonoured. If this be so, send these slabs of marble and columns by all means to Ravenna, that they may be again made beautiful and take their place in a building there.

III, 17. Theodoric to All the Gaulish Provinces (508)

During the struggle between the Franks and Visigoths in Gaul, Theodoric occupied Septimania. Hence the following edict.

Obey the Roman customs. You are now by God's blessing restored to your ancient freedom; put off the barbarian; clothe yourselves with the morals of the toga; unlearn cruelty, that you may not be unworthy to be our subjects. We are sending you . . . Gemellus, as Vicarius Praefectorum, a man of tried worth, who we trust will be guilty of no crime, because he knows he would thereby seriously displease us. Obey his commands therefore. Do not dislike the reign of Law because it is new to you, after the aimless seethings of Barbarism.

III, 23. Theodoric to Colossaeus, *Vir Illustris* and *Count* (507/11)

We delight to entrust our mandates to persons of approved character.

We are sending you 'with the dignity of the illustrious belt' to Pannonia Sirmiensis, an old habitation of the Goths. Let that Province be induced to welcome her old defenders, even as she used gladly to obey our ancestors. Show forth the justice of the Goths, a nation happily situated for praise, since it is theirs to unite the forethought of the Romans and the virtue of the Barbarians.

V, 14. Theodoric to Severianus, *Vir Illustris* (523/26)

We send you to redress the long-standing grievances of the Possessores of the Province of Suavia, to which we have not been able to apply a remedy.

(1) It appears that some of the chief Possessores are actually making a profit out of the taxes, imposing heavy burdens on their poorer neighbours and not honestly accounting for the receipts to us. See that this is put right, that the land-tax is fairly and equitably reimposed according to the ability of each Possessor, and that those who have been oppressing their neighbours heal the wounds which they have made.

(2) See also that a strict account is rendered by all Defensores, Curiales and Possessores of any receipts on behalf of the Public Treasury. If a Possessor can show that he paid his tax for the now expired eighth Indiction (514–515), and the money has not reached our Treasury, find out the defaulter and punish his crime.

(4) Men who were formerly Barbarians, who have married Roman wives and acquired property in land, are to be compelled to pay their Indictions and other taxes to the Public Treasury just like any Provincials.

IX, 2. Edict of King Athalaric (527?)

The body of the State, is so tempered together that if one member suffers all the members suffer with it. The Curiales, whose name is derived from their care and forethought, are, we are told, molested by hostile proceedings, so that what was bestowed upon them as an honour turns rather to their injury. What scandalous injustice! What an insupportable evil! that he who ought to have benefited the State by his services, should often lose both fortune and liberty.

Wherefore by this edict we decree that if any Curialis suffer oppression, if anyone, without the express warrant of ourselves or the high officers of State whose business it is, inflict upon a Curialis any injury or loss of property, he shall pay a fine of ten pounds of gold, to go to the benefit of the person thus oppressed. . . . The Curialis must then give additional diligence to the discharge of his public duties, since his debt to the State is, as it were, increased by the protection which we are thus affording him. As for the farms of the Curiales, in connection with which the greatest frauds are practised on poor men, let no one seek to obtain them by an unlawful purchase. . . . The Judges must help the Curiales against the molestations of Saiones [Gothic officials] and other officials. It is a grievous offence, when the very person to whom is entrusted the duty of defending the weak, himself turns oppressor.

IX, 4. Athalaric to Abundantius, Praetorian Prefect (527?)

The pietas of the King is happily shown in moderating the sentence of the law, where for certain reasons it bears with especial hardness on anyone. The Curiales have peculiar advantages in their opportunity of being thus liberated by the Sovereign from the performance of their duties. It is reasonable to release a Curialis whose health prevents him from fulfilling his appointed task; and a numerous Curia will never miss a few names out of so large a number.

Remitted to the ranks of mere Possessores they will now be liable to the same demands which formerly [as members of the Curia] they made upon others. They will now dread the face of the tax-collector, and will begin to fear the mandates by which formerly they made themselves feared. Still this is a sign of their past good life, that they are willing to live without office among a population whose dislike they are not conscious of having incurred, and under old colleagues whom they know that they have not incited to an abuse of their powers.

4. *Sidonius Apollinaris: Letters*

Gaius Sollius Apollinaris Sidonius (c.431–c.480) was a representative of a Gallic aristocratic family which had served the Empire for generations. Even at this late date Sidonius continued the tradition, receiving the usual education of his class and serving three emperors, Avitus (455–56), who was his father-in-law, Majorian (457–461) and Anthemius (467–72). In 469, probably while still a layman, Sidonius was elected Bishop of Clermont, then under the threat of a Visigothic siege. He heroically led the defense of his city for three years, for which he was subsequently imprisoned by King Euric. Later reinstated as bishop (476), he spent his few remaining years editing his letters for publication and ministering to his see, which revered him as a local saint for many generations afterwards.

We are largely indebted to Sidonius for our extensive knowledge of the closing years of Roman Gaul. He was the foremost literary figure of his day both as a poet and a letter writer. Since Sidonius was a man of affairs with a wide circle of friends, and since the letter was a literary genre as well as a personal means of communication, the 147 letters he prepared for publication at the end of his life give us an invaluable picture of his time.

The following selection from Sidonius' *Letters* is from the translation of O. M. Dalton, *The Letters of Sidonius,* 2 vols. (Oxford: Clarendon Press, 1915). Reprinted by permission.

I, vi. To His Friend Eutropius (467)

I HAVE long wished to write, but feel the impulse more than ever now, when by the Christ's preventing grace, I am actually on the way to Rome. My sole motive, or at least my chief one, is to drag you from the slough of your domestic ease by an appeal to you to enter the imperial service.

Moreover, by the goodness of God, your age, your health of body and mind concur to fit you for the task; you have horses, arms, wardrobe, establishment, slaves in plenty; the one thing lacking, unless I greatly err, is the courage to begin. In your own home you are energetic enough; it is only at the idea of exile from it that a dull despondency intimidates you.

How can it fairly be described as exile, for one with blood of senators in his veins and with the effigies of ancestors in the trabea daily forced upon his sight, to visit Rome once in his prime—Rome the abode of law, the training-school of letters, the fount of honours, the head of the world, the motherland of freedom, the city unique upon earth, where none but the barbarian and the slave is foreign?

Shame on you now if you bury yourself among cow-keeping rustics, or grunting swineherds, as if it were the height of your felicity to feel the plough-handle tremble above the cleft furrow, or, bowed over your scythe, to spoil the meadow of its flowery wealth, or hoe the luxuriant vines with a face bent earthwards. Have done! awake! sleek ease has unstrung the sinews of your mind; raise it to higher things. Is it a less duty in a man of your descent to cultivate himself than his estate? In fine, what you are pleased to call a young man's exercise is really a relaxation only fit for broken soldiers, when their feeble hands exchange rusty sword for belated mattock.

You will have only yourself to thank if one day you stand, you a nobleman born, obscure in your white hairs behind your juniors seated in debate, if you smart under the speech of some poor man risen to honour by office, and with anguish see yourself distanced by those in whom it would once have been presumption to follow in your train. But why say more! Take my appeal as it is meant, and you shall find me at your side ready to anticipate and share your every effort.

I, viii. To His Friend Candidianus (468)

You congratulate me on my prolonged stay at Rome, though I note the touch of irony, and your wit at my expense. You say you are glad your old friend has at last seen the sun, since on the Saône his chances of a good look at it are few and far between. You abuse my misty Lyons, and deplore the days so cloaked by morning fog that the full heat of noon can scarcely unveil them. Now does this nonsense fitly come from a native of that oven of a town Cesena? You have shown your real opinion of your charming and convenient natal soil by leaving it. The midges of Po may pierce your ears; the city frogs may croak and swarm on every side, but you know very well that you are better off in exile at Ravenna than at home. In that marsh of yours the laws of everything are always the wrong way about; the waters stand and the walls fall, the towers float and the ships stick fast, the sick man walks and the doctor lies abed, the baths are chill and the houses blaze, the dead swim and the quick are dry, the powers are asleep and the thieves wide awake, the clergy live by usury and the Syrian chants the Psalms, business men turn soldiers and soldiers business men, old fellows play ball and young fellows hazard, eunuchs take to arms and rough allies to letters. And that is the kind of city you choose to settle in, a place that may boast a territory but little solid ground. Be kinder, therefore, to Transalpines who never provoked you; their climate wins too cheap a triumph if it shines only by comparison with such as yours.

III, iv. To His Friend Magnus Felix (473)

The bearer of this is Gozolas, a Jew, and a client of your excellency, a man I should like if I could only overcome my contempt for his sect. I write in great anxiety. Our town lives in terror of a sea of tribes which find in it an obstacle to their expansion and surge in arms all round it. We are exposed as a pitiful prey at the mercy of rival peoples, suspected by the Burgundians, almost in contact with the Goths; we have to face at once the fury of our assailants and the envy of our defenders. But of this more later. Only let me know that all goes well with you, and I shall be content. For though we may be punished in the sight of all men for some obscure offence, we are still generous enough of heart to desire for others all prosperity. If a man cannot wish others well in evil times he is no better than a captive; the enemy that takes him is his own unworthy nature.

III, viii. To His Friend Eucherius

I have the highest respect for the men of antiquity, but mere priority in time shall never lead me to place the virtues and the merits of our contemporaries upon a lower plane of excellence. It may be true that the Roman state has sunk to such extreme misery that it has ceased to reward its loyal sons; but I will not therefore admit that a Brutus or a Torquatus is never born into our age. You ask the purport of this declaration? You yourself shall point my moral, most capable of men; the state owes you the rewards which history applauds when granted to the great men of the past. Men ignorant of the facts had best refrain from carelessly conceived opinions; they had best abandon the obstinate habit of looking up to the men of old time and down on those of our own day. It is abundantly clear that the recognition which the state owes you is now long overdue. Yet what is there to wonder at in this, when a race of uncivilized allies directs the Roman power, yes, and bids fair to bring it crashing to the ground? We have men of rank and valour who excel anything we ourselves could hope, or our enemies believe. Aye, and they do the old deeds; but the reward is not forthcoming.

IV, i. To His Friend Probus (461–67)

You married my cousin, whence the first and principal tie between us; the cousinly relationship often leads to a stronger, purer, and more unmixed affection than that between two brothers. For when brothers' quarrels over property are once appeased, their children have no longer cause for disagreement, and so it often happens that cousins are the more deeply attached; the enmities arising from the partition of estates are over, the tie of blood relationship remains. The second link between us is intellectual, and formed by a similarity of studies; our literary taste is identical; we praise and blame the same things; a style approved or disapproved by one produces the same impression on the other. But I am presumptuous in venturing a comparison between my judgement and yours. It is common knowledge among young and old that you were my real master, though we were nominally both pupils of another. You were everybody's teacher in every branch of literature. All of us learned from you, except those who had not the brains, or could not do themselves proper justice; our epic poets derived from you their lofty vein, our comic poets their humour, our lyric poets their musical art; from you the orator drew his rhetoric, the historian his respect for truth, the satirist his pictorial gift, the grammarian his fidelity to rule, the panegyrist his plausibility, the sophist his gravity of style, the writer of epigram his petulance and point, the commentator his lucid method, the lawyer his obscurity. Heavens! how proud our respective fathers used to be when they saw that Christ had given you grace to teach and me to learn, that you not only did what lay within your power but also enjoyed the doing of it, and so deserved a name for goodness no less than a learned reputation. And indeed in your case Eusebius' house proved a veritable mint of the sciences and arts; you were there struck on a philosophical die, and to the delight of your own instructor were able to impart to the rest of us every phase of knowledge and of eloquent expression. Just as Plato the pupil was more expert than Socrates, so did you excel our good Eusebius. While he was maturing our tender, unformed and plastic youth with ruthless floggings, or trying to ground it on wholesome principles, there you were, a dialectician born, moving with Attic ease through all the categories of Aristotle.

Yet how admirable his principles were after all, how precious in possession! If only some migratory philosopher could export them to the Sigambri on their marshes, or the Alans of the Caucasus, or the mare-milking Geloni, the horny heart of all these stark and brutal folks, yes and all their frozen fibres, were surely thawed and softened, while we should cease to sneer and scoff, and tremble by turns at their stolidity and their ferocious natures, which now brook in bestial dullness, now burst into swift flame. Since, then, our family connexion and our studies thus unite us, preserve the laws of friendship unshaken, wherever your abode may be; though my home is far from yours, let our hearts draw nearer by virtue of this affection, which I for my part will keep inviolate as long as breath remains in my body.

IV, xvii. To His Friend Arbogast (c. 477)

Your friend Eminentius, honoured Lord, has delivered a letter dictated by yourself, admirable in style, and bearing in every line the evidence of three shining virtues. The first is the friendliness which leads you to esteem the lowly talents of one so far away, and so anxious to avoid publicity. The second is the modesty which makes you hyper-sensitive to blame, but deservedly wins you praise. The third is the gentle humour which makes you in the wittiest way accuse yourself of writing wretched stuff, whereas you have drunk at the well-spring of Roman eloquence, and no draughts from the Moselle can take the taste of Tiber from your mouth. You have had your conversations among barbarians, yet you permit no barbarism to pass your lips; in eloquence and valour you equal those ancient generals whose hands could wield the stylus no less skillfully than the sword. The Roman tongue is long banished from Belgium and the Rhine; but if its splendour has anywhere survived, it is surely with you; our jurisdiction is fallen into decay along the frontier, but while you live and preserve your eloquence, the Latin language stands unshaken. As I return your greeting, my heart is glad within me that our vanishing culture has left such traces with you; continue your assiduous studies, and you will feel more surely every day that the man of education is as much above the boor as the boor in his turn above the beast. Were I to obey your wish and send you a commentary on some part of the Scriptures, it would be sorry verbiage; you would do far better to direct your request to the clergy of your own district. They are venerable in years, approved in faith, known by works; they are ready in speech and tenacious in memory, my superiors in all sublimer gifts. Even if we leave out of the account the bishop of your city, a character of supreme perfection, blessed in possession and repute of all the virtues, you may far more appropriately consult on any kind of problem the celebrated fathers of the Church in Gaul; Lupus and Auspicius are both within your reach, and however inquisitive you may be, you will not get to the bottom of a learning such as theirs. In any case, you must pardon me for disobeying you in this matter, and that not only out of kindliness, but from simple justice; for if it is fair that you should escape from incompetence, it is equally right that I should avoid conceit.

IV, xx. To His Friend Domnicius (c.470)

You take such pleasure in the sight of arms and those who wear them, that I can imagine your delight if you could have seen the young prince Sigismer [probably a Frank] on his way to the palace of his father-in-law in the guise of a bridegroom or suitor in all the pomp and bravery of the tribal fashion. His own steed with its caparisons, other steeds laden with flashing gems, paced before and after; but the conspicuous interest in the procession centered in the prince himself, as with a charming modesty he went afoot amid his bodyguard and footmen, in flame-red mantle, with much glint of ruddy gold, and gleam of snowy silken tunic, his fair hair, red cheeks and white skin according with the three hues of his equipment. But the chiefs and allies who bore him company were dread of aspect, even thus on peace intent. Their feet were laced in boots of bristly hide reaching to the heels; ankles and legs were exposed. They wore tight tunics of varied colour hardly descending to their bare knees, the sleeves covering only the upper arm. Green mantles they had with crimson borders; baldrics supported swords hung from their shoulders, and pressed on sides covered with cloaks of skin secured by brooches. No small part of their adornment consisted of their arms; in their hand they grasped barbed spears and missile axes; their left sides were guarded by shields, which flashed with tawny golden bosses and snowy silver borders, betraying at once their wealth and their good taste. Though the business in hand was wedlock, Mars was no whit less prominent in all this pomp than Venus. Why need I say more? Only your presence was wanting to the full enjoyment of so fine a spectacle. For when I saw that you had missed the things you love to see, I longed to have you with me in all the impatience of your longing soul.

V, ii. To His Friend Nymphidius (c. 472)

Claudianus Mamertus, the most accomplished of our Christian philosophers and the most learned man in the world, wrote not long ago a notable work in three volumes on the Nature of the Soul; in its embellishment and final elaboration he employed the method of the disposition and logical arrangement of profane philosophy, demonstrating that the nine Muses are not maidens at all, but Liberal Arts. The attentive reader discovers in his pages the real personified titles of the Nine, who of themselves and for themselves create their proper appellations. For in this book Grammar divides, and Rhetoric declaims; Arithmetic reckons, Geometry metes; Music balances, Logic disputes; Astrology predicts, Architecture constructs; Poetry attunes her measures. Pleased with the novelty of a theory like this, and kindled to enthusiasm by so much ripe wisdom, you had hardly seen the book before you asked to have it for a short time to examine and copy it and to make extracts; you promised to return it quickly, and your request was granted as soon as made. Now, it is far from fitting that I should be deceived in this matter, and that you should be the deceiver. It is high time for you to send the book back; if you liked it, you must have had enough of it by now; if you dislike it, more than enough. Whichever it be, you have to clear your reputation. If you mean to delay the return of a volume for which I have to ask you, I shall think you care more for the parchment than for the work.

V, v. To His Friend Syagrius

Though you descend in the male line from an ancestor who was not only consul—that is immaterial—but also (and here is the real point) a poet, from one whose literary achievement would certainly have gained him the honour of a statue, had it not been secured for him already by his official honours,—witness the finished verse that he has left us; and though on this side of his activity his descendants have proved themselves no wise degenerate; yet here we find you picking up a knowledge of the German tongue with the greatest of ease; the feat fills me with indescribable amazement.

I can recall the thoroughness of your education in liberal studies; I know with what a fervid eloquence you used to declaim before the rhetor. With such a training, how have you so quickly mastered the accent of a foreign speech, that after having your Virgil caned into you, and absorbing into your very system the opulent and flowing style of the varicose orator of Arpinum [Cicero], you soar out like a young falcon from the ancient eyrie?

You can hardly conceive how amused we all are to hear that, when you are by, not a barbarian but fears to perpetrate a barbarism in his own language. Old Germans bowed with age are said to stand astounded when they see you interpreting their German letters; they actually choose you for arbiter and mediator in their disputes. You are a new Solon in the elucidation of Burgundian law; like a new Amphion you attune a new lyre, an instrument of but three strings. You are popular on all sides; you are sought after; your society gives universal pleasure. You are chosen as adviser and judge; as soon as you utter a decision it is received with respect. In body and mind alike these people are as stiff as stocks and very hard to form; yet they delight to find in you, and equally delight to learn a Burgundian eloquence and a Roman spirit.

Let me end with a single caution to the cleverest of men. Do not allow these talents of yours to prevent you from devoting whatever time you can spare to reading. Let your critical taste determine you to preserve a balance between the two languages, holding fast to the one to prevent us making fun of you, and practising the other that you may have the laugh of us.

V, xv. To His Friend Ruricius

The usual salutations over, I at once urge upon your notice the claims of our bookseller, because I have made discriminating and unbiased trial of the man, proving him to my complete satisfaction at once loyal in sentiment and alert in service to our common master—yourself. He brings in person the manuscript of the Heptateuch all written out by his own hand with the utmost neatness and rapidity, though I read it through myself and made corrections. He also brings a volume of the Prophets; this was edited by him in my absence, and with his own hand purged of corrupt additions. The scholar who had promised him assistance in reading out from another text, was only able to perform his task in part; I fancy illness prevented him from carrying out his undertaking. It remains for you by encouragement or promise of your influence to show appropriate recognition of a servant who has done his best to satisfy, and deserves to succeed; and if this is in proportion to his arduous task, he will soon begin to look for his reward. All that I ask for the moment is your benevolence towards him; it is for you to decide what he deserves, though indeed I think the good opinion of his master is far nearer to his heart than any recompense.

V, xix. To His Friend Pudens (c.472)

The son of your nurse has eloped with the daughter of mine. It is a shameful action, and one which would have destroyed our friendly relations, had I not learned at once that you knew nothing of the man's intention. But though you are thus acquitted in advance, you yet do not scruple to ask that this crying offence should be allowed to go unpunished. I can only agree on one condition; that you promote the ravisher from his original servile state, by changing your relation to him from that of master to that of patron. The woman is already free; but she will only be regarded as a lawful wife instead of a mere concubine if our criminal, whose cause you espouse, ceases to be your dependant and becomes your client, assuming the status of a freeman in place of that of a *colonus*. Nothing short of these terms or these amends will in the least condone the affront. I only yield to your request and your protestation of friendship on condition that, if as ravisher he is not to be bound to Justice, Liberty shall make him a free bridegroom.

VI, xi. To the Lord Bishop Eleutherius (c.472)

I herewith commend a Jew to you, not because I approve a sect pernicious to those involved in its toils, but because we ought to regard none of that creed as wholly lost so long as life remains to them. For while there is any possibility of converting them, there is always a hope of their redemption. The nature of his business will be best explained by himself when admitted to your presence; for it would be imprudent to allow discursive talk to exceed the brevity proper to a letter. In the transactions and the disputes of this present world, a Jew has often as good a cause as any one; however much you may attack his heresy, you can fairly defend him as a man. Deign to hold us in remembrance, my Lord Bishop.

VII, vi. To the Lord Bishop Basilius (472–73)

I must confess that formidable as the mighty Goth may be, I dread him less as the assailant of our walls than as the subverter of our Christian laws. They say that the mere mention of the name of Catholic so embitters his countenance [Sidonius refers to Euric here] and heart that one might take him for the chief priest of his Arian sect rather than for the monarch of his nation. Omnipotent in arms, keen-witted, and in the full vigour of life, he yet makes this single mistake—he attributes his success in his designs and enterprises to the orthodoxy of his belief, whereas the real cause lies in mere earthly fortune. For these reasons I would have you consider the secret malady of the Catholic Church that you may hasten to apply an open remedy. Bordeaux, Perigueux, Limoges, Javols, Eauze, Bazas, Comminges, Auch, and many another city are all like bodies which have lost their heads through the death of their respective bishops. No successors have been appointed to fill their places, and maintain in ministry in the lower orders of the church; the boundaries of spiritual desolation are extended far and wide. Every day the ruin spreads by the death of more fathers in God; so pitiful is her state, that the very heresiarchs of former times, to say nothing of contemporary heretics, might well have looked with pity on peoples orphaned of their pontiffs and oppressed by desperation at this catastrophe of their faith.

If you examine more closely the ills of the body spiritual, you will soon perceive that for every bishop snatched from our midst, the faith of a population is imperilled. I need not mention your colleagues Crocus and Simplicius, removed alike from their thrones and suffering a common exile, if different punishments. For one of them laments that he cannot see whither he is to return; the other that he sees only too clearly where he is to return no more. You for your part have about you the most holy bishops Faustus, Leontius, and Graecus, environed by the city, your order and their fraternal love. To you these miserable treaties are submitted, the pacts and agreements of two kingdoms pass through your hands. [This refers to the commission of four bishops appointed to negotiate terms of peace between the Empire and Euric. Although this commission failed, the treaty of A.D. 475, which ceded Auvergne to the Visigoths, also guaranteed better treatment for Catholics.] Do your best, as far as the royal condescension suffers you, to obtain for our bishops the right of ordination in those parts of Gaul now included within the Gothic boundaries, that if we cannot keep them by treaty for the Roman State, we may at least hold them by religion for the Roman Church.

VIII, ii. To His Friend Johannes (478)

I should hold myself guilty of something like a crime against polite learning, most accomplished of friends, were I for a moment to defer congratulation on your own success in deferring the decease of Literature. One might almost speak of her as dead and buried; it is your glory to have revived, supported and championed her, and in this tempest of war which has wrecked the Roman power, you are the sole master in Gaul who has brought the Latin tongue safely into port. Our contemporaries and our successors should all with one accord and fervent gratitude dedicate statues or portraits to you, as to a new Demosthenes or Tully; by your example they were formed and educated, and they shall preserve in the very midst of an invincible but alien race this evidence of their ancient birthright. Since old grades of rank are now abolished which once distinguished the high birth from the low, in future culture must afford the whole criterion of nobility. None is more deeply indebted to your learning than I; for like all authors professed, who write for posterity, I shall owe to your school and your teaching the certainty of an understanding audience.

VIII, 6. To His Friend Namatius (c.480)

But, joking apart, do let me know how things go with you and your household. Just as I was on the point of ending a letter which had rambled long enough, lo and behold! a courier from Saintonges. I whiled away some time talking with him about you; and he was very positive that you had weighed anchor, and in fulfillment of those half military, half naval duties of yours were coasting the western shores on the look-out for curved ships; the ships of the Saxons, in whose every oarsman you think to detect an arch-pirate. Captains and crews alike, to a man they teach or learn the art of brigandage; therefore let me urgently caution you to be ever on the alert. For the Saxon is the most ferocious of all foes. He comes on you without warning; when you expect his attack he makes away. Resistance only moves him to contempt; a rash opponent is soon down. If he pursues, he overtakes; if he flies himself, he is never caught. Shipwrecks to him are no terror, but only so much training. His is not mere acquaintance with the perils of the sea; he knows them as he knows himself. A storm puts his enemies off their guard, preventing his preparations from being seen; the chance of taking the foe by surprise makes him gladly face every hazard of rough waters and broken rocks.

Moreover, when the Saxons are setting sail from the continent, and are about to drag their firm-holding anchors from an enemy's shore, it is their usage, thus homeward bound, to abandon every tenth captive to the slow agony of a watery end, casting lots with perfect equity among the doomed crowd in execution of this iniquitous sentence of death. This custom is all the more deplorable in that it is prompted by honest superstition. These men are bound by vows which have to be paid in victims, they conceive it a religious act to perpetrate this horrible slaughter, and to take anguish from the prisoner in place of ransom; this polluting sacrilege is in their eyes an absolving sacrifice. I am full of anxiety and apprehension about these dangers, though on the other hand there are factors which encourage me mightily. Firstly, the standard under which you sail are those of an ever-victorious nation [the Visigoths]. Secondly, men of prudence, among whose number you may be fairly included, are not in the habit of leaving anything to chance. Thirdly, very intimate friends who live far from each other are apt to feel alarm without due cause, because it is natural to be apprehensive of events at once incalculable and occurring very far away. You will perhaps argue that the cause of my uneasiness need not be taken so seriously. That may be true; but it is also true that we are most timid in regard to those whom we love best. So take the first opportunity of relieving the fears which your situation has aroused by a good account of your fortunes. I am incorrigible on this head, and shall always fear the worst for friends abroad until they contradict it themselves, especially those harassed by the watchword or the signal for attack. In accordance with your request, I send you the *Libri Logistorici* of Varro and the Chronology of Eusebius. If these models reach you safely, and you find a little leisure from the watches and the duties of the camp, you will be able, your arms once furbished, to apply another kind of polish to an eloquence which must be getting rusty.

VIII, viii. To His Friend Syagrius (c.474)

Tell me, fine flower of our Gallic youth, how much longer your ardour for country labours will bid you scorn the town? How long shall rustic implements unrightfully usurp the hands only worn before by throwing dice? How much longer is your estate of Taionnacus to weary your patrician limbs with a peasant's toil? How much longer, O cavalier turned ploughman, will you go on burying in the winter fallows the spoil of the waving meadows? How much longer ply your blunt and heavy hoe along the interminable vine-rows? Why professed rival of Serranus and Camillus, do you guide the plough, yet renounce the embroidered toga? Give up this rustic folly; cease to disgrace your birth. Who cultivates in moderation is lord of his land, who does too much is slave of it. Return to your fatherland, return to your father, return to all the loyal friends who can justly claim a place in your affections. Or, if the life of Cincinnatus the Dictator attracts you so, first wed a Ricilia to yoke your oxen for you. I don't suggest that a man of your sense should neglect his domestic affairs;

but he should use moderation and think not merely of what he ought to have but what he ought to be. If you renounce all higher interests, if your one motive in life is the increase of your property, then, what can it avail you to descend from a line of consuls and see every day their ivory curule chairs with applied ornament of gold and their calendars enriched with purple? Your plodding and obscure career will bring you rather burdens from the revenue officials than honour from the censor.

VIII, ix. To His Friend Lampridius (478)

Twice has the moon risen upon me prisoned here [after the siege of Clermont, Sidonius was imprisoned by Euric]; and but once have I been received into the presence. For scant leisure has the King even for himself, since all the subjugated earth awaits his nod. We see in his courts the blue-eyed Saxon, lord of the seas, but a timid landsman here. The razor's keen blade, content no more to hold its usual course round the head's extremity, with clean strokes shearing to the skin, drives the margin of the hair back from his brow, till the head looks smaller and the visage longer. We see thee, aged Sygambrian warrior, the back of thy head shaven in sign of thy defeat; but now thou guidest the new-grown locks to the old neck again. Here strolls the Herulian with his glaucous cheeks, inhabitant of Ocean's furthest shore, and of one complexion with its weedy deeps. Here the Burgundian bends his seven feet of stature on suppliant knee, imploring peace. Here the Ostrogoth finds a powerful patron, and crushing the Hun beyond his border, triumphs at home only through his homage to this mighty patron. And here, O Roman, thou also seekest thy protection; if the Great Bear menaces commotion, and the Scythian hordes advance, the strong arm of Euric is invoked, that Garonne, drawing power from the Mars who loves its banks, may bring defence to the dwindled stream of Tiber. Here the Parthian Arsacid a Persian king of the Sassanid dynasty himself asks grace to hold, a tributary, his high hall of Susa.

5. *The Burgundian Code*

An East German people, the Burgundians were somewhat exceptional in that they migrated south and west from their original continental settlement around the mouth of the Vistula. By the third century they were established along the Rhine frontier just north of the Main. By the fifth century, due to the general weakening of the Rhine frontier, they were established on the left bank in the Spier-Worms-Strassburg region, being recognized as *foederati* by Honorius in 413. It was this Burgundian kingdom which was destroyed by the Huns, under Roman instigation, in 436, furnishing in later centuries the historic kernel of the *Niebulungenlied*. The remnants of the debacle of 436 were assigned lands north of Lake Geneva. By 443 they had established a second federate kingdom under King Gundioc (437–74). Under Gundioc's son, Gundobad (474–516), the Burgundian kingdom rose to its height, occupying much of what would be known as Burgundy in later times. From 523 the Burgundian kingdom was under increasing pressure from the Franks who finally annexed it in 534.

In all the barbarian kingdoms there was a conflict between the original customary, personal law of the Germans and the written, territorialized law of the Romans. The necessity for reaching some *modus vivendi* between the two laws resulted, in some of the kingdoms, in the issuance of an abbreviated and debased code of Roman law on the one hand, and the writing down of tribal custom on the other. In Burgundy, it was Gundobad who was responsible for the initial compilation of both codes, the *Lex Burgundionum* for the Burgundians, the *Lex Romana Burgundionum* for the Romans.

Most of what follows is from the original *Lex Burgundionum* of King Gundobad; the titles from 88 on are later. The translation is by Katherine Fischer (Philadelphia: University of Pennsylvania Press, 1949), pp. 17–21, 23–24, 29–30, 32–35, 35, 45–46, 52–53, 53–58, 62–63, 65–66, 74–75, 84, 86.

Book of Constitutions, Preface

1. In the name of God in the second year of the reign of our lord the most glorious king Gundobad, this book concerning laws past and present,

and to be preserved throughout all future time, has been issued on the fourth day before the Kalends of April (March 29) at Lyons.

2. For the love of justice, through which God is pleased and the power of earthly kingdoms acquired, we have obtained the consent of our counts (*comites*) and leaders (*proceres*), and have desired to establish such laws that the integrity and equity of those judging may exclude all rewards and corruptions from themselves.

3. Therefore all administrators and judges must judge from the present time on between Burgundians and Romans according to our laws which have been set forth and corrected by a common method, to the end that no one may hope or presume to receive anything by way of reward or emolument from any party as the result of the suits or decisions; but let him whose case is deserving obtain justice and let the integrity of the judge alone suffice to accomplish this.

5. Therefore let all nobles (*obtimates*), counsellors (*consiliarii*), bailiffs (*domestici*), mayors of our palace (*maiores domus nostrae*), chancellors (*cancellarii*), counts (*comites*) of the cities or villages, Burgundians as well as Roman, and all appointed judges and military judges (*judices militantes*) know that nothing can be accepted in connection with those suits which have been acted upon or decided, and that nothing can be sought in the name of promise or reward from those litigating; nor can the parties (to the suit) be compelled by the judge to make a payment in order that they may receive anything (from their suit).

8. Since a similar condition has been forbidden among Romans in cases of the crime of venality, we command that Romans be judged by the Roman laws just as has been established by our predecessors; let them know that they must follow the form and statement of the written law when they render decisions so that no one may be excused on grounds of ignorance.

11. Indeed if any judge, barbarian as well as Roman, shall not render decisions according to those provisions which the laws contain because he has been prevented by ignorance or negligence, and he has been diverted from justice for this reason, let him know that he must pay thirty solidi and that the case must be judged again on behalf of the aggrieved parties.

14. Finally it is pleasing that our constitutions be confirmed with the signatures of the counts added below, so that this statement of the law which has been written as the result of our effort and with the common

consent of all may, observed throughout posterity, maintain the validity of a lasting agreement. [A list of 31 names follows, all of them I believe Burgundian.]

II. Of Murders

1. If anyone presumes with boldness or rashness bent on injury to kill a native freeman of our people of any nation or a servant of the king, in any case a man of barbarian tribe, let him make restitution for the committed crime not otherwise than by the shedding of his own blood.

2. We decree that this rule be added to the law by a reasonable provision, that if violence shall have been done by anyone to any person, so that he is injured by blows of lashes or by wounds, and if he pursues his persecutor and overcome by grief and indignation kills him, proof of the deed shall be afforded by the act itself or by suitable witnesses who can be believed. Then the guilty party shall be compelled to pay to the relatives of the person killed half his wergeld according to the status of the person; that is, if he shall have killed a noble of the highest class (*optimas nobilis*), we decree that the payment be set at one hundred fifty solidi, i.e., half his wergeld; if a person of middle class (*mediocris*), one hundred solidi; if a person of the lowest class (*minor persona*), seventy-five solidi.

3. If a slave unknown to his master presumes to kill a native freeman, let the slave be handed over to death, and let the master not be made liable for damages.

4. If the master knows of the deed, let both be handed over to death.

5. If the slave himself flees (*defuerit*) after the deed, let his master be compelled to pay thirty solidi to the relatives of the man killed for the value (wergeld) of the slave.

6. Similarly in the case of royal slaves, in accordance with the status of such persons, let the same condition about murders be observed.

7. In such cases let all know this must be observed carefully, that the relatives of the man killed must recognize that no one can be pursued except the killer; because just as we ordered the criminals to be destroyed, so we will suffer the innocent to sustain no injury.

VIII. Of the Commission of Crimes Which Are Charged against Native Freemen

1. If a native freeman, either barbarian or Roman, is accused of a crime through suspicion, let him render oath, and let him swear with his wife and sons and twelve relatives: if indeed he does not have wife and

sons and he has mother or father, let him complete the designated number with father and mother. But if he has neither father nor mother, let him complete the oath with twelve relatives.

2. But if he who must take oath wishes to take it with raised hand (*de manu*), and if those who are ordered to hear the oath—those three whom we always command to be delegated by the judges for hearing an oath—before they enter the church declare they do not wish to receive the oath, then he who was about to take oath is not permitted to do so after this statement, but they (the judges) are hereby directed by us to commit the matter to the judgment of God (i.e., to ordeal).

3. If however, having received permission, he has taken the oath, and if he has been convicted after the oath, let him know that he must make restitution by a ninefold payment (*in novigildo*) to those in whose presence the judge ordered him to give his oath.

4. But if they (those appointed to hear the oath) fail to come to the place on the appointed day, and if they shall not have been detained by any illness or public duty, let them pay a fine of six solidi. But if they were detained by any illness or duty, let them make this known to the judge or send other persons in their place whom they can trust to receive the oath for them.

5. If moreover he who is about to take the oath does not come to the place, let the other party wait until the sixth hour of the day; but if he has not come by the sixth hour, let the case be dismissed without delay.

6. But if the other (the accusing party) does not come, let him who was about to take the oath depart without loss.

XIV. Of Succession

1. Among Burgundians we wish it to be observed that if anyone does not leave a son, let a daughter succeed to the inheritance of the father and mother in place of the son.

2. If by chance the dead leave neither son nor daughter, let the inheritance go to the sisters or nearest relatives.

3. It is pleasing that it be contained in the present law that if a woman having a husband dies without children, the husband of the dead wife may not demand back the marriage price (*pretium*) which had been given for her.

4. Likewise, let neither the woman nor the relatives of the woman seek back that which a woman pays when she comes to her husband if the husband dies without children.

5. Concerning those women who are vowed to God and remain in chastity, we order that if they have two brothers they receive a third portion of the inheritance of the father, that is, of that land which the father, possessing by the right of *sors* (allotment), left at the time of his

death. Likewise, if she has four or five brothers, let her receive the portion due to her.

6. If moreover she has but one brother, let not a half, but a third part go to her on the condition that, after the death of her who is a woman and a nun, whatever she possesses in usufruct from her father's property shall go to the nearest relatives, and she will have no power of transferring anything therefrom, unless perhaps from her mother's goods, that is, from her clothing or things of the cell (*rescellulae*), or what she has acquired by her own labor.

7. We decreed that this should be observed only by those whose fathers have not given them portions; but if they shall have received from their father a place where they can live, let them have full freedom of disposing of it at their will.

XVIII. Of Those Things Which Happen by Chance

1. If any animal by chance, or if any dog by bite, causes death to a man, we order that among Burgundians the ancient rule of blame be removed henceforth: because what happens by chance ought not to conduce to the loss of discomfiture of man. So that if among animals, a horse kills a horse unexpectedly, or an ox gores an ox, or a dog gnaws a dog, so that it is crippled, let the owner hand over the animal or dog through which the loss is seen to have been committed to him who suffers the loss.

2. In truth, if a lance or any kind of weapon shall have been thrown upon the ground or set there without intent to do harm (*simpliciter*), and if by accident a man or animal impales himself thereupon, we order that he to whom the weapon belongs shall pay nothing unless by chance he held the weapon in his own hands in such a manner that it could cause harm to a man.

XXXIV. Of Divorces

1. If any woman leaves (puts aside) her husband to whom she is legally married, let her be smothered in mire.

2. If anyone wishes to put away his wife without cause, let him give her another payment such as he gave for her marriage price, and let the amount of the fine be twelve solidi.

3. If by chance a man wishes to put away his wife, and is able to prove one of these three crimes against her, that is adultery, witchcraft, or violation of graves, let him have full right to put her away; and let the judge pronounce the sentence of law against her, just as should be done against criminals.

4. But if she admits none of these three crimes, let no man be permitted to put away his wife for any other crime. But if he chooses, he may go away from the home, leaving all household property behind, and his wife with their children may possess the property of her husband.

XLV. Of Those Who Deny Those Things Charged against Them

We know that many of our people are corrupted through inability to establish . . . a case and because of instinct of greed, so that they do not hesitate frequently to offer oaths about uncertain matters and likewise to perjure themselves about known matters. To break up this criminal practice, we decree by the present law that as often as a case shall arise among our people and he who has been accused denies by offering oaths that that which is sought is owed by him, and that has been done which is charged, it is fitting that an end be made to their litigation in this manner: if the party to whom oath has been offered does not wish to receive the oath, but shall say that the truthfulness of his adversary can be demonstrated only by resort to arms, and the second party (the one accused), shall not yield (the case charged), let the right of combat not be refused; with the further provision that one of the same witnesses who came to give oath shall fight, God being the judge. For it is just that if anyone shall say without delay that he knows the truth of the matter and shall offer to take oath, he should not hesitate to fight. But if the witness of him who offered oath was overcome in that combat, let all witnesses who promised that they should take oath be compelled to pay a fine of three hundred solidi without any grant of delay. But if he who refused to receive the oath (the accuser) shall have been killed, let the victorious party be repaid ninefold the sum (debt) involved taken from his property (i.e., from the property of the dead man) as damages, so that as a result, one may delight in truth rather than falsehood.

Given the 28th of May (502), Abienus, *vir clarissimus* being consul.

LIV. Of Those Who Presume to Take a Third of the Slaves and Two Parts of the Land (of Their Host) Contrary to Public Prohibition

1. It was commanded at the time the order was issued whereby our people should receive one-third of the slaves, and two-thirds of the land, that whoever had received land together with slaves either by the gift of our predecessors or of ourselves, should not require a third of the slaves

nor two parts of the land from that place in which hospitality had been assigned him; nevertheless inasmuch as we find many unmindful of their danger because they have taken in excess of those things which we have ordered, it is necessary that the present authority issued in the image of eternal law coerce the presumptuous and provide a remedy of due security against these acts of contempt. We order then that whatever lands have been taken contrary to our official prohibition from their hosts by those who already have possession of fields and slaves through our gift shall be restored without delay.

2. Also concerning clearings, we order that the new and unjust strife and trickery of the *faramanni* which causes anxiety and disquiet to the possessors be suppressed by this law, with the result that, just as concerning forests, so also concernings made either heretofore or at the present, the Roman possessors shall have a share with the Burgundians, for as was established previously, we order half of the forests in general to belong to the Romans; likewise concerning courtyards and orchards, let this condition be followed among the *faramanni,* that is, that the Romans may lay claim to take half the property.

3. But if anyone exceeds the established provisions of this law and is not reprimanded and punished by you, do not doubt that the fervor of our wrath will be aroused to your peril.

LX. Of Employing Witnesses of Gifts

1. Since the ancient custom is often neglected in various legal matters, it is necessary that consideration be taken for future times through a new law. And because we know some barbarians are willing, with two or three witnesses present, to take possession of property in the name of gift or inheritance contrary to the ancient custom, we have first corrected their presumption by the present law, decreeing that property is not validly transmitted by means of so few witnesses (i.e., that a matter confirmed by so few witnesses is invalid).

2. Moreover, if hereafter any barbarian wishes to make a will (*testari*) or gift (*donare*), either the Roman or the Barbarian custom must be observed if he wishes his action to have any validity, that is, either let what he wishes to give to anyone be confirmed by legal written documents, or at any rate, let what he wishes to bestow or give obtain validity from the witness of five native freemen, and let the property be transferred to the jurisdiction of him to whom it has been granted.

3. If a sufficient number of native freemen is not present, we permit freedmen to render testimony. And among the native freemen, it is fitting that a number of our (royal) slaves be admitted (to give testimony), as provided that witnesses are pledged (bound) by the hand (*manus*) of him who wishes to give or transfer anything, or if a question is raised regarding the trustworthiness of a witness, according to the custom of the barbarians, let him take oath.

LI. Of Those Who Did Not Give Their Sons the Portions of Their Property Due Them

1. Although these things have been observed from of old among our people, that a father should divide his property equally by law among his sons, nevertheless we have ordered in a law established now for a long time that this practice be observed, and we have added this useful counsel to fathers that a father should have freedom to do what he wishes with that which belongs to his own portion.

But because in a recent controversy it became clear that a certain Athila had passed over the provisions of the old enactments and displayed insubordination to these most useful precepts of law and had not given his son the portion due to him but had transferred his property to other persons through illegal written title since he had wished nothing therefrom to belong to his son, and that no one may follow a bad example in this manner, we order that what he has done contrary to law shall have no legal force, and we add that all his property shall be possessed by his son. It is also the purpose of our judgment to cut off the disobedience of the transgressor, so that the justice of the general precept will be inscribed in the laws and retained.

On this account we have ordered in matters of this sort that the law be observed which was promulgated long ago to the effect that any man who will not hand over portions of his property legally belonging to his sons may do nothing adverse or prejudicial to them in writing, and if he does so, it shall be invalid.

2. Nevertheless, it is pleasing that this rule be defined thus with the force of law, that a son shall have full power of doing what he wishes with the portion he receives, with the further provision that if he dies without heirs and the decrees of fate permit his father to survive, and if he has made no gift from the property legally belonging to him during his lifetime and left no will, then his father may claim the succession to these portions in question. However, the father shall have no power of alienating them and when he has died the property of their dead brother will pass to the remaining sons.

3. The mother's ornaments and vestments belong to the daughters without any right to share on the part of the brother or brothers; further, let this legal principle be observed concerning those ornaments and vestments in the case of girls whose mothers die intestate. But if the mother shall have made any disposal of her own ornaments and vestments, there shall be no cause for action thereafter.

4. But if an unmarried girl who has sisters dies, and she has not declared her wish in writing or in the presence of witnesses, let her portion after her death belong to her sisters and, as has been stated, let her brothers have no share therein.

5. However if the girl dies and does not have a blood sister, and no clear disposition has been made concerning her property, let her brothers become her heirs.

LXXVIII. Of the Succession of Inheritance

1. Upon careful consideration of these matters, we have established that if a father shall have divided his allotment (*sors*) with his sons and afterward it happens a son dies childless while his father is still living, the father may claim the use of the entire portion by the law of usufruct in accordance with the son's wish. But upon the father's death, let him divide between sons and grandsons so that all fatherless grandsons sprung from any one son shall obtain such a portion as their father had.

2. Further, let that portion which the father had retained (for himself after the) division among his sons be left to the surviving sons, and let the grandsons not succeed to that share.

3. Nevertheless the present law pertains to male heirs only.

XCVII. Of Hounds

If anyone shall presume to steal a hound, or a hunting dog, or a running dog, we order that he be compelled to kiss the posterior of that dog publicly in the presence (*in conventu*) of all the people, or let him be compelled to pay five solidi to him whose dog he took, and a fine of two solidi.

XCVIII. Of Falcons

If anyone presumes to steal another's falcon, either let the falcon eat six ounces of meat from his breast (*super testones*), or if he does not wish, let him be compelled to pay six solidi to the owner of the falcon; moreover, let the fine be two solidi.

CII. Of Jews Who Presume to Raise Their Hands against a Christian

1. If any Jew presumes to raise a hand against a Christian with fist, shoe, club, whip, or stone, or has seized his hair, let him be condemned to the loss of a hand.

2. But if he wishes to redeem his hand, we order him to redeem it with seventy-five solidi; and let the fine be twelve solidi.

3. Besides this, we order that if he has presumed to raise a hand against a priest, let him be handed over to death, and let his property be given into our treasury.

Chapter Three

The Christian Antique

ONE of the commonplace generalizations about the beginning of the Middle Ages is that it was an amalgam of three elements, Graeco-Roman civilization, the Germans, and Christianity. The statement is true enough, although there has never been any agreement concerning the proportions of the mixture, but it needs one qualification. Is it possible to look at Christianity as an element separate from Graeco-Roman civilization? The answer to this question is no.

Christianity's birth and historical growth was in the context of Graeco-Roman civilization. Once beyond the early apostolic period its language was Greek, its literary forms were Greek—the acts, epistles, apocalypse—its first converts were Hellenized Jews and increasingly it used Greek philosophic terms to justify itself. Eastern Christianity has remained Greek. In the West, Christianity became Roman in language, structure and spirit. Christianity became the state religion of the Roman Empire, an obvious point but one whose implications are too often overlooked in this respect.

If Christianity was to become universal it had to take on the speech, forms, and thought of the Roman Empire. Its decision to do so was the governing *cultural* fact of early Christianity. Christianity emerged out of a Judaic religious environment; it would have remained a sect of Judaism if it had not assimilated Graeco-Roman civilization.

On the other hand, since Christianity did assimilate Graeco-Roman civilization it was not alien to it, at least not after the second century of the Christian era. Here is Gilbert Murray on the difference in viewpoint between Classical Greece and Christian Rome:

> Anyone who turns from the great writers of classical Athens, say Sophocles or Aristotle, to those of the Christian Era must be conscious of a great difference in tone. There is a change in the whole relation of the writer to the world about him. The new quality is not especially Christian; it is just as marked in the Gnostics and Mithra worshippers as in the Gos-

pels, in Plotinus as in Jerome. It is a rise of asceticism, of mysticism, in a sense, of pessimism, a loss of self confidence, of hope in this life and of faith in normal human effort; a despair of patient inquiry, a cry for infallible revelation; an indifference to the walfare of the state, a conversion of the soul to God. It is an atmosphere in which the aim of the good man is not so much to live justly, to help the society to which he belongs. . . ; but rather, by means of a burning faith, by contempt for the world and its standards, by ecstasy, suffering and martyrdom, to be granted pardon for his unspeakable unworthiness, his immeasurable sins. There is an intensifying of certain spiritual emotions, an increase of sensitiveness, a failure of nerve.

With this as the background, there is no mystery about the spread of Christianity although one other important element needs to be added. At the end of the third century Christianity was far stronger in the Greek-speaking areas of the Empire than the Latin and for an obvious reason. Christianity was still basically Greek in language. With two exceptions, Egypt and Africa, Christianity was predominately urban. Finally, at this time it had made relatively little progress among the educated upper classes of the Empire who were repelled by the vulgar character of Christianity socially and by the fact that it was a cruder, more uncompromising religion than it was to become. It was one particular fact which transformed Christianity from a Greek, urban, and socially vulgar religion into the state religion of the Roman Empire: the conversion of Constantine.

Whatever Constantine's motives in adopting the Christian faith, the fact that he did so was decisive. It determined that his successors would be Christian. By a natural process, the religion of the emperor must become the religion of the Empire. Further, Constantine's conversion suddenly made Christianity socially respectable and, by another natural process, made it socially essential. Despite the fact of a pagan reaction later in the fourth century, the religion of the emperor must also become the religion of the senate. The imperial conversion also meant that Christianity would not be a Greek monopoly. Independently, one wonders if Christianity would ever have gained much of a foothold in the West.

The fact that Christianity did spread to the West, in conjunction with later developments, had two important ramifications. St. Peter, the chief of the apostles, became the first bishop of the Greek-speaking Christian community at Rome and suffered martyrdom there. Because Peter was the foremost of the apostles in the Gospel tradition, by the theory of apostolic succession his Latin successors at

Rome inherited his primacy. Christianity, Greek in origin, development, and theology, now had a Latin head. Greek Christianity always regarded its western counterpart as a crude upstart and in this sense Latin and Greek Christianity has never been unified. An extension of this point was the rise of the papacy. Never accepted in the East, without rivals in the West nor embarrassed, after the fifth century, by the presence of a Roman Emperor, papal primacy developed in a vacuum.

Christianity developed within the Roman Empire and within the intellectual framework of classical civilization. From the one came the political power of the church; from the other a built-in tension between classical humanism and Christian eschatology.

For our purposes, the development of the Christian Church belongs primarily to the West and to the period following the collapse of the Western Empire. Nevertheless, even in the fourth century we see a foreshadowing of what was to follow. The Christian church quickly acquired a legal position within the state of quite a different character than that ever held by paganism, notably in the extraordinary courts possessed by Christian bishops and the obligation of the state to enforce orthodoxy. Christianity, from another point of view, made more demands on the individual than any other religion, demands that could lead to church intervention into secular affairs. St. Ambrose has been included in the selections that follow as a case in point. Theodosius may have been a Roman Emperor but he was also a Christian; Ambrose felt perfectly competent to judge his actions whether as a private individual or as a public magistrate. Finally, when the Roman state did wither away, the Christian church inherited its structure—in the older parts of the Empire the boundaries of the *civitas* were coterminous with the diocese—and some measure of its political power in the *civitas*.

The superimposition of the forms of Graeco-Roman philosophy on the Judaeo-Christian religious conception left Christianity with a permanent problem. Could purely religious conceptions such as original sin, the Incarnation, the Atonement, and the Trinity be expressed in philosophic terms? Should they be? Was reason a condition of belief? Or to twist St. Jerome's plaintive question a little bit, "What has Athens got to do with Jerusalem?" This problem was never solved even though the four great ecumenical councils of the early Christian period laid down some guide lines. Although attempting to express the supernatural content of the faith in the language of human reason, they declared, beginning with the judgment of Nicaea, that the mysteries of the faith were impenetrable to reason.

Christianity alone among the institutions of Roman civilization had the stamina to survive into the early medieval period. But it was not so much the church as a whole, it was one specific Christian institution, the monastery, which was largely instrumental in saving both the church itself and Western civilization from extinction. There is an apparent paradox here, that a movement originating through reaction against the world should eventually save it, yet the reason is simple enough. The Benedictine Rule provided Western monasticism with an immensely workable, stable, institutional form. During the centuries that followed the collapse of the Roman Empire, centuries justly called the Benedictine centuries, the Benedictine monastery constituted little self-sufficient islands of peace and piety around which secular society sought shelter. And only the monk had the leisure in these times for intellectual pursuits. The Benedictine Rule, given below almost in its entirety, gives a glimpse of the stability of this institution.

1. *The Edict of Milan*

Although not an edict and not issued at Milan, there is little point in changing the title of this famous document. Its importance lies in the fact that it grants Christianity freedom from persecution and equal status with other religions of the Empire. Thus, even though there is nothing specifically pro-Christian in its content, it marks the first step in the rise of Christianity to the state religion of the Roman Empire.

The translation is from Sidney Z. Ehler and John B. Morrall, *Church and State Through the Centuries* (Westminster, Maryland: the Newman Press, 1954), pp. 5–6.

WE, Constantinus and Licinius the Emperors, having met in concord at Milan and having set in order everything which pertains to the common good and public security, are of the opinion that among the various things which we perceived would profit men, or which should be set in order first, was to be found the cultivation of religion; we should therefore give both to Christians and to all others free facility to follow the religion which each may desire, so that by this means whatever divinity is enthroned in heaven may be gracious and favourable to us and to all who have been placed under our authority. Therefore we are of the opinion that the following decision is in accordance with sound and true reasoning: that no one who has given his mental assent to the Christian persuasion or to any other which he feels to be suitable to him should be compelled to deny his conviction, so that the Supreme Godhead ("Summa Divinitas"), whose worship we freely observe, can assist us in all things with his wonted favour and benevolence. Wherefore it is necessary for your Excellency to know that it is our pleasure that all restrictions which were previously put forward in official pronouncements concerning the sect of the Christians should be removed, and that each one of them who freely and sincerely carries out the purpose of observing the Christian religion may endeavour to practise its precepts without any fear or danger. We believed that these points should be fully brought to your attention, so that you might know that we have given free and absolute permission to practise their religion to the Christians. Now that you perceive what we have granted to them, your Excellency must also learn that for the sake of peace in our time a similar public and free right to practise their religion or cult is granted to others, so that every man may have free opportunity to worship according to his own wish. This has been done by us to avoid any appearance of disfavour to any one religion. We have decided furthermore to decree the following in respect of the Christians: if those places at which they were accustomed in former times to hold their meetings (concerning which a definite procedure was laid down for your guidance in previous communications) have been at any previous time acquired from our treasury or from any other person, let the persons concerned be willing and swift to restore them to the Christians without financial recompense and without trying to ask a price. Let those who have received such property as a gift restore whatever they have acquired to the Christians in similar manner. If those who have bought such property or received it as a gift, seek some recompense from our benevolence, let them apply to the Vicar, by whom their cases will be referred to our clemency. You are to consider it your duty that all these things shall be handed over to the Christian body immediately and without delay by your intervention. And since the aforesaid Christians are known to have possessed not only those places at which they are wont to assemble, but others also pertaining to the law of their body, that is of the churches, not of private individuals, you are to order in accordance with the law which we have described above the return of all those possessions to the aforesaid Christians, that is to their bodies and assemblies without any further hesitation or argument. Our previous statement is to be borne in mind that those who restore this property without price may, as we have said, expect some compensation from our benevolence.

You ought to bring into play your very effective intervention in all these matters concerning the aforesaid Christian body so that there may be a swift fulfilment of our Edict, in which the interests of public quiet have been consulted by our clemency. Let all this be done, so that as we stated above, the divine favour, of which we have experienced so many instances, may continue with us to bless our successors through all time with public wellbeing. In order that the character of this our perpetual benevolence can reach the knowledge of all, it will be well for you to circulate everywhere, and to bring to the awareness of all, these points which have been written to you as above, so that the enactment of this our benevolence may not be hidden.

2. *Eusebius: Life of Constantine*

The early life of Eusebius (c.260–c.340) is obscure. He was probably born in Asia Minor and certainly studied with the Christian scholar and martyr Pamphilius. After suffering through the persecution of Diocletian, Constantine appointed him Bishop of Caesarea (c.315). He became one of the intimates of Constantine, to whom he was an unofficial theological advisor, and a leading figure in the Arian controversy. Eusebius rates the title "the father of church history" on the basis of his *Ecclesiastical History* which is the foundation for our knowledge of the early Christian church. His *Life of Constantine* is also extremely valuable as the major source for the conversion of Constantine and the Arian controversy.

The translation is from *The Select Library of Nicene and Post-Nicene Fathers of the Christian Church,* second series (New York: Charles Scribner's Sons, 1925), Vol. I, pp. 511–12, 515–18, 520–23.

II, xliv. After this [The Edict of Milan] the emperor continued to address himself to matters of high importance, and first he sent governors to the several provinces, mostly such as were devoted to the saving faith; and if any appeared inclined to adhere to Gentile worship, he forbade them to offer sacrifice. This law applied also to those who surpassed the provincial governors rank and dignity, and even to those who occupied the highest station, and held the authority of the Praetorian Praefecture. If they were Christians, they were free to act consistently with their profession; if otherwise, the law required them to abstain from idolatrous sacrifices.

II, xlvi. Victor Constantinus, Maximus Augustus, to Eusebius

"Forasmuch as the unholy and willful rule of tyranny has persecuted the servants of our Saviour until this present time, I believe and have fully satisfied myself, best beloved brother, that the buildings belonging to all the churches have either become ruinous through actual neglect, or have received inadequate attention from the dread of the violent spirit of the times.

"But now, that liberty is restored, and that serpent [Licinius] driven from the administration of public affairs by the providence of the Supreme God, and our instrumentality, we trust that all can see the efficacy of the Divine power, and that they who through fear of persecution or through unbelief have fallen into any errors, will now acknowledge the true God, and adopt in future that course of life which is according to truth and rectitude. With respect, therefore, to the churches over which you yourself preside, as well as the bishops, presbyters, and deacons of other churches with whom you are acquainted, do you admonish all to be zealous in their attention to the buildings of the churches, and either to repair or enlarge those which at present exist, or, in cases of necessity, erect new ones.

"We also empower you, and the others through you, to demand what is needful for the work, both from the provincial governors and from the Praetorian Praefect. For they have received instructions to be most diligent in obedience to your Holiness's order. God preserve you, beloved brother." A copy of this charge was transmitted throughout all the provinces to the bishops of the several churches: the provincial governors received directions accordingly, and the imperial statute was speedily carried into effect.

II, xlviii. Victor Constantinus, Maximus Augustus, to the People of the Eastern Provinces

"Whatever is comprehended under the sovereign laws of nature, seems to convey to all men an adequate idea of the forethought and intelligence of the divine order. Nor can any, whose minds are directed in the true path of knowledge to the attainment of that end, entertain a doubt that the just perceptions of sound reason, as well as those of the natural vision itself, through the sole influence of genuine virtue, lead to the knowledge of God. Accordingly no wise man will ever be surprised when he sees the mass of mankind influenced by opposite sentiments. For the beauty of virtue would be useless and unperceived, did not vice display in contrast with it the course of perversity and folly. Hence it is that the one is crowned with reward, while the most high God is himself the administrator of judgment to the other.

"And now I will endeavor to lay before you all as explicitly as possible, the nature of my own hopes of future happiness."

(II, lvi) "My own desire is, for the common good of the world and the advantage of all mankind, that thy people should enjoy a life of peace and undisturbed concord. Let those, therefore, who still delight in error, be made welcome to the same degree of peace and tranquillity which they have who believe. For it may be that this restoration of equal privileges to all will prevail to lead them into the straight path. Let no one molest another, but let every one do as his soul desires. Only let men of sound judgment be assured of this, that those only can live a life of holiness and purity, whom thou callest to a reliance of thy holy laws. With regard to those who will hold themselves aloof from us, let them have, if they please, their temples of lies: *we* have the glorious edifice of thy truth, which thou hast given us as our native home. We pray, however, that they too may receive the same blessing, and thus experience that heartfelt joy which unity of sentiment inspires."

II, xli. In this manner the emperor, like a powerful herald of God, addressed himself by his own letter to all the provinces, at the same time warning his subjects against superstitious error, and encouraging them in the pursuit of true godliness. But in the midst of his joyful anticipations of the success of this measure he received tiding of the most serious disturbance which had invaded the peace of the church. This intelligence he heard with deep concern, and at once endeavoured to devise a remedy for the evil. The origin of this disturbance may be thus described. The people of God were in a truly flourishing state, and abounding in the practice of good works. No terror from without assailed them, but a bright and most profound peace, through the favor of God, encompassed his Church on every side. Meantime, however, the spirit of envy was watching to destroy our blessings, which at first crept in unperceived, but soon revelled in the midst of the assemblies of the saints. At length it reached the bishops themselves, and arrayed them in angry hostility against each other, on pretense of a jealous regard for the doctrines of Divine truth. Hence it was that a mighty fire was kindled as it were from a little spark, and which, originating in the first instance in the Alexandrian church, overspread the whole of Egypt and Libya, and the further Thebaid. Eventually it extended its ravages to the other provinces and cities of the empire; so that not only the prelates of the churches might be seen encountering each other in the strife of words, but the people themselves were completely divided, some adhering to one faction and others to another. Nay, so notorious did the scandal of these proceedings become, that the sacred matters of inspired teaching were exposed to the most shameful ridicule in the very theaters of the unbelievers.

II, lxiii. As soon as the emperor was informed of these facts, which he heard with much sorrow of heart, considering them in the light of a calamity personally affecting himself, he forthwith selected from the Christians in his train one whom he well knew to be approved for the sobriety and genuineness of his faith [Hosius, Bishop of Cordova], and who had before this time distinguished himself by the boldness of his religious profession, and sent him to negotiate peace between the dissentient parties at Alexandria. He also made him the bearer of a most needful and appropriate letter to the original movers of the strife: and this letter, as exhibiting a specimen of his watchful care over God's people, it may be well to introduce into this our narrative of his life. Its purport was as follows.

II, lxiv. Victor Constantinus, Maximus Augustus, to Alexander and Arius

"I call that God to witness as well I may, who is the helper of my endeavors, and the Preserver of all men, that I had a twofold reason for undertaking that duty which I have now performed.

"My design then was, first, to bring the diverse judgments formed by all nations respecting the Deity to a condition, as it were, of settled uniformity; and, secondly, to restore to health the system of the world, then suffering under the malignant power of a grievous distemper. Keeping these objects in view, I sought to accomplish the one by the secret eye of thought, while the other I tried to rectify by the power of military authority. For I was aware that, if I should succeed in establishing, according to my hopes, a common harmony of sentiment among all the servants of God, the general course of affairs would also experience a change correspondent to the pious desires of them all.

"Finding, then, that the whole of Africa was pervaded by an intolerable spirit of mad folly, through the influence of these who with heedless frivolity had presumed to rend the religion of the people into diverse sects; I was anxious to check this disorder, and could discover no other remedy equal to the occasion, except in sending some of yourselves to aid in restoring mutual harmony among the disputants, after I had removed the common enemy of mankind [Licinius] who had interposed his lawless sentence for the prohibition of your holy synods.

"For since the power of Divine light, and the law of sacred worship, which, proceeding in the first instance, through the favor of God, from the bosom, as it were, of the East, have illumined the world, by their sacred radiance, I naturally believed that you would be the first to promote the salvation of other nations, and resolved with all energy of thought and diligence of enquiry to seek your aid. As soon, therefore, as I had secured my decisive victory and unquestionable triumph over my enemies, my first enquiry was concerning that object which I felt to be of paramount interest and importance.

"But, O glorious Providence of God! how deep a wound did not my ears only, but my very heart receive in the report that divisions existed among yourselves more grievous still than those which continued in that country! so that you, through whose aid I had hoped to procure a remedy for the errors of others [the Donatists], are in a state which needs healing even more than theirs. And yet, having made a careful enquiry into the origin and foundations of these differences, I find the cause to be of a truly insignificant character, and quite unworthy of such fierce contention. Feeling myself, therefore, compelled to address you in this letter, and to appeal at the same time to your unanimity and sagacity, I call on Divine Providence to assist me in the task, while I interrupt your dissension in the character of a minister of peace. And with reason: for if I might expect, with the help of a higher power, to be able without difficulty, by a judicious appeal to the pious feelings of those who heard me, to recall them to a better spirit, even though the occasion of the disagreement were a greater one, how can I refrain from promising myself a far easier and more speedy adjustment of this difference, when the cause which hinders general harmony of sentiment is intrinsically trifling and of little moment?

"I understand, then, that the origin of the present controversy is this. When you, Alexander, demanded of the presbyters what opinion they severally maintained respecting a certain passage in the Divine law, or rather, I should say, that you asked them something connected with an unprofitable question, then you, Arius, inconsiderately insisted on what ought never to have been conceived at all, or if conceived, should have been buried in profound silence. Hence it was that a dissension arose between you, fellowship was withdrawn and the holy people, rent into diverse parties, no longer preserved the unity of the one body. Now therefore, do ye both exhibit an equal degree of forbearance, and receive the advice which your fellow-servant righteously gives. What then is this advice? It was wrong in the first instance to propose such questions as these, or to reply to them when propounded. For those points of discussion which are enjoined by the authority of no law, but rather suggested by the contentious spirit which is fostered by misused leisure, even though they may be intended merely as an intellectual exercise, ought certainly to be confined to the regions of our own thoughts, and not hastily produced in the popular assemblies, nor unadvisedly intrusted to the general ear. For how very few are there able either accurately to comprehend, or adequately to explain subjects so sublime and abstruse in their nature? Or, granting that one were fully competent for this, how many people will he convince? Or, who, again, in dealing with questions of such subtle nicety as these, can secure himself against a dangerous declension from the truth? It is incumbent therefore on us in these cases to be sparing of our words, lest, in case we ourselves are unable, through the feebleness of our natural faculties, to give a clear explanation of the subject before us, or, on the other hand, in case the slowness of our hearers' understandings disables them from arriving at an accurate apprehension of what we say, from one or other of these causes the people be reduced to the alternative either of blasphemy or schism.

"Let therefore both the unguarded question and the inconsiderate answer receive your mutual forgiveness, For the cause of your difference has not been any of the leading doctrines or precepts of the Divine law, nor has any new heresy respecting the worship of God arisen among you. You are in truth of one and the same judgment: you may therefore well join in communion and fellowship.

"For as long as you continue to contend about these small and very insignificant questions, it is not fitting that so large a portion of God's people should be under the direction of your judgment, since you are thus divided between yourselves. I believe it indeed to be not merely unbecoming, but positively evil, that such should be the case. But I will refresh your minds by a little illustration, as follows. You know that philosophers, though they all adhere to one system, are yet frequently at issue on certain points, and differ, perhaps, in their degree of knowledge: yet they are recalled to harmony of sentiment by the uniting power of their common doctrines. If this be true, is it not far more reasonable that you, who are the ministers of the Supreme God, should be of one mind respecting the profession of the same religion? But let us still more thoughtfully and with closer attention examine what I have said, and see whether it be right that, on the ground of some trifling and foolish verbal difference between ourselves, brethren should assume towards each other the attitude of enemies, and the august meeting of the synod be rent by profane disunion, because of you who wrangle together on points so trivial and altogether unessential? This is vulgar, and rather characteristic of childish ignorance, than consistent with the wisdom of priests and men of sense. Let us withdraw ourselves with a good will from these temptations of the devil. Our great God and common Saviour of all has granted the same light to us all. Permit me, who am his servant, to bring my task to a successful issue, under the direction of his Providence, that I may be enabled through my exhortations, and diligence, and earnest admonition, to recall his people to communion and fellowship. For since you have, as I said, but one faith, and one sentiment respecting our religion, and since the Divine commandment in all its parts enjoins on us all the duty of maintaining a spirit of concord, let not the circumstance which has led to a slight difference between you, since it does not affect the validity of the whole, cause any division or schism among you. And this I say without in any way desiring to force you to entire unity of judgment in regard to this truly idle question, whatever its real nature may be. For the dignity of your synod may be preserved, and the communion of your whole body maintained unbroken, however wide a difference may exist among you as to unimportant matters. For we are not all of us like-minded on every subject, nor is there such a thing as one disposition and judgment common to all alike. As far, then, as regards the Divine Providence, let there be one faith, and one understanding among you, one united judgment in reference to God. But as to your subtle disputation on questions of little or no significance, though you may be unable to harmonize in sentiment, such differences should be consigned to the secret custody of your own minds and thoughts. And now let the preciousness of common affection, let faith in the truth, let the honor due to God and to the observance of his law continue immovable among you. Resume, then, your mutual feelings of friendship, love, and regard: restore to the people their wonted embracings; and do ye yourselves, having purified your souls, as it were, once more acknowledge one another. For it often happens that when a reconciliation is affected by the removal of the causes of enmity, friendship becomes even sweeter than it was before."

◆ ◆ ◆

In this manner the pious emperor endeavored by means of the foregoing letter to promote the peace of the Church of God. And the excellent man to whom it was intrusted performed his part not merely by communicating the letter itself, but also by seconding the views of him who sent it; for he was, as I have said, in all respects a person of pious character. The evil, however, was greater than could be remedied by a single letter, insomuch that the acrimony of the contending parties continually increased, and the effects of the mischief extended to all the Eastern provinces. These things jealousy and some evil spirit who looked with an envious eye on the prosperity of the Church, wrought.

III, v. But before this time [of the Arian controversy] another most virulent disorder had existed, and long afflicted the Church; I mean the difference respecting the salutary feast of Easter. For while one party asserted that the Jewish custom should be observed, without following the authority of those who were in error, and strangers to gospel grace.

Accordingly, the people being thus in every place divided in respect of this, and the sacred observances of religion confounded for a long period (insomuch that the diversity of judgment in regard to the time for celebrating one and the same feast caused the greatest disagreement between those who kept it, some afflicting themselves with fastings and austerities, while others devoted their time to festive relaxation), no one appeared who was capable of devising a remedy for the evil, because the controversy continued equally balanced between both parties. To God alone, the Almighty, was the healing of these differences an easy task; and Constantine appeared to be the only one on earth capable of being his minister for this good end. For as soon as he was made acquainted with the facts which I have described, and perceived that his letter to the Alexandrian Christians had failed to produce its due effect, he at once aroused the energies of his mind, and declared that he must prosecute to the utmost this war also against the secret adversary who was disturbing the peace of the Church.

Then as if to bring a divine army against this enemy, he convoked a general council, and invited the speedy attendance of bishops from all quarters, in letters expressive of the honorable estimation in which he held them. Nor was this merely the issuing of a bare command, but the emperor's good will contributed much to its being carried into effect: for he allowed some the use of the public means of conveyance, while he afforded to others an ample supply of horses for their transport. The place, too, selected for the synod, the city of Nicaea in Bithynia (named from Victoria), was appropriate to the occasion. As soon then as the imperial injunction was generally made known, all with the utmost willingness hastened thither, as though they would outstrip one another in a race; for they were impelled by the anticipation of a happy result to the conference, by the hope of enjoying present peace, and the desire of beholding something new and strange in the person of so admirable an emperor. Now when they were all assembled, it appeared evident that the proceeding was the work of God, inasmuch as men who had been most widely separated, not merely in sentiment, but also personally, and by difference of country, place, and nation, were here brought together, and comprised within the walls of a single city, forming as it were a vast garland of priests, composed of a variety of the choicest flowers.

In effect, the most distinguished of God's ministers from all the churches which abounded in Europe, Libya, and Asia were here assembled. And a single house of prayer, as though divinely enlarged, sufficed to contain at once Syrians and Cilicians, Phoenicians and Arabians, delegates from Palestine, and others from Egypt; Thebans and Libyans, with those who came from the region of Mesopotamia. A Persian bishop too was present at this conference, nor was even a Scythian found wanting to the number. Pontus, Galatia, and Pamphylia, Cappodocia, Asia, and Phrygia, furnished their most distinguished prelates; while those who dwelt in the remotest districts of Thrace and Macedonia, of Achaia and Epirus, were notwithstanding in attendance. Even from Spain itself, one whose fame was widely spread took his seat as an individual in the great assembly [Hosius]. The prelate of the imperial city was prevented from attending by extreme old age; but his presbyters were present, and supplied his place. Constantine is the first prince of any age who bound together such a garland as this with the bond of peace, and presented it to his Saviour as a thank-offering for the victories he had obtained over every foe, thus exhibiting in our own times a similitude of the apostolic company.

Now when the appointed day arrived on which the council met for the final solution of the questions in dispute, each member was present for this in the central building of the palace, which appeared to exceed the rest in magnitude. On each side of the interior of this were many seats disposed in order, which were occupied by those who had been invited to attend, according to their rank. As soon, then, as the whole assembly had seated themselves with becoming orderliness, a general silence prevailed, in expectation of the emperor's arrival. And first of all, three of his immediate family entered in succession, then others also preceded his approach, not of the soldiers or guards who usually accompanied him, but only friends in the faith. And now, all rising at the signal which indicated the emperor's entrance, at last he himself proceeded through the midst of the assembly, like some heavenly messenger of God, clothed in raiment which glittered as it were with rays of light, reflecting the glowing radiance of a purple robe, and adorned with the brilliant splendor of gold and precious stones. Such was the external appearance of his person; and with regard to his mind, it was evident that he was distinguished by piety and godly fear. This was indicated by his downcast eyes, the blush on his countenance, and his gait. For the rest of his personal excellencies, he surpassed all present in height of stature and beauty of form, as well as in majestic dignity of mien, and invincible strength and vigor. All these graces, united to a suavity of manner, and a serenity becoming his imperial station, declared the excellence of his mental qualities to be above all praise. As soon as he had advanced to the upper end of the seats, at first he remained standing, and when a low chair of wrought gold had been set for him, he waited until the bishops had beckoned to him, and then sat down, and after him the whole assembly did the same.

The bishop who occupied the chief place [usually considered to have been Eusebius himself] in the right division of the assembly then rose, and, addressing the emperor, delivered a concise speech, in a strain of thanksgiving to Almighty God on his behalf. When he had resumed his seat, silence ensued, and all regarded the emperor with fixed attention; on which he looked serenely round on the assembly with a cheerful aspect, and, having collected his thoughts, in a calm and gentle tone gave utterance to the following words.

"It was once my chief desire, dearest friends, to enjoy the spectacle of your united presence; and now that this desire is fulfilled, I feel myself bound to render thanks to God the universal King, because, in addition to all his other benefits, he has granted me a blessing higher than all the rest, in permitting me to see you not only all assembled together, but all united in a common harmony of sentiment. I pray therefore that no malignant adversary may henceforth interfere to mar our happy state; I pray that, now the impious hostility of the tyrants has been forever removed by the power of God our Saviour, that spirit who delights in evil may devise no other means for exposing the divine law to blasphemous calumny; for, in my judgment, intestine strife within the Church of God is far more evil and dangerous than any kind of war or conflict; and these our differences appear to me more grievous than any outward trouble. Accordingly, when, by the will and with the cooperation of God, I had been victorious over my enemies, I thought that nothing more remained but to render thanks to him, and sympathize in the joy of those whom he had restored to freedom through my instrumentality; as soon as I heard that intelligence which I had least expected to receive, I mean the news of your dissension, I judged it to be of no secondary importance, but with the earnest desire that a remedy for this evil also might be found through my means, I immediately sent to require your presence. And now I rejoice in beholding your assembly; but I feel that my desires will be most completely fulfilled when I can see you all united in one judgment, and that common spirit of peace and concord prevailing amongst you all, which it becomes you as consecrated to the service of God, to commend to others. Delay not, then, dear friends: delay not ye ministers of God, and faithful servants of him who is our common Lord and Saviour: begin from this moment to discard the causes of that disunion which has existed among you, and remove the perplexities of controversy by embracing the principles of peace. For by such conduct you will at the same time be acting in a manner most pleasing to the supreme God, and you will confer an exceeding favor on me who am your fellow-servant."

As soon as the emperor had spoken these words in the Latin tongue, which another interpreted, he gave permission to those who presided in the council to deliver their opinions. On this some began to accuse their neighbors, who defended themselves, and recriminated in their turn. In this manner numberless assertions were put forth by each party, and a violent controversy arose at the very commencement. Notwithstanding this, the emperor gave patient audience to all alike, and received every proposition with steadfast attention, and by occasionally assisting the argument of each party in turn, he gradually disposed even the most vehement disputants to a reconciliation. At the same time, by the affability of his address to all, and his use of the Greek language, with which he was not altogether unacquainted, he appeared in a truly attractive and amiable light, persuading some, convincing others by his reasons, praising those who spoke well, and urging all to unity of sentiment, until at last he succeeded in bringing them to one mind and judgment respecting every disputed question.

The result was that they were not only united as concerning the faith but that the time for the celebration of the salutary feast of Easter was agreed on by all. Those points also which were sanctioned by the resolution of the whole body were committed to writing, and received the signature of each several member. Then the emperor, believing that he had thus obtained a second victory over the adversary of the Church, proceeded to solemnize a triumphal festival in honor of God.

3. *The Theodosian Code*

The nature of this document has been discussed above. Included below are some of the titles connected with the establishment of Christianity and the beginning of state persecution of heretics and pagans.

I, 27, 2 (408). The judgment of a bishop shall be valid for all persons who acquiesce in being heard by priests. For since private persons can hear those persons who have given their consent, even without the knowledge of the judge, We grant that this power shall be permitted to those persons whom We necessarily venerate and We order that such reverence must be shown toward their adjudication as must be granted to your authority, from which it is not permitted to appeal. Also, in order that such cognizance may not be without effect, execution of judgment shall be granted through a public office staff.

XI, 16, 21 (397). The privileges must not be impaired which were conferred upon the venerable Church by previous sainted Emperors. Furthermore, due enforcement shall also guard as inviolable the privileges conferred upon the Bishop of the City of Rome, so that the Church shall not assume the performance of any extraordinary public service or any compulsory public service of a menial nature.

XII, 1, 49 (361). Only a bishop shall not be compelled by anyone to deliver his property to the municipal council, just as was formerly established, but he shall remain a bishop and shall not make any surrender of his substance. Of course, if any persons have attained the rank of priest, or even of deacon or subdeacon or any other cleric, if the municipal council should be present and should issue their consent under the supervision of a judge . . . such clerics may have the heritage of their commendable way of life, so that they may retain their own property, especially if it is requested by the voices of the whole people.

XII, 1, 112 (386). In obtaining the office of chief civil priest, that person shall be considered preferable who has performed the most services for his municipality, and who has not, however, withdrawn from the cult of the temples by his observance of Christianity. Indeed it is unseemly, and further, that We may speak more truly, it is illicit, for the temples and the customary rites of the temples to belong to the care of those persons whose conscience is imbued with the true doctrine of divine religion, and who ought properly to flee such compulsory public services, even if they were not prohibited by law from performing it.

XVI, 5, 6 (381). No place for celebrating their mysteries, no opportunity for exercising the madness of their excessively obstinate minds shall be available to the heretics. All men shall know also that even if some concession has been impetrated by that kind of men through any special rescript whatever, if it has been fraudently elicited, it shall not be valid.

1. Crowds shall be kept away from the unlawful congregations of all the heretics. The name of the One and Supreme God shall be celebrated everywhere; the observance, destined to remain forever, of the Nicene faith, as transmitted long ago by Our ancestors and confirmed by the declaration and testimony of divine religion, shall be maintained. The contamination of the Photinian pestilence, the poison of the Arian sacrilege, the crime of the Eunomian perfidy, and the sectarian monstrosities, abominable because of the ill-omened names of their authors, shall be abolished even from the hearing of men.

2. On the other hand, that man shall be accepted as a defender of the Nicene faith and a true adherent of the Catholic religion who confesses that Almighty God, Light of Light, who does not violate by denial the Holy Spirit which we hope for and receive from the Supreme Author of things; that man who esteems, with the perception of inviolate faith, the undivided substance of the incorrupt Trinity, that substance which those of the orthodox faith call, employing a Greek word, *ousia*. The latter beliefs are surely more acceptable to Us and must be venerated.

3. Those persons, however, who are not devoted to the aforesaid doctrines shall cease to assume with studied deceit, the alien name of true religion, and they shall be branded upon the disclosure of their crimes. They shall be removed and completely barred from the threshold of all churches, since We forbid all heretics to hold unlawful assemblies within the towns. If factions should attempt to do anything, We order that their madness shall be banished and that they shall be driven away from the very walls of the cities, in order that Catholic churches throughout the whole world may be restored to all orthodox bishops who hold the Nicene faith.

XVI, 5, 11 (383). All persons whatsoever who are tossed about by the false doctrine of diverse heresies, namely, the Eunomians, the Arians, the Macedonians, the Pneumatomachi, the Manichaeans, the Encratites, the Apotactites, the Saccophori, and the Hydroparastatae, shall not assemble in any groups, shall not collect any multitude, shall not attract any people to themselves, shall not show any walls of private houses after the likeness of churches, and shall practice nothing publicly or privately which may be detrimental to the Catholic sanctity. Furthermore, if there should exist any person who transgresses what has been so evidently forbidden, he shall be expelled by the common agreement of all good men, and the opportunity to expel him shall be granted to all who delight in the cult and the beauty of the correct observance of religion.

XVI, 5, 29 (395). We direct Your Sublimity to investigate whether any of the heretics dare to have membership in the imperial service, in violation of Our laws, either in the bureaus or among the members of the secret service or among the palatines. According to the example of Our sainted father, We also deny the aforesaid persons all right of membership in the imperial service. Moreover, if you should apprehend any persons as accessories of this crime, you shall order that they, together with the very persons with whom they have connived, to the ruin of Our law and of religion, shall not only be removed from the imperial service but even be kept outside the walls of this city.

XVI, 4, 40 (407). We have recently published Our opinion in regard to the Donatists. Especially, however, do we prosecute with the most deserved severity the Manichaeans and the Phrygians and Priscillianists. Therefore, this class of men shall have no customs and no laws in common with the rest of mankind.

1. In the first place, indeed, it is Our will that such heresy shall be considered a public crime, since whatever is committed against divine religion redounds to the detriment of all.

2. We also pursue the aforesaid persons by the confiscation of their goods, which, however, We order to accrue to each of their next of kin, in such a way that the orders of ascendants and descendants and collateral cognates, even to the second degree, shall be observed, just as in hereditary successions. Thus, finally We permit such kinsmen to have the right to take such property, unless they themselves are polluted with an equal guilt.

3. It is also Our will that the heretics themselves shall be made ineligible to accept any gift or inheritance coming under any title whatsoever.

4. Furthermore, We do not leave to any person so convicted the power to make gifts, to buy, to sell, or finally to make contracts.

XVI, 5, 54 (414). We decree that the Donatists and the heretics, who until now have been spared by the patience of Our Clemency, shall be severely punished by legal authority, so that by this Our manifest order, they shall recognize that they are intestable and have no power of entering into contracts of any kind, but they shall be branded with perpetual infamy and separated from honorable gatherings and from public assemblies.

1. Those places in which the dire superstition has been preserved until now shall surely be joined to the venerable Catholic Church, and thus their bishops and priests, that, all their prelates and ministers shall likewise be despoiled of all their property and shall be sent into exile to separate islands and provinces.

3. Furthermore, We manifestly impose the loss of their patrimony and pecuniary penalties on each such man and woman, whether a private person or a dignitary, and the penalty must be assessed in accordance with their status. Therefore, if any person should be invested with the rank of proconsul, vicar, or count of the first order, unless he should turn his mind and purpose to the observance of the Catholic religion, he shall be compelled to pay two hundred pounds of silver which shall be added to the resources of Our fisc. No person shall suppose that the foregoing penalty alone can suffice for checking their design, but as often as any person shall be convicted of having joined such a communion, so often shall the fine be exacted of him, and if it should be proved five times that he is not recalled from his false doctrine by such fines, then he shall be referred to Our Clemency so that We may judge more rigorously concerning his entire property and his status.

4. We bind the remaining dignitaries, moreover, with conditions of this kind, namely, that if a Senator who is fortified by no additional privilege of rank should be found in the herd of the Donatists, he shall pay one hundred pounds of silver; those of the rank of civil priest shall be forced to pay the same sum; the ten chief decurions shall be assessed fifty pounds of silver; the remaining decurions shall pay ten pounds of silver if they should prefer to continue in the heresy.

XV, 5, 5 (425). On the following occasions all amusement of the theaters and the circuses shall be denied throughout all cities to the people thereof, and the minds of Christians and of the faithful shall be wholly occupied in the worship of God: namely, on the Lords' day, which is the first day of the whole week, on the Natal Day and Epiphany of Christ, and on the day of Easter and of Pentecost, as long as the vestments that imitate the light of the celestial font attest to the new light of holy baptism; at the time also when the commemoration of the Apostolic Passion, the teacher of all Christianity, is duly celebrated by everyone. If any persons even now are enslaved by the madness of the Jewish impiety or the error and insanity of stupid paganism, they must know that there is a time for prayer and a time for pleasure.

XVI, 1, 2 (380). It is Our will that all the peoples who are ruled by the administration of Our Clemency [in this case Constantinople] shall practice that religion which the divine Peter the Apostle transmitted to the Romans, as the religion which he introduced makes clear even unto this day. It is evident that this is the religion that is followed by the Pontiff Damasus and by Peter, Bishop of Alexandria, a man of apostolic sanctity; that is, according to the apostolic discipline and the evangelic doctrine, we shall believe in the single Deity of the Father, the Son, and the Holy Spirit, under the concept of equal majesty and of the Holy Trinity.

1. We command that those persons who follow this rule shall embrace the name of Catholic Christians. The rest, however, whom We adjudge demented and insane, shall sustain the infamy of heretical dogmas, their meeting places shall not receive the name of churches, and they shall be smitten first by divine vengeance and secondly by the retribution of Our own initiative, which We shall assume in accordance with the divine judgment.

XVI, 8, 9 (393). It is sufficiently established that the sect of the Jews is forbidden by no law. Hence We are gravely disturbed that their assemblies have been forbidden in certain places. Your sublime Magnitude will, therefore, after receiving this order, restrain with proper severity the excesses of those persons who, in the name of the Christian religion, presume to commit certain unlawful acts and attempt to destroy and to despoil the synagogues.

XVI, 8, 21 (412, 418, 420). No person shall be trampled upon when he is innocent, on the ground that he is a Jew, nor shall any religion cause any person to be exposed to contumely. Their synagogues and habitation shall not be burned indiscriminately, nor shall they be injured wrongfully without any reason. . . . But just as it is Our will that the foregoing provision shall be made for the persons of the Jews, so We decree that the Jews also shall be admonished that they perchance shall not become insolent and, elated by their own security, commit any rash act in disrespect of the Christian religion.

4. *The Affair of the Altar of Victory*

The altar of victory, dating back to Roman Republican days, was located in the Roman Senate. Sacrifice to it was the traditional method of opening the proceedings of the senate. As a pagan symbol it was removed twice by Christian emperors of the fourth century and restored once, by the pagan Julian. The following two letters relate the final episode in the conflict between paganism and Christianity.

The translation is by H. Walford, *The Letters of St. Ambrose* (Oxford: J. H. Parker, 1881), pp. 324–29.

a. The Memorial of Symmachus, Prefect of the City

1. As soon as the honourable Senate, ever faithful to your Majesty, learnt that offences were made amenable to law, and that the character of past times was being redeemed by pious governors, it hastened to follow the precedent of better times, and give utterance to its long repressed grief, and commissioned me once more to be the spokesman of its complaints, for I was before refused access to the deceased Emperor by evil men, because otherwise justice could never have failed me, most noble Emperors Valentinian, Theodosius and Arcadius, victorious and triumphant, ever illustrious.

2. Filling then a twofold office, as your Perfect I report the proceedings of the Senate, as the envoy of the citizens I offer to your favourable notice their requests. Here is no oppositions of wills. Men have ceased to believe that disagreement proves their superiority in courtly zeal. To be loved, to be the object of respect and affection is more than sovereignty. Who could suffer private contests to injure the commonwealth? Justly does the Senate assail those who prefer their own power to the honour of the prince.

3. It is our duty to be watchful for your Majesties. The very glory of

the present time makes it the more fitting that we should maintain the customs of our ancestors, the laws and destinies of our country; for it conduces to this glory that you should know it is not in your power to do anything contrary to the practice of your parents. We ask the restoration of that state of religion under which the Republic has so long prospered. Let the Emperors of either sect and either opinion be counted up; a late Emperor observed the rites of his ancestor, his successor did not abolish them. If the religion of older times is no precedent, let the connivance of the last Emperors be so.

4. Who is so friendly with the barbarians as not to require an altar of Victory? Hereafter we must be cautious, and avoid a display of such things. But let at least that honour be paid to the name which is denied to the Divinity. Your fame owes much, and will owe still more, to Victory. Let those detest this power, who were never aided by it, but do you not desert a patronage which favours your triumphs. Vows are due to this power from every man, let no one deny that a power is to be venerated which he owns is to be desired.

5. But even if it were wrong to avoid this omen, at least the ornaments of the Senate-house ought to have been spared. Permit us, I beseech you, to transmit in our old age to our posterity what we ourselves received when boys. Great is the love of custom. And deservedly was the act of the deified Constantius [who removed the Altar of Victory] of short duration. You ought to avoid all precedents which you know to have thus been reversed. We are solicitous for the endurance of your name and glory, and that a future age may find nothing to amend.

6. Where shall we swear to observe your laws and statutes? By what sanction shall the deceitful mind be deterred from bearing false witness? All places indeed are full of God, nor is there any spot where the perjured can be safe, but it is of great efficacy in restraining crime to feel that we are in the presence of sacred things. That altar binds together the concord of all, that altar appeals to the faith of each man, nor does any thing give more weight to our decrees than that all our decisions are sanctioned, so to speak, by an oath. A door will thus be opened to perjury, and this is to be approved of by the illustrious Emperors, allegiance to whom is guarded by a public oath!

7. But Constantius, of sacred memory, is said to have done the same thing. Be it so, let us then imitate his other actions, feeling sure that had any one committed this error before his time, he would never have fallen into it. For the fall of one is a warning to his successor, and the censure of a previous example causes amendment. It was allowable for this predecessor of your Majesties to incur offence in a novel manner, but how can the same excuse avail us, if we imitate that which we know was disapproved?

8. Will your Majesties listen to other acts of this same Emperor more

worthy of your imitation? He left uncurtailed the privileges of the sacred virgins, he filled the priestly office with men of noble birth, he allowed the cost of the Roman ceremonies, and following the joyful Senate through all the streets of the eternal city, he beheld with serene countenance the temples, reading the names of the gods inscribed on their pediments, he enquired after the origin of the sacred edifices, and admired their founders. Although he himself professed another religion he maintained the ancient one for the Empire; for every man has his own customs, his own rites. The Divine mind has distributed to cities various guardians and various ceremonies. As each man that is born receives a soul, so do nations receive a genius who guards their destiny. Here the proof from utility comes in, which is our best voucher with regard to the Deity. For since our reason is in the dark, what better knowledge of the gods can we have than from the record and evidence of prosperity? And if a long course of years give their sanction to a religion, we ought to keep faith with so many centuries, and to follow our parents, as they followed with success those who founded them.

9. Let us suppose Rome herself to approach, and address you in these terms: "Excellent Emperors, Fathers of your country, respect these years to which pious rites have conducted me. Let me use the ancient ceremonies, for I do not repent of them. Let me live in my own way, for I am free. This worship reduced the world under my laws; these sacred rites repulsed Hannibal from the walls, and the Gauls from the Capitol. Am I reserved for this, to be censured in my old age? I am not unwilling to consider the proposed decree, and yet late and ignominious is the reformation of old age."

10. We pray therefore for a respite for the gods of our fathers and our native gods. That which all venerate should in fairness be accounted as one. We look on the same stars, the heaven is common to us all, the same world surrounds us. What matters it by what arts each of us seeks for truth? We cannot arrive by one and the same path at so great a secret; but this discussion belongs rather to persons at their ease, it is prayers not arguments which we now offer.

11. What advantage accrues to your treasury from the abolition of the privilege of the Vestal virgins? Shall that be denied under princes the most munificent which the most parsimonious have granted? Their sole honour consists in their wages, so to speak, of chastity. As their fillets adorn their heads, so is it esteemed by them an honour to be free to devote themselves to the ministry of sacrifices. It is but the bare name of exemption which they ask, for their poverty exonerates them from any payment. So that he who reduces their means, contributes to their praise, for virginity dedicated to the public welfare is meritorious in proportion as it is without reward.

12. Far be such gains from the purity of your treasury. The excheq-

uer of good princes should be replenished by the spoils of enemies, not by the losses of ministers of religion. And is the gain any compensation for the odium? Those whose ancient resources are cut off only feel it the more acutely in that you are free from the charge of avarice. For under Emperors who keep their hands from other men's goods and check desire what does not excite the cupidity of the spoiler must be taken solely with a view of injuring the person robbed.

13. The Imperial Exchequer retains also lands bequeathed by the will of dying persons to the sacred virgins and priests. Implore you, as Priests of justice, to restore to the sacred functionaries of your city the right of inheritance. Let men dictate their wills in peace, knowing that under equitable princes their bequests will be undisturbed. Men are wont to take pleasure in this security, and I would have you sympathize with them, for the precedent lately set has begun to harass them on their deathbeds. Shall it be said that the religion of Rome appertains not to the Roman laws? What name shall we give to the taking away of legacies, slaves are allowed a due latitude of bequeathing by will, only the noble virgins and ministers of sacred rites are excluded from inheriting lands devised to them. What advantage is it to dedicate one's virginity to the public safety, and to support the immortality of the empire with heavenly protection, to conciliate friendly powers to your arms and eagles, to take upon oneself vows salutary for all, and to refrain from commerce with mankind in general? Slavery then is a happier condition, whose service is given to men. It is the state which is wronged, whose interest it never is to be ungrateful.

14. Let me not be supposed to be defending the cause of the ancient religions only; from acts of this kind all the calamities of the Roman nation have arisen. The laws of our ancestors provided for the Vestal virgins and the ministers of the gods a moderate maintenance and just privileges. This gift was preserved inviolate till the time of the degenerate moneychangers, who diverted the maintenance of sacred chastity into a fund for the payment of base porters. A public famine ensued on this act, and a bad harvest disappointed the hopes of all the provinces. The soil was not here in fault, we ascribe no influence to the stars, no mildew blighted the crops, nor did tares choke the corn, it was sacrilege which rendered the year barren, for it was necessary that all should lose that which they had denied to religion.

15. By all means, if there is any instance of such an evil, let us attribute this famine to the effect of the seasons. An unhealthy wind has caused this blight, and so life is supported by means of shrubs and leaves, and the peasants in their want have had resource once more to the oaks of Dodona. When did the provinces suffer such a calamity, so long as the ministers of religion were supported by the public bounty? When were oaks shaken for the food of man, when were roots dug up, when were

opposite regions of the earth cursed with sterility, so long as provisions were furnished in common to the people and to the sacred virgins? The produce of the earth was blessed by its support of the priests, and thus the gift was rather in the nature of a safeguard than of a largess. Can it be doubted that the gift was for the common benefit, now that a general scarcity has attended its discontinuance?

16. But it may be said that public aid is rightly refused to the cost of an alien religion. Far be it from good rulers to suppose that what has been bestowed from the common stock of certain individuals is within the disposal of the Imperial treasury. For as the commonwealth consists of individuals, so that which comes from it becomes again the property of individuals. You govern all, but you preserve for each his own, and justice has more power with you than arbitrary will. Consult your own generous feelings, whether that ought still to be deemed public property which has been conferred on others. Gifts once devoted to the honour of the city are placed out of the powers of the donors, and that which originally was a free-gift becomes by usage and length of time a debt. Vain therefore is the fear which they would impress upon your minds who assert that unless you incur the odijum of withdrawing the gift you share the responsibility of the donors of it.

17. May the unseen patrons of all sects be propitious to your Majesties, and may those in particular who of old assisted your ancestors, aid you and be worshipped by us. We ask for that religious condition which preserved the empire to your Majesty's father, and blessed him with lawful heirs. That venerable sire beholds from his starry seat the tears of the priests, and feels himself censured by the infraction of that custom which he readily observed.

18. I beg you also to amend for your departed brother what he did by the advice of others, to cover the act by which he unknowingly offended the Senate. For it is certain that the reason why the embassage was refused admittance was, to prevent the decision of the state from reaching him. It is due to the credit of past times to abolish without hesitation that which has been found not to have been the doing of the Emperor.

b. Bishop Ambrose to the Most Blessed Prince and Gracious Emperor, His Majesty Valentinian

The honourable Symmachus, Prefect of the city, having memorialised your Majesty that the altar, which had been removed from the Senate-house at Rome, ought to be restored to its place, and your Majesty, whose years of nonage and inexperience are not yet unfulfilled, though a veteran in the power of faith, not having sanctioned the prayer of the heathen, I also as soon as I heard of it presented a petition, in which, though it embraced all that seemed necessary to be said, I requested that a copy of the Memorial might be furnished to me.

2. Now therefore, not as doubting your faith, but as providing for the future, and assured of a righteous judgment, I will reply to the allegations of the Memorial, making this one request, that you will not look for elegance of phrases but force of facts. For as Holy Scripture teaches us, the tongue of learned and wise men is golden and endowed with highly-decked words, and glittering with splendid elegance as with the brightness of some rich colour, and so captivates and dazzles the eyes of the mind with a shew of beauty. But this gold, if closely handled, may pass current outwardly, but within is base metal. Consider well, I beseech you, and sift the sect of the Heathens; their professions are grand and lofty, but what they espouse is degenerate and effete, they talk of God but worship idols.

3. The propositions of the honourable Prefect of the city, to which he attaches weight, are these, that Rome (as he asserts) seeks the restoration of her ancient rites, and that stipends are to be assigned to her priests and Vestal virgins, and that it was owing to these being withheld that a general famine has ensued.

4. According to his first proposition, Rome utters a mournful complaint, wanting back (as he asserts) her ancient ceremonies. These sacred rites, he says, repelled Hannibal from the walls, the Gauls from the Capitol. But even here, in blazoning the efficacy of these rites, he betrays their weakness. According to this, Hannibal long insulted the Roman religion, and pushed his conquest to the very walls of the city, though the gods fought against him. Why did they for whom their gods fought, allow themselves to be besieged?

5. For why speak of the Gauls, whom the remnant of the Romans could not have prevented from entering the sanctuary of the Capitol, if the timid cackling of a goose had not betrayed them. These are the guardians of the Roman temples! Where was Jupiter then? Did he speak in a goose?

6. But why should I deny that their sacred rites fought for the Romans? Yet Hannibal also worshipped the same gods. Let them choose therefore which they will. If these rites conquered the Romans, they were vanquished in the Carthaginians, but if they were thus overcome in the case of the Carthaginians, neither did they profit the Romans.

7. Away then with this invidious complaint of the Roman people; Rome never dictated it. It is with other words that she addresses them: 'Why do you daily deluge me with the useless gore of the innocent flocks? The trophies of victory depend not on the limbs of cattle, but on the strength of warriors. It was by other powers that I subdued the world. Camillus was my soldier, who recovered the standards which had been taken from the Capitol, and slew those who had captured the Tarpeian

rock; valour overthrew those against whom religion had not prevailed. Why should I name Regulus, who gave me even the services of his death? Africanus gained his triumph not among the altars of the Capitol, but among Hannibal's ranks. Why do you produce to me the rites of our ancestors? I abhor the rites of the Neros. What shall I say of the two-month Emperors [Galba, Otho and Vitellius who had short, but not two-month reigns], and the ends of princes knit on to their accession? Or is it a thing unheard of, that the barbarians should cross their frontiers? Were those men Christians, in whose miserable and unprecedented fate, in the one case a captive Emperor, in the other a captive world proved the falsehood of the rites which promised victory? Was there then no altar of Victory? I am ashamed of my downfall, the pale cheeks of age gather redness from that disgraceful bloodshed. I do not blush to be converted in my old age along with the whole world. It is surely true that no age is too late to learn. Let then old age blush which cannot improve itself. It is not the hoary head of years but of virtue which is venerable. It is no disgrace to pass to better things. This alone had I in common with the barbarians that of old I knew not God. Your sacrifice is a rite of sprinkling yourselves with the blood of beasts. Why do you look for the voice of God in dead beasts? Come and learn here on earth a heavenly warfare; we live here, but our warfare is above. Let God Himself, the Creator, teach me the mystery of heaven, not man who knew not himself. Whom should I believe about God, sooner than God Himself? How can I believe you, who confess that you know not what you worship?'

8. By a single path, he says, we cannot arrive at so great a secret. What you are ignorant of, that we have learnt by the voice of God; what you seek after by faint surmises, that we are assured of by the very Wisdom and Truth of God. Our customs therefore and yours do not agree, You ask the Emperors to grant peace to your gods, we pray for peace for the Emperors themselves from Christ. You worship the works of your own hands, we think it sacrilege that any thing which can be made should be called God. God wills not to be worshipped under the form of stones. Nay, your very philosophers have ridiculed this.

9. But if you are led to deny that Christ is God, because you cannot believe that He died (for you are ignorant how that this was the death not of His Godhead but of His flesh, whereby it comes to pass that none of the faithful shall die), how inconsistent are you, who insult by way of worship, and disparage by way of honour. You consider your god to be a block of wood; what an insulting kind of reverence! You believe not that Christ could die; what a respectful kind of unbelief.

10. But, he says, the ancient altars and images ought to be restored, and the temples adorned as of old. This request ought to be made to one who shares the superstition; a Christian Emperor has learned to honour the altar of Christ alone. Why do they compel pious hands and faithful

lips to minister to their sacrilege? Let the voice of our Emperor speak of Christ alone, let him declare Him only Whom in heart he believes, for *the king's heart is in the Hand of God.* Did ever heathen Emperor raise an altar to God? In demanding a restoration of ancient things they remind us what reverence Christian Emperors ought to pay to the Religion which they profess, since heathen ones paid the utmost to their own superstitions.

◆ ◆ ◆

12. Let the Vestal virgins, he says, enjoy their privileges. It is for those to say this, who cannot believe in gratuitous virginity, it is for them to allure by profit who distrust virtue. But how many virgins have their promised rewards obtained them? They have barely seven Vestals. Such is the whole number whom the veiled and filleted head, the dye of the purple vest, the pompous litter surrounded by attendants, high privileges, great gains, and a prescribed period of virginity, have collected.

13. Let them turn their mental and bodily eye to us, let them behold a people of chastity, an undefiled multitude, a virgin assembly. No fillets adorn their heads, but a veil of common use though dignified by chastity; the blandishments of beauty not curiously sought out, but cast aside; no purple trappings, no luxurious delicacies, but frequent fastings; no privileges, no gains; all things in short so ordered as to repress any affection in the very exercise of their functions. But in fact by this very exercise their affection to it is conciliated. Chastity is perfected by its own sacrifices. That is not virginity which is bought for money, not preserved for love of holiness; that is not integrity which is bid for at an auction by a pecuniary equivalent, to last but for a time. The first triumph of chastity is to overcome the desire of wealth, for this desire is a temptation to modesty. But let us suppose that virginity ought to be supported by pecuniary bounty. In this case, what an abundance of gifts will overflow upon the Christians; what treasury will contain riches so great? Or do they consider that it ought to be bestowed exclusively on the Vestal virgins? Do not they, who claimed the whole under heathen Emperors, feel some shame in denying that under Christian Princes we ought to participate in the bounty?

◆ ◆ ◆

24. The last and most weighty topic remains; as to whether your Majesties should restore those aids which have been profitable to yourselves, for he says, 'Let them defend you, and be worshipped by us.' This, most faithful Princes, we cannot endure; that they should make it a taunt to us that they supplicate their gods in your name, and without your command commit an atrocious sacrilege, taking your connivance as consent. Let them keep their guardians to themselves, let these guardians, if they can, protect their own. But if they cannot protect those who worship them, how can they protect you who worship them not?

25. Our ancestral rites, he says, should be preserved. But what if all things have become better? The world itself, which at first was compacted by the gathering together of the elemental seeds through the vast void, an unconsolidated sphere, or was obscured by the thick darkness of the yet unordered work, was it not afterwards endowed with the forms of things which constitute its beauty, and were not the heaven, sea, and earth distinguished from each other? The earth rescued from dripping darkness was amazed at its new sun. In the beginning too the day shines not, but as time goes on it is bright and warm with the increase of light and heat.

◆ ◆ ◆

27. In former days, the earth knew not how to be wrought into fruitfulness; but afterwards when the careful husbandman began to till the fields, and to clothe the bare soil with vineyards, it was softened by this domestic culture, and put off its rugged nature.

28. So too the first season of the year itself, which has imparted a like habit to ourselves, is bare of produce, then, as time goes on, it blossoms out in flowers soon to fade, and in the end finds its maturity in fruits.

29. So we, while young in age, experience an infancy of understanding, but as we grow in years lay aside the rudeness of our faculties.

30. Let them say then that all things ought to have continued as at first; that the world once covered with darkness is now displeasing because it shines with the beams of the sun. And how much better is it to have dispelled the darkness of the mind than that of the body, and that the beam of faith has shone forth than that of the sun. So then the early stages of the world as of all else have been unsettled, that the venerable age of hoary faith might follow. Let those who are affected by this find fault with the harvest too, because it ripens late; or with the vintage, because it is the fall of the year; or with the olive, because it is the latest of fruits.

◆ ◆ ◆

32. If the old rites pleased, why did Rome adopt alien ones? I pass over the covering of the ground with costly buildings, and shepherds' huts glittering with the gold of a degenerate age. Why, to speak of the very subject of their complaint, have they admitted in their rivalry the images of captured cities, and of conquered gods, and the foreign rites of an alien superstition? Whence do they derive their precedent for Cybele washing her chariot in a stream to counterfeit the Almo [the allusion is to the annual ceremony commemorating the reception of Cybele into Rome]? Whence came the Phrygian seers, and the deities of faithless Carthage ever hateful to Rome, her for instance, whom the Africans worship as Caelestis, and the Persians as Mitra, the greater part of the world as Venus, the same deity under different names. So also they have believed Victory to be a goddess, which is in truth a gift not a power, is bestowed and does not rule, comes by the aid of legions not by the power of religion.

Great forsooth is the goddess whom the number of soldiers claims, or the issue of the battle confers!

◆ ◆ ◆

41. I have replied to those who harass me as though I had not been harassed: for my object has been to refute their Memorial, not to expose their superstitions. But let this very Memorial make your majesty more cautious. For by pointing out that of a series of former Emperors, those who reigned first followed the rites of their ancestors, and their successors did not remove them, and by observing upon this, that if the religion of older ones was not an example, the connivance of the more recent ones was, they have plainly shewn that you owe it to the faith which you profess not to follow the precedent of heathen rites, and to brotherly love not to violate your brothers' ordinances. For if they for the sake of their own cause have praised the connivance of those Emperors, who being Christians, have not abrogated heathen decrees, how much more are you bound to shew deference to brotherly affection, and, whereas you would be bound to wink at what perhaps you did not approve, for fear of detracting from your brothers' decrees, now to maintain what you judge to be in accordance with your own faith and the ties of brotherhood.

5. *Ambrose: To the Emperor Theodosius*

St. Ambrose is too well known a figure to need description here. Concerning the massacre of Thessolonica, this letter demonstrates one means by which the medieval church acquired political authority. The translation is by J. H. Parker, as above.

1. Very pleasant to me is the remembrance of your long friendship, and I also bear a grateful sense of those benefits which at my frequent intreaties you have most graciously extended to others. You may be sure then that it could not be from my ungrateful feeling that on your arrival, which I was wont to long for so ardently, I shunned your presence. The motives of my conduct I will now briefly explain.

2. I found that I alone in all your court was denied the natural right of hearing, in order to deprive me of the power of speaking too: for you were frequently displeased at decisions having reached me which were made in your Consistory. Thus I have been debarred from the common privilege of men, though the Lord Jesus says, "Nothing is secret which shall not be made manifest." Wherefore I did my utmost to obey with reverence your royal will, and I provided both for you and for myself; for you, that you should have no cause of disturbance, to which end I endeavoured that no intelligence should be brought me of the Imperial decrees; and as to myself, I provided against my not seeming to hear, when present, from fear of others, and thus incurring the charge of connivance, and also against hearing in such a manner that while my ears were open my mouth must be closed, and I must not utter what I heard, lest I should injure those who had fallen under suspicion of treachery.

3. What then was I to do? was I not to listen? But I could not close my ears with the wax of the old tales. Must I disclose what I heard? But then I had reason to fear that the same result which I apprehended from your commands would ensue from my own words; that they might become the cause of bloodshed. Was I then to be silent? But this would be the most miserable of all, for my conscience would be bound, my liberty of speech taken away. And what then of the text, "if the priest warn not the

wicked from his wicked way, the wicked man shall die in his iniquity," but the priest shall be liable to punishment, because he did not warn him?

4. Suffer me, gracious Emperor. You have a zeal for the faith, I own it, you have the fear of God, I confess it; but you have a vehemence of temper, which if soothed may readily be changed into compassion, but if inflamed becomes so violent that you can scarcely restrain it. If no one will allay it, let no one at least inflame it. To yourself I would willingly trust, for you are wont to exercise self-control, and by your love of mercy to conquer this violence of your nature.

5. This vehemence of yours I have preferred secretly to commend to your consideration, rather than run the risk of rousing it publicly by my acts. And so I have preferred to be lacking somewhat in duty rather than in humility, and that others should complain of my want of priestly authority, rather than that you should find any want of respect in me, who am so devoted to you; and this in order that you may restrain your emotions, and have full power of choosing what counsel to follow. I alleged as my reason, bodily sickness, which was in fact severe, and not to be mitigated but by more gentle treatment; still I would rather have died than not have waited two or three days for your arrival. But I could not do so.

6. An act has been committed in the city of Thessalonica, the like of which is not recorded, the perpetration of which I could not prevent, which in my frequent petitions before the court I had declared to be most atrocious, and which by your tardy revocation you have yourself pronounced to be very heinous: such an act as this I could not extenuate. Intelligence of it was first brought to a synod held on the arrival of the Gallican Bishops: all present deplored it, no one viewed it leniently; your friendship with Ambrose, so far from excusing your deed, would have even brought a heavier weight of odium on my head, had there been no one found to declare the necessity of your being reconciled to God.

7. Is your Majesty ashamed to do that which the Royal Prophet David did, the forefather of Christ according to the flesh? It was told him that a rich man, who had numerous flocks, on the arrival of a guest took a poor man's lamb and killed it, and recognizing in this act his own condemnation, he said, "I have sinned against the Lord." Let not your Majesty then be impatient at being told, as David was by the prophet, "Thou art the man." For if you listen thereto obediently and say, "I have sinned against the Lord," if you will use those words of the royal Prophet, "O come let us worship and fall down, and kneel before the Lord our Maker," to you also it shall be said, because thou repentest, "the Lord hath put away thy sin, thou shall not die."

8. Another time, when David had commanded the people to be numbered, his heart smote him, and he said unto the Lord, "I have sinned greatly in that I have done, and now, I beseech thee O Lord, take away

the iniquity of thy servant, for I have done very foolishly." And Nathan the prophet was sent again to him, to offer him three things, to choose one of them, which he would; seven years famine in the land, or to flee three months before his enemies, or three days pestilence in the land. "And David said, I am in a great strait, let us now fall into the hand of the Lord, for His mercies are great, and let me not fall into the hand of Man." His fault lay in wishing to know the number of all the people which were with him, a knowledge which ought to have been reserved for God.

9. And Scripture tells us that when the people were dying, on the very first day and at dinner time, David saw the Angel that smote the people, he said, "Lo, I have sinned and done wickedly; but these sheep, what have they done? let Thine hand, I pray Thee, be against me, and against my father's house." So the Lord repented, and commanded the Angel to spare the people, and that David should offer sacrifice: for there were then sacrifices for sin, but we have now the sacrifices of penitence. So by that humility he was made more acceptable to God, for it is not wonderful that man should sin, but it is indeed blameable if he does not acknowledge his error, and humble himself before God.

10. Holy Job, himself also powerful in this world, saith, "I covered not my sin, but declared it before all the people." And to the cruel king Saul, Jonathan his son said, "Let not the king sin against his servant, against David;" and "Wherefore then wilt thou sin against innocent blood to slay David without a cause?" For although he was a king he still would have sinned in slaying the innocent. Again when David was possessed of the kingdom, and heard that innocent Abner had been slain by Joab the Captain of his host, he said, "I and my kingdom are guiltless before the Lord forever from the blood of Abner, the son of Ner," and he fasted for sorrow.

11. This I have written, not to confound you, but that these royal examples may induce you to put away this sin from your kingdom; for this you will do by humbling your soul before God. You are a man; temptation has fallen upon you; vanquish it. Sin is not washed away but by tears and penitence. Neither Angel nor Archangel can do it. The Lord Himself, Who alone can say "I am with you;" even He grants the remission of sin save to the penitent.

12. I advise, I entreat, I exhort, I admonish; for I am grieved that you who were an example of singular piety, who stood so high for clemency, who would not suffer even single offenders to be put in jeopardy, should not mourn over the death of so many innocent persons. Successful as you have been in battle, and great in other respects, yet mercy was ever the crown of your actions. The devil has envied you your chief excellence: overcome him, while you still have the means. Add not to sin by acting in a manner which has injured so many.

13. For my part, debtor as I am to your clemency, which I have

found superior to that of many Emperors and equalled only by one, though I have no ground for charging you with contumacy, I have still reason for apprehension: if you purpose being present, I dare not offer the Sacrifice. That which may not be done when the blood of one innocent person has been shed, may it be done where many have been slain? I trow not.

14. Lastly, I will write with my own hand what I wish should be read by yourself only. As I hope for deliverance from all tribulation from the Lord, it has not been from man, nor by man's agency that this has been forbidden me, but by His own manifest interposition. For in the midst of my anxiety, on the very night whereon I was about to set out, I saw you in a vision coming into the Church, but I was withheld from offering Sacrifice. Other things I pass over, which I might have avoided, but I bore them for your sake, I believe. May the Lord cause all things to turn out peacefully. Our God gives us divers admonitions, by heavenly signs, by prophetic warnings; and by visions vouchsafed even to sinners, He would have us understand that we ought to beseech Him to remove from us commotions, that He would bestow peace on you, our rulers, that the Church, for whose benefit it is that we should have pious and Christian Emperors, may be kept in faith and tranquillity.

15. Doubtless you wish to be approved by God, "To every thing there is a season," as it is written; "It is time for Thee Lord," saith the prophet, "to lay to Thine hand," and it is an acceptable time to God. You shall make your oblation when you have received permission to sacrifice, when your offering will be pleasing to God. Would it not be a delight to me to enjoy your Majesty's favour, and act in accordance with your will, if the case permitted it? Prayer by itself is a sacrifice; it obtains pardon while the oblation would be rejected, for the former is evidence of humility, the latter of contempt: for God Himself tells us that He prefers the performance of His commandments to sacrifice. God proclaims this, Moses announces it to the people, Paul preaches it to them. Do that which you understand is for the time better. "I will have mercy," it is said, "and not sacrifice." Are not those therefore rather to be called Christians who condemn their own sin than those who think to excuse it? "The just accuses himself in the beginning of his words." He who, having sinned, accuses himself, not he who praises himself, is just.

16. I would that previously to this I had trusted rather to myself than to your accustomed habits. Remembering that you quickly pardon, and revoke your sentence, as you have often done, you have been anticipated, and I have not shunned that which I had no need to fear. But thanks to the Lord, Who chastises His servants, that they may not be lost. This I share with the prophets, and you shall share it with the saints.

17. Shall not I value the father of Gratian at more than my own eyes? Your other sacred pledges too claim pardon for you. On those whom I

regarded with impartial affection I conferred by anticipation a name that is dear to me. You have my love, my affection, my prayers. If you believe my words, I call on you to act according to them; if, I say, you believe, acknowledge it, but if not, excuse my conduct in that I prefer God to my sovereign. May your gracious Majesty, with your holy offspring, enjoy in happiness and prosperity perpetual peace.

6. *The Benedictine Rule*

St. Benedict (c.480–c.550) wrote this rule for his own monastery of Monte Cassino, probably with no intention of being generally applied. It has nevertheless become the fundamental rule of Western monasticism. Written in a spirit of Roman moderation and discipline, it created a workable religious institution, the most successful one, as it turned out, for the next six centuries.

The translation is from Leonard J. Doyle, *St. Benedict's Rule for Monasteries* (Collegeville, Minnesota: The Liturgical Press, 1948). It is complete except for the purely liturgical chapters nine through eighteen, and the prologue.

Chapter 1
On the Kinds of Monks

IT IS well known that there are four kinds of monks. The first kind are the Cenobites: those who live in monasteries and serve under a rule and an Abbot.

The second kind are the Anchorites or Hermits: those who, no longer in the first fervor of their reformation, but after long probation in a monastery, having learned by the help of many brethren how to fight against the devil, go out well armed from the ranks of the community to the solitary combat of the desert. They are able now, with no help save from God, to fight single-handed against the vices of the flesh and their own evil thoughts.

The third kind of monks, a detestable kind, are the Sarabaites. These, not having been tested, as gold in the furnace, by any rule or by the lessons of experience, are as soft as lead. In their works they still keep faith with the world, so that their tonsure marks them as liars before God. They live in twos or threes, or even singly, without a shepherd, in their own sheepfolds and not in the Lord's. Their law is the desire for self-gratification: whatever enters their mind or appeals to them, that they call holy; what they dislike, they regard as unlawful.

The fourth kind of monks are those called Gyrovagues. These spend their whole lives tramping from province to province, staying as guests in different monasteries for three or four days at a time. Always on the move, with no stability, they indulge their own wills and succumb to the allurements of gluttony, and are in every way worse than the Sarabaites. Of the miserable conduct of all such men it is better to be silent than to speak.

Passing these over, therefore, let us proceed, with God's help, to lay down a rule for the strongest kind of monks, the Cenobites.

Chapter 2

What Kind of Man the Abbot Ought to Be

An Abbot who is worthy to be over a monastery should always remember what he is called, and live up to the name of Superior. For he is believed to hold the place of Christ in the monastery, being called by a name of His, which is taken from the words of the Apostle: "You have received a Spirit of adoption as sons, by virtue of which we cry, 'Abba—Father!'"

Therefore the Abbot ought not to teach or ordain or command anything which is against the Lord's precepts; on the contrary, his commands and his teaching should be a leaven of divine justice kneaded into the minds of his disciples.

Let the Abbot always bear in mind that at the dread Judgment of God there will be an examination of these two matters: his teaching and the obedience of his disciples. And let the Abbot be sure that any lack of profit the master of the house may find in the sheep will be laid to the blame of the shepherd. On the other hand, if the shepherd has bestowed all his pastoral diligence on a restless, unruly flock and tried every remedy for their unhealthy behavior, then he will be acquitted at the Lord's Judgment and may say to the Lord with the Prophet: "I have not concealed Your justice within my heart; Your truth and Your salvation I have declared. But they have despised and rejected me." And then finally let death itself, irresistible, punish those disobedient sheep under his charge.

Therefore, when anyone receives the name of Abbot, he ought to govern his disciples with a twofold teaching. That is to say, he should show them all that is good and holy by his deeds even more than by his words, expounding the Lord's commandments in words to the intelligent among his disciples, but demonstrating the divine precepts by his actions for those of harder hearts and ruder minds. And whatever he has taught his disciples to be contrary to God's law, let him indicate by his example that it is not to be done, lest, while preaching to others, he himself be found reprobate, and lest God one day say to him in his sin, "Why do you declare My statutes and profess My covenant with your lips, whereas you hate discipline and have cast My words behind you?" And again, "You were looking at the speck in your brother's eye, and did not see the beam in your own."

Let him make no distinction of persons in the monastery. Let him not love one more than another, unless it be one whom he finds better in good works or in obedience. Let him not advance one of noble birth ahead of one who was formerly a slave, unless there be some other reasonable ground for it. But if the Abbot for just reason think fit to do so, let him advance one of any rank whatever. Otherwise let them keep their due places; because, whether slaves or freemen, we are all one in Christ and bear an equal burden of service in the army of the same Lord. For with God there is no respect of persons. Only for one reason are we preferred in His sight: if we be found better than others in good works and humility. Therefore let the Abbot show equal love to all and impose the same discipline on all according to their deserts.

In his teaching the Abbot should always follow the Apostle's formula: "Reprove, entreat, rebuke"; threatening at one time and coaxing at another as the occasion may require, showing now the stern countenance of a master, now the loving affection of a father. That is to say, it is the undisciplined and restless whom he must reprove rather sharply; it is the obedient, meek and patient whom he must entreat to advance in virtue; while as for the negligent and disdainful, these we charge him to rebuke and correct.

And let him not shut his eyes to the faults of offenders; but, since he has the authority, let him cut out those faults by the roots as soon as they begin to appear, remembering the fate of Heli, the priest of Silo. The well-disposed and those of good understanding let him correct with verbal admonition the first and second time. But bold, hard, proud and disobedient characters he should curb at the very beginning of their ill-doing by stripes and other bodily punishments, knowing that it is written, "The fool is not corrected with words," and again, "Beat your son with the rod and you will deliver his soul from death."

The Abbot should always remember what he is and what he is called, and should know that to whom more is committed, from him more is required. Let him understand also what a difficult and arduous task he has undertaken: ruling souls and adapting himself to a variety of characters. One he must coax, another scold, another persuade, according to each one's character and understanding. Thus he must adjust and adapt himself to all in such a way that he may not only suffer no loss in the flock committed to his care, but may even rejoice in the increase of a good flock.

Above all let him not neglect or undervalue the welfare of the souls committed to him, in a greater concern for fleeting, earthly, perishable things; but let him always bear in mind that he has undertaken the government of souls and that he will have to give an account of them.

And if he be tempted to allege a lack of earthly means, let him remember what is written: "First seek the kingdom of God and His justice, and all these things shall be given you besides." And again: "Nothing is wanting to those who fear Him."

Let him know, then, that he who has undertaken the government of souls must prepare himself to render an account of them. Whatever number of brethren he knows he has under his care, he may be sure beyond doubt that on Judgment Day he will have to give the Lord an account of all these souls, as well as of his own soul.

Thus the constant apprehension about his coming examination as shepherd concerning the sheep entrusted to him, and his anxiety over the account that must be given for others, make him careful of his own record. And while by his admonitions he is helping others to amend, he himself is cleansed of his faults.

Chapter 3

On Calling the Brethren for Counsel

Whenever any important business has to be done in the monastery, let the Abbot call together the whole community and state the matter to be acted upon. Then, having heard the brethren's advice, let him turn the matter over in his own mind and do what he shall judge to be most expedient. The reason we have said that all should be called for counsel is that the Lord often reveals to the younger what is best.

Let the brethren give their advice with all the deference required by humility, and not presume stubbornly to defend their opinions; but let the decision rather depend on the Abbot's judgment, and all submit to whatever he shall decide for their welfare.

However, just as it is proper for the disciples to obey their master, so also it is his function to dispose all things with prudence and justice.

In all things, therefore, let all follow the Rule as guide, and let no one be so rash as to deviate from it. Let no one in the monastery follow his own heart's fancy; and let no one presume to contend with his Abbot in an insolent way or even outside of the monastery. But if anyone should presume to do so, let him undergo the discipline of the Rule. At the same time, the Abbot himself should do all things in the fear of God and in observance of the Rule, knowing that beyond a doubt he will have to render an account of all his decisions to God, the most just Judge.

But if the business to be done in the interests of the monastery be of lesser importance, let him take counsel with the seniors only. It is written,

"Do everything with counsel, and you will not repent when you have done it."

Chapter 4

What Are the Instruments of Good Works

1. In the first place, to love the Lord God with the whole heart, the whole soul, the whole strength.
2. Then, one's neighbor as oneself.
3. Then not to murder.
4. Not to commit adultery.
5. Not to steal.
6. Not to covet.
7. Not to bear false witness.
8. To respect all men.
9. And not to do to another what one would not have done to oneself.
10. To deny oneself in order to follow Christ.
11. To chastise the body.
12. Not to become attached to pleasures.
13. To love fasting.
14. To relieve the poor.
15. To clothe the naked.
16. To visit the sick.
17. To bury the dead.
18. To help in trouble.
19. To console the sorrowing.
20. To become a stranger to the world's ways.
21. To prefer nothing to the love of Christ.
22. Not to give way to anger.
23. Not to nurse a grudge.
24. Not to entertain deceit in one's heart.
25. Not to give a false peace.
26. Not to forsake charity.
27. Not to swear, for fear of perjuring oneself.
28. To utter truth from heart and mouth.
29. Not to return evil for evil.
30. To do no wrong to anyone, and to bear patiently wrongs done to oneself.
31. To love one's enemies.
32. Not to curse those who curse us, but rather to bless them.
33. To bear persecution for justice' sake.
34. Not to be proud.

35. Not addicted to wine.
36. Not a great eater.
37. Not drowsy.
38. Not lazy.
39. Not a grumbler.
40. Not a detractor.
41. To put one's hope in God.
42. To attribute to God, and not to self, whatever good one sees in oneself.
43. But to recognize always that the evil is one's own doing, and to impute it to oneself.
44. To fear the Day of Judgment.
45. To be in dread of hell.
46. To desire eternal life with all the passion of the spirit.
47. To keep death daily before one's eyes.
48. To keep constant guard over the actions of one's life.
49. To know for certain that God sees one everywhere.
50. When evil thoughts come into one's heart, to dash them against Christ immediately.
51. And to manifest them to one's spiritual father.
52. To guard one's tongue against evil and depraved speech.
53. Not to love much talking.
54. Not to speak useless words or words that move to laughter.
55. Not to love much or boisterous laughter.
56. To listen willingly to holy reading.
57. To devote oneself frequently to prayer.
58. Daily in one's prayers, with tears and sighs, to confess one's past sins to God, and to amend them for the future.
59. Not to fulfil the desires of the flesh; to hate one's own will.
60. To obey in all things the commands of the Abbot, even though he himself (which God forbid) should act otherwise, mindful of the Lord's precept, "Do what they say, but not what they do."
61. Not to wish to be called holy before one is holy; but first to be holy, that one may be truly so called.
62. To fulfil God's commandments daily in one's deeds.
63. To love chastity.
64. To hate no one.
65. Not to be jealous, not to harbor envy.
66. Not to love contention.
67. To beware of haughtiness.
68. And to respect the seniors.
69. To love the juniors.
70. To pray for one's enemies in the love of Christ.
71. To make peace with one's adversary before the sun sets.
72. And never to despair of God's mercy.

These, then, are the tools of the spiritual craft. If we employ them unceasingly day and night, and return them on the Day of Judgment, our compensation from the Lord will be that wage He has promised: "Eye has not seen, nor ear heard, what God has prepared for those who love Him."

Now the workshop in which we shall diligently execute all these tasks is the enclosure of the monastery and stability in the community.

Chapter 5
On Obedience

The first degree of humility is obedience without delay. This is the virtue of those who hold nothing dearer to them than Christ; who, because of the holy service they have professed, and the fear of hell, and the glory of life everlasting, as soon as anything has been ordered by the Superior, receive it as a divine command and cannot suffer any delay in executing it. Of these the Lord says, "As soon as he heard, he obeyed Me." And again to teachers He says, "He who hears you, hears Me."

Such as these, therefore, immediately leaving their own affairs and forsaking their own will, dropping the work they were engaged in the leaving it unfinished, with the ready step of obedience follow up with their deeds the voice of him who commands. And so as it were at the same moment the master's command is given and the disciple's work is completed, the two things being speedily accomplished together in the swiftness of the fear of God by those who are moved with the desire of attaining life everlasting. That desire is their motive for choosing the narrow way, of which the Lord says, "Narrow is the way that leads to life," so that, not living according to their own choice nor obeying their own desires and pleasures but walking by another's judgment and command, they dwell in monasteries and desire to have an Abbot over them. Assuredly such as these are living up to that maxim of the Lord in which He says, "I have come not to do My own will, but the will of Him who sent Me."

But this very obedience will be acceptable to God and pleasing to men only if what is commanded is done without hesitation, delay, lukewarmness, grumbling, or objection. For the obedience given to Superiors is given to God, since He Himself has said, "He who hears you, hears Me." And the disciples should offer their obedience with a good will, for "God loves a cheerful giver." For if the disciple obeys with an ill will and murmurs, not necessarily with his lips but simply in his heart, then even though he fulfil the command yet his work will not be acceptable to God, who sees that his heart is murmuring. And, far from gaining a reward for such work as this, he will incur the punishment due to murmurers, unless he amend and make satisfaction.

Chapter 6

On the Spirit of Silence

Let us do what the Prophet says: "I said, 'I will guard my ways, that I may not sin with my tongue. I have set a guard to my mouth.' I was mute and was humbled, and kept silence even from good things." Here the Prophet shows that if the spirit of silence ought to lead us at times to refrain even from good speech, so much the more ought the punishment for sin make us avoid evil words.

Therefore, since the spirit of silence is so important, permission to speak should rarely be granted even to perfect disciples, even though it be for good, holy, edifying conversation; for it is written, "In much speaking you will not escape sin," and in another place, "Death and life are in the power of the tongue."

For speaking and teaching belong to the master; the disciples's part is to be silent and to listen. And for that reason if anything has to be asked of the Superior, it should be asked with all the humility and submission inspired by reverence.

But as for coarse jests and idle words or words that move to laughter, these we condemn everywhere with a perpetual ban, and for such conversation we do not permit a disciple to open his mouth.

Chapter 7

On Humility

Holy Scripture, brethren, cries out to us, saying, "Everyone who exalts himself shall be humbled, and he who humbles himself shall be exalted." In saying this it shows us that all exaltation is a kind of pride, against which the Prophet proves himself to be on guard when he says, "Lord, my heart is not exalted, nor are mine eyes lifted up; neither have I walked in great matters, nor in wonders above me." But how has he acted? "Rather have I been of humble mind than exalting myself; as a weaned child on its mother's breast, so You solace my soul."

Hence, brethren, if we wish to reach the very highest point of humility and to arrive speedily at that heavenly exaltation to which ascent is made through the humility of this present life, we must by our ascending actions erect the ladder Jacob saw in his dream, on which Angels appeared to him descending and ascending. By that descent and ascent we must surely understand nothing else than this, that we descend by self-exaltation and ascend by humility. And the ladder thus set up is our life in the world, which the Lord raises up to heaven if our heart is humbled. For we call our body and soul the sides of the ladder, and into these sides our divine vocation has inserted the different steps of humility and discipline we must climb.

The first degree of humility, then, is that a person keep the fear of God before his eyes and beware of ever forgetting it. Let him be ever mindful of all that God has commanded; let his thoughts constantly recur to the hell-fire which will burn for their sins, those who despise God, and to the life everlasting which is prepared for those who fear Him. Let him keep himself at every moment from sins and vices, whether of the mind, the tongue, the hands, the feet, or the self-will, and check also the desires of the flesh.

Let a man consider that God is always looking at him from heaven, that his actions are everywhere visible to the divine eyes and are constantly being reported to God by the Angels. This is what the Prophet shows us when he represents God as ever present within our thoughts, in the words "Searcher of minds and hearts is God" and again in the words "The Lord knows the thoughts of men." Again he says, "You have read my thoughts from afar" and "The thoughts of men will confess to You."

In order that he may be careful about his wrongful thoughts, therefore, let the faithful brother say constantly in his heart, "Then shall I be spotless before Him, if I have kept myself from my iniquity."

As for self-will, we are forbidden to do our own will by the Scripture, which says to us, "Turn away from your own will," and likewise by the prayer in which we ask God that His will be done in us. And rightly are we taught not to do our own will when we take heed to the warning of Scripture: "There are ways which to men seem right, but the ends of them plunge into the depths of hell"; and also when we tremble at what is said of the careless: "They are corrupt and have become abominable in their wills."

And as for the desires of the flesh, let us believe with the Prophet that God is ever present to us, when he says to the Lord, "Every desire of mine is before You."

We must be on our guard, therefore, against evil desires, for death lies close by the gate of pleasure. Hence the Scripture gives this command: "Go not after your concupiscences."

So therefore, since the eyes of the Lord observe the good and the evil and the Lord is always looking down from heaven on the children of men "to see if there be anyone who understands and seeks God," and since our deeds are daily, day and night, reported to the Lord by the Angels assigned to us, we must constantly beware, brethren, as the Prophet says in the Psalm, lest at any time God see us falling into evil ways and becoming unprofitable; and lest, having spared us for the present because in His kindness He awaits our reformation, He says to us in the future, "These things you did, and I held My peace."

The second degree of humility is that a person love not his own will nor take pleasure in satisfying his desires, but model his actions on the saying of the Lord, "I have come not to do My own will, but the will of Him who sent Me." It is written also, "Self-will has its punishment, but constraint wins a crown."

The third degree of humility is that a person for love of God submit himself to his Superior in all obedience, imitating the Lord, of whom the Apostle says, "He became obedient even unto death."

The fourth degree of humility is that he hold fast to patience with a silent mind when in this obedience he meets with difficulties and contradictions and even any kind of injustice, enduring all without growing weary or running away. For the Scripture says, "He who perseveres to the end, he it is who shall be saved"; and again, "Let your heart take courage, and wait for the Lord!"

And to show how those who are faithful ought to endure all things, however contrary, for the Lord, the Scripture says in the person of the suffering, "For Your sake we are put to death all the day long; we are considered as sheep marked for slaughter." Then, secure in their hope of a divine recompense, they go on with joy to declare, "But in all these trials we conquer, through Him who has granted us His love." Again, in another place the Scripture says, "You have tested us, O God; You have tried us as silver is tried, by fire; You have brought us into a snare; You have laid afflictions on our back." And to show that we ought to be under a Superior, it goes on to say, "You have set men over our heads."

Moreover, by their patience those faithful ones fulfil the Lord's command in adversities and injuries: when struck on one cheek, they offer the other; when deprived of their tunic, they surrender also their cloak; when forced to go a mile, they go two; with the Apostle Paul they bear with false brethren and bless those who curse them.

The fifth degree of humility is that he hide from his Abbot none of the evil thoughts that enter his heart or the sins committed in secret, but that he humbly confess them. The Scripture urges us to this when it says, "Reveal your way to the Lord and hope in Him," and again, "Confess to the Lord, for He is good, for His mercy endures forever." And the Prophet likewise says, "My offense I have made known to You, and my iniquities I have not covered up. I said: 'I will declare against myself my iniquities to the Lord'; and 'You forgave the wickedness of my heart.'"

The sixth degree of humility is that a monk be content with the poorest and worst of everything, and that in every occupation assigned him he consider himself a bad and worthless workman, saying with the Prophet, "I am brought to nothing and I am without understanding; I have become as a beast of burden before You, and I am always with You."

The seventh degree of humility is that he consider himself lower and of less account than anyone else, and this not only in verbal protestation but also with the most heartfelt inner conviction, humbling himself and saying with the Prophet, "But I am a worm and no man, the scorn of men and the outcast of the people. After being exalted, I have been humbled and covered with confusion." And again, "It is good for me that You have humbled me, that I may learn Your commandments."

The eighth degree of humility is that a monk do nothing except what is commended by the common Rule of the monastery and the example of the elders.

The ninth degree of humility is that a monk restrain his tongue and keep silence, not speaking until he is questioned. For the Scripture shows that "in much speaking there is no escape from sin" and that "the talkative man is not stable on the earth."

The tenth degree of humility is that he be not ready and quick to laugh, for it is written, "The fool lifts up his voice in laughter."

The eleventh degree of humility is that when a monk speaks he do so gently and without laughter, humbly and seriously, in few and sensible words, and that he be not noisy in his speech. It is written, "A wise man is known by the fewness of his words."

The twelfth degree of humility is that a monk not only have humility in his heart but also by his very appearance make it always manifest to those who see him. That is to say that whether he is at the Work of God, in the oratory, in the monastery, in the garden, on the road, in the fields or anywhere else, and whether sitting, walking or standing, he should always have his head bowed and his eyes toward the ground. Feeling the guilt of his sins at every moment, he should consider himself already present at the dread Judgment and constantly say in his heart what the publican in the Gospel said with his eyes fixed on the earth: "Lord, I am a sinner and not worthy to lift up my eyes to heaven"; and again with the Prophet: "I am bowed down and humbled everywhere."

Having climbed all these steps of humility, therefore, the monk will presently come to that perfect love of God which casts out fear. And all those precepts which formerly he had not observed without fear, he will now begin to keep by reason of that love, without any effort, as though naturally and by habit. No longer will his motive be the fear of hell, but rather the love of Christ, good habit and delight in the virtues which the Lord will deign to show forth by the Holy Spirit in His servant now cleansed from vice and sin.

Chapter 8

On the Divine Office during the Night

In winter time, that is from the Calends of November until Easter, the brethren shall rise at what is calculated to be the eighth hour of the night, so that they may sleep somewhat longer than half the night and rise with their rest completed. And the time that remains after the Night Office should be spent in study by those brethren who need a better knowledge of the Psalter or the lessons.

From Easter to the aforesaid Calends of November, the hour of rising should be so arranged that the Morning Office, which is to be said at daybreak, will follow the Night Office after a very short interval, during which the brethren may go out for the necessities of nature.

We strongly recommend, however, that if this distribution of the Psalms is displeasing to anyone, he should arrange them otherwise, in whatever way he considers better, but taking care in any case that the Psalter with its full number of 150 Psalms be chanted every week and begun again every Sunday at the Night Office. For those monks show themselves too lazy in the service to which they are vowed, who chant less than the Psalter with the customary canticles in the course of a week, whereas we read that our holy Fathers strenuously fulfilled that task in a single day. May we, lukewarm that we are, perform it at least in a whole week!

Chapter 19

On the Manner of Saying the Divine Office

We believe that the divine presence is everywhere and that "the eyes of the Lord are looking on the good and the evil in every place." But we should believe this especially without any doubt when we are assisting at the Work of God. To that end let us be mindful always of the Prophet's words, "Serve the Lord in fear" and again "Sing praises wisely" and "In the sight of the Angels I will sing praise to You." Let us therefore consider how we ought to conduct ourselves in the sight of the Godhead and of His Angels, and let us take part in the psalmody in such a way that our mind may be in harmony with our voice.

Chapter 20

On Reverence in Prayer

When we wish to suggest our wants to men of high station, we do not presume to do so except with humility and reverence. How much the more, then, are complete humility and pure devotion necessary in supplication of the Lord who is God of the universe! And let us be assured that it is not in saying a great deal that we shall be heard, but in purity of heart and in tears of compunction. Our prayer, therefore, ought to be short and pure, unless it happens to be prolonged by an inspiration of divine grace. In community, however, let prayer be very short, and when the Superior gives the signal let all rise together.

Chapter 21

On the Deans of the Monastery

If the community is a large one, let there be chosen out of it brethren of good repute and holy life, and let them be appointed deans. These shall take charge of their deaneries in all things, observing the commandments of God and the instructions of their Abbot.

Let men of such character be chosen deans that the Abbot may with confidence share his burdens among them. Let them be chosen not by rank but according to their worthiness of life and the wisdom of their doctrine.

If any of these deans should become inflated with pride and found deserving of censure, let him be corrected once, and again, and a third time. If he will not amend, then let him be deposed and another be put in his place who is worthy of it.

And we order the same to be done in the case of the Prior.

Chapter 22

How the Monks Are to Sleep

Let each one sleep in a separate bed. Let them receive bedding suitable to their manner of life, according to the Abbot's directions. If possible let all sleep in one place; but if the number does not allow this, let them take their rest by tens or twenties with the seniors who have charge of them.

A candle shall be kept burning in the room until morning.

Let the monks sleep clothed and girded with belts or cords—but not with their knives at their sides, lest they cut themselves in their sleep—and thus be always ready to rise without delay when the signal is given and hasten to be before one another at the Work of God, yet with all gravity and decorum.

The younger brethren shall not have beds next to one another, but among those of the older ones.

When they rise for the Work of God let them gently encourage one another, that the drowsy may have no excuse.

Chapter 23

On Excommunication for Faults

If a brother is found to be obstinate, or disobedient, or proud, or murmuring, or habitually transgressing the Holy Rule in any point and contemptuous of the orders of his seniors, the latter shall admonish him secretly a first and a second time, as Our Lord commands. If he fails to amend, let him be given a public rebuke in front of the whole community. But if even then he does not reform, let him be placed under excommunication, provided that he understands the seriousness of that penalty; if he is perverse, however, let him undergo corporal punishment.

Chapter 24

What the Measure of Excommunication Should Be

The measure of excommunication or of chastisement should correspond to the degree of fault, which degree is estimated by the Abbot's judgment.

If a brother is found guilty of lighter faults, let him be excluded from the common table. Now the program for one deprived of the fellowship of the table shall be as follows: In the oratory he shall intone neither Psalm nor antiphon nor shall he recite a lesson until he has made satisfaction; in the refectory he shall take his food alone after the community meal, so that if the brethren eat at the sixth hour, for instance, that brother shall eat at the ninth, while if they eat at the ninth hour he shall eat in the evening, until by a suitable satisfaction he obtains pardon.

Chapter 25

On Weightier Faults

Let the brother who is guilty of a weightier fault be excluded both from the table and from the oratory. Let none of the brethren join him either for company or for conversation. Let him be alone at the work assigned him, abiding in penitential sorrow and pondering that terrible sentence of the Apostle where he says that a man of that kind is handed over for the destruction of the flesh, that the spirit may be saved in the day of the Lord. Let him take his meals alone in the measure and at the hour which the Abbot shall consider suitable for him. He shall not be blessed by those who pass by, nor shall the food that is given him be blessed.

Chapter 26

On Those Who without an Order Associate with the Excommunicated

If any brother presumes without an order from the Abbot to associate in any way with an excommunicated brother, or to speak with him, or to send him a message, let him incur a similar punishment of excommunication.

Chapter 27

How Solicitous the Abbot Should Be for the Excommunicated

Let the Abbot be most solicitous in his concern for delinquent brethren, for "it is not the healthy but the sick who need a physician." And therefore he ought to use every means that a wise physician would use. Let him send "senpectae," that is, brethren of mature years and wisdom, who may as it were secretly console the wavering brother and induce him to make humble satisfaction; comforting him that he may not "be overwhelmed by excessive grief," but that, as the Apostle says, charity may be strengthened in him. And let everyone pray for him.

For the Abbot must have the utmost solicitude and exercise all prudence and diligence lest he lose any of the sheep entrusted to him. Let him know that what he has undertaken is the care of weak souls and not a tyranny over strong ones; and let him fear the Prophet's warning through which God says, "What you saw to be fat you took to yourselves, and what was feeble you cast away." Let him rather imitate the loving example of the Good Shepherd who left the ninety-nine sheep in the mountains and went to look for the one sheep that had gone astray, on whose weakness He had such compassion that He deigned to place it on His own sacred shoulders and thus carry it back to the flock.

Chapter 28

On Those Who Will Not Amend after Repeated Corrections

If a brother who has been frequently corrected for some fault, and even excommunicated, does not amend, let a harsher correction be applied, that is, let the punishment of the rod be administered to him.

But if he still does not reform or perhaps (which God forbid) even rises up in pride and wants to defend his conduct, then let the Abbot do what a wise physician would do. Having used applications, the ointments of exhortation, the medicines of the Holy Scriptures, finally the cautery of excommunication and of the strokes of the rod, if he sees that his efforts are of no avail, let him apply a still greater remedy, his own prayers and those of all the brethren, that the Lord, who can do all things, may restore health to the sick brother.

But if he is not healed even in this way, then let the Abbot use the knife of amputation, according to the Apostle's words, "Expel the evil one from your midst," and again, "If the faithless one departs, let him depart," lest one diseased sheep contaminate the whole flock.

Chapter 29

Whether Brethren Who Leave the Monastery Should Be Received Again

If a brother who through his own fault leaves the monastery should wish to return, let him first promise full reparation for his having gone away; and then let him be received in the lowest place, as a test of his humility. And if he should leave again, let him be taken back again, and so a third time; but he should understand that after this all way of return is denied him.

Chapter 30

How Boys Are to Be Corrected

Every age and degree of understanding should have its proper measure of discipline. With regard to boys and adolescents, therefore, or those who cannot understand the seriousness of the penalty of excommunication, whenever such as these are delinquent let them be subjected to severe fasts or brought to terms by harsh beatings, that they may be cured.

Chapter 31

What Kind of Man the Cellarer of the Monastery Should Be

As cellarer of the monastery let there be chosen from the community one who is wise, of mature character, sober, not a great eater, not haughty, not excitable, not offensive, not slow, not wasteful, but a God-fearing man who may be like a father to the whole community.

Let him have charge of everything. He shall do nothing without the Abbot's orders, but keep to his instructions. Let him not vex the brethren. If any brother happens to make some unreasonable demand of him, instead of vexing the brother with a contemptuous refusal he should humbly give the reason for denying the improper request.

Let him keep guard over his own soul, mindful always of the Apostle's saying that "he who has ministered well acquires for himself a good standing."

Let him take the greatest care of the sick, of children, of guests and of the poor, knowing without doubt that he will have to render an account for all these on the Day of Judgment.

Let him regard all the utensils of the monastery and its whole property as if they were the sacred vessels of the altar. Let him not think that he may neglect anything. He should be neither a miser nor a prodigal and squanderer of the monastery's substance, but should do all things with measure and in accordance with the Abbot's instructions.

Above all things let him have humility; and if he has nothing else to give let him give a good word in answer, for it is written, "A good word is above the best gift."

Let him have under his care all that the Abbot has assigned to him, but not presume to deal with what he has forbidden him.

Let him give the brethren their appointed allowance of food without any arrogance or delay, that they may not be scandalized, mindful of the Word of God as to what he deserves "who shall scandalize one of the little ones."

If the community is a large one, let helpers be given him, that by their assistance he may fulfil with a quiet mind the office committed to him. The proper times should be observed in giving the things that have to be given and asking for the things that have to be asked for, that no one may be troubled or vexed in the house of God.

Chapter 32

On the Tools and Property of the Monastery

For the care of the monastery's property in tools, clothing and other articles let the Abbot appoint brethren on whose manner of life and character he can rely; and let him, as he shall judge to be expedient, consign the various articles to them, to be looked after and to be collected again. The Abbot shall keep a list of these articles, so that as the brethren succeed one another in their assignments he may know what he gives and what he receives back.

If anyone treats the monastery's property in a slovenly or careless way, let him be corrected. If he fails to amend, let him undergo the discipline of the Rule.

Chapter 33

Whether Monks Ought to Have Anything of Their Own

This vice especially is to be cut out of the monastery by the roots. Let no one presume to give or receive anything without the Abbot's leave, or to have anything as his own—anything whatever, whether book or tablets or pen or whatever it may be—since they are not permitted to have even their bodies or wills at their own disposal; but for all their necessities let them look to the Father of the monastery. And let it be unlawful to have anything which the Abbot has not given or allowed. Let all things be common to all, as it is written, and let no one say or assume that anything is his own.

But if anyone is caught indulging in this most wicked vice, let him be admonished once and a second time. If he fails to amend, let him undergo punishment.

Chapter 34

Whether All Should Receive in Equal Measure What Is Necessary

Let us follow the Scripture, "Distribution was made to each according as anyone had need." By this we do not mean that there should be respecting of persons (which God forbid), but consideration for infirmities. He who needs less should thank God and not be discontented; but he who needs more should be humbled by the thought of his infirmity rather than feeling important on account of the kindness shown him. Thus all the members will be at peace.

Above all, let not the evil of murmuring appear for any reason whatsoever in the least word or sign. If anyone is caught at it, let him be placed under very severe discipline.

Chapter 35

On the Weekly Servers in the Kitchen

Let the brethren serve one another, and let no one be excused from the kitchen service except by reason of sickness or occupation in some important work. For this service brings increase of reward and of charity. But let helpers be provided for the weak ones, that they may not be distressed by this work; and indeed let everyone have help, as required by the size of the community or the circumstances of the locality. If the community is a large one, the cellarer shall be excused from the kitchen service; and so also those whose occupations are of greater utility, as we said above. Let the rest serve one another in charity.

The one who is ending his week of service shall do the cleaning on Saturday. He shall wash the towels with which the brethren wipe their hands and feet; and this server who is ending his week, aided by the one who is about to begin, shall wash the feet of all the brethren. He shall return the utensils of his office to the cellarer clean and in good condition, and the cellarer in turn shall consign them to the incoming server, in order that he may know what he gives out and what he receives back.

An hour before the meal let the weekly servers each receive a drink and some bread, over and above the appointed allowance, in order that at the meal time they may serve their brethren without murmuring and without excessive fatigue. On solemn days, however, let them wait until after Mass.

Immediately after the Morning Office on Sunday, the incoming and outgoing servers shall prostrate themselves before all the brethren in the oratory and ask their prayers. Let the server who is ending his week say this verse: "Blessed are You, O Lord God, who have helped me and consoled me." When this has been said three times and the outgoing server has received his blessing, then let the incoming server follow and say, "Incline unto my aid, O God; O Lord, make haste to help me." Let this also be repeated three times by all, and having received his blessing let him enter his service.

Chapter 36

On the Sick Brethren

Before all things and above all things, care must be taken of the sick, so that they will be served as if they were Christ in person; for He Himself said, "I was sick, and you visited Me," and, "What you did for one of these least ones, you did for Me." But let the sick on their part consider that they are being served for the honor of God, and let them not annoy their brethren who are serving them by their unnecessary demands. Yet they should be patiently borne with, because from such as these is gained a more abundant reward. Therefore the Abbot shall take the greatest care that they suffer no neglect.

For these sick brethren let there be assigned a special room and an attendant who is God-fearing, diligent and solicitous. Let the use of baths be afforded the sick as often as may be expedient; but to the healthy, and especially to the young, let them be granted more rarely. Moreover, let the use of meat be granted to the sick who are very weak, for the restoration of their strength; but when they are convalescent, let all abstain from meat as usual.

The Abbot shall take the greatest care that the sick be not neglected by the cellarers or the attendants; for he also is responsible for what is done wrongly by his disciples.

Chapter 37
On Old Men and Children

Although human nature itself is drawn to special kindness towards these times of life, that is towards old men and children, still the authority of the Rule should also provide for them. Let their weakness be always taken into account, and let them by no means be held to the rigor of the Rule with regard to food. On the contrary, let a kind consideration be shown to them, and let them eat before the regular hours.

Chapter 38
On the Weekly Reader

The meals of the brethren should not be without reading. Nor should the reader be anyone who happens to take up the book; but there should be a reader for the whole week, entering that office on Sunday. Let this incoming reader, after Mass and Communion, ask all to pray for him that God may keep him from the spirit of pride. And let him intone the following verse, which shall be said three times by all in the oratory: "O Lord, open my lips, and my mouth shall declare Your praise." Then, having received a blessing, let him enter on the reading.

And let absolute silence be kept at table, so that no whispering may be heard nor any voice except the reader's. As to the things they need while they eat and drink, let the brethren pass them to one another so that no one need ask for anything. If anything is needed, however, let it be asked for by means of some audible sign rather than by speech. Nor shall anyone at table presume to ask questions about the reading or anything else, lest that give occasion for talking; except that the Superior may perhaps wish to say something briefly for the purpose of edification.

The brother who is reader for the week shall take a little refreshment before he begins to read, on account of the Holy Communion and lest perhaps the fast be hard for him to bear. He shall take his meal afterwards with the kitchen and table servers of the week.

The brethren are not to read or chant in order, but only those who edify their hearers.

Chapter 39
On the Measure of Food

We think it sufficient for the daily dinner, whether at the sixth or the ninth hour, that every table have two cooked dishes, on account of individual infirmities, so that he who for some reason cannot eat of the one may make his meal of the other. Therefore let two cooked dishes suffice for all the brethren; and if any fruit or fresh vegetables are available, let a third dish be added.

Let a good pound weight of bread suffice for the day, whether there be only one meal or both dinner and supper. If they are to have supper, the cellarer shall reserve a third of that pound, to be given them at supper.

But if it happens that the work was heavier, it shall lie within the Abbot's discretion and power, should it be expedient, to add something to the fare. Above all things, however, over-indulgence must be avoided and a monk must never be overtaken by indigestion; for there is nothing so opposed to the Christian character as over-indulgence, according to Our Lord's words, "See to it that your hearts be not burdened with over-indulgence."

Young boys shall not receive the same amount of food as their elders, but less; and frugality shall be observed in all circumstances.

Except the sick who are very weak, let all abstain entirely from eating the flesh of four-footed animals.

Chapter 40
On the Measure of Drink

"Everyone has his own gift from God, one in this way and another in that." It is therefore with some misgiving that we regulate the measure of other men's sustenance. Nevertheless, keeping in view the needs of weaker brethren, we believe that a hemina of wine a day is sufficient for each. But those to whom God gives the strength to abstain should know that they will receive a special reward.

If the circumstances of the place, or the work, or the heat of summer require a greater measure, the Superior shall use his judgment in the matter, taking care always that there be no occasion for surfeit or drunkenness. We read, it is true, that wine is by no means a drink for monks; but since the monks of our day cannot be persuaded of this, let us at least agree to drink sparingly and not to satiety, because "wine makes even the wise fall away."

But where the circumstances of the place are such that not even the measure prescribed above can be supplied, but much less or none at all, let whose who live there bless God and not murmur. Above all things do we give this admonition, that they abstain from murmuring.

Chapter 41

At What Hours the Meals Should Be Taken

From holy Easter until Pentecost let the brethren take dinner at the sixth hour and supper in the evening.

From Pentecost throughout the summer, unless the monks have work in the fields or the excessive heat of summer oppresses them, let them fast on Wednesdays and Fridays until the ninth hour; on the other days let them dine at the sixth hour. This dinner at the sixth hour shall be the daily schedule if they have work in the fields or the heat of summer is extreme; the Abbot's foresight shall decide on this. Thus it is that he should adapt and arrange everything in such a way that souls may be saved and that the brethren may do their work without just cause for murmuring.

From the Ides of September until the beginning of Lent let them always take their dinner at the ninth hour.

In Lent until Easter let them dine in the evening. But this evening hour shall be so determined that they will not need the light of a lamp while eating, but everything will be accomplished while it is still daylight. Indeed at all seasons let the hour, whether for supper or for dinner, be so arranged that everything will be done by daylight.

Chapter 42

That No One Speak after Compline

Monks ought to be zealous for silence at all times, but especially during the hours of the night. For every season, therefore, whether there be fasting or two meals, let the program be as follows:

If it be a season when there are two meals, then as soon as they have risen from supper they shall all sit together, and one of them shall read the Conferences or the Lives of the Fathers or something else that may edify the hearers; not the Heptateuch or the Books of Kings, however, because it will not be expedient for weak minds to hear those parts of Scripture at that hour; but they shall be read at other times.

If it be a day of fast, then having allowed a short interval after Vespers they shall proceed at once to the reading of the Conferences, as prescribed above; four or five pages being read, or as much as time permits, so that during the delay provided by this reading all may come together, including those who may have been occupied in some work assigned them.

When all, therefore, are gathered together, let them say Compline; and when they come out from Compline, no one shall be allowed to say anything from that time on. And if anyone should be found evading this rule of silence, let him undergo severe punishment. An exception shall be made if the need of speaking to guests should arise or if the Abbot should give someone an order. But even this should be done with the utmost gravity and the most becoming restraint.

Chapter 43

On Those Who Come Late to the Work of God or to Table

At the hour for the Divine Office, as soon as the signal is heard, let them abandon whatever they may have in hand and hasten with the greatest speed, yet with seriousness, so that there is no excuse for levity. Let nothing, therefore, be put before the Work of God.

If at the Night Office anyone arrives after the "Glory be to the Father" of Psalm 94—which Psalm for this reason we wish to be said very slowly and protractedly—let him not stand in his usual place in the choir; but let him stand last of all, or in a place set aside by the Abbot for such negligent ones in order that they may be seen by him and by all. He shall remain there until the Work of God has been completed, and then do penance by a public satisfaction. The reason why we have judged it fitting for them to stand in the last place or in a place apart is that, being seen by all, they may amend for very shame. For if they remain outside of the oratory, there will perhaps be someone who will go back to bed and sleep or at least seat himself outside and indulge in idle talk, and thus an occasion will be provided for the evil one. But let them go inside, that they may not lose the whole Office, and may amend for the future.

At the day Hours anyone who does not arrive at the Work of God until after the verse and the "Glory be to the Father" of the first Psalm following it shall stand in the last place, according to our ruling above. Nor shall he presume to join the choir in their chanting until he has made satisfaction, unless the Abbot should pardon him and give him permission; but even then the offender must make satisfaction for his fault.

Anyone who does not come to table before the verse, so that all together may say the verse and the oration and all sit down to table at the same time—anyone who through his own carelessness or bad habit does not come on time shall be corrected for this up to the second time. If then he does not amend, he shall not be allowed to share in the common table, but shall be separated from the company of all and made to eat alone, and his portion of wine shall be taken away from him, until he has made satisfaction and has amended. And let him suffer a like penalty who is not present at the verse said after the meal.

And let no one presume to take any food or drink before or after the appointed time. But if anyone is offered something by the Superior and refuses to take it, then when the time comes that he desires what he formerly refused or something else, let him receive nothing whatever until he has made proper satisfaction.

Chapter 44

How the Excommunicated Are to Make Satisfaction

One who for serious faults is excommunicated from oratory and table shall make satisfaction as follows. At the hour when the celebration of the Work of God is concluded in the oratory, let him lie prostrate before the door of the oratory, saying nothing, but only lying prone with his face to the ground at the feet of all as they come out of the oratory. And let him continue to do this until the Abbot judges that satisfaction has been made. Then, when he has come at the Abbot's bidding, let him cast himself first at the Abbot's feet and then at the feet of all, that they may pray for him.

And next, if the Abbot so orders, let him be received into the choir, to the place which the Abbot appoints, but with the provision that he shall not presume to intone Psalm or lesson or anything else in the oratory without a further order from the Abbot. Moreover, at every Hour, when the Work of God is ended, let him cast himself on the ground in the place where he stands. And let him continue to satisfy in this way until the Abbot again orders him finally to cease from this satisfaction.

But those who for slight faults are excommunicated only from table shall make satisfaction in the oratory, and continue in it till an order from the Abbot, until he blesses them and says, "It is enough."

Chapter 45

On Those Who Make Mistakes in the Oratory

When anyone has made a mistake while reciting a Psalm, a responsory, an antiphon or a lesson, if he does not humble himself there before all by making a satisfaction, let him undergo a greater punishment because he would not correct by humility what he did wrong through carelessness.

But boys for such faults shall be whipped.

Chapter 46

On Those Who Fail in Any Other Matters

When anyone is engaged in any sort of work, whether in the kitchen, in the cellar, in a shop, in the bakery, in the garden, while working at some craft, or in any other place, and he commits some fault, or breaks something, or loses something, or transgresses in any other way whatsoever, if he does not come immediately before the Abbot and the community of his own accord to make satisfaction and confess his fault, then when it becomes known through another, let him be subjected to a more severe correction.

But if the sin-sickness of the soul is a hidden one, let him reveal it only to the Abbot or to a spiritual father, who knows how to cure his own and others' wounds without exposing them and making them public.

Chapter 47

On Giving the Signal for the Time of the Work of God

The indicating of the hour of the Work of God by day and by night shall devolve upon the Abbot, either to give the signal himself or to assign this duty to such a careful brother that everything will take place at the proper hours.

Let the Psalms and the antiphons be intoned by those who are appointed for it, in their order after the Abbot. And no one shall presume to sing or read unless he can fulfil that office in such a way as to edify the hearers. Let this function be performed with humility, gravity and reverence, and by him whom the Abbot has appointed.

Chapter 48

On the Daily Manual Labor

Idleness is the enemy of the soul. Therefore the brethren should be occupied at certain times in manual labor, and again at fixed hours in sacred reading. To that end we think that the times for each may be prescribed as follows.

From Easter until the Calends of October, when they come out from Prime in the morning let them labor at whatever is necessary until about the fourth hour, and from the fourth hour until about the sixth let them apply themselves to reading. After the sixth hour, having left the table, let them rest on their beds in perfect silence; or if anyone may perhaps want to read, let him read to himself in such a way as not to disturb anyone else. Let None be said rather early, at the middle of the eighth hour, and let them again do what work has to be done until Vespers.

And if the circumstances of the place or their poverty should require that they themselves do the work of gathering the harvest, let them not be discontented; for then are they truly monks when they live by the labor of their hands, as did our Fathers and the Apostles. Let all things be done with moderation, however, for the sake of the fainthearted.

From the Calends of October until the beginning of Lent, let them apply themselves to reading up to the end of the second hour. At the second hour let Terce be said, and then let all labor at the work assigned them until None. At the first signal for the Hour of None let everyone break off from his work, and hold himself ready for the sounding of the second signal. After the meal let them apply themselves to their reading or to the Psalms.

On the days of Lent, from morning until the end of the third hour let them apply themselves to their reading, and from then until the end of the tenth hour let them do the work assigned them. And in these days of Lent they shall each receive a book from the library, which they shall read straight through from the beginning. These books are to be given out at the beginning of Lent.

But certainly one or two of the seniors should be deputed to go about the monastery at the hours when the brethren are occupied in reading and see that there be no lazy brother who spends his time in idleness or gossip and does not apply himself to the reading, so that he is not only unprofitable to himself but also distracts others. If such a one be found (which God forbid), let him be corrected once and a second time; if he does not amend, let him undergo the punishment of the Rule in such a way that the rest may take warning.

Moreover, one brother shall not associate with another at unseasonable hours.

On Sundays, let all occupy themselves in reading, except those who have been appointed to various duties. But if anyone should be so negligent and shiftless that he will not or cannot study or read, let him be given some work to do so that he will not be idle.

Weak or sickly brethren should be assigned a task or craft of such a nature as to keep them from idleness and at the same time not to overburden them or drive them away with excessive toil. Their weakness must be taken into consideration by the Abbot.

Chapter 49

On the Observance of Lent

Although the life of a monk ought to have about it at all times the character of a Lenten observance, yet since few have the virtue for that, we therefore urge that during the actual days of Lent the brethren keep their lives most pure and at the same time wash away during these holy days all the negligences of other times. And this will be worthily done if we restrain ourselves from all vices and give ourselves up to prayer with tears, to reading, to compunction of heart and to abstinence.

During these days, therefore, let us increase somewhat the usual burden of our service, as by private prayers and by abstinence in food and drink. Thus everyone of his own will may offer God "with joy of the Holy Spirit" something above the measure required of him. From his body, that is, he may withhold some food, drink, sleep, talking and jesting; and with the joy of spiritual desire he may look forward to holy Easter.

Let each one, however, suggest to his Abbot what it is that he wants to offer, and let it be done with his blessing and approval. For anything done without the permission of the spiritual father will be imputed to presumption and vainglory and will merit no reward. Therefore let everything be done with the Abbot's approval.

Chapter 50

On Brethren Who Are Working Far from the Oratory or Are on a Journey

Those brethren who are working at a great distance and cannot get to the oratory at the proper time—the Abbot judging that such is the case—shall perform the Work of God in the place where they are working, bending their knees in reverence before God.

Likewise those who have been sent on a journey shall not let the appointed Hours pass by, but shall say the Office by themselves as well as they can, and not neglect to render the task of their service.

Chapter 51

On Brethren Who Go Not Very Far Away

A brother who is sent out on some business and is expected to return to the monastery that same day shall not presume to eat while he is out, even if he is urgently requested to do so by any person whomsoever, unless he has permission from his Abbot. And if he acts otherwise, let him be excommunicated.

Chapter 52

On the Oratory of the Monastery

Let the oratory be what it is called, a place of prayer; and let nothing else be done there or kept there. When the Work of God is ended, let all go out in perfect silence, and let reverence for God be observed, so that any brother who may wish to pray privately will not be hindered by another's misconduct. And at other times also, if anyone should want to pray by himself, let him go in simply and pray, not in a loud voice but with tears and fervor of heart. He who does not say his prayers in this way, therefore, shall not be permitted to remain in the oratory when the work of God is ended, lest another be hindered, as we have said.

Chapter 53

On the Reception of Guests

Let all guests who arrive be received like Christ, for He is going to say, "I came as a guest, and you received Me." And to all let due honor be shown, especially to the domestics of the faith and to pilgrims.

As soon as a guest is announced, therefore, let the Superior or the brethren meet him with all charitable service. And first of all let them pray together, and then exchange the kiss of peace. For the kiss of peace should not be offered until after the prayers have been said, on account of the devil's deceptions.

In the salutation of all guests, whether arriving or departing, let all humility be shown. Let the head be bowed or the whole body prostrated on the ground in adoration of Christ, who indeed is received in their persons.

After the guests have been received and taken to prayer, let the Superior or someone appointed by him sit with them. Let the divine law be read before the guest for his edification, and then let all kindness be shown him. The Superior shall break his fast for the sake of a guest, unless it happens to be a principal fast day which may not be violated. The brethren, however, shall observe the customary fasts. Let the Abbot give the guests water for their hands; and let both Abbot and community wash the feet of all guests. After the washing of the feet let them say this verse: "We have received Your mercy, O God, in the midst of Your temple."

In the reception of the poor and of pilgrims the greatest care and solicitude should be shown, because it is especially in them that Christ is received; for as far as the rich are concerned, the very fear which they inspire wins respect for them.

Let there be a separate kitchen for the Abbot and guests, that the brethren may not be disturbed when guests, who are never lacking in a monastery, arrive at irregular hours. Let two brethren capable of filling the office well be appointed for a year to have charge of this kitchen. Let them be given such help as they need, that they may serve without murmuring. And on the other hand, when they have less to occupy them, let them go out to whatever work is assigned them.

And not only in their case but in all the offices of the monastery let this arrangement be observed, that when help is needed it be supplied, and again when the workers are unoccupied they do whatever they are bidden.

The guest house also shall be assigned to a brother whose soul is possessed by the fear of God. Let there be a sufficient number of beds made up in it; and let the house of God be managed by prudent men and in a prudent manner.

On no account shall anyone who is not so ordered associate or converse with guests. But if he should meet them or see them, let him greet them humbly, as we have said, ask their blessing and pass on, saying that he is not allowed to converse with a guest.

Chapter 54

Whether a Monk Should Receive Letters or Anything Else

On no account shall a monk be allowed to receive letters, tokens or any little gift whatsoever from his parents or anyone else, or from his brethren, or to give the same, without the Abbot's permission. But if anything is sent him even by his parents, let him not presume to take it before it has been shown to the Abbot. And it shall be in the Abbot's power to decide to whom it shall be given, if he allows it to be received; and the brother to whom it was sent should not be grieved, lest occasion be given to the devil.

Should anyone presume to act otherwise, let him undergo the discipline of the Rule.

Chapter 55

On the Clothes and Shoes of the Brethren

Let clothing be given to the brethren according to the nature of the place in which they dwell and its climate; for in cold regions more will be needed, and in warm regions less. This is to be taken into consideration, therefore, by the Abbot.

We believe, however, that in ordinary places the following dress is sufficient for each monk: a tunic, a cowl (thick and woolly for winter, thin or worn for summer), a scapular for work, stockings and shoes to cover the feet.

The monks should not complain about the color or the coarseness of any of these things, but be content with what can be found in the district where they live and can be purchased cheaply.

The Abbot shall see to the size of the garments, that they be not too short for those who wear them, but of the proper fit.

Let those who receive new clothes always give back the old ones at once, to be put away in the wardrobe for the poor. For it is sufficient if a monk has two tunics and two cowls, to allow for night wear and for the washing of these garments; more than that is superfluity and should be taken away. Let them return their stockings also and anything else that is old when they receive new ones.

Those who are sent on a journey shall receive drawers from the wardrobe, which they shall wash and restore on their return. And let their cowls and tunics be somewhat better than what they usually wear. These they shall receive from the wardrobe when they set out on a journey, and restore when they return.

For bedding let this suffice: a mattress, a blanket, a coverlet and a pillow.

The beds, moreover, are to be examined frequently by the Abbot, to see if any private property be found in them. If anyone should be found to have something that he did not receive from the Abbot, let him undergo the most severe discipline.

And in order that this vice of private ownership may be cut out by the roots, the Abbot should provide all the necessary articles: cowl, tunic, stockings, shoes, girdle, knife, pen, needle, handkerchief, tablets; that all pretext of need may be taken away. Yet the Abbot should always keep in mind the sentence from the Acts of the Apostles that "distribution was made to each according as anyone had need." In this manner, therefore, let the Abbot consider the weaknesses of the needy and not the ill-will of the envious. But in all his decisions let him think about the retribution of God.

Chapter 56
On the Abbot's Table

Let the Abbot's table always be with the guests and the pilgrims. But when there are no guests, let it be in his power to invite whom he will of the brethren. Yet one or two seniors must always be left with the brethren for the sake of discipline.

Chapter 57

On the Craftsmen of the Monastery

If there are craftsmen in the monastery, let them practice their crafts with all humility, provided the Abbot has given permission. But if any one of them becomes conceited over his skill in his craft, because he seems to be conferring a benefit on the monastery, let him be taken from his craft and no longer exercise it unless, after he has humbled himself, the Abbot again gives him permission.

If any of the work of the craftsmen is to be sold, let those through whose hands the transactions pass see to it that they do not presume to practice any fraud. Let them always remember Ananias and Saphira, lest perhaps the death which these incurred in the body, they themselves and any others who would deal dishonestly with the monastery's property should suffer in the soul. And in the prices let not the sin of avarice creep in, but let the goods always be sold a little cheaper than they can be sold by people in the world, "that in all things God may be glorified."

Chapter 58

On the Manner of Receiving Brethren

When anyone is newly come for the reformation of his life, let him not be granted an easy entrance; but, as the Apostle says, "Test the spirits to see whether they are from God." If the newcomer, therefore, perseveres in his knocking, and if it is seen after four or five days that he bears patiently the harsh treatment offered him and the difficulty of admission, and that he persists in his petition, then let entrance be granted him, and let him stay in the guest house for a few days.

After that let him live in the novitiate, where the novices study, eat and sleep. A senior shall be assigned to them who is skilled in winning souls, to watch over them with the utmost care. Let him examine whether the novice is truly seeking God, and whether he is zealous for the Work of God, for obedience and for humiliations. Let the novice be told all the hard and rugged ways by which the journey to God is made.

If he promises stability and perseverance, then at the end of two months let this Rule be read through to him, and let him be addressed thus: "Here is the law under which you wish to fight. If you can observe it, enter; if you cannot, you are free to depart." If he still stands firm, let him be taken to the above-mentioned novitiate and again tested in all patience. And after the lapse of six months let the Rule be read to him, that he may know on what he is entering. And if he still remains firm, after four months let the same Rule be read to him again.

Then, having deliberated with himself, if he promises to keep it in its entirety and to observe everything that is commanded him, let him be received into the community. But let him understand that, according to the law of the Rule, from that day forward he may not leave the monastery nor withdraw his neck from under the yoke of the Rule which he was free to refuse or to accept during that prolonged deliberation.

He who is to be received shall make a promise before all in the oratory of his stability and of the reformation of his life and of obedience. This promise he shall make before God and His Saints, so that if he should ever act otherwise, he may know that he will be condemned by Him whom he mocks. Of this promise of his let him draw up a petition in the name of the Saints whose relics are there and of the Abbot who is present. Let him write this petition with his own hand; or if he is illiterate, let another write it at his request, and let the novice put his mark to it. Then let him place it with his own hand upon the altar; and when he has placed it there, let the novice at once intone this verse: "Receive me, O Lord, according to Your word, and I shall live: and let me not be confounded in my hope." Let the whole community answer this verse three times and add the "Glory be to the Father." Then let the novice brother prostrate himself at each one's feet, that they may pray for him. And from that day forward let him be counted as one of the community.

If he has any property, let him either give it beforehand to the poor or by solemn donation bestow it on the monastery, reserving nothing at all for himself, as indeed he knows that from that day forward he will no longer have power even over his own body. At once, therefore, in the oratory, let him be divested of his own clothes which he is wearing and dressed in the clothes of the monastery. But let the clothes of which he was divested be put aside in the wardrobe and kept there. Then if he should ever listen to the persuasions of the devil and decide to leave the monastery (which God forbid), he may be divested of the monastic clothes and cast out. His petition, however, which the Abbot has taken from the altar, shall not be returned to him, but shall be kept in the monastery.

Chapter 59

On the Sons of Nobles and of the Poor Who Are Offered

If anyone of the nobility offers his son to God in the monastery and the boy is very young, let his parents draw up the petition which we mentioned above; and at the oblation let them wrap the petition and the boy's hand in the altar cloth and so offer him.

As regards their property, they shall promise in the same petition under oath that they will never of themselves, or through an intermediary, or in any way whatever, give him anything or provide him with the opportunity of owning anything. Or else, if they are unwilling to do this, and if they want to offer something as an alms to the monastery for their advantage, let them make a donation of the property they wish to give to the monastery, reserving the income to themselves if they wish. And in this way let everything be barred, so that the boy may have no expectations whereby (which God forbid) he might be deceived and ruined, as we have learned by experience.

Let those who are less well-to-do make a similar offering. But those who have nothing at all shall simply draw up the petition and offer their son before witnesses at the oblation.

Chapter 60

On Priests Who May Wish to Live in the Monastery

If anyone of the priestly order should ask to be received into the monastery, permission shall not be granted him too readily. But if he is quite persistent in his request, let him know that he will have to observe the whole discipline of the Rule and that nothing will be relaxed in his favor, that it may be as it is written: "Friend, for what have you come?"

It shall be granted him, however, to stand next after the Abbot and to give blessings and to celebrate Mass, but only by order of the Abbot. Without such order let him not presume to do anything, knowing that he is subject to the discipline of the Rule; but rather let him give an example of humility to all.

If there happens to be question of an appointment or of some business in the monastery, let him expect the rank due him according to the date of his entrance into the monastery, and not the place granted him out of reverence for the priesthood.

If any clerics, moved by the same desire, should wish to join the monastery, let them be placed in a middle rank. But they too are to be admitted only if they promise observance of the Rule and their own stability.

Chapter 61

How Pilgrim Monks Are to Be Received

If a pilgrim monk coming from a distant region wants to live as a guest of the monastery, let him be received for as long a time as he desires, provided he is content with the customs of the place as he finds them and does not disturb the monastery by superfluous demands, but is simply content with what he finds. If, however, he censures or points out anything reasonably and with the humility of charity, let the Abbot consider prudently whether perhaps it was for that very purpose that the Lord sent him.

If afterwards he should want to bind himself to stability, his wish should not be denied him, especially since there has been opportunity during his stay as a guest to discover his character.

But if as a guest he was found exacting or prone to vice, not only should he be denied membership in the community, but he should even be politely requested to leave, lest others be corrupted by his evil life.

If, however, he has not proved to be the kind who deserves to be put out, he should not only on his own application be received as a member of the community, but he should even be persuaded to stay, that the others may be instructed by his example, and because in every place it is the same Lord who is served, the same King for whom the battle is fought.

Moreover, if the Abbot perceives that he is a worthy man, he may put him in a somewhat higher rank. And not only with regard to a monk but also with regard to those in priestly or clerical orders previously mentioned, the Abbot may establish them in a higher rank than would be theirs by date of entrance if he perceives that their life is deserving.

Let the Abbot take care, however, never to receive a monk from another known monastery as a member of his community without the consent of his Abbot or a letter of recommendation; for it is written, "Do not to another what you would not want done to yourself."

Chapter 62
On the Priests of the Monastery

If an Abbot desire to have a priest or a deacon ordained for his monastery, let him choose one of his monks who is worthy to exercise the priestly office.

But let the one who is ordained beware of self-exaltation or pride; and let him not presume to do anything except what is commanded him by the Abbot, knowing that he is so much the more subject to the discipline of the Rule. Nor should he by reason of his priesthood forget the obedience and the discipline required by the Rule, but make ever more and more progress towards God.

Let him always keep the place which he received on entering the monastery, except in his duties at the altar or in case the choice of the community and the will of the Abbot should promote him for the worthiness of his life. Yet he must understand that he is to observe the rules laid down by deans and Priors.

Should he presume to act otherwise, let him be judged not as a priest but as a rebel. And if he does not reform after repeated admonitions, let even the Bishop be brought in as a witness. If then he still fails to amend, and his offenses are notorious, let him be put out of the monastery, but only if his contumacy is such that he refuses to submit or to obey the Rule.

Chapter 63
On the Order of the Community

Let all keep their places in the monastery established by the time of their entrance, the merit of their lives and the decision of the Abbot. Yet the Abbot must not disturb the flock committed to him, nor by an arbitrary use of his power ordain anything unjustly; but let him always think of the account he will have to render to God for all his decisions and his deeds.

Therefore in that order which he has established or which they already had, let the brethren approach to receive the kiss of peace and Communion, into the Psalms and stand in choir. And in no place whatever should age decide the order or be prejudicial to it; for Samuel and Daniel as mere boys judged priests.

Except for those already mentioned, therefore, whom the Abbot has promoted by a special decision or demoted for definite reasons, all the rest shall take their order according to the time of their entrance. Thus, for example, he who came to the monastery at the second hour of the day, whatever be his age or his dignity, must know that he is junior to one who came at the first hour of the day. Boys, however, are to be kept under discipline in all matters and by everyone.

The juniors, therefore, should honor their seniors, and the seniors love their juniors.

In the very manner of address, let no one call another by the mere name; but let the seniors call their juniors Brothers, and the juniors call their seniors Fathers, by which is conveyed the reverence due to a father. But the Abbot, since he is believed to represent Christ, shall be called Lord and Abbot, not for any pretensions of his own but out of honor and love for Christ. Let the Abbot himself reflect on this, and show himself worthy of such an honor.

And wherever the brethren meet one another the junior shall ask the senior for his blessing. When a senior passes by, a junior shall rise and give him a place to sit, nor shall the junior presume to sit with him unless his senior bid him, that it may be as was written, "In honor anticipating one another."

Boys, both small and adolescent, shall keep strictly to their rank in oratory and at table. But outside of that, wherever they may be, let them be under supervision and discipline, until they come to the age of discretion.

Chapter 64

On Constituting an Abbot

In the constituting of an Abbot let this plan always be followed, that the office be conferred on the one who is chosen either by the whole community unanimously in the fear of God or else by a part of the community, however small, if its counsel is more wholesome.

Merit of life and wisdom of doctrine should determine the choice of the one to be constituted, even if he be the last in the order of the community.

But if (which God forbid) the whole community should agree to choose a person who will acquiesce in their vices, and if those vices somehow become known to the Bishop to whose diocese the place belongs, or to the Abbots or the faithful of the vicinity, let them prevent the success of this conspiracy of the wicked, and set a worthy steward over the house of God. They may be sure that they will receive a good reward for this action if they do it with a pure intention and out of zeal for God; as, on the contrary, they will sin if they fail to do it.

Once he has been constituted, let the Abbot always bear in mind what a burden he has undertaken and to whom he will have to give an account of his stewardship, and let him know that his duty is rather to profit his brethren than to preside over them. He must therefore be learned in the divine law, that he may have a treasure of knowledge from which to bring forth new things and old. He must be chaste, sober and merciful. Let him exalt mercy above judgment, that he himself may obtain mercy. He should hate vices; he should love the brethren.

In administering correction he should act prudently and not go to excess, lest in seeking too eagerly to scrape off the rust he break the vessel. Let him keep his own frailty ever before his eyes and remember that the bruised reed must not be broken. By this we do not mean that he should allow vices to grow; on the contrary, as we have already said, he should eradicate them prudently and with charity, in the way which may seem best in each case. Let him study rather to be loved than to be feared.

Let him not be excitable and worried, nor exacting and headstrong, nor jealous and over-suspicious; for then he is never at rest.

In his commands let him be prudent and considerate; and whether the work which he enjoins concerns God or the world, let him be discreet and moderate, bearing in mind the discretion of holy Jacob, who said, "If I cause my flocks to be overdriven, they will all die in one day." Taking this, then, and other examples of discretion, the mother of virtues, let him so temper all things that the strong may have something to strive after, and the weak may not fall back in dismay.

And especially let him keep this Rule in all its details, so that after a good ministry he may hear from the Lord what the good servant heard who gave his fellow-servants wheat in due season: "Indeed, I tell you, he will set him over all his goods."

Chapter 65

On the Prior of the Monastery

It happens all too often that the constituting of a Prior gives rise to grave scandals in monasteries. For there are some who become inflated with the evil spirit of pride and consider themselves second Abbots. By usurping power they foster scandals and cause dissensions in the community. Especially does this happen in those places where the Prior is constituted by the same Bishop or the same Abbots who constitute the Abbot himself. What an absurd procedure this is can easily be seen; for it gives the Prior an occasion for becoming proud from the very time of his constitution, by putting the thought into his mind that he is freed from the authority of his Abbot: "For," he will say to himself, "you were constituted by the same persons who constituted the Abbot." From this source are stirred up envy, quarrels, detraction, rivalry, dissensions and disorders. For while the Abbot and the Prior are at variance, their souls cannot but be endangered by this dissension; and those who are under them, currying favor with one side or the other, go to ruin. The guilt for this dangerous state of affairs rests on the heads of those whose action brought about such disorder.

To us, therefore, it seems expedient for the preservation of peace and charity that the Abbot have in his hands the full administration of his monastery. And if possible let all the affairs of the monastery, as we have already arranged, be administered by deans according to the Abbot's directions. Thus, with the duties being shared by several, no one person will become proud.

But if the circumstances of the place require it, or if the community asks for it with reason and with humility, and the Abbot judges it to be expedient, let the Abbot himself constitute as his Prior whomsoever he shall choose with the counsel of God-fearing brethren.

That Prior, however, shall perform respectfully the duties enjoined on him by his Abbot and do nothing against the Abbot's will or direction; for the more he is raised above the rest, the more carefully should he observe the precepts of the Rule.

If it should be found that the Prior has serious faults, or that he is deceived by his exaltation and yields to pride, or if he should be proved to be a despiser of the Holy Rule, let him be admonished verbally up to four times. If he fails to amend, let the correction of regular discipline be applied to him. But if even then he does not reform, let him be deposed from the office of Prior and another be appointed in his place who is worthy of it. And if afterwards he is not quiet and obedient in the community, let him even be expelled from the monastery. But the Abbot, for his part, should bear in mind that he will have to render an account to God for all his judgments, lest the flame of envy or jealousy be kindled in his soul.

Chapter 66

On the Porters of the Monastery

At the gate of the monastery let there be placed a wise old man, who knows how to receive and to give a message, and whose maturity will prevent him from straying about. This porter should have a room near the gate, so that those who come may always find someone at hand to attend to their business. And as soon as anyone knocks or a poor man hails him, let him answer "Thanks be to God" or "A blessing!" Then let him attend to them promptly, with all the meekness inspired by the fear of God and with the warmth of charity.

Should the porter need help, let him have one of the younger brethren.

If it can be done, the monastery should be so established that all the necessary things, such as water, mill, garden and various workshops, may be within the enclosure, so that there is no necessity for the monks to go about outside of it, since that is not at all profitable for their souls.

We desire that this Rule be read often in the community, so that none of the brethren may excuse himself on the ground of ignorance.

Chapter 67

On Brethren Who Are Sent on a Journey

Let the brethren who are sent on a journey commend themselves to the prayers of all the brethren and of the Abbot; and always at the last prayer of the Work of God let a commemoration be made of all absent brethren.

When brethren return from a journey, at the end of each canonical Hour of the Work of God on the day they return, let them lie prostrate on the floor of the oratory and beg the prayers of all on account of any faults that may have surprised them on the road, through the seeing or hearing of something evil, or through idle talk. And let no one presume to tell another whatever he may have seen or heard outside of the monastery, because this causes very great harm. But if anyone presumes to do so, let him undergo the punishment of the Rule. And let him be punished likewise who would presume to leave the enclosure of the monastery and go anywhere or do anything, however small, without an order from the Abbot.

Chapter 68

If a Brother Is Commanded to Do Impossible Things

If it happens that difficult or impossible tasks are laid on a brother, let him nevertheless receive the order of the one in authority with all meekness and obedience. But if he sees that the weight of the burden altogether exceeds the limit of his strength, let him submit the reasons for his inability to the one who is over him in a quiet way and at an opportune time, without pride, resistance, or contradiction. And if after these representations the Superior still persists in his decision and command, let the subject know that this is for his good, and let him obey out of love, trusting in the help of God.

Chapter 69

That the Monks Presume Not to Defend One Another

Care must be taken that no monk presume on any ground to defend another monk in the monastery, or as it were to take him under his protection, even though they be united by some tie of blood-relationship. Let not the monks dare to do this in any way whatsoever, because it may give rise to most serious scandals. But if anyone breaks this rule, let him be severely punished.

Chapter 70

That No One Venture to Punish at Random

Every occasion of presumption shall be avoided in the monastery, and we decree that no one be allowed to excommunicate or to strike any of his brethren unless the Abbot has given him the authority. Those who offend in this matter shall be rebuked in the presence of all, that the rest may have fear.

But boys up to 15 years of age shall be carefully controlled and watched by all, yet this too with all moderation and discretion. Anyone, therefore, who presumes without the Abbot's instructions to punish those above that age or who loses his temper with the boys, shall undergo the discipline of the Rule; for it is written, "Do not to another what you would not want done to yourself."

Chapter 71

That the Brethren Be Obedient to One Another

Not only is the boon of obedience to be shown by all to the Abbot, but the brethren are also to obey one another, knowing that by this road of obedience they are going to God. Giving priority, therefore, to the commands of the Abbot and of the Superiors appointed by him (to which we allow no private orders to be preferred), for the rest let all the juniors obey their seniors with all charity and solicitude. But if anyone is found contentious, let him be corrected.

And if any brother, for however small a cause, is corrected in any way by the Abbot or by any of his superiors, or if he faintly perceives that the mind of any Superior is angered or moved against him, however little, let him at once, without delay, prostrate himself on the ground at his feet and lie there making satisfaction until that emotion is quieted with a blessing. But if anyone should disdain to do this, let him undergo corporal punishment or, if he is stubborn, let him be expelled from the monastery.

Chapter 72

On the Good Zeal Which Monks Ought to Have

Just as there is an evil zeal of bitterness which separates from God and leads to hell, so there is a good zeal which separates from vices and leads to God and to life everlasting. This zeal, therefore, the monks should practice with the most fervent love. Thus they should anticipate one another in honor; most patiently endure one another's infirmities, whether of body or of character; vie in paying obedience one to another—no one following what he considers useful for himself, but rather what benefits another—; tender the charity of brotherhood chastely; fear God in love; love their Abbot with a sincere and humble charity; prefer nothing whatever to Christ. And may He bring us all together to life everlasting!

Chapter 73
On the Fact That the Full Observance of Justice Is Not Established in This Rule

Now we have written this Rule in order that by its observance in monasteries we may show that we have attained some degree of virtue and the rudiments of the religious life.

But for him who would hasten to the perfection of that life there are the teachings of the holy Fathers, the observance of which leads a man to the height of perfection. For what page or what utterance of the divinely inspired books of the Old and New Testaments is not a most unerring rule for human life? Or what book of the holy Catholic Fathers does not loudly proclaim how we may come by a straight course to our Creator? Then the Conferences and the Institutes and the Lives of the Fathers, as also the Rule of our holy Father Basil—what else are they but tools of virtue for right-living and obedient monks? But for us who are lazy and ill-living and negligent they are a source of shame and confusion.

Whoever you are, therefore, who are hastening to the heavenly homeland, fulfil with the help of Christ this minimum Rule which we have written for beginners; and then at length under God's protection you will attain to the loftier heights of doctrine and virtue which we have mentioned above.

Chapter Four

Merovingian and Carolingian Gaul

THE Franks were unknown to the most ancient sources on the Germans. They first appeared by name in the third century and even then they were archaeologically indistinguishable from other Germans inhabiting the continental shores of the North Sea. Even the origin of the name is unknown; apparently it was merely a term of convenience adopted by Roman historians, not an appellation native to them.

The early history of the Franks was typical of Germanic peoples on the frontiers of the Roman Empire. Franks served as individuals and in groups in the Roman army, some of them, Bauto, Ricimer, Arbogast, Merobaudes, rising to the highest ranks. Also, Franks were settled within the frontiers of the Empire as *foederati* by the middle of the fourth century. A century later, several Frankish war bands were established in *Belgica secunda,* possibly to protect the towns of the province.

Although the earliest references to the Franks show them as coastal raiders, by the early fourth century some of them were pressing inland towards what is modern Belgium. This group of Franks was called the Salians by contemporary writers. Another group, known as the Ripuarians, were still across the Rhine opposite Cologne and northwards. How distinct the two were is a matter for conjecture.

After the assassination of Aetius in 454, direct Roman power collapsed in Gaul. By that time some of the Franks were well-established in *Belgica secunda,* as we have seen, and were showing interest in expanding towards the more fertile lands to the south. Clodio, the leader of the Frankish war band around Tournai, was driven out of Gaul by Aetius in 446. Clodio's son or brother, Merovech, was the eponymous ancestor of the Merovingian dynasty. At this point we reach the fairly secure ground of Gregory of Tours' *History of the Franks.*

At the age of fifteen, Clovis succeeded to the leadership of the

Franks of Tournai, one of several Frankish kings. When he died Clovis was master of most of Roman Gaul and sole king of the Franks. The two are related. Without military successes Clovis would never have become the founder of the Merovingian dynasty or the creator of Frankish kingship. Of course, for Gregory of Tours, Clovis' greatest achievement was his conversion to the true faith. Indeed, except for Clovis' defeat of Syagrius in 484, Gregory regarded this fact as the source of all his successes, leading him to date Clovis' conversion some ten years too early. Still, Gregory may not have been far wrong. As successor to Syagrius at Soissons, Clovis could not have been unaware of the power of the Gallo-Roman episcopate. It is clear, at any rate, that even as a pagan he enjoyed their tacit support as being preferable to the heretical Burgundians and Visigoths.

Clovis created Frankish kingship and laid the territorial foundations of Frankish Gaul. He also sowed the seeds of its fragmentation. When he died he divided his kingdom, as if it were a piece of private property, among his four heirs. Even if the division was not arbitrary—it was in fact based on political divisions which harked back to Aetius' reorganization of the Gallic provinces—it did provide the maximum opportunity for the civil wars which were the despair of Gregory. Clovis did not invent the blood feud of the Franks, he merely provided it with the ideal environment in which to operate on the royal level.

Nevertheless, Clovis' successors for the next ventury were impressive for their power. It was power based on wealth; wealth derived from land, the remains of the imperial fisc, and money, the source of which, other than booty and tribute from the Byzantine Empire, was the *teloneum*, the Roman tax on commerce. With this wealth they rounded out the territorial boundaries of Frankish Gaul and modified Frankish customary law in a Roman and authoritarian direction.

Gregory does not reflect the authoritative tone of Merovingian royal documents. Admittedly, Gregory did not think much of the Merovingian kings. Yet it may have been their attitude towards the church, rather than the moral failings Gregory complains of, that incurred his wrath. In the eyes of Clovis' successors the church was growing dangerously in wealth and political power and they did everything they could to curb the latter, at least.

Frankish kings of the seventh century were more docile in respect to the church and less powerful. Even if the real period of

Merovingian decline did not set in until after the death of Dagobert I in 639, the sources of decay originated before. Discounting family degeneracy, those sources were three. If the early Merovingians were powerful because they were wealthy, it follows that the later Merovingians were weak for the opposite reason. The slow and inexorable alienation of royal estates in favor of the church and faithful followers was one factor. Yet underlying this was a more basic factor, the drying up of the sources of monetary wealth. In the seventh century, Byzantium turned its back on the West with the consequence that this source of liquid wealth ceased to flow. Simultaneously, Mediterranean commerce, and with it the *teloneum*, ground slowly to a halt. The seventh century kings, therefore, had to pay their followers in a different way. Where Clovis and his successors had kept a large following around them, rewarding them with cash, the later Merovingians were forced to disperse on them their only remaining resource, the land.

Connected with this factor is another in the decline of Merovingian kingship. If they had less land and less money, they also had fewer trained officials to work their will. Taking it as axiomatic that bureaucracy is essential to strong kingship, every grant of an estate meant a delegation and dispersal of royal authority. Further, we must look at the rise of the *major domus* in this light. They were not menial officials working the will of the king; they were landed magnates in their own right whose interests were ultimately antagonistic to those of their royal masters.

Nevertheless, the Merovingians survived a full century after they had ceased to exercise any personal authority. The real question is not to explain the rise of the *major domus*, but the longevity of the Merovingians. Perhaps too much can be made of the prestige of Merovingian blood. Still, they were of the race of Clovis, the long-haired kings, and this meant something, at least in Neustria. Certainly there was no rival royal family. Besides, kings who reign but do not rule are often a convenience. The Frankish church, the chief recipient of Merovingian largesse, seemed to feel this way.

If these things explain the longevity of the Merovingians, what explains their downfall? Merovingian power had been based on Neustria. In the eighth century, however, the balance of power in Frankland was shifting to the east, to Austrasia. There, the Merovingians had few estates and consequently few vassals. It was in Austrasia, moreover, that the Carolingians rose to prominence. They had accumulated vast estates and with them many supporters. From there they were performing royal functions in the defense of the kingdom and in the patronage of the church. Through the former the Carolingians earned their claim to royalty in the same way the Merovingians had done almost three centuries before: through success in war. Through the latter they won the Frankish church, the most important prop of the Merovingian dynasty. The Carolingian mayors were lavish in their gifts to the church, above all to the church in Neustria. And through their patronage of Anglo-Saxon missionaries, the Carolingians came into close contact with the papacy, a connection important in the transfer of dynasties in 751 and decisive for the future.

The Carolingian Revolution inaugurated a new period in Frankish history. Basically, it was a period containing four major developments. The first of them, the expansion of Frankish power, was also the most striking. From about the middle of the sixth century, by which time the successors of Clovis had rounded out the frontiers of Frankland, the Merovingians had been too preoccupied with internal feuds to take much interest in expansion. In fact, toward the end of Merovingian rule the eastern frontier contracted at the expense of the Saxons. Immediately, the Carolingians reversed this trend. Within three years of his coronation Pepin I intervened in Italy, a move consolidated by Charlemagne in 774 when he became King of the Lombards. It was also Charlemagne who took the offensive in the east against the Saxons, Slavs and Avars, the result of which was the expansion of Frankish frontiers beyond the Elbe. In the south, Charlemagne began the expansion into Spain which ultimately resulted in the creation of the Spanish March.

Charlemagne's motives in creating the most impressive political edifice in the West since the collapse of the Roman Empire was explicitly religious. He conceived of himself as the leader of a Christian Commonwealth whose duty was not only to protect the church against its enemies but also to take the offensive on her behalf. Both his success and his conceptions put him in a different relationship with the church than any previous ruler in the west had been. The Christian Commonwealth, heretofore a theoretical conception, now became a reality, one which made him the political neighbor of the papacy in Italy. Further, if Charlemagne had ever heard of the Gelasian theory of the two powers (for which see Chapter 6) he certainly rejected its implications. He interpreted his position as "protector" of the church in a way which made him absolute master of it: the arbiter of its theology, judge in its disputes, and director of its educational program.

Charlemagne's conception of the Christian Commonwealth did not accord with that of the papacy. In Roman circles the idea of papal supremacy was already being worked out. Here is the background of the second important development of the Carolingian period, the Imperial Coronation of Christmas Day, 800.

The Imperial Coronation of 800 has been called many things, the most sensible of which is "a comedy improvised by a handful of antiquarian-minded ecclesiastics." Nevertheless, the event was important, not for what it meant at the time (no one has ever established exactly what it was supposed to mean at the time), but for its future significance.

There is no reason to doubt Einhard's statement that Charlemagne was angry at being crowned by Pope Leo. Even though imperial ideas were circulating in Frankland before 800, ideas shared in some form by Charlemagne, the circumstances of the coronation offended him. Papal sanction had never been necessary to the imperial dignity nor did the implication that the pope had the power to confer it suit his conception of the Christian Commonwealth. Significantly, he only reluctantly adopted the imperial title, almost two years after his coronation, and when his son assumed it in 812 the pope was conspicuously absent from the ceremony. Charlemagne's displeasure, however, was prophetic of the future importance of the event. It set a precedent and created a situation which would trouble the future course of German and Italian history.

The third major development of the Carolingian age was the Carolingian Renaissance, the label given to the comparative flourishing of arts and letters in the period. The first thing that must be said about it is that it was self-conscious; it was deliberately fostered by Carolingian mayors and kings. The motivation was in part practical; the Palace School was to train the men who would be the administrators of the Frankish kingdom. It was in part religious, born out of an awareness of the lack of an educated clergy. It was also personal, both in the sense that the patronage of learning and the arts contributes to the prestige of a ruler, and in the sense that Charlemagne and his successors genuinely enjoyed the companionship of scholars.

Wealth and the desire to use it in this particular way is the source of culture. Once the Carolingians became wealthy, from about the middle of Charlemagne's reign, they lavished their treasure on books, buildings and men. The scholars did particularly well. Alcuin, for example, arrived in Frankland with a single companion; when he died he was lord of 20,000 men.

In keeping with its deliberate character, the Carolingian Renaissance had a well-defined educational program. It aimed first of all to preserve literacy; into this category fall the handwriting reform, the famous Carolingian minuscule, and the attempt to standardize orthography. Secondly, it attempted to increase literacy by establishing schools. Thirdly, it attempted to standardize the curriculum. Alcuin was the chief figure here. He abandoned the Roman literary approach to education with its ideal of training for the public life and substituted a curriculum which trained men for the church. The seven liberal arts, the division of knowledge into the *trivium* and *quadrivium*, became standard after Alcuin; but it was knowledge directed to the service of God.

The Carolingian Renaissance was not creative. Aside from the isolated figure of the philosopher, John the Scot, it contained no intellectual figures of the first stature. It was derivative; its outstanding scholars came mostly from outside the kingdom—Italy, Spain, and above all, England and Ireland. Nevertheless, it did make a permanent mark on the face of intellectual Europe. For one thing, the memory of Carolingian educational legislation remained even if only as an ideal to strive for. For another, the Carolingian revival of learning did not entirely die out during the uncertain times that followed. In monasteries and schools here and there the lamp of learning remained lit. Finally, and most important, if the Carolingian Renaissance was not creative it was at least preservative; it preserved the tradition of learning and in its emphasis on the careful copying and purifying of texts it preserved the materials of learning as well.

The fourth development of the Carolingian period was the disintegration of the Frankish Empire. This disintegration took place on two levels. On one, the Frankish Empire did not survive the death of Charlemagne's successor, Louis the Pious. Even if the fiction of imperial unity was maintained for a time, the partitions of 843 and 870 insured that the component parts of the Empire, East Frankland, West Frankland, and the Middle Kingdom, would go separate ways.

These partitions of the Frankish kingdom were disastrous to the material and personal basis of Carolingian kingship. The bulk of the royal estates were in Austrasia and hence passed into the Middle

Kingdom in 843. During its further fragmentation after 855, the failure of the Middle Kingdom as a viable political unit, those estates gradually dispersed into other hands. Personally, Carolingian kingship rested on the church and the royal vassals and both were affected adversely by the partitions. However, loyal they were to the idea of a unified empire, they found their loyalty torn amongst the various Carolingian kings and claimants of the later ninth century.

At a lower level, disintegration worked in a different way within each of the divisions. The Middle Kingdom was further subdivided at the death of Lothar in 855 into three sub-kingdoms, Lotharingia (Lorraine), Burgundy, and Italy. After a tortuous history, most of it was absorbed in various ways into the East Frankish kingdom. In West Frankland, subdivision proceeded even further. Since the West Frankish monarchy was materially weak, it was unable to defend the kingdom as a whole against the incessant attacks of Norse and Saracen. Hence it fell apart into smaller defensive units based on the old county system, some thirty being visible at the beginning of the tenth century, some fifty-five by the middle of that century.

East Frankland was the most fortunate of the three major divisions of the Carolingian Empire. It was fortunate in the first place to have a talented Carolingian king in the chaotic years following the deposition of Charles the Fat in 887, who kept the traditions of strong Carolingian kingship alive in Germany for another generation. This was made all the easier because the German region was less exposed to invasion than West Frankland and hence it was possible for the defense of the kingdom to remain in royal hands. Secondly, when political decentralization did begin, during the second decade of the tenth century, it did not come in the same way nor proceed as far. Although the county system had been extended to Germany during the eighth century, it was a comparatively recent innovation, never replacing older, popular forms of local government. For this reason the county would not be the basis of political fragmentation as it was in West Frankland. In Germany it would be the duchy, a new, revolutionary authority, of which only five emerged in the early tenth century.

The underlying factors in Carolingian disintegration were three. The kingship was too large and not homogeneous enough to be governed by the crude administrative machinery available to the Carolingians. Its material resources by the middle of the ninth century consisted almost exclusively of land, and a landed society inevitably produces political decentralization. Most important, the Carolingian Empire broke up under the onslaught of Norse, Magyar and Saracen.

◆ ◆ ◆

The Merovingian and Carolingian age completed the transformation of classical antiquity into the Middle Ages. It witnessed the shift of the political center of gravity northwards away from the Mediterranean. It saw the growth of the church and the papacy to political power and landed wealth. It created the medieval empire. Intellectually, it saw the decline of learning and its transformation into a clerical monopoly. And, as we shall see in the following chapter, it created new social, economic, and political forms.

1. *Gregory of Tours*

Gregory, Bishop of Tours (c.540–94), was the first and foremost historian of the Franks. Coming from an aristocratic Gallo-Roman family which had already produced several bishops, he became Bishop of Tours in 573. His education and his eminent position were, in terms of the sixth century, ideally suited for his purpose. His *History of the Franks* was begun between 586–90. In ten books, it is most valuable in book ii, the reign of Clovis, included in its entirety below, and books v–ix which constitute a detailed history of his own time.

I have used the translation of O. M. Dalton (Oxford; Clarendon Press, 1927), Vol. II, pp. 2, 65–81, 168–69, 278–80, 298–302, 310–20, 377–79, 389–92. Reprinted by permission.

IN THESE times when the practice of letters declines, nay, rather perishes in the cities of Gaul, there has been found no scholar trained in the art of ordered composition to present in prose or verse a picture of the things that have befallen. Yet there have been done good things many, and evil many; the people savagely raged; the fury of kings grew sharp; churches were assailed by heretics and protected by catholics; the faith of Christ that glowed in many hearts was lukewarm in not a few; the faithful enriched the churches while the unbelievers stripped them bare. Wherefore the voice of lament was oft times raised, and men said: 'Alas! for these our days! The study of letters is perished from us, nor is any found among our peoples able to set forth in a book the events of this present time.'

Now when I heard these and like complaints ever repeated, I was moved, with however rude an utterance, to hand down the memory of the past to future generations, in no wise leaving untold the conflicts of the wicked and those who lived in righteousness. I was the more encouraged because I often heard with surprise our people say that while the accomplished writer is understood by few, it is the man of plain speech who has the general ear.

◆ ◆ ◆

After this Childeric died, and Clovis his son reigned in his stead. In the fifth year of his reign, Syagrius, king of the Romans, son of Aegidius, had his residence in the city of Soissons, which had before been the home of the above-mentioned Aegidius. Clovis marched against him, with his relation Ragnachar, himself also a king, and called upon him to fix a field of battle. Syagrius did not seek delay nor did he fear to stand his ground. And so when the battle was joined between them, Syagrius, seeing his army crushed, turned to flight and escaped as fast as he could to Alaric at Toulouse. But Clovis sent to Alaric calling upon him to surrender the fugitive, else he must look to be himself invaded for giving him refuge. Then Alaric, lest he should incur the wrath of the Franks for his sake, was afraid, after the craven habit of the Goths, and handed him over to the messengers in bonds. When Clovis received him prisoner, he ordered him to be imprisoned; had him put to the sword in secret, while he took possession of his kingdom.

At this time many churches were plundered by the troops of Clovis, because he was yet fast held in pagan errors. Thus it happened that a ewer of great size and beauty had been taken, with other ornaments used in the service of the church. But the bishop of that church sent messengers to the king, asking that if no other of the sacred vessels might be restored, his church might at least receive back this ewer. When the king heard this he said to the envoy: 'Follow us to Soissons, for there all the booty is to be divided, and if the lot gives me the vessel, I will fulfil the desire of the bishop.' When they were at Soissons and all the spoil was laid out in open view, the king said: 'I ask you, most valiant warriors, not to refuse to cede me that vessel' (he meant the ewer of which I have spoken) 'over and above my share.' After this speech all the men of sense replied: 'All that is before our eyes, most glorious king, is thine; we ourselves are submitted to thy power. Do now that which seemeth good to thee, for none is so strong as to say thee nay.' At these words a soldier of a vain, jealous, and unstable temper raised his axe and smote the ewer, crying with a loud voice: 'Naught shalt thou receive of this but that which thine own lot giveth thee.' While all stood astounded at this act, the king suppressed his resentment at the wrong under a show of patient mildness; he then took the ewer and restored it to the bishop's envoy. But the wound remained hidden in his heart. After the lapse of a year, he commanded the whole army to assemble with full equipment, and to exhibit their arms in their brightness on the field of March. The king went round inspecting them all; but when he came to the man who struck the ewer he said: 'None hath appeared with his arms so ill-kept as thou; neither thy lance, nor thy sword, nor thy axe is fit for use.' He then seized the axe, and threw it on the ground. As the man bent down a little to take it up, the king swung his own axe high and cleft his skull, saying as he did it, 'Thus didst thou treat the ewer at Soissons.' The man lying dead, he dismissed the rest, having put great fear of him into their hearts by his act. Clovis waged many wars and won many victories. For in the tenth year of his reign he invaded the Thuringians and subjected them to his rule.

At that time the king of the Burgundians was Gundioc, of the race of the royal persecutor Athanaric whom I have before mentioned. He had four sons, Gundobad, Godigisel, Chilperic, and Gundomar. Gundobad put his brother Chilperic to the sword, and drowned his wife by tying a stone to her neck. Her two daughters he condemned to exile, the elder of whom, Chrona, had adopted the habit of a nun, while the younger was called Clotild. It happened that Clovis used often to send envoys into Burgundy, and they discovered the young Clotild. Observing her grace and understanding, and learning that she was of the blood royal, they spoke of these things to King Clovis, who straightway sent an embassy to Gundobad, asking her in marriage. Gundobad was afraid to refuse, and handed her over to the men, who received her, and with all speed brought her before the king. At sight of her he greatly rejoiced and was united to her in wedlock, having already by a concubine one son named Theuderic.

Of Queen Clotild the king had a firstborn son whom the mother wished to be baptized; she therefore persistently urged Clovis to permit it, saying: 'The gods whom ye worship are naught; they cannot aid either themselves or others, seeing that they are images carved of gold or stone, or metal. Moreover the names which ye have given them are the names of men and not of gods. Saturn was a man, fabled to have escaped by flight from his son to avoid being thrust from his kingdom; Jupiter also, the lewdest practiser of all debaucheries and of unnatural vice, the abuser of the women of his own family, who could not even abstain from intercourse with his own sister, as she herself admitted in the words "sister and spouse of Jove." What power had Mars and Mercury: They may have been endowed with magical arts; they never had the power of the divine name. But ye should rather serve Him, who at His word created out of nothing the heaven and earth, the sea and all therein; who made the sun to shine and adorned the heaven with stars; who filled the waters with fish, the earth with animals, the air with birds; at whose nod the lands are made fair with fruits, the trees with apples, the vines with grapes; by whose hand the race of man was created; by whose largess every creature was made to render homage and service to the man whom he created.' Though the queen ever argued thus, the king's mind was nowise moved towards belief, but he replied: 'It is by command of our gods that all things are created and come forth; it is manifest that thy god availeth in nothing; nay more, he is not even proven to belong to the race of gods.' But the queen, true to her faith, presented her son for baptism; she ordered the church to be adorned with hangings and curtains, that the king, whom no preaching could influence might by this ceremony be persuaded to belief. The boy was baptized and named Ingomer, but died while yet clothed in the white raiment of his regeneration. Thereupon the king was moved to bitter wrath, nor was he slow to reproach the queen, saying: 'If the child had been dedicated in the name of my gods, surely he would have survived, but now, baptized in the name of thy God, he could not live a day.' The queen replied: 'I render thanks to Almighty God, Creator of all things, who hath not judged me all unworthy, and deigneth to take into His kingdom this child born of my womb. My mind is untouched by grief at this event, since I know that they which be called from this world in the white robes of baptism shall be nurtured in the sight of God.' Afterwards she bore another son, who was baptized with the name of Chlodomer. When he too began to ail, the king said: 'It cannot but befall that this infant like his brother shall straightway die, being baptized in the name of thy Christ.' But the mother prayed, and God ordained that the child should recover.

Now the queen without ceasing urged the king to confess the true God, and forsake his idols; but in no wise could she move him to this belief, until at length he made war upon a time against the Alamanni, when he was driven of necessity to confess what of his free will he had denied. It befell that when the two hosts joined battle there was grievous slaughter, and the army of Clovis was being swept to utter ruin. When the king saw this he lifted up his eyes to heaven, and knew compunction in his heart, and, moved to tears, cried aloud: 'Jesus Christ, Thou that art proclaimed by Clotild Son of the living God, Thou that art said to give aid to those in stress, and to grant victory to those that hope in Thee, I entreat from a devout heart the glory of Thy succour. If Thou grant me victory over these enemies, and experience confirm that power which the people dedicated to Thy name claimeth to have proved, then will I also believe on Thee and be baptized in Thy name. I have called upon mine own gods, but here is proof that they have withdrawn themselves from helping me; wherefore I believe that they have no power, since they come not to the succour of their servants. Thee do I now invoke, on Thee am I fain to believe, if but I may be plucked out of the hands of mine adversaries.' And as he said this, lo, the Alamanni turned their backs, and began to flee. And when they saw that their king was slain, they yielded themselves to Clovis, saying: 'No longer, we entreat thee, let the people perish; we are now thy men.' Then the king put an end to the war, and having admonished the people, returned in peace, relating to the queen how he had called upon the name of Christ and had been found worthy to obtain the victory. This happened in the fifteenth year of his reign.

Then the queen commanded the holy Remigius, bishop of Reims, to be summoned secretly, entreating him to impart the word of salvation to the king. The bishop, calling the king to him in privity, began to instil into him faith in the true God, Maker of heaven and earth, and urged him to forsake his idols, which were unable to help either himself or others. But Clovis replied: 'I myself, most holy father, will gladly hearken to thee; but one thing yet remaineth. The people that followeth me will not suffer it that I forsake their gods; yet will I go, and reason with them according to thy word.' But when he came before the assembled people, or ever he opened his mouth, the divine power had gone forth before him, and all the people cried with one voice: 'O gracious king, we drive forth our gods that perish, and are ready to follow that immortal God whom Remigius preachest.' News of this was brought to the bishop, who was filled with great joy, and commanded the font to be prepared. The streets were overshadowed with coloured hangings, the churches adorned with white hangings, the baptistery was set in order, smoke of incense spread in clouds, perfumed tapers gleamed, the whole church about the place of baptism was filled with the divine fragrance. And now the king first demanded to be baptized by the bishop. Like a new Constantine, he moved forward to the water, to blot out the former leprosy, to wash away in this new stream the foul stains borne from old days. As he entered to be baptized the saint of God spoke these words with eloquent lips: 'Meekly bow thy proud head, Sicamber; adore that which thou hast burned, burn that which thou hast adored.' For the holy Remigius, the bishop, was of excellent learning, and above all skilled in the art of rhetoric, and so exemplary in holiness that his miracles were equal to those of the holy Silvester; there is preserved to us a book of his life, in which it is related how he raised a man from the dead. The king therefore, confessing Almighty God, three in one, was baptized in the name of the Father, the Son, and the Holy Ghost, and anointed with holy chrism, with the sign of the Cross of Christ. Of his army were baptized more than three thousand; and his sister Albofled, who not long after was taken to the Lord, was likewise baptized. And when the king was sorrowing for her death, the holy Remigius sent him a letter of consolation, beginning after this fashion: 'The cause of thy sadness doth afflict me with a great affliction, for that thy sister of fair memory hath passed away. But this shall console us, that she hath in such wise left the world as that we should rather lift up our eyes to her than mourn her.' And another of his sisters was converted, by name Lanthechild, who had fallen into the heresy of the Arians; she also received the holy chrism, having confessed the Son and the Holy Ghost equal to the Father.

At this time two brothers, Gundobad and Godigisel, possessed their kingdom about the Rhône and Saône with the territory of Marseilles. They and their people were in the thraldom of the Arian sect. And as the brothers were on terms of hostility, Godigisel, who had heard of the victories won by King Clovis, sent envoys to him by stealth, saying: 'If thou afford me aid to pursue my brother, so that I may either slay him in battle, or drive him from the kingdom, I will pay thee every year such tribute as thou mayest thyself impose.' This offer Clovis received gladly, and promised him aid whenever his necessity should demand it. At a time appointed between them he marched an army against Gundobad, who ignorant of his brother's guile, sent to him upon this news, saying: 'Come thou to my deliverance, for the Franks have risen against us, and are come up against our territory to take it. Let us therefore be of one mind against a people that hateth us, for if we hold apart we shall undergo the fate suffered by other peoples.' Godigisel made answer: 'I will come with my army, and will bring thee succour.' So all three kings set their forces in movement together, Clovis marching against Gundobad and Godigisel; they came to Dijon with all the armaments of war. But when they joined battle on the Ouche, Godigisel joined Clovis, and their united armies crushed the force of Gundobad. But he, perceiving the treachery of his brother which till that hour he never suspected, turned his back and fled along the Rhône, until he entered the city of Avignon. After his victory thus gained, Godigisel promised Clovis a part of his kingdom, and went home in peace, entering Vienne in triumph, as though he were master of the entire kingdom. But Clovis reinforced his troops, and followed Gundobad with intent to take him from Avignon and slay him. When Gundobad heard this, he was grievously afraid, dreading to be overtaken by a sudden death. Now he had with him Aridius, a man of rank, who was both strenuous and astute. Him he summoned and thus addressed: 'I am hemmed in by straits upon every side, and know not what to do, for these barbarians are fallen upon me with intent to slay us and lay waste all the land.' Aridius answered: 'Thou hadst best assuage the savagery of this man, and so preserve thy life. Now therefore, if it be pleasing in thy sight, I will feign to forsake thee and desert to him; once with him, I will bring it about that he neither ruin thee nor yet this country. Do thou only have a care to satisfy all the demands which by my advice he shall make of thee, till the Lord of His goodness deign to make thy cause triumph.' Gundobad made answer: 'I will do all that thou shalt enjoin.' Thereupon Aridius bade him farewell and departed, and came to King Clovis, to whom he said: 'Behold in me, most pious king, thy humble slave, who hath forsaken the miserable Gundobad to serve thy mightiness. If now thy piety deign to look on me, thou and thy posterity shall find in me an honest and faithful follower.' Clovis forthwith took him to himself, and kept him near his person; for he could tell lively tales, was active in counsel, just in judgement, and faithful in every trust. Clovis then continuing to invest the city with his army, Aridius said: 'O king, if in the majesty of thy high estate thou deign to hear from me a few words of humble advice, though indeed thou hast small need of counsel, I will offer them in all loyalty; and it shall be useful to thee and to the cities through which it is thy intent to pass. Wherefore dost thou keep afoot this army, when thy foe abideth in an impregnable place? Thou layest waste the fields and devourest the meadows, thou cuttest the vines, thou hewest down the olives, all of this region thou doest utterly destroy, and yet thou availest not to do him hurt. Send rather envoys to him and impose a yearly tribute, that this region be saved from ruin, and thou be always lord over thy vassal. If he should refuse, then do according to thy pleasure.' The king hearkened to this counsel, and bade his army return home. And he sent an embassy to Gundobad, commanding him yearly to pay the tribute now to be laid upon him. After he paid it forthwith, and pledged himself to pay it thereafter.

But later, when he had recovered strength, he disdained to pay the promised tribute to King Clovis, and marched an army against Godigisel his brother, besieging him in the city of Vienne. As soon as provisions began to run short among the common people, Godigisel feared the famine might extend even to him, and ordered them to be driven outside the city. It was done; but among the rest was expelled the artificer who had charge of the aqueduct. This man, indignant at his expulsion with the others, went in a fury to Gundobad, and showed him how he might break into the city and take vengeance on his brother. Under his guidance armed men were led along the aqueduct, preceded by men with iron crowbars. For there was an outlet covered by a great stone, which was moved away by the crowbars under the direction of the artificer, and so they entered the city, taking in the rear the garrison who were discharging their arrows from the walls. Then at a signal given by a trumpet from the centre of the city, the besiegers seized the gates, threw them open, and crowded in. The inhabitants were caught between two forces and cut to pieces, but Godigisel took refuge in a church of the heretics, and was there put to death with the Arian bishop. The Franks who were with him held together in a tower: Gundobad commanded that none of them should be harmed, and when they were taken, sent them into banishment to King Alaric at Toulouse; but the Gallo-Romans of senatorial family and the Burgundians who had taken part with Godigisel he slew. He restored to his dominion the whole region now known as Burgundy, and instituted milder laws among the Burgundians that there should be no undue oppression of the Romans.

Gundobad, perceiving the doctrines of the heretics to be worthless, confessed that Christ, the Son of God, and the Holy Ghost are both equal to the Father, and asked secret baptism of the holy bishop of Vienne. But the bishop replied: 'If thou verily believest, it is thy duty to follow the teaching of our Lord Himself, when He said: "If any man will confess Me before men, him will I also confess before My Father which is in heaven; but whosoever shall deny Me before men, him will I also deny before My Father which is in heaven." This also did our Lord urge even upon His holy and beloved, the blessed apostles, when He said: "But beware of men; for they will deliver you up to councils, and in their synagogues they will scourge you; yea, and before the governors and kings shall ye be brought for My sake, for a testimony to them and to the Gentiles." But thou that art a king, and needest not to fear that any shall lay hands on thee, see how thou dreadest revolt among the people, not daring to confess in public the Creator of all men. Forsake this foolishness, and that which thou professest to believe in thy heart declare with thy lips before the people. For according to the word of the blessed apostle: "With the heart man believeth unto righteousness, and with the mouth confession is made unto salvation." Likewise also the prophet saith: "I will give Thee thanks in the great congregation, I will praise Thee among much people." And again: "I will give thanks unto Thee, O Lord, among the peoples; I will sing praises unto Thee among the nations." Thou fearest the people, O king; but perceivest thou not that it is more meet for the people to follow thy belief, than for thee to indulge their weakness? For thou art the head of the people; the people is not thy head. If thou goest at warfare, it is thou that goest before the troops of thy host, which follow whither thou leadest. Wherefore it is better that thou shouldst lead them to the knowledge of the truth than that thou shouldst perish and leave them in their error. "For God is not mocked," nor doth He love the men who for an earthly kingdom refuseth to confess Him before the world.' Though troubled by these arguments, Gundobad persisted to his dying day in this madness, nor ever would publicly confess that the three Persons of the Trinity are equal. The blessed Avitus was at this time of great eloquence; for heresy springing up in Constantinople, both that taught by Eutyches and that of Sabellius, to the effect that our Lord Jesus Christ had in Him nothing of the divine nature, at the request of King Gundobad he wrote against them. There are to-day extant among us his admirable letters, which, as they once quelled heresy, so now they edify the Church of God. He wrote a book of Homilies, six metrical books on the creation of the world and on various other subjects, and nine books of Letters, including those just mentioned. In a homily composed of the Rogations, he relates that these solemnities which we celebrate before the triumph of our Lord's Ascension were instituted by Namertus, bishop of Vienne (his own see when he wrote), at a time when the city was alarmed by many portents. For it was frequently shaken by earthquakes, and wild creatures, stags and wolves, entered the gates, wandering without fear through the whole city. These things befell through the circle of the year, till at the approach of the Easter festival the whole people looked devoutly for the mercy of God, that at last this day of great solemnity might set a term to all their terror. But on the very vigil of that glorious night, while the holy rite of the Mass was being celebrated, on a sudden the royal palace within the walls was set ablaze by fire from heaven. All the congregation, stricken with fear, rushed from the church, believing that the whole city would be consumed in this fire, or that the earth would open and swallow it up. The holy bishop, prostrate before the altar, with groans and tears implored the mercy of God. What need for me to say more? The prayer of the illustrious bishop penetrated to the height of heaven; the river of his flowing tears extinguished the burning palace. When, after these events, the day of the Lord's Ascension drew near, he imposed a fast upon the people, instituted the form of prayer, the order of their repasts, and manner of their joyful almsgiving to the poor. Thereupon all these terrors ceased; the fame of this deed spread through all the provinces, putting all the bishops in mind to follow the example of his faith. And down to our day these rites are celebrated in all churches in Christ's name, in compunction of the heart and a contrite spirit.

Now when Alaric, king of the Goths, beheld the manner in which King Clovis kept steadily subduing his neighbours in war, he sent envoys to him with this message: 'If it please thee, O my brother, I am minded that we two meet by God's grace.' Clovis did not refuse, but came to him. They met on an island in the Loire near the village of Amboise in the territory of the city of Tours. There they conversed, ate and drank together, swore mutual friendship, and parted in peace. Many people in Gaul at this time ardently desired to live under the dominion of the Franks.

This was the reason why Quintianus, bishop of Rodez, incurred hatred and was driven from the city. Men said to him: 'It is because thou desirest the Franks to become masters and possess this land.' A few days afterwards there was a quarrel between him and the citizens. Those of the Gothic nation dwelling in the town were suspicious of him, and the citizens accused him of wishing to bring them under the Frankish rule. They took counsel together, and planned to put him to the sword. But the man of God was warned, and rising in the night with the most faithful of his attendants, left Rodez and came to Clermont. There he was kindly received by the holy bishop Eufrasius, successor to Aprunculus of Dijon, who kept him with him, and bestowed on him houses, lands, and vineyards, saying: 'The riches of this church suffice to support us both; only let the brotherly love preached by the blessed apostle continue among the priests of God.' The bishop of Lyons also presented him with possessions of his church in Auvergne. The remaining history of the holy Quintianus, both the treachery which he endured, and the works which the Lord deigned to perform by his hands, is written in the book containing his life.

Now King Clovis said to his men: 'It irketh me sore that these Arians hold a part of Gaul. Let us go forth, then, and with God's aid bring the land under our own sway.' This speech finding favour with all, he assembled his army, and marched on Poitiers, where King Alaric then happened to be. Part of the troops had to traverse the territory of Tours, and out of reverence for the blessed Martin the king issued an edict that none should take anything from that region but water and hay. Now a certain soldier, finding some hay belonging to a poor man, said: 'Was it not the king's order that we should take grass and nothing besides? Well, this is grass, and if we take it we shall not transgress his bidding.' So he took the hay from the poor man by force, taking advantage of his own strength. The matter came to the ears of the king, who straightway cut the man down with his own sword, saying: 'Where shall be our hope of victory, if we offend the blessed Martin?' And the army was content to take nothing more from this region. Moreover the king sent messengers to the church of the saint, with these words: 'Go now, and haply ye shall bring some good auspice of victory from that sacred house.' He entrusted them with offerings to be set in the holy place, saying: 'If Thou, O Lord, art my helper, and if Thou hast determined to deliver into my hands this unbelieving people, ever set against Thee, deign of Thy favour to give me a sign at the going in to the basilica of the blessed Martin, that I may know that Thou wilt deign to show Thy servant Thy favour.' His men, setting forth on their journey, reached Tours according to the king's command. And as they were entering the church, the precentor chanced to lead this antiphon: 'Thou hast girded me, O Lord, with strength unto the battle; Thou hast subdued under me those that rose up against me. Thou hast also made mine enemies turn their backs upon me, and Thou hast destroyed them that hate me.' The messengers, hearing these words chanted, gave thanks to God, and vowing gifts to the blessed confessor, joyfully returned with their news to the king. But when Clovis had reached the Vienne with his army he was wholly at a loss where to cross the stream, for it was swollen by heavy rains. That night he besought the Lord that He would show him where he might pass, and lo! at dawn a hind of wondrous size entered the river at God's bidding, and where she forded the host saw that it could cross. When the king came to the neighborhood of Poitiers, but was abiding at some distance in his tents, he saw a fiery beacon issue from the church of the holy Hilary and come over above his head; it signified that aided by the light of the blessed confessor Hilary he might more surely overcome the host of those heretics against whom the saint himself had so often done battle for the faith. He adjured the whole army to despoil no man, either there or upon the way, and to rob none of his goods.

In those days the abbot Maxentius, a man laudable in holiness, lived recluse for the fear of God in his monastery in the territory of Poitiers. I give no particular name to the monastery, since to our own day the place is always known as the cell of the holy Maxentius. Now when the monks beheld a dense body of soldiers drawing near the monastery, they besought the abbot to come forth out of his cell for their encouragement. He delayed to come. Then, stricken with panic, they opened the cell door and brought him out, whereupon he went forth fearlessly to meet the enemy as if to ask peace of them. One of their number unsheathed his sword to strike the abbot on the head, when lo! he found his hand held rigid at the level of his ear, while the sword fell backwards; he then fell at the feet of the holy man, and besought his pardon. When the rest saw what was done, they returned to the army in great dread, fearing that they might all perish. But the blessed confessor rubbed the man's arm with consecrated oil, and making the sign of the Cross, restored him to health; thus by his protection the monastery remained unharmed. He performed many other miracles, which whoso seeks diligently will find as he reads the history of the abbot's Life. This took place in the twenty-fifth year of Clovis.

In the mean time King Clovis encountered Alaric, king of the Goths, on the field of Vouillé at the tenth milestone out of Poitiers. Part of the combatants fought with missiles from a distance, another part hand to hand. But when, as their habit is, the Goths turned to fly, King Clovis by God's aid obtained the victory. He had with him as an ally Chloderic, son of Sigibert the Lame. This Sigibert, in the fight at Zülpich against the Alamanni, was wounded in the knee so that he limped. When the Goths were put to flight, and the king had slain Alaric, two of the enemy suddenly came up and struck at him with their spears on each side; the cuirass which he wore and the speed of his horse preserved him from death. There perished on this field a great number of the people of Auvergne who had come with Apollinaris, and the chief men of senatorial family fell. From this battle Amalaric, son of Alaric, fled into Spain and ruled with prudence his father's kingdom. Clovis sent his own son Theuderic through Albi and Rodez to Clermont. Traversing these cities he subdued beneath his father's sway the whole country from the Gothic to the Burgundian frontier. Alaric had reigned twenty-two years. Clovis, after wintering in Bordeaux, carried off all Alaric's treasures from Toulouse and came to Angoulême. And the Lord showed him such favour that the walls fell down of themselves before his eyes; he drove out the Goths and subjected the city to his own rule. Then, his victory being complete, he returned to Tours and made many offerings to the holy shrine of the holy Martin.

Clovis received letters from the emperor Anastasius conferring the consulate, and in the church of the blessed Martin he was vested in the purple tunic, and in a mantle, and set the diadem upon his head. Then, mounting his horse, he showered with his own hand in the generosity of his heart pieces of gold and silver among the people all along the road between the gate of the atrium of the holy Martin's church, and the church of the city. From that day he was hailed as consul or Augustus. He left Tours and came to Paris, where he established the seat of his government. There he was joined by Theuderic.

After the death of Eustochius, bishop of Tours, Licinius was consecrated as eighth bishop after Martin. In his time was waged the war which I have above described, and it was in his time that King Clovis came to Tours. He is said to have been in the East, to have visited the holy places, and to have even entered Jerusalem; it is related that he often saw the places of the Passion and Resurrection of our Lord, of which we read in the Gospels.

While Clovis was sojourning at Paris, he sent secretly to the son of Sigibert, saying: 'Thy father is grown old, and is lame of one foot. If he were to die, his kingdom would fall to thee of right, together with our friendship.' The prince, seduced through his ambition, plotted his father's death. One day Sigibert left Cologne and crossed the Rhine, to walk in the forest of Buchau. He was enjoying a midday repose in his tent when his son compassed his death by sending assassins against him, intending so to get possession of the kingdom. But by the judgement of God he fell himself into the pit which he had treacherously digged for his father. He sent messengers to King Clovis announcing his father's death in these terms: 'My father hath perished, and his kingdom and treasures are in my power. Come to me, and right gladly will I hand over to thee whatever things may please thee from his treasure.' Clovis answered: 'I thank thee for thy goodwill, and request of thee that thou show all to my envoys; but thou shalt keep the whole.' On the arrival of the envoys, the prince displayed his father's treasure, and while they were inspecting its various contents, said to them: 'In this coffer my father used to amass pieces of gold.' They answered: 'Plunge in thy hand to the bottom, to make sure of all.' He did so; but as he was stooping, one of them raised his two-edged axe and buried it in his brain; so was his guilt towards his father requited on himself. When Clovis heard that Sigibert was slain, and his son also, he came to Cologne and called all the people together, addressing them in these words: 'Hear ye what hath befallen. While I was sailing the Scheldt, Chloderic, son of my cousin, was harassing his father, and telling him that I desired his death. When his father fled through the forest of Buchau, he set bandits upon him, delivering him over to death. But he in his turn hath perished, striken I know not by whom, while he was showing his father's treasure. To all these deeds I was in no wise privy; for I could not bear to shed the blood of my kindred, holding it an impious deed. But since things have so fallen out, I offer you this counsel, which take, if it seemeth good to you: turn ye to me, and live under my protection.' At these words the clash of shields vied with their applause; they raised Clovis upon a shield, and recognized him as their king. Thus he became possessed of the kingdom of Sigibert and of his treasures, and submitted the people also to his dominion. For daily the Lord laid his enemies low under his hand, and increased his kingdom, because he walked before Him with an upright heart, and did that which was pleasing in His sight.

After this he marched against King Chararic. For during his war with Syagrius, this Chararic, summoned to his aid, stood aloof, joining neither side, but awaiting the issue in order to ally himself with the victor, for which cause Clovis marched against him full of wrath. And he cunningly circumvented him and took him, together with his son; he then bound them, and cut off their hair, commanding that Chararic should be ordained priest, and his son deacon. Chararic lamented his humiliation and wept; but they say that his son replied: 'These branches have been cut from a green tree, nor are they all withered, but shall soon shoot forth, and grow again. May he who has done these things as swiftly perish!' This saying reached the ears of Clovis, who thought that they threatened to let their hair grow again and compass his death. He therefore ordered both of the heads to be cut off. After their death, he took possession of their kingdom, together with their treasure and their people.

There was at that time in Cambrai a king named Ragnachar, whose wantonness was so unbridled that he hardly spared his own near kindred. He had as counsellor a certain Farron, defiled by the same foul taint, in regard to whom it was alleged that when any one brought the king a gift of food or a present, or any other kind of thing, the king would say that the gift was sufficient for him and his Farron. On this account the hearts of the Franks were swollen with the utmost indignation. Thereupon Clovis presented armlets and baldrics of spurious gold to the *leudes* of Ragnachar in order that they might call him in against their lord; the supposed gold was only copper, cunningly gilded. When he had set his army on foot against him, Ragnachar kept sending out scouts to bring in intelligence. These men were asked on their return in what strength the enemy was. They answered: 'Abundant force for thee and for thy Farron.' But Clovis came, and drew up his battle array. And when Ragnachar saw his army vanquished, he made ready to escape in flight, but he was caught by his own men, and brought before Clovis with his arms bound behind his back; so likewise was Ricchar his brother. Clovis said to him: 'Why hast thou disgraced our race by suffering thyself to be bound? It had been better for thee to die;' he then raised his axe and buried it in his head. Afterwards he turned to his brother, and said: 'If thou hadst stood by thy brother, he would not have been thus bound,' and slew him in the same way with a blow of his axe. After their death, their betrayers for the first time discovered that the gold which Clovis had given them was false. But when they remonstrated with the king, men say that he replied: 'This is the kind of gold deserved by the man who of set mind lureth his lord to his death;' adding that they ought to be content to have escaped with their lives, not expiating the betrayal of their lords by a death amid torments. When they heard this, they chose to sue for grace, declaring that it sufficed them if they were judged worthy to live. The two kings of whom I have spoken were kinsmen of Clovis. Their brother, Rignomer, was slain at Le Mans by his command, and the kingdom and treasures of all three passed into his possession. He caused many other kings to be slain and the near relatives whom he suspected of usurping his kingdom; in this way he extended his dominion over all Gaul. Upon a day when he had assembled his own people, he is said to have spoken as follows of the kinsmen whom he had destroyed: 'Woe unto me who remain as a traveller among strangers, and have none of my kin to help me in the evil day.' But he did not thus allude to their death out of grief, but craftily, to see if he could bring to light some new relative to kill.

After these events Clovis died at Paris, and was buried in the church of the Holy Apostles which he had himself built, with Clotild his queen. It was the fifth year after the battle of Vouillé that he passed away. And all the days of his reign were thirty years, and of his own age forty-five. From the passing of the holy Martin to the passing of Clovis, which was in the eleventh year of the episcopate of Licinius, bishop of Tours, there are counted one hundred and twelve years. After the death of her lord, Queen Clotild came to Tours, and, save for rare visits to Paris, here she remained all the days of her life, distinguished for her great modesty and kindliness.

◆ ◆ ◆

Now King Sigibert, seeing his brothers take to themselves unworthy wives and even wed serving-maids, sent an embassy to Spain with many gifts to demand in marriage Brunhild, daughter of King Athanagild. For she was a girl of graceful form, fair to look upon, honorable and comely, prudent in judgement, and amiable of address. Her father did not refuse her, but sent her with great treasures to the king, who, assembling the chief men of his kingdom, and making ready a feast, received her as his wife with boundless rejoicing and delight. And because she was subject to the Arian law, she was converted by the preaching of bishops and the admonitions of the king himself, so that she confessed the blessed Trinity in Unity, and received the holy chrism, remaining a Catholic in the name of Christ until this day.

At the time when King Sigibert was slain at Vitry, Queen Brunhild was dwelling with her children at Paris. When the news was brought to her, and in the tumult of her grief and anguish she knew not what she did, Duke Gundovald took Childebert, her little son, and bore him away in secret, snatching him from imminent death. Then he assembled the peoples over which his father had reigned, and proclaimed him king, his years being as yet hardly five: it was Christmas Day when Childebert began to reign. Now in the first year of his reign King Chilperic came to Paris, seized Brunhild and banished her to Rouen, took possession of treasures which she had brought to Paris, and ordered her daughters to be detained at Meaux. At this time Roccolen came to Tours with the men of Maine, took plunder, and committed many crimes. I shall shortly relate after what manner he was smitten and slain by the power of the holy Martin for all the evil which he wrought.

King Chilperic sent his son Merovech with an army to Poitiers. But the prince, disobeying his orders, came to Tours and there passed the holy days of Easter, while his army sorely devastated all that country. Then, under the pretext of visiting his mother, he betook himself to Rouen, where he joined Queen Brunhild and took her to wife. As soon as Chilperic heard that in defiance of usage and of canonical law his son had married his uncle's widow, he grew exceeding bitter against him, and in a shorter time than I can say it, set forth for the aforesaid town. But upon the news that he meant to decree their separation the pair took sanctuary in the church of the holy Martin, which is built of wooden planks, upon the city walls. The king arrived and strove by many a device to get them out; but when they would not believe him, suspecting his treacherous intent, he took an oath declaring that if that which was done was according to the will of God, he would not try to part them. When they heard his solemn oath, they came forth from the church, whereupon he embraced them and received them right worthily. But a few days afterwards he went back to Soissons, taking Merovech with him.

◆ ◆ ◆

While these men pursued their way with all this plunder, Chilperic, the Nero and Herod of our time, proceeded to the domain of Chelles, about a hundred stadia from Paris, and went a-hunting. One day, on his return from the chase as the night drew on, he was alighting from his horse, with one hand resting on a servant's shoulder, when some man unknown came up and first struck him under the armpit, then with a second blow stabbed him in the stomach. At once blood streamed both from his mouth and from the gaping wound, and so he breathed out his wicked soul.

The evil which he did is set forth in the earlier part of this History. Many a region did he lay waste and burn again and again; whereat he felt no grief, but rather pleasure, like Nero, who of old sang play-verses amid the flames of his palace. Many a time did he unjustly punish men, to confiscate their goods. In his days few priests were raised to bishoprics. He gave himself over to gluttony, and his god was his belly. No man, he would declare, was cleverer than he. He wrote two books in verse, taking Sedulius as his model; but as, in his ignorance, he put short syllables for long and long for short, his feeble lines had no feet to stand on. He wrote other short pieces, hymns and chants for the Mass; but by no possibility could they have been used. He hated the cause of the poor. Ever he spoke evil of the priests of the Lord; and in his private hours no men were more often the butt of his ridicule and his jests than the bishops. To one he imputed levity, to a second arrogance, to a third excess, to a fourth loose living; one bishop he would call a vain fool, another pompous. He hated nothing so much as the churches. He would often say: 'See how poor our treasury always is! Look how the churches have drained our riches away! Of a verity, none ruleth at all, save only the bishops. Our royal office is lost and gone; it hath passed to the bishops in their cities.' So thinking, he ever made it his habit to tear up all wills made in favour of churches; often he would trample upon the diplomas of his own father, thinking that there was left no man to carry out that king's intentions. The mind can conceive no lust or debauchery that this man did not practise. He was ever on the watch for new ways of torturing the people; when he found a man guilty, he ordered the eyes to be torn out of his head. The instructions which he issued to the judges in his own affairs he would close with this sentence: 'If any shall disregard our decrees, let him be punished by the tearing out of his eyes.' Never a soul did he love in singleness of heart; by none was he himself beloved. And so when he breathed his last all men abandoned him. Only Mallulf, bishop of Senlis, remained, who for three days had camped in his tent, waiting there for an audience. He came at news of the murder, and washed the body, putting upon it seemlier garments. He passed the night chanting hymns; on the next day, embarking the corpse in a vessel, he buried it in Paris, in the church of the holy Vincent. But Fredegund the queen remained in the cathedral church.

After these things Gundovald again sent two envoys to the king, bearing consecrated rods according to the custom of the Franks, that they might not be touched by any man, but, after setting forth the object of their mission, return with their answer. These men were heedless enough to reveal to many persons, before they were given audience of the king, what they were instructed to ask. The king soon heard talk of this, and they were brought into his presence in chains. They did not dare to deny the object of their mission, or who sent them and to whom, but delivered their message: 'Gundovald, who of late is come from the East, declareth himself the son of thy father king Lothar. We are sent to demand the portion of the kingdom which is his due. If this be not yielded up by thee, know that he will come into these regions with an army, for all the most powerful men in the parts of Gaul beyond the Dordogne have joined him. And thus speaketh he: "God's judgement will decide, when we twain encounter in a single field, whether I am Lothar's son or not."' Thereat the king, inflamed with wrath, ordered them to be stretched by the pulleys and severely flogged, that if they spoke sooth they might give yet more evident proof, or, if the depths of their hearts held further secrets, the frightful pain might drag the truth from them in their own despite. It was done, and as the agony increased, they declared that the king's niece, King

Chilperic's daughter, had been banished with Magnulf, bishop of Toulouse, and that her whole treasure had been seized by Gundovald, who had been asked to take the throne by all the chief men of King Childebert: the request had been the special object of the visit made to Constantinople a few years before by Guntram Boso, who had brought him the invitation to enter Gaul.

After the envoys had been thus flogged and cast into prison, the king summoned his nephew Childebert, thinking it well that they should hear the evidence of these men together. The two kings therefore questioned the prisoners, who repeated in their joint presence all that King Guntram had heard alone. They steadily asserted that the matter, as I have said above, was common knowledge to all the chief men in Childebert's kingdom. This was the reason why some of them were afraid to attend the present conference; they were suspected of being parties to the affair. After this, King Guntram placed his spear in the hand of King Childebert, saying: 'This is the sign that I have bestowed all my kingdom on thee. By virtue of this, take under thy dominion all my cities as if they were thine own. For by reason of my sins, no male of my line remaineth, save only thou, who art my brother's son. I shut out all others from my succession; do thou succeed as heir in all my realm.' Then, dismissing all the rest and taking the boy apart, he privily spoke with him, first earnestly adjuring him to reveal to no man the secrets of their conversation. He then indicated to him the men whom he should admit as his advisers and those whom he should keep from his counsels; those whom he might trust, and those whom he should avoid; those whom he should distinguish by rewards, and those whom he should degrade from their offices: enjoining him above all on no account to trust or have about him Egidius, bishop of Reims, who had ever been his enemy and had many a time sworn falsely both to his father and himself. Later, when they appeared together at the banquet, King Guntram exhorted all his people in these words: 'Behold, O comrades, how my son Childebert is now grown up to manhood; behold, and give heed that ye take him no more for a child. Forsake now your forwardness and your presumption; for he is now a king to whom ye owe your service.' These words he said and others like to them; and having for three whole days feasted and made merry together, exchanging many and rich gifts, the kings separated in peace. It was on this occasion that King Guntram restored to his nephew all that had belonged to Sigibert his father, adjuring him not to visit his mother, that no opening should be given her for writing to Gundovald or receiving letters from him in return.

Now when Gundovald heard that an army was approaching, he crossed the Garonne and made for Convenae with Bishop Sagittarius and the dukes Mummolus and Bladast; Walddo was also with him, but Duke Desiderius had abandoned his cause. The city crowns an isolated height, with no other mountain near. A great spring issuing from the foot of the hill is enclosed by a very strong tower; men go down to it by a covered way and thus draw water without being exposed to view. Gundovald entered the city at the beginning of Lent, and addressed the people of the town in these words: 'Ye know that I am chosen king by all men in the realm of Childebert, and that I have with me no small power. But since my brother, King Guntram, hath sent a huge army against me, ye must bring within the walls all your provisions and all your gear, that ye perish not for want before the divine goodness bringeth me increased support.' They believed his words, and collecting within the walls all that they could lay hands upon, prepared to make resistance. At this juncture King Guntram sent a letter to Gundovald in the name of Queen Brunhild, advising him to forsake and disband his army, himself keeping out of sight and passing the winter at Bordeaux: he wrote this with cunning intent, in order that he might learn of him more fully what he meant to do. But Gundovald remained at Comminges, and spoke to the people, saying: 'Behold, the army draweth nigh; sally forth now, and make resistance.' They sallied forth; but his men seized and closed the gates, shutting out the bishop and all the people, and took possession of everything which they found in the town. They discovered such quantity of corn and wine that if they had stood fast like men, provision had not failed them for the space of many years.

By this time news had reached King Guntram's dukes that Gundovald was on the farther bank of the Garonne with a great multitude of their enemies, and that he had possession of the treasures which Rigunth had taken with her. They pressed forward, and their cavalry swam the Garonne, some being drowned in the river. The rest, on reaching the far bank, went in search of Gundovald, and found camels laden with a great weight of gold and silver, and exhausted horses which he had left behind along the roads. Hearing later that Gundovald and his men were now within the walls of Convenae, they left behind their wagons and baggage with the less able-bodied, and dispatched the more active men, as they were already across the river, to follow up the enemy. Moving forward with all speed, they came to the church of the holy Vincent near the boundary of the city of Agen, where the martyr is said to have finished his fight for the name of Christ. They found it filled with all manner of treasure belonging to the inhabitants of the place, who hoped that the church of so great a martyr would never be violated by Christian men. The doors were most carefully fastened. But when the approaching troops were unable to break them open, they lit a fire and burned them down, whereupon they carried off all the property and gear that they found, and all the church plate as well. But the divine vengeance then and there filled many of them with affright. For the hands of some were supernaturally burned, and sent forth a great smoke, like that which rises above a fire.

Others were seized by an evil spirit; thus possessed, they shouted in their frenzy the martyr's name. A great number began brawling and wounded each other with their own spears. The remainder of their body proceeded on their march, not without great alarm. To cut the story short, they all came together again at Convenae (that, as I have written, was the name of the place); the whole force now pitched tents in the country about the city, and there remained encamped. They ravaged all the surrounding region; some of the soldiers, goaded more deeply than the rest by avarice, strayed too far from their comrades and were put to death by the peasants.

Many of their number would often go up the hill and speak with Gundovald, reviling him and saying: 'Art thou that painter fellow who in the days of King Lothar used to daub the walls and vaults of oratories? Art thou he whom the people of Gaul used often to call *Ballomer?* Art thou he who several times wast shorn and banished by the kings of the Franks for these very pretensions which thou makest to-day? Tell us plainly, most miserable of men, who was it that brought thee hither? Who gave thee the heart to set foot within the frontiers of our lords and kings? If any man invited thee, declare it with a loud voice. Behold, death standeth plain before thine eyes; look on the pit of thy destruction which so long thou hast sought, and into which thou shalt be cast headlong! Tell us, man by man, the names of thine abettors, and make those known to us by whom thou wert invited.' When he had listened to what they said, Gundovald drew nearer, and taking up his position above the gate, replied: 'No man is ignorant that my father Lothar ever detested me, or that my hair was cut short first by him, and later by my brothers. This was why I joined Narses, prefect of Italy, in which country I took a wife and begat two sons. Upon her death, I took my sons with me and withdrew to Constantinople. I was received right graciously by the emperors, and lived there down to the present time. Some years ago, Guntram Boso came to Constantinople, and I eagerly questioned him how it fared with my brothers; from him I learned that our royal house was grievously diminished, and that of our line no males remained but Guntram and Childebert, a brother and a brother's son; for the sons of King Chilperic had perished with him, and there was left only one young child. My brother Guntram had no sons; my nephew Childebert was without power. Guntram Boso having set these things forth at length, gave me an invitation to return, saying: 'Come; all the chief men of King Childebert's realm call for thee, and not one hath dared mutter a word against thee. It is known to us all that thou art Lothar's son. And thou come not, there is none left in Gaul to rule his kingdom.' I gave him many gifts, and in twelve sacred places received his oath that I might enter this realm in safety. I therefore came to Marseilles, where the bishop received me with the greatest kindness, for he had letters written by the chief men of my nephew's kingdom. I then went to Avignon, according to the wish of the patrician Mummolus. But Guntram Boso, regardless of his oath and promise, stole from me my treasures and took them for himself. Learn, therefore, that I am king, even as is my brother Guntram. But if too great a hatred rageth in your minds, at least conduct me to your king, and if he knoweth me for his brother, I will do according to his will. If ye will not do this, then let me return to the place whence I set out. For I will go away, and do no harm to any man. If ye would know the truth of what I say, make inquiry of Radegund at Poitiers and Ingitrude at Tours, for they will confirm my words as true.' While he made this harangue many men followed his words with reviling and with taunts.

The fifteenth day of the siege had dawned, and Leudegisel was preparing new engines for the destruction of the city. There were wagons fitted with rams covered with wattle-work and planks, under which troops could go forward to destroy the walls. But as soon as they came near they were overwhelmed with such showers of stones that all fell who approached the wall. The defenders threw down on them vessels of burning pitch and grease, and others filled with stones. When night forbade further fighting, the assailants returned to their camp.

With Gundovald was Chariulf, a citizen passing rich and powerful, who had many stores and repositories in the city, and from whose substance the garrison was for the most part fed. But Bladast, seeing the trend of events, feared that if Leudigisel captured the place he would put them all to death. He therefore set fire to the church house, and when all the besieged crowded to put out the flames, took to flight and got away. The next morning the enemy attacked again, and made fascines to fill up the deep valley which lies on the eastern side; but this device did the enemy no damage. All the time Bishop Sagittarius was going round the ramparts in arms, and with his own hand hurling stones from the walls.

When the besiegers saw that their efforts availed nothing, they sent messengers to Mummolus in secret, saying: 'Acknowledge thy true lord, and desist even at this late hour from thy forwardness. What madness constraineth thee, that thou servest a man unknown? Thy wife and thy children are taken captive; thy sons are surely slain. Whither rushest thou? To what canst thou look forward but thy ruin?' On receipt of this message he replied: 'I see that our dominion draweth already to its end, and our power declineth. But one course remaineth; and had I surety that my life should be safe, I might spare you many toils.' When the messengers were gone, Bishop Sagittarius, with Mummolus, Chariulf, and Waddo, proceeded to the church, and there they made mutual oaths that if they were assured of their lives, they would renounce their loyalty to Gundovald, and surrender his person to the enemy. The messengers came back with a promise that their lives should be spared. Mummolus said: 'Grant but that, and I will surrender this man into your hands; I will acknowledge my lord and king, and straightway seek his presence.' Thereupon they promised that if he would keep his word, they would receive him with kindliness, and if they failed to obtain his pardon from the king, they would place him in a church that he might escape punishment of death. They promised this under oath, and took their departure. Then Mummolus, with Sagittarius and Waddo, went to Gundovald and said: 'Thou knowest, thou that standest here before us, what oaths of fealty we took to thee. But hear now a wholesome counsel. Depart from this city and present thyself before thy brother, as thou hast often wished to do. For we have already held conference with these men, and they have told us that the king desireth not to lose thy support, since of the royal line so few remain alive.' Gundovald saw through their treachery, and said with many tears: 'It was by your invitation that I was brought to Gaul, and of my treasures, including an immense weight of gold, silver, and divers precious things, part is kept back in Avignon, and part was plundered by Guntram Boso. All my hope was placed in you, next to God's aid; I gave you all my confidence; by your help I ever hoped to reign. If ye now have spoken to me falsely, lay your account with God, for He shall judge my cause.' To this Mummolus made answer: 'We have said nothing with treacherous intent; and, behold, already there stand at the gate stout men of war awaiting thy coming forth. Now therefore put off my golden baldric which thou wearest, that thou seem not to go forth in bravery; gird on thy own sword, and restore me mine.' He replied: 'I see well enough the double purport of these words: that these things of thine which I have worn till now as symbols of our friendship are now to be taken from me.' Mummolus then solemnly swore that no evil should be done him.

So they went out from the gate, and Gundovald was received by Ullo, count of Bourges, and by Boso; but Mummolus and his followers drew back within the city and made the gate fast behind them. When Gundovald saw that he was betrayed into the hands of his enemies, he lifted up his hands and his eyes to heaven and cried: 'O Eternal Judge, and true avenger of the innocent, Thou God from whom all justice proceedeth, who hatest a lie, in whom is no guile nor craft of malice, to Thee do I commend my cause, that Thou avenge me swiftly on those who have betrayed me, innocent of all offence, into the hands of mine enemies.' Having said these words, and made the sign of the Lord's Cross, he went away with the men of whom I have written. When they had gone some distance from the gate, the city being surrounded by a valley with precipitous sides, Ullo pushed him down, shouting as he did so, 'Behold your *Ballomer* who declareth himself son and brother of kings!' He then thrust at him with his spear, wishing to run him through, but the rings of his hauberk turned the blow, and made it harmless. Gundovald then rose and tried to go back up the hill, but Boso hurled a stone and struck his head so that he fell and breathed his last. A crowd of men came up and pierced the body with their spears. They then bound his feet with a rope and dragged him through the whole camp; the hair of his head and his beard were plucked out, and he was left unburied on the spot where he was slain.

On the following night the chief men in the town secretly removed all the treasures which they could find, including the church plate. The next morning the gates were opened and the besieging army was admitted. All the common people within were put to the sword, and the priests of the Lord, with those who served them, were massacred before the altars. When all were dead, so that there remained not one that pisseth against a wall, they set fire to the city with all its churches and other buildings. They left nothing but the naked ground.

Now when Leudegisel returned to the camp with Mummolus and Sagittarius, Chariulf and Waddo, he sent messengers to King Guntram secretly, to ask what he would have done to these men. The king commanded that they should receive sentence of death. But Waddo and Chariulf left their sons as hostages and got away. The word ran that they had been slain, and when Mummolus heard it he girded on his arms and went off to the hut of Leudegisel, who cried on his appearance: 'Why comest thou thus as if bent on flight?' The other replied: 'I perceive that the faith plighted to me is in nothing observed; I see myself in peril of death.' Leudegisel answered: 'I will come forth, and assuage all.' Going out, he forthwith ordered the house to be surrounded that Mummolus might be slain. But Mummolus, having long and stubbornly resisted his assailants, at last came to the door. No sooner had he set foot outside, than he was pierced from right and left by two lances; thus he fell and died. At this sight the bishop was afeared and in dismay, but one who stood by said to him: 'Behold with thine own eyes, O bishop, what things are done. Cover thy head, make for the forest, and hide thee awhile; haply when this fury abateth, thou mayst escape.' The bishop followed his advice, and strove to flee with veiled head; but one drew a sword and cut off his head, hood and all. Thereafter every man of the army returned to his own place, plundering and man-slaying as they went.

At this time Queen Fredegund dispatched Chuppa to the territory of Toulouse to bring her daughter thence in whatever manner he could. There were many who declared that he was really sent to entice Gundovald, if he still lived, with many promises, and so bring him to the queen. But as he could not now do this, he took Rigunth, humbled and put to shame as she was, and brought her away from that region.

Duke Leudegisel came to the king with the treasures aforesaid, which the king afterwards distributed among the poor and among the churches. He caused the wife of Mummolus to be arrested, and inquired what had become of the treasures which she and her husband had amassed. And when she heard that her lord was slain, and that all their pride of place was utterly brought down to the dust, she revealed all, and said that in Avignon there was still much gold and silver of which the king had no knowledge. Straightway the king sent men to fetch it, with a trusted servant of Mummolus, to whose charge it had been committed. They went on their errand, and took everything which had been left in that city. It was said that there were two hundred and fifty talents of silver, and more than thirty of gold, reported to have been taken by Mummolus from an ancient treasure which had been discovered. The king divided the money with his nephew Childebert, giving away the greater part of his own share to the poor. He left the widow nothing but what she had inherited from her kinsfolk.

Then also one of the servants of Mummolus was brought to the king, a very giant, so big that he was accounted two or three feet higher than the tallest men yet known. He was a carpenter, and died soon afterwards.

After this the judges issued an order that all who had been slow in joining the late expedition should be punished. The count of Bourges sent his servants to collect the fine from such delinquents in a house belonging to the blessed Martin, situated in that territory. But the overseer of this property resisted stoutly, saying: 'These be Martin's men; do them no injury, since it is not customary for them to serve upon such occasions.' They answered: 'What care we for this Martin, of whom thou ever idly protest in such affairs? But thou and these men shall pay the fine for neglecting the king's command.' So saying, one entered the court of the house. And straightway he was stricken with great anguish, and fell down, and was in evil case. Then, turning towards the overseer, he said in a tearful voice: 'I pray thee make over me the sign of our Lord's Cross, and call on the name of the blessed Martin. Now know I how great is his power; for as I came into the court of the house, I saw an aged man hold out a tree in his hand, whose boughs spread and covered all the court. One branch thereof touched me, and smote me so that I was confounded and fell.' Then the overseer made sign to his followers to put him forth from the court. And when he was without, he began to call fervently on the name of the blessed Martin. And thereby he had ease of his pain, and was healed.

Desiderius sought safety for himself and his possessions within fortified places of his own. Waddo, former mayor of the household to Rignuth, went over to Queen Brunhild, who received him well, and dismissed him with favour and with gifts. Chariulf betook himself to the church of the holy Martin.

◆ ◆ ◆

Rauching leagued himself with the chief men in the kingdom of Lothar, son of Chilperic, under the pretext that he acted on behalf of peace, and wished to prevent quarrels and raids across the frontiers of the two kingdoms. It was really a conspiracy to slay Childebert. Rauching was then to rule in Champagne, with control over Theudebert, the king's elder son; Ursio and Berthefred were to get into their hands Theuderic, the younger son born not long since, and hold the rest of the kingdom, excluding King Guntram from power. They murmured against Queen Brunhild, and longed once more to humiliate her, as they had done before in her early widowhood.

Rauching, elated at his great power, and, so to speak, vaunting a regal state to come, now made ready for his journey; it was his purpose to have audience of King Childebert, and then carry out the design which he had planned. But the goodness of God brought the plot first to the ears of King Guntram, who sent envoys in secret to King Childebert to warn him of the conspiracy, and then to say: 'Make speed that we may meet together, for there are urgent matters to be discussed.' Childebert made inquiry as to that which was told him, and finding it to be true, sent for Rauching. As soon as he had arrived, and before he had been admitted to the presence, the king issued orders, and dispatched some of his servants with authority to travel in the king's name and take possession of all Rauching's property wherever it might be found. He then ordered the duke to be admitted to his chamber; and after a talk on various subjects, dismissed him. As he came out, two doorkeepers seized him by the legs, so that he fell upon the threshold, one part of his body lying within, the other without the chamber. Then men appointed for the work fell upon him with swords, and hacked his head so fine that the whole of it looked like a mass of brain; his death was instantaneous. The body was stripped, flung from a window, and consigned to burial. This man was a light character, beyond all human measure rapacious and greedy after the goods of others. Moreover, his very riches made him so haughty that at the time of his death he was giving himself out as the son of King Lothar. Much gold was found upon him. As soon as he was slain, one of his servants dashed away at full speed, and told the dead man's wife what had happened. At the time she was riding through a street of Soissons, with an escort of servants before and behind, pranked with fine jewels and precious stones, and covered with flashing gold, bound for the church of the saints Crispin and Crispinianus to hear Mass, for it was the day of the passion of these blessed martyrs. When she saw the messenger, she turned back by another street, cast her jewels to the ground, and took refuge in the church of the holy Médard, trusting to find safety there under the protection of that blessed confessor. The servants sent by the king to sequester the property of Rauching discovered so many precious things among his possessions that their match might not be found even in the royal treasury; all of them were brought and shown to the king. The day of Rauching's death there were a number of citizens of Tours and Poitiers with the king, of whom the conspirators had intended to make use. If the plot had succeeded, these men were to have been seized and tortured, and the charge would have been brought against them: 'It was one of you who caused the death of our king;' thereafter they would have been again tortured and put to a violent death. The conspirators would then have proclaimed themselves the avengers of the king's murder. But Almighty God confounded their designs by reason of their iniquity, and fulfilled that which is written: 'The pit which thou preparest for thy brother, thyself shalt fall therein.' Magnovald was sent as duke in place of Rauching.

Ursio and Berthefred, sure that Rauching would be able to carry out the plan which they had plotted together, had meanwhile collected an army and were on the march. But on learning of his death and the manner of it, they added more partisans to their force and, conscious of their guilt, fortified themselves in a strong place, in the Woëvre, near the estate of Ursio, with all their movable effects, determined to defend themselves with valiance against Childebert's army if he should think fit to take any action against them. Ursio was the head and the fount of all the mischief. Queen Brunhild sent a message to Berthefred to this effect: 'Separate thyself from this our enemy, and thou shalt have thy life; if not, thou shalt perish with him.' For the queen had received his daughter from the water of baptism, and for this reason was fain to have compassion on him. But he replied: 'I will never forsake him, until death rend us asunder.'

◆ ◆ ◆

'When in the name of Christ the most excellent lords King Guntram and King Childebert and the right glorious lady the queen Brunhild met together at Andelot for loving-kindness' sake, that they might take full counsel to end whatsoever causes of offence might arise between them, it was settled, approved, and agreed between them with the concourse of their bishops and chief men, the grace of God being their help and mutual love their care, that as long as Almighty God shall grant them life in this present world they shall preserve mutual faith and loving-kindness in purity and singleness of heart. Likewise that since King Guntram, in accordance with the treaty which he made with King Sigibert of good memory, claimed all the portion of the said lord Sigibert in the kingdom of Charibert, and since King Childebert sought to recover the whole part which his father had possessed; it is hereby after final deliberation decided between the parties as hereinafter followeth. All that the lord Sigibert obtained by treaty from the kingdom of Charibert, namely, the third part of the city of Paris, with its territory and its inhabitants, the castles of Châteaudun, Vendôme, and all that the said king had possessed in the territory of Étampes towards those regions, and in Chartres, with their territories and their inhabitants, shall remain in perpetuity under the lawful rule and dominion of King Guntram, in addition to all that he previously possessed of the kingdom of Charibert while the lord Sigibert was yet alive. In like manner the lord King Childebert shall from this day forward hold under his dominion the city of Meaux, two-thirds of Senlis, the cities of Tours, Poitiers, Avranches, Aire, Saint-Lizier, Bayonne, and Albi, with their territories; but on this condition, that whichever of the two kings God shall cause to survive the other, if that other pass childless from the light of this present world, shall inherit his kingdom in its entirety and for ever, and by God's aid hand it down to his descendants.

'It is especially determined, and through all things inviolably to be observed, that whatsoever the lord King Guntram hath presented to his daughter Clotild or by God's favour shall yet present to her in all kinds of property, or in men, in cities, lands or revenues, shall remain under her power and control; and if she should be fain to dispose of any part of the domain lands assigned to her, or of costly objects, or money, or to bestow them upon any person, these gifts shall with the aid of the Lord be preserved to the possessors for ever, nor shall they at any time or by any man be taken from them; and she herself, under the guardianship and protection of King Childebert, shall hold in undisturbed possession, with all honour and dignity, everything of which she shall stand possessed at the death of her sire. Likewise the lord King Guntram promiseth that if, through the frailty of our human flesh, that should befall which he would fain not live to see, and which he trusteth that God's goodness may forbid, namely, that King Childebert should depart first from the light of this world, leaving him behind, he will receive as a true father under his guardianship and protection the said king's sons, Theudebert and Theuderic as kings, and any other sons which God may have willed to give him, and will see that in all security they possess their father's kingdom; and that he will receive under his guardianship and defence in all spiritual affection the lady Queen Brunhild, mother of the lord King Childebert, and her daughter Chlodosind, sister of the lord King Childebert, as long as she shall remain in the Frankish dominions, and likewise his queen Faileuba, as it were his own dear sister, with her daughters, and shall grant them to possess in all security and quietness, with all honour and dignity, all their goods, their cities, lands, revenues, and rights, all their property, both such as they hold at this present time, and such as, with Christ's guidance, they may lawfully add hereafter, so that if of their free will they shall desire to dispose of any part of that which was given them out of the domain lands, or of their several effects, or of their moneys, or to confer such property on any person, it shall be secured to him in safe possession in perpetuity, and their wish shall at no time and by no man whatsoever be annulled. As to the cities of Bordeaux, Limoges, Cahors, Lescar, and Cieutat, which were given, whether as dowry, or as *morgengabe*, which is to say morning-gift, to Galswinth, sister of the lady Brunhild, on her coming into Francia, and which the lady Brunhild, in the lifetime of kings Chilperic and Sigibert, acquired by decision of the lord King Guntram and of the Franks, it is agreed that the lady Brunhild shall forthwith receive them in her own possession . . . ; meanwhile, so long as the lord Guntram liveth, they shall at no time and under no pretext be claimed by the lady Brunhild, or by her son King Childebert, or by his sons. It is likewise agreed that the lord Childebert shall hold Senlis in its entirety, and that the said lord Childebert shall compensate the lord Guntram for the third part of it of right belonging to him, by adding to his possessions the third part of Ressons now in the lord Childebert's possession. It is further agreed that in accordance with the compacts made between the lord Guntram and the lord Sigibert of blessed memory, those *leudes* who upon the death of King Lothar first took oaths of loyalty to the lord Guntram, and are shown thereafter to have transferred their allegiance elsewhere, shall be brought back from the places where they now dwell. Likewise those who after the death of the lord King Lothar are proved to have first taken oaths of fealty to the lord Sigibert, and then transferred their allegiance elsewhere, shall in like manner be sent back. Likewise whatsoever the above-mentioned kings have conferred upon churches and upon their own trusty adherents, or may yet by God's propitious grace decide lawfully to confer upon them, shall be preserved to them in security. And whatsoever any trusty subject of the kings in either kingdom shall of law and justice possess, he shall suffer no prejudice, but shall be permitted to hold these things which are his due. And if, during an interregnum, anything be lost to any man without any fault of his, an inquiry shall be held and it shall be restored. And that which each man hath possessed through the munificence of preceding kings down to the death of the lord King Lothar of glorious memory, let him continue to possess it in security. And that which hath thereafter been taken from our trusty subjects, let it be forthwith returned. And since the aforesaid kings are now united in the name of God in a pure and single concord, it is agreed that at no time shall a free passage through the kingdom of either be refused to their respective *leudes*, whether a man would travel upon public or upon private affairs. In like manner it is agreed that neither shall invite to him the *leudes* of the other, or receive them if they come to him of their own accord. And if haply, on the ground of some offence, a subject of one king shall deem it well to seek the territory of the other, he shall be delivered up, but treated with such lenience as the nature of the offence allows.

'Further, it was resolved to add this article to the present treaty: if either party shall by any subtle pretext, or at any time, transgress these its provisions, he shall forfeit all the benefits, as well those promised for the future as those straightway conferred, and these benefits shall profit him only who shall have observed all the above conditions; he shall be in all respects absolved from the obligation of keeping his oaths. These points being thus decided, the contracting parties swear by the name of Almighty God and the indivisible Trinity, by all things divine, and by the tremendous day of Judgement, that without any treachery or fraud they will inviolably observe all that is hereinbefore set down.

'This treaty was made on the fourth day of the kalends of December, in the twenty-sixth year of the reign of the lord King Guntram, and in the twelfth year of the lord Childebert.'

2. *Einhard*

Born about 770, Einhard studied at Fulda and with Alcuin at the Palace School. He became a member of the learned circle surrounding Charlemagne and one of his most trusted advisors. He continued in favor with Charlemagne's successor, Louis the Pious during whose reign he wrote his *Life* of Charlemagne. Modeled closely after Suetonius, Einhard's biography is a little masterpiece, one of the outstanding secular biographies of the Middle Ages.

The *Life* is given completely below in the translation of Samuel Turner (New York: Harper and Brothers, 1880).

SINCE I have taken upon myself to narrate the public and private life, and no small part of the deeds, of my lord and foster-father, the most excellent and most justly renowned King Charles, I have condensed the matter into as brief a form as possible. I have been careful not to omit any facts that could come to my knowledge, but at the same time not to offend by a prolix style those minds that despise everything modern, if one can possibly avoid offending by a new work men who seem to despise also the masterpieces of antiquity, the works of most learned and luminous writers. Very many of them, I have no doubt, are men devoted to a life of literary leisure, who feel that the affairs of the present generation ought not to be passed by, and who do not consider everything done today as unworthy of mention and deserving to be given over to silence and oblivion, but are nevertheless seduced by lust of immortality to celebrate the glorious deeds of other times by some sort of composition rather than to deprive posterity of the mention of their own names by not writing at all.

Be this as it may, I see no reason why I should refrain from entering upon a task of this kind, since no man can write with more accuracy than I of events that took place about me, and of facts concerning which I had personal knowledge, ocular demonstration, as the saying goes, and I have no means of ascertaining whether or not any one else has the subject in hand.

In any event, I would rather commit my story to writing, and hand it down to posterity in partnership with others, so to speak, than to suffer the most glorious life of this most excellent king, the greatest of all the princes of his day, and his illustrious deeds, hard for men of later times to imitate, to be wrapped in the darkness of oblivion.

But there are still other reasons, neither unwarrantable nor insufficient, in my opinion, that urge me to write on this subject, namely, the care that King Charles bestowed upon me in my childhood, and my constant friendship with himself and his children after I took up my abode at court. In this way he strongly endeared me to himself, and made me greatly his debtor as well in death as in life, so that were I, unmindful of the benefits conferred upon me, to keep silence concerning the most glorious and illustrious deeds of a man who claims so much at my hands, and suffer his life to lack due eulogy and written memorial, as if he had never lived, I should deservedly appear ungrateful, and be so considered, albeit my powers are feeble, scanty, next to nothing indeed, and not at all adapted to write and set forth a life that would tax the eloquence of a Tully.

I submit the book. It contains the history of a very great and distinguished man; but there is nothing in it to wonder at besides his deeds, except the fact that I, who am a barbarian, and very little versed in the Roman language, seem to suppose myself capable of writing gracefully and respectably in Latin, and to carry my presumption so far as to disdain the sentiment that Cicero is said in the first book of the "Tusculan Disputations" to have expressed when speaking of the Latin authors. His words are: "It is an outrageous abuse both of time and literature for a man to commit his thoughts to writing without having the ability either to arrange them or elucidate them, or attract readers by some charm of style." This dictum of the famous orator might have deterred me from writing if I had not made up my mind that it was better to risk the opinions of the world, and put my little talents for composition to the test, than to slight the memory of so great a man for the sake of sparing myself.

The Merovingian family, from which the Franks used to choose their kings, is commonly said to have lasted until the time of Childeric, who was deposed, shaved, and thrust into the cloister by command of the Roman Pontiff Stephen. But although, to all outward appearance, it ended with him, it had long since been devoid of vital strength, and conspicuous only from bearing the empty epithet Royal; the real power and authority in the kingdom lay in the hands of the chief officer of the court, the so-called Mayor of the Palace, and he was at the head of affairs. There was nothing left the King to do but to be content with his name of King, his flowing hair, and long beard, to sit on his throne and play the ruler, to give ear to the ambassadors that came from all quarters, and to dismiss them, as if on his own responsibility, in words that were, in fact, suggested to him, or even imposed upon him. He had nothing that he could call his own beyond this vain title of King and the precarious support allowed by the Mayor of the Palace in his discretion, except a single country seat, that brought him but a very small income. There was a dwelling house upon this, and a small number of servants attached to it, sufficient to perform the necessary offices. When he had to go abroad, he used to ride in a cart, drawn by a yoke of oxen, driven, peasant-fashion, by a ploughman; he rode in this way to the palace and to the general assembly of the people, that met once a year for the welfare of the kingdom, and he returned him in like manner. The Mayor of the Palace took charge of the government and of everything that had to be planned or executed at home or abroad.

At the time of Childeric's deposition, Pepin, the father of King Charles, held this office of Mayor of the Palace, one might almost say, by hereditary right; for Pepin's father, Charles, had received it at the hands of his father, Pepin, and filled it with distinction. It was this Charles that crushed the tyrants who claimed to rule the whole Frank land as their own, and that utterly routed the Saracens, when they attempted the conquest of Gaul, in two great battles—one in Aquitania, near the town of Poitiers, and the other on the River Berre, near Narbonne—and compelled them to return to Spain. This honor was usually conferred by the people only upon men eminent from their illustrious birth and ample wealth. For some years, ostensibly under King Childeric, Pepin, the father of King Charles, shared the duties inherited from his father and grandfather most amicably with his brother, Carloman. The latter, then, for reasons unknown, renounced the heavy cares of an earthly crown and retired to Rome. Here he exchanged his worldly garb for a cowl, and built a monastery on Mt. Oreste, near the Church of St. Sylvester, where he enjoyed for several years the seclusion that he desired, in company with certain others who had the same object in view. But so many distinguished Franks made the pilgrimage to Rome to fulfill their vows, and insisted upon paying their respects to him, as their former lord, on the way, that the repose which he so much loved was broken by these frequent visits, and he was driven to change his abode. Accordingly, when he found that his plans were frustrated by his many visitors, he abandoned the mountain, and withdrew to the Monastery of St. Benedict, on Monte Cassino, in the province of Samnium, and passed the rest of his days there in the exercises of religion.

Pepin, however, was raised, by decree of the Roman Pontiff, from the rank of Mayor of the Palace to that of King, and ruled alone over the Franks for fifteen years or more. He died of dropsy, in Paris, at the close of the Aquitanian war, which he had waged with William, Duke of Aquitania, for nine successive years, and left two sons, Charles and Carloman, upon whom, by the grace of God, the succession devolved.

The Franks, in a general assembly of the people, made them both kings, on condition that they should divide the whole kingdom equally between them, Charles to take and rule the part that had belonged to their father, Pepin, and Carloman the part which their uncle, Carloman, had governed. The conditions were accepted, and each entered into possession of the share of the kingdom that fell to him by this arrangement; but peace was only maintained between them with the greatest difficulty, because many of Carloman's party kept trying to disturb their good understanding, and there were some even who plotted to involve them in a war with each other. The event, however, showed the danger to have been rather imaginary than real, for at Carloman's death his widow fled to Italy with her sons and her principal adherents, and without reason, despite her husband's brother, put herself and her children under the protection of Desiderius, King of the Lombards. Carloman had succumbed to disease after ruling two years in common with his brother, and at his death Charles was unanimously elected King of the Franks.

It would be folly, I think, to write a word concerning Charles' birth and infancy, or even his boyhood, for nothing has ever been written on the subject, and there is no one alive now who can give information of it. Accordingly, I have determined to pass that by as unknown, and to proceed at once to treat of his character, his deeds, and such other facts of his life as are worth telling and setting forth, and shall first give an account of his deeds at home and abroad, then of his character and pursuits, and lastly of his administration and death, omitting nothing worth knowing or necessary to know.

His first undertaking in a military way was the Aquitanian war, begun by his father, but not brought to a close; and because he thought that it could be readily carried through, he took it up while his brother was yet alive, calling upon him to render aid. The campaign once opened, he conducted it with the greatest vigor, notwithstanding his brother withheld the assistance that he had promised, and did not desist or shrink from his self-imposed task until, by his patience and firmness, he had completely gained his ends. He compelled Hunold, who had attempted to seize Aquitania after Waifar's death, and renew the war then almost concluded, to abandon Aquitania and flee to Gascony. Even here he gave him no rest, but crossed the River Garonne, built the castle of Fronsac, and sent ambassadors to Lupus, Duke of Gascony, to demand the surrender of the fugitive, threatening to take him by force unless he were promptly given up to him. Thereupon Lupus chose the wiser course, and not only gave Hunold up, but submitted himself, with the province which he ruled, to the King.

After bringing this war to an end and settling matters in Aquitania (his associate in authority had meantime departed this life), he was induced, by the prayers and entreaties of Hadrian, Bishop of the city of

Rome, to wage war on the Lombards. His father before him had undertaken this task at the request of Pope Stephen, but under great difficulties, for certain leading Franks, of whom he usually took counsel, had so vehemently opposed his design as to declare openly that they would leave the King and go home. Nevertheless, the war against the Lombard King Astolf had been taken up and very quickly concluded. Now, although Charles seems to have had similar, or rather just the same grounds for declaring war that his father had, the war itself differed from the preceding one alike in its difficulties and its issue. Pepin, to be sure, after besieging King Astolf a few days in Pavia, had compelled him to give hostages, to restore to the Romans the cities and castles that he had taken, and to make oath that he would not attempt to seize them again: but Charles did not cease, after declaring war, until he had exhausted King Desiderius by a long siege, and forced him to surrender at discretion; driven his son Adalgis, the last hope of the Lombards, not only from his kingdom, but from all Italy; restored to the Romans all that they had lost; subdued Hruodgaus, Duke of Friuli, who was plotting revolution; reduced all Italy to his power, and set his son Pepin as king over it.

At this point I should describe Charles' difficult passage over the Alps into Italy, and the hardships that the Franks endured in climbing the trackless mountain ridges, the heaven-aspiring cliffs and ragged peaks, if it were not my purpose in this work to record the manner of his life rather than the incidents of the wars that he waged. Suffice it to say that this war ended with the subjection of Italy, the banishment of King Desiderius for life, the expulsion of his son Adalgis from Italy, and the restoration of the conquests of the Lombard kings to Hadrian, the head of the Roman Church.

At the conclusion of this struggle, the Saxon war, that seems to have been only laid aside for the time, was taken up again. No war ever undertaken by the Frank nation was carried on with such persistence and bitterness, or cost so much labor, because the Saxons, like almost all the tribes of Germany, were a fierce people, given to the worship of devils, and hostile to our religion, and did not consider it dishonorable to transgress and violate all law, human and divine. Then there were peculiar circumstances that tended to cause a breach of peace every day. Except in a few places, where large forests or mountain ridges intervened and made the bounds certain, the line between ourselves and the Saxons passed almost in its whole extent through an open country, so that there was no end to the murders, thefts, and arsons on both sides. In this way the Franks became so embittered that they at last resolved to make reprisals no longer, but to come to open war with the Saxons. Accordingly war was begun against them, and was waged for thirty-three successive years with great fury; more, however, to the disadvantage of the Saxons than of the Franks. It could doubtless have been brought to an end sooner, had it not been for the faithlessness of the Saxons. It is hard to say how often they were conquered, and, humbly submitting to the King, promised to do what was enjoined upon them, gave without hesitation the required hostages, and received the officers sent them from the King. They were sometimes so much weakened and reduced that they promised to renounce the worship of devils, and to adopt Christianity, but they were no less ready to violate these terms than prompt to accept them, so that it is impossible to tell which came easier to them to do; scarcely a year passed from the beginning of the war without such changes on their part. But the King did not suffer his high purpose and steadfastness—firm alike in good and evil fortune—to be wearied by any fickleness on their part, or to be turned from the task that he had undertaken; on the contrary, he never allowed their faithless behavior to go unpunished, but either took the field against them in person, or sent his counts with an army to wreak vengeance and exact righteous satisfaction. At last, after conquering and subduing all who had offered resistance, he took ten thousand of those that lived on the banks of the Elbe, and settled them, with their wives and children, in many different bodies here and there in Gaul and Germany. The war that had lasted so many years was at length ended by their acceding to the terms offered by the King; which were renunciation of their national religious customs and the worship of devils, acceptance of the sacraments of the Christian faith and religion, and union with the Franks to form one people.

Charles himself fought but two pitched battles in this war, although it was long protracted—one on Mount Osning, at the place called Detmold, and again on the bank of the river Hase, both in the space of little more than a month. The enemy were so routed and overthrown in these two battles that they never afterwards ventured to take the offensive or to resist the attacks of the King, unless they were protected by a strong position. A great many of the Frank as well as of the Saxon nobility, men occupying the highest posts of honor, perished in this war, which only came to an end after the lapse of thirty-two years. So many and grievous were the wars that were declared against the Franks in the meantime, and skillfully conducted by the King, that one may reasonably question whether his fortitude or his good fortune is to be more admired. The Saxon war began two years before the Italian war; but although it went on without interruption, business elsewhere was not neglected, nor was there any shrinking from other equally arduous contests. The King, who excelled all the princes of his time in wisdom and greatness of soul, did not suffer difficulty to deter him or danger to daunt him from anything that had to be taken up or carried through, for he had trained himself to bear and endure whatever came, without yielding in adversity, or trusting to the deceitful favors of fortune in prosperity.

In the midst of this vigorous and almost uninterrupted struggle with the Saxons, he covered the frontier by garrisons at the proper points, and marched over the Pyrenees into Spain at the head of all the forces that he could muster. All the towns and castles that he attacked surrendered, and up to the time of his homeward march he sustained no loss whatever; but on his return through the Pyrenees he had cause to rue the treachery of the Gascons. That region is well adapted for ambuscades by reason of the thick forests that cover it; and as the army was advancing in the long line of march necessitated by the narrowness of the road, the Gascons, who lay in ambush on the top of a very high mountain, attacked the rear of the baggage train and the rear guard in charge of it, and hurled them down to the very bottom of the valley. In the struggle that ensued, they cut them off to a man; they then plundered the baggage, and dispersed with all speed in every direction under cover of approaching night. The lightness of their armor and the nature of the battle ground stood the Gascons in good stead on this occasion, whereas the Franks fought at a disadvantage in every respect, because of the weight of their armor and the unevenness of the ground. Eggihard, the King's steward; Anselm, Count Palatine; and Roland, Governor of the March of Brittany, with very many others, fell in this engagement. This ill turn could not be avenged for the nonce, because the enemy scattered so widely after carrying out their plan that not the least clue could be had to their whereabouts.

Charles also subdued the Bretons, who live on the sea coast, in the extreme western part of Gaul. When they refused to obey him, he sent an army against them, and compelled them to give hostages, and to promise to do his bidding. He afterwards entered Italy in person with his army, and passed through Rome to Capua, a city in Campania, where he pitched his camp and threatened the Beneventans with hostilities unless they should submit themselves to him. Their duke, Aragis, escaped the danger by sending his two sons, Rumold and Grimold, with a great sum of money to meet the King, begging him to accept them as hostages, and promising for himself and his people compliance with all the King's commands, on the single condition that his personal attendance should not be required. The King took the welfare of the people into account rather than the stubborn disposition of the Duke, accepted he proffered hostages, and released him from the obligation to appear before him in consideration of his handsome gift. He retained the younger son only as hostage, and sent the elder back to his father, and returned to Rome, leaving commissioners with Aragis to exact the oath of allegiance, and administer it to the Beneventans. He stayed in Rome several days in order to pay his devotions at the holy places, and then came back to Gaul.

At this time, on a sudden, the Bavarian war broke out, but came to a speedy end. It was due to the arrogance and folly of Duke Tassilo. His wife, a daughter of King Desiderius, was desirous of avenging her father's banishment through the agency of her husband, and accordingly induced him to make a treaty with the Huns, the neighbors of the Bavarians on the east, and not only to leave the King's commands unfulfilled, but to challenge him to war. Charles' high spirit could not brook Tassilo's insubordination, for it seemed to him to pass all bounds; accordingly he straightway summoned his troops from all sides for a campaign against Bavaria, and appeared in person with a great army on the river Lech, which forms the boundary between the Bavarians and the Alemanni. After pitching his camp upon its banks, he determined to put the Duke's disposition to the test by an embassy before entering the province. Tassilo did not think that it was for his own or his people's good to persist, so he surrendered himself to the King, gave the hostages demanded, among them his own son Theodo, and promised by oath not to give ear to any one who should attempt to turn him from his allegiance; so this war, which bade fair to be very grievous, came very quickly to an end. Tassilo, however, was afterward summoned to the King's presence, and not suffered to depart, and the government of the province that he had had in charge was no longer intrusted to a duke, but to counts.

After these uprisings had been thus quelled, war was declared against the Slavs who are commonly known among us as Wilzi, but properly, that is to say in their own tongue, are called Welatabians. The Saxons served in this campaign as auxiliaries among the tribes that followed the King's standard at his summons, but their obedience lacked sincerity and devotion. War was declared because the Slavs kept harassing the Abodriti, old allies of the Franks, by continual raids, in spite of all commands to the contrary. A gulf of unknown length, but nowhere more than a hundred miles wide, and in many parts narrower, stretches off towards the east from the Western Ocean. Many tribes have settlements on its shores; the Danes and Swedes, whom we call Northmen, on the northern shore and all the adjacent islands; but the southern shore is inhabited by the Slavs and Aïsti, and various other tribes. The Welatabians, against whom the King now made war, were the chief of these; but in a single campaign, which he conducted in person, he so crushed and subdued them that they did not think it advisable thereafter to refuse obedience to his commands.

The war against the Avars, or Huns, followed, and, except the Saxon war, was the greatest that he waged; he took it up with more spirit than any of his other wars, and made far greater preparations for it. He conducted one campaign in person in Pannonia, of which the Huns then had possession. He intrusted all subsequent operations to his son, Pepin, and the governors of the provinces, to counts even, and lieutenants. Although they most vigorously prosecuted the war, it only came to a conclusion after a seven years' struggle. The utter depopulation of Pannonia, and the site of the Khan's palace, now a desert, where not a trace of human habitation is visible, bear witness how many battles were fought in those years, and how much blood was shed. The entire body of the Hun nobility perished in this contest, and all its glory with it. All the money and treasure that had been years amassing was seized, and no war in which the Franks have ever engaged within the memory of man brought them such riches and such booty. Up to that time the Huns had passed for a poor people, but so much gold and silver was found in the Khan's palace, and so much valuable spoil taken in battle, that one may well think that the Franks took justly from the Huns what the Huns had formerly taken unjustly from other nations. Only two of the chief men of the Franks fell in this war—Eric, Duke of Friuli, who was killed in Tarsatch, a town on the coast of Liburnia, by the treachery of the inhabitants; and Gerold, Governor of Bavaria, who met his death in Pannonia, slain, with two men that were accompanying him, by an unknown hand while he was marshaling his forces for battle against the Huns, and riding up and down the line encouraging his men. This war was otherwise almost a bloodless one so far as the Franks were concerned, and ended most satisfactorily, although by reason of its magnitude it was long protracted.

The Saxon war next came to an end as successful as the struggle had been long. The Bohemian and Linonian wars that next broke out could not last long; both were quickly carried through under the leadership of the younger Charles. The last of these wars was the one declared against the Northmen called Danes. They began their career as pirates, but afterward took to laying waste the coasts of Gaul and Germany with their large fleet. Their King Godfred was so puffed with vain aspirations that he counted on gaining empire over all Germany, and looked upon Saxony and Frisia as his provinces. He had already subdued his neighbors the Abodriti, and made them tributary, and boasted that he would shortly appear with a great army before Aix-la-Chapelle, where the King held his court. Some faith was put in his words, empty as they sound, and it is supposed that he would have attempted something of the sort if he had not been prevented by a premature death. He was murdered by one of his own bodyguard, and so ended at once his life and the war that he had begun.

Such are the wars, most skilfully planned and successfully fought, which this most powerful king waged during the forty-seven years of his reign. He so largely increased the Frank kingdom, which was already great and strong when he received it at his father's hands, that more than double its former territory was added to it. The authority of the Franks was formerly confined to that part of Gaul included between the Rhine and the Loire, the Ocean and the Balearic Sea; to that part of Germany which is inhabited by the so-called Eastern Franks, and is bounded by Saxony and the Danube, the Rhine and the Saale—this stream separates the Thuringians from the Sorabians; and to the country of the Alemanni and Bavarians. By the wars above mentioned he first made tributary

Aquitania, Gascony, and the whole of the region of the Pyrenees as far as the River Ebro, which rises in the land of the Navarrese, flows through the most fertile districts of Spain, and empties into the Balearic Sea, beneath the walls of the city of Tortosa. He next reduced and made tributary all Italy from Aosta to Lower Calabria, where the boundary line runs between the Beneventans and the Greeks, a territory more than a thousand miles long; then Saxony, which constitutes no small part of Germany, and is reckoned to be twice as wide as the country inhabited by the Franks, while about equal to it in length; in addition, both Pannonias, Dacia beyond the Danube, and Istria, Liburnia, and Dalmatia, except the cities on the coast, which he left to the Greek Emperor for friendship's sake, and because of the treaty that he had made with him. In fine, he vanquished and made tributary all the wild and barbarous tribes dwelling in Germany between the Rhine and the Vistula, the Ocean and the Danube, all of which speak very much the same language, but differ widely from one another in customs and dress. The chief among them are the Welatabians, the Sorabians, the Abodriti, and the Bohemians, and he had to make war upon these; but the rest, by far the larger number, submitted to him of their own accord.

He added to the glory of his reign by gaining the good will of several kings and nations; so close, indeed, was the alliance that he contracted with Alfonso, King of Galicia and Asturias, that the latter, when sending letters or ambassadors to Charles, invariably styled himself his man. His munificence won the kings of the Scots also to pay such deference to his wishes that they never gave him any other title than lord, or themselves than subjects and slaves: there are letters from them extant in which these feelings in his regard are expressed. His relations with Aaron, King of the Persians, who ruled over almost the whole of the East, India excepted, were so friendly that this prince preferred his favor to that of all the kings and potentates of the earth, and considered that to him alone marks of honor and munificence were due. Accordingly, when the ambassadors sent by Charles to visit the most holy sepulchre and place of resurrection of our Lord and Savior presented themselves before him with gifts, and made known their master's wishes, he not only granted what was asked, but gave possession of that holy and blessed spot. When they returned, he dispatched his ambassadors with them, and sent magnificent gifts, besides stuffs, perfumes, and other rich products of the Eastern lands. A few years before this, Charles had asked him for an elephant, and he sent the only one that he had. The Emperors of Constantinople, Nicephorus, Michael, and Leo, made advances to Charles, and sought friendship and alliance with him by several embassies; and even when the Greeks suspected him of designing to wrest the empire from them, because of his assumption of the title Emperor, they made a close alliance with him, that he might have no cause of offense. In fact, the power of the Franks was always viewed by the Greeks and Romans with a jealous eye, whence the Greek proverb "Have the Frank for your friend, but not for your neighbor."

This King, who showed himself so great in extending his empire and subduing foreign nations, and was constantly occupied with plans to that end, undertook also very many works calculated to adorn and benefit his kingdom, and brought several of them to completion. Among these, the most deserving of mention are the basilica of the Holy Mother of God at Aix-la-Chapelle, built in the most admirable manner, and a bridge over the Rhine at Mayence, half a mile long, the breadth of the river at this point. This bridge was destroyed by fire the year before Charles died, but, owing to his death so soon after, could not be repaired, although he had intended to rebuild it in stone. He began two palaces of beautiful workmanship—one near his manor called Ingelheim, not far from Mayence; the other at Nimeguen, on the Waal, the stream that washes the south side of the island of the Batavians. But, above all, sacred edifices were the object of his care throughout his whole kingdom; and whenever he found them falling to ruin from age, he commanded the priests and fathers who had charge of them to repair them, and made sure by commissioners that his instructions were obeyed. He also fitted out a fleet for the war with the Northmen; the vessels required for this purpose were built on the rivers that flow from Gaul and Germany into the Northern Ocean. Moreover, since the Northmen continually overran and laid waste the Gallic and German coasts, he caused watch and ward to be kept in all the harbors, and at the mouths of rivers large enough to admit the entrance of vessels, to prevent the enemy from disembarking; and in the South, in Narbonensis and Septimania, and along the whole coast of Italy as far as Rome, he took the same precautions against the Moors, who had recently begun their piratical practices. Hence, Italy suffered no great harm in his time at the hands of the Moors, nor Gaul and Germany from the Northmen, save that the Moors got possession of the Etruscan town of Civita Vecchia by treachery, and sacked it, and the Northmen harried some of the islands in Frisia off the German coast.

Thus did Charles defend and increase as well as beautify his kingdom, as is well known; and here let me express my admiration of his great qualities and his extraordinary constancy alike in good and evil fortune. I will now forthwith proceed to give the details of his private and family life.

After his father's death, while sharing the kingdom with his brother, he bore his unfriendliness and jealousy most patiently, and, to the wonder of all, could not be provoked to be angry with him. Later he married a daughter of Desiderius, King of the Lombards, at the instance of his mother; but he repudiated her at the end of a year for some reason unknown, and married Hildegard, a woman of high birth, of Suabian origin. He had three sons by her—Charles, Pepin, and Louis—and as many daughters—Hruodrud, Bertha, and Gisela. He had three other daughters besides these—Theoderada, Hiltrud, and Ruodhaid—two by his third wife, Fastrada, a woman of East Frankish (that is to say, of German) origin, and the third by a concubine, whose name for the moment escapes me. At the death of Fastrada, he married Liutgard, an Alemannic woman, who bore him no children. After her death he had three concubines—Gersuinda, a Saxon, by whom he had Adaltrud; Regina, who was the mother of Drogo and Hugh; and Ethelind, by whom he had Theodoric. Charles' mother, Berthrada, passed her old age with him in great honor; he entertained the greatest veneration for her; and there was never any disagreement between them except when he divorced the daughter of King Desiderius, whom he had married to please her. She died soon after Hildegard, after living to see three grandsons and as many granddaughters in her son's house, and he buried her with great pomp in the Basilica of St. Denis, where his father lay. He had an only sister, Gisela, who had consecrated herself to a religious life from girlhood, and he cherished as much affection for her as for his mother. She also died a few years before him in the nunnery where she had passed her life.

The plan that he adopted for his children's education was, first of all, to have both boys and girls instructed in the liberal arts, to which he also turned his own attention. As soon as their years admitted, in accordance with the custom of the Franks, the boys had to learn horsemanship, and to practice war and the chase, and the girls to familiarize themselves with cloth-making, and to handle distaff and spindle, that they might not grow indolent through idleness, and he fostered in them every virtuous sentiment. He only lost three of all his children before his death, two sons and one daughter; Charles, who was the eldest, Pepin, whom he had made King of Italy, and Hruodrud, his oldest daughter, whom he had betrothed to Constantine, Emperor of the Greeks. Pepin left one son, named Bernard, and five daughters, Adelaide, Atula, Guntrada, Berthaid, and Theoderada. The King gave a striking proof of his fatherly affection at the time of Pepin's death: he appointed the grandson to succeed Pepin, and had the granddaughters brought up with his own daughters. When his sons and his daughter died, he was not so calm as might have been expected from his remarkably strong mind, for his affections were no less strong, and moved him to tears. Again, when he was told of the death of Hadrian, the Roman Pontiff, whom he had loved most of all his friends, he wept as much as if he had lost a brother, or a very dear son. He was by nature most ready to contract friendships, and not only made friends easily, but clung to them persistently, and cherished most fondly those with whom he had formed such ties. He was so careful of the training of his sons and daughters that he never took his meals without them when he was at home, and never made a journey without them; his sons would ride at his side, and his daughters follow him, while a number of his bodyguard, detailed for their protection, brought up the rear. Strange to say, although they were very handsome women, and he loved them very dearly, he was never willing to marry any of them to a man of their own nation or to a foreigner, but kept them all at home until his death, saying that he could not dispense with their society. Hence, though otherwise happy, he experienced the malignity of fortune as far as they were concerned; yet he concealed his knowledge of the rumors current in regard to them, and of the suspicions entertained of their honor.

By one of his concubines he had a son, handsome in face, but hunchbacked, named Pepin, whom I omitted to mention in the list of his children. When Charles was at war with the Huns, and was wintering in Bavaria, this Pepin shammed sickness, and plotted against his father in company with some of the leading Franks, who seduced him with vain promises of the royal authority. When his deceit was discovered, and the conspirators were punished, his head was shaved, and he was suffered, in accordance with his wishes, to devote himself to a religious life in the monastery of Prüm. A formidable conspiracy against Charles had previously been set on foot in Germany, but all the traitors were banished, some of them without mutilation, others after their eyes had been put out. Three of them only lost their lives; they drew their swords and resisted arrest, and, after killing several men, were cut down, because they could not be otherwise overpowered. It is supposed that the cruelty of Queen Fastrada was the primary cause of these plots, and they were both due to Charles' apparent acquiescence in his wife's cruel conduct, and deviation from the usual kindness and gentleness of his disposition. All the rest of his life he was regarded by everyone with the utmost love and affection, so much so that not the least accusation of unjust rigor was ever made against him.

He liked foreigners, and was at great pains to take them under his protection. There were often so many of them, both in the palace and the kingdom, that they might reasonably have been considered a nuisance; but he, with his broad humanity, was very little disturbed by such annoyances, because he felt himself compensated for these great inconveniences by the praises of his generosity and the reward of high renown.

Charles was large and strong, and of lofty stature, though not disproportionately tall (his height is well known to have been seven times the length of his foot); the upper part of his head was round, his eyes very large and animated, nose a little long, hair fair, and face laughing and merry. Thus his appearance was always stately and dignified, whether he was standing or sitting; although his neck was thick and somewhat short, and his belly rather prominent; but the symmetry of the rest of his body concealed these defects. His gait was firm, his whole carriage manly, and his voice clear, but not so strong as his size led one to expect. His health was excellent, except during the four years preceding his death, when he was subject to frequent fevers; at the last he even limped a little with one foot. Even in those years he consulted rather his own inclinations than the advice of physicians, who were almost hateful to him, because they wanted him to give up roasts, to which he was accustomed, and to eat boiled meat instead. In accordance with the national custom, he took frequent exercise on horseback and in the chase, accomplishments in which scarcely any people in the world can equal the Franks. He enjoyed the exhalations from natural warm springs, and often practiced swimming, in which he was such an adept that none could surpass him; and hence it was that he built his palace at Aix-la-Chapelle, and lived there constantly during his latter years until his death. He used not only to invite his sons to his bath, but his nobles and friends, and now and then a troop of his retinue or bodyguard, so that a hundred or more persons sometimes bathed with him.

He used to wear the national, that is to say, the Frank, dress—next his skin a linen shirt and linen breeches, and above these a tunic fringed with silk; while hose fastened by bands covered his lower limbs, and shoes his feet, and he protected his shoulders and chest in winter by a close-fitting coat of otter or marten skins. Over all he flung a blue cloak, and he always had a sword girt about him, usually one with a gold or silver hilt and belt; he sometimes carried a jeweled sword, but only on great feastdays or at the reception of ambassadors from foreign nations. He despised foreign costumes, however handsome, and never allowed himself to be robed in them, except twice in Rome, when he donned the Roman tunic, chlamys, and shoes; the first time at the request of Pope Hadrian, the second to gratify Leo, Hadrian's successor. On great feastdays he made use of embroidered clothes and shoes bedecked with precious stones, his cloak was fastened by a golden buckle, and he appeared crowned with a diadem of gold and gems, but on other days his dress varied little from the common dress of the people.

Charles was temperate in eating, and particularly so in drinking, for he abominated drunkenness in anybody, much more in himself and those of his household; but he could not easily abstain from food, and often complained that fasts injured his health. He very rarely gave entertainments, only on great feastdays, and then to large numbers of people. His meals ordinarily consisted of four courses, not counting the roast, which his huntsmen used to bring in on the spit; he was more fond of this than of any other dish. While at table, he listened to reading or music. The subjects of the readings were the stories and deeds of olden time: he was fond, too, of St. Augustine's books, and especially of the one entitled "The City of God." He was so moderate in the use of wine and all sorts of drink that he rarely allowed himself more than three cups in the course of a meal. In summer, after the midday meal, he would eat some fruit, drain a single cup, put off his clothes and shoes, just as he did for the night, and rest for two or three hours. He was in the habit of awaking and rising from bed four or five times during the night. While he was dressing and putting on his shoes, he not only gave audience to his friends, but if the Count of the Palace told him of any suit in which his judgment was necessary, he had the parties brought before him forthwith, took cognizance of the case, and gave his decision, just as if he were sitting on the judgment seat. This was not the only business that he transacted at this time, but he performed any duty of the day whatever, whether he had to attend to the matter himself, or to give commands concerning it to his officers.

Charles had the gift of ready and fluent speech, and could express whatever he had to say with the utmost clearness. He was not satisfied with command of his native language merely, but gave attention to the study of foreign ones, and in particular was such a master of Latin that he could speak it as well as his native tongue; but he could understand Greek better than he could speak it. He was so eloquent, indeed, that he might have passed for a teacher of eloquence. He most zealously cultivated the liberal arts, held those who taught them in great esteem, and conferred great honors upon them. He took lessons in grammar of the deacon Peter of Pisa, at that time an aged man. Another deacon, Albin of Britain, surnamed Alcuin, a man of Saxon extraction, who was the greatest scholar of the day, was his teacher in other branches of learning. The King spent much time and labor with him studying rhetoric, dialectics, and especially astonomy; he learned to reckon, and used to investigate the motions of the heavenly bodies most curiously, with an intelligent scrutiny. He also tried to write, and used to keep tablets and blanks in bed under his pillow, that at leisure hours he might accustom his hand to form the letters; however, as he did not begin his efforts in due season, but late in life, they met with ill success.

He cherished with the greatest fervor and devotion the principles of the Christian religion, which had been instilled into him from infancy. Hence it was that he built the beautiful basilica at Aix-la-Chapelle, which he adorned with gold and silver and lamps, and with rails and doors of solid brass. He had the columns and marbles for this structure brought from Rome and Ravenna, for he could not find such as were suitable elsewhere. He was a constant worshipper at this church as long as his health permitted, going morning and evening, even after nightfall, besides attending mass; and he took care that all the services there conducted should be administered with the utmost possible propriety, very often warning the sextons not to let any improper or unclean thing be brought into the building or remain in it. He provided it with a great number of sacred vessels of gold and silver and with such a quantity of clerical robes that not even the doorkeepers who fill the humblest office in the church were obliged to wear their everyday clothes when in the exercise of their duties. He was at great pains to improve the church reading and psalmody, for he was well skilled in both, although he neither read in public nor sang, except in a low tone and with others.

He was very forward in succoring the poor, and in that gratuitous generosity which the Greeks call alms, so much so that he not only made a point of giving in his own country and his own kingdom, but when he discovered that there were Christians living in poverty in Syria, Egypt, and Africa, at Jerusalem, Alexandria, and Carthage, he had compassion on their wants, and used to send money over the seas to them. The reason that he zealously strove to make friends with the kings beyond seas was that he might get help and relief to the Christians living under their rule. He cherished the Church of St. Peter the Apostle at Rome above all other holy and sacred places, and heaped its treasury with a vast wealth of gold, silver, and precious stones. He sent great and countless gifts to the popes, and throughout his whole reign the wish that he had nearest at heart was to re-establish the ancient authority of the city of Rome under his care and by his influence, and to defend and protect the Church of St. Peter, and to beautify and enrich it out of his own store above all other churches. Although he held it in such veneration, he only repaired to Rome to pay his vows and make his supplications four times during the whole forty-seven years that he reigned.

When he made his last journey thither, he had also other ends in view. The Romans had inflicted many injuries upon the Pontiff Leo, tearing out his eyes and cutting out his tongue, so that he had been compelled to call upon the King for help. Charles accordingly went to Rome, to set in order the affairs of the Church, which were in great confusion, and passed the whole winter there. It was then that he received the titles of Emperor and Augustus, to which he at first had such an aversion that he declared that he would not have set foot in the Church the day that they were conferred, although it was a great feastday, if he could have foreseen the design of the Pope. He bore very patiently with the jealousy which the Roman emperors showed upon his assuming these titles, for they took this step very ill; and by dint of frequent embassies and letters, in which he addressed them as brothers, he made their haughtiness yield to his magnanimity, a quality in which he was unquestionably much their superior.

It was after he had received the imperial name that, finding the laws of his people very defective (the Franks have two sets of laws, very different in many particulars), he determined to add what was wanting, to reconcile the discrepancies, and to correct what was vicious and wrongly cited in them. However, he went no further in this matter than to supplement the laws by a few capitularies, and those imperfect ones; but he caused the unwritten laws of all the tribes that came under his rule to be compiled and reduced to writing. He also had the old rude songs that celebrate the deeds and wars of the ancient kings written out for transmission to posterity. He began a grammar of his native language. He gave the months names in his own tongue, in place of the Latin and barbarous names by which they were formerly known among the Franks. He likewise designated the winds by twelve appropriate names; there were hardly more than four distinctive ones in use before. He called January, Wintarmanoth; February, Hornung; March, Lentzinmanoth; April, Ostarmanoth; May, Winnemanoth; June, Brachmanoth; July, Heuvimanoth; August, Aranmanoth; September, Witumanoth; October, Windumemanoth; November, Herbistmanoth; December, Heilagmanoth. He styled the winds as follows; Subsolanus, Ostroniwint; Eurus, Ostsundroni; Euroauster, Sundostroni; Auster, Sundroni; Austro-Africus, Sundwestroni; Africus, Westsundroni; Zephyrus, Westroni; Caurus, Westnordroni; Circius, Nordwestroni; Septentrio, Nordroni; Aquilo, Nordostroni; Vulturnus, Ostnordroni.

Toward the close of his life, when he was broken by ill-health and old age, he summoned Louis, King of Aquitania, his only surviving son by Hildegard, and gathered together all the chief men of the whole kingdom of the Franks in a solemn assembly. He appointed Louis, with their unanimous consent, to rule with himself over the whole kingdom, and constituted him heir to the imperial name; then, placing the diadem upon his son's head, he bade him be proclaimed Emperor and Augustus. This step was hailed by all present with great favor, for it really seemed as if God had prompted him to it for the kingdom's good; it increased the King's dignity, and struck no little terror into foreign nations. After sending his son back to Aquitania, although weak from age he set out to hunt, as usual, near his palace at Aix-la-Chapelle, and passed the rest of the autumn in the chase, returning thither about the first of November. While wintering there, he was seized, in the month of January, with a high fever, and took to his bed. As soon as he was taken sick, he prescribed for himself abstinence from food, as he always used to do in case of fever, thinking that the disease could be driven off, or at least mitigated, by fasting. Besides the fever, he suffered from a pain in the side, which the Greeks call pleurisy; but he still persisted in fasting, and in keeping up his strength only by draughts taken at very long intervals. He died January twenty-eighth, the seventh day from the time that he took to his bed, at nine o'clock in the morning, after partaking of the holy communion, in the seventy-second year of his age and the forty-seventh of his reign.

His body was washed and cared for in the usual manner, and was then carried to the church, and interred amid the greatest lamentations of all the people. There was some question at first where to lay him, because in his lifetime he had given no directions as to his burial; but at length all agreed that he could nowhere be more honorably entombed than in the very basilica that he had built in the town at his own expense, for love of

God and our Lord Jesus Christ, and in honor of the Holy and Eternal Virgin, His Mother. He was buried there the same day that he died, and a gilded arch was erected above his tomb with his image and an inscription. The words of the inscription were as follows: "In this tomb lies the body of Charles, the Great and Orthodox Emperor, who gloriously extended the kingdom of the Franks, and reigned prosperously for forty-seven years. He died at the age of seventy, in the year of our Lord 814, the 7th Indiction, on the 28th day of January."

Very many omens had portended his approaching end, a fact that he had recognized as well as others. Eclipses both of the sun and moon were very frequent during the last three years of his life, and a black spot was visible on the sun for the space of seven days. The gallery between the basilica and the palace, which he had built at great pains and labor, fell in sudden ruin to the ground on the day of the Ascension of our Lord. The wooden bridge over the Rhine at Mayence, which he had caused to be constructed with admirable skill, at the cost of ten years' hard work, so that it seemed as if it might last forever, was so completely consumed in three hours by an accidental fire that not a single splinter of it was left, except what was under water. Moreover, one day in his last campaign into Saxony against Godfred, King of the Danes, Charles himself saw a ball of fire fall suddenly from the heavens with a great light, just as he was leaving camp before sunrise to set out on the march. It rushed across the clear sky from right to left, and everybody was wondering what was the meaning of the sign, when the horse which he was riding gave a sudden plunge, head foremost, and fell, and threw him to the ground so heavily that his cloak buckle was broken and his sword belt shattered; and after his servants had hastened to him and relieved him of his arms, he could not rise without their assistance. He happened to have a javelin in his hand when he was thrown, and this was struck from his grasp with such force that it was found lying at a distance of twenty feet or more from the spot. Again, the palace at Aix-la-Chapelle frequently trembled, the roofs of whatever buildings he tarried in kept up a continual crackling noise, the basilica in which he was afterwards buried was struck by lightning, and the gilded ball that adorned the pinnacle of the roof was shattered by the thunderbolt and hurled upon the bishop's house adjoining. In this same basilica, on the margin of the cornice that ran around the interior, between the upper and lower tiers of arches, a legend was inscribed in red letters, stating who was the builder of the temple, the last words of which were *Karolus Princeps.* The year that he died it was remarked by some, a few months before his decease, that the letters of the word *Princeps* were so effaced as to be no longer decipherable. But Charles despised, or affected to despise, all these omens, as having no reference whatever to him.

It had been his intention to make a will, that he might give some share in the inheritance to his daughters and the children of his concubines; but it was begun too late and could not be finished. Three years before his death, however, he made a division of his treasures, money, clothes, and other movable goods in the presence of his friends and servants, and called them to witness it, that their voices might insure the ratification of the disposition thus made. He had a summary drawn up of his wishes regarding this distribution of his property, the terms and text of which are as follows:

"In the name of the Lord God, the Almighty Father, Son, and Holy Ghost. This is the inventory and division dictated by the most glorious and most pious Lord Charles, Emperor Augustus, in the 811th year of the Incarnation of our Lord Jesus Christ, in the 43d year of his reign in France and 37th in Italy, the 11th of his empire, and the 4th Indiction, which considerations of piety and prudence have determined him, and the favor of God enabled him, to make of his treasures and money ascertained this day to be in his treasure chamber. In this division he is especially desirous to provide not only that the largess of alms which Christians usually make of their possessions shall be made for himself in due course and order out of his wealth, but also that his heirs shall be free from all doubt, and know clearly what belongs to them, and be able to share their property by suitable partition without litigation or strife. With this intention and to this end he has first divided all his substance and movable goods ascertained to be in his treasure chamber on the day aforesaid in gold, silver, precious stones, and royal ornaments into three lots, and has subdivided and set off two of the said lots into twenty-one parts, keeping the third entire. The first two lots have been thus subdivided into twenty-one parts because there are in his kingdom twenty-one recognized metropolitan cities, and in order than each archbishopric may receive by way of alms, at the hands of his heirs and friends, one of the said parts, and that the archbishop who shall then administer its affairs shall take the part given to it, and share the same with his suffragans in such manner that one third shall go to the Church, and the remaining two thirds be divided among the suffragans. The twenty-one parts into which the first two lots are to be distributed, according to the number of recognized metropolitan cities, have been set apart one from another, and each has been put aside by itself in a box labeled with the name of the city for which it is destined. The names of the cities to which this alms or largess is to be sent are as follows: Rome, Ravenna, Milan, Friuli, Grado, Cologne, Mayence, Salzburg, Treves, Sens, Besançon, Lyons, Rouen, Rheims, Arles, Vienne, Moutiers-en-Tarantaise, Embrun, Bordeaux, Tours, and Bourges. The third lot, which he wishes to be kept entire, is to be bestowed as follows: While the first two lots are to be divided into the parts aforesaid, and set aside under seal, the third lot shall be employed for the owner's daily needs, as property which he shall be under no obligation to part with in order to the fulfillment of any vow, and this as long as he shall be in the flesh, or consider it necessary for his use. But upon his death, or voluntary renunciation of the affairs of this world, this said lot shall be divided into four parts, and one thereof shall be added to the aforesaid twenty-one parts; the second shall be assigned to his sons and daughters, and to the sons and daughters of his sons, to be distributed among them in just and equal partition; the third, in accordance with the custom common among Christians, shall be devoted to the poor; and the fourth shall go to the support of the men servants and maid servants on duty in the palace. It is his wish that to this said third lot of the whole amount, which consists, as well as the rest, of gold and silver, shall be added all the vessels and utensils of brass, iron, and other metals, together with the arms, clothing, and other movable goods, costly and cheap, adapted to divers uses, as hangings, coverlets, carpets, woolen stuffs, leathern articles, pack-saddles, and whatsoever shall be found in his treasure chamber and wardrobe at that time, in order that thus the parts of the said lot may be augmented, and the alms distributed reach more persons. He ordains that his chapel—that is to say, its church property, as well that which he has provided and collected as that which came to him by inheritance from his father—shall remain entire, and not be dissevered by any partition whatever. If, however, any vessels, books, or other articles be found therein which are certainly known not to have been given by him to the said chapel, whoever wants them shall have them on paying their value at a fair estimation. He likewise commands that the books which he has collected in his library in great numbers shall be sold for fair prices to such as want them, and the money received therefrom given to the poor. It is well known that among his other property and treasures are three silver tables, and one very large and massive golden one. He directs and commands that the square silver table, upon which there is a representation of the city of Constantinople, shall be sent to the Basilica of St. Peter the Apostle at Rome, with the other gifts destined therefore; that the round one, adorned with a delineation of the city of Rome, shall be given to the Episcopal Church at Ravenna; that the third, which far surpasses the other two in weight and in beauty of workmanship, and is made in three circles, showing the plan of the whole universe, drawn with skill and delicacy, shall go, together with the golden table, fourthly above mentioned, to increase that lot which is to be devoted to his heirs and to alms.

"This deed, and the dispositions thereof, he has made and appointed in the presence of the bishops, abbots, and counts able to be present, whose names are hereto subscribed: Bishops—Hildebald, Ricolf, Arno, Wolfar, Bernoin, Laidrad, John, Theodulf, Jesse, Heito, Waltgaud. Abbots—Fredugis, Adalung, Angilbert, Irmino. Counts—Walacho,

Meginher, Otulf, Stephen, Unruoch, Burchard, Meginhard, Hatto, Rihwin, Edo, Ercangar, Gerold, Bero, Hildiger, Rocculf."

Charles' son Louis, who by the grace of God succeeded him, after examining this summary, took pains to fulfill all its conditions most religiously as soon as possible after his father's death.

3. *Charlemagne's Capitulary on Education*

The translation is from the *Pennsylvania Translations and Reprints Series*, Vol. VI, no. 5, pp. 12–14.

CHARLES, by the grace of God, King of the Franks and Lombards and Patrician of the Romans, to Abbot Baugulf and to all the congregation, also to the faithful committed to you, we have directed a loving greeting by our ambassadors in the name of omnipotent God.

Be it known, therefore, to your devotion pleasing God, that we, together with our faithful, have considered it to be useful that the bishoprics and monasteries entrusted by the favor of Christ to our control, in addition to the order of monastic life and the intercourse of holy religion, in the culture of letters also ought to be zealous in teaching those who by the gift of God are able to learn, according to the capacity of each individual, so that just as the observance of the rule imparts order and grace to honesty of morals, so also zeal in teaching and learning may do the same for sentences, so that those who desire to please God by living rightly should not neglect to please him also by speaking correctly. For it is written: "Either from thy words thou shalt be justified or from thy words thou shalt be condemned." For although correct conduct may be better than knowledge, nevertheless knowledge precedes conduct. Therefore, each one ought to study what he desires to accomplish, so that so much the more fully the mind may know what ought to be done, as the tongue hastens in the praises of omnipotent God without the hindrances of errors. For since errors should be shunned by all men, so much the more ought they to be avoided as far as possible by those who are chosen for this very purpose alone, so that they ought to be the especial servants of truth. For when in the years just passed letters were often written to us from several monasteries in which it was stated that the brethren who dwelt there offered up in our behalf sacred and pious prayers, we have recognized in most of these letters both correct thoughts and uncouth expressions; because what pious devotion dictated faithfully to the mind, the tongue, uneducated on account of the neglect of study, was not able to express in the letter without error. Whence it happened that we began to fear lest perchance, as the skill in writing was less, so also the wisdom for understanding the Holy Scriptures might be much less than it rightly ought to be. And we all know well that, although errors of speech are dangerous, far more dangerous are errors of the understanding. Therefore, we exhort you not only not to neglect the study of letters, but also with most humble mind, pleasing to God, to study earnestly in order that you may be able more easily and more correctly to penetrate the mysteries of the divine Scriptures. Since, moreover, images, tropes and similar figures are found in the sacred pages, no one doubts that each one in reading these will understand the spiritual sense more quickly if previously he shall have been fully instructed in the mastery of letters. Such men truly are to be chosen for this work as have both the will and the ability to learn and a desire to instruct others. And may this be done with a zeal as great as the earnestness with which we command it. For we desire you to be, as it is fitting that soldiers of the church should be, devout in mind, learned in discourse, chaste in conduct and eloquent in speech, so that whosoever shall seek to see you out of reverence for God, or on account of your reputation for holy conduct, just as he is edified by your appearance, may also be instructed by your wisdom, which he has learned from your reading or singing, and may go away joyfully giving thanks to omnipotent God. Do not neglect, therefore, if you wish to have our favor, to send copies of this letter to all your suffragans and fellow-bishops and to all the monasteries. . . . Farewell.

4. *Life of Louis the Pious*

The author of this work is anonymous. Internal evidence suggests that the author was a younger contemporary of his subject and an intimate of Louis' court, probably a palatine official.

The translation is from Allen Cabaniss, *Son of Charlemagne* (Syracuse: Syracuse University Press, 1961), pp. 64–67, 89–92, 95–98, 99–104, 115–17, 119–20.

THE Enemy of mankind did not endure this holy and worthy devotion of the emperor to God, but pursued him everywhere and declared war against him in all the ranks of the church. He also undertook to oppose Louis, as the latter attacked him, with an abundance of forces and through his members to harass Christ's brave warrior with what power and craft he could command. After these matters had been arranged properly, the emperor later in the same diet desired his firstborn son, Lothair, to be recognized and designated as co-emperor, and sent his other two sons, Pepin and Louis, to Aquitaine and Bavaria respectively, so that the people might know whose authority to obey. But there was immediately reported to him the defection of the Obotrites who had joined in friendship with the sons of Godefrid and who were harassing Saxony beyond the Elbe. With God's favor the emperor, directing adequate forces against them, checked their movements. Thereafter he entered the forest of the Vosges to hunt. The hunt there was completed after the manner of the Franks, and Louis returned to spend the winter at Aachen.

It was announced [818] that his nephew, Bernard, in whose behalf he had been Charles's chief adviser in making him king of Italy, had been maddened by the counsels of evil men to such a degree that he deserted him, that all the cities of the realm and the princes of Italy had conspired at this pretense, and that all the passes by which one has access to Italy they had closed with barriers and guard-posts. When Louis had ascertained this through messengers who informed him, especially Bishop Rathaldus and Suppo, he went as far as Châlon with a great number of troops, forces having been procured from both Gaul and Germany. But when Bernard observed that he himself was unequal in strength and unsuited for the things undertaken (many of his troops were daily falling away from him since matters had become desperate), he came to the emperor and laying down his arms prostrated himself at the emperor's feet, acknowledging that he had acted falsely. His magnates followed his example and also submitted to Louis's power and judgment, laying aside their arms. The questioning of the nobles betrayed how and why they had begun the rebellion, for what purpose they had sought to effect the things thus begun, and whom they alleged to have been their accomplices. The authors of this plot were Eggideo, chief of the royal friends; Reginherius, formerly a count of the emperor's palace and a son of Count Meginherius; also Reginhardus, provost of the royal chamber. A great many clerics and laymen were implicated in the crime, among whom the stormy tempest involved some bishops, Anselm of Milan, Wulfold of Cremona, and Theodulf of Orléans.

After the leaders of the conspiracy were carried out and placed in confinement, the emperor returned to winter at Aachen as he had previously decided. There he lingered until the holy solemnity of Easter. That celebration fulfilled, he remitted the harsher sentence and decreed that Bernard, the erstwhile king, and his accomplices in the crime be deprived of their eyes, although by the law and verdict of the Franks they should have been slain with a mortal blow. Many protested and sought to be revenged upon them with the full severity of the law. Yet, despite the emperor's acting more indulgently, the doom which had been remitted was brought to effect upon some. For since Bernard and Reginherius endured the destruction of their eyes with such suffering, they brought bitter death upon themselves. The emperor committed to monasteries the bishops who had been implicated in this savage revolt, after they had been deposed by the remaining bishops. Of the rest, however, he ordered that none be deprived of life or maimed by amputation of members; but according to what seemed necessary by virtue of compelling guilt, he sentenced some to be exiled, others to be tonsured.

◆ ◆ ◆

Later, during the Lenten season [830], while the emperor was traveling through the places lying close to the sea, the chiefs of the evil faction, not willing to delay any longer, displayed the sore which had been hidden for a while. First, the great nobles contrived among themselves a league, then attached the lesser ones to them. Part of them was always desirous of change after the manner of greedy dogs and birds which look for another's defeat to add to their satiety. Relying therefore upon the number and consent of many, they approached the emperor's son Pepin, alleging his being slighted, Bernard's arrogance, and the despising of others, and claiming indeed (what is wicked to relate) that Bernard was an incestuous polluter of Pepin's father's bed. They insinuated furthermore that his father was baffled by certain delusions to such a degree that he was in no way able to avenge these things nor indeed even to perceive them. It was therefore necessary, they said, that a good son suffer his father's shame with indignation and that he restore his father to reason and honor. Not only would a reputation for virtue pursue the one doing this, they asserted, but also an extension of his earthly realm—by this remark dissembling their guilt. The young man, therefore, enticed by these incentives, proceeded with them and with many of their troops to Verberie by way of the city of Orléans, since Odo had been removed from that place and Matfrid had been reinstated. But when the Emperor learned with absolute certainty about the deadly armed conspiracy against himself, his wife, and Bernard, he allowed Bernard to protect himself by flight. He requested his wife, however, to remain in Laon and to settle in the monastery of Saint Mary; but he himself hastened to Compiègne.

Those who came to Verberie with Pepin (Warinus and Lantbert having been dispatched along with as many others as possible) caused Queen Judith to be brought before them from the city and basilica of the monastery. Threatening death by torture, they compelled her to promise that, if ample opportunity were given her to speak to the emperor, she would persuade him to devote himself to a monastery, laying aside his arms and having his hair shorn, and that she herself would also do similarly, placing the veil upon her head. The more eagerly they desired this procedure, the more easily they put credence in her acquiescence. Sending some of their men with her, they brought her to the emperor. When he had given her permission to speak more privately, he allowed her to take the veil in order to escape death, but he demanded time to deliberate his tonsure. Since he always lived kindly toward others, the emperor was depressed by their unjust hatred which was so great that they loathed the very existence of him by whose favor they were alive and without whose favor they would have been justly and lawfully deprived of life. When the queen returned to them, they restrained themselves from other injuries indeed, but yielding to the shouting of the public, they had her carried away into exile and thrust into the monastery of Saint Radegunda.

Later, about the month of May, the emperor's son Lothair came from Italy and found him at Compiègne. As he was approaching, the entire faction hostile to the emperor joined itself to him. He seemed to impute nothing dishonorable to his father at that time, yet he approved what had been done. Lastly, contrary to the emperor's pledge, Bernard's brother

Heribert was sentenced to loss of his eyes and his first cousin Odo was disarmed and sent away into exile, as if they were accomplices and promoters of those things which were shouted against Bernard and the queen. Continuing there for a while, the emperor in name only passed the summer. But when autumn was drawing near, those who were of contrary opinions to the emperor wished for a general gathering to be held somewhere in Frankland. The emperor secretly resisted, distrusting the Franks and entrusting himself to the Germans. The emperor's sentiment therefore prevailed that the people come together at Nijmegen. Fearing that the multitude of opponents would overwhelm the paucity of his faithful ones, he gave order that each person coming to the diet employ a single retainer only. He enjoined Count Lambert to have a care of the frontiers reckoned to him and directed Abbot Helisachar to exercise justice there. At length therefore the assembly gathered at Nijmegen. All Germany flocked thither to serve as aid to the emperor. Wishing still further to break the power of his adversaries, the emperor accused Abbot Hilduin, asking why he approached in a hostile manner although he had been ordered to come alone. The latter, unable to answer satisfactorily, was forthwith commanded to leave the palace and spend the winter with only a few men in a campaign tent near Paderborn. Abbot Walach was commanded to retire to the monastery of Corbie and there show himself as one bound by the Rule.

When they who had gathered to oppose the emperor observed that their forces were being depleted, they surrendered to abject hopelessness. Throughout a whole night, assembling and meeting at the quarters of the emperor's son Lothair, they urged him either to go to war or to withdraw somewhere away from the emperor's influence. They spent the entire night in this deliberation. In the morning the emperor ordered his son not to confide in the common enemy, but to come to him as son to father. Heeding these words, in spite of those around him trying to dissuade him, he approached his father. He was not assailed with harsh rebuke, but was chided with moderate leniency. When Lothair entered the recesses of the royal residence, the crowd, splitting in two by instigation of the devil, began to rage. The fury would have mounted to bloodshed on both sides if imperial wisdom had not been on the watch. For while they were in an uproar and were almost ready to rush into a mad passion, the emperor appeared before them all with his son. Immediately the animal-like excitement abated. When the emperor's address had been heard, the entire popular disorder subsided. The emperor thereupon gave command that all leaders of the wicked conspiracy be kept under individual guard. When they were later brought to judgment, the emperor permitted none of them to be slain, although all the magistrates of the law and the emperor's sons had decreed by legal decision that they suffer the death penalty as persons guilty of *lèse-majesté*. But employing, as it seemed to many, a milder procedure than was fitting (although kindness and mercy were his custom), he commanded the laymen to be tonsured at suitable places and the clerics to be detained in similarly appropriate monasteries.

◆ ◆ ◆

The devil, long hostile to the human race and to peace, was in no wise tricked by the emperor's success, but was stirring up the sons through the cunning of his accomplices, persuading them that their father wished to destroy them wantonly, not reflecting that he who was very mild to foreigners could be inhuman to his own. But, since "evil communications corrupt good manners," and a gentle drop of water striking very often is wont to bore through the hardest stone, it finally came to pass that they caused the emperor's sons to form a common league and muster as large an army as they could. They invoked Pope Gregory under the pretext that he alone ought and could reconcile sons to father. Afterwards, however, the truth became obvious. Later in the month of May the emperor came to Worms with a strong force and there debated for a long time what should be done. Through designated emissaries, Bishop Bernard and others, he urged his sons to return to him. It was asked respecting the pope of the Roman see why, if he were present after the manner of his predecessors, he contrived such great delays so as not to meet the emperor. A rumor spread abroad and confirmed what was true about the others, but it alleged that the Roman pope was present to ensnare the emperor and the bishops in the toils of excommunication if there were any disobedience to his will and that of the emperor's sons. But that audacious presumption was insufficient to steal away the emperor's bishops who declared that they would in no wise yield to his judgment. For if the pope had come to excommunicate, he would have gone away himself excommunicated, since the authority of the ancient canons held otherwise.

At length the assembly was held on the festival of John [833], Christ's holy forerunner, at the place which—from what happened there—had been branded with a name of perpetual infamy, the "Field of Lies." For those who had sworn fealty to the emperor lied, and the name of the place where that occurred has remained ever since a witness of the faithlessness. When they stood, however, with ranks arrayed not far from each other and the rush to arms was imminent, it was announced to the emperor that the Roman pope was approaching. The emperor, in battle formation, received him as he came, although less fittingly than was appropriate, charging that he who had come in such an unaccustomed manner would have prepared a similar reception for him. But the pope, escorted into the field tent, pressed the emperor with oaths that he had undertaken so great a journey for no reasons other than the report that the emperor was struggling against his sons in unyielding discord and the pope's desire to sow peace between both parties. The emperor's position was then stated and the pope remained with him several days before being sent back to the sons to contrive a mutual peace. Partly distracted by bribes, partly seduced by promises, partly frightened by threats, almost all the people were surging like a torrent to the sons and their followers. The pope's efforts were in vain. With as many troops brought thither and wrested from the emperor, the defection became stronger day by day, so that on the feast of Saint Paul the populace, fawning upon his sons, was threatening to launch an attack on the emperor. Not able to resist those forces, the emperor ordered his sons not to expose themselves to popular pillaging. They in turn commanded him to abandon camp and come to them, asserting that they would eagerly go out to meet him. And so they did, but the emperor warned his sons, as they leaped from their horses to meet him, to remember their promise concerning himself, his son [Charles], and his wife, and to preserve unimpaired the things which they had formerly promised. Embracing them as they replied suitably, he proceeded to their camp. As he was going, his wife was led away and directed to the tents of Louis [of Bavaria]. But Lothair escorted the emperor along with Charles, then still a boy, to his own tents, and made them remain with a few men in a pavilion prepared for the purpose.

After these events the people were bound by oaths and the empire was partitioned among the brothers by a threefold division. Received by King Louis, his father's wife was again banished, this time to Italy, to the city of Tortona. Observing such things, Pope Gregory returned with heavy grief to Rome. Pepin went back to Aquitaine and Louis to Bavaria. Then Lothair, taking along his father, who rode behind in a private capacity with appointed deputies, came to the villa of Marlenheim where he lingered as long as he could. Arranging such matters as appeared and satisfying the people, but appointing an assembly at Compiègne, he crossed the Mediomatricus (which is Metz by another name). He moved up to Verdun and entered the city of Soissons. There he ordered his father to be held under strict surveillance in the monastery of Saint Médard and Charles committed to Prüm but not tonsured. Lothair hunted eagerly until in the season of autumn, that is, on the Kalends of October, he went to Compiègne, as had been decreed, leading his father with him.

This business completed by Martinmas, the people were granted leave to go back to their own lands, full of sadness for such deeds. Lothair, leading his father along, returned to winter at Aachen. All during the winter the people of Frankland and of Burgundy, of Aquitaine and of Germany, assembled in throngs to express indignation at the emperor's misfortune. Count Eggebard and Constable William indeed organized against Frankland an association for the purpose of reinstating the emperor. Abbot Hugo was dispatched from Germany to Aquitaine by

Louis and by those who had fled thither, by Bishop Drogo and the rest, to arouse the interest of Pepin. Bernard and Warinus were inflaming the people in Burgundy with persuasive addresses, were enticing them with promises, were binding them with oaths, and were uniting them into one will.

The winter passed and spring [834] presented its rosy face. Lothair—his father having been taken through the Haspengau countryside—set out and came to the city of Paris where he had commanded all his faithful to meet him. Against him advanced Count Eggebard and other nobles of that country with a great band collected to fight for the emperor's liberation. Matters would have reached that eventuality if the most pious emperor, on guard against the peril of the many as well as of his own, had not by command and adjuration prevented them from this undertaking. The assembly was finally held in the monastery of Saint Denis the martyr.

But Pepin, departing from Aquitaine with a great host and coming up to the Seine, halted there since demolished bridges and sunken boats prevented a crossing. Then Counts Warinus and Bernard, with a great many allies assembled from the regions of Burgundy, came up to the Marne. There, partly delayed by the severity and unseasonableness of the wind, partly checked to muster their allies, they settled for several days in the villa of Boneuil and those estates which lie around. The holy season of Lent was at hand. In the first week, on the fifth feria, legates (Abbot Atrebaldus and Count Gautselm) were sent by them to the emperor's son Lothair, demanding that the emperor be released from the bonds of confinement and handed over to them. If Lothair would heed their demand, they would place themselves at his disposal for the sake of the dignity and honor which he formerly had from his father. If otherwise, they would seek him out, at their own peril if need be, and with God as judge they would attack those resisting in this matter. To the ultimatum Lothair replied reasonably that no one suffered more in his father's calamity or rejoiced more in his father's good fortune than he did; that the blame of priority imputed to him should not be so attributed since they too had deserted and betrayed the emperor; and that the mark of prison confinement was not unlawfully imprinted upon his father since it was in accordance with an episcopal judgment. Sent forward, therefore, with this explanation, the legates returned to those who had commissioned them.

Counts Guerinus and Odo, and Abbots Fulco and Hugo, were ordered to come to consider with him [Lothair] how their demand could be fulfilled. The emperor's son Lothair also gave order that emissaries be dispatched tomorrow to learn the time of the approach of the aforesaid men, so that he could meet them on the agreed day to treat concerning the case. But the plan was changed. Leaving his father at Saint Denis, he and those induced by his favor repaired to Burgundy, to Vienne, where he chose to pitch camp. The ones who had remained with the emperor urged him to resume the imperial badges of honor, for although he was put away from communion with the church in the manner aforesaid, yet was he in no wise content with that hasty decision. On the morrow, being Sunday, he sought to be reconciled by the ministry of the bishops in the church of Saint Denis, and he agreed to be girded with arms by the hands of the prelates. In this matter the joy of the people increased so greatly that even the weather, which seemed to suffer with him as he endured injury, now rejoiced with him as he was relieved. For up to that time the force of tempests and violence of rains had beat so heavily that waters had flooded beyond wont and winds had rendered the channels of rivers impassable. But at his absolution the elements seem to have conspired, so that soon the raging winds became gentle and the face of the sky reverted to its ancient and long-impeded serenity.

The emperor undertook a journey from that place, but did not seek to pursue his departing son, although many were pressing him to do so. From that place therefore he went to Nanteuil and thereafter to the royal villa of Kierzy where remaining a while he awaited his son Pepin and the ones who were tarrying beyond the Marne. He waited also for those who had taken refuge beyond the Rhine with his son Louis and for that son Louis himself who was on his way to him. While he was there in the mid-season of Lent (when even the joyfulness of the day itself smiled and the ecclesiastical *cantilena* of the Office [Introit] encouraged, saying: "Rejoice, Jerusalem, and all you who love her, make holy day"), a great multitude of his faithful ones met him there and congratulated him with mutual rejoicing. Receiving them kindly and thanking them for the integrity of their fealty, the emperor dismissed his son Pepin to Aquitaine with joy; the others he allowed to return rejoicing to their own lands. He came, however, to Aachen, where he received Judith Augusta, Rathaldus the bishop and Boniface and Pepin bringing her back from Italy. Thereafter he kept his son Charles with him for a long time. With accustomed devotion he observed the solemnity of Easter. After the celebration he busied himself with hunting in the Ardennes forest. When the holy feast of Pentecost had passed, he gave attention to hunting and fishing in the regions of Remiremont.

Although the emperor's son Lothair had discreetly withdrawn from his father and departed to the districts mentioned above, there still remained in the domain of Neustria Count Lantbert and Matfrid and a great many others who strove to maintain control of the areas by their own strength. Count Odo and many who favored the emperor's faction tolerated that fact with impatience and gathered forces against them, endeavoring to hurl them from those places or join battle with them. This matter was managed more slowly than was fitting and was heeded less prudently and it brought upon them no little mischief. For when the enemy came upon them without warning, they, exercising less caution than occasion required, bared their backs to the foe pressing upon them.

There Odo himself and his brother William, as well as a great many others, perished; still others put their safety in flight. Since it did not seem sufficiently safe to remain there, and since they could not join themselves to Lothair, those who achieved the victory feared that the emperor would come upon them if they lingered or would surely meet them as they hastened to their own people. They sent therefore to Lothair as quickly as possible that he might bring them aid since they were surrounded and were apprehensive of their distance from him. Lothair determined to assist them. At that season Count Warinus with a great many allies fortified the castle of Châlon so that if a revolution should be attempted by the zealous ones of the hostile parties it would serve as a refuge and bulwark for himself and his men. When that had been ascertained by Lothair, he decided to advance thither, unexpectedly if possible, but it proved impossible. He did advance, however, and did invest the town, the outskirts of which were put to the torch. The battle raged bitterly for five days, but at last the city was captured, then (after the fashion of cruel conquerors) churches were pillaged, treasuries were robbed, and public supplies were plundered. Finally the city was given up to devouring fire, except one small basilica which by an outstanding miracle could not be burned although it was engulfed with roaring and lapping flames. It had been consecrated to God under the invocation of blessed George the martyr. Yet it was not Lothair's wish for the city to be set afire. After the town was taken, Count Gotselin, Count Sanila, and Madalelm, vassal of the Lord Emperor, were beheaded by a military court. Gerberga, daughter of the late Count William, was strangled by water as a witch.

When that winter had passed [probably 838], on the Kalends of January the terrible fire of a comet appeared in the sign of Scorpio not long after sunset. The death of Pepin followed soon after its menacing apparition. In the meanwhile Judith Augusta, mindful of the plan which she had initiated with the palace counselors and other nobles of the Frankish realm, persuaded the emperor to dispatch emissaries to his son Lothair intimating to him that, if he wished to be the guardian and helper, the protector and defender, of his brother Charles, he should come to his father and learn from him personally that he would obtain clemency for everything done wrongly and would at the same time secure half of the empire, Bavaria alone excepted. To Lothair as well as to his men this proposal seemed advantageous in every respect.

He came therefore to Worms, according to appointment, after the solemnity of Easter. His father received him with eagerness, ordered his men to be cared for lavishly, and did all the things that he had promised. A truce of three days having been granted Lothair, the emperor agreed to divide his whole empire with them, if it was pleasing, but so that the designation of the portions would remain with the emperor and Charles. Otherwise Lothair might rather propose the partition of the empire for the emperor and Charles. Lothair and his men, however, entrusted the apportionment of the realm to the Lord Emperor as he deemed proper, asserting that they could in no wise execute the division because of lack of knowledge of the places. The emperor and his men therefore divided, with equitable balance as it seemed to them, his entire empire, except Bavaria which he left to Louis and assigned to no one else. These things having been completed, and the sons and all the people having been summoned, Lothair chose his portion southward from the Meuse river, but left for his brother Charles the western part, signifying before all the people that he wished Charles to have it. While all the people applauded, the emperor heartily rejoiced and said that all things were pleasing to him. But the mind of Louis [of Bavaria] was grieved not a little. The emperor then gave thanks to God for these accomplishments and admonished his sons to be of one mind and to support each other, charging that Lothair indeed assume care of the younger brother whose spiritual father he was, and that Charles offer the honor due to a spiritual father and an elder brother. When the emperor, lover of true peace, had finished this and had sowed a mutual love between the brothers and as far as possible a reciprocal love between the adherents of each brother, he joyfully dismissed a rejoicing Lothair to Italy enriched with many gifts, dowered with fatherly blessings, and admonished not to forget what he [Lothair] had recently promised. The emperor therefore observed the Lord's Nativity and the solemnity of Easter very festively at Aix.

But hearing about his father's disposition toward his brothers and about the division of the realm between them, Louis [of Bavaria] did not endure it willingly. He determined to make formal demand for whatever was beyond the Rhine. When this was made known to the emperor, he judged that a decision could be postponed until the Paschal feast had been completed. When that, however, was finished, deeming that there should be no delay in such matters, the emperor crossed the Rhine and the Main and came to Tribur, where he settled for some time in order to muster his army. Then he proceeded as far as Bodman, where his son came as a reluctant suppliant. Rebuked by the emperor, Louis admitted that he had acted wickedly and he promised that he would amend the things he had done amiss. But the emperor, employing the friendly gentleness always characteristic of him, forgave his son and upbraided him, at first somewhat harshly (as was appropriate), but afterwards with softer, more caressing words. He then left him in his domain.

Having done these things he celebrated the Lord's Nativity festival at Poitiers with due and customary honor [839]. While he was lingering there and adjudicating whatever public welfare required, a messenger came, saying that his son Louis had invaded Alamannia with some Saxons and Thuringians. This matter constituted a very great misfortune for him. For in addition to being already burdened with old age, with his lung vexed more than usual with abundance of phlegm (which increased in winter) and with his chest disturbed, to him in such condition this sorrowful messenger also chanced to come. Although in nature the emperor was very mild (almost beyond human measure), in resolution magnanimous, in piety most circumspect, he was so bitterly weakened by the report that the increasing mucus hardened into an abscess, and a deadly ulcer began to grow larger within his vitals. Although he learned that God's church was being thrown into confusion and Christian people harassed by so great a bane, his unvanquished spirit did not yield to loathing or, shattered to pieces, succumb to grief. Hardly had he with his wife and son Charles begun the holy fast of Lent when he raised himself as a barrier to thwart this calamity. He who had been wont with profoundest devotion to spend the entire solemn season in the singing of Psalms, urgent prayers, celebration of Masses, and largess of alms, so that he scarcely conceded one or two days to riding for exercise, now for the sake of avoiding discord and of restoring peace, wished to have no day idle. Following the example of the Good Shepherd he did not refrain from incurring damage to his own body for the advantage of the flock entrusted to him. There should be no doubt that he received the reward which the All Highest and Prince of shepherds has promised to give those who labor.

Chapter Five

Feudalism and Manorialism

FEUDALISM, like other words we use in medieval history, including medieval, is not a medieval word. As a legal term it belongs to the seventeenth century; as a description of a state of society, it belongs to the eighteenth. The word, however, does have a medieval derivation. The best theory is that it derives from a German word which meant moveable property or cattle (the most common form of it). In Romance-speaking Gaul the Old German *vieh* came out as *fief*, Latinized as *feodum* or *feudum*. At the same time its meaning broadened, coming to mean any form of remuneration, again in its most typical form, landed property. Eventually, it developed a meaning best expressed by the Latin *beneficium*—property granted on favorable terms in return for service.

To the French and English scholars who coined the concept of feudalism, the *feudum* (the Latinized vernacular eventually superseded the Latin *beneficium*) was at the heart of the matter. Feudalism was the complex of political and social obligations contingent on the possession of fiefs. This is still the most common meaning in England and the United States. Feudalism, in this definition, was primarily a form of government, although it necessarily presupposed some economic base and certainly produced distinctive social relationships. It was an arrangement of a private rather than a public character, i.e., between lord and vassal rather than ruler and subject; political authority became a private possession.

Conceived as a primarily legal institution, feudalism had three essential elements: a personal relationship known as vassalage; a property relationship consisting of the holding of fiefs by vassals from their lords; and a governmental relationship, consisting of the exercise of political authority within the fief by the vassal. Naturally, such a system required a particular historical environment: a weak central government, a professionalization of the military art and the consequent concentration of military might into relatively few hands, a time of military necessity, and a predominantly rural society. In short, feudalism grew up a result of the historical conditions that prevailed in much of western Europe during the sixth through tenth centuries.

Each of these essential elements of feudalism had a separate origin and only gradually became intertwined. Vassalage, the personal relationship, was the earliest to develop. Both the Romans and the Germans were familiar with bodies of retainers attached to powerful men (see the extract from Tacitus in Chapter 2). The political conditions of Merovingian Gaul, particularly between the Loire and the Rhine, merely increased their incidence. Although there were at least two other words in use to describe these retainers (*antrustiones, gasindi*), the one with a future was *vassus,* which by the eighth century had the common meaning of a freeman dependent upon a lord. A man became a *vassus* through the act of commendation, a ceremony which ultimately developed into the familiar homage and fealty. The services demanded of a free man who commended himself to another were originally various; they could be domestic, economic, or military depending upon his social status.

The first significant step in the direction of feudalism was the rise in the social scale of vassals. Deriving from a Celtic word meaning slave, *vassus* gained social respectability in a very simple way, through its adoption by the early Carolingians, in preference to the older term *antrustiones,* for their retainers. As men of the highest social rank became vassals they pulled its rank up with them in the social scale. The second important development was the normal association of vassalage with the holding of fiefs. The *vassus* was originally maintained in the great man's household. However, there was an alternative method for maintaining dependents familiar to late Roman law as the *precaria* and common in Frankish Gaul. The *precaria* was simply a grant of land in return for some kind of rent. A particular form of it was known as a *beneficium* because it was held on extremely favorable terms. From the time of Charles Martel it became common to support Carolingian retainers, *vassi,* by grants of *beneficia,* on Church lands at first, from the royal patrimony later. The general imitation of this practice led to the regular association of vassalage with fief-holding.

So far only two elements of feudalism have been accounted for. The third was the exercise of governmental authority by the vassal within his fief. Now the fief was an economic unit consisting of "fields and men" rather than an uncultivated plot of land. That its possessor should control his tenants politically is such a natural development that the search for institutional origins is probably unnecessary. We have already seen how the late Roman *potentes* exercised governmental functions over their *coloni*. Still, there was an institution, the immunity, which may have served as the exemplar for later feudal rights of justice. Originating with the Merovingian kings, the immunity was a grant to monastery or church exempting them from the authority of the count. It did not remove them from royal authority, it merely delegated that authority to the abbot or bishop. Even though surviving grants of immunity, aside from some exceptional cases, are confined to ecclesiastical officials, it is easy to see how the same privilege could be usurped by a layman of sufficient status with the decay of central authority in the ninth century. Besides, as the office of count became hereditary (another ninth century development), it became difficult to distinguish his delegated royal authority from the authority he wielded as landlord.

Looked at in this way, feudalism could only exist when all three elements were present. It was not, in other words, synonymous with aristocracy or a system of great landed estates tilled by servile labor. Each element could, and did, exist separately. Feudal forms, particularly vassalage, existed widely throughout western Europe; feudalism did not. It was born in France north of the Loire and spread to England after the Norman Conquest and ultimately to parts of Germany, Italy and Spain. It also appeared, as an exotic transplant, in the Byzantine Empire and the Holy Land. But wherever central government was too effective, the terrain too difficult, or towns too strong, feudalism could not flourish.

Feudalism, other than being a specific combination of institutions, was a response to a particular historical situation. It was initially an improvisation for solving on a local basis a defensive need that larger political units could not handle. It emerged out of the failure of the West Frankish monarchy to defend northern France from the Norse invaders. In an overwhelmingly rural society, land rather than money was the principal means of securing fighting men, particularly since the military art had become a highly professional one. The dominance of the heavily-armed cavalryman, a process too complicated to describe here, had profound social results. It produced a sharp distinction between those who had the resources to equip themselves to fight (i.e., those who were vassals, had fiefs, and governed) and those who did not (i.e., those who tilled the soil and were servile either legally or economically).

If we look at feudalism as originally a military institution with important social and political ramifications, some of its secondary features become perfectly intelligible. Homage and fealty was the ceremony through which one entered into the feudal relationship, that is, became a vassal and received a fief on terms of military service. Since the fief was in one aspect an economic unit designed to support a fighting man or men, it was not feasible originally to divide it among the heirs of a deceased vassal, hence the rule of primogeniture. For the same reason, if the heir were a minor (not of fighting age) or a woman, the lord exercised rights of wardship and marriage. The original military character of the fief is also demonstrated by the relief, an inheritance tax consisting at first of the arms and armor of the dead vassal. Similarly, subinfeudation was merely one way of satisfying the military quota imposed on the fief.

◆ ◆ ◆

So far we have concentrated on the fief as a political and social unit. It was necessarily an economic unit as well; it existed so the vassal could draw an income from it. The reason for separating the two aspects of the fief under the headings feudalism and manorialism has been primarily pedagogical although it is true that the manorial or seigneurial system was older than feudalism, could exist independently of it, and did in fact long survive it.

The manor came into existence at a time when historical records fail us. Consequently the details of manorial origins are obscure and much disputed. But at least we may begin with one certainty, that the manor did not exist in Roman times. Despite the superficial resemblance between the Roman *latifundia,* with its divisions into demesne and dependent tenures, and the medieval manor, certain essentials were lacking. One was economic, consisting in the fact that where the *latifundia* produced for the market, the medieval manor did not, or at least did not until quite late in its history. Another difference was political, involving the fact that the Roman *colonus* was not in theory so completely dependent upon his lord governmentally as was the medieval serf.

The medieval manor and the Roman *latifundia* also differed in their agricultural techniques. The Roman estate was a collection of small farms cultivated individually by the peasant families holding them. There was no trace of that communal element which became prominent in later manorial development. Nor did the Roman peasant perform labor services on the demesne. Further, medieval agriculture utilized field systems, like the three- and four-course rotations, which were unknown in late Roman times. In the fields, the division into ridge and furrow was a medieval innovation as was the heavy plow which made it possible. Finally, the introduction of the horse shoe and the horse collar, which made the horse an efficient agricultural instrument for the first time, came during the medieval period.

When the developments in the preceding paragraphs took place and their exact relation to the manor are among the most serious puzzles of medieval history. To give just one example, some scholars have thought that the key to the development of the manor, technologically, was the heavy plow, invented or adopted by the Germans and imported by them into western Europe. From it, they argued, came the communal aspect of the manor (because of its expense and the number of oxen required to pull it) and its division into strips (because of the difficulty in turning the plow around). Other scholars have pointed out, however, that while the heavy plow was surely associated with strip-farming by the ridge and furrow method, there cannot be any deterministic equation of the heavy plow with the manor. Strip-farming, they point out, was not a medieval innovation even though it was much more commonly practised then. Strips could be cultivated by any kind of plow and were. Nor was the ridge and furrow pattern produced by the heavy plow invariable in manorial cultivation. Moreover, even if the introduction of the heavy plow demanded a higher degree of cooperation among the peasants than before, the really cooperative features of manorial agriculture only came with the introduction, at a late stage in manorial development, of the regulated three-course rotation.

Confusions such as the one described above stem from two causes: a false equation of the "classic" manor (heavy plow, open fields, regulated three-course rotation, single village community) with medieval agriculture as a whole, and the failure to recognize what a complicated development the manor had. In the first place, not all agricultural estates were organized as manors. We merely know more about the latter because their size required efficient organization, hence they kept records. Furthermore, there were four different types of manorial organization: the unitary manor to which all the farms in a village belonged; the manor concentrated in one village but which did not embrace all the farms in it; the manor whose farms were in several neighboring villages also containing either independent farms or farms belonging to other manors; and finally, the federative manor which was scattered over a large number of villages in each of which only a few farms belonged to the manor. The second and third types were the most common.

In the third place, the services and rents demanded of the peasants were not at all standard either from region to region or from period to period. In the Merovingian and Carolingian periods, for example, labor services on the demesne were heavy in direct proportion to the scarcity of money; in the thirteenth century, on the other hand, when the quantity of money was much greater, labor services dwindled to a few days in the year as rents in money came to constitute the bulk of the lord's revenue.

Fourthly, western Europe was not manorialized at the same time, and then never completely. The system appeared first in Frankish Gaul in the seventh century and spread from there to the Rhineland, western Germany, and England in the ninth through eleventh centuries. And many areas of Europe, mountainous regions, coastland—areas which had a specialized type of agriculture (e.g., vineyards)—were not manorialized at all. Finally, we must comment on the diversity of field systems. The three-course rotation, whether free or regulated, was very common but it was not standard. Two- and four-course rotations were in use, often interchangeably with the three course. Nor did the three-course rotation demand three separate fields any more than the two course demanded two nor the four course, four.

The historical development of the manor must have looked something like this. During the Roman period the norm was square fields cultivated in a two-course rotation by the sliding or scratch plow drawn by oxen. In the sixth century, possibly because the climate of northern Europe became damper, the square fields were subdivided into strips to afford better drainage, a process facilitated by the heavy plow whose fixed mouldboard enabled it to plow them into the ridge and furrow pattern. It was also the heavy plow which enabled the northern farmer to begin cultivation of richer and heavier lowland soils. In the eighth century the pressure of population introduced a free three-course rotation which, although it never entirely replaced the two course, produced more food for human and animal consumption. The introduction of the horse collar in the tenth century enabled the horse to be used efficiently as a draft animal especially in the areas of three-course rotation (which produced more fodder). This combination of more efficient motive power with more efficient production probably lies behind the increase of

Europe's population between the eleventh and thirteenth centuries. In turn this rise in population led, in some areas, to the introduction of the regulated three-course rotation. The operative factor here was that the pressure of population decreased the amount of pasture as opposed to arable land, hence cattle had to be pastured on the fallow. In turn, this meant, in the absence of fencing, that rotation from arable to fallow, and thus planting and sowing, had to be done at the same time by everyone.

To get back to the comparison of the medieval manor and the *latifundia,* it is easy to see how economic self-sufficiency and political domination by the landlord came about. As western Europe became more and more isolated economically, it was thrown back upon its only economic resource, the land. With the decline of towns and commerce the agricultural estate absorbed more and more of the population until it ceased to serve any substantial market outside of itself. And politically, we have already seen how, as the authority of the Roman imperial government withered away, the great landlords slowly absorbed its functions in respect to the people dependent upon them economically. Nor is it difficult to see how as feudalism evolved it powerfully reinforced this same tendency. The immunity, discussed above, was one means. Another was the voluntary submission by individuals and even entire village communities to a feudal lord for purposes of protection. And, of course, the simple usurpation of political and economic authority was very common.

Naturally, the systems just described underwent profound modifications in the later Middle Ages. As a military system, feudalism was obsolete by the end of the twelfth century although it remained as a peculiar social institution up to the eighteenth century in some areas. The manor, even though more tenacious, also lost its original *raison d'etre* in many areas of medieval Europe. The reasons are very simple: the historical conditions that brought them into being slowly disappeared. The rebirth of effective central governments, a money economy, commerce and industry—all worked against these typically medieval institutions. Not at the same time nor at the same rate, but they did work and when they did, these aspects of the Middle Ages dissolved.

1. *Creation of an Antrustio*

The following document, like several succeeding ones in this collection, comes from a Frankish formulary of the first half of the seventh century. It is not a legal instrument, merely a form for the use of scribes in the drawing up of legal documents, in this case for the appointment of an individual as a member of the king's *trustis* or bodyguard.

The translation is from Thatcher and McNeal, *A Source Book for Medieval History* (New York: Charles Scribner's Sons, 1905) pp. 34–43.

IT IS right that those who have promised us unbroken faith should be rewarded by our aid and protection. Now since our faithful subject ——— with the will of God has come to our palace with his arms and has there sworn in our hands to keep his trust and fidelity to us, therefore we decree and command by the present writing that henceforth the said ——— is to be numbered among our *antrustiones.* If anyone shall presume to slay him, let him know that he shall have to pay 600 solidi as a wergeld for him.

2. *Form for Commendation*

This document comes from a formulary about a century later in date than the one above.

The translation is from Thatcher and McNeal, pp. 343–44.

TO MY great lord, ———, I, ———. Since, as was well known, I had not wherewith to feed and clothe myself, I came to you and told you my wish, to commend myself to you and to put myself under your protection. I have now done so, on the condition that you shall supply me with food and clothing as far as I shall merit by my services, and that as long as I live I shall perform such services for you as are becoming to a freeman, and shall never have the right to withdraw from your power and protection, but shall remain under them all the days of my life. It is agreed that if either of us shall try to break this compact he shall pay ——— solidi, and the compact shall still hold. It is also agreed that two copies of this letter shall be made and signed by us, which also has been done.

3. *Two Capitularies Concerning Vassals*

The first of these documents was issued by Louis the Pious in 816; the second by his sons Lothar, Louis and Charles in 847.

The translation is from the *Pennsylvania Translation and Reprints Series,* Vol. IV, no. 3, p. 5.

IF ANYONE shall wish to leave his lord and is able to prove against him one of these crimes, that is, in the first place, if the lord has wished to reduce him unjustly into servitude; in the second place, if he has taken counsel against his life; in the third place if the lord has committed adultery with the wife of his vassal, in the fourth place if has wilfully attacked him with a drawn sword; in the fifth place, if the lord has been able to bring defense to his vassal after he commended his hands to him, and has not done so; it is allowed to the vassal to leave him. If the lord has perpetrated anything against the vassal in these five points it is allowed the vassal to leave him.

◆ ◆ ◆

We will moreover that each free man in our kingdom shall choose a lord, from us or our faithful, such a one as he wishes.

We command moreover that no man shall leave his lord without just cause, nor should any one receive him, except in such a way as was customary in the time of our predecessors.

And we wish you to know that we want to grant right to our faithful subjects and we do not wish to do anything to them against reason. Similarly we admonish you and the rest of our faithful subjects that you grant right to your men and do not act against reason toward them.

And we will that the man of each one of us in whosoever kingdom he is, shall go with his lord against the enemy, or in his other needs unless there shall have been (as may there not be) such an invasion of the kingdom as is called a *landwer,* so that the whole people of that kingdom shall go together to repel it.

4. *Capitulary of Lestinnes*

This capitulary, dated 743, contains the earliest known reference to the *precaria verbo regis.*

The translation is by the author from *The Monumenta Germanae Historica, Capitularia Regum Francorum,* Vol. I, 28.

ALSO we have established, with the advice of our clergy and the Christian people, that because of threats of war and the invasions of some of the border tribes, we shall in the future, God consenting, take possession of a part of the land belonging to the Church, on precarial tenure and with a fixed rent, for the support of our army and on these conditions. From each appropriated estate one shilling, that is twelve pence, shall be paid annually to the church or monastery. But if the person granted the property should die, the Church shall recover its own property unless, necessity requiring it, the ruler should command the *precaria* be renewed and written again. Let care be taken in each case that no church or monastery whose land has been granted in *precaria* should thus suffer poverty or want. If poverty demands it, then let the whole possession be returned to the church or house of God.

5. *Form for a Precarial Letter and a Benefice*

The following two documents are taken from the same formulary as document 1 above. The *precaria* was not exclusively associated with the Church. The high incidence of ecclesiastical documents in this chapter and in this book generally is fortuitous—the Church kept better records than most medieval institutions.

The translation is from Thatcher and McNeal, pp. 346, 347.

TO OUR lord and father in Christ, the holy and apostolic bishop———, I———, and my wife———. It is well known that we have given in the name of the Lord our villa of———, situated in the county of———, in its entirety and with all that we possessed there, by a letter of gift to the church of———, founded in honor of———, and that you have received it on behalf of the said church. And in response to our petition you have granted that as long as we or either of us shall live we shall hold the said villa as a benefice with the right of usufruct, with the understanding that we shall not diminish its value in any way or alienate anything that belongs to it, but shall hold it without prejudice to the ownership of the said church or bishop. Therefore we have written this precarial letter in witness that our possession shall not work any prejudice to your ownership or any injury to the said villa; but that we only have the use of it during our lives, and that after we are dead you shall immediately recover it with all the additions and improvements which we may have made, by virtue of this precarial letter, which shall be renewed every five years, and without requiring any judicial process or obtaining the consent of the heirs; and that thereafter you shall hold it forever, or do with it whatever may seem to you to be the best interests of the said church.

◆ ◆ ◆

I,———, and my wife,———, in the name of the Lord, give by this letter of gift, and transfer from our ownership to the ownership and authority of the monastery of———, over which the venerable abbot ——— presides, and which was founded in the honor of——— by———

in the county of ———, the following villas ——— situated in the county of ———, with all the lands, houses, buildings, tenants, slaves, vineyards, woods, fields, pastures, meadows, streams and all other belongings and dependencies, and all things movable and immovable which are found in the said villas now or may be added later; in order that under the protection of Christ they may be used for the support and maintenance of the monks who dwell in the aforesaid monastery. We do this on condition that as long as either of us shall live we may possess the aforesaid villas, without prejudice to the ownership of the monastery and without diminution of the value of them, except that we shall be allowed to emancipate any of the slaves that dwell on the lands for the salvation of our souls. After the death of both of us, the aforesaid villas with any additions or improvements which have been made, shall return immediately to the possession of the said monastery and the said abbot and his successors, without taking any judicial process or obtaining the consent of the heirs.

6. *Form for a Grant of Immunity*

The document comes from the same formulary as the previous two. In this case grants of immunity are almost exclusively associated with the church although the same powers were appropriated by secular officials and persons in a later period.

The translation is from Thatcher and McNeal, p. 352.

WE BELIEVE that our reign will best be rendered memorable, if we bestow suitable benefits on churches (or whatever you wish to insert here), with pious purpose, and if we secure these benefits under the protection of God by putting them in writing. Therefore, be it known to you that we have granted the request of that apostolic man, the bishop of ———, for the salvation of our souls; namely, that no public official may enter the lands which his church holds now, by our gift or by the gift of anyone else, or which his church may receive in the future, for the purpose of trying cases, or collecting taxes; but that the said bishop and his successors shall hold the said lands in the name of the Lord with full immunity. We decree therefore that neither you nor any of your subordinates or successors, nor any other public official shall presume to enter the lands of the said church for the purpose of trying cases, or collecting taxes or revenues, or receiving entertainment or seizing supplies or securities. All the taxes and other revenues which the royal treasury has a right to demand from the people on the lands of the said church, whether they be freemen or slaves, Romans or barbarians, we now bestow on the said church for our future salvation, to be used by the officials of the church forever for the best interests of the church.

7. *Capitulary of Kiersy*

This capitulary was published by Charles the Bald just before he left France for Italy. It was intended to regulate the affairs of the kingdom which was to be administered by his son in his absence. Dating from 877, it shows how far the practice of the inheritance of land and office had gone by the second half of the ninth century.

The excerpt is from Thatcher and McNeal, pp. 355–56.

IF A count whose son accompanies us shall die during our absence, our son with the advice of our faithful subjects shall appoint one of the near relatives of the deceased count to govern the county with the aid of the officials of the county and the bishop in whose diocese it is, until we are notified of the case and have an opportunity to give the son of the count his father's honors. But if the deceased count shall leave a minor son, that son shall govern the county with the aid of the officials and the bishop in whose diocese it is, until the death of the said count has been brought to our notice and we endow the son with his father's honors. But if the count shall not leave a son, our son with the advice of our faithful subjects shall appoint someone to govern the county with the aid of the officials of the county and the bishop, until our commands in respect to it are made known. And no one shall feel aggrieved, if we give the county to another than the one who governed it up to the time of our appointment. The same procedure shall be observed in regard to our vassals; and the bishops, abbots, and counts of our kingdom, and our other faithful subjects, shall do the same toward their men.

8. *Capitulary to the Missi*

This capitulary indicates some of the abuses the royal benefices were subject to and how they were already becoming absorbed into the private property of individuals. It dates from 806.

The excerpt is from Thatcher and McNeal, pp. 358–59.

WE HAVE heard that counts and other men who hold benefices from us have improved their own property at the expense of the benefices, and have made the serfs on the benefices labor on their own land, so that our benefices are waste and those dwelling on them in many places suffer great evils.

We have heard that some sell the benefices which they hold from us to other men in full ownership, and then, having received the price in the public court, they buy back the lands as allodial lands. This must not be done, for those who do this break the faith which they promised us.

9. *Various Capitularies on the Growth of Feudal Dependence*

The following four capitularies, dating between 805 and 829, illustrate the simplification of Carolingian society as great men gradually brought lesser into subjection.

The excerpts are from Thatcher and McNeal, pp. 359–60.

CONCERNING the oppression of poor freemen: that they are not to be unjustly oppressed by more powerful persons on any pretext, and forced to sell or give up their property.

◆ ◆ ◆

Poor men complain that they are despoiled of their property, and they make this complaint equally against bishops and abbots and their agents, and against counts and their subordinates.

◆ ◆ ◆

Freemen who have no lands of their own, but live on the land of a lord, are not to be received as witnesses, because they hold land of another; but they are to be accepted as compurgators, because they are free. Those who have land of their own, and yet live on the land of a lord, are not to be rejected as witnesses because they live on the land of a lord, but their testimony shall be accepted, because they have land of their own.

◆ ◆ ◆

No one shall leave his senior, after he has received from him the value of a solidus, unless his senior attempts to kill him, to beat him with a club, to violate his wife or his daughter, or to take his hereditary possession from him.

10. *Homage and Fealty*

a. Homage and Fealty to the Count of Flanders (1127)

(*Pennsylvania Translations and Reprints Series*, Vol. IV, no. 3, p. 18)

THROUGHOUT the whole remaining part of the day those who had previously enfeoffed by the most pious count Charles, did homage to the count, taking up now again their fiefs and offices and whatever they had before rightfully and legitimately obtained. On Thursday the seventh of April, homages were again made to the count being completed in the following order of faith and security.

First they did their homage thus, the count asked if he was willing to become completely his man, and the other replied, "I am willing"; and with clasped hands, surrounded by the hands of the count, they were bound together by a kiss. Secondly, he who had done homage gave his fealty to the representative of the count in these words, "I promise on my faith that I will in future be faithful to count William and will observe my homage to him completely against all persons in good faith and without deceit," and thirdly he took his oath to this upon the relics of the saints. Afterward, with a little rod which the count held in his hand, he gave investitures to all who by this agreement had given their security and homage and accompanying oath.

b. Charter of Homage and Fealty (1110)

(*Ibid.*, pp. 18–20)

In the name of the Lord, I, Bernard Atton, Viscount of Carcassonne, in the presence of my sons, Roger and Trencavel, and of Peter Roger of Barbazan, and William Hugo, and Raymond Mantellini, and Peter de Vitry, nobles, and of many other honorable men, who had come to the monastery of St. Mary of Grasse, to the honor of the festival of the august St. Mary; since lord Leo, abbot of the said monastery, has asked me, in the presence of all those above mentioned, to acknowledge to him the fealty and homage for the castles, manors, and places which the patrons, my ancestors, held from him and his predecessors and from the said monastery, as a fief, and which I ought to hold as they held, I have made to the lord abbot Leo acknowledgment and homage as I ought to do.

Therefore, let all present and to come know that I the said Bernard Atton, lord and viscount of Carcassonne, acknowledge verily to thee my lord Leo, by the grace of God, abbot of St. Mary of Grasse, and to thy successors that I hold and ought to hold as a fief, in Carcassonne, the following: that is to say, the castles of Confoles, of Leoque, of Capendes . . . ; and the manors of Mairac, of Albars and of Musso; also, in the valley of Aquitaine, Rieux, Traverina, Herault, Archas, Servians, Villatritoes, Tansiraus, Presler, Cornelles. Moreover, I acknowledge that I hold from thee and from the said monastery as a fief the castle of Termes in Narbonne; and in Minerve the castle of Tentaion, and the manors of Cassanolles, and of Ferral and Aiohars; and in Le Roges, the little village of Longville; for each and all of which I make homage and fealty with hands and with mouth to thee my said lord abbot Leo and to thy successors, and I swear upon these four gospels of God that I will always be a faithful vassal to thee and to thy successors and to St. Mary of Grasse in all things in which a vassal is required to be faithful to his lord, and I will defend thee, my lord, and all thy successors, and the said monastery and the monks present and to come and the castles and manors and all your men and their possessions against all malefactors and invaders, at my request and that of my successors at my own cost; and I will give to thee power over all the castles and manors above described, in peace and in war, whenever they shall be claimed by thee or by thy successors.

Moreover I acknowledge that, as a recognition of the above fiefs, I and my successors ought to come to the said monastery, at our own expense, as often as a new abbot shall have been made, and there do homage and return to him the power over all the fiefs described above. And when the abbot shall mount his horse I and my heirs, viscounts of Carcassonne, and our successors ought to hold the stirrup for the honor of the dominion of St. Mary of Grasse; and to him and all who come with him to as many as two hundred beasts, we should make the abbot's purveyance in the borough of St. Michael of Carcassonne, the first time he enters Carcassonne, with the best fish and meat and with eggs and cheese, honorably according to his will, and pay the expense of the shoeing of the horses, and for straw and fodder as the season shall require.

And if I or my sons or their successors do not observe to thee or to thy successors each and all the things declared above, and should come against these things, we wish that all the aforesaid fiefs should by that very fact be handed over to thee and to the said monastery of St. Mary of Grasse and to thy successors.

I, therefore, the aforesaid lord Leo, by the grace of God, abbot of St.

Mary of Grasse, receive the homage and fealty for all the fiefs of castles and manors and places which are described above; in the way and with the agreements and understandings written above; and likewise I concede to thee and thy heirs and their successors, the viscounts of Carcassonne, all the castles and manors and places aforesaid, as a fief, along with this present charter, divided through the alphabet. And I promise to thee and thy successors, viscounts of Carcassonne, under the religion of my order, that I will be a good and faithful lord concerning all those things described.

Moreover, I, the aforesaid viscount, acknowledge that the little villages of Cannetis, Maironis, Villamagna, Aiglino, Villadasas, Villafrancos, Villadenz, Villaudriz, St. Genese, Gauart, Conguste and Mata, with the farm-house of Mathus and the chateaux of Villalauro and Claromont, with the little villages of St. Stephen of Surlac, and of Upper and Lower Agrifolio, ought to belong to the said monastery, and whoever holds anything there holds from the same monastery, as we have seen and have heard read in the privileges and charters of the monastery, and as was there written.

Made in the year of the Incarnation of the Lord 1110, in the reign of Louis. Seal of Bernard Atton, viscount of Carcassonne, seal of Raymond Mantellini, seal of Peter Roger of Barbazon, seal of Roger, son of the said viscount of Carcassonne, seal of William Hugo, seal of lord abbot Leo, who has accepted this acknowledgment of the homage of the said viscount.

And I, the monk John, have written this charter at the command of the said lord Bernard Atton, viscount of Carcassonne and of his sons on the day and year given above, in the presence and witness of all those named above.

c. Letter of Bishop Fulbert of Chartres (1020)

(*Ibid.*, pp. 23–24)

To William most glorious duke of the Aquitanians, bishop Fulbert the favor of his prayers.

Asked to write something concerning the form of fealty, I have noted briefly for you on the authority of the books the things which follow. He who swears fealty to his lord ought always to have these six things in memory; what is harmless, safe, honorable, useful, easy, practicable. Harmless, that is to say that he should not be injurious to his lord in his body; safe, that he should not be injurious to him in his secrets or in the defenses through which he is able to be secure; honorable, that he should not be injurious to him in his justice or in other matters that pertain to his honor; useful, that he should not be injurious to him in his possessions;

easy or practicable, that that good which his lord is able to do easily, he make not difficult, nor that which is practicable he make impossible to him.

However, that the faithful vassal should avoid these injuries is proper, but not for this does he deserve his holding; for it is not sufficient to abstain from evil, unless what is good is done also. It remains, therefore, that in the same six things mentioned above he should faithfully counsel and aid his lord, if he wishes to be looked upon as worthy of his benefice and to be safe concerning the fealty which he has sworn.

The lord also ought to act toward his faithful vassal reciprocally in all these things. And if he does not do this he will be justly considered guilty of bad faith, just as the former, if he should be detected in the avoidance of or the doing of or the consenting to them, would be perfidious and perjured.

I would have written to you at greater length, if I had not been occupied with many other things, including the rebuilding of our city and church which was lately entirely consumed in a great fire; from which loss though we could not for a while be diverted, yet by the hope of the comfort of God and of you we breathe again.

11. *Marriage*

The following are all taken from the English Exchequer Rolls between the years 1140–1282.

The translation is from the *Pennsylvania Translations and Reprints Series*, Vol. IV, no. 3, pp. 25–26.

RALPH son of William owes 100 marks as a fine, to be allowed to marry Margery who was wife of Nicholas Corbet who held of the king *in capite,* and that the same Margery may be allowed to marry him.

Walter de Cancy renders account of £15 to be allowed to marry a wife as he shall choose.

Wiverone wife of Iverac of Ipswich renders account of £4 and 1 mark of silver that she may not have to take any husband except the one she wishes.

Emma de Normanville and Roheisa and Margaret and Juliana, her sister, render account of 10 marks for license to marry where they wish.

Roheisa de Doura renders account of £450 to have half of all the lands which belonged to Richard de Lucy, her grandfather, and which the brother of the same Roheisa had afterward as well in England as in Normandy, and for license to marry where she wishes so long as she does not marry herself to any of the enemies of the king.

Alice, countess of Warwick, renders account of £1000 and 10 palfreys to be allowed to remain a widow as long as she pleases, and not to be forced to marry by the king. And if perchance she should wish to marry, she shall not marry except with the assent and on the grant of the king, where the king shall be satisfied; and to have the custody of her sons whom she has from the earl of Warwick her late husband.

Hawisa, who was wife of William Fitz Robert renders account of 130 marks and 4 palfreys that she may have peace from Peter of Borough to whom the king has given permission to marry her; and that she may not be compelled to marry.

Geoffrey de Mandeville owes 20,000 marks to have as his wife Isabella, countess of Gloucester, with all the lands and tenements and fiefs which fall to her.

12. *Wardship, Relief and Aids*

The following entries are also taken from the English Exchequer Rolls.

Translation as above, pp. 26–27, 28.

THOMAS DE COLVILLE renders an account of 100 marks for having the custody of the sons of Roger Torpel and their land until they come of age.

William, bishop of Ely, owes 220 marks for having the custody of Stephen de Beauchamp with his inheritance and for marrying him when he wishes.

William of St. Mary's church, renders an account of 500 marks for having the custody of the heir of Robert Young, son of Robert Fitzharding, with all his inheritance and all its appurtenances and franchises; that is to say with the services of knights and gifts of churches and marriages of women, and to be allowed to marry him to whatever one of his relatives he wishes; and that all his land is to revert to him freely when he comes of age.

Bartholomew de Muleton renders an account of 100 marks for having the custody of the land of the heiress of Lambert of Ibtoft, and for marrying the wife of the same Lambert to whomsoever he wishes where she shall not be disparaged and that he may be able to confer her upon whom he wishes.

Walter Hait renders an account of 5 marks of silver for the relief of the land of his father.

Walter Brito renders an account of £66, 13s. and 4d. for the relief of his land.

Richard of Estre renders an account of £15 for his relief for 3 knights' fees which he holds from the honor of Mortain.

Walter Fitz Thomas, of Newington, owes 28s. 4d. for having the fourth part of one knight's fee which has been seized into the hand of the king for default of relief.

John of Venetia renders an account of 300 marks for the fine of his land and for the relief of the land which was his father's and he does homage to the king against all mortals.

Ralph, son and heir of Ralph of Sullega renders an account of £100 for his relief for the lands which were Ralph his father's which he held from the king *in capite.*

John de Balliol owes £150 for the relief of 30 knights' fees which Hugh de Balliol his father held from the king *in capite,* that is 100s. for each fee.

Peter de Bruce renders an account of £100 for his relief for the barony which was of Peter his father.

Aid granted to the king (Henry III) for the knighting of eldest son, that is to say from each fee 40s. The sheriff (of Hereford) renders account of 40s. from John de Balun for one fee, and of £30 from John de Munemul for fifteen fees; the bishop of Hereford renders account of £30 for fifteen fees.

The earl of Clare renders account of £94, 11s. 10d. for the aid for the daughter of the king, for 131 knights and two-thirds of a knight, and a third and a fourth and an eighth and a ninth and a tenth of a knight, and two-thirtieths of a knight of his fee; and for nine knights and the fourth part of a knight of the fee of the countess, his wife.

The abbot of St. Edmund's renders account of 40 marks for the same aid for 40 knights whom he acknowledges he owes to the king.

Of the scutage of knights for the ransom of the lord king. Constance, countess of Brittany, renders account of 140 knights whom Thomas of Borough, steward of the same countess acknowledges before the barons to pertain to the honor of the count of Brittany in England.

13. *Military Service*

a. An Early Feudal Summons (c.1072)

The translations in this section are as above, pp. 28, 30, 31.

W. KING of the English to Aethelwig, abbot of Evesham, greeting. I command you to summon all those who are under your charge and jurisdiction to have armed before me by the week after Whitsunday at Clarendon all the knights which are due to me. And do you also come to me on that day and bring with you armed those five knights which you owe to me from your abbey. Witness, Eudo, the steward, at Winchester.

b. Grant of a Fief (1100)

Abbot Faritius also granted to Robert, son of William Mauduit, the land of four hides in Weston which his father had held from the former's predecessor, to be held as a fief. And he should do this service from it, to wit: that whenever the church of Abingdon should perform its knight's service he should do the service of half a knight for the same church; that is to say in castle ward, in military service beyond and on this side of the sea, and in giving money in proportion to the knights on the capture of the king, and in the rest of the services which other knights of the church perform. He also does homage to the abbot. This land previously did the service of three weeks yearly only.

c. Etablissements de St. Louis (1270)

The barons and all vassals of the king are bound to appear before him when he shall summon them, and to serve him at their own expense for forty days and forty nights, with as many knights as each one owes; and he is able to exact from them these services when he wishes and when he has need of them. And if the king wishes to keep them more than forty days at their own expense, they are not bound to remain if they do not wish it. And if the king wishes to keep them at his expense for the defense of the realm, they are bound to remain. And if the king wishes to lead them outside of the kingdom, they need not go unless they wish to, for they have already served their forty days and forty nights.

d. Military Tenants Summoned to the Royal Army

In the year 1272 the bishop of Paris came to Tours at the citation of the lord king and presented himself in the king's house on the second Sunday after Easter, before Ferrario de Verneuil, knight, Marshall of France, saying that he had come at the citation of the lord king prepared to fulfill his duty; who replied to him that he should come again or send at the first hour of the next day, because in the meanwhile he could not speak or respond to him, since Gregory of St. Martin of Tours was absent, on account of his weakness, and because, moreover, he was expecting new instructions from the king. On the next day and on Tuesday the aforesaid bishop presented himself before the said marshall, saying that he had come ready for the service of the king with three knights, whose names were John de Marchiaco, John de Juliaco and Adam de Blesum. He said that if he was held to send more he was ready to do what he ought; and if he had furnished more than he owed, that this should not bind either him or the church of Paris for the future.

The bishop of Troyes appeared for his see, saying that he owed two knights, whose names were Ralph and Droco de Pratellis.

John de Rouvraye, knight, lord of Yneto, appeared for himself acknowledging that he owed one knight by reason of his land of Rouvraye, whom he brought with him, that is to say John de Caim.

Reginald Trihan, knight, appeared for himself and goes.

Henry d'Eauville did not appear, but he sent for himself knight, William de Petra.

William Bacon, knight, appeared for Geoffrey de Foret, who owes military service for forty days; he goes to the army.

William de Coyneres, knight, sends for himself Thomas Chocquet, for ten days.

Thomas de Cugry, esquire, appeared saying that he owes four days; he sent instead of himself Richard de St. Germain, who will complete these four days after his own service.

Nicholas Bourdet, esquire, appeared for himself, and goes to the army; and he will be a knight there, or will provide another knight.

John de Chanteleu, knight, appeared saying that he owed ten days for himself, and that he also appeared for Godardus de Godardville, knight, who owes forty days.

Robert de Morville, knight, appeared for himself, owing military service for twenty days for half a fee.

The count of Soissons appeared and went to the army with three other knights whom he acknowledges he owes to the king, and led with him six knights besides his service.

Hugh de Conflans, knight, marshal of Champagne, appeared for the king of Navarre and led with him sixty knights for service owed to the king.

John Doré, knight, appeared for the lady of Chapelle, on account of her land of Berry which owes military service; and he goes in place of her.

William de Chantelon, knight, appeared for himself saying that he owed military service to the lord king for thirty days, for three-quarters of a knight's fee.

14. *Feudal Justice*

a. English Customs of the Eleventh Century

The translations in this section are as above.

TO EVERY lord it is allowed to summon his man that he may be at right to him in his court; and even if he is resident at the most distant manor of that honor from which he holds, he shall go to the plea if his lord summons him. If his lord holds different fiefs the man of one honor is not compelled by law to go to another plea, unless the cause belongs to the other to which his lord has summoned him.

If a man holds from several lords and honors, however much he holds from others, he owes most and will be subject for justice to him to whom he is the liege man.

Every vassal owes to his lord fidelity concerning his life and members and earthly honor and keeping of his counsel in what is honorable and useful saving the faith of God and of the prince of the land. Theft, however, and treason and murder and whatever things are against the Lord and the catholic faith are to be required or performed by no one; but faith shall be held to all lords, saving the faith of the earlier, and the more to the one of which he is the liege. And let permission be given him, if any of his men seek another lord for himself.

b. Etablissements de St. Louis

If a baron is summoned to the court of the king for any question of an inheritance and shall say, "I am not willing to be judged in this matter except by my peers" then at least three others ought to be summoned, and the king's justice shall try the suit along with these and other nobles.

c. Condemnation by a Feudal Court

Raymond by the grace of God count of Toulouse, marquis of Provence, to the nobleman Arnold Atton, viscount of Lomagne, greeting.

Let it be known to your nobility, by the tenor of these presents what has been done in the matter of the complaints which we have made about you before the court of Agen; that you have not taken the trouble to keep or fulfil the agreements sworn by you to us, as is more fully contained in the instrument drawn up there, sealed with our seal by the public notary; and that you have refused contemptuously to appear before the said court for the purpose of doing justice; and otherwise committed multiplied and great delinquencies against us. As your faults have required, the aforesaid court of Agen has unanimously and concordantly pronounced sentence against you, and for these matters has condemned you to hand over and restore to us the chateau of Auvillars and all that land which you hold from us in fee, to be had and held by us by right of the obligation by which you have bound it to us for fulfilling and keeping the said agreements.

Likewise it has declared that we are to be put into possession of the said land and that it is to be handed over to us, on account of your contumacy, because you have not been willing to appear before the same court on the days which were assigned to you. Moreover, it has been declared that you shall be held and required to restore the said land in whatsoever way we wish to receive it, with few or many, in peace or anger, in our own person, by right of lordship. Likewise it has declared that you shall restore to us all the expenses which we have incurred or the court itself has incurred on those days which were assigned to you or because of those days, and has condemned you to repay these to us.

Moreover, it has declared that the nobleman Gerald d'Armagnac, whom you hold captive, you shall liberate, and deliver him free to us. We will, moreover, by right of our lordship that you liberate him.

We call, therefore, upon your discretion in this matter, strictly requiring you and commanding that you obey the aforesaid sentence in all things and fulfil them in all respects and in no way defer the fulfillment of them. For making the announcement, the demand and the reception of these things, we have appointed as our representatives our beloved and faithful noblemen Gaston de Gontaud and R. Bernard de Balencs, promising that whatever shall be done by them in the aforesaid matters, we will hold as settled and firm forever. In testimony of which we have caused these present letters to be corroborated by the strength of our seal. Similar letters, divided through the alphabet, for a perpetual memory of this matter we have cause to be retained with us. Given at Agen, the third of the Kalends of July, A.D. 1249.

15. *Polyptyque de l'abbé Irminon*

This is an excerpt from the most famous of the early French manorial documents, a ninth century survey of the estates of the great abbey of St. Germain near Paris.

The translation is by the author from the edition of B. Guérard, Vol. II (1844), pp. 6 ff.

IN PALAISEAU there is a demesne manse with a house and other sufficient buildings. There are six fields of arable land containing 287 *bunuaria* (992.65 acres) where 1300 *modios* (about 2250 bushels) of wheat can be sown. There are 127 *aripennos* (127 acres) of vine which provide 800 *modios* (11,088 gallons) of wine.

It has 100 *aripennos* (100 acres) of meadow which provides 150 cartloads of hay.

The woodland measures as a whole one league in circumference and can fatten 50 pigs.

It has three mills which pay a rent of 153 *modios* (about 2580 bushels).

It has a church, carefully-constructed and completely furnished. Pertaining to it are 17 *bunuaria* (about 58 acres) of arable land and 5½ *aripennos* (henceforth acres) of vine and 3 acres of meadow. However, it has a free manse (*mansum ingenuilem*) consisting of 4 *bunuaria* (13.8 acres) of arable land and 1½ acres of vine and 3 acres of meadow. There are 6 tenants who each have a *jornalem* (?) of arable land and who owe for that a day's work a week, a hen and 5 eggs.

It also has a church in Gito held by the priest Warodus. Seven tenants belong to it. They work one day a week with food and owe one hen, 5 eggs and 3 *denarios.* It also demands, in gift, one horse.

Walafredus, a *colonus* and mayor, and his wife, a *colona* . . . , dependents (*homines*) of St. Germain; they have 2 children. . . . He holds 2 free manses having 7 *bunuaria* (about 24 acres) of arable land, 6 acres of vine and 4 of meadow. He owes for each manse a cow one year, a pig the next, 4 *denarios* for the right to use the wood, 2 *modios* of wine (almost 28 gallons) for the right to use the pasture, a ewe and a lamb. He plows 4 perches (⅓ of an acre?) for winter wheat, 2 perches for spring wheat. He owes *corvées,* cartage, manual labor, tree-felling when ordered, 3 hens and 15 eggs.

Hairmundus, a *colonus,* and his wife, a *colona* . . . , dependents of St. Germain; they have 5 children. He holds one free manse having 10 *bunuaria* (33½ acres) of arable land, 2 acres of vine and 1½ acres of meadow. He owes the same (as Walafredus).

Turpius, a *colonus* of St. Germain; he has 3 children. Regenulfus, a *colonus,* and his wife, a *colona,* dependents of St. Germain; they have one child. . . . These two hold a free manse having 4 *bunuaria* (13.8 acres) of arable land, 2 acres of vine and 2 of meadow. They owe the same.

◆ ◆ ◆

Aclemandus, a *colonus,* and his wife, a *colona,* dependents of St. Germain; they have 6 children. Ermenricus, *colonus* of St. Germain; Amicus, *colonus* of St. Germain; Ratboldus, a *colonus,* and his wife, a *colona,* . . . dependents of St. Germain; they have 6 children. Wineboldus, a *colonus,* and his wife, a *colona* . . . , dependents of St. Germain; they have 4 children. . . . These 5 hold one free manse, having 8 *bunuaria* (27½ acres) of arable land, 3 acres of vine and 2 of meadow. They owe the same. . . .

Ebrulfus, a *colonus,* and his wife, a slave, . . . dependents of St. Germain; they have 4 children. Ermenoldus, a slave, and his wife, a *colona,* . . . dependents of St. Germain; they have 4 children. . . . Teutgardis, slave of St. Germain; she has one child. . . . These three hold a free manse having 4 *bunuaria* and one *antsingam*(?) of arable land, 4 acres of vine and 2 of meadow. They work 8 acres (of the lord's) vine. They owe 2 *modios* (almost 28 gallons) of wine for right of pasture and 2 *sestarios* (1½ gallons?) of mustard.

Berneharius, a *colonus,* and his wife, a *colona,* . . . . dependents of St. Germain; they have 5 children. He holds half a manse having 4 *bunuaria* (13.8 acres) of arable land and 1½ acres of vine. He owes for half a manse.

Maurus, a slave, and his wife, a freedwoman, . . . dependents of St. Germain; they have 2 children. . . . Guntoldus, a *colonus* of St. Germain. These two hold one servile manse, having 2 *bunuaria* (about 7 acres) of arable land, 2½ acres of vine and 1½ of meadow. They work 8 acres (of the lord's) vine and owe 4 *modios* (about 55½ gallons) of wine for right of pasture; 2 *sestarios* (1½ gallons?) of mustard, three hens and 15 eggs; also manual labor, corvees and cartage.

Leodardus, freedman of St. Germain, holds a quarter of a manse, having 2 *bunuaria* (about 7 acres) of arable land and ½ acre of vine. He works 4 acres (of the lord's) vine. He owes 1 *modius* (almost 14 gallons) of wine for right of pasture, one *sestarios* (¾ gallon?) of mustard, one hen and five eggs.

Nadalfredus, a slave, and his wife, a *colona,* . . . dependents of St. Germain; they have 3 children. . . . Electulfs, a slave, and his wife, a *colona,* dependents of St. Germain; they have 3 children. . . . Todoinus, a slave, and his wife, a *colona,* . . . dependents of St. Germain. These three hold one servile manse having 1 *bunuaria* (about 2⅓ acres) of arable land, 1 acre of vine and ½ acre of meadow. They work 8 acres (of the lord's) vine. They owe 3 *modios* (41½ gallons) of wine for right of pasture and 3 *sestarios* (about 2 gallons) of mustard.

16. *Extent of the Manor of Bernehorne*

Bernehorne was a Sussex manor of Battle Abbey. This document is extracted from a survey made in 1307.

The translation is from *Pennsylvania Translations and Reprints, Series,* Vol. III, no. 5, pp. 8–13.

EXTENT of the manor of Bernehorne, made in Wednesday next after the feast of St. Gregory the Pope, in the thirty-fifth year of the reign of King Edward, in the presence of Brother Thomas, keeper of Marley, John de la More, and Adam de Thruhlegh, clerks, on the oath of William de Gocecoumbe, Walter le Parker, Richard le Knyst, Richard the son of the latter, Andrew of Estone, Stephen Morsprich, Thomas Brembel, William de Swynham, John Pollard, Roger le Glide, John Syward and John de Lillingewist, who say etc., that there are there all the following things:

The jurors say that the principal messuage and its garden with the herbage and curtilage are worth yearly 6s. 8d.; and the dovecote is worth yearly 5s.; and the windmill is worth yearly 20s.

And there are there 12 acres of thick undergrowth whence the pannage and herbage are worth yearly 2s.

And there are there 42 acres of maritime land (salt marsh?) in a certain place called Scotsmarsh, each acre of which is worth yearly 12d., the sum being 42s.

And there are there 7 acres and 1 rood of maritime land in a certain place called Aldithewisse; and 47 acres and 3 roods of maritime land in a certain place called Flittermarsh, each acre of which is worth yearly 12d. the sum being 55s.

And there are there 22 acres of maritime land in two places called Pundfold and Longrech; and 7 acres of maritime land in a certain place called Wyssh, and 8 acres and 3 roods of maritime land in a certain place called Upcroft marsh, and 3 acres and a half of maritime land in a certain place called Redewysshe; and each acre is worth yearly 12d.: the sum being 41s. 3d.

And there are there 19 acres, 1 rood of maritime land in a certain place called Berghamsmarsh, and 7 acres in a certain place called Pammarsh, and 3 acres and 1 rood of maritime land beyond the wall of Flittermarsh and Longreche; and each acre is worth yearly 12d.: the sum being 28s. 6d.

And there are 15 acres of marshy land in a certain place called Swyhamme and 66 acres of marshy land in a certain place called Hoobrokes, each acre of which is worth now 4d. a year; and the foresaid marshy lands, if they should be properly drained will be worth 10d. per acre yearly; the sum being 4£ 4s. 2d.

And there are there 18 acres of waste land in the fields called Welleland and Hammes, and 21 acres of land in the fields called Panden and Panylond, each acre of which is worth yearly 6d.: the sum being 19s. 6d.

And there are 24½ acres in the field of Berghamme, and each acre is worth yearly 6d.: the sum being 12s. 3d.

And there are there 34 acres of land in a certain place called Swynhamme, and 56 acres of land in a certain field called Hoolonde, of which each acre is worth yearly 3d. and the sum is 22s. 6d.

And there are there 30½ acres of land in the fields called Eldeton and Furneyslland, and 12 acres of land in the fields called Pleme and Schebbecroft and Robertsmarsh, and each acre is worth yearly 3d.; the sum being 10s. 7½d.

And there are there 6 acres and 1 rood of meadow in a certain place called Hoolonde, and 6 acres of meadow in a certain place called Robertsmarsh, and 1 acre of meadow near Robertswood, otherwise called Rokeswood, each acre of which is worth 18d. a year; and the sum is 19s. 10½d.

The total of the acres of woods is 12 acres.

The total of the acres of arable land is 444 acres and 3 roods, of which 147 acres 4 roods are maritime land, 101 acres marshy land, and 180 acres waste ground.

The total of the acres of meadow is 13 acres 1 rood.

The total of the whole preceding extent 18£. 10s. 4d.

John Pollard holds a half acre in Aldithewisse and owes 18d. at four terms, and owes from it relief and heriot.

John Suthinton holds a house and 40 acres of land and owes 3s. 6d. at Easter and Michaelmas.

William of Swynhamme holds 1 acre of land in Pinden and owes 3s. at Easter and Michaelmas, and attendance at the court in the manor every three weeks, relief and heriot.

Richard Knyst of Swynhamme holds 2 acres and a half of land and owes yearly 4s.

William at Knelle holds 2 acres of land in Aldithewisse and owes yearly 4s.

Roger le Glede holds a cottage and 3 roods of land and owes 2s. 6d. at Easter and Michaelmas.

Alexander Hamound holds a little piece of land near Aldewisse and owes 1 goose, of the value of 2d.

The sum of the whole rent of the free tenants, with the value of the goose, is 18s. 9d.

They say moreover that John of Cayworth holds a house and 30 acres of land, and owes yearly 2s. at Easter and Michaelmas; and he owes a cock and two hens at Christmas, of the value of 4d.

And he ought to harrow for 2 days at the Lenten sowing with one man and his own horse and his own harrow, the value of the work being 4d.; and he is to receive from the lord on each day 3 meals, of the value of 5d., and then the lord will be at a loss of 1d. Thus his harrowing is of no value to the service of the lord.

And he ought to carry the manure of the lord for 2 days with one cart, with his own 2 oxen, the value of the work being 8d.: and he is to receive from the lord each 3 meals of the price as above. And thus the service is worth 3d. clear.

And he shall find one man for 2 days for mowing the meadow of the lord, who can mow, by estimation, 1 acre and a half, the value of the mowing of an acre being 6d.: the sum is therefore 9d. and he is to receive each day 3 meals of the value given above; and thus that mowing is worth 4d. clear.

And he ought to gather and carry that same hay which he has cut, the price of the work being 3d.

And he shall have from the lord 2 meals for 1 man, of the value of 1½d. Thus the work will be worth 1½d. clear.

And he ought to carry the hay of the lord for 1 day with a cart and 3 animals of his own, the price of the work being 6d. And he shall have from the lord 3 meals of the value of 2½d. And thus the work is worth 3½d. clear.

And he ought to carry in autumn beans or oats for 2 days with a cart and 3 animals of his own, the value of the work being 12d. And he shall receive from the lord each day 3 meals of the value given above: and thus the work is worth 7d. clear.

And he ought to carry wood from the woods of the lord as far as the manor for two days in summer with a cart and three animals of his own, the value of the work being 9d. And he shall receive from the lord each day 3 meals of the price given above, and thus the work is worth 4d. clear.

And he ought to carry the heath which he has cut, the value of the work being 4d. and he shall have three meals each day of the value given above; and thus the lord will lose, if he receives the service, 3d. Thus that mowing is worth nothing to the service of the lord.

And he ought to carry the heath which he has cut, the value of the work being 5d. And he shall receive from the lord 3 meals at the price of 2½d. And thus the work will be worth 2½d. clear.

And he ought to carry to Battle twice in the summer season, each time half a load of grain, the value of the service being 4d. And he shall receive in the manor each time 1 meal of the value of 2d. And thus the work is worth 2d. clear.

The total of the rents, with the value of the hens, is 2s. 4d.

The total of the value of the works is 2s. 3½d.; owed from the said John yearly.

William of Cayworth holds a house and 30 acres of land and owes at Easter and Michaelmas 2s. rent. And he shall do all customs just as the foresaid John of Cayworth.

William atte Grene holds a house and 30 acres of land and owes in all things just as the said John.

Alan atte Felde holds a house and 16 acres of land (for which the sergeant pays to the court of Bixley 2s.), and he owes at Easter and Michaelmas 4s., attendance at the manor court, relief and heriot.

John Lyllingwyst holds a house and 4 acres of land and owes at the two terms 2s., attendance at the manor court, relief and heriot.

The same John holds one acre of land in the fields of Hoo and owes at the two periods 2s., attendance, relief and heriot.

Reginald atte Denne holds a house and 18 acres of land and owes at the said periods 18d., attendance, relief and heriot.

Robert of Northehou holds 3 acres of land at Saltcote and owes at the said period attendance, relief and heriot.

Total of all the works of these three villeins, 6s. 10½d.

And it is to be noted that none of the above named villeins can give their daughters in marriage nor cause their sons to be tonsured, nor can they cut down timber growing on the lands they hold, without license of the bailiff or sergeant of the lord, and then for building purposes and not otherwise. And after the death of any one of the foresaid villein the lord shall have as a heriot his best animal, if he had any; if however he have no living beast the lord shall have no heriot, as they say. The sons or daughters of the foresaid villeins shall give for entrance into the holding after the death of their predecessors as much as they give of rent per year.

Silvester the priest holds 1 acre of meadow adjacent to his house, and owes yearly 3s.

Total of the rents of tenants for life, 3s.

Petronilla atte Holme holds a cottage and a piece of land and owes at Easter and Michaelmas . . . ; attendance, relief, and heriot.

Walter Herying holds a cottage and a piece of land and owes at Easter and Michaelmas 18d., attendance, relief, and heriot.

Isabella Mariner holds a cottage and owes at the feast of St. Michael 12d., attendance, relief and heriot.

Jordan atte Melle holds a cottage and 1 acre of land and half and owes at Easter and Michaelmas 2s., attendance, relief, and heriot.

William of Batelesmere holds 1 acre of land with a cottage and owes at the feast of St. Michael 3d., and 1 cock and 1 hen at Christmas, of the value of 3d., attendance, relief, and heriot.

John le Man holds half an acre of land with a cottage, and owes at the feast of St. Michael 2s., attendance, relief, and heriot.

John Werthe holds 1 rood of land with a cottage and owes at the said term 18d., attendance, relief, and heriot.

Geoffrey Caumbreis holds half an acre and a cottage and owes at the said term 18d., attendance, relief, heriot.

The same man holds 3½ acres of land and owes yearly at the feast of St. Michael 3s. for all.

Roger Doget holds half an acre of land and a cottage which were those of R. the miller, and owes at the feast of St. Michael 18d., attendance, relief, and heriot.

Thomas le Brod holds 1 acre and a cottage and owes at the said term 18d., attendance, relief, and heriot.

Agnes of Cayworth holds a half acre and a cottage and owes at the said term 18d., attendance, relief, and heriot.

Agnes of Badlesmere holds 1 acre of land and a cottage and owes at the said term 3s., attendance, relief, and heriot.

William atte Whaunne holds one acre of land and owes at Easter and Michaelmas 2s., and relief.

Total of the rents of the said cottagers, with the value of the hens, 34s. 6d.

And it is to be noted that all the said cottagers shall do as regards giving their daughters in marriage, having their sons tonsured, cutting down timber, paying heriot, and giving fines for entrance just as John of Cayworth and the rest of the villeins formerly mentioned.

Note, fines and penalties, with heriots and reliefs are worth yearly 5s.

Chapter Six

The Investiture Controversy

BEFORE we examine the issues connected with the Investiture Controversy we must deal with two matters which form a part of their essential background: the relations between church and state prior to the eleventh century, and the Cluniac reform movement.

The salient fact about the relations between church and state prior to the eleventh century was that their spheres of jurisdiction had become hopelessly confused. There were two reasons. One was a purely practical one, the absorption by the church of secular duties. Even under the Roman Empire, Christian bishops performed governmental functions. With the withering away of Roman civil authority in the West they took on many more, notably the governing of towns. Finally, from the ninth century or so, the church became inextricably bound up with feudalism.

The other reason for the confusion of church and state was a theoretical and much more complicated one. The starting point was St. Augustine. Although his *City of God* was not primarily a work of political theory, the nature of it obliged him to examine the relation of the Christian to earthly political authority. For Augustine, the state was the result of sin; man prior to the fall did not need government. Afterwards, as the result of his innate moral defect, he could not get along peacefully with his fellows, hence the necessary disciplinary authority of the state. To this extent the state has its source in God. However, a true state (*res publica* = commonwealth) must be a just one and it cannot be just unless it is Christian. The latter qualification put the state in a humbler position than it enjoyed in classical political theory besides leaving a door wide open for future developments.

Only two generations after Augustine's death the famous letter of Pope Gelasius showed how his ideas had been developed into a fully formed concept of a Christian Commonwealth. "There are," wrote Gelasius, "two powers by which this world is chiefly ruled: the sacred authority of the Popes and the royal power." Now this statement did two things. It dissolved, for all practical purposes, the classical idea of the state with its single source of sovereignty (Gelasius' terminology technically maintained it since in Roman law "authority" was the source of sovereignty while "power" was the delegated exercise of it; the distinction did not survive very far into the Middle Ages). Further, in saying this, Gelasius gave the priestly power (*sacerdotium*) a status it had never enjoyed before. It would never have occurred to Augustine, for example, to say that the church ruled anything; for him the church was a spiritual communion of souls rather than an administrative hierarchy. Thus subsequent to Gelasius the idea of the state in the West disappeared, although the idea of the state as a *res publica* remained in the Carolingian period. We speak henceforth of a Christian Commonwealth composed of two powers, the *sacerdotium* and *regnum*.

The confusion between *sacerdotium* and *regnum* was also working in another direction. Although an institution of great antiquity in the East, the sacral anointing of kings first appeared in the West between the sixth and eighth centuries. Presumably its introduction was connected with the accession of a powerful but technically illegitimate ruler who sought legitimacy through supernatural sanction. Such at least was the case with the first fully known example, the anointing of the Frankish king Pepin I in 751.

Ecclesiastical consecrations of kings cut both ways. Since the act was sacramental in character, similar to the consecration of a priest, it transformed the king from a layman into a quasi-priest, *rex et sacerdos* in the fully developed phrase of the tenth century. As "the Lord's Anointed," the king received a strong claim for the allegiance of his subjects. At the same time he was given a justification for a control of the church which, if not very important at the time since few questioned it, would be useful later, when many would. On the other hand, if the *regnum* gained from sacral anointing, so did the *sacerdotium*. It was essential to the sacrament; was it therefore the source of royal authority? and could it refuse its sanction on the ground that the candidate was not worthy?

Two more matters will round out the theoretical background of the Investiture Controversy. One is both theoretical and historical—the creation of the Frankish Empire under Charlemagne. The nature of that Empire has been a much disputed subject in our own day nor was there any consistent view of it in its own. The actual relations between *sacerdotium* and *regnum* under Charlemagne have never been in dispute, however. He was protector and arbiter of the church; nothing concerning it, even doctrinal matters, was beyond his authority. This was borne out by his actions and given explicit statement in a letter he wrote to Pope Leo III. "It is our part with the help of divine holiness to defend by armed strength the holy Church of Christ everywhere from the onslaught of pagans and the ravages of infidels, and to strengthen within it the knowledge of the Catholic faith. It is your part, most Holy Father, to help our armies with your hands uplifted to God like Moses. . . ."

Within a few years of Charlemagne's letter to Pope Leo (written in 796) other documentary evidence showed that quite different ideas were being entertained in papal circles. The coronation of Charlemagne on Christmas Day, 800, whatever it meant to Charlemagne and his advisers, did express the papal belief that popes could confer the Empire. We may say this with confidence because of the famous document printed below known as the *Donation of Constantine*. It was forged in the papal chancery within a half century either way of the coronation and is obviously connected with it. Neither forgery nor coronation were important at the time except insofar as they indicated the willingness of some churchmen to reverse the existing relations between *sacerdotium* and *regnum*. Under different and future circumstances both would become potent weapons in the papal arsenal.

With the dissolution of the Carolingian Empire and the resulting fragmentation of society, the rival claims of the papacy and the Frankish emperor to hegemony within the Christian Commonwealth lost all substance. On the local level the *regnum* continued to dominate the *sacerdotium*, or it might be better to say they became so intermingled that they were scarcely distinguishable. Partly due to this, the spiritual vitality of western Christendom on every level was very low in the ninth and tenth centuries. The first signs of a revival which would become general in the eleventh century were first visible in a remarkable monastic reform movement which began at Cluny early in the tenth.

The monastery of Cluny was founded in 909 or 910 by William the Pious, Duke of Aquitaine. From the beginning it set a high standard of monastic observance. Because of this and a succession of long-lived and able abbots, Cluniac influence spread rapidly until under St. Odilo (c.942–1048) and St. Hugh (1024–1109) it became an international religious force, numbering at least sixty-five houses under its own observance and by its example raising the general level of Benedictine monasticism.

In the monastic reform movement inspired by Cluny we see the most striking characteristic of the religious life of the eleventh century: and how far western monasticism had developed from the original Benedictine Rule. One notable difference was the increased emphasis on the choir office. The simple psalmody and chant of early monasticism became an elaborate liturgy of Hours, Masses, ceremonials, and prayers. Manual labor, so important to St. Benedict, virtually disappeared as a normal monastic occupation, being replaced by the intellectual labor of reading, writing, and the copying or illumination of manuscripts. Most important, however, was a changed relation of the monastery to the world.

The monastery was now an integral part of the social community. In fact, until the middle of the twelfth century the cloister was the real center of medieval Christendom. It is well known that it was the center of learning and piety. But it was also the center of much more. To quote Friedrich Heer: "It was in the shelter of the monasteries that folk art was preserved and cherished, in the Romanesque animal symbolism which harks back to the period of the migrations and older centuries still, or in the recording of folk ballads and poetry. The monks lived in the midst of the people and shared their joys and sorrows; it was to the monasteries that peasants fled for refuge, to escape the pangs of hunger and the feuds of their aristocratic overlords." It was also the monastery which was at the center of popular religious life. Medieval people were convinced they could not live in the world and still be good Christians—Heer rightly calls this the most deeply held belief of medieval Christendom. Notice the words of William of Aquitaine in his foundation charter for Cluny. "If I cannot myself despise the things of this world, at least by sustaining those who despise the world, those whom I believe to be righteous in the eyes of God, I may myself receive the reward of the righteous." So the monk in his cloister lived the perfect Christian life, vicariously, for those around him. Everyone, therefore, had a vested interest in monasticism. Here is the explanation for the foundation and enrichment of monasteries by laymen, and their interest in monastic reform. This in turn explains the elaborate round of ceremonials carried out in them for their dead benefactors. The importance of liturgies for the dead is another important contrast between original and later Benedictine monasticism.

By the middle of the twelfth century the monastery had ceased to be at the center of medieval Christendom in the old way. Intellectually, it was replaced by the cathedral school and the university;

spiritually by a revitalized secular hierarchy headed by the papacy. For the latter change, the Investiture Controversy is responsible.

The basic ideas behind the Investiture Controversy appeared quite suddenly in the writings of Cardinal Humbert of Silva Candida (d. 1061) who, along with St. Peter Damian (1007–1072) and Hildebrand (the future Pope Gregory VII), was among the reform leaders in the papal curia. For Humbert the so-called Cluniac reform movement was not enough. Cluny had wanted to reform monastic morals in particular and clerical morals in general. Hence, as far as the latter was concerned, the issues were simony and clerical marriage. What Humbert sought was not reform but revolution. He would have drastically altered two things, the relation of the church to the world and its internal constitution. The one demanded complete ecclesiastical independence from lay control; the other the organization of the church into a strict hierarchy controlled by the papacy. In advocating this Humbert was challenging two views of Christian society; the monastic, based on the accumulation of merit by the individual and focused on the hereafter, and the monarchical, in which it was the duty of the king to lead church and people towards God.

Humbert saw the matter quite differently. His was what Tellenbach calls the sacramental conception of Christian society which "bases the worth of the individual on the nature of his service at the sacrament, that is, on the measure of Christ's presence within him, and sees the hierarchy as an institution with its face turned towards the world since its task was to raise the world to eternal life." It is clear from this that while the monastic and monarchical views of Christian society were quite compatible (witness the ardent championing of the monastic reform movement by secular rulers), the monarchical and sacramental conceptions of Christian society were hopelessly incompatible. For the *sacerdotium* to perform its function under the sacramental conception, it had to be independent of the *regnum;* for the *regnum* to perform its function under the monarchical conception it had to control the *sacerdotium.* This incompatibility is explicit in Humbert's work *Against the Simoniacs* (1055) in which he extends the definition of simony to include not only the buying and selling of spiritual offices but any time the free working of the Holy Spirit is interfered with, i.e., as in the case of lay investiture.

The concept of papal supremacy had more to do with Gregory VII than Humbert and more with practical situations than theory. The Bishop of Rome had always enjoyed a sentimental primacy in the West and at times a good deal of authority. Immediately prior to the Investiture Controversy, however, papal influence had sunk to its lowest point. Only just before mid-century did it revive, particularly during the pontificate of Leo IX (1048–1052) who used the papal primacy in quite a spectacular way in the interest of general clerical reform. One of the first indications that a new order of things was approaching was the papal decree of 1059, freeing the selection of the pope from the control of the German Emperor. Then, with the pontificate of Gregory VII (1073–85) came the full statement of papal claims for supremacy as well as an attempt to implement them.

Gregory's position rested on the Petrine theory, that as successor to St. Peter he was the direct representative of God on earth. As such he was custodian of the spirit of Christ, perpetually present in the sacraments, and of the purity of the faith. On this rested his dominance over the *sacerdotium*. As for the *regnum*, Gregory used St. Augustine and Gelasius to demonstrate its inferiority to the *sacerdotium* (cf. the letter to Hermann of Metz below). The power he claimed to interfere with the affairs of the *regnum* stemmed in part from the general superiority of priests, because of their care of souls, over laymen; particularly, he rested his case on historical precedent: St. Ambrose and Theodosius, the anointing of Pepin, and the coronation of Charlemagne.

Gregory's enemies accused him of being an innovator, which indeed he was. Even though he cited scripture and history to justify his position, the simple fact is that he was flying in the face of what had been the actual relations between *sacerdotium* and *regnum* for three centuries past. In company with a good deal of personal abuse, his opponents also attacked the fundamentals of the Gregorian conceptions of the sacramental hierarchy and the papal supremacy. All of the monarchical defenders emphasized the divine character of kingship as symbolized in sacral anointing. Some used an analogical argument, likening society to the human body with the *regnum* as the head and the lower parts subordinate to it. The most unique of the monarchical arguments strikes at the very root of the Gregorian position by equating the church of God with the body of believing Christians rather than with the priestly hierarchy, in effect denying the concept of the Christian Commonwealth while giving the *regnum* complete control of human society.

The Investiture Controversy, however, was not only or even primarily a clash of rival conceptions of the nature of the Christian

Commonwealth. It was also a four-way political struggle involving a secularized episcopate, the royal power, the feudal nobility, and the papacy. Here we see why it is misleading to call the Investiture Controversy a matter of church vs. state or even of *sacerdotium* vs. *regnum.* The secularized episcopate, not quite uniformly resentful of the growth of papal power and the consequent diminution of their own, was as often as not found in the royal camp. The feudal nobility of Germany and to some extent England, and the towns of northern Italy, were equally resentful of the growth of royal authority and hence were frequently supporters of the papacy.

Finally, we must recognize that the term Investiture Controversy, however imbedded in the historical vocabulary (and used here for that reason) describes only an episode (and the least important part of that episode) in a continuing struggle. The issue of lay investiture itself was one easily compromised. With the essentials of the Gregorian reform movement no compromise was possible.

1. *Letter of Pope Gelasius I (492-96)*

The following is an extract from one of the most famous medieval documents on the relationship between church and state. The occasion for the letter, written to the Byzantine Emperor Anastasius I in 494, was Anastasius' support of the schismatic attitude of the Patriarchs of Constantinople in regard to the Monophysite heresy.

The translation is by Sidney Z. Ehler and John Morrall, *Church and State Through the Centuries* (Westminster, Maryland: The Newman Press, 1959), pp. 10–11.

I BEG your Piety not to judge duty to Divine truth as arrogance. I hope that it will not have to be said of a Roman Emperor that he resented the truth being brought home to him. There are indeed, most august Emperor, two powers by which this world is chiefly ruled: the sacred authority of the Popes and the royal power. Of these the priestly power is much more important, because it has to render account for the kings of men themselves at the Divine tribunal. For you know, our very clement son, that although you have the chief place in dignity over the human race, yet you must submit yourself faithfully to those who have charge of Divine things, and look to them for the means of your salvation. You know that it behooves you, in matters concerning the reception and reverent administration of the Sacraments, to be obedient to the ecclesiastical authority rather than to control it. So in such matters you ought to depend on ecclesiastical judgment, instead of seeking to bend it to your own will. For if in matters pertaining to the administration of public discipline, the bishops of the Church, knowing that the Empire has been conferred on you by Divine instrumentality, are themselves obedient to your laws, lest in purely material matters contrary opinions may seem to be voiced, with what willingness, I ask you, should you obey those to whom is assigned the administration of Divine mysteries? So just as there is great danger for the Popes in not saying what is necessary in matters of the Divine honour, so there is no small peril for those who are obstinate in resistance (which God forbid) at the time when they ought to be obedient. And if the hearts of the faithful ought to be submitted to all priests in general, who administer holy things in a right manner, how much more ought assent to be given to him who presides over that See which the Supreme Godhead Itself desired to be pre-eminent over all priests, and which the pious judgment of the whole Church was honoured ever since?

2. *The Donation of Constantine*

This document purports to be an edict of Constantine conferring on Pope Sylvester I and his successors supremacy over the other four patriarchs and overlordship over the western portion of the Roman Empire. In fact it is a forgery produced in the papal chancery sometime between 750 and 850 although it was generally accepted as genuine throughout the Middle Ages.

The translation is from Ehler and Morrall, *Church and State Through the Centuries*, pp. 16–22.

IN THE name of the Holy and Undivided Trinity. The Emperor Caesar Flavius Constantinus in Christ Jesus (our Saviour and our God, a Member of the same Holy Trinity), the faithful, merciful, great, beneficent, conqueror of the Alamanni, Goths, Sarmatians, Germans, Britons and Huns, pious, fortunate, victor and conqueror, ever august: to the most holy and blessed Father of fathers, Sylvester, Bishop of the City of Rome and Pope, and to all his successors, the Pontiffs who shall occupy the See of the blessed Peter until the end of time; also to all the most reverend and God-loved Catholic bishops, subjected by this our Imperial enactment to the same most holy Roman Church throughout the whole world, to all who have been appointed now or who will be appointed at any future time; grace, peace, love, joy, long-suffering, and mercy from God the Father Almighty and Jesus Christ His Son and the Holy Spirit be with you all.

Our most merciful Serenity desires to bring to the knowledge of peoples throughout the whole world in a clear narrative, through the page of this our Imperial enactment, the things which the Saviour and Redeemer our Lord Jesus Christ, Son of the Most High Father, has deigned miraculously to work through His holy Apostles Peter and Paul by the intervention of our father Sylvester, Supreme Pontiff and universal Pope. But first we put forward with a sincere confession of the heart, for the instruction of your minds, our faith, which we learnt from the above-mentioned most blessed father, our confessor, Sylvester the Universal Pontiff, and then at last we announce the mercy of God which has been poured forth upon us.

[The document goes on to a lengthy statement of Christian belief and then resumes:]

Our Lord God Himself, having pity on me a sinner, sent His holy Apostles to visit us and shed the light of His splendour upon us. Therefore rejoice with me that I have been rescued from darkness and brought into the true light and knowledge of truth. For while a powerful and sordid leprosy has taken possession of all the flesh of my body, and after I had received the attention of many assembled physicians, obtaining no cure from any of them, the priests of the Capitol came here, telling me that I ought to make a bath in the Capitol and fill it with the blood of innocent children and that I could be cleansed by bathing in it when it was warm. According to their instructions many innocent children were assembled, but when the unholy pagan priests were about to slaughter them and fill the bath with their blood, our Serenity noticed the tears of their mothers and immediately was seized with horror at the outrage. Having mercy on them, I ordered their sons to be restored to them and sent them back to their own homes with transport provided and with presents.

At the end of that same day, when the silence of night had fallen upon us, when the time of sleep had come, the Apostles St. Peter and St. Paul appeared, saying to me: "Since you have put a stop to your crimes and have shunned the shedding of innocent blood, we have been sent by Christ our Lord God to give you advice on the recovery of your health. Hear our injunctions, therefore, and do whatever we tell you. Sylvester, Bishop of the City of Rome, has fled from your persecutions to Mount Serapte and has found an obscure hiding-place with his clergy in the caverns of the rocks. When you have summoned him to you, he will show you a holy pool, in which he will immerse you three times and then all the strength of the leprosy will leave you. When this has been done, make this recompense to your Saviour, that all the churches throughout the world may be restored by your order and that you purify yourself in this respect that, laying aside all vain worship of idols, you adore and worship the living and true God, who is alone true; in this way you will succeed in doing His Will."

Arising from sleep, I immediately carried out what I had been instructed to do by the holy Apostles. I summoned the excellent and beneficent father, or enlightener Sylvester, Universal Pope, and told him all the words imparted to me by the holy Apostles and I asked him who were these gods Peter and Paul. But he said they were not really to be called gods, but Apostles of our Saviour the Lord God Jesus Christ. And again we began to ask that same most blessed Pope, whether he had any accurate picture of those Apostles, so that we might learn from the picture that they were those whom revelation had shown to us. Then the venerable father commanded that the pictures of those Apostles should be shown by his deacon. When I looked at them I recognized the faces of those, whom I had seen in my dream, depicted in those pictures, and I confessed with a great cry in the presence of all my satraps that they were those which I had seen in my dream.

At this the most blessed Sylvester our father, Bishop of the City of Rome, placed upon us a period of penance within our Lateran palace in a hair shirt, so that we might beg pardon from our Lord God Jesus Christ by watching, fasting, tears and prayers for everything which has been wickedly performed and unjustly commanded by us. Then after the clergy had laid their hands on me I came to the Bishop himself. There, renouncing the pomps of Satan and his works and all idols made with hands, I freely acknowledged before all the people that I believed in God the Father, Almighty Creator of heaven and earth, of things visible and invisible, and in Jesus Christ His only Son, our Lord, who was born of the Holy Spirit and the Virgin Mary. Then, after the font had been blessed, the water of salvation purified me with a triple immersion. There, when I was placed in the depths of the font, I saw with my own eyes a hand from heaven touch me. Learn that when I rose from the font I was cleansed from all the filthiness of leprosy. And after I had been raised from the venerable font the Bishop put on white vestments and administered to me the sign of the sevenfold Holy Spirit, the unction of the Holy Oil and he traced the emblem of the Holy Cross on my brow, saying : "God seals you with the sign of His faith in the name of the Father and the Son and the Holy Spirit in recognition of your faith." All the clergy replied: "Amen." The Bishop added: "Peace be with you."

On the first day, then, after receiving the mystery of holy Baptism and after the cure of my body from the filth of leprosy I recognized that there was no other God except the Father and the Son and the Holy Spirit, whom the most blessed Pope Sylvester preaches, Trinity in Unity, Unity in Trinity. For all the gods of the heathen which up to now I have worshipped, have been proved to be demons, the hand-made work of men. That same venerable father told very plainly to us the great power in heaven and earth which our Saviour had committed to the blessed Apostle Peter when, finding him faithful under questioning, he said: "Thou art Peter and upon this rock I will build my Church and the gates of hell shall not prevail against it." Take note, O mighty sovereigns, and incline the attention of your heart to what the good Master and Lord gave in addition to His disciple when He said: "And I will give unto thee the keys of the kingdom of heaven; whatsoever thou shalt bind on earth shall be bound also in heaven and whatsoever thou shalt loose on earth shall be loosed also in heaven." It is a very wonderful and glorious thing to bind and loose on earth and to have that sentence of binding and loosing carried out in heaven.

While the blessed Sylvester was preaching these things I understood them and found that I was restored to full health by the beneficence of the same blessed Peter. So we, together with all our satraps and the whole Senate and all the nobles and the whole Roman people which is subject to the glory of our Empire, judged it in the public interest that, because St. Peter was made Vicar of the Son of God on earth, the Pontiffs also, who are the successors of the same Prince of the Apostles, may obtain from us and our Empire greater governmental power than the earthly clemency of our Imperial serenity has so far conceded to them; thus we chose the same Prince of the Apostles and his Vicar to be our powerful patrons with God. And because our Imperial power is earthly, we have decided to honour reverently his most holy Roman Church, and to exalt the most holy See of blessed Peter in glory above our own Empire and earthly throne, ascribing to it power and glorious majesty and strength and Imperial honour.

And we command and decree that he should have primacy over the four principal Sees of Antioch, Alexandria, Constantinople and Jerusalem, as well as over all the Churches of God throughout the whole world; and the Pontiff who occupies at any given moment the See of that same most holy Roman Church shall rank as the highest and chief among all the priests of the whole world and by his decision all things are to be arranged concerning the worship of God or the security of the faith of Christians. For it is just that the holy law should have its centre of government at the place where the institutor of the holy laws, our Saviour, commanded blessed Peter to set up the chair of his apostolate, where also, bearing the agony of the cross, he received the cup of a holy death and appeared as an imitator of his Master and Lord; there also it should be that the Gentiles should bow their necks in acknowledgement of the name of Christ where their teacher blessed Paul the Apostle stretched out his neck for Christ and was crowned with martyrdom; let them until the end seek their teacher there, where the holy body of that teacher rests; and there, where they proudly acted as slaves to the empire of an earthly king, let them, prostrate and humble, carry out the service of the King of Heaven, our God and Saviour Jesus Christ.

Meanwhile we wish all the people of every race and nation throughout the whole world to know that we have built from its foundations, together with a baptistery, a church consecrated to that same Saviour, our Lord Jesus Christ, within our Lateran palace, and you are to know that we have carried on our own shoulders twelve baskets heavy with soil from the foundations according to the number of the twelve Apostles; we decree that this most holy church is to be called, honoured, venerated and proclaimed as the head and summit of all the churches in the whole world, just as we have ordered by other Imperial decrees. We have built also the churches of blessed Peter and Paul, princes of the Apostles, and have enriched them with gold and silver; there also we have buried with great honour their most holy bodies and have made the coffins of amber, against which no elemental force may prevail. And we have placed on each of their coffins a cross of purest gold and adorned with precious stones and we have locked them with golden keys. We have bestowed on these churches the revenues of estates to provide lights, and have enriched them in various respects. And through our sacred Imperial orders we have conceded to them lands in the East as well as in the West and even on the northern and southern coasts, that is to say in Judaea, Greece, Asia, Thrace, Africa and Italy and the various islands under the condition that all shall be governed by the instrumentality of our most blessed father Sylvester the Pontiff and his successors.

Let every people and the nations of the Gentiles in all the world rejoice therefore with us; we exhort you all that you return thanks abundantly to our God and Saviour Jesus Christ, because He is God in Heaven above and on earth beneath, Who, visiting us through His holy Apostles made us worthy to receive the holy Sacrament of Baptism and bodily health. In recompense for this we concede to those same holy Apostles, my lords the most blessed Peter and Paul and through them also to blessed Sylvester our father, Supreme Pontiff and Universal Pope of the City of Rome, and to all his successors, the Pontiffs who will preside over the See of blessed Peter until the end of the world, and by this present document we confer, our Imperial palace of the Lateran, which surpasses and excels all palaces in the whole world, then a diadem which is the crown of our head, and at the same time the tiara; also the shoulder covering, that is the strap which is wont to surround our Imperial neck; also the purple cloak and the crimson tunic and all our Imperial garments. They shall also receive the rank of those who preside over the Imperial cavalry. We confer on them also the Imperial sceptres and at the same time the spears and standards, also the banners and various Imperial decorations and all the prerogatives of our supreme Imperial position and the glory of our authority.

We decree that those very reverend men, the clerics who serve the most holy Roman Church in various orders, shall have the same dignity, distinction, power and pre-eminence, by the glory of which our Senate is decorated; and we decree that the clergy of the most holy Roman Church shall be adorned as are the soldiers of the Empire; and just as the Imperial power receives dignity from various offices, chamberlains, doorkeepers and all the guards, so also we wish the holy Roman Church to be adorned; and so that the Pontifical dignity may shine forth more clearly, we decree this also, that the clerics of the same holy Roman Church shall decorate their horses with saddle-cloths of linen of the very whitest colour, and thus the horses are to be equipped for riding; and just as our Senate uses sandals with fur covering, so let the clerics be distinguished by their very white linen; then shall terrestrial as well as celestial things be adorned to God's glory. Above all, in addition, we grant to the same our most holy father Sylvester, Bishop of the City of Rome and Pope, and to all the most blessed Pontiffs who shall come after him in succession for ever, for the honour and glory of Christ our God, to add to the numbers in that same great Catholic and Apostolic Church of God any one from our court who shall wish of his own free choice to become a cleric, and to add any to the number of monastic clergy. Let no one presume to act arrogantly in all these matters.

So we have decreed this also, that our venerable father Sylvester, the Supreme Pontiff, and all his successors should use and wear upon their heads to the praise of God for the honour of blessed Peter a diadem, that is a crown of purest gold and precious gems, a crown which we have transferred from our own head; but the most holy Pope would by no means allow that golden crown to be worn above the crown of the priesthood, which he wears to the glory of the blessed Peter, so we placed upon his most holy head, with our own hands, a sparklingly bright tiara depicting the Lord's glorious Resurrection. And, holding the bridle of his horse, we performed the office of groom for him, decreeing that all the Pontiffs, his successors, might alone use that tiara in processions.

To correspond to our own Empire and so that the supreme Pontifical authority may not be dishonoured, but may rather be adorned with glorious power greater than the dignity of any earthly empire, behold, we give to the often-mentioned most holy Pontiff, our father Sylvester, the Universal Pope, not only the above-mentioned palace, but also the city of Rome and all the provinces, districts and cities of Italy and the Western regions, relinquishing them to the authority of himself and his successors as Pontiffs by a definite Imperial grant. We have decided that this should be laid down by this our divine, holy and lawfully framed decree and we grant it on a permanent legal basis to the holy Roman Church.

Therefore we have seen it to be fitting that our Empire and the power of the kingdom should be transferred and translated to the Eastern regions and that in the province of Byzantium in the most suitable place a city should be built in our name and our Empire established there; because it is not just that an earthly Emperor should exercise authority where the government of priests and the Head of the Christian religion have been installed by the heavenly Emperor.

We decree also that all the things which we have established and approved by this our holy Imperial edict and by other divine decrees shall remain uninjured and unbroken until the end of the world; so, in the presence of the living God, Who ordered us to reign, and in the presence of His terrible judgement, we solemnly warn, by this our Imperial enactment, all our successors as Emperors and all our nobles, the satraps, the most honourable Senate and all people throughout the world, now and in the future and in all times previously subject to our Empire, that none of them will be permitted in any way to oppose or destroy or to take away any of these privileges, which have been conceded by our Imperial decree to the most holy Roman Church and to its Pontiffs. But if anyone (which we do not believe) does show himself as bold or presumptuous in this matter, he shall be handed over to undergo eternal condemnation, and he shall feel the hostility of the Saints of God, the Princes of the Apostles, Peter and Paul, against him in this life and the next, and he shall perish with the devil and all the wicked by burning in the lowest hell.

We have confirmed the parchment of this Imperial decree with our own hands and have placed it over the venerable body of blessed Peter, the Prince of the Apostles, promising to that same Apostle of God that we will observe inviolably all things stated in it, and that we will hand down in our commands to our successors instructions to preserve it. We then handed it over to our most blessed father Sylvester, the Supreme Pontiff and Universal Pope, and through him to all the Pontiffs who succeed him, to be possessed in perpetuity and happiness, with the consent of our Lord God and Saviour Jesus Christ.

The Imperial signature follows: May the Godhead preserve you for many years, most holy and blessed fathers.

Given at Rome of the third day before the Kalends of April, when our lord Flavius Constantinus the Emperor (in his fourth term of office) and Galliganus, those most illustrious men, were consuls.

3. *Foundation Charter of the Abbey of Cluny*

Given at Bourges by Duke William IX of Aquitaine (September 11, 910), this foundation charter is quite typical in its motivation and details. The charter of Cluny was chosen for obvious reasons.

The translation is that of Joan Evans, *Monastic Life at Cluny* (London: Humphrey Milford for the Oxford University Press, 1931), pp. 4–6.

TO THOSE who consider things sanely it is evident that Divine Providence counsels the rich to use well those goods that they possess in transitory fashion, if they wish for eternal recompense. And Holy Writ shows this to be possible, for such counsel is manifest in the saying: "The ransom of a man's life is his riches." Wherefore I, William, by the grace of God count and duke, having pondered these things and wishing while there is yet time to make provision for my salvation, have found it right, yea necessary, to dispose for the good of my soul of some of the temporal possessions which have been bestowed upon me. For since I appear to have increased them much, I would not wish to deserve the reproach in the hour of death that I had used them only for the needs of my body, but would rather, when my last moment shall take them all from me, give myself the joy of having used a part for my soul: the which may not be better done than by following the precept of our Lord: "I will make myself friends among the poor." That this benefaction may endure not only for a time, but may last for ever, I will provide at my expense for men living together under monastic vows, with this faith and hope that if I cannot myself despise all the things of this world, at least by sustaining those who despise the world, those whom I believe to be righteous in the eyes of God, I may myself receive the reward of the righteous.

To all those who live in the unity of the faith and who implore the mercy of Christ, to all who shall succeed them and shall be living so long as the world endures, I make known that for the love of God and of our Saviour Christ Jesus I give and deliver to the Apostles Peter and Paul the village of Cluny, on the river Grosne, with its curtilage and its house, with the Chapel that is dedicated in honour of St. Mary Mother of God and of St. Peter, Prince of the Apostles, with all the property that depends thereon, cottages, chapels, serfs both men and women, vines, fields, meadows, forests, water and watercourses, mills, crops and revenues, land tilled and untilled, with no reservations. All these things are situate in the country of Mâcon or near it, each enclosed within its bounds. I, William, with my wife Ingelberge, give these things to the aforesaid Apostles, first for the love of God, then for the soul of my lord the King Eudes, for the souls of my father and mother, for me and my wife, that is for the salvation of our souls and bodies, for the soul of Ava my sister who left me these properties by will, for the souls of our brothers and sisters, our nephews and of all our kindred, men and women, for our faithful servants, and for the maintenance and integrity of the Catholic faith. Finally, since as Christians we are all bound together by the bonds of our faith and charity, may this gift be made also for the faithful of times past, present and to come.

I give on condition that a Regular Monastery be established at Cluny in honour of the apostles Peter and Paul; that monks shall form a congregation there living under the rule of St. Benedict; that they shall for ever possess, hold and order the property given in such wise that this honourable house shall be unceasingly full of vows and prayers, that men shall seek there with a lively desire and an inner fervour the sweetness of converse with Heaven, and that prayers and supplications shall be addressed thence without ceasing to God, both for me and for those persons commemorated above.

We ordain that our foundation shall serve forever as a refuge for those who having renounced the world as poor men bring nothing with them but their good will, and we desire that our superfluity shall become their abundance. May the monks and all the aforesaid possessions be under the power and dominion of Abbot Berno, who shall rule according to his knowledge and power so long as he shall live. After his death may the monks have the power and liberty to elect as abbot and ruler the monk of their order whom they shall prefer, according to the good pleasure of God and the rule laid down by St. Benedict, with no contradiction or impediment of this election by our power or that of any man. Nevertheless every five years they shall pay to Rome twelve pieces of gold for the upkeep of the candles of the Church of the Apostles. May they have as protectors the Apostles themselves, and for defender the Pontiff of Rome. Out of the fullness of their hearts and souls may they themselves build a monastery in this place, according to their knowledge and capacity. We also desire that in our time and in the time of our successors, as much at least as the circumstances of the time and the situation of the place admit, they may each day perform with fervent zeal works of mercy to the poor, to beggars, strangers and travellers.

It has pleased us to set forth in this testament that from this day forward the monks united in congregation of Cluny shall be wholly freed from our power, from that of our kindred, and from the jurisdiction of royal greatness, and shall never submit to the yoke of any earthly power. I beg and pray that no secular Prince, no Count, no Bishop, no Pontiff of the Roman Church, by God and through God and all his saints, under threat of the awful day of judgment, may ever invade the possessions of these servants of God. Let him not sell, nor diminish, nor exchange, nor take any things which is theirs; let him set up no ruler over them against their will. That this prohibition may bind the bold and evil with straiter bonds, once again I say it, and add: I conjure you, ye Holy Apostles and glorious Princes of the Earth, Peter and Paul; and thou, Pontiff of Pontiffs of the Apostolic See, do ye cut off from the communion of the Holy Catholic Church and from life eternal, by the canonical and apostolic authority received from God, those who steal, invade or sell these things which I give to you with eager wish and a joyful heart. Be ye the guardians and defenders of Cluny and of the servants of God who shall dwell there, and of their goods that are destined for the giving of alms, for the imitation of the loving-kindness and mercy of our most Holy Redeemer. . . .

4. *Decree of Pope Nicholas II*

This decree marked an important development in the relations of empire and papacy. It reserved the right of papal election to the Cardinal bishops of Rome, giving to the German King, and then only to Henry IV personally, a vague right of cooperation. It did not establish the College of Cardinals, which already existed, nor did it completely outline the procedures for papal elections which were subsequently elaborated by a decree of Alexander III in 1179. It did, however, declare the theoretical independence of the papacy, in this important sphere, from both the Roman aristocratic families and the Emperor.

The translation is from Ehler and Morrall, *Church and State Through the Centuries,* pp. 25–27.

IN THE name of the Lord God our Saviour Jesus Christ, in the year of His incarnation 1059, in the month of April, in the twelfth indiction, the Holy Gospel being placed before the assembly presided over by the most reverend and blessed Apostolic Pope Nicholas and attended by the most reverend archbishops, bishops, abbots, and venerable priests and deacons in the patriarchal basilica of Lateran, called the basilica of Constantine, the same venerable Pontiff, speaking with Apostolic authority, said this about the election of the Supreme Pontiff:

You know, most blessed and beloved brothers and fellow-bishops—nor has it been concealed from the lower members also—how much adversity this Apostolic See, in which by God's will I serve, endured since the death of the lord Stephen, our predecessor of blessed memory, to how many hammering blows and frequent wounds it was subjected by the traffickers in simoniacal heresy; it almost seemed as if the column of the living God was about to stagger and the net of the chief fisher to be submerged in the depths of shipwreck by the swelling blasts. Therefore, if it please you, Brethren, we should, with the help of God, wisely foresee future cases and provide for the constitution of the Church in future, lest—which God forbid—the same and revived evil may prevail. Consequently, strengthened by the authority of our predecessors and of other holy Fathers, we decide and decree:

That, when the Pontiff of the Universal Roman Church dies, the Cardinal-Bishops shall first take counsel together with most diligent consideration, thereupon call in to themselves the Cardinal-Clerics and then, in the same manner, the remaining clergy and people shall approach to express their consent to the new election.

That—to be sure that the disease of venality will have no opportunity to creep in—the churchmen shall have the leading part in effecting the election of the Pope, and the others shall only be followers. And certainly this order of the election will be found right and legitimate, if, after the rules and acts of the various Fathers have been considered, the dictum of our blessed predecessor Leo be also recalled: "No reason allows," he says, "that they who have neither been elected by clerics, nor desired by the people, nor consecrated by the bishops of their provinces with the approval of the Metropolitan should be accounted as bishops." But because the Apostolic See is raised above all Churches throughout the whole world and thus can have no Metropolitan above itself, the Cardinal-Bishops undoubtedly function in the place of the Metropolitan; that is to say, they raise their elected Pontiff to the summit of the Apostolic eminence.

Let them make their choice from the Roman Church itself, if a suitable person is to be found there; if not, a person from elsewhere may be elected.

Saving due honour and reverence for our beloved son Henry, who is at present called king and who, if God wills, is expected to be future Emperor; in so far as we have made such concessions to himself and his successors, who shall personally have obtained this right from this holy Apostolic See.

But if the perversity of corrupt and evil men shall so prevail, that an uncorrupted, genuine and free election may not be made in the City, the Cardinal-Bishops together with the clerics of the Church and Catholic laity, however few, may be legally empowered to elect a Pontiff to the Apostolic See wherever they shall judge to be more suitable.

After an election shall have been definitely made, if a warlike disturbance or the attempt of any man whatever who may be inspired by an evil disposition, shall not allow the person who has been elected to the Apostolic See to be enthroned according to custom, nevertheless the person elected shall, as Pope, obtain authority to rule the holy Roman Church and to dispose of all its prerogatives, as we know blessed Gregory did before his consecration.

But if anyone, contrary to this our statute promulgated by decision of the Synod, shall by discord or usurpation or any trickery whatsoever be elected, consecrated and enthroned, let him be held and accounted by all not as Pope but as Satan, not as an Apostle but as an apostate, and let him undergo, as Antichrist and the ravager and destroyer of all Christendom, separation by perpetual excommunication from the threshold of the holy Church of God together with his instigators, supporters and followers; nor shall any hearing be allowed him in this case, but he shall be deposed permanently from every ecclesiastical office, which he formerly held. Whosoever shall take his part or shall show him any reverence as Pontiff whatsoever or shall dare to defend him in any way, shall be penalized with the same sentence. And whoever shall show himself contemptuous of the verdict of this our statute and shall attempt in his temerity to throw into disorder and to disturb the Roman Church in infringement of this statute, shall be condemned to perpetual anathema and excommunication and shall be reckoned with the wicked who do not rise at the Judgment. He shall perceive that the anger of the Omnipotent God, Father, Son and Holy Spirit, is turned against him and both in this life and in the life to come he shall experience the fury of the holy Apostles Peter and Paul, whose Church he dares to throw into disorder. "Let his habitation be desolate, and let there be no one to dwell in his tents. Let his children be orphans and his wife a widow." In tumult he shall be swept away and his sons also "shall become beggars and shall be cast out of their habitations. The usurer shall take stock of all his property and strangers shall wipe out his labours." The whole world shall fight against him, and all the elements shall be adverse to him, and the merits of all the saints now at rest shall put him to confusion and in this life shall take open vengeance upon him.

But the grace of Almighty God shall protect those who are faithful to this our statute, and through the authority of the blessed Apostles Peter and Paul He will absolve them of all their sins.

5. *Dictatus Papae Gregorii VII*

This set of propositions, more like a private memorandum than an official document, may not actually be the work of Gregory VII. They could be, insofar as they express the principal papal prerogatives claimed by him, and must be, at any rate, the product of his circle.

The translation is from Ehler and Morrall, *Church and State Through the Centuries*, pp. 43–44.

1. That the Roman Church was founded by God alone.
2. That the Roman Pontiff alone is rightly to be called universal.
3. That he alone can depose or reinstate bishops.
4. That his legate, even if of lower grade, takes precedence, in a council, of all bishops and may render a sentence of deposition against them.
5. That the Pope may depose the absent.
6. That, among other things, we also ought not to stay in the same house with those excommunicated by him.
7. That for him alone it is lawful to enact new laws according to the needs of the time, to assemble together new congregations, to make an abbey of a canonry; and, on the other hand, to divide a rich bishopric and unite the poor ones.
8. That he alone may use the imperial insignia.
9. That the Pope is the only one whose feet are to be kissed by all princes.
10. That his name alone is to be recited in churches.
11. That his title is unique in the world.
12. That he may depose Emperors.
13. That he may transfer bishops, if necessary, from one See to another.
14. That he has power to ordain a cleric of any church he may wish.
15. That he who has been ordained by him may rule over another church, but not be under the command of others; and that such a one may not receive a higher grade from any bishop.

16. That no synod may be called a general one without his order.

17. That no chapter or book may be regarded as canonical without his authority.

18. That no sentence of his may be retracted by any one; and that he, alone of all, can retract it.

19. That he himself may be judged by no one.

20. That no one shall dare to condemn a person who appeals to the Apostolic See.

21. That to this See the more important cases of every church should be submitted.

22. That the Roman Church has never erred, nor ever, by the witness of Scripture, shall err to all eternity.

23. That the Roman Pontiff, if canonically ordained, is undoubtedly sanctified by the merits of St. Peter; of this St. Ennodius, Bishop of Pavia, is witness, many Holy Fathers are agreeable and it is contained in the decrees of Pope Symmachus the Saint.

24. That, by his order and with his permission, subordinate persons may bring accusations.

25. That without convening a synod he can depose and reinstate bishops.

26. That he should not be considered as Catholic who is not in conformity with the Roman Church.

27. That the Pope may absolve subjects of unjust men from their fealty.

6. *Letter of Gregory VII to Henry IV*

This letter was written in December of 1075 upbraiding him for not obeying a papal decree forbidding lay investiture and excommunicating five of Henry's bishops (the text of which has been lost).

The translation is from J. H. Robinson, *Readings in European History* (Boston: Ginn and Co., 1904) I, pp. 276–78.

FOR we cannot but hesitate to send thee our benediction when we seriously consider the strictness of the Judge to whom we shall have to render account for the ministry intrusted to us by St. Peter, chief of the apostles. For thou art said knowingly to associate with men excommunicated by a judgment of the apostolic chair and by sentence of a synod. If this be true, thou thyself dost know that thou mayst not receive the favor of the divine, nor of the apostolic benediction, unless those who have been excommunicated be separated from thee and compelled to do penance, and thou, with condign repentance and satisfaction, obtain absolution and pardon for thy misdeeds. Therefore we counsel thy Highness that, if thou dost feel thyself guilty in this matter, thou shouldst seek the advice of some devout bishop, with prompt confession. He, with our permission, enjoining on thee a proper penance for this fault, shall absolve thee, and shall take care to inform us by letter, with thy consent, of the exact measure of thy penance.

In the next place, it seems strange to us that although thou dost so often send us such devoted letters; and although thy legates,—calling thyself the son of holy mother Church and of ourselves, subject in the faith, foremost in love and devotion;—although, in short, thou dost commend thyself with all the sweetness of devotion and reverence, yet in conduct and action thou dost show thyself most stubborn, and in opposition to the canonical and apostolic decrees in those matters which the religion of the Church deems of chief importance. For, not to mention other things, in the affair of Milan the actual outcome shows with what intent thou didst make, and how thou didst carry out, the promises made through thy mother and through our brothers the bishops whom we sent to thee. And now, indeed, inflicting wound upon wound, thou hast, contrary to the rules of the apostolic chair, given the churches of Fermo and Spoleto—if indeed a church can be given or granted by a mere man—to certain persons not even known to us, on whom, unless they are previously well known and proven, it is not lawful regularly to perform the laying on of hands.

It would have beseemed thy royal dignity, since thou dost confess thyself a son of the Church, to have treated more respectfully the master of the Church,—that is, St. Peter, the chief of the apostles. For to him, if thou art of the Lord's sheep, thou wast given over by the Lord's voice and authority to be fed; Christ himself saying, "Peter, feed my sheep." And again: "To thee are given over the keys of the kingdom of heaven; and whatsoever thou shalt bind on earth shall be bound in heaven; and whatsoever thou shalt loose on earth shall be loosed in heaven."

Inasmuch as in his seat and apostolic ministration we, however sinful and unworthy, do, by the providence of God, act as the representative of his power, surely he himself is receiving whatever, in writing or by word of mouth, thou hast sent to us. And at the very time when we are either perusing thy letters or listening to the voices of those who speak for thee, he himself is observing, with discerning eye, in what spirit the instructions were issued. Wherefore thy Highness should have seen to it that no lack of good will should appear toward the apostolic chair in thy words and messages. . . .

In this year a synod was assembled about the apostolic chair, over which the heavenly dispensation willed that we should preside, and at which some of thy faithful subjects were present. Seeing that the good order of the Christian religion has now for some time been disturbed, and that the chief and proper methods of winning souls have, at the instigation of the devil, long been neglected and suppressed, we, struck by the danger and impending ruin of the Lord's flock, reverted to the decrees and teachings of the holy fathers,—decreeing nothing new, nothing of our own invention. . . .

Lest these things should seem unduly burdensome or unjust to thee, we did admonish thee, through thy faithful servants, that the changing of an evil custom should not alarm thee; that thou shouldst send to us wise and religious men from thy land, to demonstrate or prove, if they could, by any reasoning, in what respects, saving the honor of the Eternal King and without danger to our soul, we might moderate the decree as passed by the holy fathers, and we would yield to their counsels. Even without our friendly admonitions it would have been but right that, before thou didst violate apostolic decrees, thou shouldst reasonably have appealed to us in cases where we oppressed thee or infringed thy prerogatives. But how little thou didst esteem our commands or the dictates of justice is shown by those things which thou afterwards didst.

But since the long-suffering patience of God still invites thee to amend thy ways, we have hopes that thy understanding may be awakened, and thy heart and mind be bent to obey the mandates of God: we exhort thee with paternal love to recognize the dominion of Christ over thee and to reflect how dangerous it is to prefer thine own honor to his.

7. *Letter of Henry IV Summoning the German Bishops to the Diet of Worms (1076)*

This represents Henry's angry response to his excommunication and deposition by Gregory VII (February 1076). It is an important statement of Henry's conception of the relations between *sacerdotium* and *regnum* and interesting for its novel use of the Gelasian theory of the two swords.

The translation is from Ehler and Morrall, *Church and State Through the Centuries*, pp. 45–47.

HENRY, king by the grace of God, sends favour, greeting and affection—but not to all, only to a few.

In great affairs the wisest counsels of the most outstanding men are necessary—of such men who are both externally able and inwardly do not lack the will to give good counsel on a matter for which they have interest; for ability without will or will without ability can never bring advantage in any matter. We are sure that both of these you possess equally, our most faithful one; or, better to say, although you have ability adequate to your greatness, nonetheless—if we know you properly and if we have noted your faithfulness with proper care—you abound with a good will to be useful to us and to the kingdom which is even greater than your great ability. For from the faithful services of the past we are led to hope for still more faithful services in the future. We rely on your love that your loyalty will not be inferior to our expectations. From the fidelity of no other prince in the realm do we expect greater things than from yours, as we are pleased not only with its showing in the past but also with what it promises in hopes for the future. Let, therefore, your timely good will be coupled now with your ability; because it is greatly required not only by our own strait but also by those of all your fellow-bishops and brothers, indeed of all the oppressed Church.

You are certainly not ignorant of this oppression. Therefore, see to it that you do not withdraw your help and consolation from the oppressed Church, but that you give your sympathy to the kingdom and the priesthood. The Church had been so far exalted in both of these, but it is now humiliated in both and bereaved. For assuredly one man who has claimed them both for himself, disintegrated them both; he could not bring advantage to one of them who was neither able nor willing to be of benefit to any of them. But we should not keep from you any longer the name, which is well known to you, of the person about whom we are talking: it is Hildebrand, a monk in appearance and called Pope, but sitting on the Apostolic chair rather through the violence of an invader than through the care of a shepherd and, from the seat of Catholic and universal peace, sundering the chain of this peace—as you yourself know very well. For, to mention only a few things among many: he usurped for himself the kingdom and the priesthood without God's sanction; by this doing he despised the holy ordination of God according to which the kingdom and the priesthood should not be in the hands of one, but, as two, in the hands of two. The Saviour Himself intimated this symbolically in His Passion as the meaning of the sufficiency of the two swords. When they told Him: "Behold, Lord, here are two swords," He replied: "It is enough." He meant by this sufficing duality that a spiritual and a carnal sword were to be wielded inside the Church by which all the harmful things should be cut off and amputated; by the sacerdotal sword, namely, in order that the king, for God's sake, should be obeyed; by the royal one in order that the external enemies of Christ should be defeated and that internally all people should be bound to obey the priesthood. So He taught and He also taught that affection should be extended from the one to the other so that the kingdom would not be deprived of the honour due to the priesthood, nor the priesthood of the honour due to the kingdom.

You know very well—if you are willing to know—in what way the madness of Hildebrand confounded this ordination of God. For in his judgment no one is a rightful priest unless he obtained a sanction of it by begging from his haughtiness. He also endeavoured to deprive me whom God called to the kingdom—not having, however, called him to the priesthood—of my royal power; this he did because he saw that I wanted to hold my rule from God and not from him who had not constituted me king; at the same time he menaced me that he would take away from me my kingdom and my soul, neither of which he had granted. Although he so often instigated and heaped against us this and other similar contumelies—as you know well—he apparently has not considered that as sufficient because from day to day he attacked us with fresh and gratuitous assaults and confusing manoeuvres—as he recently showed in the case of our envoys. A page would not suffice to tell how he treated these our envoys, how he mishandled them using disgraceful methods, put them in jail and afflicted them, while in prison, with nakedness, cold, hunger, thirst and blows; and finally how he ordered them to be led around like martyrs in the middle of the town, thus providing a spectacle for all; so that you would say and believe that he is mad like Decius the tyrant, and a burner of saints.

Therefore, do not hesitate, my dearest, and may all of us not hesitate, to fulfil my request and that of your fellow-bishops and do not fail to come to Worms at Pentecost; there you will hear, together with the other princes, about many things of which only a few are mentioned in this letter and your view will be requested as to what is to be done. You are asked for love of your fellow-bishops, called upon for the good of the Church and bound for the honour of our life and of the whole kingdom to do this.

8. *Letter of Gregory VII to Hermann, Bishop of Metz*

This is the second of two letters Gregory wrote to Hermann, one of his German supporters. It is the best single statement of Gregory's position regarding papal supremacy.

The translation is from Robinson, *Readings,* Vol. I, pp. 284–89.

IT IS doubtless through God's grace that thou art ready, as we hear, to endure trials and dangers in the defense of the truth. . . . However, thy request to be supported and fortified by a letter from us directed against those persons who are constantly asserting, with perverse tongues, that the holy and apostolic see had no authority to excommunicate Henry—the scorner of Christian law, the destroyer of churches and of the empire, the patron and companion of heretics—nor to absolve any one from the oath of fidelity to him, hardly seems necessary to us when so many and such absolutely decisive warrants are to be found in the pages of Holy Scriptures. . . .

Shall not an office instituted by laymen—by those even who did not know God—be subject to that office which the providence of God Almighty has instituted for his own honor, and in compassion given to the world? For his Son, even as he is unquestioningly believed to be God and man, so is he considered the chief of priests, sitting on the right hand of the Father and always interceding for us. Yet he despised a secular kingdom, over which the men of this world swell with pride, and came of his own will to the priesthood of the cross. Whereas all know that kings and princes are descendants of men who were ignorant of God, and who, by arrogance, robbery, perfidy, murder,—in a word by almost every crime,—at the prompting of the prince of this world, the devil, strove with blind avarice and intolerable presumption to gain the mastery over their equals, that is, over mankind.

To whom, indeed, can we better compare them, when they seek to make the priests of God bend to their feet, than to him who is chief of all the sons of pride and who tempted the highest Pontiff himself, the chief of priests, the Son of the Most High, and promised to him all the kingdoms of the world, saying, "All these will I give thee, if thou wilt fall down and worship me"?

Who doubts that the priests of Christ should be regarded as the fathers and masters of kings and princes, and of all the faithful? Is it not evidently hopeless folly for a son to attempt to domineer over his father, a pupil over his master, or for any one, by iniquitous exactions, to claim power over him by whom he himself, as he acknowledges, can be bound and loosed both on earth and in heaven? Constantine, the great lord of all kings and princes thoughout nearly the whole world, plainly understood this, as the blessed Gregory observes in a letter to the emperor Mauritius, for Constantine took his seat after all the bishops in the holy Council of Nicaea; he presumed to issue no decisions superior to theirs, but addressed them as gods, and declared that they should not be subject to his judgment, but that he was dependent upon their will. . . .

Armed accordingly with such decrees and authority, many bishops have excommunicated, in some cases kings, in others emperors. If the names of such princes are asked for, it may be said that the blessed pope Innocent excommunicated the emperor Arcadius for consenting to the expulsion of St. John Chrysostom from his see. Likewise another Roman pontiff, Zacharias, deposed a king of the Franks, not so much for his iniquities, as for the reason that he was not fitted to exercise his great power. And he substituted Pippin, father of the emperor Charles the Great, in his place,—releasing all the Franks from the oath of fealty which they had sworn to him,—as, indeed, the holy Church frequently does, by its abundant authority, when it absolves servitors from the fetters of an oath sworn to such bishops as are deposed by apostolic sentence from their pontifical rank.

The blessed Ambrose—who, although a saint, was yet not bishop over the whole Church—excommunicated and excluded from the Church the emperor Theodosius the Great for a fault which was not looked upon as very grave by other priests. He shows, too, in his writings that gold does not so far excel lead in value as the priestly dignity transcends the royal power. He speaks in this fashion near the beginning of his pastoral letter: "The honor and sublimity of bishops, brethren, is beyond all comparison. To compare them to resplendent kings and diademed princes would be far more unworthy than to compare the base metal lead to gleaming gold. For one may see how kings and princes bow their necks before the knees of priests, and kiss their right hands so as to believe themselves protected by their prayers. . . ."

Furthermore every Christian king, when he comes to die, seeks as a poor suppliant the aid of a priest, that he may escape hell's prison, may pass from the darkness into the light, and at the judgment of God may appear absolved from the bondage of his sins. Who, in his last hour, whether layman or priest, has ever implored the aid of an earthly king for the salvation of his soul? And what king or emperor is able, by reason of the office he holds, to rescue a Christian from the power of the devil through holy baptism, to number him among the sons of God, and to fortify him with the divine unction? Who of them can by his own words make the body and blood of our Lord,—the greatest act in the Christian religion? Or who of them possesses the power of binding and loosing in heaven and on earth? From all of these considerations it is clear how greatly the priestly office excels in power.

Who of them can ordain a single clerk in the holy Church, much less depose him for any fault? For in the ranks of the Church a greater power is needed to depose than to ordain. Bishops may ordain other bishops, but can by no means depose them without the authority of the apostolic see. Who, therefore, of even moderate understanding, can hesitate to give priests the precedence over kings? Then, if kings are to be judged by priests for their sins, by whom should they be judged with better right than by the Roman pontiff?

In short, any good Christian whatsoever might far more properly be considered as a king than might a bad prince; for the former, seeking the glory of God, strenuously governs himself, whereas the latter, seeking the things which are his own and not the things of God, is an enemy to himself and a tyrannical oppressor of others. Faithful Christians constitute the body of the true king, Christ; evil rulers, that of the devil. The former rule themselves in the hope that they will eternally reign with the Supreme Emperor, but the sway of the latter ends in their destruction and eternal damnation with the prince of darkness, who is king over all the sons of pride.

It is certainly not strange that wicked bishops are of one mind with a bad king, whom they love and fear for the honors which they have wrongfully obtained from him. Such men, simoniacally ordaining whom they please, sell God even for a paltry sum. As even the elect are indissolubly united with their Head, so also the wicked constitute a pertinacious league with him who is the head of evil, with the special purpose of resisting the good. But surely we ought not so much to inveigh against them as to mourn for them with tears and lamentations, beseeching God Almighty to snatch them from the snares of Satan in which they are held captive, and after their period to bring them at last to a knowledge of the truth.

We refer to those kings and emperors who, too much elated by worldly glory, rule not for God but for themselves. Now, since it belongs to our office to admonish and encourage every one as befits the special rank or dignity which he enjoys, we endeavor, by God's grace, to implant in emperors and kings and other princes the virtue of humility, that they may be able to allay the gusts of passion and the floods of pride. For we know that mundane glory and worldly cares usually foster pride, especially in those who are in authority, and that, in consequence, they forget humility and seek ever their own glory, and dominion over their brethren. Wherefore it is well for kings and emperors, particularly when they grow haughty in spirit and delight in their own pomp, to discover a means by which they may be humbled and be brought to realize that the cause of their complacency is the very thing that they should most fear.

Let them, therefore, diligently consider how dangerous and how much to be dreaded are the royal and imperial offices. For in them very few are saved, and those who, through the mercy of God, do attain to salvation are not so glorified in the holy Church by the will of the Holy Spirit as are many of the poor. From the beginning of the world to this our own day, in the whole extent of recorded history, we do not find seven emperors or kings whose lives were as distinguished for piety and as beautified by the gift of miracles as were those of an innumerable multitude who despised the world; yet, notwithstanding this, we believe that many of them achieved salvation through the almighty God of mercy.

What emperor or king was ever honored by miracles as were St. Martin, St. Anthony, and St. Benedict, not to mention the apostles and the martyrs? What emperor or king raised the dead, cleansed lepers, or gave sight to the blind? Observe how the holy Church praises and reveres the emperor Constantine of blessed memory, Theodosius, Honorius, Charles, and Louis, lovers of justice, promoters of Christian religion, defenders of the churches; yet it does not ascribe even to them such resplendent and glorious miracles. Furthermore, how many emperors or kings have chapels or altars dedicated to them by order of the holy Church, or masses celebrated in their honor?

Let kings and princes fear lest the more they exult in their sway over men in this life, the more they shall be subjected to eternal fires; for of them it is written, "The mighty shall suffer mightily in torment." They must needs render account to God for as many as they had under their dominion, and if it be no slight task for any devout person in a private station to guard his single soul, how much labor devolves upon them who rule over many thousands of souls?

Moreover if the judgment of the holy Church severely punishes a sinner for the slaying of one man, what will become of them who, for the sake of worldly renown, send many thousands of souls to death? Such men, though after a great slaughter they may say with their lips, "We have sinned," nevertheless inwardly rejoice that they have extended their so-called fame. They would not undo what they have done, nor do they grieve that they have sent their brethren down to Tartarus. And so long as they do not repent with their whole heart, and refuse to let go what they have gained or kept through the shedding of human blood, their repentance fails in the sight of God to bring forth the true fruit of repentance.

They should, therefore, be in constant apprehension and should frequently recall to mind that, as we have already said, from the beginning of the world very few of the multitude of kings in the various realms of the earth are known to have been holy, whereas in one see alone, the Roman,—where bishops have succeeded one another in an unbroken line,—almost a hundred, since the time of St. Peter the apostle, are reckoned among the most holy. Why is this, except that kings and princes of the earth, seduced by vain glory, prefer, as has been said, the things that are their own to the things that are spiritual, whereas the bishops of the Church, despising vain glory, prefer to carnal things the things that are of God? The former punish promptly offenders against themselves and are indifferent to sinners against God. The latter pardon readily those who sin against themselves, but do not spare those who are remiss toward God. The former, too much bent on earthly achievements, think slightingly of spiritual ones; the latter, sedulously meditating upon heavenly things, despise the things of earth.

9. *Letter of Pope Paschal II*

The drastic proposal contained in this letter of Paschal II (1099–1118) to Henry V (1106–25) was never carried out since it was damaging to too many vested interests, both secular and ecclesiastical. It also ran counter to the whole aim of the Gregorian reform movement.

The translation is from Robinson, *Readings*, Vol. I, pp. 290–292.

Bishop Paschal, Servant of the Servants of God, to His Beloved Son Henry and His Successors Forever:

IT IS forbidden by the provisions of divine law, and interdicted by the holy canons, that priests should busy themselves with secular concerns or should attend the public tribunals except to rescue the condemned or bear aid to those who are suffering wrong. Wherefore, also, the apostle Paul says, "If ye have judgments of things pertaining to this life, set them to judge who are least esteemed in the church." Nevertheless in portions of your kingdom bishops and abbots are so absorbed in secular affairs that they are obliged regularly to appear at court and to perform military service, pursuits rarely, if ever, carried on without plunder, sacrilege, or arson.

Ministers of the altar are become ministers of the king's court, inasmuch as they receive cities, duchies, margravates, mints, and other things which have to do with the king's service. Hence the custom has grown up, intolerable for the Church, that bishops should not receive consecration until they have first been invested by the hand of the king. From this has sprung the prevalent vices, simoniacal heresy and ambition, at times so strong that episcopal sees were filled without any previous election. Occasionally investiture has even taken place while the bishop holding the office was still alive.

Alarmed by these and many other evils which had come about, owing chiefly to the method of investiture, our predecessors, the pontiffs Gregory VII and Urban II of blessed memory, in the councils of the bishops which they frequently held, condemned investitures by lay hands, and decreed that those who had obtained churches in this manner should be deposed and the donors also should be excluded from the communion, in accordance with that chapter of the Apostolic Canons which runs: "If any bishop do employ the powers of the world to obtain a church, he shall be deposed and isolated, as well as all who communicate with him." We also, following in the path of these examples, have confirmed their decision in an episcopal council.

So, most beloved son, King Henry,—now through our sanction, by the grace of God, emperor of the Romans,—we decree that those royal appurtenances are to be restored to thee and to thy kingdom which clearly belonged to that kingdom in the time of Charles, Louis, and of thy other predecessors. We forbid and prohibit, under penalty of anathema, any bishop or abbot, present or future, from intruding upon these same royal appurtenances; in which are included the cities, duchies, margravates, counties, mints, tolls, market rights, manors, rights of royal bailiffs, and rights of the judges of the courts of the hundreds, which manifestly belong to the king, together with what pertains to them, the military posts and camps of the kingdom. Nor shall they henceforth, unless by favor of the king, have aught to do with these royal appurtenances. Neither shall it be allowable for our successors, who shall follow us in the apostolic chair, to disturb thee or thy kingdom in this matter.

In addition we decree that the churches, with their offerings and hereditary possessions which plainly do not belong to the kingdom, shall remain free; as on the day of thy coronation, before the whole church, thou didst promise they should be. It is right that the bishops, freed from secular cares, should take charge of their people and no longer be absent from their churches; for, as the apostle Paul says, let them watch, as men about to render an account for the souls of the people.

10. *Eadmer: Life of St. Anselm*

Eadmer, brought up from childhood as a monk at Christ Church, Canterbury, was one of the foremost historians (*Historia Novorum in Anglia*) and hagiographers (lives of Wilfrid, Dunstan and Oswald) of his time (c.1055–c.1124). A close friend and constant companion of Anselm, his *Vita Anselmi* is authoritative within the limits of the boundless admiration Eadmer felt for Anselm. It is also authorized to the extent that Anselm read the greater part of it and contributed details to it (even though he later, obviously unsuccessfully, forbade its publication).

The selection below is from Book II which begins with events leading up to Anselm's election as Archbishop of Canterbury in 1093 and extends to his death in 1109. Through considerations of space I have omitted those chapters devoted chiefly to the miraculous.

The translation is from R. W. Southern, *The Life of St. Anselm Archbishop of Canterbury by Eadmer* in the Nelson Medieval Texts Series (London: Thomas Nelson and Sons, 1962).

1. How Anselm Came to England and Was Received by King William the Younger

WHEN the renowned William king of the English died, his son William inherited his kingdom. Then the venerable father Lanfranc departed this life, and William oppressed the churches and monasteries throughout England most harshly. In the fourth year of this oppression Anselm was invited, nay urgently entreated and required to come to England [1092] by Hugh earl of Chester and many other noblemen of the English kingdom, who had chosen him as their spiritual physician and protector; and being moreover constrained by the prayer and command laid upon him by his own church for their common good, he came to England. Thus on the eve of the Nativity of the Blessed and ever Virgin Mother of God he arrived at Canterbury. Here many of the monks and laity, as if foretelling the future, acclaimed him as archbishop; wherefore he left the place early next morning and on no account would consent to celebrate the Feast there, as they besought him to do. Moreover when he came to the royal court all the nobility eagerly met him and received him with great honour. The king himself rose from his throne, and met him at the door of his hall with joy; he fell on his neck and led him by the hand to his seat. They sat down, and for a while exchanged cheerful conversation. Then Anselm asked the others to go apart so that he could talk privately with the king. He put aside the business of the monastery, which was supposed to be his chief reason for coming there, and began to rebuke the king for those things which were reported about him: nor did he pass over in silence anything which he knew ought to be said to him. For almost everyone in the whole kingdom daily talked about him, in private and in public, saying such things as by no means befitted the dignity of a king. When they had finished talking they parted, and Anselm said nothing on that occasion about the business of his church. Then he went off to the earl at Chester and was obliged to remain a considerable time in those parts.

ii.

Meanwhile King William was stricken with a serious illness and came to the point of death. His barons persuaded him, among other things, to take thought for the mother of his whole kingdom, namely the church of Canterbury, and to relieve her long widowhood and misfortune by the appointment of an archbishop. He acquiesced in this advice, and declared that Anselm was the man most fitted for this work. There was universal acclamation, and both clergy and people commended the king's judgement without a single voice being raised in contradiction. When Anselm heard this, he wore himself almost to death in his objections, and in resisting and fighting against it. But the united body of the Church of God prevailed. So he was seized, and forcibly carried rather than led into the neighbouring church with hymns and rejoicings. This took place in the year of our Lord's Incarnation 1093, on 6 March, being the first Sunday in Lent.

iv.

Now Anselm, because of many obstacles which stood in the way, had not yet consented to the election which had put him forward into the archbishopric. But he stayed in England at the instance of the king, who ordered the aforesaid Gundulf bishop of Rochester to stay with him and see that he had everything he needed. At last the reasons which held him back were dissipated, and after a long delay both obedience and necessity compelled him to give his consent, and he was consecrated with due honour at Canterbury by all the bishops of England on 4 December. At his consecration, this was the sentence in the Gospels which fell to his lot:

. . . he bade many: And sent his servant at supper time to say to them that were bidden, Come; for all things are now ready. And they all with one consent began to make excuse.'

v.

Afterwards he presented himself at the royal court at Christmas time, and was honourably received by the king. He passed the first three days of the Feast pleasantly with the king. But then the king's mind was turned against him, at the instigation of the devil and of evil men, because he refused to despoil his tenants in order to give the king £1,000 as a thank-offering for his munificence. So, having angered his lord, he left the court.

vii.

A few days later, Anselm was sent for to go to the court and speed the king, who was about to cross the sea, with his blessing. The crossing was delayed by a contrary wind, and Anselm—thinking that he had found a suitable opportunity—began to solicit the King for the relief of the churches which were daily going to ruin, for the revival of the Christian law which was being violated in many ways, and for the reform of morals which every day and in every class of people showed too many corruptions. The king listened to all this with the greatest displeasure, and declared that he would do nothing about any of these things to please him. Then in his anger he ordered him to go, and to wait no longer for the beginning of his voyage.

viii.

When Anselm began now to think of all the peace he had lost and all the labour he had found, his spirit was torn and tormented with bitter anguish. For he saw in his mind's eye the life which he had been accustomed to lead as prior and as abbot,—how joyfully he had reposed and delighted in the love of God and of his neighbour, how devoutly he had been heard by all to whom he ministered the words of life, how still more devoutly his hearers had hastened to put into practice what he taught, and thereby (as he hoped) added to the sum of his reward. And now how different it was! As a bishop he ought to have gone on to better things; but he saw his days and nights taken up with secular business; he saw himself unable to devote his attention either to God or to his neighbour in God's name as he had formerly done; and he saw no-one willing to listen to the Word of Life from his lips or to carry it out; and thereby he lost (as he thought) his reward. To add to these evils of his own, the cruel oppression of his men daily afflicted his ears; and he was deafened by the threats of worse to follow, made by malicious men on all sides. For it was well-known that the king's mind was worked up into a fury against him, and as a result every wicked man thought himself happy if he could hit on any device to exasperate him further. Thus he was tossed by the storms of injuries of many kinds, without having the consolation of any flattering caresses of worldly honour or prosperity. Nevertheless, he preserved a pure conscience in all things and towards all men; and he even had some relief from these trials, finding his chief consolation in burying himself in the cloister with the monks and talking to them of things pertaining to their rule of life. He referred to this once when he was presiding in their chapter. He had as usual been discoursing freely about matters which concerned their rule, and when he came to the end of his discourse he made a joking comparison, saying with cheerful good-humour: 'Just as an owl is glad when she is in her hole with her chicks and (in her own fashion) all is well with her; and just as she is attacked and torn to pieces when she is among crows and rooks and other birds, and everything then is far from well with her; so it is with me. For when I am with you, all is well with me, and this is the joy and consolation of my life. But when I am separated from you, and my ways lie among men who are in the world, then I am torn this way and that by the onrush of disputes of many kinds and I am harassed by secular business which I hate. Then indeed I am in an ill state, and I tremble with horror at the great danger to my soul which may ensue.' Although he had begun, as I said, in jest, he broke into most bitter tears as he spoke, adding 'But you at least my friends, do you, at least, take pity on me, for the hand of the Lord is upon me.' Since his chief recreation was in such companionship, when he was deprived of it he was grievously afflicted. God knows I often heard him most vehemently protest that he would rather be one of the boys in the monastic community, trembling under the master's rod, than sit aloft in the pontifical throne among the congregation of the people having the pastoral care of the whole of Britain. Perhaps someone may ask; If he found it so good and joyful a thing to live with the monks, why did he not always live at Canterbury with his retinue? To which I answer: If only this had been possible for him, he would have thought it a great consolation. But he was deprived of this consolation partly by the remoteness of his manors, partly by the traditional usage of his predecessors, and partly by the large retinue which his episcopal dignity and the custom of the country did not allow him to be without: all this obliged him to keep on the move and to live on his manors. Besides, if he had stayed at Canterbury all the time, his men would have had the burden of bringing food to the town, and, if he had never been present on his manors to hear their complaints, his reeves would have oppressed them in many ways (as often happened) until, as the oppression got worse and worse, they were utterly destroyed.

x.

As often as an opportunity occurred, he was in the habit of withdrawing to an inner room in his chamber, and there in solitude he gave himself up to divine studies. It was thus that, being moved by his zeal for the Christian faith, he wrote an excellent—and in the circumstances of his time most necessary—work *On the Incarnation of the Word.* This work was written in the form of a letter addressed to the venerable Pope Urban, supreme pontiff of the Holy Roman Church, and it was sent to him. He received it with thanks, and having understood the true and invincible reasoning on which it was founded, he held it in such esteem that he afterwards (as will be related in due course) used it as the basis of his argument in the dispute with Greeks at the Council of Bari, showing how damnable was their error in denying that the Holy Spirit proceeded from the Son. But we shall pass this over here and, proceeding with our narrative, we shall describe how Anselm talked at meal-times. While he sat to refresh his body, he sometimes took as his subject-matter the holy lesson which was being read in his presence and spoke to the edification of those at table; sometimes, instead of the lesson, he himself gave a holy discourse for the instruction of those who were present; and sometimes, being asked about some subject of useful or necessary business, he satisfied both the enquirer and all who heard him with the wonderful graciousness of his replies. In this connection an incident comes readily to my mind, and I insert it here as an example—not as an illustration of the power of his teaching, but simply to show in a small way how he was accustomed to employ his tongue at meal-times.

xvi.

Now when the king returned from across the sea, Anselm went to him, and humbly sought permission to go to Pope Urban at Rome for his archepiscopal pallium. But the king flared up at the name of Urban, and said that he did not recognise him as pope, and that it was contrary to established usage to allow anyone in his kingdom to nominate a pope not of his choosing. Hence there arose a serious difference of opinion, but the discussion of it was put off till another time. The order went out therefore to the bishops, abbots, and barons of all England that they should come together at the castle of Rockingham to discuss this difference. They did as they were bidden, and assembled in the third week of Lent. The case was brought forward, and Anselm was attacked from all sides on various pretexts. Many—but above all the bishops—wishing to be on the king's side and having no regard for justice and equity, tried to prove that Anselm could not recognize Urban, the bishop of the apostolic see, as pope within the king's realms without breaking the faith which he owed to the king. Many arguments, supported by reason, were brought forward against these men, and Anselm altogether confounded them with the words of the Lord 'Render unto Caesar the things which are Caesar's, and to God the things which are God's,' and with some other passages which no argument could refute. Then they, having nothing that they could answer, raised a loud clamour that he was blaspheming against the king, simply because in his kingdom and without his consent he had dared to ascribe anything even to God. Therefore, at one word of royal indignation, some of the bishops made haste to throw off all submission and the obedience which they had promised to their archbishop and primate, and in the same breath the wretches renounced all brotherly intercourse with him. Others of them simply refused to obey him in any orders which he gave them on behalf of Pope Urban. So by one means or another all the bishops who were present, with the single exception of the bishop of Rochester, renounced the submission and obedience due to him. The king moreover for his part withdrew from him all assurance of security in his affairs, and swore that he would no longer treat him as archbishop or Father unless he immediately renounced his obedience to the vicar of Saint Peter. Three days, heavily charged with outcries and insults against Anselm, were spent on this business, and in the end the conclusion of them was as I have described. Then Anselm, unshaken in his resolve, sent intermediaries to the king asking for a safe conduct to leave the kingdom. The barons saw that this would be injurious to many people, and they begged for and obtained a truce on both sides until Pentecost in the hope of restoring peace: and so they stopped him leaving the kingdom. The king therefore promised that he would leave all his goods in full peace and tranquillity until the date fixed for the end of the truce; and that he would then out of respect for him make some considerable concession to his wishes in the business which had arisen. But everything in fact turned out quite differently, and Anselm was grievously molested,—Dom Baldwin being driven from the kingdom, his men seized and plundered, and his lands devastated. And yet, after all this, the king recognised Urban as pope through the agency of Walter, bishop of Albano, who brought the pallium for Anselm from Rome to Canterbury; and, acting on the advice of his barons, he extended his friendship at least in appearance to Anselm.

xvii.

But after a certain time this same king returned victoriously from Wales with his anger once more kindled against Anselm, because of the knights whom Anselm had sent on the expedition, who were falsely reported by malicious tongues to have been badly equipped. At this Anselm reflected that this sort of thing could crop up all the time about nothing, so that he would always be thus occupied and unable to carry out his episcopal duties. So he decided that he must go to Rome and seek advice about these things from the See of St. Peter. Therefore at the Feast of Pentecost, when he went to the court at Windsor, he sent some members of his household to the king to say that it was very necessary for him to go to Rome, and, if he agreed, he would be glad to have his permission to go. But the king refused, 'For,' he said, 'we have not found him to go to Rome, and if he agreed, he would be glad to have his consult the pope, nor subject to any grave sin, for which he must implore his absolution.' And so the matter rested for the time being.

XX.

After this Anselm came once more to the court, and he again sought permission from the king to go to Rome, but in vain. Afterwards, in the month of October he went to Winchester at the king's invitation, and a third time and more insistently he asked through intermediaries for what he had twice already sought. The king was vexed and querulously complained that he was being troubled by him too much. At this Anselm broke out: 'Now truly it is for the sake of the holy estate of the Christian religion which I have undertaken to rule in this land, and for the health of my own soul, and also—if he would believe it—for his own honour and advantage, that I have decided to go to Rome. If then he will give me permission to go with a good will, I shall gladly accept it. But if not, I least of all should put aside the commands of God, for it is written, "We ought to obey God rather than man."' When the king heard this, he angrily ordered him either to desist from this enterprise and promise on his oath that he would never again on any account appeal to St. Peter or his See; or leave the kingdom without delay and give up all hope of returning. And he added: 'If this frightens him, and he chooses to drop his plan and remain rather than go, then I require him to pay such a fine as my court shall decide; for he has asked me three times to grant him something in which he had no assurance that he should persevere.' Anselm answered: 'He is lord; his word is law. But I know to what end I have been chosen, and what I undertook in assuming authority in England; and I declare that it would not be honourable for me in the desire for temporal gain to omit anything which I hope, with the aid of God's mercy, will be useful to his Church in time to come.' Many more things than these took place over this affair, but since we have written about them elsewhere, we shall here shortly dispose of them. The king, then, and all the members of the court were moved to anger against Anselm, but Anselm came to him with unruffled countenance and sat down at his customary place at his right hand, saying: 'My lord, I go as I have determined; but first, if you do not refuse it, I shall give you my blessing.' The king replied that he had no wish to refuse it, and as he bent forward for it, Anselm raised his right hand and blessed him; and so, leaving the court, he came to Canterbury.

xxi.

The next day, he called together the monks who served the Lord Christ in that church, and spoke these words to them: 'My dearest brethren and children, as you have heard and already know, I am shortly to leave this kingdom. The long drawn-out dispute between our lord king and myself about the reform of Christian discipline has at last come to this, that either I shall have to do things which are against God and my honour, or leave the kingdom without delay. For my own part I go willingly, trusting that by the workings of God's mercy my journey will be of some use to the liberty of the church in time to come. But for you, whom I am leaving for the time being, I am filled with compassion, seeing what tribulations and sufferings, what oppressions and insults—even worse than usual—you will suffer when I am away. For though these have never wholly been absent even when I was present, still, when they arose, I was able to be some sort of a shelter for you against them, and I placed myself as a shield for your protection so that they did not hurt you beyond measure. And I truly think that you enjoyed greater peace and security after I came among you, than you had done between the death of our Father Lanfranc of blessed memory and my arrival. But from this fact also I seem to perceive that those who used to injure you will be the more violent against you in my absence, because so long as I have been present they have seen themselves cast down from that lordship with which they used to oppress you. You, however, are not so raw or dull in the Lord's service, that you need to be told how to conduct yourselves in circumstances like this if they arise. Nevertheless, since you have come together to serve God within the precincts of this monastery, I shall add a few words to keep you in mind of the nature of your service. For not all men serve in the same fashion, as we see clearly in the courts of secular princes. For a prince has different kinds of soldiers at his court: he has some who are active in his service in return for the lands which they hold from him; he has others who bear arms and toil on his behalf for pay; and he has yet others who labour with unbroken fortitude to obey his will for the sake of receiving back again an inheritance of which they bewail the loss through their parents' fault. Those then who serve him for the lands which they hold, are already rooted and grounded, and have no fear of being torn up so long as they conform themselves to their lord's will. Those on the other hand who have entered military service for pay, sometimes are wearied by their exertions and idly fall away from the service they have undertaken, thinking maybe that the wages and rewards are not equal to the amount of toil and exertion. But those who have submitted to the conditions of service for the sake of recovering their inheritance—although they are ground down by toil of one kind or another, and suffer insults of every description—yet bear everything with steadfast minds so long as they have a firm desire to recover their inheritance and are supported by a sure hope. This is clearly the case among men, and one may gather from this what happens in the court of the Ruler of all men. For God, to whom all things belong, has his court divided into these three classes of those who do his will. He has angels who minister to him: they are firmly grounded in eternal blessedness. But also he has men who serve him like mercenary soldiers for worldly gain. Then in addition he has some men who keep to their purpose day and night, and strive to reach the heavenly kingdom which, being theirs by inheritance, they lost through the fault of their father Adam. Our task however is rather to press forward to the company of the spirits of the blessed, than to discourse at present about the order in which they stand unchangeably before God. So let us turn to God's mercenary soldiers. You may see very many men leading a secular life, who have the appearance of loving God in the midst of their possessions, and who in certain good works which they do are active in his service. Then by the judgement of God some trial befalls them; they lose their goods. What follows? They straightway face about, rush away from the love of God, abandon the good works which they were doing, grumble and accuse God of injustice. What are we to say about these men? They are mercenaries and the words of the Psalmist are fulfilled in them: "A man will praise thee when thou doest well to him." So much for men living in the world. But we who are monks—let us not be such as they are! For if men refuse to stand in the straight path of that profession which they have undertaken unless all things which minister to their wants are present in abundance, and if they are unwilling to suffer any kind of privation or strictness of rule on God's behalf, what arguments, pray, can save them from being such as those others? They simply seek the reward for all they do before carrying out the service for which the reward is due. Shall such men as these inherit the Kingdom of Heaven? I say certainly not, unless they repent of being like this. For he whose aim in serving is directed towards the recovering of the kingdom of eternal life, strives to stick to God through thick and thin, and with unshakeable perseverance to place his whole trust in him. No adversity tears him away from God's service, and no earthly pleasure holds him back from his love. Through difficulties and adversities he follows the way of his commandments; he warms his heart with an undying fire of love in the hope of the reward in store for him; and thus, strong in patience, he rejoices in all things, and says with the Psalmist: "Great is the glory of the Lord." This glory, even in this earthly pilgrimage, he has a taste of; he savours it; and, as he savours, he desires it; and with great desire he salutes it while yet far off. Thus he is supported by the hope of attaining it, and consoled by it in the midst of all earthly dangers, and he sings with joy "Great is the glory of the Lord." And you may be sure that he will by no means be cheated of this glory of the Lord; for his whole being is subject to the Lord's will and is directed to obtaining this glory. But now, oh now, I see I must make an end of talking of these things with you. My brethren, I beseech you, I beseech you, if here and now we part in grief, press on, so that in the future we may be joined together before God in gladness. Act like men who truly desire to become heirs of God.' At these words, tears which prevented him from saying more broke from his eyes; and who can describe the anguish of the brethren which followed? They were so overcome with weeping that they had no voice for words. At last the Father, breaking through his sobs, said; 'You know, my dearest friends, what I wish you to do, and whither I wish you to direct your course. But the hour forbids more talk. I commend you to Almighty God, and to the most blessed Prince of the Apostles, Peter, that God may number you among his sheep, and Saint Peter may receive you into his keeping as God's sheep committed to his care. With your permission and blessing I go, and I pray that the God of Peace and love may remain with you.' Having said this, he rose and, after giving the kiss of peace to all, he went into the church to speak such words of consolation and encouragement to the people who awaited his holy exhortation as the urgency of the situation allowed. This he excellently performed; and in the presence of the monks, clerks and a large concourse of people, he took his scrip and staff like a pilgrim from the altar; then he commended them all to Christ, and, setting forth with much weeping and lamentation, he left them. On the same day, we came to Dover and there we found a certain clerk called William, sent to Anselm from the king. We were detained there for a fortnight by a wind which made our crossing impossible. While we were delayed, this William was constantly with us and ate daily at the Father's table, but he revealed to no-one the purpose for which he had been sent.

xxii.

Then on the fifteenth day you might have seen a pitiful spectacle. When the sailors urged us to go abroad, and we in our eagerness to get away were straining ourselves to do so, the Father of his country, the Primate of all Britain, was detained on the sea-shore like a fugitive and a common criminal. This same William, on behalf of his lord, forbade him to cross the sea until he had shown him piece by piece everything that he was taking with him. So the bags and baggages were brought and opened before him, and all his belongings were turned out and searched in the hope of finding money, while a huge crowd of people, astonished at the novelty of the proceedings, stood round watching and abominating the nefarious deed. When everything had been turned out and none of the things for which the search was instituted had been found—the officiousness of the searcher being thus derided—Anselm and his party were allowed to depart.

xxvi.

Thence we hastened day by day on the journey we had undertaken, but the report of his coming flew ahead much faster and spread varying rumours among the people. So wherever he came he was met by crowds of people, gatherings of clergy and armies of monks, who acclaimed him with joy and enthusiasm, and showed forth their praise to God for his arrival with banners and melodious song.

xxvii.

But a few days after he had come to Lyons and had been splendidly received by the archbishop of that city, he sent letters to the lord pope asking his advice about his business, and indicating to him that he was unable to go further than Lyons, partly because of his bodily weakness and partly because of many other hindrances. He therefore settled down at Lyons and awaited the return of his messengers. After a time the messengers returned from Rome and reported that the pope had ordered him to put aside every objection and to make haste to come to him. He obeyed the pontifical commands without any thought of delay, and, being unafraid of death in God's service, he exposed himself to the perils of the road.

xxviii.

From here we came to Susa and presented ourselves to the abbot of the place. We were just three monks: our lord and father Anselm, Dom Baldwin, and myself, brother Eadmer, who writes this. We journeyed as if we were equals, showing by no external sign to others who was the superior or who the inferior. Therefore when we were asked by the abbot who we were and whence we came, we replied in a few words. When he heard that some of us were monks of Bec, he enquired: 'Tell me, brethren, I beg you, does that friend of God and of all good men, Anselm, the abbot of that monastery and a man approved and acceptable in every religious work, still live?' To this Baldwin replied: 'He has been carried off to an archbishopric in another kingdom.' 'So I have heard,' he said. 'But now, tell me, how is he? Is he well?' 'To tell the truth,' he replied, 'I haven't seen him at Bec since he became archbishop; but they say that he is very well where he is.' Then the abbot said, 'And I pray that he may continue so.' Anselm heard these things being said about himself, and covering his head hastily in the hood of his cowl, he sat with downcast face. For we were unwilling to be recognised, in case the report of the coming of so great a man should go before us and cause us to run into danger by our carelessness.

xxix.

After this we celebrated the festivals of our Lord's Passion and Resurrection in the monastery of St. Michael the Archangel, which is called Chiusa and lies in the mountains. Then we returned to our road and hurried on to Rome. It is worthy of remark, that though we were few and unknown, journeying in a foreign land, knowing no-one, and telling no-one who we were or whence we came, nevertheless the mere appearance of Anselm stirred people's admiration for him and they pointed him out as a man of God. Hence, though we were now travelling among those whose molestations we feared, it sometimes happened that men and women entered our lodgings, earnestly begging to see this man and to receive his blessing. With such marks of popular esteem, then, he progressed as far as Rome, and went to the Lateran, where the supreme pontiff was at that time staying. When the arrival of the Father was announced to the pope, he joyfully ordered him to be lodged in a part of his palace and to spend the day quietly. The next morning the Roman nobility flocked to the pope and the talk turned on the arrival of the new guest. He was conducted into the assembly with marks of respect, and a chair was placed for him in which he could conveniently sit facing the pope. On entering he humbled himself in the customary way at the feet of the supreme pontiff, who immediately raised him up and kissed him. He sat down, and the successor of the Apostles said that he and the whole Roman curia rejoiced at his arrival. At this the court applauded. Then, when silence was restored, the pope said many things in his praise, affirming that he was a man of high religion and virtue. 'And indeed,' he said 'so he is. For though we consider him as a master steeped in all branches of the liberal arts, and though we justly regard him as one to be venerated almost as our equal —for he is the apostolic patriarch of that other world—, nevertheless so excellent a humility and constancy rules his mind, that he could not be frightened away by the perils of the sea or by the vast expanses of foreign soil from presenting himself at the feet of St. Peter for the service of our humble selves, or from coming to us—who rather need his counsel than he ours—to consult us about his affairs. Consider therefore with what love and honour we ought to receive and embrace him.' Anselm himself often used to confess that when he heard these and many other things said about himself in his own praise, he was greatly embarrassed, for in his heart he recognised that he was not such as he was made out to be by so great a man. However he remained silent during the talk, deeming it more fitting to say nothing about such a subject than to speak. After this the pope asked him about the cause of his coming, and he explained it to him in a manner which met the demands of both truth and discretion. The pope was astonished at what he heard and promised his full support. He ordered therefore that Anselm should stay near him till he gave effect to this support. But since the heat of summer in those parts scorches everything, and living in the city is very unhealthy especially for foreigners, a former monk of Bec, John by name, who was then abbot of the monastery of Holy Saviour at Telese, entertained him, with the pope's permission, as if he were his own father. He took him to his village called Liberi, which, being on the top of a mountain, has always a healthy and cool air agreeable to those living there.

xxx.

Thus we took up our abode on the mountain top, as far removed from the thronging crowd as it were in a desert. When Anselm saw this, his spirits rose with the hope of future quiet, and he said: 'This is my resting-place: here I shall live.' He ordered his life therefore on the lines of his early routine before he became abbot, which he deplored more than ever having had to give up since he became archbishop: day and night his mind was occupied with acts of holiness, with divine contemplation, and with the unravelling of sacred mysteries. Being then moved by his love of the Christian faith, he put out a remarkable book which he entitled *Cur Deus Homo*. He had begun this work, as he explains in the prologue to it, in England; but he finished it while living in this place, in the province, that is, of Capua.

xxxiii.

After this, Urban, the bishop of the apostolic See arrived. He was met by Anselm and by the leaders of the whole army and conducted with an immense display of worldly glory to a tent where we were, which was more splendidly made than the others. Thus the lord pope and Anselm were neighbours at the siege until the city surrendered, so that their households seemed rather to be one than two, nor did anyone willingly come to visit the pope without turning aside to Anselm. For the pope was reverenced by all as their general father and pastor; but Anselm was loved by all as a mild and gentle man to whom—in his own eyes—nobody owed anything. In the pope moreover there shone forth supreme power and the authority of high position; but in Anselm a wonderful and pure humility and simplicity which won all hearts. Many therefore who were afraid to approach the pope, hurried to come to Anselm, being led by the love which knows no fear. The majesty of the pope gave access only to the rich: the humanity of Anselm received all without any acceptance of persons. And whom do I mean by *all?* Even pagans—not to speak of Christians. There were indeed some pagans, for the count of Sicily, a vassal of duke Roger, had brought many thousands of them with him on the expedition.

Some of them, I say, were stirred by the report of his goodness which circulated among them to frequent our lodging. They gratefully accepted offerings of food from Anselm and returned to their own people making known the wonderful kindness which they had experienced at his hands. As a result he was from this time held in such veneration among them, that when we passed through their camp—for they were all encamped together—a huge crowd of them, raising their hands to heaven, would call down blessings on his head; then kissing their hands as they are wont, they would do him reverence on their bended knees giving thanks for his kindness and liberality. Many of them even, as we discovered, would willingly have submitted themselves to his instruction and would have allowed the yoke of the Christian faith to be placed by him upon their shoulders, if they had not feared that the cruelty of their count would have been let loose against them on this account. For in truth he was unwilling to allow any of them to become Christian with impunity. With what policy—if one can use that word—he did this, is no concern of mine: that is between God and himself.

xxxiv.

Afterwards, when the siege was ended, Anselm tried to persuade the pope with many prayers to relieve him from his episcopal burden and allow him to live in peace and freedom. But, so far as any practical result went, he laboured in vain, and with the pope's blessing he returned to Liberi to wait there until the time of the council, which the pope was going to hold at Bari on 1 October. When Anselm had presented himself at the Council, he was induced by the pope to confute the Greeks, who erred on the procession of the Holy Spirit, in asserting that He proceeded from the Father but not the Son. Having accomplished this in a reasoned and catholic disquisition, he was held in great honour by all and established as a man worthy of the highest veneration. Then, the Council being finished, we returned to Rome with the pope.

xxxv.

After some days, the same William whom we mentioned in connection with our departure from England came to Rome. Among other things he induced the pope to grant a delay to the king of England in the matter of Anselm till the Feast of St. Michael the Archangel. When Anselm learnt this, he wanted to return to Lyons at once, but the pope forbade him because of a Council which he had decided to hold at Rome in the third week after Easter. So we stayed at Rome for almost half a year, being constantly with the pope and living almost as one household. The pope on his side sometimes called on Anselm, making himself agreeable to him and paying his court to him. Moreover he gave him the lodging where we stayed with the privilege that if ever he returned to Rome he could claim it as his own against all men. In gatherings of the nobility, in processions and in *stationes,* he always and everywhere had second place after the pope, being held in honour before all men, acceptable to all, and subject to all in simplicity and humility.

xxxvi.

Moreover the Englishmen who came to Rome at that time wished to honour him by prostrating themselves at his feet, as at the feet of a Roman pontiff. But this he would by no means allow, and he retired to a private part of the house, where he would not allow them to come to him for such a purpose on any account. When this was told to the pope, he marvelled at the humility of the man and his contempt for worldly things, and he asked him to restrain this impulse and to forbid no-one who in future wished to do him honour, but patiently to admit all who came with such a purpose. But he was overcome with a certain bashful modesty, and would certainly have disregarded these orders, had he not feared to be tainted with the fault of disobedience.

xxxvii.

And what shall I say about some of the citizens of Rome? A great number of these were hostile to the pope because of their loyalty to the emperor. More than once, when Anselm was going with his companions from the Lateran to Saint Peter's, they banded themselves together and wanted to capture him because of their hostility to the pope. But as soon as they saw his face, they were filled with fear and, throwing down their arms, they prostrated themselves on the ground and asked him to favour them with his blessing. Everywhere he was followed by similar marks of popular honour and good-will, for in all his actions his life was spent in the service of God. Hence scarcely anyone in Rome referred to him simply as that 'man' or 'archbishop,' but—as if it were his own name—as 'the Saint.' And all we who served him were likewise held in universal love and honour.

xxxviii.

When the Council I have mentioned came on, and had dealt with whatever seemed to need correction or decision, the pope and the whole Council launched a sentence of excommunication both against laymen who give investiture of churches and against those who receive them from their hands. He also pronounced the same sentence against those who consecrate anyone to an office obtained in this way.

xxxix.

When the Council was over, we obtained permission and left Rome. Our return journey was beset with many dangers but, by God's protection, we escaped them all and came to Lyons without harm. Here we were received with great honour and joy, and invited to stay by the venerable archbishop of the city, Hugh; so we fixed our abode here, having lost all hope of returning to England while king William was alive. In this place, Anselm was treated not like a guest or a foreigner, but like a native and lord of the place. Hence the prelate of the city himself never willingly presided in his own see while Anselm was present, but with amazing humility and goodness he assumed the position and performed the offices of an inferior, and almost of a suffragan. Besides this he ordained that Anselm should perform episcopal functions throughout his diocese whenever he wished and saw fit. When this became known in the surrounding countryside the people frequently flocked to him, asking to be anointed with the holy oil in the laying on of his hands. For his part he admitted them all to the benefit of this sacrament, so that the whole day was very often spent in its administration, and we who assisted him were overcome with weariness, while he remained bright and cheerful to the end. Out of this there grew up a wonderful and unbelievable love for him among all the people, and his goodness was the talk of the whole neighbourhood.

xlv.

Meanwhile Urban, the bishop of the Apostolic See, departed this life before the period of grace which he had granted the king in the Anselm affair had ended. At this time also many things were prophesied by many people about the king's death, and it was said—both because of the strange and unusual signs which were seen throughout England and because of the revelations which were made to many religious persons in visions—that the Divine vengeance was soon going to fall on him for his persecution of Anselm. But Anselm gave no heed to these things and daily prayed God for the king's conversion and safety.

xlvi.

Thereafter, in the third year of our exile, and in the second year after our coming from Rome to Lyons, Anselm went to Marcigny to speak with Hugh, the lord abbot of Cluny, and with the nuns. When we were there and were sitting together in the presence of the abbot, certain things passed to and fro in conversation, as usually happens, about the proceedings between Anselm and the king up to that date. Then the venerable abbot interjected, as a matter of assured truth, that during the previous night the king had been accused before the throne of God, judged, and had sentence of damnation passed upon him. At these words we were not a little startled, but—considering the speaker's eminent sanctity and the respect due to him—we were obliged to have faith in what he said; and so we were content to trust his words alone, and omitted to ask him how he knew this.

xlvii.

The next day, we departed and came to Lyons. On the following day, being the Feast of St. Peter which is observed on 1 August, we had said matins, and those of us who were in constant attendance on Anselm wanted to settle down to rest. Then suddenly a young man, comely in dress and appearance, stood beside our fellow clerk, who was lying near the chamber door, not yet asleep but with his eyes shut ready for sleep. He called him by his name. 'Adam,' he said, 'are you asleep?' 'No,' he replied. Then he said, 'Do you want to hear some news?' 'Gladly,' he replied. 'Then know for certain,' he said 'that the whole dispute between Archbishop Anselm and King William is at an end and settled.' At this he became more wide-awake, raised his head and looked round with wide open eyes. But he saw no-one. Then on the next night during matins, one of us was standing singing the psalms with closed eyes. Suddenly someone put a rather small piece of parchment before him for him to read. He looked at it, and on it he found written, 'King William has died.' Immediately he opened his eyes, but he saw no-one except his companions.

xlix.

After this, two of his own monks came to Anselm announcing the death of the aforesaid king. In fact, on 2 August—the second day to dawn after the first vision at Lyons which I have just described, and the day following the second vision—the king went hunting in a wood in the morning, and there an arrow pierced his heart and killed him instantly. At this Anselm was utterly stupefied and soon burst into bitter tears. We onlookers were somewhat surprised. But he declared, in words broken with sobs, that if it had been possible he would much rather that his own body had died than that the king had died in his present state.

We then returned to Lyons, and messengers came to Anselm one after the other bringing letters with requests from the mother church of the English, from the new king, Henry, who had succeeded his brother, and also from the barons of the kingdom, begging him with all earnestness to return quickly, asserting that the whole land was on tip-toe for his arrival, and that all the business of the kingdom was at a stand-still, hanging on his wishes.

l.

But when he came to the king at Salisbury and told him plainly what he had heard in the Council at Rome about investitures of churches, the king was disturbed and troubled beyond measure, and he showed no desire to defer to Anselm's wishes in anything, as the messengers had said. Whoever wants to know about the negotiations which took place between them on this subject during the next two and a half years, and the many great injuries and tribulations which Anselm suffered, not to mention the two occasions on which messengers were sent to Rome to obtain a change in these decrees and what they achieved, should read the work which is mentioned in the prologue of this little book; and there he will find, I think, everything plainly set forth. After all this the king asked Anselm to go himself to Rome with the messenger whom he would send to lend his assistance in safeguarding the royal honour in the dispute which had arisen. The bishops, abbots and barons of the whole of England agreed to this, crying out that he should let nothing stand in the way of his going in a matter of so much importance. He replied that he would certainly go, but he openly declared that he would never ask or advise the pope to do anything which could injure either the liberty of the churches or his own honour.

lii.

When Anselm then had continued his journey and was approaching Lyons, the aforesaid William desired to leave his company, and forbade him on behalf of his lord the king to return to England unless he would definitely promise to ignore his submission and obedience to the Apostolic See, and to observe towards the king all the customs of his father and brother. When he heard this he was astonished, for he knew that he had left England on quite different terms. But when he reached Lyons he settled down there, living as of old in peace and quietness in the house of the already mentioned and revered archbishop of the city, Hugh; and not an hour passed in which he was not engaged either in word or deed in the things which belong to God.

liv.

Now King Henry, when he heard that the pope was firm in his decision, at once took the archbishopric into his own hands and deprived Anselm of all his possessions. There were many negotiations between them over this, and the king's anger was not appeased for a year and a half.

lvi.

Afterwards Anselm left Burgundy and went to France, in order to bring into force the rigour of ecclesiastical discipline, and to relieve the condition of the churches in England. When this was made known to Henry, king of the English, he invited him to come to Normandy; and then the king—moved both by the fear and the love of God—reinvested him with his possessions and received him into his friendship.

lvii.

Henceforth Anselm lived in Normandy, until the return of Baldwin and William, who had been sent to Rome by the king and archbishop to complete the business which still remained unsettled between them over church investitures. William went on to the king in England and soon returned to Anselm at Bec, requesting him on behalf of the king—now that the former quarrels were settled—to come with all speed to England. Anselm promptly agreed to do this and set out on his way as far as Jumieges, but here he was detained by sickness and unable to continue his journey. When he was better, he returned to Bec to wait there till the king of England crossed over to him. But here, when the expectation of his return filled all men with an extraordinary joy, suddenly Anselm's illness came on again and confined him to his bed, putting an end to the rejoicing and filling everyone with sorrow and heaviness. As a result he could neither eat or do anything which would give us hope for his recovery, and we looked forward only to his death with an immense dread. Meanwhile with anxious care we besought him to take some food, but he, drawing his breath with difficulty, said that he had no stomach for anything. Nevertheless we urged him repeatedly, and at last he agreed rather than burden us further by an absolute refusal. 'Perhaps' he said 'I might eat some partridge, if I had some.' There was no need to say more. All his people dispersed through the fields and woods, and a whole day was spent in the lost labour of seeking a partridge. But it happened that one of the servants of the monastery was going that same day through a neighbouring wood, with no thought of the business which was occupying the others; and suddenly a little animal which they call a marten appeared on the road along which he was walking with a partridge in its mouth. When the animal saw the man, it dropped its prey and saved itself by flight. He picked up the partridge and brought it to us. Our invalid took some nourishment from it, and at once he began to recover from his sickness; and he got better from day to day until at length he was restored to perfect health.

11. *The Concordat of Worms* (*1122*)

The translation is from Ehler and Morrall, *Church and State Through the Centuries*, pp. 48–49.

I, BISHOP Calixtus, servant of the servants of God, concede to you, beloved son Henry—by the grace of God August Emperor of the Romans—that the election of those bishops and abbots in the German kingdom who belong to the kingdom shall take place in your presence without simony and without any violence; so that if any discord occurs between the parties concerned, you may—with the counsel or judgment of the metropolitan and the co-provincials—give your assent and assistance to the party which appears to have the better case. The candidate elected may receive the "regalia" from you through the sceptre and he shall perform his lawful duties to you for them. But he who is elected in the other parts of the Empire shall, within six months, receive the "regalia" from you through the sceptre and shall perform his lawful duties for them, saving all things which are known as pertaining to the Church. If you complain to me in any of these matters and ask for help, I will furnish you the aid, if such is the duty of my office. I grant true peace to you and to all those who are or have been of your party during this discord.

In the name of the Holy and Indivisible Trinity, I, Henry, by the grace of God August Emperor of the Romans, for the love of God and the Holy Roman Church and of the lord Pope Calixtus and for healing of my soul, do surrender to God, to the Holy Apostles of God, Peter and Paul, and to the Holy Roman Church all investiture through ring and staff; and do agree that in all churches throughout my kingdom and empire there shall be canonical elections and free consecration. I restore to the same Roman Church all the possessions and temporalities which have been abstracted until the present day either in the lifetime of my father or in my own and which I hold; and I will faithfully aid in the restoration of those which I do not hold. The possessions also of all other churches and princes and of every one else, either cleric or laymen, which had been lost in that war, I will restore, so far as I hold them, according to the counsel of the princes or according to justice; and I will faithfully aid in the restoration of those that I do not hold. And I grant a true peace to the lord Pope Calixtus and to the Holy Roman Church and to all who are or have been on its side. In matters where the Holy Roman Church would seek assistance I will faithfully grant it; and in those where she shall complain to me, I will duly grant justice to her.

Chapter Seven

The Crusades

IN ITS broadest sense, the word *crusade* applies to any military expedition undertaken by Christians, with papal sanction, against infidels or heretics. Thus it applies to a variety of medieval episodes, from the *reconquista* of Spain to the papal vendetta against Frederick II of Germany. Most commonly, however, the word refers to the great western European attempt to recover the Holy Land from the Muslims.

The origins of the crusading movement are both general and specific. Generally, the Crusades were the product of the "openness" of the twelfth century. That century had two frontiers; an internal one of forest and marsh which the rapid growth of population forced it to exploit, and an external one for which population growth is only a partial explanation. That frontier pointed toward the east, against the Slavs beyond the Elbe and Oder, and toward the south, where the Mediterranean soon ceased to be a Muslim lake.

Also in the category of general motives behind the Crusading movement was the religious revival of the later eleventh and twelfth centuries. The two motives were obviously related. Although the conception of violence in the service of religion is not uniquely western, the expansionist tendency of the twelfth century offered it an ideal environment in which to operate. Here the specifically religious practice of pilgrimage played an important role. The people of western Europe became noticeably more mobile during the eleventh century. Granted the religious revival, one natural outcome of this was the increase in the practice of pilgrimage.

The desire to visit holy places of the Christian religion might seem natural to the pious, but it was not much practiced until the fourth century. The motivating factors were more the development of a Christian penitential system, the difficulty of travel and the growth of a popular veneration for relics. In western Europe itself, St. James of Compostella and Rome were the prime objects of pilgrimage; in the East, the scenes of the birth, life and passion of

Christ, although the Holy Land, even before the Muslim conquest, was increasingly difficult to visit. The eleventh century established a balance. It was difficult and expensive to reach Palestine, but possible. At the same time desire to reach it and the rewards, thanks to the penitential system, increased. At this point some of the specific factors in the Crusading movement began to operate.

In the East, the advent of the Turks curtailed pilgrimages to the Holy Land during the second half of the eleventh century. Further, through their conquest of most of Asia Minor, the Turks threatened the existence of the Byzantine Empire. In the West, these developments corresponded ideally with the internal situation. The growth of population had, among other things, made it difficult for the nobility to provide for their younger sons. The result of this particular form of land hunger was internal strife, in recognition of which the Church erected the Peace and Truce of God. Simultaneously (this was the age of the Investiture Controversy), the Papacy saw in the Crusading movement a way to assert its claims to the moral leadership of Europe, besides offering the tempting possibility of a reunification of the Eastern and Western Churches.

All of these factors are explicit in the speech Urban II gave at the Council of Clermont in 1095 and manifested in the response to it. Within a year a formidable army was on its way to the East. Even before that, however, the Crusading movement bore the first of a series of unexpected results. Urban's appeal was directed towards the nobility of France; the expected result was an organized, armed force of knights which would relieve the Holy Land. He did not foresee that the combination of enticements offered in his speech would appeal generally to all classes. Although the Peasants' Crusade was a failure, it illustrates the basically religious motivation behind the Crusades without, however, negating the element of violence.

The Barons' Crusade was not a failure. The establishment of the Latin Kingdom of Jerusalem, and the circumstances under which it was established, governed the later history of the Crusades. On the one hand it produced an implacable hostility between East and West which eventually bore fruit in the Fourth Crusade and the failure of the Crusading movement. On the other, it committed the West to a sporadic and unsuccessful defense of its initial creation.

Without very much question, the united forces of western Europe could have maintained the Latin Kingdom of Jerusalem. This, of course, is the point. Almost any page of the Crusading chronicles reveals the lack of cooperation which made failure inevitable. The religious zeal which governed the whole movement could not submerge secular ambitions and rivalries. Furthermore, by the thirteenth century, medieval piety had other outlets than the Holy Land.

The popular religious movements of the thirteenth century provided an alternative outlet for religious zeal. And, insofar as some of them were heretical, they provided a domestic opportunity for a Crusade. Besides, the Slavs on the German frontier and the Moors in Spain offered more convenient outlets for conversion and aggrandizement. Even in papal circles, the concept of a *crux cismarina,* a crusade on the home front, gained popularity. There were many pagans and heretics locally whose conversion or suppression would have a more beneficial effect on papal authority than futile attempts to maintain the Latin Kingdom.

The failure of the Crusading movement in the Holy Land and its diversion from its proper aim caused a popular reaction. Even at the middle of the twelfth century the failure of the Second Crusade caused a wave of criticism in Germany. In the thirteenth, after the debacle of the Fourth Crusade and the horrors of the Albigensian Crusade, the Crusade against Frederick II, and the pitiful example of Louis IX, the revulsion became general. For the secular minded, there were more important things to do at home; for the religious, the question arose, why not "worship God just as well in Paris as in Jerusalem?" Although the Mongol invasions opened up for some the tantalizing opportunity of a world empire governed by the Roman Church, the Crusading ideal died long before the final conquest of Acre in 1291.

It remains to assess the significance of the Crusades. At one time almost everything connected with the High Middle Ages was ascribed to the Crusades—the revival of towns and commerce, the decline of feudalism, the rise of national monarchies, and many other things. Now, the Crusades are seen as merely one aspect of a general European revival.

Intellectually, the Crusades made very little contribution to medieval life. No doubt the Crusading experience broadened the intellectual horizons of many people as it undoubtedly increased their geographical knowledge. Particularly in the thirteenth century, thanks to the Mongol invasions, the Crusades paved the way for European contacts with India and China. But as for the positive contribution of new ideas, the Crusades contributed nothing. And the Crusades, as we shall see, took place at a time when western Europe was busily absorbing new ideas—most of them from Islamic sources. Byzantium, Sicily and Spain was their source, not the Holy Land.

Economically, the contribution of the Crusades was much greater. If they did not cause, they certainly contributed to the demand for oriental spices and luxuries. And thereby they contributed to the prosperity of the Italian maritime states which served as the *entrepôts* between East and West, both for pilgrims and goods. The Crusades further stimulated economic life through the liquidation of assets necessary for participation in them

In the military field the influence of the Crusades was patent, especially in military architecture in which the Arabs and Byzantines were much more advanced than the West. Also from the East came the practice of wearing a surcoat over armor to soften the effect of sun on metal. And most probably heraldic devices and coats of arms were imports from the Holy Land.

For the papacy, the Crusades were initially a source of great prestige and always a great source of military power. On the other hand, the failure of the Crusades and the papal perversion of the Crusading ideal ultimately diminished the moral authority of the papacy and in that respect contributed to the defeat of the medieval papacy at the hands of secular monarchies. The practice of granting indulgences, which later came to be so abused, first became widespread during and as a result of the Crusades.

In sum, the Crusading movement, except for some specific and relatively minor contributions, was merely the product of, or an agent in, forces already at work in western Europe. For most people, however, it remains the most romantic episode of the Middle Ages and the one most written about both by contemporaries and modern historians.

1. *Speech of Urban II at Clermont*

There are four contemporary versions of the famous speech that Urban II gave at the Council of Clermont on November 27, 1095. All are in substantial agreement as to its content; the one given below, by Robert the Monk, is the only eyewitness account.

The translation is from Robinson's *Readings,* Vol. I, 312–16.

IN THE year of our Lord's Incarnation one thousand and ninety-five, a great council was celebrated within the bounds of Gaul, in Auvergne, in the city which is called Clermont. Over this Pope Urban II presided, with the Roman bishops and cardinals. This council was a famous one on account of the concourse of both French and German bishops, and of princes as well. Having arranged the matters relating to the Church, the lord pope went forth into a certain spacious plain, for no building was large enough to hold all the people. The pope then, with sweet and persuasive eloquence, addressed those present in words something like the following, saying:

"Oh, race of Franks, race from across the mountains, race beloved and chosen by God,—as is clear from many of your works,—set apart from all other nations by the situation of your country as well as by your Catholic faith and the honor which you render to the holy Church: to you our discourse is addressed, and for you our exhortations are intended. We wish you to know what a grievous cause has led us to your country, for it is the imminent peril threatening you and all the faithful which has brought us hither.

"From the confines of Jerusalem and from the city of Constantinople a grievous report has gone forth and has repeatedly been brought to our ears; namely, that a race from the kingdom of the Persians, an accursed race, a race wholly alienated from God, 'a generation that set not their heart aright, and whose spirit was not steadfast with God,' has violently invaded the lands of those Christians and has depopulated them by pillage and fire. They have led away a part of the captives into their own country, and a part they have killed by cruel tortures. They have either destroyed the churches of God or appropriated them for the rites of their own religion. They destroy the altars, after having defiled them with their uncleanness. . . . The kingdom of the Greeks is now dismembered by them and has been deprived of territory so vast in extent that it could not be traversed in two months' time.

"On whom, therefore, is the labor of avenging these wrongs and of recovering this territory incumbent, if not upon you,—you, upon whom, above all other nations, God has conferred remarkable glory in arms, great courage, bodily activity, and strength to humble the heads of those who resist you? Let the deeds of your ancestors encourage you and incite your minds to manly achievements: —the glory and greatness of King Charlemagne, and of his son Louis, and of your other monarchs, who have destroyed the kingdoms of the Turks and have extended the sway of the holy Church over lands previously pagan. Let the holy sepulcher of our Lord and Saviour, which is possessed by the unclean nations, especially arouse you, and the holy places which are now treated with ignominy and irreverently polluted with the filth of the unclean. Oh, most valiant soldiers and descendants of invincible ancestors, do not degenerate, and recall the valor of your progenitors.

"But if you are hindered by love of children, parents, or wife, remember that the Lord says in the Gospel, 'He that loveth father or mother more than me is not worthy of me.' 'Every one that hath forsaken houses, or brethren, or sisters, or father, or mother, or wife, or children, or lands, for my name's sake, shall receive an hundred fold, and shall inherit everlasting life.' Let none of your possessions retain you, nor solicitude for your family affairs. For this land which you inhabit, shut in on all sides by the seas and surrounded by the mountain peaks, is too narrow for your large population; nor does it abound in wealth; and it furnishes scarcely food enough for its cultivators. Hence it is that you murder and devour one another, that you wage war, and that very many among you perish in intestine strife.

"Let hatred therefore depart from among you, let your quarrels end, let wars cease, and let all dissensions and controversies slumber. Enter upon the road to the Holy Sepulcher; wrest that land from the wicked race, and subject it to yourselves. That land which as the Scripture says, 'floweth with milk and honey' was given by God into the power of the children of Israel. Jerusalem is the center of the earth; the land is fruitful above all others, like another paradise of delights. This spot the Redeemer of mankind has made illustrious by his advent, has beautified by his sojourn, has consecrated by his passion, has redeemed by his death, has glorified by his burial.

"This royal city, however, situated at the center of the earth, is now held captive by the enemies of Christ and is subjected, by those who do not know God, to the worship of the heathen. She seeks, therefore, and desires to be liberated and ceases not to implore you to come to her aid. From you especially she asks succor, because as we have already said, God has conferred upon you above all other nations great glory in arms. Accordingly, undertake this journey eagerly for the remission of your sins, with the assurance of the reward of imperishable glory in the kingdom of heaven."

When Pope Urban had urbanely said these and very many similar things, he so centered in one purpose the desires of all who were present that all cried out, "It is the will of God! It is the will of God!" When the venerable Roman pontiff heard that, with eyes uplifted to heaven, he gave thanks to God and, commanding silence with his hand, said:

"Most beloved brethren, today is manifest in you what the Lord says in the Gospel, 'Where two or three are gathered together in my name, there am I in the midst of them'; for unless God had been present in your spirits, all of you would not have uttered the same cry; since, although the cry issued from numerous mouths, yet the origin of the cry was one. Therefore I say to you that God, who implanted this in your breasts, has drawn it forth from you. Let that then be your war cry in combats, because it is given to you by God. When an armed attack is made upon the enemy, let this one cry be raised by all the soldiers of God: 'It is the will of God! It is the will of God!'

"And we neither command nor advise that the old or feeble, or those incapable of bearing arms, undertake this journey. Nor ought women to set out at all without their husbands, or brothers, or legal guardians. For such are more of a hindrance than aid, more of a burden than an advantage. Let the rich aid the needy; and according to their wealth let them take with them experienced soldiers. The priests and other clerks, whether secular or regular, are not to go without the consent of their bishop; for this journey would profit them nothing if they went without permission. Also, it is not fitting that laymen should enter upon the pilgrimage without the blessing of their priests.

"Whoever, therefore, shall determine upon this holy pilgrimage, and shall make his vow to God to that effect, and shall offer himself to him for sacrifice, as a living victim, holy and acceptable to God, shall wear the sign of the cross of the Lord on his forehead or on his breast. When, indeed, he shall return from his journey, having fulfilled his vow, let him place the cross on his back between his shoulders. Thus shall ye, indeed, by this twofold action, fulfill the precept of the Lord, as he commands in the Gospel, 'He that taketh not his cross, and followeth after me, is not worthy of me.'"

2. *Gesta Francorum*

The author of this contemporary account of the First Crusade is anonymous. It is clear, however, that he was a vassal of Bohemond and that he accompanied him on the Crusade. He was a Sicilian Norman therefore, and a knight, not a cleric. He writes from the point of view of the simple soldier. Our anonymous author had no pretensions to learning or literary background; he wrote a simple, straightforward and extremely valuable account.

The translation is by Rosalind Hill in the *Nelson's Medieval Texts Series* (London: 1962), pp. 1–17, 72–101.

Book I

(i) When that time had already come, of which the Lord Jesus warns his faithful people every day, especially in the Gospel where he says, 'If any man will come after me, let him deny himself, and take up his cross, and follow me,' there was a great stirring of heart throughout all the Frankish lands, so that if any man, with all his heart and all his mind, really wanted to follow God and faithfully to bear the cross after him, he could make no delay in taking the road to the Holy Sepulchre as quickly as possible. For even the pope set out across the Alps as soon as he could, with his archbishops, bishops, abbots and priests, and he began to deliver eloquent sermons and to preach, saying, 'If any man wants to save his soul, let him have no hesitation in taking the way of the Lord in humility, and if he lacks money, the divine mercy will give him enough.' The lord pope said also, 'Brothers, you must suffer for the name of Christ many things, wretchedness, poverty, nakedness, persecution, need, sickness, hunger, thirst and other such troubles, for the Lord says to his disciples, "You must suffer many things for my name," and "Be not ashamed to speak before men, for I will give you what you shall say" and afterwards "Great will be your reward."' And when these words had begun to be rumoured abroad through all the duchies and countries of the Frankish lands, the Franks, hearing them, straightway began to sew the cross on the right shoulders of their garments, saying that they would all with one accord follow in the footsteps of Christ, by whom they had been redeemed from the power of hell. So they set out at once from their homes in the lands of the Franks.

(ii) The Franks ordered themselves in three armies. One, which entered into Hungary, was led by Peter the Hermit and Duke Godfrey, Baldwin his brother and Baldwin, count of Hainault. These most valiant knights and many others (whose names I do not know) travelled by the road which Charlemagne, the heroic king of the Franks, had formerly caused to be built to Constantinople.

The aforesaid Peter was the first to reach Constantinople on 1 August, and many Germans came with him. There they found men from northern and southern Italy and many others gathered together. The emperor ordered such provisions as there were in the city to be given to them, and he said, 'Do not cross the Hellespont until the great army of the Christians arrives, for there are not enough of you to fight against the Turks.' But those Christians behaved abominably, sacking and burning the palaces of the city, and stealing the lead from the roofs of the churches and selling it to the Greeks, so that the emperor was angry, and ordered them to cross the Hellespont. After they had crossed they did not cease from their misdeeds, and they burned and laid waste both houses and churches. At last they reached Nicomedia, where the Italians and Germans broke away from the Franks, because the Franks were intolerably proud. The Italians chose a leader called Rainald; the Germans also chose a leader, and they all went into Rum and travelled for four days' journey beyond the city of Nicea, where they found a deserted castle named Xerigordo which they took, finding therein plenty of corn and wine and meat and abundance of all good things. But when the Turks heard that the Christians were in the castle, they came and besieged it. Before its gate was a well, and beneath its walls a spring, where Rainald went out to lay an ambush for the Turks, but when they arrived on Michaelmas Day they caught Rainald and his company, and killed many of them. The survivors fled into the castle, which the Turks at once besieged, cutting off the water-supply. Our men were therefore so terribly afflicted by thirst that they bled their horses and asses and drank the blood; others let down belts and clothes into a sewer and squeezed out the liquid into their mouths; others passed water into one another's cupped hands and drank; others dug up damp earth and lay down on their backs, piling the earth upon their chests because they were so dry with thirst. The bishops and priests encouraged our men and told them not to despair. This miserable state of affairs went on for eight days. Then the leader of the Germans made an agreement to betray his comrades to the Turks, and pretending that he was going out to fight he fled to them, and many men went with him. Of the remainder, those who would not renounce God were killed; others, whom the Turks captured alive, were divided among their captors like sheep, some were put up as targets and shot with arrows, others sold and given away as if they were brute beasts. Some of the Turks took their prisoners home to Khorasan, Antioch or Aleppo or wherever they happened to live. These men were the first to endure blessed martyrdom for the Name of our Lord Jesus.

Afterwards, when the Turks heard that Peter the Hermit and Walter the Penniless were in Kivotos, which is beyond the city of Nicea, they came thither full of glee intending to kill them and their comrades, and when they had come they found Walter and his men, and killed them at once. Peter the Hermit, however, had gone off to Constantinople a little before this happened, for he could not control such a mixed company of people who would not obey him or listen to what he said. The Turks fell upon his men and killed most of them—some they found asleep, others naked, and all these they slaughtered. Among the rest they found a priest saying mass, and they killed him at once upon the altar. Those who managed to escape fled to Kivotos. Some leapt into the sea, and others hid in the woods and mountains. The Turks chased some of our men into the castle, and piled up wood so that they could burn them and the castle together, but the Christians in the castle set fire to the pile of wood, and the flames were blown back against the Turks and burned some of them, but God delivered our men from that fire. At last the Turks took them alive and apportioned them as they had done with the others, sending them away through all the neighbouring lands, some to Khorasan and some to Persia. All this happened in October. When the emperor heard that the Turks had inflicted such a defeat on our men he rejoiced greatly, and gave orders for the survivors to be brought back over the Hellespont. When they had crossed over he had them completely disarmed.

(iii) Our second army came through the Dalmatian lands, and it was led by Raymond, count of Saint Gilles, and the bishop of Le Puy. The third came by way of the old Roman road. In this band were Bohemond and Richard of the Principality, Robert count of Flanders, Robert the Norman, Hugh the Great, Everard of Puiset, Achard of Montmerle, Isard of Mouzon and many others. Some of them came to the port of Brindisi, others to Bari or Otranto. Hugh the Great and William son of the Marquis embarked at Bari and sailed to Durazzo, but the governor of that place, hearing that warriors of such experience were arriving, immediately devised a treacherous plan, and he arrested them and sent them under guard to the emperor at Constantinople, so that they might swear fealty to him.

After this Duke Godfrey was the first of all our leaders to reach Constantinople with a great army, and he arrived two days before Christmas, and encamped outside the city until that wretch of an emperor gave orders that quarters were to be assigned to him in the suburbs. When the duke had settled in, he sent his squires out each day, quite confidently, to get straw and other things necessary for the horses; but, when they thought that they could go out freely whenever they liked, the wretched Emperor Alexius ordered his Turcopuli and Patzinaks to attack and kill them. So Baldwin, the duke's brother, hearing of this, lay in ambush, and when he found the enemy killing his men he attacked them bravely and by God's help defeated them. He took sixty prisoners, some of whom he killed and others he presented to the duke his brother. When the emperor heard of this he was very angry, and the duke, realising this, led his men out of the city and encamped outside the walls. Late that evening the miserable emperor ordered his men to attack the duke and the Christian army, but our unconquered leader with his Christian knights drove back the imperial troops, killing seven men and driving the rest to the gates of the city. Afterwards he came back to his camp and stayed there for five days, until he came to an agreement with the emperor, who told him to cross the Hellespont and promised that he would have as good provision there as he had in Constantinople; moreover the emperor promised to give alms to the poor so that they could live.

(iiii) As for Bohemond, that great warrior, he was besieging Amalfi when he heard that an immense army of Frankish crusaders had arrived, going to the Holy Sepulchre and ready to fight the pagans. So he began to make careful inquiries as to the arms they carried, the badge which they wore in Christ's pilgrimage and the war-cry which they shouted in battle. He was told, 'They are well-armed, they wear the badge of Christ's cross on their right arm or between their shoulders, and as a war-cry they shout all together "God's will, God's will, God's will!"' Then Bohemond, inspired by the Holy Ghost, ordered the most valuable cloak which he had to be cut up forthwith and made into crosses, and most of the knights who were at the siege began to join him at once, for they were full of enthusiasm, so that Count Roger was left almost alone, and when he had gone back to Sicily he grieved and lamented because he had lost his army. My lord Bohemond went home to his own land and made careful preparations for setting out on the way to the Holy Sepulchre. Thereafter he crossed the sea with his army, and with him went Tancred son of the Marquis, Richard of the Principality and Ranulf his brother, Robert of Anse, Herman of Cannes, Robert of Sourdeval, Robert Fitz-Toustan, Humphrey Fitz-Ralph, Richard son of Count Ranulf, the count of Russignolo and his brothers, Boel of Chartres, Aubré of Cagnano and Humphrey of Monte Scaglioso. All these crossed at Bohemond's expense, and reached western Macedonia, where they found plenty of corn and wine and other things to eat, and going down into the valley of Andronopolis they waited for their men, until all had crossed over. Then Bohemond called a council to encourage his men, and to warn them all to be courteous and refrain from plundering that land, which belonged to Christians, and he said that no one was to take more than sufficed for his food.

Then we set out and travelled through very rich country from one village to another, and from one city to another and from one castle to another, until we came to Castoria, where we held the feast of Christmas and stayed for some days trying to buy provisions, but the inhabitants would sell us none, because they were much afraid of us, taking us to be no pilgrims but plunderers come to lay waste the land and to kill them. So we seized oxen, horses and asses, and anything else we could find, and leaving Castoria we went into Palagonia, where there was a castle of heretics. We attacked this place from all sides and it soon fell into our hands, so we set fire to it and burnt the castle and its inhabitants together. After this we reached the river Vardar, and my lord Bohemond crossed over with some of his men, but not all, for the count of Russignolo and his brothers stayed behind. The emperor's army came up and attacked the count and his brothers and all their men, so when Tancred heard of this he went back and, diving into the river, he swam across to the others, with two thousand men following him. They found Turcopuli and Patzinaks fighting with our men, so they made a sudden and gallant attack and, since they were men of experience, they defeated the enemy and took many prisoners whom they bound and led before my lord Bohemond. He said to them, 'You scoundrels, why do you kill Christ's people and mine? I have no quarrel with your emperor!' They answered, 'We cannot do anything else. We are at the emperor's command, and whatever he orders, that we must do.' Bohemond let them go scot-free. This battle was fought on the fourth day of the week, which was Ash Wednesday. Blessed be God in all his works! Amen.

Book II

(v) The wretched emperor commanded one of his own men, who was very dear to him and whom they call the *kyriopalatios*, to accompany our messengers so that he might guide us safely through his country until we came to Constantinople. Whenever we passed by any of their cities this man used to tell the people of the land to bring us provisions, as those whom we have mentioned before used to do. It was clear that they were so much afraid of my lord Bohemond's strong army that they would not allow any of our men to go inside the walls of the cities. Our men wanted to attack one of the castles and take it, because it was full of goods of all kinds, but the valiant Bohemond would not allow this, for he wished to treat the country justly and to keep faith with the emperor, so he was furious with Tancred and all the others. This happened one evening, and the next morning the inhabitants of the castle emerged in procession, carrying crosses in their hands, and came into the presence of Bohemond, who received them with joy and let them also go away rejoicing. After this we reached a town called Serres, where we encamped and had provisions good enough for Lent. While we were there Bohemond made an agreement with two of the *kyriopalatioi*, and because of his friendship with them and his desire to treat the country justly he ordered all the animals which our men had stolen and kept to be given back. Thereafter we reached the city of Rusa. The Greek inhabitants came out and approached my lord Bohemond rejoicing, bringing us plenty of provisions, so we pitched our tents there on the Wednesday in Holy Week. While we were there Bohemond left his army, and went ahead to Constantinople with a few knights to take counsel with the emperor. Tancred stayed behind with the army of Christ, and when he saw that the pilgrims were buying food he had the idea of turning aside from the road and bringing the people where they could live in plenty; so that he went into a certain valley full of all kinds of things which are good to eat, and there we kept the festival of Easter with great devotion.

(vi) When the emperor had heard that Bohemond, that most distinguished man, had come, he ordered him to be received with proper ceremony, but took care to lodge him outside the city. After Bohemond had settled in, the emperor sent to invite him to a secret conference. Duke Godfrey and his brother were also present, and the count of St. Gilles was near the city. Then the emperor, who was troubled in mind and fairly seething with rage, was planning how to entrap these Christian knights by fraud and cunning, but by God's grace neither he nor his men found place or time to harm them. At last all the elders of Constantinople, who were afraid of losing their country, took counsel together and devised a crafty plan of making the dukes, counts and all the leaders of our army swear an oath of fealty to the emperor. This our leaders flatly refused to do, for they said, 'Truly, this is unworthy of us, and it seems unjust that we should swear to him any oath at all.'

Perhaps, however, we were fated to be misled often by our leaders, for what did they do in the end? They may say that they were constrained by need, and had to humble themselves willy-nilly to do what that abominable emperor wanted.

Now the emperor was much afraid of the gallant Bohemond, who had often chased him and his army from the battlefield, so he told Bohemond that he would give him lands beyond Antioch, fifteen days' journey in length and eight in width, provided that he would swear fealty with free consent, and he added this promise, that if Bohemond kept his oath faithfully he would never break his own. But why did such brave and determined knights do a thing like this? It must have been because they were driven by desperate need.

The emperor for his part guaranteed good faith and security to all our men, and swore also to come with us, bringing an army and a navy, and faithfully to supply us with provisions both by land and sea, and to take care to restore all those things which we had lost. Moreover he promised that he would not cause or permit anyone to trouble or vex our pilgrims on the way to the Holy Sepulchre.

The count of St. Gilles was encamped outside the city in the suburbs, and his army had stayed behind, so the emperor ordered him to do homage and swear fealty as the others had done; but when the emperor sent him this message the count was planning how to revenge himself on the imperial army. Duke Godfrey and Robert, count of Flanders, and the other leaders, however, told him that it would be improper to fight against fellow Christians, and the valiant Bohemond said that if Count Raymond did any injustice to the emperor, or refused to swear fealty to him, he himself would take the emperor's part. Therefore the count took the advice of his friends and swore that he would respect the life and honour of Alexius, and neither destroy them nor permit anyone else to do so; but when he was asked to do homage he said that he would not, even at the peril of his life. After this my lord Bohemond's army came up to Constantinople.

(vii) Tancred and Richard of the Principality crossed the Hellespont secretly, because they did not want to take the oath to the emperor, and nearly all Bohemond's forces went with them. Soon afterwards the count of St. Gilles approached Constantinople, and he stayed on there with his forces. Bohemond stayed with the emperor in order to consult him about the supply of provisions to the people who had gone on beyond Nicea, so Duke Godfrey was the first to go to Nicomedia, taking with him Tancred and all the others. They stayed there for three days, and when the duke saw that there was no road by which he could lead these people to Nicaea (for there were so many of them that they could not go by the route which the other crusaders had followed) he sent ahead three thousand men with axes and swords so that they could go on and hack open a route for our pilgrims as far as the city of Nicaea. This route led over a mountain, steep and very high, so the pathfinders made crosses of metal and wood, and put them upon stakes where our pilgrims could see them. Eventually we came to Nicaea, which is the capital of Rum, on Wednesday the sixth of May, and there we encamped. Before my lord the valiant Bohemond came to us we were so short of food that a loaf cost twenty or thirty pence, but after he came he ordered plenty of provisions to be brought to us by sea, so goods poured in both by land and sea, and all Christ's army enjoyed great abundance.

(viii) On Ascension Day we began to lay siege to the town, and to build siege-engines and wooden towers by means of which we could knock down the towers on the wall. We pressed the siege so bravely and fiercely for two days that we managed to undermine the wall of the city, but the Turks who were inside sent messengers to the others who had come to their help, telling them that they might come and enter, fearlessly and safely, by way of the south gate, for there was no-one there to stand in their way or attack them. This gate, however, was blocked on that very day (the Saturday after Ascension Day) by the count of St. Gilles and the bishop of Le Puy. The count, who came from the other side of the city with a very strong army, trusting in God's protection and glorious in his earthly weapons, found the Turks coming towards the gate against our men. Protected on all sides by the sign of the Cross, he made a fierce attack upon the enemy and defeated them so that they took to flight and many of them were killed. The survivors rallied with the help of other Turks and came in high spirits, exulting in their certainty of victory, bringing with them ropes with which to lead us bound into Khorasan. They came along gleefully and began to descend a little way from the top of the mountain, but as many as came down had their heads cut off by our men, who threw the heads of the slain into the city by means of a sling, in order to cause more terror among the Turkish garrison.

After this the count of St. Gilles and the bishop of Le Puy took counsel together how they could undermine a tower which stood over against their camp, so they set men to sap it, with arbalists and archers to protect them. The sappers dug down to the foundations of the wall and inserted beams and pieces of wood, to which they set fire, but because all this was done in the evening it was already night when the tower fell, and since it was dark our men could not fight with the defenders. That night the Turks arose in haste and rebuilt the wall so strongly that at daybreak there was no chance of defeating them at that point.

Soon afterwards Robert count of Normandy and Count Stephen arrived with many others, and Roger of Barneville followed them. Then Bohemond took up his station in front of the city, with Tancred next to him, then Duke Godfrey and the count of Flanders, next to whom was Robert of Normandy, and then the count of St. Gilles and the bishop of Le Puy. The city was therefore so closely besieged by land that no-one dared go out or in. Our men were all, for the first time, collected together in this place, and who could count such a great army of Christians? I do not think that anyone has ever seen, or will ever see, so many valiant knights.

On one side of the city was a great lake, on which the Turks launched boats, and they went in and out bringing fodder and wood and many other things, so our leaders took counsel together and sent messengers to Constantinople to ask the emperor to have boats brought to Kivotos, where there is a harbour, and to have oxen collected to drag these boats over the mountains and through the woods until they reached the lake. The emperor had this done immediately, and sent his Turcopuli with them. His men would not launch the boats at once on the day on which they arrived, but they put out on the lake at nightfall, with the boats full of Turcopuli who were well armed. At daybreak there were the boats, all in very good order, sailing across the lake towards the city. The Turks, seeing them, were surprised and did not know whether it was their own fleet or that of the emperor, but when they realised that it was the emperor's they were afraid almost to death, and began to wail and lament, while the Franks rejoiced and gave glory to God. Then the Turks, realising that their armies could do no more to help them, sent a message to the emperor saying that they would surrender the city to him if he would let them go free with their wives and children and all their goods. The emperor, who was a fool as well as a knave, told them to go away unhurt and without fear; he had them brought to him at Constantinople under safe-conduct, and kept them carefully so that he could have them ready to injure the Franks and obstruct their crusade.

We besieged this city for seven weeks and three days, and many of our men suffered martyrdom there and gave up their blessed souls to God with joy and gladness, and many of the poor starved to death for the Name of Christ. All these entered Heaven in triumph, wearing the robe of martyrdom which they have received, saying with one voice, 'Avenge, O Lord, our blood which was shed for thee, for thou art blessed and worthy of praise for ever and ever. Amen.'

Book X

(xxx) When all our enemies had been resoundingly defeated (high praise be to God Almighty, the Three in One) they fled hither and thither, some of them half dead, others wounded, and they fell down and died in the valleys and woods and fields and by the roadside. Christ's people, the conquering pilgrims, went back into the city after their enemies had been defeated, exulting in their joyful triumph. Without delay all our leaders, Duke Godfrey, Raymond, count of St. Gilles, Bohemond, the count of Normandy and the count of Flanders, and all the others, sent the high-born knight Hugh the Great to the emperor at Constantinople, asking him to come and take over the city and fulfil the obligations which he had undertaken towards them. Hugh went, but he never came back.

After all these things were done, all our leaders assembled and held a council to decide how best to guide and lead the people until they should complete their journey to the Holy Sepulchre, for which they had already suffered so many perils. In this council they decided that they dared not yet enter into the land of the pagans, because in summer it is very dry and waterless, and that they would therefore wait until the beginning of November. So our leaders separated and each went off into his own territory until it should be time to resume the march. They had it announced throughout the city that if there were any poor man, lacking gold and silver, who wished to take service with them and stay on, they would gladly enrol him.

There was in the army of the count of St. Gilles a certain knight whose name was Raymond Pilet. He took into his service many knights and foot-soldiers, and set out boldly, with the army which he had collected, into the land of the Saracens. He passed by two cities and came to a castle named Tell-Mannas. The occupants of this castle, who were Syrians, surrendered it to him at once, and when his men had all been there for eight days messengers came to him, saying, 'There is a castle full of Saracens near at hand.' The knights and pilgrims of Christ went straight to that castle and besieged it on all sides, and by Christ's help they took it at once. They captured all the peasants of the district and killed those who would not be christened, but those who preferred to acknowledge Christ they spared. When this was done, our Franks came back with great joy to the first castle. On the third day they set out and came to a city named Marra which was not far off, in which were assembled many Turks and Saracens from the city of Aleppo and from all the cities and castles round about. The barbarians came out to fight with our men who, resolving to do battle with them, put them to flight, yet the enemy rallied and went on attacking our men all through the day, and their onslaught lasted until the evening. The heat was unspeakable, and our men could not endure such fearful thirst, for they could find no water to drink, so they wanted to get back safely to their castle. The Syrians and poor pilgrims, for their sins, got into a blind panic and began to retreat in a hurry. When the Turks saw them drawing back, they began to pursue them, and victory increased their strength, so that many of our people gave up their souls to God, for love of whom they had come thither. This massacre took place on 5 July. The surviving Franks withdrew into the castle, and Raymond with his men stayed there for several days. The other crusaders, who remained in Antioch, stayed there with joy and great gladness, having the bishop of Le Puy as their ruler and shepherd. But, as God would have it, he fell very sick, and by God's will he departed from this world, and resting in peace he fell asleep in the Lord on the feast of St. Peter's Chains. Therefore there was grief and sorrow and great mourning throughout the whole army of Christ, for the bishop was a helper of the poor and a counsellor of the rich, and he used to keep the clergy in order and preach to the knights, warning them and saying, 'None of you can be saved if he does not respect the poor and succour them; you cannot be saved without them, and they cannot survive without you. They ought every day to pray that God will show mercy towards your sins, by which you daily offend him in many ways, and therefore I beseech you, for the love of God, to be kind to them, and to help them as much as you can.'

(xxxi) Not long afterwards the noble Raymond, count of St. Gilles, came and entered into the land of the Saracens and reached a city called al-Bara, which he attacked with his army and captured at once. He killed all the Saracens whom he found in it, both men and women, great and small, and after he had established his power there he restored the town to the Christian faith, and took counsel with his most trustworthy advisers as to how he might, with due devotion, have a bishop set up in the city, to recall it to the worship of Christ, and to consecrate the house of the devil to be a temple of the true and living God, and a church dedicated to his saints. Eventually they chose an honourable and learned man and took him to Antioch to be consecrated, and this was done. The rest of the army, which was in Antioch, stayed there with joy and gladness.

When the appointed day (the feast of All Saints) approached, all our leaders returned together to Antioch and began to discuss how they should continue their journey to the Holy Sepulchre, for, said they, 'The appointed day is at hand, and it is no time for any further quarrels,' for Bohemond had been asking every day for the recognition of the agreement by which all the leaders had formerly promised to give him the city, but the count of St. Gilles would make no agreement and did not want to give way to Bohemond, because he was afraid of breaking his oath to the emperor. Many meetings were held in the church of St. Peter in order to come to a just conclusion. Bohemond recited his agreement and showed a list of his expenses, and likewise the count of St. Gilles repeated the words and the oath which he had sworn to the emperor on Bohemond's advice. The bishops, with Duke Godfrey, the counts of Flanders and Normandy and the other leaders, went apart from the rest, and entered that part of the church where stands St. Peter's chair, so that they might give judgement between the two parties; but afterwards, fearing lest the journey to the Holy Sepulchre might be interrupted, they would not give a clear judgement. Then said the count of St. Gilles, 'Rather than abandon the journey to the Holy Sepulchre, and provided that Bohemond will come with us, I will faithfully promise to do whatever is approved by our peers, Duke Godfrey and the count of Flanders and Robert the Norman and the other leaders, saving the faith which I owe to the emperor.' Bohemond agreed to all this, and the two of them promised, putting their hands into those of the bishops, that the journey to the Holy Sepulchre should in no wise be interrupted by them. Then Bohemond took counsel with his men as to how he could garrison and victual the citadel on top of the mountain. Likewise the count of St. Gilles took counsel with his men as to how he could garrison and victual the palace of Yaghi Siyan the amir, and the tower which is over the Bridge Gate (which lies on the side of the city nearest to St. Simeon's Port), so that it could hold out for a long time.

(xxxii) *Description of the city of Antioch.* The city of Antioch is a very fine and distinguished place. Within its walls are four great mountains which are exceedingly high. The citadel, a wonderful building which is exceedingly strong, stands on the highest of them. Down below lies the city, which is impressive and well-planned, adorned with all kinds of splendid buildings, for there are many churches, and three hundred and sixty monasteries. Its patriarch is metropolitan over a hundred and fifty-three bishops.

This city is surrounded by two walls, the greater of which is very high and amazingly broad, built of great stones, and there are set upon it four hundred and fifty towers. Everything about this city is beautiful. On the east it is shut in by four great mountains, on the west, beside the city walls, runs a river called the Orontes. This city is the centre of great authority, for it was formerly established by seventy-five kings, of whom the chief was King Antiochus, from whom it gets its name of Antioch. The Franks besieged this city for eight months and a day, and thereafter they themselves were besieged for three weeks by the Turks and other pagans, in greater number than have ever before been gathered together, whether of Christian men or pagans. Finally, by the help of God and the Holy Sepulchre, they were defeated by the Christians, and we rested in Antioch, with joy and gladness, for five months and eight days.

(xxxiii) When this time came to an end, Raymond count of St. Gilles set out from Antioch with his army in the month of November, and came to a city called Riha and thence to one called al-Bara. On 28 November he reached the city of Marra, in which was assembled a great number of Saracens, Turks, Arabs and other pagans, and the count attacked it next day. Bohemond and his army followed the other counts soon afterwards, and joined forces with them on a Sunday. On the Monday they attacked the town very bravely from all sides, and pressed on with such eagerness and courage that scaling-ladders were set up against the wall, but such was the power of the pagans that on that day it was not possible to come to grips with them or to do them any harm. When our leaders saw that they could do nothing, and that they were labouring in vain, Raymond count of St. Gilles caused a wooden siege-tower to be built, and it was strong and lofty, so engineered and constructed that it ran upon four wheels. On the top storey stood many knights and Everard the Huntsman, who blew loud blasts on his horn, and underneath were armed knights who pushed the tower up to the city wall, over against one of its towers. When the pagans saw this they immediately made an engine by which they threw great stones upon our siege-tower, so that they nearly killed our knights. Moreover they threw Greek fire upon the siege-tower, hoping to burn and destroy it, but this time Almighty God would not let the siege-tower burn, and it was higher than all the walls of the city. Our knights who were on its upper storey (William of Montpellier and many others) threw great stones down upon those who stood on the city wall, and struck them upon their shields; so that shield and man fell backward into the city, and the man was killed. While they were doing this others held in their hands spears adorned with pennants, and tried to pull the enemy towards them with lances and hooks of iron. Thus they fought until the evening. Behind the siege-tower stood the priests and clerks, clad in their holy vestments, praying and beseeching God to defend his people, and to exalt Christendom and cast down idolatry.

On the other side of the city our knights were fighting every day with the enemy, putting up scaling-ladders against the city wall, but the might of the pagans was such that they could gain no advantage. At last Geoffrey of Lastours was the first to get up the ladder on to the wall; the ladder broke at once under the weight of the crowd who followed him, but nevertheless he and some others succeeded in reaching the top of the wall. Those who had gone up cleared a space around them on the wall. Others found a fresh ladder and put it up quickly, and many knights and foot-soldiers went up it at once, but the Saracens attacked them so fiercely, from the wall and from the ground, shooting arrows and fighting hand-to-hand with spears, that many of our men were terrified and jumped off the wall. While those very gallant men who stayed on the wall were resisting the enemy attack, others, protected by the siege-tower, were undermining the defences of the city. When the Saracens saw that our men had undermined the wall they were panic-stricken and fled into the city. (This all happened on a Saturday, at the hour of vespers, when the sun was setting. It was 11 December.)

Then Bohemond sent an interpreter to the Saracen leaders to tell them that if they, with their wives and children and goods, would take refuge in a palace which lies above the gate he would save them from death. Our men all entered the city, and each seized his own share of whatever goods he found in houses or cellars, and when it was dawn they killed everyone, man or woman, whom they met in any place whatsoever. No corner of the city was clear of Saracen corpses, and one could scarcely go about the city streets except by treading on the dead bodies of the Saracens. Then Bohemond took those whom he had ordered to enter the palace, and stripped them of all their belongings, gold, silver and other valuables, and some of them he caused to be killed, others to be taken to Antioch and sold as slaves.

The Franks stayed in that city for one month and four days, during which time the bishop of Orange died. While we were there some of our men could not satisfy their needs, either because of the long stay or because they were so hungry, for there was no plunder to be had outside the walls. So they ripped up the bodies of the dead, because they used to find bezants hidden in their entrails, and others cut the dead flesh into slices and cooked it to eat.

(xxxiiii) Bohemond could not reach an agreement about his claims with the count of St. Gilles, so he was angry and went back to Antioch.

Count Raymond, without much delay, sent messengers to Antioch, asking Duke Godfrey and the count of Flanders and Robert the Norman and Bohemond to come and hold a conference with him at Riha. All the leaders came thither, and took counsel as to how they should continue on their way to the Holy Sepulchre, for which they had set out and towards which they had marched until this time, but they could not reconcile Bohemond with Raymond, unless Count Raymond would surrender Antioch to Bohemond, and this the count was unwilling to do, because of the oath which he had sworn to the emperor. Then the other counts and duke returned to Antioch with Bohemond, but Count Raymond returned to Marra, where the poor pilgrims were, and he ordered his knights to fortify the palace, and the castle which was above the gate by the city bridge.

When Raymond saw that he was the cause why none of the other leaders would set out on the way to the Holy Sepulchre, he went out barefoot from Marra on the thirteenth of January and reached Kafartab, where he stayed for three days and the count of Normandy joined him. The king of Shaizar had sent many messengers to Count Raymond while he was at Marra and Kafartab, because he wanted a treaty of peace, and he swore to pay an indemnity, and to be kind to the Christian pilgrims, so that while they were within his territory they should not suffer the least offence, and he said that he would be glad to sell them horses and food. So our men went out and came to encamp near Shaizar, on the river Orontes. When the king of Shaizar saw the Frankish camp so near to the city he was anxious, and ordered merchandise to be withheld from them unless they moved further off from the city boundary. Next day he sent two Turks, his messengers, to go with them and show them the ford over the river, and to lead them where they could find booty, so they came into a valley guarded by a castle, and seized there more than five thousand animals and plenty of corn and other goods, which were a great refreshment to the whole army of Christ. The garrison of the castle surrendered to the count, and gave him horses and refined gold, and swore on the Koran that they would do no harm to the pilgrims. We stayed there for five days, and when we set out we came rejoicing and took up our quarters in a castle belonging to Arabs, for its lord came out and made an agreement with the count. After leaving this place we reached a city which was very beautiful and full of all kinds of good things; it was called Kephalia and stood in a valley. Its inhabitants, on hearing of the approach of the Franks, left the city, and their gardens full of vegetables and houses full of food, and took to flight. On the third day we left this city and crossed a mountain which was very high and broad, and entered the valley of Sem, which was extremely fertile, and there we stayed for nearly fifteen days. Nor far off there was a castle, in which a great multitude of pagans had assembled. Our men attacked it, and would have taken it by force if the Saracens had not turned out of the gates an immense number of beasts, so that our men returned to the camp with all the good things which they had captured. At dawn our men struck their tents and came to besiege that castle, proposing to encamp there, but the pagans had fled and left the castle empty. Our men entered and found plenty of corn, wine, oil, flour and whatever they needed, so we celebrated the feast of Candlemas there with great devotion. While we were there messengers came from the city of La Chamelle, the king of which sent to the count horses and gold, and made an agreement with him that he would not do the Christians the least harm, but that he would be kind to them and respect them. Also the king of Tripoli sent to the count, proposing to make a faithful treaty of friendship with him, if he agreed, and he sent ten horses and four mules and some gold; but the count said that he would make no treaty at all with him, unless he would be christened.

When we left that valley (which was a very good place) we came on Monday in the second week in February to a castle which is called Arqa and pitched our tents around it. This castle was full of an immense horde of pagans, Turks, Saracens, Arabs and Paulicians, who had made its fortifications exceedingly strong and defended themselves bravely. While we were there fourteen of our knights rode over to the city of Tripoli, which was quite near, and found about sixty Turks and others who had rounded up men and beasts to the number of more than fifteen hundred. Our men made the Sign of the Cross and attacked them, killing six men and capturing six horses, and by God's help they won a marvellous victory.

Raymond Pilet and Raymond vicomte of Turenne left the main army of Count Raymond and came to the city of Tortosa, which they attacked bravely, for it was garrisoned by many of the pagans. When night fell they withdrew into a corner where they encamped and lit many fires, so that it might appear that the whole host was there. The pagans were terrified and fled secretly in the night, leaving the city full of provisions. (It has also an excellent harbour.) Next morning our men came and attacked it from all sides, but they found it empty, so they entered it and stayed there until the siege of Arqa began. There is another city, called Marakia, not far from this one; the amir who governed it made a treaty with our men, admitted them to the city, and put up our banner.

(xxxv) Meanwhile Duke Godfrey, Bohemond and the count of Flanders came to the city of Laodicea, where Bohemond broke away and went back to Antioch. The others came and laid siege to a city called Gibel. But when Raymond count of St. Gilles heard that an immense force of pagans was speeding towards us, determined to fight, he took counsel with his followers and decided to summon those of our leaders who were besieging Gibel to come to his aid. When they heard this news they made a treaty with the amir at once, and agreed with him on terms of peace, receiving a tribute of horses and gold, and so they left the city and came to our help; but the threatened attack did not come, so the said counts encamped on the other side of the river and took part in the siege of Arqa.

Not long afterwards our men rode against Tripoli, and came upon Turks, Arabs and Saracens outside the city. Our men scared them off and put them to flight, killing many of the leading men of the city. So great were the slaughter of pagans and the bloodshed that even the stream which flowed into the city ran red and stained the water in the citizen's tanks, for which reason they were full of grief and lamentation, and so frightened that none of them dared to go outside the city gate.

Another day our men rode over beyond Sem and found oxen, sheep, asses and many other beasts, and they also carried off nearly three thousand camels. We went on besieging Arqa for three months, all but one day, and celebrated Easter there on 10 April. While the siege was going on our ships put into a port near at hand, and they were laden with plenty of provisions, corn, wine, meat, cheese, barley and oil, so that the whole army was very well supplied. Many of our men, including Anselm of Ribemont, William the Picard and many others whose names I do not know, suffered blessed martyrdom in the course of this siege. The king of Tripoli sent frequent messengers to our leaders, asking them to raise the siege and make a treaty with him. When Duke Godfrey and Raymond, count of St. Gilles, and Robert the Norman and the count of Flanders heard this, and saw that the season of harvest was come, for we were eating spring beans in the middle of March and corn in the middle of April, they took counsel together and decided that it would be a very good thing to finish the journey to Jerusalem while the harvest was being gathered in.

(xxxvi) Therefore we left the castle and came to Tripoli on Friday the thirteenth of May, and there we stayed for three days. The king of Tripoli finally made an agreement to set free at once more than three hundred pilgrims who had been captured there, and to give us fifteen thousand bezants and fifteen horses of great value. He also sold us plenty of horses, asses and provisions, so that the whole army of Christ was well supplied. The treaty also stated that if we could defeat the army which the amir of Cairo was preparing against our men, and could take Jerusalem, then the king of Tripoli would be christened and hold his land from our leaders. This was the lawful agreement.

We departed from the city one Monday in the month of May and travelled all that day and night, by a narrow and steep path, until we came to a castle called Bethelon, and thence to a city on the coast called Gibelon, where we suffered badly from thirst, so that we were exhausted by the time that we reached the river called Braym. After this we spent the night and the following day (which was Ascension Day) in crossing a cliff where the path is very narrow, and we expected to find our enemies lying in ambush, but by God's grace none of them dared to come near us. Then our knights went on ahead of us, clearing the way, and we reached a city called Beyrut which lies on the coast. From thence we came to another city called Sagitta, and so to another called Sur, and from Sur to Acre. From Acre we came to a castle named Haifa, and afterwards we encamped near Caesarea, where we celebrated Whit Sunday on 30 May. Thence we came to the city of Ramleh, which the Saracens had evacuated for fear of the Franks. Near Ramleh is a church worthy of great reverence, for in it rests the most precious body of St. George, who there suffered blessed martyrdom at the hands of the treacherous pagans for the name of Christ. While we were there our leaders took counsel together to choose a bishop who might protect and build up this church, and they paid him tithes and endowed him with gold and silver, horses and other animals, so that he and his household might live in a proper and religious manner.

(xxxvii) He stayed there gladly, but we, rejoicing and exulting, came to the city of Jerusalem on Tuesday 6 June and established a very thorough siege. Robert the Norman took up his station on the north, next to the church of St. Stephen the Protomartyr, who was stoned there for the name of Christ, and Robert count of Flanders was next to him. Duke Godfrey and Tancred besieged the city from the west. The count of St. Gilles was on the south, that is to say on Mount Sion, near the church of St. Mary the Mother of the Lord, where the Lord shared the Last Supper with his disciples.

On the third day some of our men—Raymond Pilet, Raymond of Turenne and many others—went off to fight, and found two hundred Arabs. The knights of Christ fought against these misbelievers, and by God's help bravely defeated them, killing many and capturing thirty horses. On the Monday we pressed upon the city in such a vigorous assault that if our scaling-ladders had been ready we should have taken it. We did indeed destroy the curtain-wall, and against the great wall we set up one ladder, up which our knights climbed and fought hand-to-hand with the Saracens and those who were defending the city, using swords and spears. We lost many men, but the enemy lost more. During this siege we could not buy bread for nearly ten days, until a messenger arrived from our ships, and we suffered so badly from thirst that we had to take our horses and other beasts six miles to water, enduring great terror and apprehension on the way. The pool of Siloam, at the foot of Mount Sion, kept us going, but water was sold very dearly in the army.

After the messenger from our ships arrived, our leaders took counsel and decided to send knights who might provide a faithful guard for the men and ships who were in the harbour of Jaffa. At dawn a hundred knights set out from the army of Raymond, count of St. Gilles. They included Raymond Pilet, Achard of Montmerle and William of Sabran, and they rode confidently towards the port. Then thirty of our knights got separated from the others, and fell in with seven hundred Arabs, Turks and Saracens from the army of the amir. The Christian knights attacked them bravely, but they were such a mighty force in comparison with ours that they surrounded our men and killed Achard of Montmerle and some poor foot-soldiers. While our men were thus surrounded and all expecting death, a messenger reached the others, saying to Raymond Pilet, 'Why are you staying here with your knights? Look! All our men are trapped by the Arabs and Turks, and perhaps at this very moment they are all dead, so bring help, bring help!' When our men heard this they rode at once as hard as they could, and came quickly to where the others were fighting. When the pagans saw the Christian knights they split up into two bands, but our men called upon the Name of Christ and charged these misbelievers so fiercely that every knight overthrew his opponent. When the enemy saw that they could not stand up to the brave attack of the Franks they turned tail, panic-stricken, and our men pursued them for the space of nearly four miles, killing many of them, but they spared the life of one so that he could give them information. They also captured one hundred and three horses.

During this siege, we suffered so badly from thirst that we sewed up the skins of oxen and buffaloes, and we used to carry water in them for the distance of nearly six miles. We drank the water from these vessels, although it stank, and what with foul water and barley bread we suffered great distress and affliction every day, for the Saracens used to lie in wait for our men by every spring and pool, where they killed them and cut them to pieces; moreover they used to carry off the beasts into their caves and secret places in the rocks.

(xxxviii) Our leaders then decided to attack the city with engines, so that we might enter it and worship at our Saviour's Sepulchre. They made two wooden siege-towers and various other mechanical devices. Duke Godfrey filled his siege-tower with machines, and so did Count Raymond, but they had to get the timber from far afield. When the Saracens saw our men making these machines, they built up the city wall and its towers by night, so that they were exceedingly strong. When, however, our leaders saw which was the weakest spot in the city's defences, they had a machine and siege-tower transported round to the eastern side one Saturday night. They set up these engines at dawn, and spent Sunday, Monday and Tuesday in preparing the siege-tower and fitting it out, while the count of St. Gilles was getting his engine ready on the southern side. All this time we were suffering so badly from the shortage of water that for one penny a man could not buy sufficient to quench his thirst.

On Wednesday and Thursday we launched a fierce attack upon the city, both by day and by night, from all sides, but before we attacked our bishops and priests preached to us, and told us to go in procession round Jerusalem to the glory of God, and to pray and give alms and fast, as faithful men should do. On Friday at dawn we attacked the city from all sides but could achieve nothing, so that we were all astounded and very much afraid, yet, when that hour came when our Lord Jesus Christ deigned to suffer for us upon the cross, our knights were fighting bravely on the siege-tower, led by Duke Godfrey and Count Eustace his brother. At that moment one of our knights, called Lethold, succeeded in getting on to the wall. As soon as he reached it, all the defenders fled along the walls and through the city, and our men went after them, killing them and cutting them down as far as Solomon's Temple, where there was such a massacre that our men were wading up to their ankles in enemy blood.

Count Raymond was bringing up his army and a siege-tower from the south to the neighbourhood of the wall, but between the wall and the tower there was a deep pit. Our leaders discussed how they should fill the pit, and they had it announced that if anyone would bring three stones to cast into that pit he should have a penny. It took three days and nights to fill the pit, and when it was full they took the siege-tower up to the wall. The defenders fought against our men with amazing courage, casting fire and stones. But when the count heard that the Franks were in the city he said to his men, 'Why are you so slow? Look! All the other Franks are in the city already!' Then the amir who held David's Tower surrendered to the count, and opened for him the gate where the pilgrims used to pay their taxes, so our men entered the city, chasing the Saracens and killing them up to Solomon's Temple, where they took refuge and fought hard against our men for the whole day, so that all the Temple was streaming with their blood. At last, when the pagans were defeated, our men took many prisoners, both men and women, in the Temple. They killed whom they chose, and whom they chose they saved alive. On the roof of the Temple of Solomon were crowded great numbers of pagans of both sexes, to whom Tancred and Gaston of Bearn gave their banners.

After this our men rushed round the whole city, seizing gold and silver, horses and mules, and houses full of all sorts of goods, and they all came rejoicing and weeping from excess of gladness to worship at the Sepulchre of our Saviour Jesus, and there they fulfilled their vows to him. Next morning they went cautiously up on to the Temple roof and attacked the Saracens, both men and women, cutting off their heads with drawn swords. Some of the Saracens threw themselves down headlong from the Temple. Tancred was extremely angry when he saw this.

(xxxix) Our leaders then took counsel and ordered that every man should give alms and pray the God would choose for himself whomsoever he wished, to rule over the others and to govern the city. They also commanded that all the Saracen corpses should be thrown outside the city because of the fearful stench, for almost the whole city was full of their dead bodies. So the surviving Saracens dragged the dead ones out in front of the gates, and piled them up in mounds as big as houses. No-one has ever seen or heard of such a slaughter of pagans, for they were burned on pyres like pyramids, and no-one save God alone knows how many there were. Count Raymond, however, caused the amir and those who were with him to be taken to Ascalon, safe and sound.

On the eighth day after the city was taken they chose Duke Godfrey as its ruler, so that he might fight against the pagans and protect the Christians. Likewise a most experienced and distinguished man called Arnulf was chosen as Patriarch, on the Feast of St. Peter's Chains. (This city was captured by God's Christians on the fifteenth of July, which was a Friday.)

While all this was happening, a messenger came to Tancred and Count Eustace, asking them to make ready and go to receive the surrender of the town of Nablus; so they set out, taking with them many knights and foot-soldiers, and came to the city, the inhabitants of which surrendered at once. Then Duke Godfrey summoned them to come quickly, for the amir of Cairo was getting ready to fight with us at Ascalon, so they went quickly into the mountains, looking for Saracens to fight, and came to Caesarea, from whence they came along the coast towards Ramleh, where they found many Arabs who had been sent as scouts before the main army. Our men chased them and captured several, who gave us a full report as to where their army was, and its numbers, and where it was planning to fight with the Christians. When Tancred heard this, he sent a messenger straight off to Jerusalem to Duke Godfrey and the patriarch and all the other leaders, saying, 'There is going to be a battle at Ascalon, so come quickly with all the forces you can muster!' Then the duke had everyone summoned so that they might go faithfully prepared to fight our enemies at Ascalon. He himself, with the patriarch, Robert count of Flanders and the bishop of Martirano, went with them on Tuesday, but the count of St. Gilles and Robert the Norman said that they would not go unless they knew for certain that there would be a battle, so they ordered their knights to go out and see whether the battle was really going to take place, and to come back as soon as possible, for they themselves were all ready to set out. The knights went out, saw the preparations for the battle and came straight back to report what they had seen with their own eyes. The duke at once summoned the bishop of Martirano and bade him go to Jerusalem to tell the knights there to get ready to come to the field of battle.

On Wednesday those lords went out and rode to battle. The bishop of Martirano was returning from Jerusalem, bearing messages to the duke and the patriarch, when the Saracens met him, and they captured him and took him away with them. Peter the Hermit stayed in Jerusalem to admonish and encourage all the Greek and Latin priests and the clerks to go in procession devoutly to the honour of God, and to pray and give alms, so that God might grant his people victory. The clerks and priests put on their holy vestments and led the procession to the Temple of our Lord, where they sang masses and orisons, praying that God would defend his people.

Meanwhile the patriarch and the bishops and the other leaders were assembled at the river which lies on this side of Ascalon. They carried off from thence many animals, oxen, camels and sheep, and other goods. About three hundred Arabs came up, and our men attacked them and captured two, driving the rest back to their own army. When evening came, the patriarch had it announced throughout all the host that every man should be ready for battle at dawn, and that anyone who turned aside for plunder before the battle was finished should be excommunicated, but that thereafter they might return with great joy to take whatever the Lord should grant.

At daybreak on Friday our men entered into a beautiful valley near the coast and drew up their lines of battle. The duke, the count of Normandy, the count of St. Gilles, the count of Flanders, Count Eustace, Tancred and Gaston each drew up his own men, and foot-soldiers with archers were ordered to precede the knights. All this was thus arranged, and they joined battle at once in the Name of our Lord Jesus Christ. Duke Godfrey with his men fought on the left wing, the count of St. Gilles on the right (near the sea), while the counts of Normandy and Flanders, with Tancred and all the rest, rode in the centre, and thus our men began gradually to advance. The pagans, for their part, stood ready for battle. Each of them had, hanging round his neck, a bottle from which he could drink while he was pursuing us, by God's grace this was not to be.

The count of Normandy, seeing that the amir's standard had a golden apple on the top of the pole, which was covered with silver, rushed straight at its bearer and gave him a mortal wound. The count of Flanders made a determined attack from the other side, and Tancred charged straight into the middle of the enemy camp. When the pagans saw this, they began to flee at once. (There was an innumerable multitude of pagans, and nobody knows how many there were save God alone.) The battle was terrible, but the power of God was with us, so mighty and so strong that we gained the victory at once. The enemies of God stood about blinded and bewildered; although their eyes were open they could not see the knights of Christ and they dared not stand fast against them, for they were terror-stricken by the power of God. Some in their panic climbed up trees, hoping to hide, but our men killed them with arrows and spears and swords, and cast them down to the ground. Others threw themselves flat on the ground, not daring to stand up against us, so our men slaughtered them as one slaughters beasts in a shambles. The count of St. Gilles, who was near the sea, killed any number of them. Some jumped into the sea and others fled hither and thither.

So the amir reached the city, grieving and lamenting, and saying as he wept, 'O spirits of the gods! Who has ever seen or heard of such things as these? Such power, such courage, such an army as has never been overcome by anyone, to be defeated by such a wretched little force of Christians! Woe's me, sad and miserable man that I am! What more can I say? I have been beaten by a force of beggars, unarmed and poverty-stricken, who have nothing but a bag and a scrip. And this is the army which is now pursuing the Egyptians, who often used to give alms to these people when they went round our country begging. I led two hundred thousand soldiers hither to battle, and now I see them all fleeing with slack reins down the road to Cairo, and they have not the courage to rally against the Franks. I swear by Mohammed and by the glory of all the gods that I will never raise another army, because I have been defeated by a strange people. I brought all sorts of weapons and engines to besiege these men in Jerusalem, and it is they who have attacked me two days' march outside the city. Woe's me! What more can I say? I shall be held up to everlasting scorn in the land of Cairo.'

Our men captured the amir's standard, which the count of Normandy redeemed for twenty marks of silver and gave to the patriarch in honour of God and the Holy Sepulchre. The amir's sword was bought for sixty bezants. So by God's will our enemies were defeated. All the ships from the lands of the pagans were there, but when the crews saw the amir fleeing with his army they hoisted sail at once and made for the open sea. Our men went back to the enemy camp and found innumerable spoils of gold and silver, piles of riches, and all kinds of animals, weapons and tools. They took what they wanted and burnt the rest.

Then our men came back to Jerusalem rejoicing, bearing with them all sorts of provisions which they needed. This battle was fought on 12 August, by the mercy of our Lord Jesus Christ, to whom be honour and glory, now and for ever, world without end. May every soul say 'Amen'!

3. *The Chronicle of Geoffry de Villehardouin*

All we know about this author is what he tells us himself, namely, that he was Constable of the County of Champagne and a participant, at the highest levels, in the events he describes. The chronicle was written, or rather dictated, in Old French. That notwithstanding it is probably the greatest of the crusading chronicles and one of the great monuments of the early French language.

The translation is by Sir Frank Marzials (London: J. M. Dent, Co., 1908), pp. 1–7, 12–16, 17–18, 19–21, 22–24, 26, 29–33, 34–35, 37–40, 41–48, 52–57, 58–65.

BE IT known to you that eleven hundred and ninety-seven years after the Incarnation of our Lord Jesus Christ, in the time of Innocent, Pope of Rome, and Philip, King of France, and Richard, King of England, there was in France a holy man named Fulk of Neuilly—which Neuilly is between Lagni-sur-Marne and Paris—and he was a priest and held the cure of the village. And this said Fulk began to speak of God throughout the Isle of France, and the other countries round about; and you must know that by him the Lord wrought many miracles.

Be it known to you further, that the fame of this holy man so spread, that it reached the Pope of Rome, Innocent; and the pope sent to France, and ordered the right worthy man to preach the cross (the Crusade) by his authority. And afterward the Pope sent a cardinal of his, Master Peter of Capua, who himself had taken the cross, to proclaim the indulgence of which I now tell you, viz., that all who should take the cross and serve in the host for one year, would be delivered from all the sins they had committed, and acknowledged in confession. And because this indulgence was so great, the hearts of men were much moved, and many of them took the cross for the greatness of the pardon.

The other year after that right worthy man Fulk had so spoken of God, there was held a tourney in Champagne, at a castle called Ecri, and by God's grace, it so happened that Thibaut, Count of Champagne and

Brie, took the cross, and the Count Louis of Blois and Chartres likewise; and this was at the beginning of Advent (28th November 1199). Now you must know that this Count Thibaut was but a young man, and not more than twenty-two years of age and the Count Louis not more than twenty-seven. . . .

With these two counts there took the cross two very high and puissant Barons of France, Simon of Montfort, and Renaud of Montmirail. Great was the fame thereof throughout the land when these two high and puissant men took the cross. . . .

Afterward the Barons held a parliament at Soissons, to settle when they should start, and whither they should wend. But they could come to no agreement, because it did not seem to them that enough people had taken the cross. So during all that year (1200) no two months passed without assemblings in parliament at Compeigne. There met all the counts and barons who had taken the cross. Many were the opinions given and considered; but in the end it was agreed that envoys should be sent, the best that could be found, with full powers, as if they were the lords in person, to settle such matters as needed settlement. . . .

To these six envoys the business in hand was fully committed, all the Barons delivering to them valid charters, with seals attached, to the effect that they would undertake to maintain and carry out whatever conventions and agreements the envoys might enter into, in all sea ports, and whithersoever else the envoys might fare.

Thus were the six envoys despatched, as you have been told; and they took counsel among themselves, and this was their conclusion: that in Venice they might expect to find a greater number of vessels than in any other port. So they journeyed day by day, till they came thither in the first week of Lent (February 1201).

The Doge of Venice, whose name was Henry Dandolo, and who was very wise and very valiant, did them great honor, both he and the other folk, and entertained them right willingly, marveling, however, when the envoys had delivered their letters, what might be the matter of import that had brought them to that country. For the letters were letters of credence only and declared no more than that the bearers were to be accredited as if they were the Counts in person, and that the said Counts would make good whatever the six envoys should undertake.

So the Doge replied: "Signors, I have seen your letters; well do we know that of men uncrowned your lords are the greatest, and they advise us to put faith in what you tell us, and that they will maintain whatsoever you undertake. Now, therefore, speak and let us know what is your pleasure."

And the envoys answered: "Sire, we would that you should assemble your council; and before your council we will declare the wishes of our lords; and let this be tomorrow, if it so pleases you." And the Doge replied asking for respite till the fourth day, when he would assemble his council, so that the envoys might state their requirements.

The envoys waited then till the fourth day, as had been appointed them, and entered the palace, which was passing rich and beautiful; and found the Doge and his council in a chamber. There they delivered their message after this manner: "Sire, we come to thee on the part of the high Barons of France, who have taken the sign of the cross to avenge the shame done to Jesus Christ, and to reconquer Jerusalem, if so be that God will suffer it. And because they know that no people have such great power to help them as you and your people, therefore we pray you by God that you take pity on the land oversea, and the shame of Christ, and use diligence that our lords have ships for transport and battle."

"And after what manner should we have diligence?" said the Doge. "After all manners that you may advise and propose," replied the envoys, "in so far as what you propose may be within our means." "Certes," said the Doge, "it is a great thing that our lords require of us, and well it seems that they have in view a high enterprise. We will give you our answer eight days from today. And marvel not if the term be long, for it is meet that so great a matter be fully pondered."

When the term appointed by the Doge was ended, the envoys returned to the palace. Many were the words then spoken which I cannot now rehearse. But this was the conclusion of that parliament: "Signors," said the Doge, "we will tell you the conclusions at which we have arrived, if so be that we can induce our great council and the commons of the land to allow of them; and you, on your part, must consult and see if you can accept them and carry them through.

"We will build transports to carry four thousand five hundred horses, and nine thousand squires, and ships for four thousand five hundred knights, and twenty thousand sergeants of foot. And we will agree also to purvey food for these horses and people during nine months. This is what we undertake to do at the least, on condition that you pay us for each horse four marks, and for each man two marks.

"And the covenants we are now explaining to you, we undertake to keep, wheresoever we may be, for a year, reckoning from the day on which we sail from the port of Venice in the service of God and of Christendom. Now the sum total of the expenses above named amounts to 85,000 marks.

"And this we do moreover. For the love of God, we will add to the fleet fifty armed galleys on condition that, so long as we act in company, of all conquests in land or money, whether at sea or on dry ground, we shall have the half, and you the other half. Now consult together to see if you, on your parts, can accept and fulfill these covenants."

The envoys then departed, and said that they would consult together and give their answer on the morrow. They consulted, and talked together that night, and agreed to accept the terms offered.

◆ ◆ ◆

After Easter and towards Whitsuntide (June 1202) began the pilgrims to leave their own country. And you must know that at their departure many were the tears shed for pity and sorrow, by their own people and by their friends. So they journeyed through Burgundy, and by the mountains of Mont-Joux (? Jura) by Mont Cenis, and through Lombardy, and began to assemble at Venice, where they were lodged on an island which is called St. Nicholas in the port.

At that time started from Flanders a fleet that carried a great number of good men-at-arms. Of this fleet were Captains John of Nêle, Castellan of Bruges, Thierri, who was the son of Count Philip of Flanders, and Nicholas of Mailly. And these promised Count Baldwin, and swore on holy relics, that they would go through the straits of Morocco, and join themselves to him, and to the host of Venice, at whatsoever place they might hear that the count was faring. And for this reason the Count of Flanders and Henry his brother had confided to them certain ships loaded with cloth and food and other wares.

Very fair was this fleet, and rich, and great was the reliance that the Count of Flanders and the pilgrims placed upon it, because very many of their good sergeants were journeying therein. But ill did these keep the faith they had sworn to the count, they and others like them, because they and such others of the same sort became fearful of the great perils that the host of Venice had undertaken.

Thus did the Bishop of Autun fail us, and Guignes the Count of Forez, and Peter Bromont, and many people besides, who were greatly blamed therein; and of little worth were the exploits they performed there where they did go. And of the French failed us Bernard of Moreuil, Hugh of Chaumont, Henry of Araines, John of Villers, Walter of Saint-Denis, Hugh his brother, and many others, who avoided the passage to Venice because of the danger, and went instead to Marseilles—whereof they received shame, and much were they blamed—and great were the mishaps that afterwards befell them.

Now let us for this present speak of them no further, but speak of the pilgrims, of whom a great part had already come to Venice. Count Baldwin of Flanders had already arrived there, and many others, and thither were tidings brought to them that many of the pilgrims were travelling by other ways, and from other ports. This troubled them greatly, because they would thus be unable to fulfill the promise made to the Venetians, and find the moneys that were due.

So they took counsel together, and agreed to send good envoys to meet the pilgrims, and to meet Count Lewis of Blois and Chartres, who had not yet arrived, and to put them in good heart, and beseech them to have pity of the Holy Land beyond the sea, and show them that no other passage, save that from Venice, could be of profit.

For this embassage they made choice of Count Hugh of Saint-Paul and Geoffry the Marshal of Champagne, and these rode till they came to Pavia in Lombardy. There they found Count Lewis with a great many knights and men of note and worth; and by encouragements and prayers prevailed on many to proceed to Venice who would otherwise have fared from other ports, and by other ways.

Nevertheless from Placentia many men of note proceeded by other ways to Apulia. Among them were Villain of Neuilly, who was one of the best knights in the world, Henry of Arzillières, Renaud of Dampierre, Henry of Longchamp, and Giles of Trasegnies, liegeman to Count Baldwin of Flanders and Hainault, who had given him, out of his own purse, five hundred *livres* to accompany him on this journey. With these went a great company of knights and sergeants, whose names are not recorded.

Thus was the host of those who went by Venice greatly weakened; and much evil befell them therefrom, as you shall shortly hear.

Thus did Count Lewis and the other barons wend their way to Venice; and they were there received with feasting and joyfully, and took lodging in the Island of St. Nicholas with those who had come before. Goodly was the host, and right worthy were the men. Never did man see goodlier or worthier. And the Venetians held a market, rich and abundant, of all things needful for horses and men. And the fleet they had got ready was so goodly and fine that never did Christian man see one goodlier or finer; as well galleys as transports, and sufficient for at least three times as many men as were in the host.

Ah! the grievous harm and loss when those who should have come thither sailed instead from other ports! Right well, if they had kept their tryst, would Christendom have been exalted, and the land of the Turks abased! The Venetians had fulfilled all their undertakings, and above measure, and they now summoned the barons and counts to fulfil theirs and make payment, since they were ready to start.

The cost of each man's passage was now levied throughout the host; and there were people enough who said they could not pay for their passage, and the barons took from them such moneys as they had. So each man paid what he could. When the barons had thus claimed the cost of the passages, and when the payments had been collected, the moneys came to less than the sum due—yea by more than one half.

Then the barons met together and said: "Lords, the Venetians have well fulfilled all their undertakings, and above measure. But we cannot fulfil ours in paying for our passages, seeing we are too few in number; and this is the fault of those who have journeyed by other ports. For God's sake therefore let each contribute all that he has, so that we may fulfil our convenant; for better is it that we should give all that we have, than lose what we have already paid, and prove false to our covenants; for if this host remains here, the rescue of the land oversea comes to naught."

Great was then the dissension among the main part of the barons and the other folk, and they said: "We have paid for our passages, and if they will take us, we shall go willingly; but if not, we shall inquire and look for other means of passage." And they spoke thus because they wished that the host should fall to pieces and each return to his own land. But the other party said, "Much rather would we give all that we have and go penniless with the host, than that the host should fall to pieces and fail; for God will doubtless repay us when it so pleases Him."

Then the Count of Flanders began to give all that he had and all that he could borrow, and so did Count Lewis, and the Marquis, and the Count of Saint-Paul, and those who were of their party. Then might you have seen many a fine vessel of gold and silver borne in payment to the palace of the Doge. And when all had been brought together, there was still wanting, of the sum required, 34,000 marks of silver. Then those who had kept back their possessions and not brought them into the common stock, were right glad, for they thought now surely the host must fail and go to pieces. But God, who advises those who have been ill-advised, would not so suffer it.

Then the Doge spoke to his people, and said unto them: "Signors, these people cannot pay more; and in so far as they have paid at all, we have benefited by an agreement which they cannot now fulfil. But our right to keep this money would not everywhere be acknowledged; and if we so kept it we should be greatly blamed, both us and our land. Let us therefore offer them terms.

"The King of Hungary has taken from us Zara in Sclavonia, which is one of the strongest places in the world; and never shall we recover it with all the power that we possess, save with the help of these people. Let us therefore ask them to help us to reconquer it, and we will remit the payment of the debt of 34,000 marks of silver, until such time as it shall please God to allow us to gain the moneys by conquest, we and they together." Thus was agreement made. Much was it contested by those who wished that the host should be broken up. Nevertheless the agreement was accepted and ratified.

Now give ear to one of the greatest marvels, and most wonderful adventures that you have ever heard tell of. At that time there was an emperor in Constantinople, whose name was Isaac, and he had a brother, Alexius by name, whom he had ransomed from captivity among the Turks. This Alexius took his brother the emperor, tore the eyes out of his head, and made himself emperor by the aforesaid treachery. He kept Isaac a long time in prison, together with a son whose name was Alexius. This son escaped from prison, and fled in a ship to a city on the sea, which is called Ancona. Thence he departed to go to King Philip of Germany, who had his sister for wife; and he came to Verona in Lombardy, and lodged in the town, and found there a number of pilgrims and other people who were on their way to join the host.

And those who had helped him to escape, and were with him, said: "Sire, here is an army in Venice, quite near to us, the best and most valiant people and knights that are in the world, and they are going oversea. Cry to them therefore for mercy, that they have pity on thee and on thy father, who have been so wrongfully dispossessed. And if they be willing to help thee, thou shalt be guided by them. Perchance they will take pity on thy estate." And Alexius said he would do this right willingly, and that the advice was good.

Thus he appointed envoys, and sent them to the Marquis Boniface of Montferrat, who was chief of the host, and to the other barons. And when the barons saw them, they marvelled greatly, and said to the envoys: "We understand right well what you tell us. We will send an envoy with the prince to King Philip, whither he is going. If the prince will help to recover the land oversea, we will help him to recover his own land, for we know that it has been wrested from him and from his father wrongfully." So were envoys sent into Germany, both to the heir of Constantinople and to King Philip of Germany.

Then were the ships and transports apportioned by the barons. Ah, God! what fine war-horses were put therein. And when the ships were fulfilled with arms and provisions, and knights and sergeants, the shields were ranged round the bulwarks and castles of the ships, and the banners displayed, many and fair.

And be it known to you that the vessels carried more than three hundred petraries and mangonels, and all such engines as are needed for the taking of cities, in great plenty. Never did finer fleet sail from any port. And this was in the octave of the Feast of St. Remigius (October) in the year of the Incarnation of Jesus Christ twelve hundred and two. Thus did they sail from the port of Venice, as you have been told.

On the Eve of St. Martin (10th November) they came before Zara in Sclavonia, and beheld the city enclosed by high walls and high towers; and vainly would you have sought for a fairer city, or one of greater strength, or richer. And when the pilgrims saw it, they marvelled greatly, and said one to another, "How could such a city be taken by force, save by the help of God himself?"

The first ships that came before the city cast anchor, and waited for the others; and in the morning the day was very fine and very clear, and all the galleys came up with the transports, and the other ships which were behind; and they took the port by force, and broke the chain that defended it and was very strong and well-wrought; and they landed in such sort that the port was between them and the town. Then might you have seen many a knight and many a sergeant swarming out of the ships, and taking from the transports many a good war-horse, and many a rich tent and many a pavilion. Thus did the host encamp. And Zara was besieged on St. Martin's Day (11th November 1202).

At this time all the barons had not yet arrived. Thus the Marquis of Montferrat had remained behind for some business that detained him. And Stephen of the Perche had remained at Venice sick, and Matthew of Montmorency. When they were healed of their sickness Matthew of Montmorency came to rejoin the host at Zara; but Stephen of the Perche dealt less worthily, for he abandoned the host, and went to sojourn in Apulia. With him went Rotrou of Montfort and Ives of the Jaille, and many others, who were much blamed therein; and they journeyed to Syria in the following spring.

On the day following the feast of St. Martin, certain of the people of Zara came forth, and spoke to the Doge of Venice who was in his pavilion, and said to him that they would yield up the city and all their goods—their lives being spared—to his mercy. And the Doge replied that he would not accept these conditions, nor any conditions, save by consent of the counts and barons, with whom he would go and confer.

While he went to confer with the counts and barons, that party, of whom you have already heard, who wished to disperse the host, spoke to the envoys and said, "Why should you surrender your city? The pilgrims will not attack you—have no care of them. If you can defend yourselves against the Venetians, you will be safe enough." And they chose one of themselves, whose name was Robert of Boves, who went to the walls of the city, and spoke the same words. Therefore the envoys returned to the city, and the negotiations were broken off.

The Doge of Venice, when he came to the counts and barons, said to them: "Signors, the people who are therein desire to yield the city to my mercy, on condition only that their lives are spared. But I will enter into no agreement with them—neither this nor any other—save with your consent." And the barons answered: "Sire, we advise you to accept these conditions, and we even beg of you so to do." He said he would do so; and they all returned together to the pavilion of the Doge to make the agreement, and found that the envoys had gone away by the advice of those who wished to disperse the host.

Then rose the abbot of Vaux, of the order of the Cistercians, and said to them: "Lords, I forbid you, on the part of the Pope of Rome, to attack this city; for those within it are Christians, and you are pilgrims." When the Doge heard this, he was very wroth, and much disturbed, and he said to the counts and barons: "Signors, I had this city, by their own agreement, at my mercy, and your people have broken that agreement; you have covenanted to help me to conquer it, and I summon you to do so."

Whereon the counts and barons all spoke at once, together with those who were of their party, and said: "Great is the outrage of those who have caused this agreement to be broken, and never a day has passed that they have not tried to break up the host. Now are we shamed if we do not help to take the city." And they came to the Doge, and said: "Sire, we will help you to take the city in despite of those who would let and hinder us."

Thus was the decision taken. The next morning the host encamped before the gates of the city, and set up their petraries and mangonels, and other engines of war, which they had in plenty, and on the side of the sea they raised ladders from the ships. Then they began to throw stones at the walls of the city and at the towers. So did the assault last for about five days. Then were the sappers set to mine one of the towers, and began to sap the wall. When those within the city saw this, they proposed an agreement, such as they had before refused by the advice of those who wished to break up the host.

A fortnight after came to Zara the Marquis Boniface of Montferrat, who had not yet joined, and Matthew of Montmorency, and Peter of Bracieux, and many another man of note. And after another fortnight came also the envoys from Germany, sent by King Philip and the heir of Constantinople. Then the barons, and the Doge of Venice assembled in a palace where the Doge was lodged. And the envoys addressed them and said: "Lords, King Philip sends us to you, as does also the brother of the king's wife, the son of the Emperor of Constantinople.

" 'Lords,' says the king, 'I will send you the brother of my wife; and I commit him into the hands of God—may He keep him from death!—and into your hands. And because you have fared forth for God, and for right, and for justice, therefore you are bound, in so far as you are able, to restore to their own inheritance those who have been unrighteously despoiled. And my wife's brother will make with you the best terms ever offered to any people, and give you the most puissant help for the recovery of the land oversea.

" 'And first, if God grant that you restore him to his inheritance, he will place the whole empire of Roumania in obedience to Rome, from which it has long been separated. Further, he knows that you have spent of your substance, and that you are poor, and he will give you 200,000 marks of silver, and food for all those of the host, both small and great. And he, of his own person, will go with you into the land of Babylon, or, if you hold that that will be better, send thither 10,000 men, at his own charges. And this service he will perform for one year. And all the days of his life he will maintain, at his own charges, five hundred knights in the land oversea, to guard that land.' "

"Lords, we have full power," said the envoys, "to conclude this agreement, if you are willing to conclude it on your parts. And be it known to you, that so favourable an agreement has never before been offered to any one; and that he that would refuse it can have but small desire of glory and conquest."

The barons and the Doge said they would talk this over; and a parliament was called for the morrow. When all were assembled, the matter was laid before them.

Then arose much debate. The abbot of Vaux, of the order of the Cistercians, spoke, and that party that wished for the dispersal of the host; and they said they would never consent: that it was not to fall on Christians that they had left their homes, and that they would go to Syria.

And the other party replied: "Fair lords, in Syria you will be able to do nothing; and that you may right well perceive by considering how those have fared who abandoned us, and sailed from other ports. And be it known to you that it is only by way of Babylon, or of Greece, that the land oversea can be recovered, if so be that it ever is recovered. And if we reject this covenant we shall be shamed to all time."

There was discord in the host, as you hear. Nor need you be surprised if there was discord among the laymen, for the white monks of the order of Cîteaux were also at issue among themselves in the host. The abbot of Loos, who was a holy man and a man of note, and other abbots who held with him, prayed and besought the people, for pity's sake, and the sake of God, to keep the host together, and agree to the proposed convention, in that "It afforded the best means by which the land oversea might be recovered;" while the abbot of Vaux, on the other hand, and those who held with him, preached full oft, and declared that all this was naught, and that the host ought to go to the land of Syria, and there do what they could.

Then came the Marquis of Montferrat, and Baldwin Count of Flanders and Hainault, and Count Lewis, and Count Hugh of St. Paul, and those who held with them, and they declared that they would enter into the proposed covenant, for that they should be shamed if they refused. So they went to the Doge's hostel, and the envoys were summoned, and the covenant, in such terms as you have already heard, was confirmed by oath, and by charters with seals appended.

And the book tells you that only twelve persons took the oaths on the side of the Franks, for more (of sufficient note) could not be found. Among the twelve were first the Marquis of Montferrat, the Count Baldwin of Flanders, the Count Lewis of Blois and of Chartres, and the Count of St. Paul, and eight others who held with them. Thus was the agreement made, and the charters prepared, and a term fixed for the arrival of the heir of Constantinople; and the term so fixed was the fifteenth day after the following Easter.

Then the barons spoke together and said that they would send to Rome, to the Pope, because he had taken the capture of Zara in evil part. And they chose as envoys such as they knew were fitted for this office, two knights, and two clerks. Of the two clerks one was Nevelon, Bishop of Soissons, and the other Master John of Noyon, who was chancellor to

Count Baldwin of Flanders; and of the knights one was John of Friaize, the other Robert of Boves. These swore on holy relics that they would perform their embassage loyally and in good faith, and that they would come back to the host.

Three kept their oath right well, and the fourth evilly, and this one was Robert of Boves. For he executed his office as badly as he could, and perjured himself, and went away to Syria as others had done. But the remaining three executed their office right well, and delivered their message as the barons had directed, and said to the Pope: "The barons cry mercy to you for the capture of Zara, for they acted as people who could do no better, owing to the default of those who had gone to other ports, and because, had they not acted as they did, they could not have held the host together. And as to this they refer themselves to you, as to their good Father, that you should tell them what are your commands, which they are ready to perform."

And the Pope said to the envoys that he knew full well that it was through the default of others that the host had been impelled to do this great mischief, and that he had them in great pity. And then he notified to the barons and pilgrims that he sent them his blessing, and absolved them as his sons, and commanded and besought them to hold the host together, inasmuch as he well knew that without that host God's service could not be done. And he gave full powers to Nevelon, Bishop of Soissons, and Master John of Noyon, to bind and to unloose the pilgrims until the cardinal joined the host.

Then did they sail from the port of Corfu on the eve of Pentecost (24th May), which was twelve hundred and three years after the Incarnation of our Lord Jesus Christ. And there were all the ships assembled, and all the transports, and all the galleys of the host, and many other ships of merchants that fared with them. And the day was fine and clear, and the wind soft and favourable, and they unfurled all their sails to the breeze.

And Geoffry, the Marshal of Champagne, who dictates this work, and has never lied therein by one word to his knowledge, and who was moreover present at all the councils held—he bears witness that never was yet seen so fair a sight. And well might it appear that such a fleet would conquer and gain lands, for, far as the eye could reach, there was no space without sails, and ships, and vessels, so that the hearts of men rejoiced greatly.

Thus they sailed over the sea till they came to Malea, to straits that are by the sea. And there they met two ships with pilgrims, and knights and sergeants returning from Syria, and they were of the parties that had gone to Syria by Marseilles. And when these saw our fleet so rich and well-appointed, they conceived such shame that they dared not show themselves. And Count Baldwin of Flanders sent a boat from his ship to ask what people they were; and they said who they were.

And a sergeant let himself down from his ship into the boat, and said to those in the ship, "I cry quits to you for any goods of mine that may remain in the ship, for I am going with these people, for well I deem that they will conquer lands." Much did we make of the sergeant, and gladly was he received in the host. For well may it be said, that even after following a thousand crooked ways a man may find his way right in the end.

The host fared forward till it came to Nigra (Negropont). Nigra is a very fair island, and there is on it a very good city called Negropont. Here the barons took council. Then went forward the Marquis Boniface of Montferrat, and Count Baldwin of Flanders and Hainault, with a great part of the transports and galleys, taking with them the son of the Emperor Isaac of Constantinople; and they came to an island called Andros, and there landed. The knights took their arms, and over-rode the country; and the people of the land came to crave mercy of the son of the Emperor of Constantinople, and gave so much of their goods that they made peace with him.

Then they returned to the ships, and sailed over the sea; when a great mishap befell, for a great lord of the host, whose name was Guy, Castellan of Coucy, died, and was cast into the sea.

The other ships, which had not sailed thitherward, had entered the passage of Abydos, and it is there that the straits of St. George (the Dardanelles) open into the great sea. And they sailed up the straits to a city called Abydos which lies on the straits of St. George, towards Turkey, and is very fair, and well situate. There they took port and landed, and those of the city came to meet them, and surrendered the city, as men without stomach to defend themselves. And such guard was established that those of the city lost not one stiver current.

They sojourned there eight days to wait for the ships, transports, and galleys that had not yet come up. And while they thus sojourned, they took corn from the land, for it was the season of harvest, and great was their need thereof, for before they had but little. And within those eight days all the ships and barons had come up. God gave them fair weather.

All started from the port of Abydos together. Then might you have seen the Straits of St. George (as it were) in flower with ships and galleys sailing upwards, and the beauty thereof was a great marvel to behold. Thus they sailed up the Straits of St. George till they came, on St. John the Baptist's Eve, in June (23rd June 1203) to St. Stephen, an abbey that lay three leagues from Constantinople. There had those on board the ships and galleys and transports full sight of Constantinople; and they took port and anchored their vessels.

Now you may know that those who had never before seen Constantinople looked upon it very earnestly, for they never thought there could be in all the world so rich a city; and they marked the high walls and strong towers that enclosed it round about, and the rich palaces, and mighty churches—of which there were so many that no one would have believed it who had not seen it with his eyes—and the height and the length of that city which above all others was sovereign. And be it known to you, that no man there was of such hardihood but his flesh trembled; and it was no wonder, for never was so great an enterprise undertaken by any people since the creation of the world.

Then landed the counts and barons and the Doge of Venice, and a parliament was held in the church of St. Stephen. There were many opinions set forth, this way and that. All the words then spoken shall not be recorded in this book; but in the end the Doge rose on his feet and said: "Signors, I know the state of this land better than you do, for I have been here erewhile. We have undertaken the greatest enterprise, and the most perilous, that ever people have undertaken. Therefore it behoves us to go to work warily. Be it known to you that if we go on dry ground, the land is great and large, and our people are poor and ill-provided. Thus they will disperse to look for food; and the people of the land are in great multitude, and we cannot keep such good watch but that some of ours will be lost. Nor are we in case to lose any, for our people are but few indeed for the work in hand.

"Now there are islands close by which you can see from here, and these are inhabited, and produce corn, and food, and other things. Let us take port there, and gather the corn and provisions of the land. And when we have collected our supplies, let us go before the city, and do as our Lord shall provide. For he that has supplies, wages war with more certainty than he that has none." To this counsel the lords and barons agreed, and all went back to their ships and vessels.

They rested thus that night. And in the morning, on the day of the feast of our Lord St. John the Baptist in June (24th June 1203), the banners and pennants were flown on the castles of the ships, and the coverings taken from the shields, and the bulwarks of the ships garnished. Every one looked to his arms, such as he should use, for well each man knew that full soon he would have need of them.

The sailors weighed the anchors, and spread the sails to the wind, and God gave them a good wind, such as was convenient to them. Thus they passed before Constantinople, and so near to the walls and towers that we shot at many of their vessels. There were so many people on the walls and towers that it seemed as if there could be no more people (in the world).

Then did God our Lord set to naught the counsel of the day before, and keep us from sailing to the islands: that counsel fell to naught as if none had ever heard thereof. For lo, our ships made for the mainland as straight as ever they could, and took port before a palace of the Emperor Alexius, at a place called Chalcedon. This was in face of Constantinople, on the other side of the straits, towards Turkey. The palace was one of the most beautiful and delectable that ever eyes could see, with every delight therein that the heart of man could desire, and convenient for the house of a prince.

The counts and barons landed and lodged themselves in the palace; and in the city round about, the main part pitched their tents. Then were the horses taken out of the transports, and the knights and sergeants got to land with all their arms, so that none remained in the ships save the mariners only. The country was fair, and rich, and well supplied with all good things, and the sheaves of corn (which had been reaped) were in the fields, so that all—and they stood in no small need—might take thereof.

They sojourned thus in that palace the following day; and on the third day God gave them a good wind, and the mariners raised their anchors, and spread their sails to the wind. They went thus up the straits, a good league above Constantinople, to a palace that belonged to the Emperor Alexius, and was called Scutari. There the ships anchored, and the transports, and all the galleys. The horsemen who had lodged in the palace of Chalcedon went along the shore by land.

The host of the French encamped thus on the Straits of St. George, at Scutari, and above it. And when the Emperor Alexius saw this, he caused his host to issue from Constantinople, and encamp over against us on the other side of the straits, and there pitched his tents, so that we might not take land against him by force. The host of the French sojourned thus for nine days, and those obtained supplies who needed them, and that was every one in the host.

The next day after, the Emperor Alexius sent an envoy with letters to the counts and to the barons. This envoy was called Nicholas Roux, and he was a native of Lombardy. He found the barons in the rich palace of Scutari, where they were holding council, and he saluted them on the part of the Emperor Alexius of Constantinople, and tendered his letters to the Marquis of Montferrat—who received them. And the letters were read before all the barons; and there were in them words, written after various manners, which the book does not (here) relate, and at the end of the other words so written, came words of credit, accrediting the bearer of the letters, whose name was Nicholas Roux.

"Fair sir," said the barons, "we have seen your letters, and they tell us that we are to give credit to what you say, and we credit you right well. Now speak as it pleases you."

And the envoy was standing before the barons, and spoke thus: "Lords," said he, "the Emperor Alexius would have you know that he is well aware that you are the best people uncrowned, and come from the best land on earth. And he marvels much why, and for what purpose, you have come into his land and kingdom. For you are Christians, and he is a Christian, and well he knows that you are on your way to deliver the Holy

Land oversea, and the Holy Cross, and the Sepulchre. If you are poor and in want, he will right willingly give you of his food and substance, provided you depart out of his land. Neither would he otherwise wish to do you any hurt, though he has full power therein, seeing that if you were twenty times as numerous as you are, you would not be able to get away without utter discomfiture if so be that he wished to harm you."

By agreement and desire of the other barons, and of the Doge of Venice, then rose to his feet Conon of Béthune, who was a good knight, and wise, and very eloquent, and he replied to the envoy: "Fair sir, you have told us that your lord marvels much why our signors and barons should have entered into his kingdom and land. Into his land they have not entered, for he holds this land wrongfully and wickedly, and against God and against reason. It belongs to his nephew, who sits upon a throne among us, and is the son of his brother, the Emperor Isaac. But if he is willing to throw himself on the mercy of his nephew; and to give him back his crown and empire, then we will pray his nephew to forgive him, and bestow upon him as much as will enable him to live wealthily. And if you come not as the bearer of such a message, then be not so bold as to come here again." So the envoy departed and went back to Constantinople, to the Emperor Alexius.

The day was fixed on which the host should embark on the ships and transports to take the land by force, and either live or die. And be it known to you that the enterprise to be achieved was one of the most redoubtable ever attempted. Then did the bishops and clergy speak to the people, and tell them how they must confess, and make each one his testament, seeing that no one knew what might be the will of God concerning him. And this was done right willingly throughout the host, and very piously.

The term fixed was now come; and the knights went on board the transports with their war-horses; and they were fully armed, with their helmets laced, and the horses covered with their housings, and saddled. All the other folk, who were of less consequence in battle, were on the great ships; and the galleys were fully armed and made ready.

The morning was fair a little after the rising of the sun; and the Emperor Alexius stood waiting for them on the other side, with great forces, and everything in order. And the trumpets sound, and every galley takes a transport in tow, so as to reach the other side more readily. None ask who shall go first, but each makes the land as soon as he can. The knights issue from the transports, and leap into the sea up to their waists, fully armed, with helmets laced, and lances in hand; and the good archers, and the good sergeants, and the good crossbowmen, each in his company, land so soon as they touch ground.

The Greeks made a goodly show of resistance; but when it came to the lowering of the lances, they turned their backs, and went away flying, and abandoned the shore. And be it known to you that never was port more proudly taken. Then began the mariners to open the ports of the transports, and let down the bridges, and take out the horses; and the knights began to mount, and they began to marshal the divisions of the host in due order.

Count Baldwin of Flanders and Hainault, with the advanced guard, rode forward, and the other divisions of the host after him, each in due order of march; and they came to where the Emperor Alexius had been encamped. But he had turned back towards Constantinople, and left his tents and pavilions standing. And there our people had much spoil.

Our barons were minded to encamp by the port before the tower of Galata, where the chain was fixed that closed the port of Constantinople. And be it known to you, that any one must perforce pass that chain before he could enter into the port. Well did our barons then perceive that if they did not take the tower, and break the chain, they were but as dead men, and in very evil case. So they lodged that night before the tower, and in the Jewry that is called Stenon, where there was a good city, and very rich.

Well did they keep guard during the night; and on the morrow, at the hour of tierce, those who were in the tower of Galata made a sortie, and those who were in Constantinople came to their help in barges; and our people ran to arms. There came first to the onset James of Avesnes and his men on foot; and be it known to you that he was fiercely charged, and wounded by a lance in the face, and in peril of death. And one of his knights, whose name was Nicholas of Jenlain, gat to horse, and came to his lord's rescue, and succoured him right well, and so won great honour.

Then a cry was raised in the host, and our people ran together from all sides, and drove back the foe with great fury, so that many were slain and taken. And some of them did not go back to the tower, but ran to the barges by which they had come, and there many were drowned, and some escaped. As to those who went back to the tower, the men of our host pressed them so hard that they could not shut the gate. Then a terrible fight began again at the gate, and our people took it by force, and made prisoners of all those in the tower. Many were there killed and taken.

So was the tower of Galata taken, and the port of Constantinople won by force. Much were those of the host comforted thereby, and much did they praise the Lord God; and greatly were those of the city discomforted. And on the next day, the ships, the vessels, the galleys and the transports were drawn into the port.

Then did those of the host take council together to settle what thing they should do, and whether they should attack the city by sea or by land. The Venetians were firmly minded that the scaling ladders ought to be planted on the ships, and all the attack made from the side by the sea. The French, on the other hand, said that they did not know so well how to help themselves on sea as on land, but that when they had their horses and their arms they could help themselves on land right well. So in the end it was devised that the Venetians should attack by sea, and the barons and those of the host by land.

They sojourned thus for four days. On the fifth day, the whole host were armed, and the divisions advanced on horseback, each in the order appointed, along the harbour, till they came to the palace of Blachernae; and the ships drew inside the harbour till they came over against the self-same place, and this was near to the end of the harbour. And there is at that place a river that flows into the sea, and can only be passed by a bridge of stone. The Greeks had broken down the bridge, and the barons caused the host to labour all that day and all that night in repairing the bridge. Thus was the bridge repaired, and in the morning the divisions were armed, and rode one after the other in the order appointed, and came before the city. And no one came out from the city against them; and this was a great marvel, seeing that for every man that was in the host there were over two hundred men in the city.

Then did the barons decide that they should quarter themselves between the palace of Blachernae and the castle of Boemond, which was an abbey enclosed with walls. So the tents and pavilions were pitched—which was a right proud thing to look upon; for of Constantinople, which had three leagues of front towards the land, the whole host could attack no more than one of the gates. And the Venetians lay on the sea, in ships and vessels, and raised their ladders, and mangonels, and petaries, and made order for their assault right well. And the barons for their part made ready their petaries and mangonels on land.

And be it known to you that they did not have their time in peace and quiet; for there passed no hour of the night or day but one of the divisions had to stand armed before the gate, to guard the engines, and provide against attack. And, notwithstanding all this, the Greeks ceased not to attack them, by this gate and by others, and held them so short that six or seven times a day the whole host was forced to run to arms. Nor could they forage for provisions more than four bow-shots' distance from the camp. And their stores were but scanty, save of flour and bacon, and of those they had a little; and of fresh meat none at all, save what they got from the horses that were killed. And be it known to you that there was only food generally in the host for three weeks. Thus were they in very perilous case, for never did so few people besiege so many people in any city.

Thus their peril and toil lasted for nearly ten days, until, on a Thursday morning (17th July 1203) all things were ready for the assault, and the ladders in trim; the Venetians also had made them ready by sea. The order of the assault was so devised, that of the seven divisions, three were to guard the camp outside the city, and other four to give the assault. The Marquis Boniface of Montferrat guarded the camp towards the fields, with the division of the Burgundians, the division of the men of Champagne, and Matthew of Montmorency. Count Baldwin of Flanders and Hainault went to the assault with his people, and Henry his brother; and Count Lewis of Blois and Chartres, and Count Hugh of St. Paul, and those who held with them, went also to the assault.

They planted two ladders at a barbican near the sea; and the wall was well defended by Englishmen and Danes; and the attack was stiff and good and fierce. By main strength certain knights and two sergeants got up the ladders and made themselves masters of the wall; and at least fifteen got upon the wall, and fought there, hand to hand, with axes and swords, and those within redoubled their efforts, and cast them out in very ugly sort, keeping two as prisoners. And those of our people who had been taken were led before the Emperor Alexius; much was he pleased thereat. Thus did the assault leave matters on the side of the French. Many were wounded and many had their bones broken, so that the barons were very wroth.

Meanwhile the Doge of Venice had not forgotten to do his part, but had ranged his ships and transports and vessels in line, and that line was well three crossbow-shots in length; and the Venetians began to draw near to the part of the shore that lay under the walls and the towers. Then might you have seen the mangonels shooting from the ships and transports, and the crossbow bolts flying, and the bows letting fly their arrows deftly and well; and those within defending the walls and towers very fierce; and the ladders on the ships coming so near that in many places swords and lances crossed; and the tumult and noise were so great that it seemed as if the very earth and sea were melting together. And be it known to you that the galleys did not dare to come to the shore.

Now may you hear of a strange deed of prowess; for the Doge of Venice, who was an old man, and saw naught (seeing he was blind), stood, fully armed, on the prow of his galley, and had the standard of St. Mark before him; and he cried to his people to put him on land, or else that he would do justice upon their bodies with his hands. And so they did, for the galley was run aground, and they leapt therefrom, and bore the standard of St. Mark before him on to the land.

And when the Venetians saw the standard of St. Mark on land, and the galley of their lord touching ground before them, each held himself for shamed, and they all gat to the land; and those in the transports leapt forth, and landed; and those in the big ships got into barges, and made for the shore, each and all as best they could. Then might you have seen an assault, great and marvellous; and to this bears witness Geoffry of Villehardouin, who makes this book, that more than forty people told him for sooth that they saw the standard of St. Mark of Venice at the top of one of the towers, and that no man knew who bore it thither.

Now hear of a strange miracle: those who are within the city fly and abandon the walls, and the Venetians enter in, each as fast and as best he can, and seize twenty-five of the towers, and man them with their people. And the Doge takes a boat, and sends messengers to the barons of the host to tell them that he has taken twenty-five towers, and that they may know for sooth that such towers cannot be retaken. The barons are so overjoyed that they cannot believe their ears; and the Venetians begin to send to the host in boats the horses and palfreys they have taken.

When the Emperor Alexius saw that our people had thus entered into the city, he sent his people against them in such numbers that our people saw they would be unable to endure the onset. So they set fire to the buildings between them and the Greeks; and the wind blew from our side, and the fire began to wax so great that the Greeks could not see our people, who retired to the towers they had seized and conquered.

Then the Emperor Alexius issued from the city, with all his forces, by other gates which were at least a league from the camp; and so many began to issue forth that it seemed as if the whole world were there assembled. The emperor marshalled his troops in the plain, and they rode towards the camp; and when our Frenchmen saw them coming, they ran to arms from all sides. On that day Henry, the brother of Count Baldwin and Flanders, was mounting guard over the engines of war before the gate of Blachernae, together with Matthew of Walincourt, and Baldwin of Beauvoir, and their followers. Against their encampment the Emperor Alexius had made ready a great number of his people, who were to issue by three gates, while he himself should fall upon the host from another side.

Then the six divisions issued from our camp as had been devised, and were marshalled in ranks before the palisades: the sergeants and squires on foot behind the horses, and the archers and crossbowmen in front. And there was a division of the knights on foot, for we had at least two hundred who were without horses. Thus they stood still before the palisades. And this showed great good sense, for if they had moved to the attack, the numbers of the enemy were such that they must have been overwhelmed and (as it were) drowned among them.

It seemed as if the whole plain was covered with troops, and they advanced slowly and in order. Well might we appear in perilous case, for we had but six divisions, while the Greeks had full forty, and there was not one of their divisions but was larger than any of ours. But ours were ordered in such sort that none could attack them save in front. And the Emperor Alexius rode so far forward that either side could shoot at the other. And when the Doge of Venice heard this, he made his people come forth, and leave the towers they had taken, and said he would live or die with the pilgrims. So he came to the camp, and was himself the first to land, and brought with him such of his people as he could.

Thus, for a long space, the armies of the pilgrims and of the Greeks stood one against the other; for the Greeks did not dare to throw themselves upon our ranks, and our people would not move from their palisades. And when the Emperor Alexius saw this, he began to withdraw his people, and when he had rallied them, he turned back. And seeing this, the host of the pilgrims began to march towards him with slow steps, and the Greek troops began to move backwards, and retreated to a palace called Philopas.

And be it known to you, that never did God save any people from such peril as He saved the host that day; and be it known to you further that there was none in the host so hardy but he had great joy thereof. Thus did the battle remain for that day. As it pleased God nothing further was done. The Emperor Alexius returned to the city, and those of the host to their quarters—the latter taking off their armour, for they were weary and overwrought; and they ate and drank little, seeing that their store of food was but scanty.

Now listen to the miracles of our Lord—how gracious are they whithersoever it pleases Him to perform them! That very night the Emperor Alexius of Constantinople took of his treasure as much as he could carry, and took with him as many of his people as would go, and so fled and abandoned the city. And those of the city remained astonied, and they drew to the prison in which lay the Emperor Isaac, whose eyes had been put out. Him they clothed imperially, and bore to the great palace of Blachernae, and seated on a high throne; and there they did to him obesiance as their lord. Then they took messengers, by the advice of the Emperor Isaac, and sent them to the host, to apprise the son of the Emperor Isaac, and the barons, that the Emperor Alexius had fled, and that they had again raised up the Emperor Isaac as emperor.

When the young man knew of this he summoned the Marquis Boniface of Montferrat, and the marquis summoned the barons throughout the host. And when they were met in the pavilion of the Emperor Isaac's son, he told them the news. And when they heard it, their joy was such as cannot be uttered, for never was greater joy in all this world. And greatly and most devoutly was our Lord praised by all, in that He had succoured them within so short a term, and exalted them so high from such a low estate. And therefore well may one say: "Him whom God will help can no man injure."

Then the day began to dawn, and the host to put on their armour; and all gat them to their arms throughout the host, because they did not greatly trust the Greeks. And messengers began to come out from the city, two or three together, and told the same tale. The barons and counts, and the Doge of Venice had agreed to send envoys into the city, to know how matters really stood; and, if that was true which had been reported, to demand of the father that he should ratify the covenants made by the son; and, if he would not, to declare that they on their part should not suffer the son to enter into the city. So envoys were chosen: one was Matthew of Montmorency, and Geoffry the Marshal of Champagne was the other, and two Venetians on the part of the Doge of Venice.

The envoys were conducted to the gate, and the gate was opened to them, and they dismounted from their horses. The Greeks had set Englishmen and Danes, with their axes, at the gate and right up to the palace of Blachernae. Thus were the envoys conducted to the great palace. There they found the Emperor Isaac, so richly clad that you would seek in vain throughout the world for a man more richly apparelled than he, and by his side the empress, his wife, a most fair lady, the daughter of the King of Hungary; and of great men and great ladies there were so many, that you could not stir foot for the press, and the ladies were so richly adorned that richer adornment might not be. And all those who, the day before, had been against the emperor were, on that day, subject in everything to his good pleasure.

The envoys came before the Emperor Isaac, and the emperor and all those about him did them great honour. And the envoys said that they desired to speak to him privily, on the part of his son, and of the barons of the host. And he rose and entered into a chamber, and took with him only the empress, and his chancellor, and his dragoman (interpreter) and the four envoys. By consent of the other envoys, Geoffry of Villehardouin, the Marshal of Champagne, acted as spokesman, and he said to the Emperor Isaac: "Sire, thou seest the service we have rendered to thy son, and how we have kept our covenants with him. But he cannot come hither till he has given us surety for the covenants he has made with us. And he asks of thee, as thy son, to confirm those covenants in the same form, and the same manner, that he has done." "What covenants are they?" said the emperor. "They are such as we shall tell you," replied the envoys: "In the first place to put the whole empire of Roumania in obedience to Rome, from which it has been separated this long while; further to give 200,000 marks of silver to those of the host, with food for one year for small and great; to send 10,000 men, horse and foot—as many on foot as we shall devise and as many mounted—in his own ships, and at his own charges, to the land of Babylon, and keep them there for a year; and during his lifetime to keep, at his own charges, five hundred knights in the land oversea, so that they may guard that land. Such is the covenant that your son made with us, and it was confirmed by oath, and charters with seals appended, and by King Philip of Germany who has your daughter to wife. This covenant we desire you to confirm."

"Certes," said the emperor, "this covenant is very onerous, and I do not see how effect can be given to it; nevertheless, you have done us such service, both to my son and to myself, that if we bestowed upon you the whole empire, you would have deserved it well." Many words were then spoken in this sense and that, but, in the end, the father confirmed the covenants, as his son had confirmed them, by oath and by charters with gold seals appended. These charters were delivered to the envoys. Then they took their leave of the Emperor Isaac, and went back to the host, and told the barons that they had fulfilled their mission.

Then did the barons mount their horses, and led the young man, with great rejoicings, into the city, to his father; and the Greeks opened the gate to him, and received him with very much rejoicing and great feasting. The joy of the father and of the son was very great, because of a long time they had not seen one another, and because, by God's help and that of the pilgrims, they had passed from so great poverty and ruin to such high estate. Therefore the joy was great inside Constantinople; and also without, among the host of the pilgrims, because of the honour and victory that God had given them.

And on the morrow the emperor and his son also besought the counts and the barons, for God's sake, to go and quarter themselves on the other side of the straits, toward Estanor and Galatas; for, if they quartered themselves in the city, it was to be feared that quarrels would ensue between them and the Greeks, and it might well chance that the city would be destroyed. And the counts and barons said that they had already served him in so many ways that they would not now refuse any request of his. So they went and quartered themselves on the other side, and sojourned there in peace and quiet, and with great store of good provisions.

Now you must know that many of those in the host went to see Constantinople, and the rich palaces and great churches, of which there were many, and all the great wealth of the city—for never was there city that possessed so much. Of relics it does not behove me to speak, for at that day there were as many there as in all the rest of the world. Thus did the Greeks and French live in good fellowship in all things, both as regards trafficking and other matters.

By common consent of Franks and Greeks, it was settled that the new emperor should be crowned on the feast of our Lord St. Peter (1st August 1203). So was it settled, and so it was done. He was crowned full worthily and with honour according to the use for Greek emperors at that time. Afterwards he began to pay the moneys due to the host; and such moneys were divided among the host, and each repaid what had been advanced in Venice for his passage.

The Emperor Alexius remained for a long time on progress, till St. Martin's Day, and then he returned to Constantinople. Great was the joy at his home-coming, and the Greeks and ladies of Constantinople went out to meet their friends in great cavalcades, and the pilgrims went out to meet their friends, and had great joy of them. So did the emperor re-enter Constantinople and the palace of Blachernae; and the Marquis of Montferrat and the other barons returned to the camp.

The emperor, who had managed his affairs right well and thought he had now the upper hand, was filled with arrogance towards the barons and those who had done so much for him, and never came to see them in the camp, as he had done aforetime. And they sent to him and begged him to pay them the moneys due, as he had covenanted. But he led them on from delay to delay, making them, at one time and another, payments small and poor; and in the end the payments ceased and came to naught.

The Marquis Boniface of Montferrat, who had done more for him than any other, and stood better in his regard, went to him oftentimes, and showed him what great services the Crusaders had rendered him, and that greater services had never been rendered to any one. And the emperor still entertained them with delays, and never carried out such things as he had promised, so that at last they saw and knew clearly that his intent was wholly evil.

Then the barons of the host held a parliament with the Doge of Venice, and they said that they now knew that the emperor would fulfil no covenant, nor ever speak sooth to them; and they decided to send good envoys to demand the fulfilment of their covenant, and to show what services they had done him; and if he would now do what was required, they were to be satisfied; but, if not, they were to defy him, and right well might he rest assured that the barons would by all means recover their due.

For this embassage were chosen Conon of Béthune and Geoffry of Villehardouin, the Marshal of Champagne, and Miles the Brabant of Provins; and the Doge also sent three chief men of his council. So these envoys mounted their horses, and, with swords girt, rode together till they came to the palace of Blachernae. And be it known to you that, by reason of the treachery of the Greeks, they went in great peril, and on a hard adventure.

They dismounted at the gate and entered the palace, and found the Emperor Alexius and the Emperor Isaac seated on two thrones, side by side. And near them was seated the empress, who was the wife of the father, and stepmother of the son, and sister to the King of Hungary—a lady both fair and good. And there were with them a great company of people of note and rank, so that well did the court seem the court of a rich and mighty prince.

By desire of the other envoys Conon of Béthune, who was very wise and eloquent of speech, acted as spokesman: "Sire, we have come to thee on the part of the barons of the host and of the Doge of Venice. They would put thee in mind of the great service they have done to thee—a service known to the people and manifest to all men. Thou hast sworn, thou and thy father, to fulfil the promised covenants, and they have your charters in hand. But you have not fulfilled those covenants well, as you should have done. Many times have they called upon you to do so, and now again we call upon you, in the presence of all your barons, to fulfil the covenants that are between you and them. Should you do so, it shall be well. If not, be it known to you that from this day forth they will not hold you as lord or friend, but will endeavour to obtain their due by all the means in their power. And of this they now give you warning, seeing that they would not injure you, nor any one, without first defiance given; for never have they acted treacherously, nor in their land is it customary to do so. You have heard what we have said. It is for you to take counsel thereon according to your pleasure."

Much were the Greeks amazed and greatly outraged by this open defiance; and they said that never had any one been so hardy as to dare defy the Emperor of Constantinople in his own hall. Very evil were the looks now cast on the envoys by the Emperor Alexius and by all the Greeks, who aforetime were wont to regard them very favourably.

Great was the tumult there within, and the envoys turned about and came to the gate and mounted their horses. When they got outside the gate, there was not one of them but felt glad at heart; nor is that to be marvelled at, for they had escaped from very great peril, and it held to very little that they were not all killed or taken. So they returned to the camp, and told the barons how they had fared.

Thus did the war begin; and each side did to the other as much harm as they could, by sea and by land. The Franks and the Greeks fought often; but never did they fight, let God be praised therefor! that the Greeks did not lose more than the Franks. So the war lasted a long space, till the heart of the winter.

Then the Greeks bethought themselves of a very great device, for they took seven large ships, and filled them full of big logs, and shavings, and tow, and resin, and barrels, and then waited until such time as the wind should blow strongly from their side of the straits. And one night, at midnight, they set fire to the ships, and unfurled their sails to the wind. And the flames blazed up high, so that it seemed as if the whole world were a-fire. Thus did the burning ships come towards the fleet of the pilgrims; and a great cry arose in the host, and all sprang to arms on every side. The Venetians ran to their ships, and so did all those who had ships in possession, and they began to draw them away out of the flames very vigorously.

And to this bears witness Geoffry the Marshal of Champagne, who dictates this work, that never did people help themselves better at sea than the Venetians did that night; for they sprang into the galleys and boats belonging to the ships, and seized upon the fire ships, all burning as they were, with hooks, and dragged them by main force before their enemies, outside the port, and set them into the current of the straits, and left them to go burning down the straits. So many of the Greeks had come down to the shore that they were without end and innumerable, and their cries were so great that it seemed as if the earth and sea would melt together. They got into barges and boats, and shot at those on our side who were battling with the flames, so that some were wounded.

All the knights of the host, as soon as they heard the clamour, armed themselves; and the battalions marched out into the plain, each according to the order in which they had been quartered, for they feared lest the Greeks should also attack them on land.

They endured thus in labour and anguish till daylight; but by God's help those on our side lost nothing, save a Pisan ship, which was full of merchandise, and was burned with fire. Deadly was the peril in which we stood that night, for if the fleet had been consumed, all would have been lost, and we should never have been able to get away by land or sea. Such was the guerdon which the Emperor Alexius would have bestowed upon us in return for our services.

Then the Greeks, being thus embroiled with the Franks, saw that there was no hope of peace; so they privily took counsel together to betray their lord. Now there was a Greek who stood higher in his favour than all others, and had done more to make him embroil himself with the Franks than any other. This Greek was named Mourzuphles.

With the advice and consent of the others, one night towards midnight, when the Emperor Alexius was asleep in his chamber, those who ought to have been guarding him—and especially Mourzuphles—took him in his bed and threw him into a dungeon in prison. Then Mourzuphles assumed the scarlet buskins with the help and by the counsel of the other Greeks (January 1204). So he made himself emperor. Afterwards they crowned him at St. Sophia. Now see if ever people were guilty of such horrible treachery!

When the Emperor Isaac heard that his son was taken and Mourzuphles crowned, great fear came upon him, and he fell into a sickness that lasted no long time. So he died. And the Emperor Mourzuphles caused the son, whom he had in prison, to be poisoned two or three times; but it did not please God that he should thus die. Afterwards the emperor went and strangled him, and when he had strangled him, he caused it to be reported everywhere that he had died a natural death, and had him mourned for, and buried honourably and as an emperor, and made great show of grief.

But murder cannot be hid. Soon was it clearly known, both to the Greeks and to the French, that this murder had been committed, as has just been told to you. Then did the barons of the host and the Doge of Venice assemble in parliament, and with them met the bishops and the clergy. And all the clergy, including those who had powers from the Pope, showed to the barons and to the pilgrims that any one guilty of such a murder had no right to hold hands, and that those who consented thereto were abettors of the murder; and beyond all this, that the Greeks had withdrawn themselves from obedience to Rome. "Wherefore we tell you," said the clergy, "that this is lawful and just, and that if you have a right intention in conquering this land, to bring it into the Roman obedience, all those who die after confession shall have part in the indulgence granted by the Pope." And you must know that by this the barons and pilgrims were greatly comforted.

Dire was the war between the Franks and the Greeks, for it abated not, but rather increased and waxed fiercer, so that few were the days on which there was not fighting by sea or land. Then Henry, the brother of Count Baldwin of Flanders rode forth and took with him a great part of the good men in the host. With him went James of Avesnes, and Baldwin of Beauvoir, Odo of Champagne of Champlitte, William his brother, and the people of their country. They started at vesper time and rode all night, and on the morrow, when it was full day, they came to a good city, called Phile, and took it; and they had great gain, beasts, and prisoners, and clothing, and food, which they sent in boats down the straits to the camp, for the city lies on the sea of Russia.

So they sojourned two days in that city, with food in great plenty, enough and to spare. The third day they departed with the beasts and the booty, and rode back towards the camp. Now the Emperor Mourzuphles heard tell how they had issued from the camp, and he left Constantinople by night, with a great part of his people, and set himself in ambush at a place by which they must needs pass. And he watched them pass with their beasts and their booty, each division, the one after the other, till it came to the rear-guard. The rear-guard was under the command of Henry, the brother of Count Baldwin of Flanders, and formed of his people, and the Emperor Mourzuphles fell upon them at the entrance to a wood; whereupon they turned against him. Very fiercely did the battle rage there.

By God's help the Emperor Mourzuphles was discomfited, and came near to being taken captive; and he lost his imperial banner and an Eikon that was borne before him, in which he and the other Greeks had great confidence—it was an Eikon that figured our Lady—and he lost at least twenty knights of the best people that he had. Thus was discomfited the Emperor Mourzuphles, as you have just heard; and fiercely did the war rage between him and the Franks; and by this time a great part of the winter had already passed, and it was near Candlemas (2nd February 1203), and Lent was approaching.

Now let us leave speaking of those who avoided the host, and speak of those before Constantinople. Well had these prepared all their engines, and mounted their petraries, and mangonels on the ships and on the transports, and got ready all such engines of war as are needful for the taking of a city, and raised ladders from the yards and masts of the vessels, so high that they were a marvel to behold.

And when the Greeks saw this, they began, on their side, to strengthen the defences of the city which was enclosed with high walls and high towers. Nor was any tower so high that they did not raise thereon two or three stages of wood to heighten it still more. Never was city so well fortified. Thus did the Greeks and the Franks bestir themselves on the one side and the other during the greater part of Lent.

Then those of the host spoke together, and took counsel what they should do. Much was advanced this way and that, but in the end, they devised that if God granted them entry into the city by force, all the booty taken was to be brought together, and fittingly distributed; and further, if the city fell into their power, six men should be taken from among the Franks, and six from among the Venetians, and these twelve should swear, on holy relics, to elect as emperor the man who, as they deemed, would rule with most profit to the land. And whosoever was thus elected emperor, would have one quarter of whatever was captured, whether within the city or without, and moreover would possess the palace of Bucoleon and that of Blachernae; and the remaining three parts would be divided into two, and one of the halves awarded to the Venetians and the other to those of the host.

And there should be taken twelve of the wisest and most experienced men among the host of the pilgrims, and twelve among the Venetians, and those twenty-four would divide fiefs and honours, and appoint the service to be done therefor to the emperor.

This covenant was made sure and sworn to on the one side and the other by the Franks and the Venetians; with provision that at the end of March, a year thence, any who so desired might depart hence and go their way, but that those who remained in the land would be held to the service of the emperor in such manner as might be ordained. Thus was the covenant devised and made sure; and such as should not observe it were excommunicated by the clergy.

The fleet was very well prepared and armed, and provisions were got together for the pilgrims. On the Thursday after mid-Lent (8th April 1204), all entered into the vessels, and put their horses into the transports. Each division had its own ships, and all were ranged side by side; and the ships were separated from the galleys and transports. A marvellous sight it was to see; and well does this book bear witness that the attack, as it had been devised, extended over full half a French league.

On the Friday morning the ships and the galleys and the other vessels drew near to the city in due order, and then began an assault most fell and fierce. In many places the pilgrims landed and went up to the walls, and in many places the scaling ladders on the ships approached so close, that those on the towers and on the walls and those on the ladders crossed lances, hand to hand. Thus lasted the assault, in more than a hundred places, very fierce, and very dour, and very proud, till near upon the hour of nones.

But, for our sins, the pilgrims were repulsed in that assault, and those who had landed from the galleys and transports were driven back into them by main force. And you must know that on that day those of the host lost more than the Greeks, and much were the Greeks rejoiced thereat. And some there were who drew back from the assault, with the ships in which they were. And some remained with their ships at anchor so near to the city that from either side they shot at one another with petraries and mangonels.

Then, at vesper time, those of the host and the Doge of Venice called together a parliament, and assembled in a church on the other side of the straits—on the side where they had been quartered. There were many opinions given and discussed; and much were those of the host moved for the mischief that had that day befallen them. And many advised that they should attack the city on another side—the side where it was not so well fortified. But the Venetians, who had fuller knowledge of the sea, said that if they went to that other side, the current would carry them down the straits, and that they would be unable to stop their ships. And you must know that there were those who would have been well pleased if the current had borne them down the straits, or the wind, they cared not whither, so long as they left that land behind, and went on their way. Nor is this to be wondered at, for they were in sore peril.

Enough was there spoken, this way and in that; but the conclusion of their deliberation was this: that they would repair and refit on the following day, which was Saturday, and during the whole of Sunday, and that on the Monday they would return to the assault; and they devised further that the ships that carried the scaling ladders should be bound together, two and two, so that two ships should be in case to attack one tower; for they had perceived that day how only one ship had attacked each tower, and that this had been too heavy a task for the ship, seeing that those in the tower were more in number than those on the ladder. For this reason was it well seen that two ships would attack each tower with greater effect than one. As had been settled, so was it done, and they waited thus during the Saturday and Sunday.

Before the assault the Emperor Mourzuphles had come to encamp, with all his power, in an open space, and had there pitched his scarlet tents. Thus matters remained till the Monday morning, when those on the ships, transports, and galleys were all armed. And those of the city stood in much less fear of them than they did at the beginning, and were in such good spirits that on the walls and towers you could see nothing but people. Then began an assault proud and marvellous, and every ship went straight before it to the attack. The noise of the battle was so great that it seemed to rend the earth.

Thus did the assault last for a long while, till our Lord raised a wind called Boreas which drove the ships and vessels further up on to the shore. And two ships that were bound together, of which the one was called the *Pilgrim* and the other the *Paradise*, approached so near to a tower, the one on the one side and the other on the other—so as God and the wind drove them—that the ladder of the *Pilgrim* joined on to the tower. Immediately a Venetian, and a knight of France, whose name was Andrew of Urboise, entered into the tower, and other people began to enter after them, and those in the tower were discomfited and fled.

When the knights see this, who are in the transports, they land, and raise their ladders against the wall, and scale the top of the wall by main force, and so take four of the towers. And all begin to leap out of the ships and transports and galleys, helter-skelter, each as best he can; and they break in some three of the gates and enter in; and they draw the horses out of the transports; and the knights mount and ride straight to the quarters of the Emperor Mourzuphles. He had his battalions arrayed before his tents, and when his men see the mounted knights coming, they lose heart and fly; and so goes the emperor flying through the streets to the castle of Bucoleon.

Then might you have seen the Greeks beaten down; and horses and palfreys captured, and mules, and other booty. Of killed and wounded there was neither end nor measure. A great part of the Greek lords had fled towards the gate of Blachernae. And vesper-time was already past, and those of the host were weary of the battle and of the slaying. And they began to assemble in a great open space that was in Constantinople, and decided that they would take up their quarters near the walls and towers they had captured. Never had they thought that in a whole month they should be able to take the city, with its great churches, and great palaces, and the people that were in it.

As they had settled, so was it done, and they encamped before the walls and before the towers by their ships. Count Baldwin of Flanders and Hainault quartered himself in the scarlet tents that the Emperor Mourzuphles had left standing, and Henry his brother before the palace of Blachernae; and Boniface, Marquis of Montferrat, he and his men, towards the thickest part of the city. So were the host encamped as you have heard, and Constantinople taken on the Monday after Palm Sunday (12th April 1204).

Now Count Lewis of Blois and Chartres had languished all the winter with a quartan fever, and could not bear his armour. And you must know that this was a great misfortune to the host, seeing he was a good knight of his body; and he lay in one of the transports.

Thus did those of the host, who were very weary, rest that night. But the Emperor Mourzuphles rested not, for he assembled all his people, and said he would go and attack the Franks. Nevertheless he did not do as he had said, for he rode along other streets, as far as he could from those held by the host, and came to a gate which is called the Golden Gate, whereby he escaped, and avoided the city; and afterwards all who could fled also. And of all this those of the host knew nothing.

During the night, towards the quarters of Boniface, Marquis of Montferrat, certain people, whose names are unknown to me, being in fear lest the Greeks should attack them, set fire to the buildings between themselves and the Greeks. And the city began to take fire, and to burn very direfully; and it burned all that night and all the next day, till vesper-time. And this was the third fire there had been in Constantinople since the Franks arrived in the land; and more houses had been burned in the city than there are houses in any three of the greatest cities in the kingdom of France.

That night passed and the next day came, which was a Tuesday morning (13th April 1204); and all armed themselves throughout the host, both knights and sergeants, and each repaired to his post. Then they issued from their quarters, and thought to find a sorer battle than the day before, for no word had come to them that the emperor had fled during the night. But they found none to oppose them.

The Marquis Boniface of Montferrat rode all along the shore to the palace of Bucoleon, and when he arrived there it surrendered, on condition that the lives of all therein should be spared. At Bucoleon were found the larger number of the great ladies who had fled to the castle, for there were found the sister of the King of France, who had been empress, and the sister of the King of Hungary, who had also been empress, and other ladies very many. Of the treasure that was found in that palace I cannot well speak, for there was so much that it was beyond end or counting.

At the same time that this palace was surrendered to the Marquis Boniface of Montferrat, did the palace of Blachernae surrender to Henry, the brother of Count Baldwin of Flanders, on condition that no hurt should be done to the bodies of those who were therein. There too was found much treasure, not less than in the palace of Bucoleon. Each garrisoned with his own people the castle that had been surrendered to him, and set a guard over the treasure. And the other people, spread abroad throughout the city, also gained much booty. The booty gained was so great that none could tell you the end of it: gold and silver, and vessels and precious stones, and samite, and cloth of silk, and robes vair and grey, and ermine, and every choicest thing found upon the earth. And well does Geoffry of Villehardouin, the Marshal of Champagne, bear witness, that never, since the world was created, had so much booty been won in any city.

Every one took quarters where he pleased, and of lodgings there was no stint. So the host of the pilgrims and of the Venetians found quarters, and greatly did they rejoice and give thanks because of the victory God had vouchsafed to them—for those who before had been poor were now in wealth and luxury. Thus they celebrated Palm Sunday and the Easter Day following (25th April 1204) in the joy and honour that God had bestowed upon them. And well might they praise our Lord, since in all the host there were no more than twenty thousand armed men, one with another, and with the help of God they had conquered four hundred thousand men, or more, and in the strongest city in all the world—yea, a great city—and very well fortified.

Chapter Eight

The Twelfth Century Awakening

THE title of this chapter indicates clearly enough that I am rejecting the concept of a "Twelfth Century Renaissance." The principal reason is that I do not believe the multiplication of "Renaissances" serves any useful purpose. Something did happen in the twelfth century, whatever name we call it, but it was not the same as the movement which began in Italy in the fourteenth century. There are parallels between the two and certain well-known continuities. However, the parallels inhere more in a basic similarity of type rather than of kind. Both involved a general quickening of intellectual and every other kind of pace. Both sought innovation and new forms and institutions to express them. Nevertheless, the forms were not the same.

One specific example may serve to illustrate this similarity of type and divergence of kind. Both what I call the Twelfth Century Awakening and the Renaissance drew inspiration from classical antiquity; in both cases it was a matter of occasion rather than cause. But the "humanism" of the twelfth century was of a different nature than the "humanism" of the fifteenth. Although one could scarcely improve on John of Salisbury's knowledge of the classics, in the fifteenth century or at any other time, his attitude towards them was not the same as say, Petrarch or Poggio. Essentially, the difference is that John saw the ancients he admired through the powerful but distorting lens of medieval Christianity; this meant that he failed to see their incompatibility with his own values. Petrarch and Poggio did see the incompatibility and for this reason they could comprehend that a different civilization intervened between themselves and classical antiquity. They called that civilization the Middle Ages. Intellectually, the difference between the twelfth and the fifteenth centuries lies precisely in this historical perspective.

Most historians agree that the twelfth was the most medieval century. From the standpoint of intellectual history specifically, and this is the viewpoint of this chapter, the statement probably would not survive sustained analysis. Yet it is as true of the twelfth century generally as most sweeping statements are likely to be.

Joseph Strayer, in his *Western Europe in the Middle Ages,* gives five broad characteristics of the twelfth century. In the first place, it was primarily western European in its focus rather than Mediterranean, as was classical civilization, or "oceanic," as modern civilization has become. Secondly, its political organization differed from ancient or modern types. The twelfth century did not have the concept, or reality, of the state; this meant that men were subject to a variety of overlapping and sometimes conflicting authorities rather than to a single sovereign authority. On the other hand, the absence of the state increased the cohesiveness of smaller groups like the guild, town and manor. Thirdly, the twelfth century was unique in its religious structure. In the ancient world, religion was thoroughly subordinate to the state; in the modern, church and state are usually entirely separate. In the twelfth century, the church was an independent public authority claiming complete freedom of action and complete immunity for its personnel from lay control. And, in another sphere, it played a much greater role in determining the values of society. Fourthly, economic and social institutions rested on a different basis. Group effort rather than individual effort was the norm. It conceived of society in hierarchical terms in which each class (estate) had separate functions and a separate status. The individual was subordinate to a society conceived of in corporate terms. Finally, in the intellectual sphere, the twelfth century certainly began to develop forms neither ancient in structure nor modern in spirit and content—Gothic architecture, scholasticism, and the university, just to name a few.

The following selections attempt to reveal the major intellectual characteristics of the twelfth century. As I see them they were four in number. One of the most salient ones is the cosmopolitan character of intellectual life. Even though the twelfth century was a formative period in the development of the nation state, the fluidity of intellectual frontiers was quite amazing. The material that follows, especially the autobiography of Abelard and chapter ten of John of Salisbury's *Metalogicon,* gives striking illustration of this point. Place of origin mattered little for students and masters, or for prelates of the church. This is the century that saw the only English pope, Arnold of Brescia dominating Rome, and an Italian as Archbishop of Canterbury. There was an international community of scholars tied together by a common language and a common education.

If place of origin mattered little in respect of personalities, it mattered no more in terms of ideas. Europe was willing to absorb the pagan Aristotle, what it understood of Plato, the Roman Law, and, later on, the works of Arabian and Jewish philosophers. Because of this eclecticism the twelfth century could not very well be called dogmatic. People did run afoul of religious conservatism, again amply illustrated in the pages that follow, but the repressive disciplinary machinery of the following century did not yet exist.

The freemasonry of scholars and ideas was matched by a desire to learn. Students flocked to the schools, monastic at first, then cathedral, and finally, by the end of the century, the university. Here we run head on into the central and mysterious question about the Twelfth Century Awakening. Why? The standard answers to questions of this sort do not serve us very well. Political stability *per se* has never been a criterion of intellectual affluence. Perhaps the hardening of political forms made communication easier; yet it is just as likely that the desire to get people, letters and books from one place to another may be cause rather than result. Similarly, the undoubted and explosive growth of population, equally mysterious in origin, provided the human raw material for our phenomenon. No doubt the surplus of humanity caused men to search for new lines of endeavor. Yet this line of reasoning does not explain Abelard who, as eldest son, renounced his inheritance for a life of scholarship.

Again, to return to a point made in a former chapter, wealth, and the tastes and leisure it brings, has a great deal to do with culture. Just as surely as this helps to explain the phenomenon we are describing, it does not explain it all. If John of Salisbury was able to find patrons, Arnold of Brescia was not; his students begged their daily bread for themselves and their master. Yet it is true that scholars and artists did find employment with secular and ecclesiastical princes; one could make a living by one's wits in the twelfth century, whereas before only the monastery provided the leisure for scholarly and artistic activity.

Finally, outside influences are not satisfactory as even a partial explanation of the Twelfth Century Awakening. Even if the twelfth century was "open," the broadening of its intellectual horizons originated from a receptiveness that came from within its own resources. Notice, for example, that the "Old Logic" of Aristotle had been available in the West ever since the time of Boethius. It was not the discovery of dialectic, it was the willingness to use it that made the difference.

Only two things are certain. We know what the new enthusiasm for learning was about and we know that it was profitable. The enthusiasm was about dialectic, a point as difficult as it is important to grasp, since the modern student seldom shares it. "The works of Boethius," in the words of R. W. Southern, "gave the eleventh century a glimpse of what was by far the most impressive body of systematic teaching about the world, which was accessible to men of those generations. The world of nature was chaotic—a playground of supernatural forces . . . over which the mind had no control." Logic, then, "opened a window on to an orderly and systematic view of the world and of man's mind." Beginning with Porphyry's *Introduction* to Aristotle, the student learned how to classify objects external to the mind under the terms genus, species, difference, property, and accident, and to use them in argument. Turning to Aristotle's *Categories*, in Boethius' translation, he learned how objects are described using the nine categories of Quantity, Quality, Relation, Position, Place, Time, State, and Affection. Then from Aristotle's *On Interpretation* he learned to classify the kinds of statement that can be made on any subject. And so it went. By the time the full corpus of Aristotelian logical works was available, at the middle of the twelfth century, the student was in possession of a precise and orderly discipline with which to bring order into the undisciplined world about him. This is also the explanation of an intellectual sub-characteristic of the twelfth century, the confidence many had in the power of human reason in general and their own in particular.

The new learning was not only exciting, it was lucrative. Training at a cathedral school or university became the avenue for preferment in the administrative hierarchies of the church and secular governments. Not long past mid-century, the prelates and officials of the church were almost all products of the schools. It is said that over fifty of Abelard's known pupils became high ecclesiastical officials of some sort. The feeling of this change can be gotten from two parallel episodes related below. In 1121 Abelard was summarily condemned by a church council without being heard in his own defense; in 1148, Gilbert of La Porré, also facing the redoubtable St. Bernard, was acquitted under precisely parallel circumstances. The schoolmen were closing ranks against outsiders.

The latter remarks bring us to another major theme of twelfth century intellectual life, the conflict between faith and reason. To quote Friedrich Heer:

> The intellectual world of the twelfth century looked both to the past and the future. Looking to the past meant allegiance to the thousand-year-long tradition of a circuitous approach to the mysteries of the triune God, in a spirit of awe and love. Such divine mysteries were 'comprehensible' only through symbolism and the reverent interpretation of symbols: they could be revealed to human experience in images and allegory, but might never be completely exposed to view. Looking to the future meant embracing boldly and without prejudice a philosophy which included in one system God, nature, the world and man.

St. Bernard's complaint against Abelard was not that he was a heretic, it was pride, pride in thinking he could understand by his own reason the mysteries of God. He was one of the "little men with little dialectical gimlets offering to open all the safes in the theological world." For St. Bernard, the attempt to understand the faith rationally was in itself subversive of it.

For Abelard, on the other hand, as for St. Anselm, once grounded in the faith it was criminal not to attempt to understand it. As Abelard remarked of his students:

> . . . They were always seeking for rational and philosophical explanations, asking rather for reasons they could understand than for mere words, saying that it was futile to utter words which the intellect could not possibly follow, that nothing could be believed unless it could first be understood, and that it was absurd for anyone to preach to others a thing which neither he himself nor those whom he sought to teach could comprehend.

Abelard and his followers conceived of no conflict between reason and faith although occasionally there might be between reason and authority. Abelard was not, most agree now, a rationalist in any modern sense. He was confident, obviously so, in his own intellectual powers. But he never attempted to use reason as a judge of faith as if its truth depended upon its conformity with reason. He was content, as he said himself, to place the buttress of reasoning on the foundation of authority.

Although defeated in his clash with St. Bernard, the future lay with Abelard. Even the saintly Cistercian, in the letter given below, tried to meet Abelard on his own ground. Some would be more conservative, reverential of authority, than others, but they would all accept Abelard's approach.

By mid-century the first phase of the Twelfth Century Awakening was over. Most of the characteristics described above were well under way. It became possible, at this point, to consolidate the intellectual gains that had been made. The passion for systematizing was already there, the method was already fully developed. So from about the 1140's we see the dialectical approach reaching out into substantive bodies of knowledge; theology, canon law, biblical studies, grammar and rhetoric. A rash of new works appeared, similar in method and intent: in canon law the *Concordance of Discordant Canons* of Gratian (better known as the *Decretum*); in theology the *Four Books of Sentences* of Peter Lombard; in biblical studies the *Glossa Ordinaria,* compiled by the school of Laon, and the *Historia Scholastica* of Petrus Comestor; in grammar the *Summa* of Petrus Helias, in rhetoric several *Summae* from the schools of Bologna and Orleans. All of them, in their attempt to summarize the state of knowledge in a given field, expressed a newly found confidence in human reason. Likewise, the method used in most of these compilations expressed the same confidence. The method was that of Abelard in his *Sic et Non;* a statement of the question, the conflicting views of authority and the personal solution, in dialectical terms, of the compiler. It was not a new method; it had long been in use among the canonists and had been utilized by Aristotle in his *Topics, Analytics* and *Sophistics,* all of which were in general use by mid-century.

The principal intellectual achievement of the twelfth century was the absorption of the Aristotelian logical corpus and the consequent systematizing of thought and knowledge. This had been achieved by the third quarter of the century. Two other developments under way by this time, the rise of universities and the reception of the New Aristotle, since they culminated in the next century, I shall deal with them in a subsequent chapter.

1. *St. Anselm of Canterbury*

Anselm (c.1033–1109) was born in Aosta, then in the Kingdom of Burgundy, of a Lombard landowner and a Burgundian woman of noble rank. He became an early example of what would be a typical phenomenon of the twelfth century awakening, the wandering scholar. In 1056, after a quarrel with his father, he crossed the Alps to study in Burgundy and France. By 1059 he was at the famous monastic school of Bec which, under Lanfranc, was the most important school of its time. He became a monk (1060) and an assistant to Lanfranc in the school. When Lanfranc left to become abbot at Caen, Anselm succeeded him as Prior and, presumably, as chief teacher in the monastic school. On the death of Abbot Herlwin (1078) he became Abbot of Bec. For his later life see Eadmer's *Life* in Chapter 6.

Aside from his career as Archbishop of Canterbury, Anselm is significant as the most prominent philosopher and theologian of his time. The following two selections illustrate only one aspect of that prominence, his ontological proof of the existence of God.

The translations from his *Proslogium* and *An Appendix in Behalf of the Fool* are by S. N. Deane (LaSalle, Illinois: The Open Court Publishing Company, 1903), pp. 7–10, 153–70.

a. Proslogium

AND so, Lord, do thou, who dost give understanding to faith, give me, so far as thou knowest it to be profitable, to understand that thou art as we believe; and that thou art that which we believe. And, indeed, we believe that thou art a being than which nothing greater can be conceived. Or is there no such nature, since the fool hath said in his heart, there is no God? But, at any rate, this very fool, when he hears of this being of which I speak—a being than which nothing greater can be conceived—understands what he hears, and what he understands is in his understanding; although he does not understand it to exist.

For, it is one thing for an object to be in the understanding, and another to understand that the object exists. When a painter first conceives of what he will afterwards perform, he has it in his understanding, but he does not yet understand it to be, because he has not yet performed it. But after he has made the painting, he both has it in his understanding, and he understands that it exists, because he has made it.

Hence, even the fool is convinced that something exists in the understanding, at least, than which nothing greater can be conceived. For, when he hears of this, he understands it. And whatever is understood, exists in the understanding. And assuredly that, than which nothing greater can be conceived, cannot exist in the understanding alone: then it can be conceived to exist in reality; which is greater.

Therefore, if that, than which nothing greater can be conceived, exists in the understanding alone, the very being, than which nothing greater can be conceived, is one, than which a greater can be conceived. But obviously this is impossible. Hence, there is no doubt that there exists a being, than which nothing greater can be conceived, and it exists both in the understanding and in reality.

And it assuredly exists so truly, that it cannot be conceived not to exist. For, it is possible to conceive of a being which cannot be conceived not to exist; and this is greater than one which can be conceived not to exist. Hence, if that, than which nothing greater can be conceived, can be conceived not to exist, it is not that, than which nothing greater can be conceived. But this is an irreconcilable contradiction. There is, then, so truly a being than which nothing greater can be conceived to exist, that it cannot even be conceived not to exist; and this being thou art, O Lord, our God.

So truly, therefore, dost thou exist, O Lord, my God, that thou canst not be conceived not to exist; and rightly. For if a mind could conceive of a being better than thee, the creature would rise above the Creator; and this is most absurd. And, indeed, whatever else there is, except thee alone, therefore, it belongs to exist more truly than all other beings, and hence in a higher degree than all others. For whatever else exists does not exist so truly, and hence in a less degree it belongs to it to exist. Why, then, has the fool said in his heart, there is no God, since it is so evident, to a rational mind, that thou dost exist in the highest degree of all? Why except that he is dull and a fool.

But how has the fool said in his heart what he could not conceive; or how is it that he could not conceive what he said in his heart? since it is the same to say in the heart and to conceive.

But, if really, nay, since really, he both conceived, because he said in his heart; and did not say in his heart, because he could not conceive; there is more than one way in which a thing is said in the heart or conceived. For, in one sense, an object is conceived when the word signifying it is conceived; and in another, when the very entity, which the object is, is understood.

In the former sense, then, God can be conceived not to exist; but in the latter, not at all. For no one who understands what fire and water are can conceive fire to be water, in accordance with the nature of the facts themselves, although this is possible according to the words. So, then, no one who understands what God is can conceive that God does not exist; although he says these words in his heart, either without any, or with some foreign, signification. For, God is that than which a greater cannot be conceived. And he who thoroughly understands this, assuredly understands that this being so truly exists, that not even in concept can it be non-existent. Therefore, he who understands that God so exists, cannot conceive that he does not exist.

I thank thee, gracious Lord, I thank thee; because what I formerly believed by thy bounty, I now so understand by thine illumination, that if I were unwilling to believe that thou dost exist, I should not be able to understand this to be true.

b. An Appendix in Behalf of the Fool

It was a fool against whom the argument of my Proslogium was directed. Seeing, however, that the author of these objections is by no means a fool, and is a Catholic, speaking in behalf of the fool, I think it sufficient that I answer the Catholic.

You say—whosoever you may be, who say that a fool is capable of making these statements—that a being than which a greater cannot be conceived is not in the understanding in any other sense than that in which a being that is altogether inconceivable in terms of reality, is in the understanding. You say that the inference that this being exists in reality, from the fact that it is in the understanding, is no more just than the inference that a lost island most certainly exists, from the fact that when it is described the hearer does not doubt that it is in his understanding.

But I say: if a being than which a greater is inconceivable is not understood or conceived, and is not in the understanding or in concept, certainly either God is not a being than which a greater is inconceivable, or else he is not understood or conceived, and is not in the understanding or in concept. But I call on your faith and conscience to attest that this is most false. Hence, that then which a greater cannot be conceived is truly understood and conceived, and is in the understanding and in concept. Therefore either the grounds on which you try to controvert me are not true, or else the inference which you think to base logically on those grounds is not justified.

But you hold, moreover, that supposing that a being than which a greater cannot be conceived is understood, it does not follow that this being is in the understanding; nor, if it is in the understanding, does it therefore exist in reality.

In answer to this, I maintain positively: if that being can be even conceived to be, it must exist in reality. For that than which a greater is inconceivable cannot be conceived except as without beginning. But whatever can be conceived to exist, and does not exist, can be conceived to exist through a beginning. Hence what can be conceived to exist, but does not exist, is not the being than which a greater cannot be conceived. Therefore, if such a being can be conceived to exist, necessarily it does exist.

Furthermore: if it can be conceived at all, it must exist. For no one who denies or doubts the existence of a being than which a greater is inconceivable, denies or doubts that if it did exist, its non-existence, either in reality or in the understanding, would be impossible. For otherwise it would not be a being than which a greater cannot be conceived. But as to whatever can be conceived, but does not exist—if there were such a being, its non-existence, either in reality or in the understanding, would be possible. Therefore if a being than which a greater is inconceivable can be even conceived, it cannot be non-existent.

But let us suppose that it does not exist, even if it can be conceived. Whatever can be conceived, but does not exist, if it existed, would not be a being than which a greater is inconceivable. If, then, there were a being a greater than which is inconceivable, it would not be a being than which a greater is inconceivable: which is most absurd. Hence, it is false to deny that a being than which a greater cannot be conceived exists, if it can be even conceived; much the more, therefore, if it can be understood or can be in the understanding.

Moreover, I will venture to make this assertion: without doubt, whatever at any place or at any time does not exist—even if it does exist at some place or at some time—can be conceived to exist nowhere and never, as at some place and at some time it does not exist. For what did not exist yesterday, and exists to-day, as it is understood not to have existed yesterday, so it can be apprehended by the intelligence that it never exists. And what is not here, and is elsewhere, can be conceived to be nowhere, just as it is not here. So with regard to an object of which the individual parts do not exist at the same places or times: all its parts and therefore its very whole can be conceived to exist nowhere or never.

For, although time is said to exist always, and the world everywhere, yet time does not as a whole exist always, nor the world as a whole everywhere. And as individual parts of time do not exist when others exist, so they can be conceived never to exist. And so it can be apprehended by the intelligence that individual parts of the world exist nowhere, as they do not exist where other parts exist. Moreover, what is composed of parts can be dissolved in concept, and be non-existent. Therefore, whatever at any place or at any time does not exist as a whole, even if it is existent, can be conceived not to exist.

But that than which a greater cannot be conceived, if it exists, cannot be conceived not to exist. Otherwise, it is not a being than which a greater cannot be conceived: which is non-existent. By no means, then, does it at any place or at any time fail to exist as a whole: but it exists as a whole everywhere and always.

Do you believe that this being can in some way be conceived or understood, or that the being with regard to which these things are understood can be in concept or in the understanding? For if it cannot, these things cannot be understood with reference to it. But if you say that it is not understood and that it is not in the understanding, because it is not thoroughly understood; you should say that a man who cannot face the direct rays of the sun does not see the light of day, which is none other than the sunlight. Assuredly a being than which a greater cannot be conceived exists, and is in the understanding, at least to this extent—that these statements regarding it are understood.

I have said, then, in the argument which you dispute, that when the fool hears mentioned a being than which a greater is inconceivable, he understands what he hears. Certainly a man who does not understand when a familiar language is spoken, has no understanding at all, or a very dull one. Moreover, I have said that if this being is understood, it is in the understanding. Is that in no understanding which has been proved necessarily to exist in the reality of fact?

But you will say that although it is in the understanding, it does not follow that it is understood. But observe that the fact of its being understood does necessitate its being in the understanding. For as what is conceived, is conceived by conception, and what is conceived by conception, as it is conceived, so is in conception; so what is understood, is understood by understanding, as it is understood, so is in the understanding. What can be more clear than this?

After this, I have said that if it is even in the understanding alone, it can be conceived also to exist in reality, which is greater. If, then, it is in the understanding alone, obviously the very being than which a greater cannot be conceived is one than which a greater can be conceived. What is more logical? For if it exists even in the understanding alone, can it not be conceived also to exist in reality? And if it can be so conceived, does not he who conceives of this conceive of a thing greater than that being, if it exists in the understanding alone? What more consistent inference, then, can be made than this: that if a being than which a greater cannot be conceived is in the understanding alone, it is not that than which a greater cannot be conceived?

But, assuredly, in no understanding is a being than which a greater is conceivable a being than which a greater is inconceivable. Does it not follow, then, that if a being than which a greater cannot be conceived is in any understanding, it does not exist in the understanding alone? For if it is in the understanding alone, it is a being than which a greater can be conceived, which is inconsistent with the hypothesis.

But, you say, it is as if one should suppose an island in the ocean, which surpasses all lands in its fertility, and which, because of the difficulty, or rather the impossibility, of discovering what does not exist, is called a lost island; and should say that there can be no doubt that this island truly exists in reality, for this reason, that one who hears it described easily understands what he hears.

Now I promise confidently that if any man shall devise anything existing either in reality or in concept alone (except that than which a greater cannot be conceived) to which he can adapt the sequence of my reasoning, I will discover that thing, and will give him his lost island, not to be lost again.

But it now appears that this being than which a greater is inconceivable cannot be conceived not to be, because it exists on so assured a ground of truth; for otherwise it would not exist at all.

Hence, if any one says that he conceives this being not to exist, I say that at the time when he conceives of this either he conceives of a being than which a greater is inconceivable, or he does not conceive at all. If he does not conceive, he does not conceive of the non-existence of that of which he does not conceive. But if he does conceive, he certainly conceives of a being which cannot be even conceived not to exist. For if it could be conceived not to exist, it could be conceived to have a beginning and an end. But this is impossible.

He, then, who conceives of this being conceives of a being which cannot be even conceived not to exist; but he who conceives of this being does not conceive that it does not exist; else he conceives what is inconceivable. The non-existence, then, of that than which a greater cannot be conceived is inconceivable.

You say, moreover, that whereas I assert that this supreme being cannot be *conceived* not to exist, it might better be said that its non-existence, or even the possibility of its non-existence, cannot be *understood.*

But it was more proper to say, it cannot be conceived. For if I had said that the object itself cannot be understood not to exist, possibly you yourself, who say that in accordance with the true meaning of the term what is unreal cannot be understood, would offer the objection that nothing which is can be understood not to be, for the non-existence of what exists is unreal: hence God would not be the only being of which it could be said, it is impossible to understand its non-existence. For thus one of those beings which most certainly exist can be understood not to exist in the same way in which certain other real objects can be understood not to exist.

But this objection, assuredly, cannot be urged against the term *conception,* if one considers the matter well. For although no objects which exist can be understood not to exist, yet all objects, except that which exists in the highest degree, can be conceived not to exist. For all those objects, and those alone, can be conceived not to exist, which have a beginning or end or composition of parts: also, as I have already said, whatever at any place or at any time does not exist as a whole.

That being alone, on the other hand, cannot be conceived not to exist, in which any conception discovers neither beginning nor end nor composition of parts, and which any conception finds always and everywhere as a whole.

Be assured, then, that you can conceive of your own non-existence, although you are most certain that you exist. I am surprised that you should have admitted that you are ignorant of this. For we conceive of the non-existence of many objects which we know to exist, and of the existence of many which we know not to exist; not by forming the opinion that they so exist, but by imagining that they exist as we conceive of them.

And indeed, we can conceive of the non-existence of an object, although we know it to exist, because at the same time we can conceive of the former and know the latter. And we cannot conceive of the non-existence of an object, so long as we know it to exist, because we cannot conceive at the same time of existence and non-existence.

If, then, one will thus distinguish these two senses of this statement, he will understand that nothing, so long as it is known to exist, can be conceived not to exist; and that whatever exists, except that being than which a greater cannot be conceived, can be conceived not to exist, even when it is known to exist.

So, then, of God alone it can be said that it is impossible to conceive of his non-existence; and yet many objects, so long as they exist, in one sense cannot be conceived not to exist. But in what sense God is to be conceived not to exist, I think has been shown clearly enough in my book.

The nature of the other objections which you, in behalf of the fool, urge against me it is easy, even for a man of small wisdom, to detect; and I had therefore thought it unnecessary to show this. But since I hear that some readers of these objections think they have some weight against me, I will discuss them briefly.

In the first place, you often repeat that I assert that what is greater than all other beings is in the understanding; and if it is in the understanding, it exists also in reality, for otherwise the being which is greater than all would not be greater than all.

Nowhere in all my writings is such a demonstration found. For the real existence of a being which is said to be *greater than all other beings* cannot be demonstrated in the same way with the real existence of one that is said to be a *being than which a greater cannot be conceived.*

If it should be said that a being than which a greater cannot be conceived has no real existence, or that it is possible that it does not exist, or even that it can be conceived not to exist, such an assertion can be easily refuted. For the non-existence of what does not exist is possible, and that whose non-existence is possible can be conceived not to exist. But whatever can be conceived not to exist, if it exists, is not a being than which a greater cannot be conceived; but if it does not exist, it would not, even if it existed, be a being than which a greater cannot be conceived. But it cannot be said that a being than which a greater is inconceivable, if it exists, is not a being than which a greater is inconceivable; or that if it existed, it would not be a being than which a greater is inconceivable.

It is evident, then, that neither is it non-existent, nor is it possible that it does not exist, nor can it be conceived not to exist. For otherwise, if it exists, it is not that which it is said to be in the hypothesis; and if it existed, it would not be what it is said to be in the hypothesis.

But this, it appears, cannot be so easily proved of a being which is said to be *greater than all other beings.* For it is not so evident that what can be conceived not to exist is not greater than all existing beings, as it is evident that it is not a being than which a greater cannot be conceived. Nor is it so indubitable that if a being greater than all other beings exists, it is no other than the being than which a greater cannot be conceived; or that if it were such a being, some other might not be this being in like manner; so it is certain with regard to a being which is hypothetically posited as one than which a greater cannot be conceived.

For consider: if one should say that there is a being greater than all other beings, and that this being can nevertheless be conceived not to exist; and that a being greater than this, although it does not exist, can be conceived to exist: can it be so clearly inferred in this case that this being is therefore not a being greater than all other existing beings, as it would be most positively affirmed in the other case, that the being under discussion is not, therefore, a being than which a greater cannot be conceived?

For the former conclusion requires another premise than the predication, *greater than all other beings.* In my argument, on the other hand, there is no need of any other than this very predication, *a being than which a greater cannot be conceived.*

If the same proof cannot be applied when the being in question is predicated to be greater than all others, which can be applied when it is predicated to be a being than which a greater cannot be conceived, you have unjustly censured me for saying what I did not say; since such a predication differs so greatly from that which I actually made. If, on the other hand, the other argument is valid, you ought not to blame me so for having said what can be proved.

Whether this can be proved, however, he will easily decide who recognizes that this being than which a greater cannot be conceived is demonstrable. For by no means can this being than which a greater cannot be conceived be understood as any other than that which alone is greater than all. Hence, just that than which a greater cannot be conceived is understood, and is the understanding, and for that reason is asserted to exist in the reality of fact: so what is said to be greater than all other beings is understood and is in the understanding, and therefore it is necessarily inferred that it exists in reality. You see, then, with how much justice you have compared me with your fool, who, on the sole ground that he understands what is described to him, would affirm that a lost island exists.

Another of your objections is that any unreal beings, or beings whose existence is uncertain, can be understood and be in the understanding in the same way with that being which I discussed. I am surprised that you should have conceived this objection, for I was attempting to prove what was still uncertain, and contented myself at first with showing that this being is understood in any way, and is in the understanding. It was my intention to consider, on these grounds, whether this being is in the understanding alone, like an unreal object, or whether it also exists in fact, as a real being. For if unreal objects, or objects whose existence is uncertain, in this way are understood are in the understanding, because, when they are spoken of, the hearer understands what the speaker means, there is no reason why that being of which I spoke should not be understood and be in the understanding.

How, moreover, can these two statements of yours be reconciled: (1) the assertion that if a man should speak of any unreal objects, whatever they might be, you would understand, and (2) the assertion that on hearing of that being which does exist, and not in that way in which even unreal objects are held in concept, you would not say that you conceive of it or have it in concept; since, as you say, you cannot conceive of it in any other way than by understanding it, that is, by comprehending in your knowledge its real existence?

How, I ask, can these two things be reconciled: that unreal objects are understood, and that understanding an object is comprehending in knowledge its real existence? The contradiction does not concern me: do you see to it. But if unreal objects are also in some sort understood, and your definition is applicable, not to every understanding, but to a certain sort of understanding, I ought not to be blamed for saying that a being than which a greater cannot be conceived is understood and is in the understanding, even before I reached the certain conclusion that this being exists in reality.

Again, you say that it can probably never be believed that this being, when it is spoken of and heard of, cannot be conceived not to exist in the same way in which even God may be conceived not to exist.

Such an objection could be answered by those who have attained but little skill in disputation and argument. For is it compatible with reason for a man to deny the existence of what he understands, because it is said to be that being whose existence he denies because he does not understand it? Or, if at some times its existence is denied, because only to a certain extent is it understood, and that which is not at all understood is the same to him: is not what is still undetermined more easily proved of a being which exists in some understanding than of one which exists in no understanding?

Hence it cannot be credible that any man denies the existence of a being than which a greater cannot be conceived, which, when he hears of it, he understands in a certain degree: it is incredible, I say, that any man denies the existence of this being because he denies the existence of God, the sensory perception of whom he in no wise conceives of.

Or if the existence of another object, because it is not at all understood, is denied, yet is not the existence of what is understood in some degree more easily proved than the existence of an object which is in no wise understood?

Not irrationally, then, has the hypothesis of a being a greater than which cannot be conceived been employed in controverting the fool, for the proof of the existence of God: since in some degree he would understand such a being, but in no wise could he understand God.

Moreover, your so careful demonstration that the being than which a greater cannot be conceived is not analogous to the not yet executed picture in the understanding of the painter, is quite unnecessary. It was not for this purpose that I suggested the preconceived picture. I had no thought of asserting that the being which I was discussing is of such a nature; but I wished to show that what is not understood to exist can be in the understanding.

Again, you say that when you hear of a being than which a greater is inconceivable, you cannot conceive of it in terms of any real object known to you either specifically or generally, nor have it in your understanding. For, you say, you neither know such a being in itself, nor can you form an idea of it from anything like it.

But obviously this is not true. For everything that is less good, in so far as it is good, is like the greater good. It is therefore evident to any rational mind, that by ascending from the lesser good to the greater, we can form a considerable notion of a being than which a greater is inconceivable.

For instance, who (even if he does not believe that what he conceives of exists in reality) supposing that there is some good which has a beginning and an end, does not conceive that a good is much better, which, if it begins, does not cease to be? And that as the second good is better than the first, so that good which has neither beginning nor end, though it is ever passing from the past through the present to the future, is better than the second? And that far better than this is a being—whether any being of such a nature exists or not—which in no wise requires change or motion, nor is compelled to undergo change or motion?

Is this inconceivable, or is some being greater than this conceivable? Or is not this to form a notion from objects than which a greater is conceivable, of the being than which a greater cannot be conceived? There is, then, a means of forming a notion of a being than which a greater is inconceivable.

So easily, then, can the fool who does not accept sacred authority be refuted, if he denies that a notion may be formed from other objects of a being than which a greater is inconceivable. But if any Catholic would deny this, let him remember that the invisible things of God, from the creation of the world, are clearly seen, being understood by the things that are made, even his eternal power and Godhead. (Romans, i. 20.)

But even if it were true that a being than which a greater is inconceivable cannot be conceived or understood; yet it would not be untrue that a being than which a greater cannot be conceived is conceivable and intelligible. There is nothing to prevent one's saying *ineffable,* although what is said to be ineffable cannot be spoken of. *Inconceivable* is conceivable, although that to which the word *inconceivable* can be applied is not conceivable. So, when one says, *that than which nothing greater is conceivable,* undoubtedly what is heard is conceivable and intelligible, although that being itself, than which a greater is inconceivable, cannot be conceived or understood.

Or, though there is a man so foolish as to say that there is no being than which a greater is inconceivable, he will not be so shameless as to say that he cannot understand or conceive of what he says. Or, if such a man is found, not only ought his words to be rejected, but he himself should be contemned.

Whoever, then, denies the existence of a being than which a greater cannot be conceived, at least understands and conceives of the denial which he makes. But this denial he cannot understand or conceive of without its component terms; and a term of this statement is *a being than which a greater cannot be conceived.* Whoever, then, makes this denial, understands and conceives of that than which a greater is inconceivable.

Moreover, it is evident that in the same way it is possible to conceive of and understand a being whose non-existence is impossible; but he who conceives of this conceives of a greater being than one whose non-existence is possible. Hence, when a being than which a greater is inconceivable is conceived, if it is a being whose non-existence is possible that it is conceived, it is not a being than which a greater cannot be conceived. But an object cannot be at once conceived and not conceived. Hence he who conceives of a being than which a greater is inconceivable, does not conceive of that whose non-existence is possible, but of that whose non-existence is impossible. Therefore, what he conceives of must exist; for anything whose non-existence is possible, is not that of which he conceives.

I believe that I have shown by an argument which is not weak, but sufficiently cogent, that in my former book I proved the real existence of a being than which a greater cannot be conceived; and I believe that this argument cannot be invalidated by the validity of any objection. For so great force does the signification of this reasoning contain in itself, that this being which is the subject of discussion, is of necessity, from the very fact that it is understood or conceived, proved also to exist in reality, and to be whatever we should believe of the divine substance.

For we attribute to the divine substance anything of which it can be conceived that it is better to be than not to be that thing. For example: it is better to be eternal than not eternal; good, than not good; nay, goodness itself, than not goodness itself. But it cannot be that anything of this nature is not a property of the being than which a greater is inconceivable. Hence, the being than which a greater is inconceivable must be whatever should be attributed to the divine essence.

I thank you for your kindness both in your blame and in your praise for my book. For since you have commended so generously those parts of it which seem to you worthy of acceptance, it is quite evident that you have criticised in no unkind spirit those parts of it which seemed to you weak.

2. *Peter Abelard (1079-1142)*

The existence of this unique autobiography makes it unnecessary to describe the man.

The following is excerpted from the translation by Henry Adams Bellows (St. Paul: T. A. Boyd, 1922).

The *Story* of My Misfortunes

Chapter I

KNOW, then, that I am come from a certain town which was built on the way into lesser Brittany, distant some eight miles, as I think, eastward from the city of Nantes, and in its own tongue called Palets. Such is the nature of that country, or, it may be, of them who dwell there—for in truth they are quick in fancy—that my mind bent itself easily to the study of letters. Yet more, I had a father who had won some smattering of letters before he had girded on the soldier's belt. And so it came about that long afterwards his love thereof was so strong that he saw to it that each son of his should be taught in letters even earlier than in the management of arms. Thus indeed did it come to pass. And because I was his first born, and for that reason the more dear to him, he sought with double diligence to have me wisely taught. For my part, the more I went forward in the study of letters, and ever more easily, the greater became the ardour of my devotion to them, until in truth I was so enthralled by my passion for learning that, gladly leaving to my brothers the pomp of glory in arms, the right of heritage and all the honours that should have been mine as the eldest born, I fled utterly from the court of Mars that I might win learning in the bosom of Minerva. And since I found the armory of logical reasoning more to my liking than the other forms of philosophy, I exchanged all other weapons for these, and to the prizes of victory in war I preferred the battle of minds in disputation. Thenceforth, journeying through many provinces, and debating as I went, going whithersoever I heard that the study of my chosen art most flourished, I became such an one as the Peripatetics.

Chapter II

I came at length to Paris, where above all in those days the art of dialectics was most flourishing, and there did I meet William of Champeaux, my teacher, a man most distinguished in his science both by his renown and by his true merit. With him I remained for some time, at first indeed well liked of him; but later I brought him great grief, because I undertook to refute certain of his opinions, not infrequently attacking him in disputation, and now and then in these debates I was adjudged victor. Now this, to those among my fellow students who were ranked foremost, seemed all the more insufferable because of my youth and the brief duration of my studies.

Out of this sprang the beginning of my misfortunes, which have followed me even to the present day; the more widely my fame was spread abroad, the more bitter was the envy that was kindled against me. It was given out that I, presuming on my gifts far beyond the warranty of my youth, was aspiring despite my tender years to the leadership of a school; nay, more, that I was making ready the very place in which I would undertake this task, the place being none other than the castle of Melun, at that time a royal seat. My teacher himself had some foreknowledge of this, and tried to remove my school as far as possible from his own. Working in secret, he sought in every way he could before I left his following to bring to nought the school I had planned and the place I had chosen for it. Since, however, in that very place he had many rivals, and some of them men of influence among the great ones of the land, relying on their aid I won to the fulfillment of my wish; the support of many was secured for me by reason of his own unconcealed envy. From this small inception of my school, my fame in the art of dialectics began to spread abroad, so that little by little the renown, not alone of those had been my fellow students, but of our very teacher himself, grew dim and was like to die out altogether. Thus it came about that, still more confident in myself, I moved my school as soon as I well might to the castle of Corbeil, which is hard by the city of Paris, for there I knew there would be given more frequent chance for my assaults in our battle of disputation.

No long time thereafter I was smitten with a grievous illness, brought upon me by my immoderate zeal for study. This illness forced me to turn homeward to my native province, and thus for some years I was as if cut off from France. And yet, for that very reason, I was sought out all the more eagerly by those whose hearts were troubled by the lore of dialectics. But after a few years had passed, and I was whole again from my sickness, I learned that my teacher, that same William Archdeacon of Paris, had changed his former garb and joined an order of the regular clergy. This he had done, or so men said, in order that he might be deemed more deeply religious, and so might be elevated to a loftier rank in the prelacy, a thing which, in truth, very soon came to pass, for he was made bishop of Châlons. Nevertheless, the garb he had donned by reason of his conversion did nought to keep him away either from the city of Paris or from his wonted study of philosophy; and in the very monastery wherein he had shut himself up for the sake of religion he straightway set to teaching again after the same fashion as before.

To him did I return, for I was eager to learn more of rhetoric from his lips; and in the course of our many arguments on various matters, I compelled him by most potent reasoning first to alter his former opinion on the subject of the universals, and finally to abandon it altogether. Now, the basis of this old concept of his regarding the reality of universal ideas was that the same quality formed the essence alike of the abstract whole and of the individuals which were its parts: in other words, that there could be no essential differences among these individuals, all being alike save for such variety as might grow out of the many accidents of existence. Thereafter, however, he corrected this opinion, no longer maintaining that the same quality was the essence of all things, but that, rather, it manifested itself in them through diverse ways. This problem of universals is ever the most vexed one among logicians, to such a degree, indeed, that even Porphyry, writing in his "Isagoge" regarding universals, dared not attempt a final pronouncement thereon, saying rather: "This is the deepest of all problems of its kind." Wherefore it followed that when William had first revised and then finally abandoned altogether his views on this one subject, his lecturing sank into such a state of negligent reasoning that it could scarce be called lecturing on the science of dialectics at all; it was as if all his science had been bound up in this one question of the nature of universals.

Thus it came about that my teaching won such strength and authority that even those who before had clung most vehemently to my former master, and most bitterly attacked my doctrines, now flocked to my school. The very man who had succeeded to my master's chair in the Paris school offered me his post, in order that he might put himself under my tutelage along with all the rest, and this in the very place where of old his master and mine had reigned. And when, in so short a time, my master saw me directing the study of dialectics there, it is not easy to find words to tell with what envy he was consumed or with what pain he was tormented. He could not long, in truth, bear the anguish of what he felt to be his wrongs, and shrewdly he attacked me that he might drive me forth. And because there was nought in my conduct whereby he could come at me openly, he tried to steal away the school by launching the vilest calumnies against him who had yielded his post to me, and by putting in his place a certain rival of mine. So then I returned to Melun, and set up my school there as before; and the more openly his envy pursued me, the greater was the authority it conferred upon me. Even so held the poet

"Jealousy aims at the peaks; the winds storm the loftiest summits." (Ovid, *Remedia Amoris,* I, 369)

Not long thereafter, when William became aware of the fact that almost all his students were holding grave doubts as to his religion, and were whispering earnestly among themselves about his conversion, deeming that he had by no means abandoned this world, he withdrew himself and his brotherhood, together with his students, to a certain estate far distant from the city. Forthwith I returned from Melun to Paris, hoping for peace from him in the future. But since, as I have said, he had caused my place to be occupied by a rival of mine, I pitched the camp, as it were, of my school outside the city on Mont Ste. Geneviève. Thus I was as one laying siege to him who had taken possession of my post. No sooner had my master heard of this than he brazenly returned post haste to the city, bringing back with him such students as he could, and reinstating his brotherhood in their former monastery, much as if he would free his soldiery, whom he had deserted, from my blockade. In truth, though, if it was his purpose to bring them succour, he did nought but hurt them. Before that time my rival had indeed a certain number of students, of one sort and another, chiefly by reason of his lectures on Priscian, in which he was considered of great authority. After our master had returned, however, he lost nearly all of these followers, and thus was compelled to give up the direction of the school. Not long thereafter, apparently despairing further of worldly fame, he was converted to the monastic life.

Following the return of our master to the city, the combats in disputation which my scholars waged both with him himself and with his pupils, and the successes which fortune gave to us, and above all to me, in these wars, you have long since learned through your own experience. The boast of Ajax, though I speak it more temperately, I still am bold enough to make:

> . . . if fain you would learn now
> How victory crowned the battle, by him was
> I never vanquished. (Ovid, *Metamorphoses,* XIII, 89)

But even were I to be silent, the fact proclaims itself, and its outcome reveals the truth regarding it.

While these things were happening, it became needful for me again to repair to my old home, by reason of my dear mother, Lucia, for after the conversion of my father, Berengarius, to the monastic life, she so ordered her affairs as to do likewise. When all this had been completed, I returned to France, above all in order that I might study theology, since now my oft-mentioned teacher, William, was active in the episcopate of Châlons. In this field of learning Anselm of Laon, who was his teacher therein, had for long years enjoyed the greatest renown.

Chapter III

I sought out, therefore, this same venerable man, whose fame, in truth, was more the result of long-established custom than of the potency of his own talent or intellect. If any one come to him impelled by doubt on any subject, he went away more doubtful still. He was wonderful, indeed, in the eyes of these who only listened to him, but those who asked him questions perforce held him as nought. He had a miraculous flow of words, but they were contemptible in meaning and quite void of reason. When he kindled a fire, he filled his house with smoke and illuminated it not at all. He was a tree which seemed noble to those who gazed upon its leaves from afar, but to those who came nearer and examined it more closely was revealed its barrenness. When, therefore, I had come to this tree that I might pluck the fruit thereof, I discovered that it was indeed the fig tree which Our Lord cursed (Matthew, xxi, 19, Mark, xi, 13), or that ancient oak to which Lucan likened Pompey, saying:

> . . . he stands, the shade of a name once
> mighty,
> Like to the towering oak in the midst of the
> fruitful field. (Lucan, *Pharsalia,* IV, 135)

It was not long before I made this discovery, and stretched myself lazily in the shade of that same tree. I went to his lectures less and less often, a thing which some among his eminent followers took sorely to heart, because they interpreted it as a mark of contempt for so illustrious a teacher. Thenceforth they secretly sought to influence him against me, and by their vile insinuations made me hated of him. It chanced, moreover, that one day, after the exposition of certain texts, we scholars were jesting among ourselves, and one of them, seeking to draw me out, asked me what I thought of the lectures on the Books of Scripture. I, who had as yet studied only the sciences, replied that following such lectures seemed to me the most useful in so far as the salvation of the soul was concerned, but that it appeared quite extraordinary to me that educated persons should not be able to understand the sacred books simply by studying them themselves, together with the glosses thereon, and without the aid of any teacher. Most of those who were present mocked at me, and asked whether I myself could do as I had said, or whether I would dare to undertake it. I answered that if they wished, I was ready to try it. Forthwith they cried out and jeered all the more. "Well and good," said they; "we agree to the test. Pick out and give us an exposition of some doubtful passage in the Scriptures, so that we can put this boast of yours to the proof." And they all chose that most obscure prophecy of Ezekiel.

I accepted the challenge, and invited them to attend a lecture on the very next day. Whereupon they undertook to give me good advice, saying that I should by no means make undue haste in so important a matter, but that I ought to devote a much longer space to working out my exposition and offsetting my inexperience by diligent toil. To this I replied indignantly that it was my wont to win success, not by routine, but by ability. I added that I would abandon the test altogether unless they would agree not to put off their attendance at my lecture. In truth at this first lecture of mine only a few were present, for it seemed quite absurd to all of them that I, hitherto so inexperienced in discussing the Scriptures, should attempt the thing so hastily. However, this lecture gave such satisfaction to all those who heard it that they spread its praises abroad with notable enthusiasm, and thus compelled me to continue my interpretation of the sacred text. When word of this was bruited about, those who had stayed away from the first lecture came eagerly, some to the second and more to the third, and all of them were eager to write down the glosses which I had begun on the first day, so as to have them from the very beginning.

Chapter IV

Now this venerable man of whom I have spoken was acutely smitten with envy, and straightway incited, as I have already mentioned, by the insinuations of sundry persons, began to persecute me for my lecturing on the Scriptures no less bitterly than my former master, William, had done for my work in philosophy. At that time there were in this old man's school two who were considered far to excel all the others: Alberic of Rheims and Lotulphe the Lombard. The better opinion these two held of themselves, the more they were incensed against me. Chiefly at their suggestion, as it afterwards transpired, yonder venerable coward had the impudence to forbid me to carry on any further in his school the work of preparing glosses which I had thus begun. The pretext he alleged was that if by chance in the course of this work I should write anything containing blunders—as was likely enough in view of my lack of training—the thing might be imputed to him. When this came to the ears of his scholars, they were filled with indignation at so undisguised a manifestation of spite, the like of which had never been directed against any one before. The more obvious his rancour became, the more it redounded to my honour, and his persecution did nought save to make me more famous.

Chapter V

And so, after a few days, I returned to Paris, and there for several years I peacefully directed the school which formerly had been destined for me, nay, even offered to me, but from which I had been driven out. At the very outset of my work there, I set about completing the glosses on Ezekiel which I had begun at Laon. These proved so satisfactory to all who read them that they came to believe me no less adept in lecturing on theology than I had proved myself to be in the field of philosophy. Thus my school was notably increased in size by reason of my lectures on subjects of both these kinds, and the amount of financial profit as well as glory which it brought me cannot be concealed from you, for the matter was widely talked of. But prosperity always puffs up the foolish, and worldly comfort enervates the soul, rendering it an easy prey to carnal temptations. Thus I, who by this time had come to regard myself as the only philosopher remaining in the whole world, and had ceased to fear any further disturbance of my peace, began to loosen the rein on my desires, although hitherto I had always lived in the utmost continence. And the greater progress I made in my lecturing on philosophy or theology, the more I departed alike from the practice of the philosophers and the spirit of the divines in the uncleanness of my life. For it is well known, methinks, that philosophers, and still more those who have devoted their lives to arousing the love of sacred study, have been strong above all else in the beauty of chastity.

Thus did it come to pass that while I was utterly absorbed in pride and sensuality, divine grace, the cure for both diseases, was forced upon me, even though I, forsooth, would fain have shunned it. First was I punished for my sensuality, and then for my pride. For my sensuality I lost those things whereby I practiced it; for my pride, engendered in me by my knowledge of letters—and it is even as the Apostle said: "Knowledge puffeth itself up" (1 Cor., viii, 1)—I knew the humiliation of seeing burned the very book in which I most gloried. And now it is my desire that you should know the stories of these two happenings, understanding them more truly from learning the very facts than from hearing what is spoken of them, and in the order in which they came about. Because I had ever held in abhorrence the foulness of prostitutes, because I had diligently kept myself from all excesses and from association with the women of noble birth who attended the school, because I knew so little of the common talk of ordinary people, perverse and subtly flattering chance gave birth to an occasion for casting me lightly down from the heights of my own exaltation. Nay in such case not even divine goodness could redeem one who, having been so proud, was brought to such shame, were it not for the blessed gift of grace.

Chapter VI

Now there dwelt in that same city of Paris a certain young girl named Héloïse, the niece of a canon who was called Fulbert. Her uncle's love for her was equalled only by his desire that she should have the best education which he could possibly procure for her. Of no mean beauty, she stood out above all by reason of her abundant knowledge of letters. Now this virtue is rare among women, and for that very reason it doubly graced the maiden, and made her the most worthy of renown in the entire kingdom. It was this young girl whom I, after carefully considering all those qualities which are wont to attract lovers, determined to unite with myself in the bonds of love, and indeed the thing seemed to me very easy to be done. So distinguished was my name, and I possessed such advantages of youth and comeliness, that no matter what woman I might favour with my love, I dreaded rejection of none. Then, too, I believed that I could win the maiden's consent all the more easily by reason of her knowledge of letters and her zeal therefor; so, even if we were parted, we might yet be together in thought with the aid of written messages. Perchance, too, we might be able to write more boldly than we could speak, and thus at all times could we live in joyous intimacy.

Thus, utterly aflame with my passion for this maiden, I sought to discover means whereby I might have daily and familiar speech with her, thereby the more easily to win her consent. For this purpose I persuaded the girl's uncle, with the aid of some of his friends, to take me into his household—for he dwelt hard by my school—in return for the payment of a small sum. My pretext for this was that the care of my own household was a serious handicap to my studies, and likewise burdened me with an expense far greater than I could afford. Now, he was a man keen in avarice, and likewise he was most desirous for his niece that her study of letters should ever go forward, so, for these two reasons, I easily won his consent to the fulfillment of my wish, for he was fairly agape for my money, and at the same time believed that his niece would vastly benefit by my teaching. More even than this, by his own earnest entreaties he fell in with my desires beyond anything I had dared to hope, opening the way for my love; for he entrusted her wholly to my guidance, begging me to give her instruction whensoever I might be free from the duties of my school no matter whether by day or by night, and to punish her sternly if ever I should find her negligent of her tasks. In all this the man's simplicity was nothing short of astounding to me; I should not have been more smitten with wonder if he had entrusted a tender lamb to the care of a ravenous wolf. When he had thus given her into my charge, not alone to be taught but even to be disciplined, what had he done save to give free scope to my desires, and to offer me every opportunity, even if I had not sought it, to bend her to my will with threats and blows if I failed to do so with caresses? There were, however, two things which particularly served to allay any foul suspicion: his own love for his niece, and my former reputation for continence.

Why should I say more? We were united first in the dwelling that sheltered our love, and then in the hearts that burned with it. Under the pretext of study we spent our hours in the happiness of love, and learning held out to us the secret opportunities that our passion craved. Our speech was more of love than of the books which lay open before us; our kisses far outnumbered our reasoned words. Our hands sought less the book than each other's bosoms; love drew our eyes together far more than the lesson drew them to the pages of our text. In order that there might be no suspicion, there were, indeed, sometimes blows, but love gave them, not anger; they were the marks, not of wrath but of a tenderness surpassing the most fragrant balm in sweetness. What followed? No degree in love's progress was left untried by our passion, and if love itself could imagine any wonder as yet unknown, we discovered it. And our inexperience of such delights made us all the more ardent in our pursuit of them, so that our thirst for one another was still unquenched.

In measure as this passionate rapture absorbed me more and more, I devoted ever less time to philosophy and to the work of the school. Indeed it became loathsome to me to go to the school or to linger there; the labour, moreover, was very burdensome, since my nights were vigils of love and my days of study. My lecturing became utterly careless and lukewarm; I did nothing because of inspiration, but everything merely as a matter of habit. I had become nothing more than a reciter of my former discoveries, and though I still wrote poems, they dealt with love, not with the secrets of philosophy. Of these songs you yourself well know how some have become widely known and have been sung in many lands, chiefly, methinks, by those who delighted in the things of this world. As for the sorrow, the groans, the lamentations of my students when they perceived the preoccupation, nay, rather the chaos, of my mind, it is hard even to imagine them.

A thing so manifest could deceive only a few, no one, methinks, save him whose shame it chiefly bespoke, the girl's uncle, Fulbert. The truth was often enough hinted to him, and by many persons, but he could not believe it, partly, as I have said, by reason of his boundless love for his niece, and partly because of the well-known continence of my previous life. Indeed we do not easily suspect shame in those whom we most cherish, nor can there be the blot of foul suspicion on devoted love. Of this St. Jerome in his epistle to Sabinianus (Epist., 48) says: "We are wont to be the last to know the evils of our own households, and to be ignorant of the sins of our children and our wives, though our neighbours sing them aloud." But no matter how slow a matter may be in disclosing itself, it is sure to come forth at last, nor is it easy to hide from one what is known to all. So, after the lapse of several months, did it happen with us. Oh, how great was the uncle's grief when he learned the truth, and how bitter was the sorrow of the lovers when we were forced to part! With what shame was I overwhelmed, with what contrition smitten because of the blow which had fallen on her I loved, and what a tempest of misery burst over her by reason of my disgrace! Each grieved most, not for himself, but for the other. Each sought to allay, not his own sufferings, but those of the one he loved. The very sundering of our bodies served but to link our souls closer together; the plenitude of the love which was denied to us inflamed us more than ever. Once the first wildness of shame had passed, it left us more shameless than before, and as shame died within us the cause of it seemed to us ever more desirable. And so it chanced with us as, in the stories that the poets tell, it once happened with Mars and Venus when they were caught together.

It was not long after this that Héloïse found that she was pregnant, and of this she wrote to me in the utmost exultation, at the same time asking me to consider what had best be done. Accordingly, on a night when her uncle was absent, we carried out the plan we had determined on, and I stole her secretly away from her uncle's house, sending her without delay to my own country. She remained there with my sister until she gave birth to a son, whom she named Astrolabe. Meanwhile her uncle, after his return, was almost mad with grief; only one who had then seen him could rightly guess the burning agony of his sorrow and the bitterness of his shame. What steps to take against me, or what snares to set for me, he did not know. If he should kill me or do me some bodily hurt, he feared greatly lest his dear-loved niece should be made to suffer for it among my kinsfolk. He had no power to seize me and imprison me somewhere against my will, though I make no doubt he would have done so quickly enough had he been able or dared, for I had taken measures to guard against any such attempt.

At length, however, in pity for his boundless grief, and bitterly blaming myself for the suffering which my love had brought upon him through the baseness of the deception I had practiced, I went to him to entreat his forgiveness, promising to make any amends that he himself might decree. I pointed out that what had happened could not seem incredible to any one who had ever felt the power of love, or who remembered how, from the very beginning of the human race, women had cast down even the noblest men to utter ruin. And in order to make amends even beyond his extremest hope, I offered to marry her whom I had seduced, provided only the thing could be kept secret, so that I might suffer no loss of reputation thereby. To this he gladly assented, pledging his own faith and that of his kindred, and sealing with kisses the pact which I had sought of him—and all this that he might the more easily betray me.

Chapter VII

Forthwith I repaired to my own country, and brought back thence my mistress, that I might make her my wife. She, however, most violently disapproved of this, and for two chief reasons: the danger thereof, and the disgrace which it would bring upon me. She swore that her uncle would never be appeased by such satisfaction as this, as, indeed, afterwards proved only too true. She asked how she could ever glory in me if she should make me thus inglorious, and should shame herself along with me.

What penalties, she said, would the world rightly demand of her if she should rob it of so shining a light! What curses would follow such a loss to the Church, what tears among the philosophers would result from such a marriage! How unfitting, how lamentable it would be for me, whom nature had made for the whole world, to devote myself to one woman solely, and to subject myself to such humiliation! She vehemently rejected this marriage, which she felt would be in every way ignominious and burdensome to me.

Besides dwelling thus on the disgrace to me, she reminded me of the hardships of married life, to the avoidance of which the Apostle exhorts us, saying: "Art thou loosed from a wife? seek not a wife. But and if thou marry, thou hast not sinned; and if a virgin marry, she hath not sinned. Nevertheless such shall have trouble in the flesh: but I spare you." (1 Cor., vii, 27). And again: "But I would have you to be free from cares" (1 Cor., vii, 32). But if I would heed neither the counsel of the Apostle nor the exhortations of the saints regarding this heavy yoke of matrimony, she bade me at least consider the advice of the philosophers, and weigh carefully what had been written on this subject either by them or concerning their lives. Even the saints themselves have often and earnestly spoken on this subject for the purpose of warning us. Thus St. Jerome, in his first book against Jovinianus, makes Theophrastus set forth in great detail the intolerable annoyances and the endless disturbances of married life, demonstrating with the most convincing arguments that no wise man should ever have a wife, and concluding his reasons for this philosophic exhortation with these words: "Who among Christians would not be overwhelmed by such arguments as these advanced by Theophrastus?"

Again, in the same work, St. Jerome tells how Cicero, asked by Hircius after his divorce of Terentia whether he would marry the sister of Hircius, replied that he would do no such thing, saying that he could not devote himself to a wife and to philosophy at the same time. Cicero does not, indeed, precisely speak of "devoting himself," but he does add that he did not wish to undertake anything which might rival his study of philosophy in its demands upon him.

Then, turning from the consideration of such hindrances to the study of philosophy, Héloïse bade me observe what were the conditions of honourable wedlock. What possible concord could there be between scholars and domestics, between authors and cradles, between books or tablets and distaffs, between the stylus or the pen and the spindle? What man, intent on his religious or philosophical meditations, can possibly endure the whining of children, the lullabies of the nurse seeking to quiet them, or the noisy confusion of family life? Who can endure the continual untidiness of children? The rich, you may reply, can do this, because they have palaces or houses containing many rooms, and because their wealth takes no thought of expense and protects them from daily worries. But to this the answer is that the condition of philosophers is by no means that of the wealthy, nor can those whose minds are occupied with riches and worldly cares find time for religious or philosophical study. For this reason the renowned philosophers of old utterly despised the world, fleeing from its perils rather than reluctantly giving them up, and denied themselves all its delights in order that they might repose in the embraces of philosophy alone. One of them, and the greatest of all, Seneca, in his advice to Lucilius, says: "Philosophy is not a thing to be studied only in hours of leisure; we must give up everything else to devote ourselves to it, for no amount of time is really sufficient thereto" (Epist., 73).

It matters little, she pointed out, whether one abandons the study of philosophy completely or merely interrupts it, for it can never remain at the point where it was thus interrupted. All other occupations must be resisted; it is vain to seek to adjust life to include them, and they must simply be eliminated. This view is maintained, for example, in the love of God by those among us who are truly called monastics, and in the love of wisdom by all those who have stood out among men as sincere philosophers. For in every race, gentiles or Jews or Christians, there have always been a few who excelled their fellows in faith or in the purity of their lives, and who were set apart from the multitude by their continence or by their abstinence from worldly pleasures.

◆ ◆ ◆

Her final argument was that it would be dangerous for me to take her back to Paris, and that it would be far sweeter for her to be called my mistress than to be known as my wife; nay, too, that this would be more honourable for me as well. In such case, she said, love alone would hold me to her, and the strength of the marriage chain would not constrain us. Even if we should by chance be parted from time to time, the joy of our meeting would be all the sweeter by reason of its rarity. But when she found that she could not convince me or dissuade me from my folly by these and like arguments, and because she could not bear to offend me, with grievous sighs and tears she made an end of her resistance, saying: "Then there is no more left but this, that in our doom the sorrow yet to come shall be no less than the love we two have already known." Nor in this, as now the whole world knows, did she lack the spirit of prophecy.

So, after our little son was born, we left him in my sister's care, and secretly returned to Paris. A few days later, in the early morning, having kept our nocturnal vigil of prayer unknown to all in a certain church, we were united there in the benediction of wedlock, her uncle and a few friends of his and mine being present. We departed forthwith stealthily and by separate ways, nor thereafter did we see each other save rarely and in private, thus striving our utmost to conceal what we had done. But her uncle and those of his household, seeking solace for their disgrace, began to divulge the story of our marriage, and thereby to violate the pledge they had given me on this point. Héloïse, on the contrary, denounced her own kin and swore that they were speaking the most absolute lies. Her uncle, aroused to fury thereby, visited her repeatedly with punishments. No sooner had I learned this than I sent her to a convent of nuns at Argenteuil, not far from Paris, where she herself had been brought up and educated as a young girl. I had them make ready for her all the garments of a nun, suitable for the life of a convent, excepting only the veil, and these I bade her put on.

When her uncle and his kinsmen heard of this, they were convinced that now I had completely played them false and had rid myself forever of Héloïse by forcing her to become a nun. Violently incensed, they laid a plot against me, and one night, while I, all unsuspecting was alseep in a secret room in my lodgings, they broke in with the help of one of my servants, whom they had bribed. There they had vengeance on me with a most cruel and most shameful punishment, such as astounded the whole world, for they cut off those parts of my body with which I had done that which was the cause of their sorrow. This done, straightway they fled, but two of them were captured, and suffered the loss of their eyes and their genital organs. One of these two was the aforesaid servant, who, even while he was still in my service, had been led by his avarice to betray me.

Chapter IX

It so happened that at the outset I devoted myself to analysing the basis of our faith through illustration based on human understanding, and I wrote for my students a certain tract on the unity and trinity of God. This I did because they were always seeking for rational and philosophical explanations, asking rather for reasons they could understand than for mere words, saying that it was futile to utter words which the intellect could not possibly follow, that nothing could be believed unless it could first be understood, and that it was absurd for any one to preach to others a thing which neither he himself nor those whom he sought to teach could comprehend. Our Lord Himself maintained this same thing when He said: "They are blind leaders of the blind (Matthew, xv, 14).

Now, a great many people saw and read this tract, and it became exceedingly popular, its clearness appealing particularly to all who sought information on this subject. And since the questions involved are generally considered to be the most difficult of all, their complexity is taken as the measure of the subtlety of him who succeeds in answering them. As a result, my rivals became furiously angry, and summoned a council to take action against me, the chief instigators therein being my two intriguing enemies of former days, Alberic and Lotulphe. These two, now that both

William and Anselm, our erstwhile teachers, were dead, were greedy to reign in their stead, and, so to speak, to succeed them as heirs. While they were directing the school at Rheims, they managed by repeated hints to stir up their archbishop, Rodolphe, against me, for the purpose of holding a meeting, or rather an ecclesiastical council, at Soissons, provided they could secure the approval of Conon, Bishop of Praeneste, at that time papal legate in France. Their plan was to summon me to be present at this council, bringing with me the famous book I had written regarding the Trinity. In all this, indeed, they were successful, and the thing happened according to their wishes.

Before I reached Soissons, however, these two rivals of mine fouly slandered me with both the clergy and the public that on the day of my arrival the people came near to stoning me and the few students of mine who had accompanied me thither. The cause of their anger was that they had been led to believe that I had preached and written to prove the existence of three gods. No sooner had I reached the city, therefore, than I went forthwith to the legate; to him I submitted my book for examination and judgment, declaring that if I had written anything repugnant to the Catholic faith, I was quite ready to correct it or otherwise to make satisfactory amends. The legate directed me to refer my book to the archbishop and to those two rivals of mine to the end that my accusers might also be my judges. So in my case was fulfilled the saying: "Even our enemies are our judges" (Deut., xxxii, 31).

These men, then, took my book and pawed it over and examined it minutely, but could find nothing therein which they dared to use as the basis for a public accusation against me. Accordingly they put off the condemnation of the book until the close of the council, despite their eagerness to bring it about. For my part, every day before the council convened I publicly discussed the Catholic faith in the light of what I had written, and all who heard me were enthusiastic in their approval alike of the frankness and the logic of my words. When the public and the clergy had thus learned something of the real character of my teaching, they began to say to one another: "Behold, now he speaks openly, and no one brings any charge against him. And this council, summoned, as we have heard, chiefly to take action upon his case, is drawing toward its end. Did the judges realize that the error might be theirs rather than his?"

As a result of all this, my rivals grew more angry day by day. On one occasion Alberic, accompanied by some of his students, came to me for the purpose of intimidating me, and, after a few bland words, said that he was amazed at something he had found in my book, to the effect that, although God had begotten God, I denied that God had begotten Himself, since there was only one God. I answered unhesitatingly: "I can give you an explanation of this if you wish it." "Nay," he replied, "I care nothing for human explanation or reasoning in such matters, but only for the words of authority." "Very well," I said; "turn the pages of my book and you will find the authority likewise." The book was at hand, for he had brought it with him. I turned to the passage I had in mind, which he had either not discovered or else passed over as containing nothing injurious to me. And it was God's will that I quickly found what I sought. This was the following sentence, under the heading "Augustine, On the Trinity, Book I": "Whosoever believes that it is within the power of God to beget Himself is sorely in error; this power is not in God, neither is it in any created thing, spiritual or corporeal. For there is nothing that can give birth to itself."

When those of his followers who were present heard this, they were amazed and much embarrassed. He himself, in order to keep his countenance, said: "Certainly, I understand all that." Then I added: "What I have to say further on this subject is by no means new, but apparently it has nothing to do with the case at issue, since you have asked for the word of authority only, and not for explanations. If, however, you care to consider logical explanations, I am prepared to demonstrate that, according to Augustine's statement, you have yourself fallen into a heresy in believing that a father can possibly be his own son." When Alberic heard this he was almost beside himself with rage, and straightway resorted to threats, asserting that neither my explanations nor my citations of authority would avail me aught in this case. With this he left me.

On the last day of the council, before the session convened, the legate and the archbishop deliberated with my rivals and sundry others as to what should be done about me and my book, this being the chief reason for their having come together. And since they had discovered nothing either in my speech or in what I had hitherto written which would give them a case against me, they were all reduced to silence, or at the most to maligning me in whispers. Then Geoffroi, Bishop of Chartres, who excelled the other bishops alike in the sincerity of his religion and in the importance of his see, spoke thus:

"You know, my lords, all who are gathered here, the doctrine of this man, what it is, and his ability, which has brought him followers in every field to which he has devoted himself. You know how greatly he has lessened the renown of other teachers, both his masters and our own, and how he has spread as it were the offshoots of his vine from sea to sea. Now if you impose a lightly considered judgment on him, as I cannot believe you will, you well know that even if mayhap you are in the right there are many who will be angered thereby, and that he will have no lack of defenders. Remember above all that we have found nothing in this book of his that lies before us whereon any open accusation can be based. Indeed it is true, as Jerome says: 'Fortitude openly displayed always creates rivals, and the lightning strikes the highest peaks.' Have a care, then, lest by violent action you only increase his fame, and lest we do more hurt to ourselves through envy than to him through justice. A false report, as that same wise man reminds us, is easily crushed, and a man's later life gives testimony as to his earlier deeds. If, then, you are disposed to take canonical action against him, his doctrine or his writings must be brought forward as evidence, and he must have free opportunity to answer his questioners. In that case, if he is found guilty or if he confesses his error, his lips can be wholly sealed. Consider the words of the blessed Nicodemus, who, desiring to free Our Lord Himself, said: 'Doth our law judge any man before it hear him and know what he doeth?' " (John, vii, 51).

When my rivals heard this they cried out in protest, saying: "This is wise counsel, forsooth, that we should strive against the wordiness of this man, whose arguments, or rather, sophistries, the whole world cannot resist!" And yet, methinks, it was far more difficult to strive against Christ Himself, for Whom, nevertheless, Nicodemus demanded a hearing in accordance with the dictates of the law. When the bishop could not win their assent to his proposals, he tried in another way to curb their hatred, saying that for the discussion of such an important case the few who were present were not enough, and that this matter required a more thorough examination. His further suggestion was that my abbot, who was there present, should take me back with him to our abbey, in other words to the monastery of St. Denis, and that there a large convocation of learned men should determine, on the basis of a careful investigation, what ought to be done. To this last proposal the legate consented, as did all the others.

Then the legate arose to celebrate mass before entering the council, and through the bishop sent me the permission which had been determined on, authorizing me to return to my monastery and there await such action as might be finally taken. But my rivals, perceiving that they would accomplish nothing if the trial were to be held outside of their own diocese, and in a place where they could have little influence on the verdict, and in truth having small wish that justice should be done, persuaded the archbishop that it would be a grave insult to him to transfer the case to another court, and that it would be dangerous for him if by chance I should thus be acquitted. They likewise went to the legate, and succeeded in so changing his opinion that finally they induced him to frame a new sentence, whereby he agreed to condemn my book without any further inquiry, to burn it forthwith in the sight of all, and to confine me for a year in another monastery. The argument they used was that it sufficed for the condemnation of my book that I had presumed to read it in public without the approval either of the Roman pontiff or of the Church, and that, furthermore, I had given it to many to be transcribed. Methinks it would be a notable blessing to the Christian faith if there were more who displayed a like presumption. The legate, however, being less skilled in law that he should have been, relied chiefly on the advice of the archbishop, and he, in turn, on that of my rivals. When the Bishop of

Chartres got wind of this, he reported the whole conspiracy to me, and strongly urged me to endure meekly the manifest violence of their enmity. He bade me not to doubt that this violence would in the end react upon them and prove a blessing to me, and counseled me to have no fear of the confinement in a monastery, knowing that within a few days the legate himself, who was now acting under compulsion, would after his departure set me free. And thus he consoled me as best he might, mingling his tears with mine.

3. *St. Bernard*

Bernard of Clairvaux was the dominant ecclesiastical figure of the first half of the twelfth century. He was the chief force in the rapidly growing Cistercian Order, the personal instigator of the Second Crusade and one of the founders of western mysticism. Besides, in numerous works of biblical interpretation and theology and in his extensive series of letters, he was also one of the great medieval masters of language. The following selection, although classed as a letter, is a full-scale treatise against Abelard.

The translation is by Samuel J. Eales, *The Life and Works of St. Bernard* (London: J. Hodges, 1889), II, pp. 565–73, 574–80, 583–85.

Letter to Pope Innocent II against Abelard (1140)

TO HIS most loving Father and Lord, Innocent, Supreme Pontiff, Brother Bernard, called Abbot of Clairvaux, sends humble greeting.

The dangers and scandals which are coming to the surface in the Kingdom of God, especially those which touch the faith, ought to be referred to your apostolic authority. For I judge it fitting that there most of all, the losses suffered by the faith should be repaired, where faith cannot suffer defect. This, truly, is the prerogative of your see. For to what other person [than Peter] has it ever been said, *I have prayed for thee, Peter, that thy faith fail not?* (Luke, xxii, 32). Therefore that which follows is required from the successor of Peter: *And when thou art converted strengthen thy brethren.* That, indeed, is necessary now. The time is come, most loving Father, for you to recognize your primacy, to prove your zeal, to do honour to your ministry. In this plainly you fulfil the office of Peter, whose seat you occupy, if by your admonition you strengthen the hearts that are wavering in the faith, if by your authority you crush the corrupters of the faith.

Chapter I

1. We have in France an old teacher turned into a new theologian, who in his early days amused himself with dialectics, and now gives

utterance to wild imaginations upon the Holy Scriptures. He is endeavouring again to quicken false opinions, long ago condemned and put to rest, not only his own, but those of others; and is adding fresh ones as well. I know not what there is in heaven above and in the earth beneath which he deigns to confess ignorance of: he raises his eyes to Heaven, and searches the deep things of God, and then returning to us, he brings back unspeakable words which it is not lawful for a man to utter, while he is presumptuously prepared to give a reason for everything, even of those things which are above reason; he presumes against reason and against faith. For what is more against reason than by reason to attempt to transcend reason? And what is more against faith than to be unwilling to believe what reason cannot attain? For instance, wishing to explain that saying of the wise man: *He who is hasty to believe is light in mind* (Eccles., xix, 4), he says that a hasty faith is one that believes before reason; when Solomon says this not of faith towards God, but of mutual belief amongst ourselves. For the blessed Pope Gregory denies plainly that faith towards God has any merit whatever if human reason furnishes it with proof. But he praises the Apostles, because they followed their Saviour when called but once. He knows doubtless that this word was spoken as praise: *At the hearing of the ear he obeyed me* (Ps., xviii, 44), that the Apostles were directly rebuked because they had been slow in believing (Mark, xvi, 14). Again, Mary is praised because she anticipated reason by faith, and Zacharias punished because he tempted faith by reason (Luke, i, 20, 45), and Abraham is commended in that *against hope he believed in hope* (Romans, iv, 18).

2. But on the other hand our theologian says: "What is the use of speaking of doctrine unless what we wish to teach can be explained so as to be intelligible?" And so he promises understanding to his hearers, even on those most sublime and sacred truths which are hidden in the very bosom of our holy faith; and he places degrees in the Trinity, modes in the Majesty, numbers in the Eternity. He has laid down, for example, that God the Father is a full power, the Son a certain kind of power, the Holy Spirit no power. And that the Son is related to the Father as force in particular to force in general, as species to genus, as a thing formed of material, to matter, as man to animal, as a brazen seal to brass. Did Arius ever go further? Who can endure this? Who would not shut his ears to such sacrilegious words? Who does not shudder at such novel profanities of words and ideas? He says also that "the Holy Spirit proceeds indeed from the Father or of the Son." Whence then? Perhaps from nothing, like everything created. But the Apostle does not deny that they are of God, nor is he afraid to say: *Of whom are all things* (Romans, xi, 36). Shall we say then that the Holy Spirit proceeds from the Father and the Son in no other way than all things do, that is, that He exists not essentially but by way of creation, and is therefore a creature like all other things. Or will

this man, who is always seeking after new things, who invents what he does not find, affirms those things which are not, as though they are, will he find for himself some third way, in which he may produce Him from the Father and the Son? But, he says, "if He were of the substance of the Father, He would surely have been begotten, and so the Father would have two Sons." As though everything which is from any substance has always as its father that from which it is. For lice and phlegm and such things, are they sons of the flesh, and not rather of the substance of the flesh? Or worms produced by rotten wood, whence derive they their substance but from the wood? yet are they not sons of the wood. Again, moths have their substance from the substance of garments, but not their generation. And there are many instances of this kind.

3. Since he admits that the Holy Spirit is consubstantial with the Father and the Son, I wonder how an acute and learned man (as at least he thinks himself) can yet deny that He proceeds in substance from the Father and the Son, unless perchance he thinks that the two first persons proceed from the substance of the third. But this is an impious and unheard of opinion. But if neither He proceeds from their substance, nor They from His, where, I pray, is the consubstantiality? Let him then either confess with the Church that the Holy Spirit is of their substance, from whom He does not deny that He proceeds, or let him with Arius deny His consubstantiality, and openly preach His creation. Again he says, if the Son is of the substance of the Father, the Holy Spirit is not; they must differ from each other, not only because the Holy Spirit is not begotten, as the Son is, but also because the Son is of the substance of the Father, which the Holy Spirit is not. Of this last distinction the Catholic Church has hitherto known nothing. If we admit it, where is the Trinity? where is the Unity? If the Holy Spirit and the Son are really separated by this new enumeration of differences, and if the Unity is split up, then especially let it be made plain that that distinction which he is endeavouring to make is a difference of substance. Moreover, if the Holy Spirit does not proceed from the substance of the Father and the Son, no Trinity remains, but a duality. For no Person is worthy to be admitted into the Trinity whose substance is not the same as that of the others. Let him, therefore, cease to separate the procession of the Holy Spirit from the substance of the Father and the Son, lest by a double impiety he both take away number from the Trinity and attribute it to the Unity, each of which the Christian faith abhors. And, lest I seem in so great a matter to depend on human reasonings only, let him read the letter of Jerome to Avitus, and he will plainly see, that amongst the other blasphemies of Origen which he confutes, he also rejects this one, that, as he said, the Holy Spirit is not of the substance of the Father. The blessed Athanasius thus speaks in his book on the Undivided Trinity: "When I spoke of God alone I meant not

the Person only of the Father, because I denied not that the Son and the Holy Spirit are of this same Substance of the Father."

Chapter II

4. Your holiness sees how in this man's scheme, which is not reasoning but raving, the Trinity does not hold together and the Unity is rendered doubtful, and that this cannot be without injury to the Majesty. For whatever That is which is God, it is without doubt That than which nothing greater can be conceived. If, then, in this One and Supreme Majesty we have found anything that is insufficient or imperfect in our consideration of the Persons, or if we have found that what is assigned to one is taken from another, the whole is surely less than That, than which nothing greater can be conceived. For indubitably the greatest which is a whole is greater than that which consists of parts. That man thinks worthily, as far as man can, of the Divine Majesty who thinks of no inequality in It where the whole is supremely great; of no separation where the whole is one; of no chasm where the whole is undivided; in short, of no imperfection or deficiency where the whole is a whole. For the Father is a whole, as are the Father, the Son and the Holy Spirit; the Son is a whole, as are He Himself and the Father and the Holy Spirit; the Holy Spirit is a whole, as are He Himself and the Father and the Son. And the whole Unity is a whole neither superabounding in the Three, nor diminished in Each Person. For they do not individually divide between Them that real and highest Good which they are, since they do not possess It in the way of participation, but are essentially the very Good. For those phrases which we most rightly use, as One from Another, or One to Another, are designations of the Persons, not divisions of the Unity. For although in this ineffable and incomprehensible essence of the Deity we can, by the requirements of the properties of the Persons, say One and Another in a sober and Catholic sense, yet there is not in the essence One and Another, but simple Unity; nor in the confession of the Trinity any derogation to the Unity, nor is the true assertion of the Unity any exclusion of the *propria* of the Persons. May that execrable similitude of genus and species be accordingly as far from our minds as it is from the rule of truth. It is not a similitude, but a dissimilitude, as is also that of brass and the brazen seal; for since genus and species are to each other as higher and lower, while God is One, there can never be any resemblance between equality so perfect and disparity so great. And again, with regard to his illustration of brass, and the brass which is made into a seal, since it is used for the same kind of similitude, it is to be similarly condemned. For since, as I have said, species is less than and inferior to genus, far be it from us to think of such diversity between the Father and the Son. Far be it from us to agree with him who says that the Son is related to the Father as species to genus, as man to animal, as a brazen

seal to brass, as force to force absolutely. For all these several things by the bond of their common nature are to each other as superiors and inferiors, and therefore no comparison is to be drawn from these things with That in which there is no inequality, no dissimilarity. You see from what unskilfulness or impiety the use of these similitudes descends.

Chapter III

5. Now notice more clearly what he thinks, teaches, and writes. He says that Power properly and specially belongs to the Father, Wisdom to the Son, which, indeed, is false. For the Father both is, and is most truly called, Wisdom, and the Son Power, and what is common to Both is not the *proprium* of Each singly. There are certainly some other names which do not belong to Both, but to One or the Other alone, and therefore His own Name is peculiar to Each, and not common to the Other. For the Father is not the Son, nor the Son the Father, for He is designated by the name of Father, not because He is the Father with regard to Himself, but with regard to His Son, and in like manner by the name of Son is expressed not that He is Son with regard to Himself, but to the Father. It is not so with power and many other attributes which are assigned to the Father and the Son in common, and not singly to Each taken by Himself. But he says, "No; we find that omnipotence belongs especially to the *proprium* of the Person of the Father, because He not only can do all things in union with the other two Persons, but also because He alone has His existence from Himself, so has He His power." O, second Aristotle! By parity of reasoning, if such were reasoning, would not Wisdom and Kindness belong properly to the Father, since equally the Father has his Wisdom and Kindness from Himself, and not from another, just as He has His Being and His Power? And if he does not deny this, as he cannot reasonably do, what, I ask, will he do with that famous partition of his in which, as he has assigned Power to the Father and Wisdom to the Son, so he has assigned Loving Kindness to the Holy Spirit properly and specially? For one and the same thing cannot well be the *proprium* of two, that is, to be the exclusive property of each. Let him choose which alternative he will: either let him give Wisdom to the Son and take It from the Father, or assign It to the Father and deny It to the Son; and again, let him assign Loving Kindness to the Spirit without the Father or to the Father without the Spirit; or let him cease to call attributes which are common, *propria;* and though the Father has his Power from Himself, yet let him not dare to concede It to Him as being a *proprium,* lest on his own reasoning, he be obliged to assign Him Wisdom and Loving Kindness which He has in precisely the same way, as His *propria* also.

6. But let us now wait and see in how theoretic a manner our theologian regards the invisible things of God. He says, as I have pointed

out, that omnipotence properly belongs to the Father, and He makes it to consist in the fulness and perfection of Rule and discernment. Again, to the Son he assigns Wisdom, and that he defines to be not Power simply, but a certain kind of Power in God, namely the Power of discernment only. Perhaps he is afraid of doing an injury to the Father if he gives as much to the Son as to Him, and since he dares not give Him complete power, he grants Him half. And this that he lays down he illustrates by common examples, asserting that the Power of discernment which the Son is, is a particular kind of Power, just as a man is a kind of animal, and a brazen seal a particular form of brass, which means that the power of discernment is to the power of Rule and discernment, i.e., the Son is to the Father, as a man to an animal, or as a brazen seal to brass. For, as he says, "a brazen seal must first be brass, and a man to be a man must first be an animal, but not conversely. So Divine Wisdom, which is the power of discernment, must first be Divine Power, but not conversely." Do you, then, mean that, like the preceding similitudes, your similitude demands that the Son to be the Son must first be the Father, i.e., that He who is the Son is the Father, though not conversely? If you say this you are a heretic. If you do not your comparison is meaningless.

7. For why do you fashion for yourself the comparison, and with such beating about the bush, apply it to questions long ago settled and ill-fitted for debate? Why do you bring it forward with such waste of energy, impress it on us with such a useless multiplicity of words, produce it with such a flourish, if it does not effect the purpose for which it was adduced, viz., that the members be harmonized with each other in fitting proportions? Is not this a labour and a toil, to teach us by means of it, the relation which exists between the Father and the Son? We hold according to you, that a man being given an animal is given, but not conversely, at least by the rule of your logic; for by it it is not that when the genus is given we know the species, but the species being given we know the genus. Since, then, you compare the Father to the genus, the Son to the species, does not the condition of your comparison postulate, that in like manner, when the Son is known you declare the Father to be known and not conversely; that, as he who is a man is necessarily an animal, but not conversely, so also, He who is the Son is necessarily the Father, but not conversely? But the Catholic faith contradicts you on this point, for it plainly denies both, viz., that the Father is the Son, and that the Son is the Father. For indubitably the Father is one Person, the Son another; although the Father is not of a different substance from the Son. For by this distinction the godliness of the Faith knows how to distinguish cautiously between the *propria* of the Persons, and the undivided unity of the Essence; and holding a middle course, to go along the royal road, turning neither to the right by confounding the Persons, nor looking to the left by dividing the

Substance. But if you say that it rightly follows as a necessary truth that He who is the Son is also the Father, this helps you nothing; for an identical proposition is necessarily capable of being converted in such a way that what was true of the original proposition is true of the converse; and your comparison of genus and species, or of brass and the brazen seal does not admit of this. For as it does not follow as a necessary consequence that the Son is the Father, and the Father the Son, so neither can we rightly produce a convertible consequence between man and animal, and between a brazen seal and brass. For though it be true to say, "If he is a man he is an animal," still the converse is not true, "If he is an animal he is a man." And again, if we have a brazen seal it necessarily follows that it is brass; but if we have brass it does not necessarily follow that it is a brazen seal. But now let us proceed to his other points.

Chapter IV

9. It is no wonder if a man who is careless of what he says should, when rushing into the mysteries of the Faith, so irreverently assail and tear asunder the hidden treasures of godliness, since he has neither piety nor faith in his notions about the piety of faith. For instance, on the very threshold of his theology (I should rather say his stultology) he defines faith as private judgment; as though in these mysteries it is to be allowed to each person to think and speak as he pleases, or as though the mysteries of our faith are to hang in uncertainty amongst shifting and varying opinions, when on the contrary they rest on the solid and unshakeable foundation of truth. Is not our hope baseless if our faith is subject to change? Fools then were our martyrs for bearing so cruel tortures for an uncertainty, and for entering, without hesitation, on an everlasting exile, through a bitter death, when there was a doubt as to the recompense of their reward. But far be it from us to think that in our faith or hope anything, as he supposes, depends on the fluctuating judgment of the individual, and that the whole of it does not rest on sure and solid truth, having been commended by miracles and revelations from above, founded and consecrated by the Son of the Virgin, by the Blood of the Redeemer, by the glory of the risen Christ. These infallible proofs have been given us in superabundance. But if not, the Spirit itself, lastly, bears witness with our spirit that we are the sons of God. How, then, can any one dare to call faith opinion, unless it be that he has not yet received the Spirit, or unless he either knows not the Gospel or thinks it to be a fable? *I know in whom I have believed, and I am confident* (2 Tim., i, 12), cries the Apostle, and you mutter in my ears that faith is only an opinion. Do you prate to me that that is ambiguous than which there is nothing more certain? But Augustine says otherwise: "Faith is not held by any one in whose heart it is, by conjectures or opinions, but it is sure knowledge and has the assent of the conscience." Far be it from us, then, to

suppose that the Christian faith has as its boundaries those opinions of the Academicians, whose boast it is that they doubt of everything, and know nothing. But I for my part walk securely, according to the saying of the teacher of the Gentiles, and I know that I shall not be confounded. I am satisfied, I confess, with his definition of faith, even though this man stealthily accuses it. *Faith,* he says, *is the substance of things hoped for, the evidence of things not seen* (Heb., xi, 1). The substance, he says of things hoped for, not a phantasy of empty conjectures. You hear, that it is a substance; and therefore it is not allowed you in our faith, to suppose or oppose at your pleasure, nor to wander hither and thither amongst empty opinions, through devious errors. Under the name of substance something certain and fixed is put before you. You are enclosed in known bounds, shut in within fixed limits. For faith is not an opinion, but a certitude.

10. But now notice other points. I pass over his saying that the spirit of the fear of the Lord was not in the Lord; that there will be no holy fear of the Lord in the world to come; that after the consecration of the bread and of the cup the former accidents which remain are suspended in the air; that the suggestions of devils come to us, as their sagacious wickedness knows how, by the contact of stones and herbs; and that they are able to discern in such natural objects strength suited to excite various passions; the Holy Spirit is the *anima mundi;* that the world, as Plato says, is so much a more excellent animal, as it has a better soul in the Holy Spirit. Here while he exhausts his strength to make Plato a Christian, he proves himself a heathen. All these things and his other numerous silly stories of the same kind I pass by, I come to graver matters. To answer them all would require volumes. I speak only of those on which I cannot keep silence.

Chapter V

I find in a book of his sentences, and also in an exposition of his of the Epistle to the Romans, that this rash inquirer into the Divine Majesty attacks the mystery of our Redemption. He admits in the very beginning of his disputation that there has never been but one conclusion in our ecclesiastical doctors on this point, and this he states only to spurn it, and boasts that he has a better; not fearing, against the precept of the Wise Man, *To cross the ancient boundaries which our fathers have marked out* (Prov., xxi, 28). It is needful to know, he says, that all our doctors since the Apostles agree in this, that the devil had power and dominion over man, and that he rightly possessed it, because man, by an act of the free will which he had, voluntarily consented to the devil. For they say that if any one conquers another, the conquered rightly becomes the slave of his conqueror. Therefore, he says, as the doctors teach, the Son of God became incarnate under this necessity, that since man could not otherwise be freed, he might, by the death of an innocent man, be set free from the yoke of the devil. But as it seems to us, he says, neither had the devil ever any power over man, except by the permission of God, as a jailer might, nor was it to free man that the Son of God assumed flesh. Which am I to think the more intolerable in these words, the blasphemy or the arrogance? Which is the more to be condemned, his rashness or his impiety? Does not he whose hand is against every man, rightly provoke every man's hand to be raised against him? All, he says say so, but so do not I. What, then, do you say? What better statement have you? What more secret revelation do you boast of which has passed by the Saints and escaped from the wise? He, I suppose, will give us secret waters and bidden bread.

12. Tell us, nevertheless, that truth which has shown itself to you and to none else. Is it that it was not to free man that the Son of God became man? No one, you excepted, thinks this; you stand alone. For not from a wise man, nor prophet, nor apostle, nor even from the Lord Himself have you received this. The teacher of the Gentiles *received from the Lord what he has handed down to us* (1 Cor., xi, 23). The Teacher of all confesses that His doctrine is not His own, for *I do not,* He says, *speak of Myself* (John, vii, 16 and xiv, 10), while you give us of your own, and what you have received from no one. *He who speaketh a lie speaketh of his own* (John, viii, 44). Keep for yourself what is your own. I listen to Prophets and Apostles, I obey the Gospel, but not the Gospel according to Peter. Do you found for us a new Gospel? The Church does not receive a fifth Evangelist. What other Gospel do the Law, the Prophets, Apostles, and apostolic men preach to us than that which you alone deny, viz., that God became man to free man? And if an angel from heaven should preach to us any other Gospel, let him be anathema.

13. But you do not accept the Doctors since the Apostles, because you perceive yourself to be a man above all teachers. For example, you do not blush to say that all are against you, when they all agree together. To no purpose, therefore, should I place before the faith and doctrine of those teachers whom you have just proscribed. I will take you to the Prophets. Under the type of Jerusalem the prophet speaks, or rather the Lord in the prophet speaks to His chosen people: *I will save you and deliver you, fear not* (Wisdom, iii, 16). You ask, from what power? For you do not admit that the devil has or ever has had power over man. Neither, I confess, do I. It is not, however, that he has it not because you and I wish it not. If you do not confess it, you know it not; they whom *the Lord has redeemed out of the hand of the enemy,* they know it and confess it. And you would by no means deny it, if you were not under the

hand of the enemy. You cannot give thanks with the redeemed, because you have not been redeemed. For if you had been redeemed you would recognize your Redeemer, and would not deny you redemption. Nor does the man, who knows not himself to be a captive, seek to be redeemed. Those who knew it called unto the Lord, and the Lord heard them, and redeemed them from the hand of the enemy. And that you may understand who this enemy is, He says: *Those whom He redeemed from the hand of the enemy He gathered out of all lands* (Ps., xvii, 2, 3). But first, indeed, recognize Him Who gathered them, of Whom Caiaphas in the Gospel prophesied, saying that Jesus should die for the people, and the Evangelist proceeds thus: *And not for the nation only, but that He might gather together into one all the children of God which were scattered abroad* (John, xi, 51, 52). Whither had they been scattered? Into all lands, therefore those whom He redeemed he gathered together from all lands. He first redeemed, then gathered them. For they were not only scattered, but also taken captive. He redeemed and gathered them; but redeemed them from the hand of the enemy. He does not say of the enemies, but of the enemy. The enemy was one, the lands many. Indeed, he gathered them not from one land, but from the lands, from the east and from the west, from the north and from the south. What Lord was there so powerful, who governed not one land but all lands? No other, I suppose, than He who by another prophet is said to drink up a river, that is, the human race, and not to wonder; and to trust that he can also draw up into his mouth Jordan, i.e., the elect. Blessed are they who so flow in that they can flow out, who so enter that they can go out.

14. But now perhaps you do not believe the Prophets, thus speaking with one accord of the power of the devil over man. Come with me then to the Apostles. You said, did you not? that you do not agree with those who have come since the Apostles; may you agree then with the Apostles; and perhaps that may happen to you which one of them describes, speaking of certain persons: *If God, peradventure, will give them repentance to the acknowledging of the truth, and that they may recover themselves out of the snare of the devil, who are taken captive by him at his will* (2 Tim., ii, 25, 26). It is Paul who thus asserts that men are taken captive by the devil at his own will. Do you hear? "at his will"; and do you deny his power? But if you do not believe Paul, come now the Lord Himself, if perchance you may listen to Him and be put to silence. By Him the devil is called *the prince of this world* (John, xiv, 30), and the *strong man armed* (Luke, xi, 21), and the *possessor of goods* (Matt., xii, 29), and yet you say that he has no power over men. Perhaps you think the house in this place is not to be understood of the world, nor the goods of men. But if the world is the house of the devil and men his goods, how can it be said he has no power over men? Moreover, the Lord said to those who took Him: *This is your*

hour and the power of darkness (Luke, xxi, 53). That power did not escape him who said: *Who hath delivered us from the power of darkness, and hath translated us into the kingdom of His dear Son* (Col., i, 13). The Lord then neither denied the power of the devil even of Him, nor that of Pilate who was a member of the devil. He said: *Thou couldst have no power against me at all except it were given thee from above* (John, xix, 11). But if that power given from above so violently raged against the green tree, how is it that it did not dare touch the dry? Nor I suppose will he say, that it was an unjust power which was given from above. Let him, therefore, learn that not only have the devil power over man, but also a just power, and in consequence let him see this, that the Son of God came in the flesh to set man free. But though we say that the power of the devil was a just one we do not say that his will was. Whence it is not the devil who usurped the power, who is just, nor man who deservedly was subjected to it; but the Lord is just, who permitted the subjection. For anyone is called just and unjust, not from his power but from his will. This power of the devil over man though not rightly acquired, but wickedly usurped, was yet justly permitted. And in this way man was justly taken captive, viz., that the justice was neither in the devil, nor in man, but in God.

Chapter VII

17. This is the righteousness of man in the blood of the Redeemer: which this son of perdition, by his scoffs and insinuations, is attempting to render vain; so much so, that he thinks and argues that the whole fact that the Lord of Glory emptied Himself, that He was made lower than the angels, that He was born of a woman, that He lived in the world, that He made trial of our infirmities, that He suffered indignities, that at last He returned to His own place by the way of the Cross, that all this is to be reduced to one reason alone, viz., that it was done merely that He might give man by His life and teaching a rule of life, and by His suffering and death might set before him a goal of charity. Did He, then, teach righteousness and not bestow it? Did He show charity and not infuse it, and did He so return to His heaven? Is this, then, the whole of the great *mystery of godliness, which was manifested in the flesh, justified in the Spirit, seen of angels, preached unto the Gentiles, believed on in the world, received up into glory* (1 Tim., iii, 16). O, incomparable doctor! he lays bare to himself the deep things of God, he makes them clear and easy to every one, and by his false teaching he so renders plain and evident the most lofty sacrament of grace, the mystery hidden from the ages, that any uncircumcised and unclean person can lightly penetrate to the heart of it: as though the wisdom of God knew not how to guard or neglected to guard against what Itself forbade, but had Itself given what is holy to the dogs and cast its pearls before swine. But it is not so, for though it was

manifested in the flesh, yet it was justified in the Spirit: so that spiritual things are bestowed upon spiritual men, and the natural man does not perceive the things which are of the Spirit of God. Nor does our faith consist in wisdom of words but in the power of God. And, therefore, the Saviour says: *I thank Thee, O Father, Lord of heaven and earth, because Thou hast hid these things from the wise and prudent, and hast revealed them unto babes* (Matt., xi, 25). And the Apostle says: *If our Gospel be hid, it is hid to them that are lost.* (2 Cor., iv, 3).

18. But see this man scoffing at the things which are of the Spirit of God, because they seem to him folly, and insulting the Apostle who speaks the hidden wisdom of God in a mystery, inveighing against the Gospel and even blaspheming the Lord. How much more prudent would he be if he would deign to believe what he has no power to comprehend, and would not dare to despise or tread under foot this sacred and holy mystery! It is a long task to reply to all the follies and calumnies which he charges against the Divine counsel. Yet I take a few, from which the rest may be estimated. "Since," he says, "Christ set free the elect only, how were they more than now, whether in this world or the next, under the power of the devil?" I answer: It was just because they were under the power of the devil, by whom, says the Apostle, *they were taken captive at his will* (2 Tim., ii, 26), that there was need of a liberator in order that the purpose of God concerning them might be fulfilled. But it behooved Him to set them free in this world, that He might have them as freeborn sons in the next. Then he rejoins: "Well, did the devil also torture the poor man who was in the bosom of Abraham as he did the rich man who was condemned, or had he power over Abraham himself and the rest of the elect?" No, but he would have had if they had not been set free by their faith in a future Deliverer, as of Abraham it is written: *Abraham believed God, and it was counted unto him for righteousness* (Gen., xv, 6). Again: *Abraham rejoiced to see My day, and he saw it and was glad* (John, viii, 56). Therefore even then the Blood of Christ was bedewing Lazarus, that he might not feel the flames, because he had believed on Him who should suffer. So are we to think of all the saints of that time, that they were born just as ourselves under the power of darkness, because of original sin, but rescued before they died, and that by nothing else but the Blood of Christ. For it is written: *The multitudes that went before and that followed, cried saying, Hosanna to the Son of David, Blessed is He that cometh in the Name of the Lord* (Matt., xxi, 9). Therefore blessing was given to Christ coming in the flesh, both before he came and afterwards, by multitudes of those who had been blessed by Him, although those who went before did not obtain a full blessing, this, of course, having been kept as the prerogative of grace.

4. *John of Salisbury*

John of Salisbury (c.1115–80) was in many ways a typical figure of his period. An Englishman by birth, he studied at Paris under Abelard, William of Conches, and Gilbert of la Porrée, and perhaps at Chartres. After his formal education he was at Rome in some uncertain capacity but one which gave him enough access to papal records to enable him to continue the *Historia Pontificalis*. Then through the good offices of St. Bernard he became secretary to Theobald, Archbishop of Canterbury, and his successor Thomas Becket. He was made Bishop of Chartres in 1176. John had wide-ranging interests. The greatest classicist of his time, he was not too much in sympathy with the current preoccupation with dialectic, although he defended its use in his *Metalogicon* and was the first man we know of to utilize the full *Organon* (the corpus of Aristotelian logical writings). He was an historian of merit and, in his *Policraticus*, a political theorist of note. Besides the works mentioned above he left behind an extensive series of letters.

The following selections from the *Historia Pontificalis* and the *Metalogicon* are taken from the translations of Marjorie Chibnall in the *Nelson's Medieval Texts Series* (London: 1956), pp. 15–27, 62–65, and Daniel D. McGarry, *The Metalogicon of John of Salisbury* (Berkeley and Los Angeles: California University Press, 1962), pp. 95–100.

a. Historia Pontificalis

MASTER GILBERT, bishop of Poitiers, the most learned man of our day, was summoned to the court to answer the abbot of Clairvaux—a man of the greatest eloquence and highest repute—on certain matters which had been brought up the year before at Paris [1147], but postponed until then. For certain statements had been found in the bishop's commentary on the *De Trinitate* of Boethius and the writings of his pupils which seemed reprehensible to the learned, either because they were inconsistent with accepted beliefs or because, through novelty of expression, they seemed inconsistent. Many attacked him, but the fiercest assailants were Suger, abbot of St. Denis, a learned and eloquent man, and two canons of Poitiers, Calo who later became bishop of the same church, and master Arnold nicknamed 'straightface': the master of the schools also, Peter Lombard later bishop of Paris, and Robert of Melun afterwards bishop of Hereford, led an embittered attack on him. I cannot say whether they acted out of zeal for the faith, or jealousy of his fame and merit, or a desire to propitiate the abbot [St. Bernard of Clairvaux], whose influence was then at its height and whose counsel was most weighty in the affairs of church and state alike.

Various opinions are held of the abbot himself, some saying one thing and some another, because he attacked the two men most famous for their learning—Peter Abailard and this same Gilbert—and pursued them with such zeal that he secured the condemnation of Peter and only just failed to have the other condemned. For my part I cannot believe that a man of such sanctity was not guided by the love of God, or that a bishop of such prudence and learning should commit to writing anything whose meaning was not clear to him, however obscure it might seem to others. For he was a man of the very keenest intelligence, who had read most things and who, I may say from intimate knowledge, after spending almost sixty years in reading and close study, was so learned in the liberal arts that no one could surpass him in all subjects; nay rather he was held to surpass all in every subject. And I am sure that now he no longer disagrees with the abbot and the other saints, for they both see face to face the truth they spent their lives in seeking. But of all the doctors of the church he was most conversant with the works of blessed Hilary and Augustine, and often used words from their writings which are uncommon in modern works. One thing is certain: that now several terms are hackneyed in the schools which, when he introduced them, seemed to be 'impious novelties.'

Before the abbot of Clairvaux met Gilbert publicly in court, he sent asking all the leading churchmen, those who were distinguished by their learning or sanctity or office, to meet him privately in his lodging. I speak and write what I myself have seen, knowing that I would imperil my immortal soul and my worldly reputation if I should either relate or write anything untrue in a manner such as this. There will be some, too, ready to refute me if I do not speak the truth; for several men of high repute and weighty judgment are yet living who were certainly present at this meeting. Those present included the late Theobald archbishop of Canterbury and Geoffrey of Bordeaux and Henry of York, and the abbots Suger of St. Denis and Baldwin of Châtillon-sur-Seine; and of those now living Thomas archbishop of Canterbury and Roger of York and many others whom it would be tedious to enumerate. The abbot, the most pious and learned among them, then delivered a short and eloquent discourse, concluding that it was their duty to remove all scandals from the church of God, and beseeching them to correct him if they thought he was mistaken in the case he had brought against master Gilbert. If he had pressed his argument foolishly, it was because he had been carried away by charity and zeal for the faith. But if he was not mistaken, he asked them to do their duty and preserve the purity of the faith. For cases such as this were the business not of monks and hermits, but of the prelates of the church who were bound to lay down their lives for their sheep. And to help them in judging whether he was right or wrong, he asked them to listen to the articles in which he differed from the bishop, and then approve or reject them. On their agreeing, he said he believed that 'God is deity, and the converse.' As he made this statement Geoffrey of Auxerre, one of his monks, wrote it down word for word and then read it out with the question, 'Do you accept this?' after the fashion when decretals or laws are promulgated. And they replied, 'We do.' Proceeding, the abbot said he believed that 'three Persons are one God and the converse.' This too was recorded, put to the vote and accepted as before. The more thoughtful men did not approve of this method: but they feared offending the abbot and his followers if they did not fall in with his wishes. Then the abbot went on, 'I believe that the essence or substance of God was incarnate.' This was treated in the same way. Fourthly he propounded that, 'Since God is simple and whatever is in God is God, the properties of the Persons are the Persons themselves, and so the Father is paternity, the Son, filiality, the Spirit, proceeding; and the converse.'

When this, like the other propositions, had been written down and put to the vote, a certain archdeacon of Châlons, master Robert de Bosco by name, rose holding up his hand and calling out for silence, and besought them not to give a hasty answer. He had heard, he said, that this had been propounded in the schools of the renowned doctors, brothers Anselm and Ralph of Laon, but rejected by them because they were unwilling to go beyond the definitions of the Fathers. For the same reason neither Gilbert the Universal, who later became bishop of London, nor Alberic of Rheims, afterwards raised to the archbishopric of Bourges, had been prepared to accept it. He knew this because he had heard them lecture, and questioned them on the subject. Again, Gilbert abbot of Westminster near London, whom he considered even more learned than the others, had never been willing to admit this. Consequently his advice was that they should not make a hasty judgment on so weighty a matter, especially as such men had expressly declined to make this definition: the pope and the cardinals should be present and the most distinguished men in the western world had met to discuss it. His advice was followed, and the assembly broke up.

When the news came to the hearing of the cardinals they were very wrath with the abbot and those who had assembled at his request: they agreed among themselves to support the cause of the bishop of Poitiers, saying that the abbot had attacked master Peter in exactly the same way; but he had not had access to the apostolic see, which was accustomed to confound schemes of this kind and snatch the weak from the clutches of the strong. They suspected, or made a show of suspecting, that the abbot wished to win the English and Gallic parts of the church to his side and induce them to follow him; so that the papacy should be powerless to pronounce any sound judgment in opposition to them—especially at that time and in that place—or clear master Gilbert if the church in England and Gaul were against him without provoking sedition. As far as I recall there was not a single cardinal except Alberic of Ostia of holy memory who was not wholeheartedly opposed to the abbot in spirit and deed; saying—falsely as I believe—that the abbot of St. Denis, who was acting as regent for the king in France, and the leading men of the church had been called together for the express purpose of forcing the papacy to accept the abbot's views under threat of schism. But as the abbot could not fail to hear of the cardinals' conspiracy he forestalled them all, and going to the pope as a friend, urged him to put on zeal and manly courage in the Lord's cause, lest the weakness of the body of Christ and wounds of the faith should be found to be in the head. He explained his beliefs about the articles set out in the proposition, and persuaded the pope to keep in step with him. For he was a man mighty in deed and word, with God as some believe, and with men as we all know. Once given the chance of speaking, he almost always made his will prevail. Besides, it was certain that some of the cardinals were filled with envy of him, and could not refrain from slander.

The bishop, trusting in the support and advice of the cardinals, joined conflict with confidence, and though many men questioned him searchingly he supported his answers with such sound arguments and authorities that he could not be tripped up verbally. However, the disputation was prolonged, and when issue was joined fiercely on a statement he was unwilling to admit, he replied that he had not even read it, but would accept the faith and doctrine of the apostolic see in all matters. I cannot recall that anyone boasted there of having read anything he had not read. Finally they left the court, the cardinals and several others saying of the bishop that never had a man spoken like this man. Another day, when the lord pope was sitting in consistory, he himself questioned the bishop again on the same chapters, and ordered one of the subdeacons of the court, called Henry of Pisa, to read aloud the book which was said to contain the bishop's errors. Whereat the bishop cried out that he ought to be judged on his own works, not the works of others; and that no one, least of all a bishop, ought to be condemned unless he had either confessed or been convicted of a crime. He was not, he said, a heretic and would never be one, for he was ready and always had been to recognise truth and respect apostolic doctrine; for it was not ignorance of truth that made a heretic, but pride of spirit giving rise to contumacy and presuming to cause disputes and schisms: he said he had spoken openly to the world in schools and churches, and had taught nothing in secret: he had written on the Psalms and the epistles of Paul, and if there was error in these works he was willing submit himself to correction or punishment. Likewise he had written on the *De Trinitate* of Boethius: and if any error should be found in that he admitted it would be his, and would be at pains to make amends. There was nothing of his, he said, in that book. However the subdeacon read on, and in the first chapter was the statement that baptism does not bring remission of sin to the foredoomed, and has not the virtue of a sacrament for such persons, but is no more value than a bath to them. Whereat the bishop flared up and exclaimed to the pope: 'You see, Father, how you treat me when the errors of others are recited in your holy consistory to my shame. I avow that I have several pupils who, admittedly have all heard me lecture, though some of them have not understood a word I said; what they have written is their interpretation, not my meaning. Amongst them were two who stand out for their eccentricity: one hothead still living in France and another no less hotheaded who has crossed over to England. You would do better to summon them and their kind to answer for this pamphlet and others like it. What more can I say? Like you I pronounce anathema on this book and all the heresies written in it, and on its author; whoever he is may be condemned to eternal death on the Judgment Day with all other heretics, unless he first repent and return to the Catholic faith.'

The cardinals and others cried out that this should be sufficient defence for the bishop against accusations based on this book; and the pope commanded it to be destroyed. At once, in the sight of all, the subdeacon cut it into tiny fragments and scattered them. But as a great crowd of the laity was present the pope explained in the vernacular on the bishop's behalf that this had not been done to his discredit, for the book was not his; and indeed he had been found orthodox on all points and faithful to apostolic doctrine, and was at one with the Roman church in condemning these and all other heresies.

Then the pope turned to the bishop and charged him with certain statements which were said to occur in his commentary on the *De Trinitate* of Boethius, and ordered that the book be given to him for correction. He said too that he would erase anything that needed erasing and change anything that ought to be changed. To which the bishop answered: 'Forbid it, master, that anyone else should undergo a toil that is rightly mine. It is just that if I have erred in writing I should be punished by expurgating, and deleting my own errors will be a part of my penance: do you rather command what should be erased, and I will carry out your instructions to the last letter.' The cardinals and others, who approved this reply, demanded that nothing more should be required of him. So the pope expounded the four propositions just as they had been written down in the abbot's chamber—as I have already related—and as the abbot had recorded them: and commanded the bishop to bring his book into conformity with them, and make other corrections as he should instruct him. They have been formulated in this way, possibly with the pope's cognisance, by master Geoffrey of Auxerre, who later became the fourth abbot of Clairvaux after St. Bernard:

'We believe that the simple essence of divinity is God, and that it cannot be denied in any orthodox way that divinity is God and God divinity. And if it is said that God is wise by wisdom, great by greatness, eternal by eternity, one by unity, God by divinity and so on, we believe that He is wise only by that wisdom which is God Himself, great only by that greatness which is God Himself, eternal only by that eternity which is God Himself, one only by the unity which is God Himself; that is, that He in His own essence is wise, great, eternal, indivisible. God.

'When we speak of three persons, the Father, Son and Holy Spirit, we understand them to be one God and one divine substance; and conversely, when we speak of one God or one divine substance we profess that one God and one divine substance are three persons.

'We believe that only God the Father, Son and Holy Spirit is eternal, and that no things whatsoever, whether they are called relations or properties, singularities or unities or anything of the kind exist and have existed eternally in God, unless they are God.

'We believe that that divinity whether it is called divine substance or essence, is incarnate, but only in the Son.'

To these propositions the bishop agreed; and the pope commanded him to correct any conflicting statements that might occur in his book forbidding any copy already made to be kept, or any further copy to be made until it had been brought into line with this formula. As the bishop entirely concurred, he was acquitted of the charge and stigma of his opponents. These propositions were promulgated, not during the council, but a fortnight after its dissolution, in a room called Tau in the archbishop's palace, before the archbishops and bishops of various provinces, who had remained to settle this case. Consequently I have never been able to find these propositions either among the records of the council or in the register of Pope Eugenius, though I was present and heard them published. But they can be found in the writings of that same Geoffrey who later, as abbot Igny, when the bishop was already dead, wrote a book refuting him: a book elegant in style and rightly pleasing to readers, except that it seems to have the character of a polemic and embodies a certain spleen. However no human judgment is competent to decide this, for no one knows fully the things of a man save the spirit of man which is in him, and the Judge of consciences, who alone knows the secrets of the heart. What is certain is that the saintly abbot of Clairvaux often spoke openly against the bishop, and after this enquiry wrote many things to his discredit, both in letter and in his book *De Consideratione* to Pope

Eugenius, and also in that most subtle and precious exposition of the *Song of Songs*, which assuredly the Holy Spirit dictated through his mouth: but he at least seems to have been inspired by zeal for the faith and ardent charity in all he wrote.

Some people believed that the bishop was not as sincere as he professed to be and was making a false show of humility (for on that occasion he showed the great moderation always habitual to him); and because his adversaries had difficulty in understanding him, many declared that he was taking advantage of verbal subtleties and cunningly deceiving the orthodoxy of his judge. Peace made between him and the abbot, and though many tempted him under the pretext of learning from him, he was able to escape their tentacles by referring to the authorities he had to his hand, St. Hilary in particular. I recall that I myself on behalf of the abbot entreated the bishop to meet him in some religious house in Poitou, or France, or Burgundy, wherever he preferred, to discuss the writings of the blessed Hilary amicably and without rancour. He however replied that they had already disputed sufficiently on the matter, and if the abbot wished to reach a full understanding of Hilary he should first seek further instruction in the liberal arts and other preliminary studies. For though they were both exceptionally learned and eloquent men, they excelled in different branches of learning. The abbot for his part, as his works show, was so distinguished a preacher that I can think of no one after St. Gregory comparable to him: he surpassed all in the elegance of his style and was so saturated in the Holy Scriptures that he could fully expound every subject in the words of the prophets and apostles. For he had made their speech his own, and could hardly converse or preach or write a letter except in the language of scripture. I cannot recall any writer who more aptly illustrated this verse:

> How fine your style, if by a skilful turn you make old words seem new (Horace, *De Arte Poetica*, 47, 48).

But he had little knowledge of secular learning, in which the bishop, it is believed, had no equal in our own day. Both were keenly intelligent and gifted interpreters of scripture: but the abbot was more experienced and effective in transacting business. And though the bishop had not the text of the Bible quite so much at his fingertips, it is common knowledge that he was more thoroughly conversant with the doctors—Hilary, for example, Jerome, Augustine and others like them. His doctrine seemed obscure to beginners, but all the more compendious and profound to advanced scholars. He made use of every branch of learning as occasion demanded, knowing that all were consistent with each other, and mutually illuminating. (For he held that the disciplines are interrelated, and made them minister to theology, yet applied all rules strictly to their own class; for individual rules apply only to their own class, and are misused whenever they are more widely applied.) Even in theology he explained the properties and qualities of words by quotations from philosophers and orators as well as poets. Slow to be roused, he could be stimulated by discussion, and if attacked became fuller and more intelligible in his argument. It was best to find him stirred, to win light and heat from his force and fire of mind! Both these men had many would-be imitators, but I cannot call to mind one could touch either of them.

◆ ◆ ◆

Negotiations for peace were proceeding between the pope and the Romans, and numerous legations sped to and fro between the two parties. But there were many obstacles in the way of peace, the greatest of all being the refusal of the Romans to expel Arnold of Brescia, who was said to have bound himself by oath to uphold the honour of the city and Roman republic. The Romans in their turn promised him aid and counsel against all men, and explicitly against the lord pope; for the Roman church had excommunicated him and ordered him to be shunned as a heretic. This man was a priest by office, a canon regular by profession, and one who had mortified the flesh with fasting and coarse raiment: of keen intelligence, persevering in his study of the scriptures, eloquent in speech, and a vehement preacher against the vanities of the world. Nevertheless he was reputed to be factious and a leader of schism, who wherever he lived prevented the citizens from being at peace with the clergy. He had been abbot of Brescia, and when the bishop was absent on a short visit to Rome had so swayed the minds of the citizens that they would scarcely open their gates to the bishop on his return. For this he was deposed by Pope Innocent and expelled from Italy; crossing the Alps into France he became a disciple of Peter Abailard, and together with Master Hyacinth, who is now a cardinal, zealously fostered his cause against the abbot of Clairvaux. After Master Peter had set out for Cluny, he remained at Paris on the Mont Sainte Geneviève, expounding the scriptures to scholars at the church of St. Hilary where Peter had been lodged. But he had no listeners except poor students who publicly begged their bread from door to door to support themselves and their master. He said things that were entirely consistent with the law accepted by Christian people, but not at all with the life they led. To the bishops he was merciless on account of their avarice and filthy lucre; most of all because of stains on their personal lives, and their striving to build the church of God in blood. He denounced the abbot [St. Bernard] whose name is renowned above all others for his many virtues, as a seeker after vainglory, envious of all who won distinction in learning or religion unless they were his own disciples. In consequence the abbot prevailed on the most Christian king to expel him from the Frankish kingdom; from there he returned to Italy after Pope Innocent's death and, after promising reparation and obedience to the Roman Church, was received at Viterbo by Pope Eugenius. Penance was imposed on him, which he claimed to have performed in fasts, vigils and prayers in the holy places of the city; and again he took a solemn oath to show obedience. Whilst dwelling in Rome under pretext of penance he won the city to his side, and preaching all the more freely because the lord pope was occupied in Gaul, he built up a faction known as the heretical sect of the Lombards. He had disciples who imitated his austerities and won favour with the populace through outward decency and austerity of life, but found their chief supporters amongst pious women. He himself was frequently heard on the Capitol and in public gatherings. He had already publicly denounced the cardinals, saying that their college, by its pride, avarice, hypocrisy and manifold shame was not the church of God, but a place of business and den of thieves, which took the place of the scribes and Pharisees amongst Christian peoples. The pope himself was not what he professed to be—an apostolic man and shepherd of souls—but a man of blood who maintained his authority by fire and sword, a tormentor of churches and oppressor of the innocent, who did nothing in the world save gratify his lust and empty other men's coffers to fill his own. He was, he said, so far from apostolic that he imitated neither the life nor the doctrine of the apostles, wherefore neither obedience nor reverence was due to him: and in any case no man could be admitted who wished to impose a yoke of servitude on Rome, the seat of empire, fountain of liberty and mistress of the world.

b. The Metalogicon

When, still but a youth, I first journeyed to Gaul for the sake of study, in the year following the death of the illustrious King of the English, Henry (1136), "the Lion of Justice." I betook myself to the Peripatetic of Pallet, who was then teaching at Mont Ste. Geneviève. The latter was a famed and learned master, admired by all. At his feet I learned the elementary principles of this art, drinking in, with consuming avidity, and to the full extent of my limited talents, every word that fell from his lips. After his departure, which seemed to me all too soon, I became the disciple of Master Alberic, who had a very high reputation as the best of the other dialecticians. Alberic was in fact a most bitter opponent of the Nominalist sect. After thus passing almost two full years at the Mont, I had, as instructors in this art, Alberic and also Master Robert of Melun (the latter being the cognomen he had attained in the scholastic regime, although he belonged to the English nation by birth). Alberic was always most meticulous, and everywhere found something to question. For him, not even a plain surface that was polished smooth could be entirely free from objectionable roughness. According to the saying, for him "the very bulrush would not be free of nodes." For, even in the bulrush, he would be sure to discover knots in need of untying. Conversely, Robert of Melun was ever ready with the answers. For purposes of subterfuge, he would never complete his discussion of a proposed point without [first] choosing to take up the contradictory side, or showing with deliberate variety of speech that there was more than one answer. In short, while Alberic was full of subtle questions, Robert was penetrating, concise, and to-the-point in his replies. If anyone were to have the qualities of Alberic and Robert combined, in the degree that they possessed them separately, it would be impossible in our age to find his match as a disputant. Both had keen minds and were diligent scholars. I am confident that each of them would have been outstanding as great and illustrious students of nature, had they but possessed a broad foundation of literary learning, and kept to the footsteps of their predecessors as much as they took delight in their own inventions. Such was the case during the period when I was their disciple. Afterwards Alberic departed for Bologna, where he "unlearned" what he had formerly taught; and subsequently, on returning "untaught" it. Let them judge who heard his lectures both before his departure and after his return. But Robert became proficient in divine learning, and acquired the glory of a still higher philosophy and greater renown. After working with the aforesaid masters for two full years, I became so accustomed to pointing out the topics, rules, and other elementary principles, with which teachers stock youthful minds, and of which the aforesaid doctors were skilled masters, that these seemed as familiar to me as my own nails and fingers. For I had learned the subject so thoroughly that, with youthful lack of reflection, I unduly exaggerated my own knowledge. I took myself to be a young sage, inasmuch as I knew the answers to what I had been taught. However, I recovered my senses, and took stock of my powers. I then transferred, after deliberation and consultation, and with the approval of my instructors, to the grammarian of Conches (i.e., William of Conches who was teaching at Chartres). I studied under the latter for three years, during which I learned much. Nor will I ever regret the time thus spent. Following this I became a disciple of Richard, known as "the Bishop." Richard is familiar with practically every branch of knowledge. His breast is larger than his mouth, and his [scientific] knowledge exceeds his eloquence. He is honest rather than vain, virtuous rather than ostentatious. With Richard, I reviewed all that I had studied under the others, as well as learned certain additional points concerning the Quadrivium, to which I had been previously introduced by Hardewin the German. I also reviewed rhetoric, of which, together with certain other subjects, I had already learned a little in previous studies under Master Theodoric (i.e., Thierry of Chartres), but of which, as of these, I did not understand a great deal. Later, however, I learned more rhetoric from Peter Helias. Meanwhile I took as pupils the children of nobles, who in return provided for my material necessities. For I lacked the help of friends and relatives, and God thus aided me and relieved my poverty. In this capacity, because of my duties and the insistent questions raised by the youths, I was forced frequently to recall what I had previously heard. Consequently I had recourse to Master Adam (i.e., Adam du Petit Pont), with whom I became very intimate. Adam is a man of very keen intellect, and also, regardless of what others may think, a person of wide learning. He was especially devoted to the study of Aristotle. Even though I was not one of his own disciples, he would graciously share with me his goods [of knowledge], and very clearly explained to me his doctrines: something he never or rarely did with outsiders. He was [in fact] reputed to suffer from the affliction of jealousy. Meanwhile I taught the first principles of logic to William of Soissons. William later, according to his followers, invented a device to revolutionize the old logic by constructing unacceptable conclusions and demolishing the authoritative opinions of the ancients. After instructing William, I sent him on to the aforesaid teacher. Perhaps it was there that he learned that the same conclusion may be inferred from either of two contradictories, although Aristotle teaches the contrary, saying: "It is impossible that both the existence and the non-existence of something should [each] alike necessitate the existence and the non-existence of something else." Nothing can eventuate from [both sides of] a contradiction, and it is impossible for [both sides of] a contradiction to eventuate from something. Not even by the [reasoning] process devised by a friend could I be brought to believe that, because one thing is inconceivable, all things become inconceivable. My pinched finances, the entreaties of my associates, and the advice of friends [had] induced me to assume the office of teacher. At the end of three years I returned and sought out Master Gilbert (i.e., Gilbert of Poitiers), whose disciple I became in dialectical and theological subjects. But all too soon Gilbert was transferred. His successor was Robert Pullen, a man commendable alike for his virtue and his knowledge. Next, Simon of Poissy, a dependable lecturer but rather dull in disputes, took me as his student. The last-mentioned two [Robert and Simon] only instructed me in theology. I [had] thus spent almost twelve years engaged in various studies. Accordingly, I felt that it would be pleasant to revisit my old associates, whom I had previously left behind, and whom dialectic still detained at the Mont. I wanted to confer with them concerning matters that had previously appeared ambiguous to us, and to estimate our progress by mutual comparison. I found them just as, and where, they were when I had left them. They did not seem to have progressed as much as a hand's span. Not a single tiny [new] proposition had they added toward the solution of the old problems. They themselves remained involved in and occupied with the same question whereby they used to stir their students. They had changed in but one regard: they had unlearned moderation: they no longer knew restraint. And this to such an extent that their recovery was a matter of despair. I was accordingly convinced by experience of something which can easily be inferred [by reason]: that just as dialectic expedites other studies, so, if left alone by itself, it lies powerless and sterile. For if it is to fecundate the soul to bear the fruits of philosophy, logic must conceive from an external source.

Chapter Nine

The Church in the High Middle Ages

THERE were four major developments in church affairs during the two centuries covered by this chapter (1100–1300). In the order I shall discuss them they are (1) the growth of papal government (2) the decline of monasticism (3) the emergence of popular heresies and (4) the appearance of the mendicant orders.

The Investiture Controversy ended in what was ostensibly a compromise. In fact, it was a victory for the papacy. Even if Gregory VII was a personal failure and the *regnum* continued to play a large role in the affairs of the *sacerdotium*, papal power was established in a way that it had never been before. The real loser was the episcopate, which had always felt the immediate force of royal power and which now was subject to the jurisdictional authority of the papacy.

The growth of papal government took place along two lines. One, already visible in the eleventh century, was the vastly increased activity and authority of papal legates. Although all archbishops came to be considered representatives of the papacy by virtue of their office, the custom grew up of commissioning special legates whose authority, if temporary, superseded that of all local ecclesiastical officials. This device, whose general acceptance came out of the reforming activity of the eleventh century, was an effective means of exerting papal authority in what had been a largely autonomous sphere of ecclesiastical activity.

The other principal vehicle for the growth of papal authority was its enhanced judicial activity. Although the judicial authority of the papacy, to this degree, was new, it was the outgrowth of two older customs, the practice of holding annual councils at Rome and of sending out legates. The former provided the initial means of referring disputes to Rome; the latter the occasion, again initially, for judging them.

The judicial machinery of the papacy already existed in its rudiments by the time of Gregory VII. In the twelfth century that machinery became elaborately organized under the pressure of a flood of judicial business. From this came two important developments. Since administrative authority follows judicial authority, the establishment of the Roman curia as the highest ecclesiastical court of appeal tightened up papal control over the episcopate. Further, since papal government had become such a complicated affair, the monkish types who had held the papal throne for two centuries past were replaced by university-trained theologians and canonists.

As papal authority waxed its prestige waned. The once sentimental affinity for the distant and impotent primacy of the papacy hardened into satire as it became very potent and present in medieval life. "Satire," as R. W. Southern writes, "is an unwilling tribute to power. . . ." The main charge in the satirical writings against the papacy was avarice. As the scope of papal business widened, its financial needs increased beyond the point where feudal economics could satisfy them. Consequently, the papacy developed an efficient and quite modern system of taxation which, even though it piled expedient on expedient, never equalled its demands. To a feudally oriented Europe this seemed strange and crass, hence the multitude of satires.

In the thirteenth century the reality of papal power almost caught up with its theoretical claims for supremacy. Probably for this reason the theoretical basis laid by Humbert and Gregory VII proved adequate. As the papacy moved from success to success there was no need to buttress its ideological foundations. Innocent III, the archetype of papal monarchs, when he felt the need to justify his power at all, customarily reverted to the old Gregorian formula: the pope is the only universal power because he is the head of the sacramental hierarchy; i.e., he alone is responsible to God for all Christians. Only at the end of the thirteenth century, as papal authority as well as prestige was waning was there further elaboration of the theory of papal supremacy.

The popular regard for monasticism, such an outstanding feature of medieval religious life in the tenth and eleventh centuries, underwent sharp modifications in the twelfth and thirteenth centuries. The first noticeable change was the decline of the Benedictines. Although the Black monks retained their vast possessions, they ceased to perform any social functions commensurate with them. Monasteries were no longer the center of medieval intellectual life, a change marked, as we have seen, by the flourishing of cathedral schools at the expense of monastic. Nor did monks any longer rise to the highest offices in church and state. Finally, and perhaps a reflection of the former two points, the monasteries, at least the Benedictine were no longer at the center of popular religious life. The latter, no doubt, had something to do with an increasing laxity in the Benedictine observance of the rule; primarily, we suspect, it was due to a change in fashion. A different type of monasticism captured lay religious enthusiasm in the twelfth century.

The Cistercian order and similar ones like the Carthusian, were offshoots from the parent stem of Benedictinism. They differed from the Cluniac norm in being much closer to the original aims of St. Benedict—withdrawal from the world, manual labor, utter simplicity in food and dress. But if they reverted to the old, the new orders also reflected something new in medieval life, a spirit of religious romanticism.

The new spirit was not confined to the new monastic orders although it found its typical expression in them. It is best described through two of its forms, mysticism and the cult of the Virgin. Since the new monasticism had withdrawn from the world there was more time for the cultivation of personal spiritual life; this was its justification. The result was a great outpouring of devotional works whose theme was the mystical personal search for God. That this was taking place at the same time as the rise of dialectic was certainly not fortuitous. It was a reaction against the increased formalization of thought as well as the product of monastic isolation.

The romanticism of mystical religious experience had a counterpart in lay as well as monastic piety in the cult of the Virgin. Although an important devotional figure from at least the fourth century on, in the twelfth the Virgin assumed a significance far beyond what she had enjoyed before. The difference was not merely quantitative; the conventional veneration paid the Mother of God in a former age gave way to an emotional attachment which can only be described in terms of romantic love. Indeed, the literary manifestations of the Virgin cult, like those of twelfth century mysticism, were so couched in the language of eroticism that they proved embarrassing to later, less romantic generations.

The Cistercian order, the chief representative of these forms of religious romanticism, was enormously popular in the twelfth century. In the thirteenth, like Cluny before, it fell into disrepute. Being popular, it became wealthy; being successful it found that however much it withdrew from society, society always followed. And since it expanded so rapidly—there were 530 Cistercian abbeys by the end of the twelfth century—it proved impossible to administer it adequately. So for these reasons, and another I shall suggest shortly, the Cistercians lost their popular appeal and began to suffer from the same sort of criticism as the Benedictines before them.

There were several reasons why popular heresies, which had not troubled the church since the fifth century, reappeared in the twelfth and thirteenth. One certainly was that the church did not adjust its organization and intellectual outlook as rapidly as society changed during these centuries. With its predominately rural organization the church was poorly equipped to cope with the growth of population in the towns. Further, the church was ill-prepared to adjust itself to a new popular religious attitude which appeared in those towns and spread to the countryside.

The laity had hitherto been content to play a passive religious role, letting the regular and secular clergy work out their salvation for them. By the twelfth century a wave of personal piety had swept through those towns, another facet of the religious romanticism of the twelfth century. Its appearance may be connected with the successful economic activities of the merchant and artisan classes who received a new sense of individual worth from it. At any rate the phenomenon was there and the established church not very well disposed to deal with it.

The growth of lay piety had two effects. One was that laymen became increasingly critical of clerical morals as their own personal conceptions of morality improved. Out of this came a spirit of anticlericalism, criticism of the clergy for not performing their proper functions. Certainly there was occasion for criticism since administrative efficiency rather than piety was the style of the prelates of the post-Gregorian church. Anticlericalism opened the path for a much more destructive attitude on the part of the laity. Criticizing the church for not performing its functions was one thing, denying that those functions had value because of the character of the person performing them was quite another. The latter was the old Donatist heresy which received a notable reincarnation among the Albigensians and Waldensians.

These two heresies were fundamentally similar. Both were centered in southern France with affiliations in the Rhineland and northern Italy; southern France in particular being a region where the clergy were notoriously corrupt. Both heresies were critical of the existing church because of its wealth and worldliness. Both equated the true church with a priesthood of believers (to use an anachronistic but descriptive phrase); it was the quality of individual religious experience that mattered rather than the efficacy of the sacrament. Consequently, both rejected the authority of the papacy as the custodian of the sacramental hierarchy and the intermediacy of the priesthood. And for both the secret of their appeal lay not so much in the quality of their doctrines as in the quality of their leaders. The "Poor men of Lyons" and the *perfecti* of the Albigensians actually lived holy lives in contrast to the orthodox clergy around them. In brief, lay piety was looking for emotional religious experience. Some achieved this through the Virgin cult; some through the sermons of itinerant preachers; and some, of course through the popular heresies. No doubt the popularity of the Cistercians in the twelfth century had to do with this also.

The established church was unable to cope with the aberrant forms of lay piety. Since both the Albigensians and Waldensians proved intractable to persuasion, this left repression as the only immediate solution. Until now the church had no machinery to handle popular heresy as opposed to individual lapses from orthodoxy. Now it was forced to set up the Inquisition which helped to bring the Waldensians within manageable proportions and, with the aid of a crusade, enabled it to stamp out the Albigensians.

Out of the same environment which produced the popular heresies came the mendicant orders. Both the Franciscans and Dominicans originated outside the established church; and both, as the products of popular piety themselves, proved effective agents for dealing with it once they were incorporated within the church. It was uncertain, indeed, it was quite fortuitous, that the Franciscans would be incorporated within the church. The original aim of St. Francis was precisely that of Peter Waldo—to renounce the world yet serve it by preaching a simple but emotional Christianity to the spiritually-starved laity and ministering to the poor and sick. Francis, however, sought and received papal approval (as did Peter Waldo initially); besides, his only criticism of the church was the indirect one of his own personal life and those of the swarm of followers he immediately attracted. He quickly lost control of his own order (he was not interested in maintaining it) which then fell into the hands of men for whom the original ideals of absolute poverty, itinerant preaching, and manual labor were not very attractive. In justice, it is difficult to see how a movement so immediately successful in attracting recruits (there were 1583 Francisan houses in Europe by 1282), could have been maintained with those original ideals. The only Franciscan group which did eventually secured papal condemnation.

The Dominicans, although originating in much the same way and at the same time as the Franciscans, and although individual poverty and itinerant preaching were among their original aims, were entirely different in spirit. Where the Franciscans emerged from the same milieu as the popular heresies, the Dominicans were a militant reaction against it. From the beginning they were concerned with an intellectual defense of the faith and for that reason were used to staff the Inquisition. (The intellectual turn the Franciscan order took—we have seen that between them they dominated the intellectual life of the thirteenth century—was in direct violation of St. Francis' wishes.) The Dominicans not only combated heresy, they helped to absorb it, although to a lesser degree than the Franciscans.

The early fourteenth century marked a turning point in ecclesiastical affairs as it did in several other aspects of medieval life. Then, developments began which culminated in the Reformation. For the most part the changes were merely intensifications of what had gone before, the renewed mysticism, the increased popular agitation for church reform and the increasing criticism of the papacy and the clergy. Yet there is one dimension visible in the early fourteenth century which definitely points in a new direction. That century saw the most extreme papal claims to temporal supremacy; it also saw their frustration at the hands of the secular state. The victory of the *regnum* over the *sacerdotium* would not be complete until the sixteenth century. Its beginning, however, provides a convenient place to end this aspect of the Middle Ages.

1. *Innocent III: Letters*

The great Innocent (1160–1216), was born Lothair of Segni, son of Count Trasimond of Segni, a member of one of the aristocratic families which dominated the affairs of Rome in the twelfth century. His uncle was Pope Clement III (1187–1191). He studied theology at Paris and law at Bologna. At the age of thirty his uncle appointed him cardinal; at the unprecedented age of thirty-seven (in 1198) he became Pope Innocent III.

The pretensions of Innocent were not as great as some of his successors; his power was probably superior. He regarded himself as the arbiter of Christendom, all of it, temporal as well as spiritual. For him the reason was clear; he alone was responsible to God for all Christians. As he said at his consecration: "Only St. Peter was invested with the plenitude of power. See then what manner of servant is this, appointed over the household; he is indeed the vicar of Jesus Christ, the successor of Peter, the Lord's anointed . . . set in the midst between God and man . . . less than God but greater than man, judge of all men and judged by none." The following letters, although they deal with but a small segment of his activity, show how consistent he was in this claim. Events show how nearly he came to achieving it.

The translation is by C. R. Cheney and W. H. Semple, *Selected Letters of Pope Innocent III* (London: Thomas Nelson and Sons, Ltd., 1953).

XVII

TO THE illustrious king of England.

Holy scripture testifies that a father rebukes and chastens the son whom he loves: and so if your Majesty, whom we love with sincere affection in the Lord, is rebuked in our apostolic letter, and even upbraided, for the sins which you are known to have committed against the head and members, that is, against us and the Roman Church, the clergy and the churches, it should be pleasant and welcome to you to realise that our rebuke springs from love and not from anger—especially as, in administering this rebuke, we obey the decree of the Apostle who, in his instructions for bishops, says to Timothy, 'Be constant in season, out of season, reprove, plead, upbraid with all long-suffering and doctrine.'

Your brother of renowned memory, Richard, king of England, supplicated the Holy See with many urgent prayers that it would deign effectively to support the advancement of our well-beloved son in Christ, the illustrious king Otto, his nephew and yours, then Roman emperor elect; and he promised to contribute effective help to that end. When King Richard by God's will departed this life, you who succeeded to the throne pleaded urgently with us and our brethren on behalf of the same business, sending several letters and envoys both with petitions and promises, and declaring that you would sacrifice yourself and your territory to attain this object. We believed that you meant to fulfil in deed what you promised in word; and we earnestly set ourselves to support the king's advancement—as, by the grace of God, may be seen from the result. But as for you—O that others did not know what we could not help knowing: how you later failed even the Roman Church, and withdrew your helping hand from the king, and swore an oath against him; and thus you placed the Apostolic See in the greatest difficulty within your power: but the One, who never fails His own Church and declares that He will be with it even unto the end of the world, looked down on it from heaven and graciously relieved it of such a heavy burden, and, to the surprise of many, prospered its undertaking with ever greater success. We welcome it, however, if (as we have recently heard) you have again made a treaty with the king for a genuine peace: and we will welcome it still more if you have set yourself to keep the treaty undeviatingly.

Another matter: you sent our venerable brother the bishop of Bath and certain abbots to appear before us on behalf of the Crusaders; and when we, having regard to the nature of the business, consented to hear your Majesty on such points only as with divine approval we could, then, because contrary to your wish we ruled (as we were bound to rule) that your royal petitions were not *all* admissible, on the return of the envoys to your presence you broke into such a fury that you publicly prohibited any citizen of your realm from attempting to receive a legate or nuncio of the Apostolic See anywhere in your kingdom and especially in England. True, you afterwards withdrew this decree as being thoughtlessly issued: but, as it is unheard of for any prince to act in such a manner, a king of your understanding must be well aware how deep was the offense given to the Apostolic See by the publication of the decree.

Another point: we regard it as most serious that, when in your kingdom we commit the cognizance of ecclesiastical cases to delegates, you prevent the delegates from proceeding to try them, thus impeding our jurisdiction—though (if you remember) we have always been careful to safeguard your jurisdiction.

As regards the clergy and churches, we cannot recall without sorrow, nor report without pain, how you have behaved towards them in many matters since you came to the throne, and how, forgetting the true clemency of a king, you have caused them to be dishonourably treated. For you expelled from his see our venerable brother the bishop of Limoges, and you have violently appropriated the revenues of his church —a shameful thing for you to do. Also, by oppressing and offending in many points our venerable brother the bishop of poitiers, you have almost completely destroyed his church and his diocese.

Next, take the conduct of episcopal elections: you are claiming for yourself power beyond your rights, you are applying the revenues of the churches to your own uses, you are attempting to prevent elections, and in the end by your unlawful persecution you are forcing the rightful electors to choose in accordance with your arbitrary decision—as you are known to have done in the church of Lincoln, where you refuse to allow an election to be held, so that you may keep its large revenues still longer in your own hands; and similarly in the case of the canons of the church of Séez, where you caused the canons' property to be seized by your servants and the canons themselves to be treated with much indignity, because in conducting the election they did not proceed in accordance with your mandate; and even to this day you do not permit the bishop of Séez to enjoy peaceful possession of his own see. We are perfectly well aware, too, of what you have done to the church of Coutances, though perhaps you think that this has not come to our knowledge.

And further: before your advancement to the throne you conceived against our venerable brother the archbishop of Dublin an unmerited resentment and compelled him to remain exiled from his church; and though often warned by the Roman Church, you did not trouble to receive him back into your favour. Later, when the Lord, regarding you from on high, had raised you to the throne, we imagined that your royal Magnificence, for whom Divine Providence had thus so magnificently provided, would from gratitude to God provide for the archbishop: but we have been disappointed in our hope because, considering neither God nor the prayers which you have often received from us on the archbishop's behalf, you have not troubled to restore him to the royal favour; and, because you would not, you could not be moved by any entreaties to let him return to his own church and to restore to him his sequestrated property; so in the end, banned from your whole realm, he is compelled to beg the necessaries of life—he, a feeble old man, for whose age you ought to have had a special pity.

If you seriously reflect how deeply on all these scores you have offended your Creator who has granted you such great power on earth, you may well fear that He, who declares himself to be honoured and despised in the persons of His servants (as is said in the Gospel, 'Whosoever receiveth you, receiveth me,' and, 'Whosoever despiseth you, despiseth me,') will in part now punish the wrongs done to His servants (in the hope that trouble, if nothing else, may give you understanding), and will also reserve other punishment for a future time.

Therefore, as the responsibility of our office requires, we wish by paternal warnings to recall from evil a king of your humanity and earnestly to encourage you towards goodness; and so we beg your Majesty, we warn you, we exhort you in the Lord, enjoining it on you for the remission of your sins, to give more serious thought than in the past to what conduct becomes you or does not become you, and to set yourself with more purpose of heart to revere the Roman Church which by divine appointment is the mother and teacher of all the faithful and which with sincere affection in the Lord embraces you as a specially loved son; and to love and honour all churches and ecclesiastical persons in your kingdom, and desist from troubling them, and make adequate compensation to them for the wrongs which you are known to have inflicted on them—so that God, by whose will kings rule and time's seasons move, may be rendered propitious and favourable to you, and so that, in the churches of your kingdom, loyal prayers may be continually offered to Him for your Majesty's health and the increase of your kingdom.

But be assured that, if you do not personally undertake to correct the wrongs herein stated and to abstain from similar wrongs, we, who on your account have delayed exercising our duty perhaps longer than we should (and by our silence we fear that we may have incurred Divine displeasure), will by no means hesitate to carry out our duty as is fitting—after such prolonged waiting and such fatherly warning.

The Lateran, the 20th of February. [1203]

XXI

To the archbishops and bishops of France.

He, to whom nothing is unknown, who is the searcher of hearts and diviner of secrets, knows that 'out of a pure heart and of a pure conscience and of faith unfeigned' we love our dear son in Christ, Philip illustrious king of the French, and that we greatly desire his honour, success, and increase, regarding the exaltation of the French kingdom as the exaltation of the Apostolic See, because this kingdom, blessed by God, has always remained steadfast in devotion to Him and will never, we believe, depart from that devotion; for, though occasionally wicked angels make incursions from this quarter or that, we who know Satan's wiles will apply ourselves to outwit his artifices, confident that the king will not let himself be deceived by Satan's snares.

Let no man, therefore, imagine that we intend to diminish or disturb the king's jurisdiction and power, when he is obliged not to hinder or curb our jurisdiction and power. When we cannot fully discharge our own jurisdiction, why should we wish to usurp another's? But because the Lord says in the Gospel, 'If thy brother shall trespass against thee, go and rebuke him between thee and him alone; if he shall hear thee, thou hast gained thy brother. But if he will not hear thee, then take with thee one or two more, that in the mouth of two or three witnesses every word may be established. And if he shall neglect to hear them, tell it unto the church. But if he neglect to hear the church let him be unto thee as an heathen man and a publican'; and because the king of England is ready (as he alleges) to produce ample evidence that the king of the French is trespassing against him and that he has himself proceeded by the Gospel rule in rebuking him; and because, having so far achieved nothing, he is now telling it to the church: how can we, who have been called by divine decree to govern the universal church—how can we obey the Lord's command except by proceeding as it appoints, unless king Philip, appearing before us or our delegate, shews sufficient reason to the contrary? For we do not intend to judge concerning a fief, judgment on which belongs to him, except where the application of the common law is limited by special privilege or contrary custom—but concerning sin, a judgment which unquestionably belongs to us, and which we can and should exercise against anyone.

His Majesty, therefore, should not think it damaging if he submits in this matter to the apostolic judgment; for we read that the renowned Emperor Valentinian said to the suffragans of the church of Milan: 'Take care to place in the episcopal see a man to whom even we who govern the Empire may unfeignedly bow our head, one whose admonishments when as a man we have sinned we may unquestioningly accept like a physician's medicines.' There is also the decree of the Emperor Theodosius, reissued by Charles, from whose line King Philip is himself descended: 'If any man who has received leave to bring a suit into court shall at any stage in the proceedings (when he is making his plaint either at the beginning of the case or after some lapse of time, or when the case is being closed, or when the judge has already begun to deliver sentence) choose to be tried by the pontiff of the Most Holy See, then immediately, without question, and in spite of objections from the other side, he is to be sent, with the statements of the litigants, to the bishops' court'; but in humility we pass this over, for we depend not on any human decree but on the divine law, our authority being not of man but of God. There is no man of sound mind but knows that it belongs to our office to rebuke any Christian for any mortal sin and to coerce him by ecclesiastical penalty if he has spurned our reproof; and that we have the duty and power to rebuke is evident from both the Old and New Testaments, for the Lord proclaims by the prophet, 'Cry aloud, spare not, lift up thy voice like a trumpet, and shew my people their transgressions,' and also in the Old Testament he adds, 'If thou speakest not to the wicked man of his wicked way, he shall die in the iniquity which he has wrought, but his blood will I require at thine hand.' The Apostle also warns us 'to rebuke them that are unruly,' and elsewhere he adds, 'Reprove, rebuke, exhort with all longsuffering and doctrine.' That we have also the power and duty to coerce is evident from what the Lord says to the prophet who was of the priests that were in Anathoth, 'See, I have this day set thee over the nations and over the kingdoms, to root out, and to pull down and to destroy, and to throw down, to build and to plant': obviously, all mortal sin must be rooted out, destroyed and thrown down. Furthermore, when the Lord gave the keys of the kingdom of Heaven to St Peter, he said to him, 'Whatsoever thou shalt bind on earth, shall be bound also in heaven: and whatsoever thou shalt loose on earth, shall be loosed also in heaven.' Now, no man doubts but that everyone who commits mortal sin is bound before God: therefore, that Peter may copy the divine judgment, he should bind on earth those who are undeniably bound in heaven.

But perhaps it will be said that kings should be treated differently from other men: but we know that it is written in the law of God, 'Thou shalt judge the great in the same way as the small: thou shalt not respect persons in judgment.' This respect of persons St James declares to occur if one says to a man clothed in goodly apparel, 'Sit thou here in a good place'; but to the poor man, 'Stand thou there, or sit here under my footstool.'

Though we are empowered to proceed thus in respect of any criminal sin so that we may recall the sinner from error to truth and from vice to virtue, yet we are specially so empowered when it is a sin against peace,—peace, which is the bond of love and about which Christ specially directed the apostles, 'Into whatsoever house ye enter, first say "Peace be to this house"; and if the son of peace be there, your peace will rest on him'; and again, 'Whosoever will not receive you nor hear your words, when ye depart thence shake off the dust from your feet for a testimony against them.' For the apostles to depart from such people, what is it but to deny them apostolic communion? And to shake off the dust from their feet, what is it but to apply ecclesiastical punishment? For this is the dust which, when Moses sprinkled ashes from the furnace, became a plague of ulcers on all the land of Egypt. The heavy sentence and penalty which at the Last Judgment will smite those who do not receive the messengers of peace nor hear their words is shewn immediately afterwards by the Truth when it declares, not simply, but with a forceful emphasis, 'Verily, I say unto you, it shall be more tolerable for the land of Sodom and Gomorrha in the day of judgment than for that city'—by city meaning citizens, from whose number it does not exclude kings.

Moreover, since (according to the rules of law) any right which one man has established against another may be used by another man against the first, and since the wise Cato declares, 'Submit to the law you have made,' and since in time of war the king of the French availed himself of our office and good-will against Richard of renowned memory, formerly king of the English, who was not of inferior status to himself (with all respect to King Philip be it spoken, for we say it not to shame him but to justify ourselves), how will he refuse to allow on King John's behalf against himself what he once allowed on his own behalf against King Richard? Ought there to be in our court 'divers weights and divers measures, both of which are alike abomination to the Lord'? And lastly, when a treaty of peace was made between the kings and confirmed on both sides by an oath and yet was not kept for its full duration, how can we fail to take cognizance of a sworn obligation (which unquestionably belongs to the Church's jurisdiction) so that the broken treaty of peace may be remade?

Wherefore, that we may not seem by apathy to encourage so serious a breach, or to ignore the destruction of religious houses, or disregard the slaughter of Christian people, we have odered our beloved son, the abbot of Casamari, that—unless King Philip either remakes a stable peace with King John, or concludes a suitable truce, or at least humbly allows the said abbot and our venerable brother the archbishop of Bourges informally to ascertain whether the complaint, which the king of the English has lodged against him before the Church, is a just one or whether the exception which King Philip has chosen to state against King John in his letter to us is a lawful one,—he is to proceed in accordance with the instructions we have given him. And so, by apostolic letter we command you all and strictly charge you in virtue of your obedience, that, when the abbot has discharged the apostolic mandate in this matter, you should humbly receive his, or rather our, sentence, and observe it yourselves and see that it is observed by others; and know that, if you act otherwise, we will punish your disobedience.

The Lateran, April. [1204]

XXVIIII

Innocent to John, illustrious king of the English.

On the matter of the church of Canterbury we wrote to you meekly and kindly, requesting and exhorting: but you (with respect be it said) wrote back to us insolently and impudently as though threatening and expostulating. We are careful to defer to you beyond what the law requires: but you are not careful to defer to us even as far as the law requires—giving less heed than is fitting to the fact that, while your devotion to us is most essential, our favour to you is far from inopportune; and though in such a case we have paid to no prince so much honour as to you, you are trying to diminish our honour more than any prince, in a like case, has ever before presumed to do—offering, as you do, certain paltry reasons which, you aver, prevent you from granting your consent to the election (recently celebrated by the monks of Canterbury) of our beloved son, Stephen, cardinal priest of the title of St. Chrysogonus,—such paltry reasons as that he has lived among your enemies and that his person is entirely unknown. But, as Solomon's proverb has it, 'Surely in vain the net is spread in the sight of any bird'; for we know that it should be counted to him for credit, not imputed for blame, that for a long time at Paris he devoted himself to the study of literature and made such progress that he acquired the status of Doctor not only in the liberal arts but also in theological learning; and as a result (for his life was as good as his learning) he was judged worthy to hold a prebend of Paris. We are surprised, therefore, that a man of so great a name, a native of your own kingdom, could have remained unknown to you at least in reputation, especially since after his promotion to the cardinalate you wrote to him that, though you had planned to summon him to the service of your household, you rejoiced at his elevation to a greater office. But you might more fittingly have considered this—that he was born in your land, of parents loyal and devoted to you, and that he had been a predenbary in the church of York, which is a church far greater and more worthy than that of Paris. So, from reasons both of flesh and blood, and of ecclesiastical benefice and office, he is proved to love you and your kingdom with a sincere affection.

Your envoys told us another reason for your not granting your consent to the election—namely, that your consent had never been sought by those who should have asked for it; and they stated that you had never had our letter instructing you to send to us suitable agents to conduct the business, and that the monks of Canterbury, though appearing before you on other matters, had not sent either letter or deputation to ask your consent. And so, because from the time when we decided to reserve for you the compliment of being asked by the monks of Canterbury for the royal assent this had not been done, your envoys begged most earnestly that we would deign to grant a suitable delay within which it could be done, in order that no affront to your rights might occur. They thus ended by stating something against the person of the archbishop elect, about which, since it is manifestly false, they should have kept shut the door of their lips, especially because, even supposing it true, it could not now impede his promotion. Though it has not been usual to wait for the prince's assent in elections celebrated at the Apostolic See, yet two monks had been especially deputed to go to you to request your assent; but they were detained at Dover and so could not discharge their commission. The letter (mentioned above) about the despatch of agents to our presence, was given to your own envoys to be faithfully delivered to you. We also, who have plenary authority over the church of Canterbury, deigned in a letter to entreat your royal favour in this matter: and our courier who delivered to you this apostolic letter also delivered to your Majesty a letter requesting your assent from the prior and monks who by mandate from the whole chapter of Canterbury had celebrated the aforesaid election.

Wherefore, we do not think it necessary to ask again for the king's consent after all these approaches; but, swerving neither to the right hand nor to the left, we have resolved to follow the course appointed by the canonical decrees of the holy fathers—namely, that no delay or difficulty should be allowed to thwart good arrangements, lest the Lord's flock should for a long time be without pastoral care.

Wherefore, let not anyone suggest to a king of your prudence that we can in any degree be recalled from completing this business: for, when without violence or chicanery the canonical election of a suitable person has been unanimously celebrated, we could not desist without loss of reputation and peril to our conscience.

So therefore, well-beloved son, to whose honour we have been careful to defer beyond what is required by law, be zealous in deferring to our honour as the law requires, that you may richly merit both the divine favour and ours; lest perchance, if you act otherwise, you may involve yourself in a difficulty from which you could not easily be freed, for in the end He must win 'to whom every knee bows, of things in heaven, and things in earth, and things under the earth,' whose power, however unworthily, we as Vicar exercise on earth.

Do not therefore fall in with the plans of those who always desire your trouble that they may be better able to fish in troubled water, but entrust yourself to our good pleasure which will turn out to your credit and glory and honour. To fight against God and the Church in this cause for which St. Thomas, that glorious martyr and archbishop, recently shed his blood, would be dangerous for you—the more so, as your father and brother of illustrious memory, when they were kings of the English, adjured that evil custom at the hands of legates of the Apostolic See. But, if you will humbly agree with us, we will take care to provide adequately for you and your successors, so that in this matter no prejudice may be created to your disadvantage.

The Lateran, the 26th of May, in the tenth year of our Pontificate. [1207]

XXX

To the bishops of London, Ely, and Worcester.

We invoke the testimony of Him who is a faithful witness in heaven, that ever with the most sincere affection we have loved our very dear son in Christ, John, king of the English, and that the plenitude of our favour has so abounded towards him that not only have many princes become less fervent in their loyalty to the Sacrosanct Roman Church, but some have actually become disloyal. For whenever the noise of disturbance grew strong against him or his kingdom, the Apostolic See, bearing towards him a heart of love, mightily aided him and, to the envy of many, delivered him from many difficulties. But—and with sorrow we state it—he shews himself so unthankful for our favour that, instead of winning him by kindnesses, we would seem to have provoked him by wrongs; for he opposes our decisions, or rather God's decisions, and led on by foolish advice he does not hesitate to use methods which may result in his serious peril. What these methods are, we hardly think we need state, as they are better known to you than to us. But though we regard the king's devotion as very necessary to us, he can and ought to consider our favour as not less serviceable, perhaps more serviceable, to himself; and (if he recalls aright) he has already clearly perceived this to be so. But oblivious of everything, he is trying not only to thwart our jurisdiction but actually to nullify it, though we have endeavoured always to protect his jurisdiction, never to diminish it. He ought to be reflecting on this—that those princes who, by attacking ecclesiastical liberty, have tried to seize an unauthorised power over churches, by divine judgment have almost utterly failed, whereas those who support Holy Church in her liberty and venerate her with due honour, ever advance from good to better success. But he never considers to what end he might come as a result of the persecution he has started; if he wisely considered that end, he would undoubtedly abandon his project—for, in addition to the divine displeasure, unless he comes quickly to his senses, he will incur serious loss: for 'it is hard for him to kick against the pricks.' God forbid that the English people, who are truly Christian and zealous for the orthodox faith, should in this wicked project follow their earthly king in opposition to the Heavenly King, preferring the corporeal to the spiritual, for there are not only clergy but also laity who are men of such wisdom and devotion that they have both the knowledge and the will to distinguish between the things which should be rendered to Caesar and those which should be rendered to God.

We believe, therefore, that no more useful provision can at this time be made for the king's honour and salvation than that the church of Canterbury should have a prelate who, being renowned in reputation, knowledge and life, should be able by proofs and instances to summon him to the things which are of God and, cleaving to him with the whole affection of his mind, should give him sound advice on spiritual and temporal benefits; and since we know these qualities to reside in our venerable brother, Stephen, archbishop of Canterbury, cardinal of the Holy Roman Church (grievous through it was to detach him from our side so that, having been as it were a joint governor with us of the Universal Church, he should be specially preferred to the metropolis of Canterbury according to the vocation made concerning him), yet because we desire to promote the king's benefit and salvation and also intend to provide for Stephen's advancement, we have with our hands consecrated him archbishop, canonically postulated and elected as he was by the community of the church of Canterbury: and, giving him a pall from the body of St. Peter as a symbol of the plenitude of his episcopal office, we have thought fit to send him to the government of the church committed to his care.

Therefore, although we unfeignedly love the king (with God as our witness we say it) and desire to defer to his honour, yet because in the execution of justice there ought not to be respect or choice of persons, we earnestly warn and exhort you as our brethren, strictly directing and charging you by apostolic letter, that, diligently minding the saying of the Wise Man, 'They that rebuke shall be praised and a blessing shall come upon them,' and endued with the power of the Spirit from on high, and girding on the sword of the Spirit which is the word of God, you should together approach the king and in the spirit of freedom should respectfully exhort him as king, and diligently persuade him as a son, to submit to wise counsels, thus providing salvation for souls, peace for the peoples, honour to God and liberty to the Church. You should also advise him to pay meet reverence and due honour to the archbishop (whom we know to be faithful and devoted to the king, in spite of anything that wicked slander has suggested to the king about him) and, recognising that this thing has been done by God rather than by man, to consent to the divine ordinance with ready approval, so that the archbishop, attached to him with sincere loyalty, may effectively discharge his office towards the flock entrusted to him by the Lord.

But if not, then laying aside all earthly fear and forbidding any opposition or appeal, you are to publish throughout England the general sentence of Interdict, permitting no ecclesiastical office except the baptism of infants and the confession of the dying to be celebrated there. This sentence you must yourselves fully observe, and by ecclesiastical censure you must cause it to be inviolably observed by all. For be assured that, on the incredible chance that any persons shall presume in a rebellious spirit to gainsay it, we will make certain that their presumption is signally punished; and because the terror of it will descend to later generations, their rebellion will never become a precedent, but their punishment will strike fear into all mankind.

But if affliction shall not even thus have given the king understanding, then because 'a father scourgeth every son whom he receiveth and whom the Lord loveth He rebuketh and chasteneth,' we shall begin to make our hands heavier against him, so that in the end he may be cured by the hand of healing and rise up to render us thanksgiving. But as for those who make fat his head with the oil of a sinner, pampering him in evil—let him despise them as flatterers and expel them as corrupters. We also, who have some knowledge of such men's corruptness will under God's guidance endeavour to repay them according to their merits.

See to it that in discharging this mandate you shew yourselves such as may be found to regard God rather than man. And do not be of those who 'are dumb dogs and cannot bark.'

If you cannot all take part in this business, let two of you discharge it, notwithstanding.

Viterbo, the 27th of August, in the tenth year of our Pontificate. [1207]

XXXVII

Innocent to the bishops of London, Ely, and Worcester.

On the matter of the church of Canterbury we write as follows to our well-beloved son in Christ, John, illustrious king of the English:

'We had hoped that, arising from the special privilege of affection with which the Apostolic See loved you among all other princes, you on your side would repay it with respect and honour; but we have been grieved at heart and deeply troubled because you return hatred for love and, as though a conspirator against yourself, will not heed your own honour if only you can impair ours—nay further, ignoring your reputation and salvation, to the prejudice of both you rashly rebel against an ordinance from us and the Church, or rather from God, never reflecting that it is useless to try and invalidate this ordinance, since no one can deflect the outstretched hand of the Most High and no one can change what He has decreed.

'Indeed the extent and the manner of the deference we have shewn to your Majesty in the matter of the church of Canterbury is something which (though you, being ungrateful, may perhaps forget it) cannot easily be obliterated from the memory of the universal Church which, as good fails to defeat evil, marvels at our extraordinary patience towards you.

'Alas! dearly beloved son, what hardness stopped your hearing that you did not catch the salutary warnings we so often impressed upon you? What hardness engrossed your understanding that often you did not observe the wise counsels we suggested to you? Now you are manifestly so hardened that you do not feel the illimitably spreading sore of your wound. You seem so bewitched that you will not permit either the help of medicine or the work of the physician—so that the prophet's words almost exactly fit our complaint about you: "To whom shall we speak, and whom shall we further summon as witness? His ears are uncircumcised and cannot hear." You are irked by the words which are suggested to you for your own salvation: you are wearied of the good which is recommended to you for your own honour; but you do not regret the loss of your own soul, and you are not ashamed even of your earthly fame, not to say ill-fame. Hence we pity you all the more for this great hardness inasmuch as you have turned cruel against yourself and have so far piteously shunned taking pity on yourself.

'Though the fatherly affection which prompts us to tell you this may perhaps be hateful to you, yet in dealing with you we perform the part of a wise and loving doctor who sometimes uses surgery and cautery to heal an unwilling and improvidently obstinate patient. And so if we find your disease unamenable (which Heaven forbid!), you will force us to insist on a more drastic remedy, as the necessary treatment requires; and though perhaps at the moment you may shrink from such harshness, yet when your health is restored you will praise its results and bless too the experienced physician. We are still applying the ointment of gentleness; but if you are soothed by it and do not expect harsher measures, we earnestly beg and warn your Majesty (appealing in the name of Him who will come to judge the quick and the dead) to take wiser counsel and withdraw from this great error, at least proceeding in the present matter as is set out in the letter which our beloved son the abbot of Beaulieu obtained from us in your name some time ago—because undoubtedly it can be reckoned against you as a second sin in addition to the first, if you seem to go back on the request so insistently urged and so unmistakably attested by your own letter: namely, the letter in which you humbly begged us to trust absolutely whatever the abbot in your name should say to us about this business. For this reason you ought without any difficulty to implement what the abbot obtained by his careful mediation, especially as you had once seemed to accept this: for, having first carefully heard and shrewdly considered the abbot's report, you arranged for our delegates to come before you, as though to complete the business.

'Wherefore, dearly beloved son, be not obstinate and do not for the future raise any difficulty in this business, lest you bring yourself (which Heaven forbid!) into a difficulty from which you could not easily be freed. Otherwise, though in the Lord we sincerely love your person, and though you yourself will perhaps receive canonical discipline with anger, nevertheless (because, when a loved friend is chastised, the motive is a pious affection, love's blows having this peculiarity—that, the more sharply laid on, the more friendly they are) if within three months of accepting or rejecting this present letter you have not implemented the terms already sent to you, from that date on behalf of God Almighty, Father, Son, and Holy Spirit and of SS Peter and Paul His apostles, whose authority, though unworthily, we hold, we declare you to be accursed and cut off from communion with the faithful, and we firmly instruct our venerable brethren, the bishops of London, Ely, and Worcester, that setting aside any appeal they should forthwith publish this sentence, causing it to be solemnly repeated on successive Sundays and feast-days, with tolling of bells and candles lit, until adequate satisfaction is made. Moreover, by divine authority we ourselves with our own lips will solemnly publish it, that thus the whole Church may more surely and effectively know the punishment of one whose sin is known to have offended the Church at large; and we intend, by the help of the Most High, to proceed against you in still other ways, if, even after this, you have not made speed to correct your error.

'Look, the bow is at the stretch; beloved son, avoid an arrow which turns not back—lest, wounded by it, you be so seriously crippled that, far from being able to advance to better things, you barely have strength to recover your former position: truly, a wound from this arrow cannot be healed without leaving an ugly scar.'

Wherefore, by apostolic letter we command and firmly instruct you that, if within the stated time the king has not implemented the conditions set out above, you will thereupon proceed promptly in this matter according to the form previously notified, admitting no objection or appeal whatsoever. If you cannot all etc., let two of you etc.

The Lateran, the 12th of January, in the eleventh year of our Pontificate. [1209]

LIII

To the illustrious king of England.

To Him, who from evil is able to bring forth good, we render thanks for having mercifully inspired you to make fitting reparation for the losses and wrongs inflicted upon the Church: for you have both accepted the form of reparation which had been prepared after much consideration, and you have also put your person and territory under apostolic suzerainty—by right of lordship making over in perpetuity to the Holy Roman Church your kingdoms of England and Ireland, to be held through the Church and of the Church, subject to an annual payment of 700 marks for England and 300 marks for Ireland, as is more fully and explicitly contained in your legally framed charter. Who but that Divine Spirit, that 'bloweth where it listeth and one knoweth not whence it cometh or whither it goeth' and that apportioneth its gifts to men as it willeth, instructed and guided you, so prudently and so piously at once to promote your own interests and to provide for those of the Church? Lo! You now hold your kingdoms by a more exalted and surer title than before, for the kingdom is become a royal priesthood and the priesthood a kingdom of priests as stated by Peter in the Epistle and Moses in the Law. Come, then, exalted prince, fulfil the promises given and confirm the concessions offered, so that God Almighty may ever fulfil any righteous desire of yours and confirm any honourable purpose, enabling you so to walk amid temporal blessings as not to fail of winning the eternal.

Therefore, in accordance with your urgent petition, we now send a legate to you from our presence, as it were an angel of salvation and peace, namely our venerable brother the cardinal-bishop of Tusculum, a man pleasing to God and acceptable among men, and one whom we hold in special affection among our brethren for his piety and integrity—so that in the person of the envoy you may recognise the feelings of the sender. As we have proved him prompt and eager (as far as he could with God's approval) to promote your advantage and honour, do you receive him kindly and treat him honourably, submitting to his warnings and counsels which, if respectfully accepted, will assuredly work to your good—in this world to your peace and in the next to your salvation. And through the One who desireth not the death of a sinner but rather that he should turn from his wickedness and live, we hope that, as He has begun mercifully and wonderfully to change you into a different man, He will likewise inspire in you a pious feeling of devotion, so that with a reverence comparable to the violence with which in enmity to Him you formerly attacked the Holy Church you will now for His sake honour Holy Church, having already so far progressed as by your good beginning to give promise of an excellent ending. The aforesaid legate, having full knowledge of our mind, will instruct and reassure you as to our good pleasure: to him we have deputed our authority so that, in the words of the prophet, he may root out and pull down and may build and plant all that, conformably with God's will, he shall deem to need rooting out and pulling down or building and planting; and he has been given plenary power effectively to discharge, without contradiction from anyone, all matters pertaining to the office of legate. For it is our command that any sentence duly pronounced by him against the rebellious shall be valid and inviolably observed.

The Lateran, the 6th of July, in the sixteenth year of our Pontificate. [1213]

LXVII

Innocent to His Well-Beloved Son in Christ, John Illustrious King of the English, and to His Legitimate Free-Born Heirs For Ever.

The King of kings and Lord of lords, Jesus Christ, a priest for ever after the order of Melchisedech, has so established in the Church His kingdom and His priesthood that the one is a kingdom of priests and the other a royal priesthood, as is testified by Moses in the Law and by Peter in his Epistle; and over all He has set one whom He has appointed as His Vicar on earth, so that, as every knee is bowed to Jesus, of things in heaven, and things in earth, and things under the earth, so all men should obey His Vicar and strive that there may be one fold and one shepherd. All secular kings for the sake of God so venerate this Vicar, that unless they seek to serve him devotedly they doubt if they are reigning properly. To this, dearly beloved son, you have paid wise attention; and by the merciful inspiration of Him in whose hand are the hearts of kings which He turns whithersoever He wills, you have decided to submit in a temporal sense yourself and your kingdom to him to whom you knew them to be spiritually subject, so that kingdom and priesthood, like body and soul, for the great good and profit of each, might be united in the single person of Christ's Vicar. He has deigned to work this wonder, who being alpha and omega has caused the end to fulfil the beginning and the beginning to anticipate the end, so that those provinces which from of old have had the Holy Roman Church as their proper teacher in spiritual matters should now in temporal things also have her as their peculiar sovereign. You, whom God has chosen as a suitable minister to effect this, by a devout and spontaneous act of will and on the general advice of your barons have offered and yielded, in the form of an annual payment of a thousand marks, yourself and your kingdoms of England and Ireland, with all their rights and appurtenances, to God and to SS Peter and Paul His apostles and to the Holy Roman Church and to us and our successors, to be our right and our property—as is stated in your official letter attested by a golden seal, the literal tenor of which is as follows:

'John, by the grace of God king of England, lord of Ireland, duke of Normandy and Aquitaine, count of Anjou, to all the faithful of Christ who may see this charter, greeting in the Lord.

'By this charter attested by our golden seal we wish it to be known to you all that, having in many things offended God and Holy Church our mother and being therefore in the utmost need of divine mercy and possessing nothing but ourselves and our kingdoms that we can worthily offer as due amends to God and the Church, we desire to humble ourselves for the sake of Him who for us humbled Himself even unto death; and inspired by the grace of the Holy Spirit—not induced by force nor compelled by fear, but of our own good and spontaneous will and on the general advice of our barons—we offer and freely yield to God, and to SS Peter and Paul His apostles, and to the Holy Roman Church our mother, and to our lord Pope Innocent III and his catholic successors, the whole kingdom of England and the whole kingdom of Ireland with all their rights and appurtenances for the remission of our sins and the sins of our whole family, both the living and the dead. And now, receiving back these kingdoms from God and the Roman Church and holding them as feudatory vassal, in the presence of our venerable father, lord Nicholas, bishop of Tusculum, legate of the Apostolic See, and of Pandulf, subdeacon and member of household to our lord the Pope, we have pledged and sworn our fealty henceforth to our lord aforesaid, Pope Innocent, and to his catholic successors, and to the Roman Church, in the terms hereinunder stated; and we have publicly paid liege homage for the said kingdoms to God, and to the Holy Apostles Peter and Paul, and to the Roman Church, and to our lord aforesaid, Pope Innocent III, at the hands of the said legate who accepts our homage in place and instead of our said lord, the Pope; and we bind in perpetuity our successors and legitimate heirs that without question they must similarly render fealty and acknowledge homage to the Supreme Pontiff holding office at the time and to the Roman Church. As a token of this our perpetual offering and concession we will and decree that out of the proper and special revenues of our said kingdoms, in lieu of all service and payment which we should render for them, the Roman Church is to receive annually, without prejudice to the payment of Peter's pence, one thousand marks sterling—five hundred at the feast of St. Michael and five hundred at Easter—that is, seven hundred for the kingdom of England and three hundred for the kingdom of Ireland, subject to the maintenance for us and our heirs of our jurisdiction, privileges, and regalities. Desiring all these terms, exactly as stated, to be forever ratified and valid, we bind ourselves and our successors not to contravene them; and if we or any of our successors shall presume to contravene them, then, no matter who he be, unless on due warning he come to his senses, let him lose the title to the kingdom, and let this document of our offer and concession remain ever valid.

'I, John, by grace of God king of England and lord of Ireland, will from this hour henceforward be faithful to God and Saint Peter and the Roman Church and my lord Pope Innocent III and his catholic successors. I will not take part in deed, word, agreement, or plan whereby they should lose life or limb or be treacherously taken prisoners; any injury to them, if aware of it, I will prevent and will check if I can; and otherwise, I will notify them as soon as possible, or inform a person whom I can trust without fail to tell them; any counsel they have entrusted to me either personally or by envoys or by letter I will keep secret, nor will I wittingly divulge it to anyone to their disadvantage. I will help in maintaining and defending, to the utmost of my power, against all men, the patrimony of Saint Peter, and particularly the kingdom of England and the kingdom of Ireland. So help me God and the Holy Gospels of God whereon I swear.

'To prevent any questioning of these terms at any time in the future, and for the greater surety of our offer and concession, we have caused this charter to be made and to be sealed with our golden seal; and as tribute for this the first year we pay a thousand marks sterling to the Roman Church by the hand of the said legate.

'Witnessed by his lordship Stephen archbishop of Canterbury, and by their lordships William bishop of London, Peter bishop of Winchester, Eustace bishop of Ely, and Hugh bishop of Lincoln, and by our Chancellor, Walter de Gray, our brother William earl of Salisbury, Ranulf earl of Ferrers, Saer earl of Winchester, Robert de Ros, William Briwerre, Peter FitzHerbert, Matthew FitzHerbert, and Brian de Lisle our steward.

'By the hand of Master Richard Marsh archdeacon of Richmond and Northumberland, at St. Paul's London, the third of October A.D. 1213, in the fifteenth year of our reign.'

This offer and concession so piously and wisely made we regard as acceptable and valid, and we take under the protection of Saint Peter and of ourselves your person and the persons of your heirs together with the said kingdoms and their appurtenances and all other goods which are now reasonably held or may in future be so held: to you and to your heirs, according to the terms set out above and by the general advice of our brethren, we grant the said kingdoms in fief and confirm them by this privilege, on condition that any of your heirs on receiving the crown will publicly acknowledge this as a fief held of the Supreme Pontiff and of the Roman Church, and will take an oath of fealty to them. Let no man, therefore, have power to infringe this document of our concession and confirmation, or presume to oppose it. If any man dare to do so, let him know that he will incur the anger of Almighty God and of SS Peter and Paul, His apostles. Amen, amen, Amen.

LXXXII

Innocent, bishop, servant of the servants of God, to all the faithful of Christ who will see this document, greeting and apostolic benediction.

Although our well-beloved son in Christ, John illustrious king of the English, grievously offended God and the Church—in consequence of which we excommunicated him and put his kingdom under ecclesiastical interdict—yet, by the merciful inspiration of Him who desireth not the death of a sinner but rather that he should turn from his wickedness and live, the king at length returned to his senses, and humbly made to God and the Church such complete amends that he not only paid compensation for losses and restored property wrongfully seized, but also conferred full liberty on the English church; and further, on the relaxation of the two sentences, he yielded his kingdom of England and of Ireland to St. Peter and the Roman Church, and received it from us again as fief under an annual payment of one thousand marks, having sworn an oath of fealty to us, as is clearly stated in his privilege furnished with a golden seal; and desiring still further to please Almighty God, he reverently assumed the badge of the life-giving Cross, intending to go to the relief of the Holy Land—a project for which he was splendidly preparing. But the enemy of the human race, who always hates good impulses, by his cunning wiles stirred up against him the barons of England so that, with a wicked inconsistency, the men who supported him when injuring the Church rebelled against him when he turned from his sin and made amends to the Church. A matter of dispute had arisen between them: several days had been fixed for the parties to discuss a settlement: meanwhile, formal envoys had been sent to us: with them we conferred diligently, and after full deliberation we sent letters by them to the archbishop and the English bishops, charging and commanding them to devote earnest attention and effective effort to restoring a genuine and full agreement between the two sides; by apostolic authority they were to denounce as void any leagues and conspiracies which might have been formed after the outbreak of trouble between the kingdom and the priesthood: they were to prohibit, under sentence of excommunication, any attempt to form such leagues in future: and they were prudently to admonish the magnates and nobles of England, and strongly to enjoin on them, to strive to conciliate the king by manifest proofs of loyalty and submission; and then, if they should decide to make a demand of him, to implore it respectfully and not arrogantly, maintaining his royal honour and rendering the customary services which they and their predecessors paid to him and his predecessors (since the king ought not to lose these services without a judicial decision), that in this way they might the more easily gain their object. For we in our letters, and equally through the archbishop and bishops, have asked and advised the king, enjoining it on him as he hopes to have his sins remitted, to treat these magnates and nobles kindly and to hear their just petitions graciously, so that they too might recognise with gladness how by divine grace he had had a change of heart, and that thereby they and their heirs should serve him and his heirs readily and loyally; and we also asked him to grant them full safe conduct for the outward and homeward journey and the time between, so that if they could not arrive at agreement the dispute might be decided in his court by their peers according to the laws and customs of the kingdom. But before the envoys bearing this wise and just mandate had reached England, the barons threw over their oath of fealty; and though, even if the king had wrongfully oppressed them, they should not have proceeded against him by constituting themselves both judges and executors of the judgment in their own suit, yet, openly conspiring as vassals against their lord and as knights against their king, they leagued themselves with his acknowledged enemies as well as with others, and dared to make war on him, occupying and devastating his territory and even seizing the city of London, the capital of the kingdom, which had been treacherously surrendered to them. Meantime the aforesaid envoys returned to England and the king offered, in accordance with the terms of our mandate, to grant the barons full justice. This they altogether rejected and began to stretch forth their hands to deeds still worse. So the king, appealing to our tribunal, offered to grant them justice before us to whom the decision of this suit belonged by reason of our lordship: but this they utterly rejected. Then he offered that four discreet men chosen by him and four more chosen by themselves should, together with us, end the dispute, and he promised that, first in his reforms, he would repeal all abuses introduced into England in his reign: but this also they contemptuously refused. Finally, the king declared to them that, since the lordship of the kingdom belonged to the Roman Church, he neither could nor should, without our special mandate, make any change in it to our prejudice: and so he again appealed to our tribunal, placing under apostolic protection both himself and his kingdom with all his honour and rights. But making no progress by any method, he asked the archbishop and the bishops to execute our mandate, to defend the rights of the Roman Church, and to protect himself in accordance with the form of the privilege granted to Crusaders. When the archbishop and bishops would not take any action, seeing himself bereft of almost all counsel and help, he did not dare to refuse what the barons had dared to demand. And so by such violence and fear as might affect the most courageous of men he was forced to accept an agreement which is not only shameful and demeaning but also illegal and unjust, thereby lessening unduly and impairing his royal rights and dignity.

But because the Lord has said to us by the prophet Jeremiah, 'I have set thee over the nations and over the kingdoms, to root out, and to destroy, to build and to plant,' and also by Isaiah, 'Loose the bands of wickedness, undo the heavy burdens,' we refuse to ignore such shameless presumption, for thereby the Apostolic See would be dishonoured, the king's rights injured, the English nation shamed, and the whole plan for a Crusade seriously endangered; and as this danger would be imminent if concessions, thus extorted from a great prince who has taken the cross, were not cancelled by our authority, even though he himself should prefer them to be upheld, on behalf of Almighty God, Father, Son, and Holy Spirit, and by the authority of SS Peter and Paul His apostles, and by our own authority, acting on the general advice of our brethren, we utterly reject and condemn this settlement, and under threat of excommunication we order that the king should not dare to observe it and that the barons and their associates should not require it to be observed: the charter, with all undertakings and guarantees whether confirming it or resulting from it, we declare to be null, and void of all validity for ever. Wherefore, let no man deem it lawful to infringe this document of our annulment and prohibition, or presume to oppose it. If anyone should presume to do so, let him know that he will incur the anger of Almighty God and of SS Peter and Paul His apostles.

Anagni, the 24th of August, in the eighteenth year of our Pontificate. [1215]

2. *The Gospel According to the Marks of Silver*

This is the oldest and shortest version of a famous medieval satire on the papacy.

The translation is by John A. Yunck from his article "Economic Conservatism, Papal Finance, and the Medieval Satires on Rome," reprinted in *Change in Medieval Society* (New York: Appleton-Century-Crofts, 1954), pp. 73–74.

THE beginning of the Gospel according to the Marks of Silver: At that time the pope said to the Romans: "When the son of man shall come to the seat of our majesty, first say to him 'Friend, whereto art thou come?' Yet if he shall continue knocking without giving you anything, cast him out into the exterior darkness." And it chanced that a certain poor man came to the court of the Lord Pope, and cried out, saying "Have mercy on me, at least you, dispensers of the pope, because the hand of poverty hath touched me. I am needy and poor; therefore I beg that you relieve my calamity and misery." And they hearing it were moved with indignation and said: "Friend, keep thy poverty to thyself, to perish with thee. Go behind me, Satan, because thou savourest not of the things that are of money. Amen Amen I say to thee, thou shalt not enter into the joy of thy lord till thou pay thy last farthing." And the poor man went his way and sold his mantle and his tunic and all that he had and gave to the cardinals and the dispensers and the treasurers. But they said: "And this, what is this among so many?" And they cast him out; and going forth he wept bitterly, and would not be consoled. But later there came to the court a certain wealthy clerk, fat and thick and gross, who in the sedition had committed murder. He first gave to the dispenser, second to the treasurer, third to the cardinals. But they thought among themselves that they should receive more. The Lord Pope, hearing that his cardinals had received many gifts, was sick, nigh unto death. But the rich man sent to him a couch of gold and silver and immediately he was made whole. Then the Lord Pope called his cardinals and ministers to him and said to Them: "Brethren, look, lest anyone deceive you with vain words. For I have given you an example: as I have grasped, so you grasp also."

3. *The Chronicle of Jocelin of Brakelond*

The author of this chronicle was a native of Bury St. Edmunds and presumably lived there until he entered the monastery of St. Edmunds in 1173. We know he held several monastic offices; chaplain to the prior, to the abbot, guestmaster, almoner, and that he wrote one other work, on the martydom of St. Robert, a boy allegedly murdered by the Jews of Bury in 1181. This practically exhausts the known details of his life. The man, however, we know almost intimately from his chronicle.

His chronicle is unique in one respect since it gives an unvarnished description of monastic life as it was rather than what it ought to have been. Perhaps St. Edmunds had fallen away from the strict observance of Lanfranc's day; I doubt it. At any rate we may safely say that the medieval monastery was a livelier place than the austerities of monastic constitutions suggest. Besides this, Jocelin gives us an illuminating glimpse of a great English feudal barony in action.

The following excerpts are from the translation of H. E. Butler in the *Nelson Medieval Classics Series* (London: 1949), pp. 1–19, 20–23, 26–27, 28–31, 33–34, 39–41.

WHILE the abbacy was vacant, we often besought God and his holy martyr, St. Edmund, as was meet and right, to give us a fitting shepherd for our Church, thrice every week prostrating ourselves in the choir after leaving the chapter house, and singing the seven penitential psalms; and some there were who, if they had known who was to be our Abbot, would not have prayed so devoutly. As to the choice of an Abbot, should the King grant us a free election, divers persons spoke in divers manners, some in public, some in private, and every man had his own opinion. And one said of another, "That brother is a good monk, a person worthy of approval: he knows much concerning the Rule and the customs of the Church; though he be not so perfect a philosopher as certain others he might well fill the office of Abbot. Abbot Ording was an illiterate man, and yet he was a good Abbot and ruled this house wisely; moreover, we read in the Fables that it proved better for the frogs to choose a log for their king, in whom they could trust, than a serpent who hissed venomously and after hissing devoured his subjects." To this another made answer, "How may that be? How can he, a man who has no knowledge of letters, preach a sermon in Chapter, or on feast days to the people? How shall he who does not understand the Scriptures, have knowledge how to bind and how to loose? seeing that 'the rule of souls is the art of arts and the science of sciences.' God forbid that a dumb image should be set up in the Church of St. Edmund, where it is known that there are many men of learning and of industry." Again another said of yet another, "That brother is literate, eloquent and prudent, strict in his observance of the Rule; he has greatly loved the Convent, and has endured many ills for the possessions of the Church; he is worthy to be made Abbot." And another replied, "From all good clerks, O Lord deliver us; that it may please Thee to preserve us from all Norfolk barrators [i.e., in American slang, shyster], we beseech Thee to hear us." Again one said of a certain brother, "That brother is a good manager, as is proved by the performance of his tasks and by the offices that he has filled so well, and the buildings and repairs that he has made. He knows how to work hard and to defend our house, and he is something of a clerk, though 'much learning maketh him not mad.' He is worthy to be Abbot." The other made answer, "God forbid that a man who cannot read or sing or celebrate the holy offices, a wicked man and unjust, a flayer of the poor—God forbid that such an one would be made Abbot!" Again a certain brother said of someone, "that brother is a kindly man, affable and amiable, peaceful and composed, bountiful and generous, a literate man and eloquent, a very proper man in aspect and bearing, who is loved by many both within and without. And such a man, God willing, might be made Abbot to the great honour of the Church." The other made answer, "Nay; it would be an onus rather than a honour to have such a man; for he is over nice about his food and drink, thinks it a virtue to sleep long, knows how to spend much and gain little, snores when others keep vigil, would always be in the midst of abundance and gives no thought to the debts that grow from day to day, nor that the expenditure, how it may be met; hating all toil and anxiety and caring for naught, provided that one day go and another come,—a man that loves and cherishes flatterers and liars, and himself says one thing and does another. From such a ruler may the Lord defend us!" Again one said of his comrade, "That man is wiser almost than any of us, both in the things of the world and the things of the Church: a man of great wisdom, strict in observance of the Rule, literate and eloquent and personable in bearing. Such a ruler would beseem our Church." Another replied, "True, if only he were of sound and approved repute. But his reputation is deemed unsound, perhaps truly, perhaps falsely. And though he be a wise man, humble in Chapter, devout in the singing of Psalms, and strict in the cloister, yet if he chances to hold any office, he is apt to be disdainful, scorning monks and loving men of the world more than he should; and if he should happen to be angry, he will not say a word in answer to any of the brethren, not even if he be asked a question." And in truth I heard another brother condemned by certain persons, because he had an impediment in his speech, wherefore it was said of him that he had draff or paste in his mouth, when he was called upon to speak. And I indeed, being a young man, "understood as a child and spoke as a child," and I said that I would not agree to any man being made Abbot, unless he knew something of dialectic and could distinguish between false argument and true. Again another, who thought himself wise said, "May God Almighty give us for our shepherd one who is a fool and ignorant, so that he will have to ask us to help him!" And I heard indeed that a certain man who was industrious and literate and of noble birth, was condemned by certain of our seniors because he was a novice, while the novices said of the seniors that they were decrepit old men, unfit to rule the Abbey. And so, many men said many things, and each of them "was fully persuaded in his own mind." I once saw Samson, the sub-sacrist sitting by at gatherings of this kind at the time of blood-letting, when the cloister monks are wont to reveal the secrets of their hearts, each to each, and to confer with one another—I saw him sitting by and smiling, without a word, and noting the words of each; and I heard him repeat some of the aforesaid opinions after twenty years had passed. And as he listened, I used to reply to those who passed judgment after this fashion, saying that if we had to wait to elect an Abbot until we found someone who was free of all blame and without spot, we should never find such an one, since no one lives wholly without censure, and "naught is in all things blest." On one occasion I could not contain my spirit, but blurted out what I thought, thinking that I spoke to faithful ears, and I said that a certain brother was unworthy to be Abbot, though he had loved me and conferred many benefits upon me; and said I thought another worthy to be made Abbot, and named a man whom I loved less. I spake as my conscience bade me, considering the common good rather than my own advancement, and I spake the truth, as the sequel proved. And behold! one of the sons of Belial revealed what I had said to my benefactor and friend: for which cause to this very day I have never either by prayer or gift been able to recover his favour to the full.

After the death of Abbot Hugh, when a year and three months were gone, our lord the king sent letters to us, commanding that our Prior and twelve of the Convent, unanimously chosen by our whole body, should appear before him on an appointed day to elect an Abbot. On the day after we had received these letters we assembled in the chapterhouse to deal with the matter. First of all the King's letters were read before the Convent: after this we asked the prior and charged him on the peril of his soul to nominate according to his conscience the twelve whom he should take with him, men whose life and character made it clear that they would refuse to stray from the right way. And he, granting our petition and inspired by the Holy Spirit, chose six from one side of the choir and six from the other, and satisfied us, not a voice being raised against his choice.

But one of us said, "What will happen, if those thirteen, when they come before the King, are unable to agree in their choice of an Abbot?" And one made answer, "This will be an everlasting reproach to us and to our Church." Therefore a number of us were for electing an Abbot at home before the others departed, in order that by thus taking forethought there might be no disagreement in the presence of the King. But it seemed to us to be foolish and unseemly to do this without the King's assent, since we did not yet know whether we should be able to secure a free election from our lord the king. Samson the sub-sacrist, speaking in the spirit, said, "Let us take a middle course that we may avoid peril on this side and on that. Let four confessors be chosen from the Convent and two from among the elder of our seniors, who are of good repute; and let them when they have looked upon the holy mysteries and laid their hands upon the Gospels, choose three men from the Convent whom they think best fitted for the office according to the Rule of St. Benedict; and let them set down the names in writing and enclose what they have written under seal; and thus enclosed let it be consigned to those of us who are to go to the Court. And when we are come into the King's presence and have been assured of a free election, then at last let the seal be broken, and thus we shall ascertain who are the three whom we are to nominate before the King. If our lord the King refuse to grant us one of our own house, the seal shall be carried back unbroken and handed to the six that have been sworn, so that their secret shall, on peril of their souls, be hidden for ever. To this counsel we all gave our assent: and four confessors were nominated. . . . This done, we went out singing "Verba mea," and the aforesaid six remained behind, having the Rule of St. Benedict ready to hand; and thus they carried out the business according to their instructions.

But the Prior and the twelve with him, after much toil and delay, at length stood before the King at Waltham, a manor of the Bishop of Winchester, on the second Sunday in Lent. Our lord the King received them kindly and declaring that he wished to act according to God's will and for the honour of the Church, he commanded the brethren by the mouth of his intermediaries, Richard, Bishop of Winchester and Geoffrey the Chancellor, afterwards Archbishop of York, that they should nominate three of our Convent. Whereupon the Prior and the brethren went aside, as though to speak on this matter, and drew out the seal and broke it, and found the names in the following order: Samson the sub-sacrist, Roger the Cellarer and Hugh the third prior. Whereat the brothers who were of higher rank blushed. Moreover, all marvelled that the same Hugh was both elector and elect. But since they could not change the facts, by common consent they changed the order, putting Hugh first, because he was third prior, Roger the Cellarer second, and Samson third, making, on the face of it, the first last and the last first. But the King, after first enquiring whether those nominated were born in his realm and within whose domain, said that he did not know them and ordered that three others of the Convent should be nominated as well as those three. This being agreed, William the Sacrist said, "Our Prior should be nominated because he is our head." This was readily allowed. Then said the Prior, "William the Sacrist is a good man." The same was said of Denys, and it was allowed. These being nominated without delay before the King, he marvelled saying, "They have done this quickly; God is with them." Afterwards the King demanded that for the honour of his realm they should nominate three more from other houses. Hearing this the brethren were afraid, suspecting guile. At length they agreed to name three, but on this condition that they should accept none of them without the counsel of those of the Convent who remained at home. And they nominated three: Master Nicholas of Wallingford, later and at the present time Abbot of Malmesbury, Bertrand, Prior of St. Faith, afterwards Abbot of Chertsey, and the Lord H. of St. Neots, a monk of Bec, a man of great religion and very circumspect both in matters temporal and spiritual. This done, the King thanked them and gave orders that three out of the nine should be struck off the list, whereupon the three aliens were at once removed, . . . William the Sacrist withdrew of his own free will: two of the remaining five were struck off by order of the King, and then one of the three remaining, two only being left, namely the Prior and Samson. Finally the intermediaries of our lord the King whom I have mentioned above, were called in to take counsel with the brethren. And Denys, speaking for us all, began to commend the persons of the Prior and Samson, saying that both were literate, both good, both of praiseworthy life and of unblemished reputation; but always in the corner of his speech thrusting Samson forward, multiplying the words he uttered in his praise and saying that he was a man strict in his behaviour, stern in chastising transgressions, a hard worker, prudent in worldly business, and proved in divers offices. The Bishop of Winchester replied, "We understand clearly what you mean; from your words we gather that your Prior seems to you to be somewhat slack and that you desire him whom you call Samson." Denys replied, "Both of them are good, but we should like, God willing to have the better." The Bishop made answer, "Of two good men you must choose the better. Tell me openly, do you wish to have Samson?" And a number, making a majority, answered clearly, "We want Samson," not a voice being raised against them, though some of set purpose said nothing, because they wished to offend neither the one or the other. Samson then having been nominated in the presence of the King, and the latter having taken brief counsel with his advisers, all the rest were summoned, and the King said, "You have presented Samson to me: I do not know him. If you had presented your Prior, I should have accepted him; for I have seen him and know him. But, as it is, I will do what you desire. But have a care; for by the very eyes of God, if you do ill, I will be at you!"

◆ ◆ ◆

After he had received their homage, the Abbot demanded an aid from his knights, who promised him twenty shillings each; but they had no sooner done so than they took counsel together and withdrew twelve pounds in respect of twelve knights, saying that those twelve ought to help the other forty in respect of castleward and scutages and likewise of aids to the Abbot. When the Abbot heard this, he was angry and said to his friends that, if he lived, he would render them like for like, and trouble for trouble. After this the Abbot caused an inquiry to be made as to the annual rents due from the free men in each manor and as to the names of the peasants and their holdings and the services due from each; and he had them all set down in writing. But he restored old halls and ruinous houses, through which kites and crows were flying; he built new chapels and lodgings and chambers in many places, where there had never before been buildings save only barns. He also made a number of parks which he filled with beasts, and kept a huntsman and hounds; and when any distinguished guest came to him, he would sit at times with his monks in some woodland glade and watch the hounds run; but I never saw him taste venison. He also cleared many lands and brought them back into cultivation, but would that he had shown like zeal and vigilance in his bestowal of the manors of the Convent. None the less he took our manors of Bradfield and Rougham into his own hands for the time being, making good the deficit in the rent by the expenditure of forty pounds; these manors he afterwards returned to us, having heard that there were murmurs in the Convent because he kept our manors in his own hands. Also to rule these same manors and all others, he appointed both monks and laymen who were wiser than their former wardens, that they might make more prudent provision for ourselves and our lands. He kept eight hundreds in his own hands, and after the death of Robert de Cockfield he recovered the hundred of Cosford—all of which hundreds he handed over to the custody of his sergeants who ate at his own board, keeping the more important questions for himself and settling those of lesser importance through the agency of others, and turning everything to his own profit. At his bidding a general inventory was made, in each hundred of leets and suits, hidages and corn-dues, payments of hens, and other customs, revenues and expenses, which had hitherto been largely concealed by the tenants: and he had all these things set down in writing, so that within four years from his election there was not one who could deceive him concerning the revenues of the Abbey to a single pennyworth, and this although he had not received anything in writing from his predecessors concerning the administration of the Abbey, save for one small sheet containing the names of the knights of St. Edmund, the names of the manors and the rent due from each tenancy. Now this book, in which were also recorded the debts which he had paid off, he called his Kalendar, and consulted it almost every day, as though he could see therein the image of his own efficiency as in a mirror.

On the first day on which he held a Chapter, he confirmed to us with his new seal sixty shillings from Southrey, which his predecessors had unjustly taken for themselves, having received it in the first instance from Edmund, styled "the golden monk," that he might hold the said township all the days of his life. And he issued an edict that henceforth no man should pledge any of the ornaments of the church without the consent of the Convent, as was commonly done, and that no charter should be sealed with the seal of the Convent save in Chapter in the presence of the Convent. And he made Hugh sub-sacrist, giving orders that William the Sacrist should do nothing in the sacristy in respect either of revenues or expenses, save with his assent. After this, but not on the same day, he transferred the former guardians of the oblations to other offices. And last of all he deposed William himself; whereat some who loved William said, "Behold the Abbot! Behold the wolf of the dream! Behold how he ravens!" and some wished to make a conspiracy against the Abbot. But this being revealed to the Abbot, since he did not wish to keep wholly silent on the matter nor yet to disquiet the Convent, he entered the Chapter on the morrow, drawing forth a bag full of cancelled bonds, with their seals still hanging from them, to wit, bonds given some by his predecessor, some by the Prior, some by the Sacrist, and some by the Chamberlain and other officials—the total amounting to three thousand and fifty-two pounds and one mark, all of capital alone apart from the accumulated interest, the amount of which could never be determined. For all these bonds he had come to terms within a year of the election, and within twelve years he had paid them all. "Behold," he said, "the wisdom of your Sacrist William! Behold all these bonds sealed with his seal, in which he has pledged silken copes, dalmatics, silver thuribles and Gospels bound in gold without leave of the Convent; and all these things I have redeemed and restored to you." And he added much else to show why he had deposed William; but the chief cause he did not mention, not wishing to make a scandal of him. And when he had appointed Samson the Precentor in his place, a man who pleased all of us and was beyond all blame, all was peace again. But the Abbot caused the houses of the Sacristan in the cemetery to be razed to the ground, as being unworthy to stand upon the earth, on account of the frequent wine-bibbing and other things of which it is best to say nothing, which willy-nilly he had witnessed when he was sub-sacrist; and so he ordered all to be leveled to the ground, so that within a year, in the place where a fine building had stood, we saw beans sprouting, and nettles in abundance where once had lain jars of wine.

◆ ◆ ◆

Seven months had not passed since his election, when lo and behold! letters of the Lord Pope were brought to him, offering to appoint him judge delegate for the hearing of causes, a task of which he had neither knowledge nor experience, though he was learned in the liberal arts and in the Holy Scriptures, being a literate man, brought up in the schools and once a schoolmaster, well known and approved in his country. He forthwith called to him two clerks skilled in the law and associated them with himself, making use of their counsel in ecclesiastical business, and studying the decrees and decretal letters, whenever he had time, so that within a short time by reading of books and practice in causes he came to be regarded as a wise judge, proceeding in court according to the form of law. Wherefore one said, "A curse upon the court of this Abbot, where neither gold or silver may help me for the confounding of my adversary!" In process of time when he had acquired some practice in secular cases, being guided by his native power of reasoning, he showed himself so subtle of understanding, that all marvelled, and the Undersheriff Osbert FitzHervey said of him, "This Abbot is a fine disputer: if he goes on as he has begun, he will blind us all, every one." And having approved himself in causes of this kind, he was made a justice errant, though he erred not, but was careful not to wander from the right way. But "Envy assails the earth's highest!" When his men complained to him in the court of St. Edmund, because he would not give judgment hastily nor "believe every spirit," but proceeded in the order prescribed by law, knowing that the merits of causes are revealed by the statements of the parties, it was said that he was unwilling to do justice to any complainant, unless money were first given or promised; and because his glance was sharp and penetrating, and his brow worthy of Cato and rarely relaxed into a smile, he was said to be more inclined to severity than kindness. And when he took amercements for any offence, he was said to exalt justice above mercy, because, as it seemed to many, when it was a matter of getting money, he rarely remitted what he might justly receive.

Abbot Samson was of middle height, and almost entirely bald; his face was neither round nor long, his nose prominent, his lips thick, his eyes clear as crystal and of penetrating glance; his hearing of the sharpest; his eyebrows grew long and were often clipped; a slight cold made him soon grow hoarse. On the day of his election he was forty-seven years old, and had been a monk for seventeen. He had a few white hairs in a red beard and a very few in the hair of his head, which was black and rather curly;

but within fourteen years of his election he was white as snow. He was a man of extreme sobriety, never given to sloth, extremely strong and ever ready to go either on horseback or on foot, until old age prevailed and tempered his eagerness. When he heard of the capture of the Cross and the fall of Jerusalem, he began to wear drawers of haircloth, and a shirt of hair instead of wool, and to abstain from flesh and meat; none the less he desired that meat should be placed before him when he sat at table, that so our alms might be increased. He preferred fresh milk and honey and the like to any other food. He hated liars and drunkards and wordy fellows, since virtue loves itself and hates its opposite. He condemned those who murmur at their food and drink, especially if they were monks, and preserved the old way of life that he had followed as a cloister monk; but he had this virtue, that he never liked to have a dish changed when it had once been placed before him. When I was a novice, I wished to try if this were true, and, chancing to be a server in the refectory, I thought in my heart that I would place before him a dish that was very black and broken. And when he saw this, he was as one that saw not. But after a time I repented that I had done this, and forthwith seizing the platter, I changed both dish and platter for the better and carried them away; but he was angry and vexed and took the improvement ill. He was eloquent both in French and Latin, having regard rather to the sense of what he had to say than to ornaments of speech. He read English perfectly, and used to preach in English to the people, but in the speech of Norfolk, where he was born and bred, and to this end he ordered a pulpit to be set up in the church for the benefit of his hearers and as an ornament to the church. The Abbot seemed also to love the active life better than the contemplative; he had more praise for good obedientiaries than for good cloister monks; and rarely did he approve of any man solely for his knowledge of literature, unless he were also wise in worldly affairs. And when he heard of any prelate that he grew faint beneath the burden of his pastoral cares and turned anchorite, he did not praise him for so doing.

4. *St. Bernard: Apologia*

This document was written in 1124 and directed against Cluny which had just suffered the rule of the worst abbot in its history. The following excerpt consists of chapters viii–xiii.

The translation is by G. G. Coulton in *Life in the Middle Ages* (New York: Cambridge University Press, 1954), Vol. IV, pp. 169–74.

I MARVEL how monks could grow accustomed to such intemperance in eating and drinking, clothing and bedding, riding abroad and building, that, wheresoever these things are wrought most busily and with most pleasure and expense, there Religion is thought to be best kept. For behold! spare living is taken for covetousness, sobriety for austerity, silence for melancholy; while, on the other hand, men rebaptize laxity as "discretion," waste as "liberality," garrulousness as "affability," giggling as "jollity," effeminacy in clothing and bedding as "neatness.". . . Who, in those first days when the monastic Order began, would have believed that monks would ever come to such sloth? . . . Dish after dish is set on the table; and instead of the mere flesh-meat from which men abstain, they receive twofold in mighty fishes. Though thou have eaten thy fill of the first course, yet when thou comest to the second thou shalt seem not even to have tasted the first; for all is dressed with such care and art in the kitchen that, though thou hast swallowed four or five dishes, the first are no hindrance to the last, nor doth satiety lessen thine appetite. . . . For (to say nothing of the rest) who may tell of the eggs alone, in how many ways they are tossed and vexed, how busily they are turned and turned again, beaten to froth or hard-boiled or minced, now fried and now baked, now stuffed and now mixed, or again brought up one by one? . . . What shall I say of water-drinking, when watered wine is on no account admitted? All of us, forsooth, in virtue of our monkish profession, have infirm stomachs, and are justified in not neglecting the Apostle's salutary advice as to "drinking wine"; yet (I know not why) we omit that word "little" wherewith he begins. . . . Men seek for their garments, not the most useful stuff they may find, but the most delicately woven. . . . "Yet," sayest thou, "Religion is not in the dress, but in the heart." Well said. But thou, when thou wilt buy a frock, thou goest from city to city, scourest the markets, searchest the fairs from booth to booth, scannest the merchants' shops, turnest over each man's store, unrollest vast bales of cloth, touchest with thy fingers, bringest close to thine eyes, holdest up to the sunlight, and rejectest whatsoever is seen to be too coarse or too slight; on the other hand, whatsoever taketh thee with its purity and gloss, that thou seekest to buy forthwith at any price: I ask thee, therefore, doest thou this from thy heart, or in mere simplicity? . . . Yet I marvel, since the Rule saith that all faults of the Disciple concern the Master, and our Lord through His prophet threateneth to require the blood of such as die in their sins at the hands of their Pastors—I marvel how our Abbots suffer such things to be done; unless it be perchance (if I may risk the word) that no man confidently rebuketh that wherein he trusteth not himself to be without blame. . . . I lie, if I have not seen an Abbot with a train of sixty horses and more; on seeing such pass by, thou wouldst say that they are not fathers of monasteries but lords of castles, not rulers of souls but princes of provinces. . . .

But these are small things; I will pass on to matters greater in themselves, yet seeming smaller because they are more usual. I say naught of the vast height of your churches, their immoderate length, their superfluous breadth, the costly polishings, the curious carvings and paintings which attract the worshipper's gaze and hinder his attention, and seem to me in some sort a revival of the ancient Jewish rites. Let this pass, however: say that this is done for God's honour. But I, as a monk, ask of my brother monks as the pagan [poet Persius] asked of his fellow-pagans: "Tell me, ye poor men" (for I break the verse to keep the sense) "Tell me, ye poor (if, indeed, ye be poor), what doeth this gold in *your* sanctuary?" And indeed the bishops have an excuse which monks have not; for we know that they, being debtors both to the wise and the unwise, and unable to excite the devotion of carnal folk by spiritual things, do so by bodily adornments. But we [monks] who have now come forth from the people; we who have left all the precious and beautiful things of the world for Christ's sake; who have counted but dung, that we may win Christ, all things fair to see or soothing to hear, sweet to smell, delightful to taste, or pleasant to touch—in a word, all bodily delights—whose devotion, pray, do we monks intend to excite by these things? What profit, I say, do we expect therefrom? The admiration of fools, or the oblations of the simple? Or, since we are scattered among the nations, have we perchance learnt their works and do we yet serve their graven images? To speak plainly, doth the root of all this lie in covetousness, which is idolatry, and do we seek not profit, but a gift? If thou askest: "How?" I say: "In a strange fashion." For money is so artfully scattered that it may multiply; it is expended that it may give increase, and prodigality giveth birth to plenty: for at the very sight of these costly yet marvellous vanities men are more kindled to offer gifts than to pray. Thus wealth is drawn up by ropes of wealth, thus money bringeth money; for I know not how it is that, wheresoever more abundant wealth is seen, there do men offer more freely. Their eyes are feasted with relics cased in gold, and their purse-strings are loosed. They are shown a most comely image of some saint who they think all the more saintly that he is the more gaudily painted. Men run to kiss him, and are invited to give; there is more admiration for his comeliness than veneration for his sanctity. Hence the church is adorned with gemmed crowns of light—nay, with lustres like cartwheels, girt all round with lamps, but no less brilliant with the precious stones that stud them. Moreover we see candelabra standing like trees of massive bronze, fashioned with marvellous subtlety of art, and glistening no less brightly with gems than with the lights they carry. What, think you, is the purpose of all this? The compunction of penitents, or the admiration of beholders? O vanity of vanities, yet no more vain than insane! The church is resplendent in her walls, beggarly in her poor; she clothes her stones in gold, and leaves her sons naked; the rich man's eye is fed at the expense of the indigent. The curious find their delight here, yet the needy find no relief. Do we not revere at least the images of the Saints, which swarm even in the inlaid pavement whereon we tread? Men spit oftentimes in an Angel's face; often, again, the countenance of some Saint is ground under the heel of a passer-by. And if he spare not these sacred images, why not even the fair colours? Why dost thou make that so fair which will soon be made so foul? Why lavish bright hues upon that which must needs be trodden under foot? What avail these comely forms in places where they are defiled with customary dust? And, lastly, what are such things as these to you poor men, you monks, you spiritual folk? Unless perchance here also ye may answer the poet's question in the words of the Psalmist: "Lord, I have loved the habitation of Thy House, and the place where Thine honour dwelleth." I grant it, then, let us suffer even this to be done in the church; for, though it be harmful to vain and covetous folk, yet not so to the simple and devout. But in the cloister, under the eyes of the Brethren who read there, what profit is there in those ridiculous monsters, in that marvellous and deformed comeliness, that comely deformity? To what purpose are those unclean apes, those fierce lions, those monstrous centaurs, those half-men, those striped tigers, those fighting knights, those hunters winding their horns? Many bodies are there seen under one head, or again, many heads to a single body. Here is a four-footed beast with a serpent's tail; there, a fish with a beast's head. Here again the forepart of a horse trails half a goat behind it, or a horned beast bears the hinder quarters of a horse. In short, so many and so marvellous are the varieties of divers shapes on every hand, that we are more tempted to read in the marble than in our books, and to spend the whole day in wondering at these things rather than in meditating the law of God. For God's sake, if men are not ashamed of these follies, why at least do they not shrink from the expense?

The abundance of my matter suggested much more for me to add; but from this I am distracted both by my own anxious business and by the too hasty departure of Brother Oger [the bearer of this letter]. . . . This is my opinion of your Order and mine; nor can any man testify more truly than you, and those who know me as you do, that I am wont to say these things not about you but to your faces. What in your Order is laudable, that I praise and publish abroad; what is reprehensible, I am wont to persuade you and my other friends to amend. This is no detraction, but rather attraction: wherefore I wholly pray and beseech you to do the same by me. Farewell.

5. *A Waldensian Catechism*

This catechism is of uncertain date; it may not be medieval at all. It is included here because it splendidly illustrates the anti-sacramental basis of the Waldensian heresy.

The translation is by Ray C. Petry, *A History of Christianity* (Englewood Cliffs, N.J.: Prentice-Hall, 1962), pp. 352–54.

QUESTION, Pastor. What is the foundation of the commandments by which one must enter into life, without which foundation one is incapable of following worthily or observing the commandments?

Answer, Child. The Lord Jesus Christ, of whom the Apostle says (I Cor. 3:11): No one is able to lay any other foundation. . . .

Q. This God in whom you believe, how do you adore and serve him?

A. By the adoration of prayers (*latria*) external and internal. Outwardly by bowing the knees, raising the hands, by inclining the body, by hymns, by spiritual songs, by fasts and by invocations. But inwardly, I adore with pious affection, by a will surrendered to everything He wishes, but I serve by faith, hope and charity, according to His commandments.

Q. Do you believe in the holy church?

A. No, for it is a creature, but I believe that it exists.

Q. What do you believe regarding the holy church?

A. I say that the church must be thought of in two ways: one in terms of its substance or nature, the other in terms of the ministry. As for its substance, the holy catholic (universal) church is made up of all God's elect, from the beginning to the end, who have, according to the grace of God by the merits of Christ, been gathered together by the Holy Spirit and previously ordained to eternal life, their number and names being known only to the one having chosen them. . . . But the church with regard to the ministry, comprises the ministers of Christ with the people submitted to them, profiting from the ministry of faith, hope and charity.

Q. By what mark do you recognize the church of Christ?

A. By proper ministers and by a people who participate in the truth together with them.

Q. But by what thing do you know worthy ministers?

A. By the true sense of the faith, by a holy doctrine, by an exemplary life, by the preaching of the Gospel, and by a proper administration of the sacraments.

Q. How do you detect false ministers?

A. By their fruits, by their blindness, by wicked conduct, by perverse teaching and by an improper administration of the sacraments.

Q. By what do you know blind ministers?

A. It is when, not apprehending the truth necessary to salvation, they guard human inventions. . . .

Q. By what may we know bad doctrine?

A. This is when it teaches against faith and hope; to wit, in the case of idolatry rendered variously to the creature whether rational or non-rational, sensible, visible, or invisible. For the Father, with his Son and Holy Spirit must be served, and not any creature whatever. But contrary to these, one attributes to man, to the work of his hands, or to his words or to his authority, in such wise that the man believing blindly, judges these things added by God and by a false religion and by the avaricious simony of priests.

Q. By what may one discern the improper administration of the sacraments?

A. This happens when the priests do not understand the mind of Christ and, not knowing his purpose in the sacraments, say that grace and truth are bound up with external ceremonies alone, thus leading men to receive these same sacraments without the truth of faith, hope and charity; and the Lord protects his followers from such false priests, saying: "Beware of false prophets. . . ."

Q. How many things belong to the minister?

A. Two, the preaching of the Gospel word and the sacraments.

Q. How many sacraments are there?

A. Two, namely baptism and the eucharist.

Q. What of the blessed virgin, for she is full of grace, according to the angel?

A. The blessed virgin was and is full of grace as regards her own need, but not as involving communication to others. For God's Son alone is full of grace in the sense of participation, as it is said of him, "and we receive grace on grace from his fullness."

Q. Do you not believe in the communion of saints?

A. I believe that there are two kinds of things in which the saints have communion with each other. The one kind is substantial, the other ministerial. They have communion in things substantial by the Holy Spirit in God, by the merits of Jesus Christ. But they have communion in ministerial or ecclesiastical things by virtue of the ministries duly performed, such as those effected by words, sacraments and prayers. I believe in both of these meanings of the communion of saints, the first being only in God, and in Jesus Christ, and in the Holy Spirit, spiritually; this taking place in the church of Christ.

6. *Bernard of Gui on the Albigensians*

This brief excerpt comes from the early fourteenth century *Inquisitor's Guide* by Bernard of Gui.

The translation is from Robinson's *Readings,* Vol. I, 381–383.

IT WOULD take too long to describe in detail the manner in which these same Manichaean heretics preach and teach their followers, but it must be briefly considered here.

In the first place, they usually say of themselves that they are good Christians, who do not swear, or lie, or speak evil of others; that they do not kill any man or animal, nor anything having the breath of life, and that they hold the faith of the Lord Jesus Christ and his gospel as Christ and his apostles taught. They assert that they occupy the place of the apostles, and that, on account of the above-mentioned things, they of the Roman Church, namely the prelates, clerks, and monks, and especially the inquisitors of heresy, persecute them and call them heretics, although they are good men and good Christians, and that they are persecuted just as Christ and his apostles were by the Pharisees.

Moreover they talk to the laity of the evil lives of the clerks and prelates of the Roman Church, pointing out and setting forth their pride, cupidity, avarice, and uncleanness of life, and such other evils as they know. They invoke, with their own interpretation and according to their abilities, the authority of the Gospels and the Epistles against the condition of the prelates, churchmen, and monks, whom they call Pharisees and false prophets, who say, but do not.

Then they attack and vituperate, in turn, all the sacraments of the Church, especially the sacrament of the eucharist, saying that it cannot contain the body of Christ, for had this been as great as the largest mountain Christians would have entirely consumed it before this. They assert that the host comes from straw, that it passes through the tails of horses, to wit, when the flour is cleaned by a sieve (of horse hair); that, moreover, it passes through the body and comes to a vile end, which, they say, could not happen if God were in it.

Of baptism, they assert that water is material and corruptible, and is therefore the creation of the evil power and cannot sanctify the soul but that the churchmen sell this water out of avarice, just as they sell earth for the burial of the dead, and oil to the sick when they anoint them, and as they sell the confession of sins as made to the priests.

Hence they claim that confession made to the priests of the Roman Church is useless, and that, since the priests may be sinners, they cannot loose nor bind, and, being unclean themselves, cannot make others clean. They assert, moreover, that the cross of Christ should not be adored or venerated, because, as they urge, no one would venerate or adore the gallows upon which a father, relative, or friend had been hung. They urge, further, that they who adore the cross ought, for similar reasons, to worship all thorns and lances, because as Christ's body was on the cross during the passion, so was the crown of thorns on his head and the soildier's lance in his side. They proclaim many other scandalous things in regard to the sacraments.

Moreover they read from the Gospels and the Epistles in the vulgar tongue, applying and expounding them in their favor and against the condition of the Roman Church in a manner which it would take too long to describe in detail; but all that relates to this subject may be read more fully in the books they have written and infected, and may be learned from the confessions of such of their followers as have been converted.

7. *The Rule of St. Francis*

This is the third of the rules of St. Francis, known as the *Regula bullata*, promulgated by Honorius III in 1223. The story behind it is too long to tell here. Suffice it to say that it is much less rigorous than the original rule of 1210 (*regula primitiva*) or even the *Regula prima* of 1221. It reflects the victory of the relaxing party now in power within the order rather than the original ideals of St. Francis.

The translation is from Thatcher and McNeal, pp. 499–504.

1. This is the rule and life of the Minor Brothers, namely, to observe the holy gospel of our Lord Jesus Christ by living in obedience, in poverty, and in chastity. Brother Francis promises obedience and reverence to pope Honorius and to his successors who shall be canonically elected, and to the Roman Church. The other brothers are bound to obey brother Francis, and his successors.

2. If any, wishing to adopt this life, come to our brothers [to ask admission], they shall be sent to the provincial ministers, who alone have the right to receive others into the order. The provincial ministers shall carefully examine them in the catholic faith and the sacraments of the church. And if they believe all these and faithfully confess them and promise to observe them to the end of life, and if they have no wives, or if they have wives, and the wives have either already entered a monastery, or have received permission to do so, and they have already taken the vow of chastity with the permission of the bishop of the diocese [in which they live], and their wives are of such an age that no suspicion can rise against them, let the provincial ministers repeat to them the word of the holy gospel, to go and sell all their goods and give to the poor [Matt. 19:21]. But if they are not able to do so, their good will is sufficient for them. And the brothers and provincial ministers shall not be solicitous about the temporal possessions of those who wish to enter the order; but let them do with their possessions whatever the Lord may put into their minds to do. Nevertheless, if they ask the advice of the brothers, the provincial ministers may send them to God-fearing men, at whose advice they may give their possessions to the poor. Then the ministers shall give them the dress of a novice, namely: two robes without a hood, a girdle, trousers, a

hood with a cape reaching to the girdle. But the ministers may add to these if they think it necessary. After the year of probation is ended they shall be received into obedience [that is, into the order], by promising to observe this rule and life forever. And according to the command of the pope they shall never be permitted to leave the order and give up this life and form of religion. For according to the holy gospel no one who puts his hand to the plough and looks back is fit for the kingdom of God [Luke 9:62]. And after they have promised obedience, those who wish may have one robe with a hood and one without a hood. Those who must may wear shoes, and all the brothers shall wear common clothes, and they shall have God's blessing if they patch them with coarse cloth and pieces of other kinds of cloth. But I warn and exhort them not to despise nor judge other men who wear fine and gay clothing, and have delicious foods and drinks. But rather let each one judge and despise himself.

3. The clerical brothers shall perform the divine office according to the rite of the holy Roman church, except the psalter, from which they may have breviaries. The lay brothers shall say 24 Paternosters at matins, 5 at lauds, 7 each at primes, terces, sexts, and nones, 12 at vespers, 7 at completorium, and prayers for the dead. And they shall fast for All Saints' day [November 1] to Christmas. They may observe or not, as they choose, the holy Lent which begins at epiphany [January 6] and lasts for 40 days, and which our Lord consecrated by his holy fasts. Those who keep it shall be blessed of the Lord, but those who do not wish to keep it are not bound to do so. But they shall all observe the other Lent [that is, from Ash-Wednesday to Easter]. The rest of the time the brothers are bound to fast only on Fridays. But in times of manifest necessity they shall not fast. But I counsel, warn, and exhort my brothers in the Lord Jesus Christ that when they go out into the world they shall not be quarrelsome or contentious, nor judge others. But they shall be gentle, peaceable, and kind, mild and humble, and virtuous in speech, as is becoming to all. They shall not ride on horseback unless compelled by manifest necessity or infirmity to do so. When they enter a house they shall say, "Peace be to this house." According to the holy gospel, they may eat of whatever food is set before them.

4. I strictly forbid all the brothers to accept money or property either in person or through another. Nevertheless, for the needs of the sick, and for clothing the other brothers, the ministers and guardians may, as they see that necessity requires, provide through spiritual friends, according to the locality, season, and the degree of cold which may be expected in the region where they live. But, as has been said, they shall never receive money or property.

5. Those brothers to whom the Lord has given the ability to work shall work faithfully and devotedly, so that idleness, which is the enemy of the soul, may be excluded and not extinguish the spirit of prayer and devotion to which all temporal things should be subservient. As the price

of their labors they may receive things that are necessary for themselves and the brothers, but not money or property. And they shall humbly receive what is given them, as is becoming to the servants of God and to those who practise the most holy poverty.

6. The brothers shall have nothing of their own, neither house, nor land, nor anything, but as pilgrims and strangers in this world, serving the Lord in poverty and humility, let them confidently go asking alms. Nor let them be ashamed of this, for the Lord made himself poor for us in this world. This is that highest pitch of poverty which has made you, my dearest brothers, heirs and kings of the kingdom of heaven, which has made you poor in goods, and exalted you in virtues. Let this be your portion, which leads into the land of the living. Cling wholly to this, my most beloved brothers, and you shall wish to have in this world nothing else than the name of the Lord Jesus Christ. And wherever they are, if they find brothers, let them show themselves to be of the same household, and each one may securely make known to the other his need. For if a mother loves and nourishes her child, how much more diligently should one nourish and love one's spiritual brother? And if any of them fall ill, the other brothers should serve them as they would wish to be served.

7. If any brother is tempted by the devil and commits a mortal sin, he should go as quickly as possible to the provincial minister, as the brothers have determined that recourse shall be had to the provincial ministers for such sins. If the provincial minister is a priest, he shall mercifully prescribe the penance for him. If he is not a priest, he shall, as may seem best to him, have some priest of the order prescribe the penance. And they shall guard against being angry or irritated about it, because anger and irritation hinder love in themselves and in others.

8. All the brothers must have one of their number as their general minister and servant of the whole brotherhood, and they must obey him. At his death the provincial ministers and guardians shall elect his successor at the chapter held at Pentecost, at which time all the provincial ministers must always come together at whatever place the general minister may order. And this chapter must be held once every three years, or more or less frequently, as the general minister may think best. And if at any time it shall be clear to the provincial ministers and guardians that the general minister is not able to perform the duties of his office and does not serve the best interests of the brothers, the aforesaid brothers, to whom the right of election is given, must, in the name of the Lord, elect another as general minister. After the chapter at Pentecost, the provincial ministers and guardians may, each in his own province, if it seems best to them, once in the same year, convoke the brothers to a provincial chapter.

9. If a bishop forbids the brothers to preach in his diocese, they shall obey him. And no brother shall preach to the people unless the general minister of the brotherhood has examined and approved him and given

him the right to preach. I also warn the brothers that in their sermons their words shall be chaste and well chosen for the profit and edification of the people. They shall speak to them of vices and virtues, punishment and glory, with brevity of speech, because the Lord made the word shortened over the earth [Rom. 9:28].

10. The ministers and servants shall visit and admonish their brothers and humbly and lovingly correct them. They shall not put any command upon them that would be against their soul and this rule. And the brothers who are subject must remember that for God's sake they have given up their own wills. Wherefore I command them to obey their ministers in all the things which they have promised the Lord to observe and which shall not be contrary to their souls and this rule. And whenever brothers know and recognize that they cannot observe this rule, let them go to their ministers, and the ministers shall lovingly and kindly receive them and treat them in such a way that the brothers may speak to them freely and treat them as lords speak to, and treat, their servants. For the ministers ought to be the servants of all the brothers. I warn and exhort the brothers in the Lord Jesus Christ to guard against all arrogance, pride, envy, avarice, care, and solicitude for this world, detraction, and murmuring. And those who cannot read need not be anxious to learn. But above all things let them desire to have the spirit of the Lord and his holy works, to pray always to God with a pure heart, and to have humility, and patience in persecution and in infirmity, and to love those who persecute us and reproach us and blame us. For the Lord says, "Love your enemies, and pray for those who persecute and speak evil of you" [cf. Matt. 5:44]. "Blessed are they who suffer persecution for righteousness' sake, for theirs is the kingdom of heaven" [Matt. 5:10]. He that endureth to the end shall be saved [Matt. 10:22].

11. I strictly forbid all the brothers to have any association or conversation with women that may cause suspicion. And let them not enter nunneries, except those which the pope has given them special permission to enter. Let them not be intimate friends of men or women, lest on this account scandal arise among the brothers or about brothers.

12. If any of the brothers shall be divinely inspired to go among Saracens and other infidels they must get the permission to go from their provincial minister, who shall give his consent only to those who he sees are suitable to be sent. In addition, I command the ministers to ask the pope to assign them a cardinal of the holy Roman church, who shall be the guide, protector, and corrector of the brotherhood, in order that, being always in subjection and at the feet of the holy church, and steadfast in the catholic faith, they may observe poverty, humility, and the holy gospel of our Lord Jesus Christ, as we have firmly promised to do. Let no man dare act contrary to this confirmation. If anyone should, and so on.

8. *The Testament of St. Francis*

The Testament of St. Francis probably belongs to the year 1224; at any rate it was written shortly after the *Regula bullata* was promulgated. It is the Saint's last appeal to the brethren, asking them not to abandon the original inspiration of the order.

The translation is from Thatcher and McNeal, pp. 504–507.

1. While I was still in my sins, the Lord enabled me to begin to do penance in the following manner: It seemed to me bitterly unpleasant to see lepers, but the Lord led me among them and gave me pity for them. And when I left them, that which had been bitter to me was turned into sweetness of soul and body. And a short time afterward I left the world [that is, began the religious life].

2. And the Lord gave me such faith in churches that I knelt in simplicity and said, "We adore thee, most holy Lord Jesus Christ, and all thy churches which are in the world, and we bless thee because thou hast redeemed the world through thy holy cross."

3. Afterward the Lord gave, and still gives me, such faith in priests who live according to the form of the holy Roman church, because of their clerical character, that if they should persecute me I would still have recourse to them. And if I were as wise as Solomon and should find a poor priest in this world, I would not preach against his will in his church. And I wish to fear, love, and honor all priests as my lords. I am unwilling to think of sins in them, because I discern in them the Son of God, and they are my lords. And on this account, I wish to perceive in this world nothing of the most high Son of God except his most holy body and his most holy blood which they [the priests] receive in the sacraments, and they alone administer to others.

4. And these most holy mysteries I wish to honor and venerate above all things, and to put them up in honorable places.

5. And his most holy names and words, wherever I shall find them, in improper places, I wish to collect, and I ask that they be collected and put up in honorable places.

6. We ought to honor and venerate all theologians, who minister to us the divine word, as those who minister to us the spirit of life.

7. And afterward the Lord gave me brothers [that is, followers], and no one showed me what I ought to do, but the Lord himself revealed to me that I ought to live according to the form of the holy gospel, and I caused it to be written in a few simple words.

8. And the pope confirmed the rule. And those who came to adopt this life gave all they had to the poor. And we were content with one robe, mended within and without, and those who wished had a girdle and trousers.

9. We said the office as other clergymen, the laymen said Paternosters, and we gladly remained in the churches and we were simple and obedient.

10. And I labored with my hands, and I wish to labor. And I wish all my brothers to engage in some honest work. And those who do not know how, shall learn; not because of the desire to receive wages for their labor, but to set a good example and to escape idleness.

11. And when the wages for our labors are not given us, let us go to the table of the Lord and ask alms from door to door.

12. The Lord revealed to me this salutation that we should use it: "May the Lord give thee peace."

13. The brothers shall guard against receiving the churches and dwellings which are built for us, unless, as becomes the holy poverty which we have promised to observe in our rule, they always live there as pilgrims and strangers.

14. By their oath of obedience I firmly forbid the brothers, wherever they are, to ask for a letter from the papal court, either themselves or through another, in order to secure a church or any position, either in the hope of securing a place to preach, or because of persecution which they may suffer. But wherever they shall not be received, they shall flee to another place to do penance with the blessing of the Lord.

15. And I earnestly wish to obey the general minister of this brotherhood, and that guardian whom he may put over me. And I wish to be so entirely in his hands and so subject to his control that I cannot go, or do anything, contrary to his will, because he is my lord.

16. And although I am simple and infirm, I wish always to have a clergyman who may perform the office for me as is contained in the rule. And all other brothers are bound by their oaths to obey the guardians, and perform the office according to the rule.

17. And if any do not perform the office according to the rule, but wish to change it in some way, or if there are any who are not catholic, all the brothers are bound by their oath of obedience to report all such, wherever they may find them, to the nearest guardian. And the guardian must watch them night and day, as a man in chains, so that they cannot escape, until he delivers them into the hands of the general minister. And the general minister shall send them with brothers who shall guard them

night and day, as a man in chains, until they deliver them to the cardinal bishop of Ostia, who is the protector and corrector of this brotherhood.

18. And the brothers shall not say that this is another rule, because it is only a reminder, an admonition, an exhortation, and my testament, which I, your poor brother, Franciscus, make for you, my dear brothers, that we wholly observe the rule which we have promised to the Lord.

19. And the general minister and all the other ministers and guardians are bound by their oath of obedience not to add to, or take from, these words. But they shall always have this writing in addition to the rule, and in all the chapters when they read the rule they shall also read this. I strictly forbid all the brothers, clerical and lay, to put glosses [explanations] into the rule or this testament in order to change the simple meaning of their words. But as the Lord enabled me to say and to write the rule and these words simply and plainly, so you shall understand them simply and plainly and without gloss. And with holy works you shall observe them to the end.

20. And whoever shall observe them shall be filled in heaven with the blessing of the most high heavenly Father, and in the earth he shall be filled with the benedictions of His Son, with the most holy Spirit, the Paraclete, and with all the virtues of heaven and of all the saints. And I, your poor brother and servant, Franciscus, as far as I can, confirm to you, within and without, that most holy benediction. Amen.

Chapter Ten

The Triumph of Scholasticism

BETWEEN what I have termed the Twelfth Century Awakening and what I am here terming the Triumph of Scholasticism, there was a natural gap of about sixty years in the sense that between Gilbert of la Porrée and Robert Grosseteste (c.1175–1253) there is no outstanding intellectual figure. To be sure, much was happening in these years, but it was a type of activity which required a long period of germination before it bore fruit. Specifically, there were two agencies of change at work.

The most important of these changes, the product of the physical and intellectual expansion of the twelfth century, was the reception of the New Aristotle. The phrase is a broad one, including not only the natural philosophy of Aristotle but also the products of a thousand years of commentary and criticism as well as certain Neoplatonic works which passed for a time as Aristotelian. The intellectual difference between the twelfth and thirteenth centuries, in terms of content, lies precisely here. Where one absorbed Aristotle the logician, the other was forced to cope with Aristotle the metaphysician.

One of the first documents of this chapter shows the beginning of this great intellectual effort. Aristotle had immense prestige; already he was styled "the philosopher." Hence the new Aristotelian metaphysical works and their commentaries created a dilemma. The new works revealed "the philosopher" to have compounded a naturalistic world view which seemed to rival and on some points antithetical to traditional Christian beliefs. Within the first decade of the thirteenth century the New Aristotle had seduced Amaury of Béne and David of Dinant into heresy, and he would trouble the orthodoxy of many more before the century was out. The trouble was the New Aristotle could not merely be suppressed, Aristotle was too deeply imbedded in the curriculum of the schools; indeed, the church never attempted to do so. (The so-called prohibitions of the study of Aristotle, two of which appear below, have been misunderstood. With one exception they applied only to Paris, the showplace of medieval orthodoxy. And they did not prohibit private reading, only public teaching until such a time as his "errors" could be clearly marked out.) The New Aristotle could not be suppressed, it had to be dealt with; this was the governing intellectual fact of the thirteenth century.

The other force of change working to form the intellectual world of the thirteenth century was the formalization of higher education. The free and open educational system described by Abelard and John of Salisbury have hardened drastically by the time of the regulations of Robert de Courçon in 1215. No one ever asked Abelard for a degree nor did he, apparently, ever ask anyone for permission to teach. All this changed as the courses of study, times, dress—everything, became subject to precise regulation. One word describes this change: *universitas,* by definition a formalized, organized something, in this case a guild of masters or students.

The hardening of the curriculum, in the form it took, confirmed the worst fears of John of Salisbury. Dialectic, originally only a means to the end of eloquence and knowledge, now almost encompassed the curriculum. Except for a minimal grounding in grammar, the Old and New Logic prepared the student for the licentiate, and for the ambitious, a mastership in theology or one of the two laws. Both the *trivium* and *quadrivium* withered away as dialectic swallowed up the other liberal arts. Even grammar was treated in its logical aspects; rhetoric disappeared or was transformed into the *ars dictaminis,* a course in letter-writing and business forms. The effect of this may be seen not only in the general decline in the knowledge of foreign languages, mathematics and classical literature, but also in the effect it had on the Latin of the thirteenth century. Even in translation one should see that there is really no stylistic difference between Bonaventure, Aquinas, or Matthew of Aquasparta. Latin became a remarkably lucid scholarly instrument; for the same reason it became a poor literary vehicle, justly condemned by Renaissance humanists.

One other word sums up the intellectual tone of the thirteenth century: scholasticism. Despite the various definitions given the concept, scholasticism was surely at bottom the techniques and preoccupations of the men who taught at and were the products of the medieval university. I say university rather than school because I wish to retain that sense of rigidity and system which characterized it. The word scholasticism ought to call to mind the Gothic cathedral, the syllogism and the *summa;* in short, a passion for organization. It was a discipline, moreover, applied to the Christian faith. "It was an outlook," to quote Gordon Leff, "in which rational enquiry was governed by the assumptions of faith, the faith was supported by the powers of reason."

The dominating intellectual problem of the thirteenth century, as we have seen, was the attempt to reconcile the New Aristotle with the Christian faith. From a broader point of view this attempt was merely the last phase in a process which began two centuries before. It seemed possible, at last, to combine the natural knowledge of man and the revealed knowledge of faith into a coherent system, a *summa.* This was the aim of scholasticism.

The evolutionary character of the process, however, does not prevent us from labeling it "the philosophical revolution of the thirteenth century." For nearly a thousand years the Christian outlook had been exclusively theological. Now, although retaining in its fullness the supernatural life of the soul, the Christian world-view "admitted as a primary and valid, autonomous field of mental exercise, the realm of Nature, which included man, as grasped by the faculties given man at his creation as part of his natural endowment by the God of Nature."

The victory of the naturalistic philosophy based on Aristotle was not easy nor was it complete at the end of the century. There were three responses to the New Aristotle. The first, more a general attitude than a fixed body of belief, we shall call Augustinianism. The core of Augustinian thought, represented in the following selections by the Franciscan St. Bonaventure, was a theory (or attitude) of knowledge. Truth was immaterial, stemming ultimately from God rather than sensory impressions. The soul was a formally separate spiritual substance in which, once illumined by God, truth was innate. From this follows a distinctive attitude towards faith. Augustinians rejected the separation of philosophy from theology. The source of all truth was the same, God, therefore all knowledge was of the same order. Once the soul was illuminated by faith, the Christian could confidently examine its mysteries through reason since, God again being the sole source of truth, there could be no incompatibility between natural knowledge and revealed truth.

The second response, represented below by the Dominican Thomas Aquinas, is usually known as Christian Aristotelianism. In the hands of Aquinas it was a much more consistent position than Augustinianism both in its relation to Aristotle and in its doctrine of knowledge. What Aquinas did was to radically separate two spheres of knowledge—the natural knowledge man could have about the world and the revelations of the Christian faith. With Aristotle, Aquinas held that the sole source of human knowledge was sensory perception. This, while vindicating man's natural knowledge in its own sphere, philosophy, severely limited it in another, theology. It was not possible for man to know rationally such Christian mysteries as the Incarnation and the Trinity. Since man's natural knowledge came from contact with external reality, he could not by that means penetrate the mysteries of the faith.

The third position in respect to the New Aristotle used to be called Latin Averroism. Now it bears the unwieldy but more precise label of "integral, radical and unorthodox" Aristotelianism. Whereas the above positions stem from professional theologians of the mendicant orders, this one had its source from the arts faculty at Paris, i.e., from scholars interested primarily in pure philosophy. Their avowed aim was simply to expound the pure teaching of Aristotle in isolation from—their enemies at the time would have said regardless of—the Christian religion. Beyond this there is very little agreement. Whatever the motives and precise opinions of Siger of Brabant (c.1240–c.1283) and Boethius of Sweden, the best known of them, at least we may say that they aroused the wrath of the theological faculty at Paris, moved partly no doubt by professional jalousy, and the Papacy, concerned for orthodoxy. The memorable dispute which followed tore the university apart for about a decade beginning in 1266 and ended with the wholesale condemnation of integral Aristotelianism in 1277.

The principal intellectual features of the thirteenth century are apparent from the foregoing remarks. There was a general hardening of form. Where the twelfth century had been free and open, the thirteenth was closed and disciplined. The tendency to construct syntheses, already visible previously, took on greater scope. With its passion for order, the thirteenth century attempted to reconcile or at least define the limits of things which proved to be irreconcilable, only one of which, faith vs. reason, has been touched on above. Others were sacerdotal authority vs. individual religious experience and ecclesiastical authority vs. the sovereign national state. And, in keeping with the disciplined character of the century, its intellectual leaders were not the individualistic teachers and scholars of the preceding age; they were members of the mendicant orders.

The attempt at synthesis failed, and with that failure the Middle

Ages came to an end. In the next century, south of the Alps, the germ of a new civilization is visible. In the north, the Middle Ages merely fell apart. Where the thirteenth century had sought balance, the fourteenth sought extremes. Faith *or* reason was the cry, not a compromise between the two. There was a general breakdown of structure intellectually, socially, economically, as well as politically.

1. *University Life and Regulations*

The following are all taken from the translation of Lynn Thorndike, *University Records and Life in the Middle Ages* (New York: Columbia University Press, 1944), pp. 23–24, 26–27, 27–30, 33–35, 35–39, 52–56, 64–66, 66–67, 70–72, 75–78.

a. Bishop Stephen of Tournai to the Pope

Formerly abbot of Ste. Geneviève, Stephen became bishop of Tournai in 1192. The following letter was written to either Celestine III or Innocent III sometime between 1192 and his death in 1203.

HAVING obtained indulgence, let us speak to our lord, whose gentleness emboldens us, whose prudence sustains our inexperience, whose patience promises impunity. To this the authority of our ancestors compels us and a disease gradually insinuating whose ills, if not met at the start, will be incurable in the end. Nor do we say this, father, as if we wished to be censors of morals, or judges of doctors, or debaters of doctrines. This load requires stouter shoulders, and this battle awaits the robust frames of spiritual athletes. We merely wish to indicate the sore spot to your holy paternity, to whom God has given both the power to uproot errors and the knowledge to correct them.

The studies of sacred letters among us are fallen into the workshop of confusion, while both disciples applaud novelties alone and masters watch out for glory rather than learning. They everywhere compose new and recent *summulae* and commentaries, by which they attract, detain, and deceive their hearers, as if the works of the holy fathers were not still sufficient, who, we read, expounded holy scripture in the same spirit in which we believe the apostles and prophets composed it. They prepare strange and exotic courses for their banquet, when at the nutials of the son of the king of Taurus his own flesh and blood are killed and all prepared, and the wedding guests have only to take and eat what is set before them. Contrary to the sacred canons there is public disputation as to the incomprehensible deity; concerning the incarnation of the Word, verbose flesh and blood irreverently litigates. The indivisible Trinity is cut up and wrangled over in the trivia, so that now there are as many errors as doctors, as many scandals as classrooms, and as many blasphemies as squares. Again, if a case comes up which would be settled by canon law either under your jurisdiction or within that of the ordinary judges, there is produced from the vendors an inextricable forest of decretals presumably under the name of pope Alexander of sacred memory, and older canons are cast aside, rejected, expunged. When this plunder has been unrolled before us, those things which were wholesomely instituted in councils of holy fathers neither imposed form on councils nor an end to cases, since letters prevail which perchance advocates for hire invented and forged in their shops or cubicles under the name of Roman pontiffs. A new volume composed of these is solemnly read in the schools and offered for sale in the forum to the applause of a horde of notaries, who rejoice that in copying suspect opuscula both their labor is lessened and their pay increased. Two woes are the aforesaid, and lo, a third remains: faculties called liberal having lost their pristine liberty are sunk in such servitude that adolescents with long hair impudently usurp their professorships, and beardless youths sit in the seat of their seniors, and those who don't yet know how to be disciples strive to be named masters. And they write their *summulae* moistened with drool and dribble but unseasoned with the salt of philosophers. Omitting the rules of the arts and discarding the authentic books of the artificers, they seize the flies of empty words in the sophisms like the claws of spiders. Philosophy cries that her garments are torn and disordered and, modestly concealing her nudity by a few specific tatters, neither is consulted nor consoled as of old. All these things, father, call for the hand of apostolic correction, that the disorder in teaching, learning and disputing may be reduced to due form by your authority, that the divine word be not cheapened by vulgar handling, that it be not said on the street corners, "Lo Christ is here or lo He is there," lest what is holy be given to dogs and pearls be trodden under foot by swine.

b. Decree of the Bishops of Sens, Paris, etc., against Heretics and the Natural Philosophy of Aristotle (1210)

[Amaury de Bène, a theological doctor of Paris, died of chagrin, it is said, when he was forced to retract his doctrine that every believer was a member of Christ. His followers, presumably named above, were even more radical. David of Dinant was accused of interpreting Aristotle in a materialistic and pantheistic sense. The prohibition against Aristotle, involving the *Physics, On The Soul* and the *Metaphysics,* seems only to have involved public or private teaching, not personal reading.]

Let the body of master Amaury be removed from the cemetery and cast into unconsecrated ground, and the same be excommunicated by all the churches of the entire province. Bernard, William of Arria the goldsmith, Stephen priest of Old Corbeil, Stephen priest of Cella, John priest of Occines, Master William of Poitiers, Dudo the priest, Dominicus de Triangulo, Odo and Elinans clerks of St. Cloud—these are to be degraded and left to the secular arm. Urricus priest of Lauriac and Peter of St. Cloud, now a monk of St. Denis, Guarinus priest of Corbeil, and Stephen the clerk are to be degraded and imprisoned for life. The writings of David of Dinant are to be brought to the bishop of Paris before the Nativity and burned.

Neither the books of Aristotle on natural philosophy nor their commentaries are to be read at Paris in public or secret, and this we forbid under penalty of excommunication. He in whose possession the writings of David of Dinant are found after the Nativity shall be considered a heretic.

As for the theological books written in French we order that they be handed over to the diocesan bishops, both *Credo in deum* and *Pater noster* in French except the lives of the saints, and this before the Purification, because [then] he who shall be found with them shall be held a heretic.

c. Rules of the University of Paris (1215)

Robert, servant of the cross of Christ by divine pity cardinal priest of the title, St. Stephen in Mons Caelius, legate of the apostolic see, to all the masters and scholars of Paris eternal greeting in the Lord. Let all know that, since we have had a special mandate from the pope to take effective measures to reform the state of the Parisian scholars for the better, wishing with the counsel of good men to provide for the tranquillity of the scholars in the future, we have decreed and ordained in this wise:

No one shall lecture in the arts at Paris before he is twenty-one years of age, and he shall have heard lectures for at least six years before he begins to lecture, and he shall promise to lecture for at least two years, unless a reasonable cause prevents, which he ought to prove publicly or before examiners. He shall not be stained by any infamy, and when he is ready to lecture, he shall be examined according to the form which is contained in the writing of the lord bishop of Paris, where is contained the peace confirmed between the chancellor and scholars by judges delegated by the pope. . . . And they shall lecture on the books of Aristotle on dialectic old and new in the schools ordinarily and not *ad cursum* ["ordinary" lectures were the regular, formal morning lectures, "cursory" lectures, or "extraordinary" lectures were given later in the day; *cursor,* however, was frequently used to describe a bachelor giving a lecture course for practice in less depth than an ordinary one—this is probably the sense meant here]. They shall also lecture on both Priscians ordinarily or at least on one. They shall not lecture on feast days except on philosophers and rhetoric and the quadrivium and *Barbarismus* [the third book of the *Ars maior* of Donatus] and ethics, if it please them, and the fourth book of the *Topics*. They shall not lecture on the books of Aristotle on metaphysics and natural philosophy or on summaries of them or concerning the doctrine of master David of Dinant or the heretic Amaury or Mauritius of Spain [otherwise unknown unless *Mauri* is a corruption of Averroës.]

In the *principia* and meetings of the masters and in the responsions of oppositions of the boys and youths there shall be no drinking. They may summon some friends or associates, but only a few. Donations of clothing or other things as has been customary, or more, we urge should be made, especially to the poor. None of the masters lecturing in arts shall have a cope except one round, black and reaching to the ankles, at least while it is new. Use of the pallium is permitted. No one shall wear with the round cope shoes that are ornamented or with elongated pointed toes. If any scholar in arts or theology dies, half of the masters of arts shall attend the funeral at one time, the other half the next time, and no one shall leave until the sepulture is finished, unless he has reasonable cause. If any master in arts or theology dies, all the masters shall keep vigils, each shall read or cause to be read the Psalter, each shall attend the church where is celebrated the watch until midnight or the greater part of the night, unless reasonable cause prevent. On the day when the master is buried, no one shall lecture or dispute.

We fully confirm to them the meadow of St. Germain in that condition in which it was adjudicated to them.

Each master shall have jurisdiction over his scholar. No one shall occupy a classroom or house without asking the consent of the tenant, provided one has a chance to ask it. No one shall receive the licentiate from the chancellor or another for money given or promise made or other condition agreed upon. Also, the masters and scholars can make both between themselves and with other persons obligations and constitutions supported by faith or penalty or oath in these cases: namely, the murder or mutilation of a scholar or atrocious injury done a scholar, if justice should not be forthcoming, arranging the prices of lodgings, costume, burial, lectures and disputations, so, however, that the university be not thereby dissolved or destroyed.

As to the status of the theologians, we decree that no one shall lecture at Paris before his thirty-fifth year and unless he has studied for eight years at least, and has heard the books faithfully and in classrooms, and has attended lectures in theology for five years before he gives lectures himself publicly. And none of these shall lecture before the third hour on days when masters lecture. No one shall be admitted at Paris to formal lectures or to preachings unless he shall be of approved life and science. No one shall be a scholar at Paris who has no definite master.

Moreover, that these decrees may be observed inviolate, we by virtue of our legatine authority have bound by the knot of excommunication all who shall contumaciously presume to go against these our statutes, unless within fifteen days after the offense they have taken care to emend their presumption before the university of masters and scholars or other persons constituted by the university. Done in the year of Grace 1215, the month of August.

c. Invitation to Toulouse (1229)

After the Albigensian Crusade, Count Raymond of Toulouse agreed to establish a university to combat any further outbreak of heresy. The following advertisement was directed mostly towards Paris where the university had dissolved itself after a dispute with local authorities.

To all Christ's faithful and especially to masters and scholars studying in any land who may see this letter, the university of masters and scholars of Toulouse, about to plant a new studium, wish continued good life with a blessed end. No undertaking has a stable foundation which is not firmly placed in Christ, the foundation of holy mother church. We therefore with this in mind are trying in Christ with all our might to lay the permanent foundation of a philosophic school at Toulouse, on which others may build with us whose good will is lighted to this by luminous rays of the Holy Spirit. For blessed Augustine says, "God prepares good will to be aided and aids it when prepared. He indeed causes the unwilling to will and aids the willing lest he will in vain." Therefore, most cherished, do ye will with us to prepare good will for the Lord which, when he finds prepared, he will lead on to holy works, so that where once swords cleaved a path for you, you shall fight with a sharp tongue; where war waged carnage, you shall militate with peaceful doctrine; where the forest of heretical depravity scattered thorns, the cedar of catholic faith shall be reared by you to the stars.

And lest the approach of so much labor terrify you, we have prepared the way for you, we have sustained the first hardships, we offer you the standard of security so that, with us preceding as your armbearers, you soldiers of philosophy may be able to fight the more safely with the art of Mercury, the weapons of Phoebus, and lance of Minerva. That ye may again have hope for the stability of the new university we have undertaken the load enjoined by the authority of the church. For our Moses was the lord cardinal and legate in the realm of France, leader and protector and author after God and the pope of so arduous a beginning, who decreed that all studying at Toulouse, both masters and disciples, should obtain plenary indulgence of all their sins. Therefore for this cause and because of the continuity of lecturing and disputing which the masters exercise more diligently and frequently than they did at Paris, many scholars are flocking to Toulouse, seeing that flowers have already appeared in our land and the time of putation is at hand.

Therefore let no Deidamia detain our Achilles going forth to philosophic war, that he attain not this second Troy, of which our Toulousan Statius might sing once more:

> All honor there, there great names strive;
> Fearful mothers and groups of virgins
> With difficulty remain idle.
> Here he is condemned to many sterile years
> And hateful to God, if sluggishly
> He lets this new glory pass him by.

So let each upright man put on the warlike mien of Achilles, lest meticulous Thersites take the laurel promised to the magnanimous Ajax, so that at least, the war finished, he may admire the zeal of the militant and the zeal of the philosophizing. And that the studious may more willingly know the glory of Toulouse and its university, let them know that this is the second land of promise flowing with milk and honey, green with lush pastures, where fruit trees are leafing, where Bacchus reigns in vineyards, where Ceres rules in fields, where the temperate air was preferred by the ancient philosophers to other stations of earth. O, how incomprehensible are the greatnesses of almighty God!

> Here is peace, elsewhere Mars rages in all the world.
> But this place received Mars and death formerly.

Further, that ye may not bring hoes to sterile and uncultivated fields, the professors at Toulouse have cleared away for you the weeds of the rude populace and thorns of sharp sterility and other obstacles. For here theologians inform their disciples in pulpits and the people at the crossroads, logicians train the tyros in the arts of Aristotle, grammarians fashion the tongues of the stammering on analogy, organists smooth the popular ears with the sweet-throated organ, decretists extol Justinian, and physicians Galen. Those who wish to scrutinize the bosom of nature to the inmost can hear here the books of Aristotle which were forbidden at Paris.

What then will you lack? Scholastic liberty? By no means, since tied to no one's apron strings you will enjoy your own liberty. Or do you fear the malice of the raging mob or the tyranny of an injurious prince? Fear not, since the liberality of the count of Toulouse affords us sufficient security both as to our salary and our servants coming to Toulouse and returning home. But if they suffer loss of their property through the hands of brigands in the domain of the count, he will pursue our malefactors with forces of the capitol of Toulouse, the same as on behalf of the citizens of Toulouse. To what has been said we add further that, as we hope truly, the lord legate will summon other theologians and decretists here to enlarge the university and will set a time when scholars ought to spend at Toulouse to receive the indulgence, if that prevaricator envious of the human race does not impede their stay, which God forbid, that henceforth they may magnify the place and the folk of Romanus, fighting by the salubrious triumphal mystery of the cross.

As for prices, what has already been said should reassure you [of] the fact that there is no fear of a failure of crops. On this point you may trust both report and the nuncio and these verses:

> For a little, wine, for a little, bread is had;
> For a little, meat, for a little, fish is bought.

The courtesy of the people should not be passed over. For here is seen that courtly good humor has struck a covenant with knighthood and clergy. So if you wish to marvel at more good things than we have mentioned, leave home behind, strap your knapsack on your back, and make your motto the words of Seneca: "I shall see all lands as mine, mine as of all; I shall so live that I shall know I am known to others, for to aim high and have enlarged ideas is characteristic of a noble soul."

d. Regulations for the University of Paris (1231)

During the carnival of 1228–29 a riot broke out between some of the students and townsmen of Paris. Although the students were mostly at fault, during the course of it the prévôt of Paris and his men massacred a group of students innocently playing games outside the walls. When it failed to get retribution the university disbanded for almost two years until Gregory IX, squarely on the side of the university, gave it virtual immunity from local secular and ecclesiastical officials. The following bull, *Parens scientiarum,* the last of a series, has been called the Magna Carta of the university.

Gregory, bishop, servant of the servants of God, to his cherished sons, the masters and scholars of Paris, greeting and apostolic benediction. Paris, parent of sciences, like another Cariath Sepher, city of letters, shines clear, great indeed but raising still greater hopes in teachers and pupils, where, as it were in wisdom's special workshop, veins of silver have their beginning and there is a proper place for forging gold, from which those prudent in mystic eloquence stamp golden earrings vermiculated with silver, fabricate necklaces adorned with precious stones, nay fit and decorate the spouse of Christ with priceless jewels. There iron is mined, whose earthy fragility is solidified by firmness, and from which is made the breastplate of faith, sword of the spirit, and other armor of Christian soldiery, potent against the powers aerial. And the ore dissolved by heat is turned to copper, because while stony hearts flame with the fervor of the Holy Spirit, they take fire and are made to herald praises of Christ in sounding preaching. Wherefore there is no doubt that he would gravely please God and men who in the said city should strive in any way to disturb such signal grace or who should not openly oppose those disturbing it with all his might and main. Hence, since concerning dissension arisen there by instigation of the devil, greatly disturbing the university, we have diligently considered that they should be quieted by moderate provision rather than judicial sentence.

Concerning the state therefore of schools and scholars we decree that these things are to be observed: namely, that every chancellor of Paris to be named henceforth shall swear in good faith on his conscience, at the time and place according to the state of the city and honor and respect of the faculties, that he will not bestow the licentiate to teach theology or decretals except to the worthy nor admit the unworthy, ratification by persons and nations being abolished. But before he shall license anyone, within three months from the time of the petty license, in the presence of all masters of theology in the city and other respectable and learned men by whom the truth can be learned, he shall make diligent inquiry as to the life, knowledge, facility, and also the promise and hope of success and other points which are required in such cases, and, having made such inquiry, according to what seems proper and expedient he shall give or deny according to his conscience the license asked for. The masters, moreover, of theology and decretals, when they begin to lecture, shall publicly take oath that they will furnish faithful testimony on the aforesaid points. The chancellor shall also swear that he will in no wise reveal the advice of the masters to their hurt, maintaining in their integrity the Parisian rules, liberty and law which obtain in incepting.

Concerning the medical men and artists and others the chancellor promises to examine the masters in good faith, to repel the unworthy and admit only the deserving.

But because, where there is no order, horror easily creeps in, we have conceded to you the functions of making due constitutions or ordinances as to the method and hour of lectures and disputations, as to the costume to be worn, as to funerals of the dead, and also, concerning the bachelors, who should lecture and at what hour and on what subject, as to rentals of lodgings or even their prohibition, and of duly punishing rebels against those constitutions or ordinances by expulsion from your society. And if it chance that the rental of lodgings is taken from you or that—which God forbid—injury or enormous excess be inflicted on you or any of you, such as death or mutilation of a limb, unless, after due complaint has been lodged, satisfaction is given within fifteen days, it shall be permitted you to suspend lectures until condign satisfaction is given. And if any of you shall have been unjustly imprisoned, it shall be right for you, unless the injury ceases when complaint is made, to stop lectures immediately, if it shall seem expedient.

We order, moreover, that the bishop of Paris so punish the excesses of delinquents that the honor of the scholars is preserved and crimes do not remain unpunished; but because of delinquents the innocent shall not suffer, nay, if probable suspicion shall arise against anyone, after honorable detention on furnishing suitable bail he shall be dismissed and exactions of the jailers cease. But if he has committed a crime which calls for imprisonment, the bishop shall retain the culprit in prison, it being utterly forbidden to the chancellor to have a prison of his own. We further prohibit that a scholar henceforth be arrested for debt, since this is forbidden by the canons and lawful sanctions. But neither the bishop nor his official nor the chancellor shall require a fine for raising an excommunication or any other censure, nor shall the chancellor demand from licentiates an oath or obedience or other pledge, nor shall he receive any emolument or promise for conceding the licence, abiding by the terms of his oath named above.

Furthermore, the summer vacation shall henceforth not exceed a month, and in vacation time the bachelors may continue their lectures if they wish. Moreover, we expressly enjoin that scholars shall not go about town armed, and that the university shall not defend disturbers of the peace and of studies. And those who pretend to be scholars but do not attend classes or have any master shall by no means enjoy the privileges of scholars.

We further order that masters of arts always give one ordinary reading of Priscian and one other afterwards, and those books on nature which were prohibited in provincial council for certain cause they shall not use at Paris until these shall have been examined and purged from all suspicion of errors. Moreover, the masters and scholars of theology shall strive to exercise themselves praiseworthily in the faculty which they profess and not show themselves philosophers but endeavor to know God, nor speak in the vernacular nor confound the Hebrew popular language with the Azotic, but dispute in the schools concerning those questions only which can be settled by theological works and the treatises of the holy fathers.

Furthermore, concerning the goods of scholars who die intestate or do not commit the care of their affairs to others, we have decided to provide thus, namely, that the bishop and one of the masters whom the university shall ordain for this, receiving all the goods of the defunct and depositing them in a safe and fit place, shall set a day by which his death can have been announced in his native place and those upon whom the succession to his goods devolves can come to Paris or delegate an appropriate messenger; and if they come or send, the goods shall be restored to them with a security which has been determined. But if no one appears, then the bishop and master shall use the goods for the soul of the defunct as they see fit, unless it chance that the heirs for some just cause cannot come, in which case the disposition shall be deferred to a suitable time.

But since the masters and scholars who suffered injury and damage from the breaking of the oath made to them by the city of Paris have departed from the university, they seem to have pled not so much their own case as the common cause. We, with the general need and utility of the church in view, will and order that henceforth the privileges shall be shown to the masters and scholars by our dearest son in Christ, the illustrious king of France, and fines inflicted on their malefactors, so that they may lawfully study at Paris without any further delay or return of infamy or irregularity of notation. To no man then be it licit to infringe or with rash daring to contradict this page of our provision, constitution and inhibition. If anyone shall presume to attempt this, let him know that he will incur the wrath of almighty God and of the blessed apostles Peter and Paul. Given at the Lateran on the Ides of April, the fifth year of our pontificate.

f. Statutes of the English Nation Concerning Bachelors of Arts Who Are to Determine during Lent (1252)

Determining was the first stage on the road to becoming a Master of Arts. As a bachelor the student merely applied himself to the lectures and texts prescribed above. After passing the examination on them he then determined, i.e., held public disputations during the first half of Lent which signified his change in status from scholar to part-time teacher under the direction of his master, with whom he continued to study.

In the year since the Incarnation, 1251, the masters of the English nation, teaching in arts at Paris and for the good of the university and of learning taking multifold measures, and by God's grace continuing in the future without diminution, decreed by their common counsel and that of good men the form noted below for bachelors in arts determining in Lent, as is the custom. In the first place the proctor, touching the Bible, shall select two persons whom he believes qualified to choose examiners of those determining, who, touching the Bible, shall swear that without hate or love of any person or any part of their nation, they will choose three masters, whom they know to be strict and qualified in examining faithfully, more intent on the promotion and advantage of the university, less susceptible to prayer or bribe. These three when chosen shall similarly swear on the Bible that they will faithfully examine and proceed with rigor of examination, licentiating the worthy and conducting themselves without hate of any person or group of their nation, also without envy or any rancor of mind or other sinister perturbation. Moreover, those who have insufficient standing in the examination and are unworthy to pass they shall fail, sparing no one, moved neither by prayer nor bribe nor fear nor love or any other occasion or indirect favor of persons.

The masters presenting candidates, moreover, and the bachelors themselves shall give personal security that they will make no entreaties on behalf of bachelors nor seek favor from the examiners or from the nation or from the university, either by themselves or through others, but will accept the simple statement of the examiners. By the same token, if it happens that bachelors are failed, that they will not bring contumely or complaints or threats or other evils against the examiners, either by themselves or through others, because they ought to suppose that the examiners have acted according to their consciences and good faith for the honor of the university and the nation.

Moreover, a bachelor coming up for the licentiate in arts at Paris should be twenty years old or at least in his twentieth year, and of honorable life and laudable conversation. He should not have a cope without a hood of the same cloth or a hood with knots. He should not wear a mitre on his head in the classrooms while he is determining. If he has the right to the tonsure, he may have the tonsure, nor may he or should he be blamed on this account. Also before he is admitted to examination he shall give personal security that he has his own classroom of a master under whom he seeks the license of determining, or a bachelor about to incept in arts at the latest before Lent, in whose classroom he will determine. Further, that he has attended lectures in arts for five years or four at least at Paris continuously or elsewhere in a university of arts. Further, that he has heard the books of Aristotle on the Old Logic, name the *Praedicamenta* and *Periarmeniae* at least twice in ordinary lectures and once cursorily, the *Six Principles* at least once in ordinary lectures and once cursorily, the three first books of the *Topics* and the *Divisions* once in ordinary lectures or at least cursorily, the *Topics* of Aristotle and *Elenchi* twice in ordinary lectures and once at least cursorily or if not in cursorily at least thrice in ordinary, the *Prior Analytics* once in ordinary lectures and once cursorily, or, if he is now attending, so that he has heard half before Lent and is to continue, the *Posterior Analytics* once in ordinary lectures completely. Also that he shall have heard *Priscian minor* (books 17–18) and the *Barbarismus* twice in ordinary lectures and at least once cursorily, *Priscian major* (books 1–6) once cursorily. Also he shall have heard *De anima* once or be hearing it as aforesaid. Also he shall give satisfaction that he has diligently attended the disputations of masters in a recognized university for two years and for the same length of time has answered concerning sophisms in class. Also he shall promise that he will respond to question for a full year from the beginning of one Lent to the beginning of the next.

If moreover, a bachelor shall be found sufficiently qualified in knowledge according to the examiners and shall not have completed the required number of years or books or lectures, the nation reserves to itself the power to dispense with these, as shall seem expedient to it. And in such case only it shall be permissible for his master to petition the nation for him.

Also, if after the exercise of cursory lectures has been made and finally completed, he shall have transgressed in the said exercise in any way, he shall in no case be admitted to the examination for determination. Nor similarly shall a master, whether now teaching or not, who, after the said exercise has been made as stated and finally confirmed by the masters, shall have transgressed in the said exercise, be accepted as presenting a bachelor, until full satisfaction shall have been made to the rector or proctors for the university by the master or the bachelor who has transgressed.

Also the bachelor licensed to determine shall begin to determine at the latest on the next day after Brandons [i.e., the first week in Lent]. If he shall not have begun to determine then, he shall not be allowed to do so during Lent. And from the said Monday he shall determine continuously till the middle of Lent, unless he shall have lawful case excusing him. And then let it be licit for no one to determine for him as a substitute, unless such substitute has the license to teach in arts at Paris or has determined elsewhere through Lent or is licensed to determine in that present Lent, always providing that the same shall have determined continuously from the said Monday following Brandons until the middle of Lent. Also if a bachelor shall have been licensed to determine in the arts at Paris in one year and from a legitimate cause shall have failed to determine in that Lent in which he was licensed, which sometimes happens, he may afterwards determine in some subsequent Lent, regularly however and as others do, but he shall not substitute for others unless he shall have first determined during Lent in a fixed place. Also, until he shall have paid for the university a sum such and so great as he offered for personal security, and another for the nation, he shall not be given the license to determine. Also if at the latest he shall not have been licensed before the last Sunday before Lent, he shall not be admitted later that year to the examination for determination.

Also, it shall be enjoined on him that all through Lent, and thereafter so long as he shall belong to the faculty of arts as student or teacher, he shall obey the mandate of rector and proctor in lawful and honorable matters. Also he shall not give drinks except on the first day he begins to determine and the last, unless this is done by the permission of the rector or the proctor of his nation, who can give him a dispensation in this regard as shall seem expedient to them, considering nevertheless the many factors about the determiners which are here involved.

Also, the examiners shall diligently collect from the bachelors the money to be paid to the university and nation and faithfully keep what is collected, and at the summons of the rector and proctors of the four nations deposit it at the day set in the common chest of the university of artists. Also the money received for the nation they shall deposit in the common chest before the Sunday after Ash Wednesday. Also none of the said examiners can by himself, without his associates deputed with him for determinations, license anyone or presume alone to examine.

Also, in addition to the aforesaid, after the candidates shall have been licensed, let them be present every Friday at the Vespers of the blessed Virgin and at mass the Saturday following, until Palm Sunday, under the penalty by which masters are bound.

But inasmuch as by this form it is not right nor will be for rich or poor, noble or ignoble, to put it off later, if they do not appear to seek license of determining in the aforesaid manner, therefore, to notify them it is provided by the masters that the present form be twice announced in classes each year, so that the first time it shall be read in the classrooms of masters between Purification and Lent, and the other time between the feast of St. Remy and All Saints or thereabouts when there shall be a general meeting. Moreover, individual masters shall be bound on their honor to observe this ordinance. Also, however, if anyone is found acting contrary to the said ordinance, he shall be suspended from lecturing for a month.

g. The Arts Course at Paris (1255)

In the year of the Lord 1254. Let all know that we, all and each, masters of arts by our common assent, no one contradicting, because of the new and incalculable peril which threatens in our faculty—some masters hurrying to finish their lectures sooner than the length and difficulty of the texts permits, for which reason both masters in lecturing and scholars in hearing make less progress—worrying over the ruin of our faculty and wishing to provide for our status, have decreed and ordained for the common utility and the reparation of our university to the honor of God and the church universal that all and single masters of our faculty in the future shall be required to finish the texts which they shall have begun on the feast of St. Remy [i.e., October 1] at the times below noted, not before.

The Old Logic, namely the book of Porphyry, the *Praedicamenta, Periarmeniae, Divisions* and *Topics* of Boethius, except the fourth, on the feast of the Annunciation of the blessed Virgin [i.e., March 25] or the last day for lectures preceding. *Priscian minor* and *major, Topics* and *Elenchi, Prior* and *Posterior Analytics* they must finish in the said or equal time. The *Ethics* through four books in twelve weeks, if they are read with another text; if *per se,* not with another, in half that time. Three short texts, namely *Sex principia, Barbarismus,* Priscian on accent, if read together and nothing else with them, in six weeks. The *Physics* of Aristotle, *Metaphysics,* and *De animalibus* on the feast of St. John the Baptist [i.e., June 24], *De caelo et mundo,* first book of *Meteorology* with the fourth, on Ascension day [i.e., a moveable feast, 40 days after Easter]; *De anima,* if read with the books on nature, on the feast of the Ascension, if with the logical texts, on the feast of the Annunciation of the blessed Virgin; *De generatione* on the feast of the Chair of St. Peter [i.e., February 22]; *De causis* in seven weeks; *De sensu et sensato* in six weeks; *De sompno et vigilia* in five weeks; *De plantis* in five weeks; *De memoria et Reminiscentia* in two weeks; *De morte et vita* in one week. Moreover, if masters begin to read the said books at another time than the feast of St. Remy, they shall allow as much time for lecturing on them as is indicated above. Moreover, each of the said texts, if read by itself, not with another text, can be finished in half the time of lecturing assigned above. It will not be permitted anyone to finish the said texts in less time, but anyone may take more time. Moreover, if anyone reads some portion of a text, so that he does not wish, or is unable, to complete the whole of it, he shall read that portion in a corresponding amount of time.

If a bachelor shall incept before the feast of St. Denis [i.e., October 9] he may end his lectures with those resuming on the feast of the blessed Remy. Those who begin after the feast of St. Denis shall finish their texts by as much later as they began later than others. Each in good faith shall according to his estimate portion out his text proportionally to the time allowed for his lectures. Further, no one shall be allowed to give more than two ordinary lectures, nor to make them extraordinary, nor to give them except at the ordinary hour and in ordinary wise.

Moreover, from the feast of St. John the Baptist till the feast of St.

Remy each shall arrange his lectures as shall seem most convenient for himself and his auditors. Also no one shall presume to give more than two cursory lectures on any day when lectures are held, nor more than three on a day when there are not regular lectures, nor to begin any course until he has finished the preceding course, unless he shall have been detained by serious illness over fifteen days or shall have been out of town for good reason more than fifteen days, or if the scholars do not want to hear him further. Also, no one shall be permitted to deliver any lectures on the days of the apostles and evangelists or on the three days immediately following Christmas, Easter, and Pentecost, or after the third hour on the eve of those three days. These things, moreover, we have decreed and ordained to be observed inviolate. Let no one, therefore, infringe this page of our ordinance or rashly go against it. But should anyone presume to attempt this, let him know that he will incur the wrath of the whole university and suspension of lectures for a year. In testimony and support of which thing we have decreed that the present letter be sealed with the seals of the four nations by their consent. Given in the year 1254 on the Friday before Palm Sunday.

h. Odofredus Announces His Law Lectures at Bologna

If you please, I will begin the *Old Digest* on the eighth day or thereabouts after the feast of St. Michael [i.e., September 29] and I will finish it entire with all ordinary and extraordinary, Providence permitting, in the middle of August or thereabouts. The *Code* I will always begin within about a fortnight of the feast of St. Michael and I will finish it with all ordinary and extraordinary, Providence permitting, on the first of August or thereabouts. The extraordinary lectures used not to be given by the doctors. And so all scholars including the unskilled and novices will be able to make good progress with me, for they hear their text as a whole, nor will anything be left out, as was once done in this region, indeed was the usual practice. For I shall teach the unskilled and novices but also the advanced students. For the unskilled will be able to make satisfactory progress in the position of the case and exposition of the letter; the advanced students can become more erudite in the subtleties of questions and contrarieties. I shall also read all the glosses, which was not done before my time.

For it is my purpose to teach you faithfully and in a kindly manner, in which instruction the following order has customarily been observed by the ancient and modern doctors and particularly by my master, which method I shall retain. First, I shall give you the summaries of each title before I come to the text. Second, I shall put forth well and distinctly and in the best terms I can the purport of each law. Third, I shall read the text in order to correct it. Fourth, I shall briefly restate the meaning. Fifth, I shall solve conflicts, adding general matters (which are commonly called *brocardica*) and subtle and useful distinctions and questions with the solutions, so far as divine Providence shall assist me. And if any law is deserving of a review by reason of its fame or difficulty, I shall reserve it for an afternoon review.

i. Statutes Concerning Studies in the Dominican Order (1259)

At Paris, license of lecturing in theology should not be sought for any brother, nor should one licensed incept, nor one lecturing leave off, except by advice of the master, if he shall be in the province of France, or by advice of the provincial prior of France, if the master of the order in not in France.

At Valenciennes in the year of the Lord 1259 by mandate of the master and those on the committee for education it was ordained by brothers Bonhomme, Florentius, Albertus Teutonicus [i.e., Albertus Magnus], Thomas Aquinas, Petrus de Tarantasia [later Pope Innocent V], masters of theology at Paris, who were present at the said chapter, that lecturers should not be occupied with acts and business by which they would be taken from their lectures.

Also, that provincial priors should seek diligently for youths apt for study, who could make rapid progress, and promote them in the university.

Also, that such a search be made annually by visitors in single convents and reported to the provincial chapter.

Also, that brothers should not be sent to universities, except those of good character and likely to make progress.

Also, that, if in any province lecturers cannot be had in all convents, it shall at least be provided that brothers, and especially youths, do not remain always in those convents but be sent to places where there are lecturers.

Also, that, if lecturers cannot be found qualified to lecture publicly, at least some be provided to give private lectures or histories or a *Summa* of cases, or something else of that sort, so that the brothers may not be idle.

Also, that young brothers apt for study be spared from discourses and other occupations, so as not to withdraw them from study.

Also, that there be established in provinces which require it some school of arts or place where youth are instructed.

Also, that brothers who stay away from classes be severely punished.

Also, that the brothers at the hour of lecture shall not be occupied in celebrating masses or other things of this sort nor go to town except for real necessity.

Also, that even the priors attend classes, like the other brothers, when they conveniently can.

Also, that lecturers on vacation attend classes and especially disputations.

Also, that lecturers be not made either preachers or confessors, unless they are capable of performing offices of this sort without notable peril.

Also, that priors and visitors and the masters of the brothers take pains to inquire carefully how the brothers and especially the young are occupied with study and what progress they are making, and punish the negligent.

Also, that lecturers continue their lectures as much as possible.

Also, that the visitors each year diligently inquire of the lecturers how much they lecture in a year and how many questions they have disputed and also determined, and how many convents of their visitation lack lecturers. And that whatever they shall find about this they shall report to the provincial chapter; and also the more notable defects which they have found the provincial prior and representatives shall refer afterwards to the chapter general.

Also, that in every province each year in each provincial chapter it be ordained how to provide for the students of their province who are sent to some university.

Also, the visitors shall diligently inquire how provision is made for the students and report notable defects to the provincial chapter by which an efficacious remedy shall be applied.

Also, provision shall be made that every lecturer occupying a professorial chair shall have a bachelor who shall lecture under him.

Also, that brothers carry to class the books which are read in class, if they have them, and no others.

Also, that in every convent where there is a lecturer there be instituted some brother who shall diligently repeat, provided there is anyone qualified in the convent.

Also, that repetitions be made concerning questions and collations concerning questions once a week, where this can be conveniently observed.

j. Foundation and Regulations for the College of the Treasurer at Paris (1268 and 1280)

To all who shall see these, William of Sâone, treasurer of the church of Rouen, greeting in the Lord. You should know that, since I have acquired, both in the city of Rouen and outside, possessions and rents to the amount of £120 17s. 5d. of Tours, of which express mention is made in letters of the lord king, to be committed to pious uses and the good of the poor, I, of healthy body and sane mind, wishing, from the wealth given me by God and acquired, to apply some to the uses of the church universal and the advantage of the poor, especially in those things which seem directly to regard the profit of souls, of the said good thus ordain and dispose even by donation while living, namely, that twelve students of theology, if the amount of goods and time permit, remaining together in one house at Paris or elsewhere where a university is located, shall have each three solidi of Paris per week through 45 weeks, the term beginning from the feast of St. Denis or thereabouts. Also, that twelve other poor students in liberal arts, if sometime there may be, shall have from the said rents 25 pounds of Tours for housing and for bread with the goodwill of the said theologians. I will further ordain that all the said scholars be chosen, when the need arises, by the two archdeacons of Grand-Caux and Petit-Caux, if in those two places they find sufficient and fit persons, or if not from the two Caux, at least from the whole diocese of Rouen. And such shall be chosen, so far as the theologians are concerned, as have taught well in liberal arts, and, so far as both are concerned, as are praiseworthy and upright in morals.

I further will and ordain that, if the said theologians or any of them shall have studied theology six years or have secured some sufficient benefice, then others shall be chosen in their place . . . , unless one of them reaches such a repute for knowledge that he can give public lectures in the classroom of some master of theology, in which case let him remain, if he will, until he is able to ascend the magisterial throne. . . .

I further will and ordain that two of the said theologians, to be selected similarly, remain during the vacation period, namely for seven weeks, to guard the house and its contents.

Moreover, for the support of the said theologians I give by donation, while living, the house which I bought at Paris from William called Fructuarius near the Harp in the parish of St. Severinus. I give to the same for the use of all and each a complete theological *Corpus:* namely, Bibles with text only but complete, also all the books glossed and some in duplicate, with sufficient *Postillae* and lectures, and certain moral *Summae,* with sermons of varied compilation. Also several volumes of the *Sentences* with *Summae* and several sets of *Questions.* Also several originals and many other writings of which all the names are contained in a letter sealed with my seal.

And the said theologians shall stay together for convenience in using the library and making collations in turn and for many other reasons. And the liberal arts students, if there are any, shall likewise stay together both for convenience in study and for good behavior and in token of probity. Also, the said theologians, shall swear annually to keep the statutes which I have made for them, as is contained more fully in my letters giving them in detail. . . .

August 18, 1280

To all who shall see these, William of Sâone, treasurer of Rouen, greeting in the Lord. Know that we have regulated the life of our scholars studying at Paris in this way which follows. First, we will that those who have scholarships give all their time to theology and make visible progress, having the proper books and other things essential. And if they have clerics working for them in town or if they labor for others in another subject of study, we do not wish to give them a scholarship, since our intention is to provide merely for true and pure poor students who study assiduously and to support them. We say the same of those who have acquired some sufficient benefice, on receiving which they should give way to the poverty of others. Also, if any one of them should be contentious or quarrelsome, impeding the others and disturbing the peace, we do not wish to continue his scholarship, unless he shall speedily correct himself. We say the same of those who have been of evil life or repute, and we wish that the others be required to reveal such to us or to someone by whom we may be informed, because we have no intention of providing for the perverse and unstudious and ribald and gamesters or haunters of whores and taverns, but for good and true scholars, through whom provision may be made for the church and salvation of souls.

Also, we do not want any rich student to live with them, who may provoke them to spending too much or impede their progress. If, however, our said scholars receive some quiet rich student among them, we will that they be required to pay twenty solidi Parisian for his room. Also, we do not want anyone to live with them who does not give all his time to theology. Also, we are unwilling that the books be lent about town to be copied or even studied, because thus they might be lost or mutilated or soiled, and we want the care of them entrusted to persons who can answer for them fully and who shall distribute and divide them among the rest as shall seem expedient.

We also will and ordain that the senior scholar, once a week on Sunday or other feast day, shall interview the rest at some hour convenient to him and, when all have gathered in his presence, shall see and hear how they have been doing and shall correct them, if he finds any excess among them. And if any one of them ought to be expelled, this should be done with the counsel of the rest, and if he shall have found anyone rebellious or not making progress, they shall expel him with severity.

And we wish that all, at least while in the house, speak Latin. And we want the others to be required to tell the truth about each equal or to accuse others, unless of their own accord these recognize and confess their fault, in which case they shall be dealt with more gently and leniently.

So far as food is concerned, they should not be divided but should receive together what the house provides, and he who has done contrary shall be expelled.

Also, we will that after they have been licensed in theology, they lecture only two years, because beyond that we are unwilling to give them anything, since our intention is merely to put them in a position to attain the degree of master of theology. Also, if any one of them binds himself to the service of any rich man or other, we do not wish to give him any thing, because our intention is to aid good students and not those who are not apt to advance in theology. . . .

2. The Philosophical Revolution of the Thirteenth Century

a. St. Bonaventure

Giovanni di Fidanza (1221–74) was an Italian by birth. Entering the Franciscan order between 1238 and 1243, he studied at Paris under Alexander of Hales and taught there from 1248–55. In 1257 he became the first Franciscan to receive the doctorate in theology at Paris. In the same year he was elected governor general of his order. Intellectually, he was the chief representative of the Augustinian position in theology.

The following selection is from his *Disputed Questions Concerning Christ's Knowledge*. The translation is by Eugene R. Fairweather, *A Scholastic Miscellany: Anselm to Ockham* (Philadelphia: Westminster Press, 1956), pp. 379–401. Used by permission.

Question Four: *Whether Whatever is Known by Us with Certitude is Known in the Eternal Reasons Themselves.*

I

Arguments for and against the Thesis

It is presupposed that the eternal reasons are really indistinct in the divine art of knowledge. The question is whether they are the grounds of knowing in all certain knowledge. To ask this is to ask whether whatever is known by us with certitude is known in the eternal reasons themselves. And that this is so is evident from manifold authority.

1. Augustine, *On the Teacher:* "Referring to all the things which we understand, we consult, not the speaker who utters words, but the guardian-truth within the mind itself. . . . Moreover, he who is consulted teaches; for he who is said to reside in the inner man is Christ, . . . the unchangeable excellence of God and his everlasting wisdom, which every rational soul does indeed consult."

2. Again, the same, *On the True Religion:* "It is clear that there

exists, above our mind, a norm which is called truth. It is already incontestable that this immutable nature, which is above the human mind, is God. . . . For this is that immutable truth, which is rightly called the norm of all the arts and the art of the almighty Artificer."

3. Again, Augustine, in the second book of *On Free Will:* "That beauty of wisdom and truth . . . neither passes with time or changes with locality. It is not interrupted by night or shut off by shadow, nor is it subject to the bodily senses. To all those turned to it from the whole world, who love it, it is near; to all it is everlasting; it is in no place, it is never lacking; it warns without, it teaches within. . . . No one judges it, and without it no one judges rightly; and thus it is manifest, without doubt, that it is greater than our minds, since by it alone each mind is made wise, and judges, not concerning it, but through it concerning other things." But if you say that it follows from this that we see *by* the reasons, but not *in* the truth or *in* the reasons, there is Augustine to the contrary, in the twelfth book of the *Confessions:* "Suppose that both of us see that what you say is true, and both again see that what I say is true, where, I ask you, do we see it? In truth, I do not see it in you, or you in me, but both of us see it in the selfsame unchangeable Truth, which is above our minds."

4. Again, in the eighth book of *The City of God,* speaking of the philosophers, he says: "Those whom we rightly prefer to all . . . declared that the light of our minds for learning all things was the very God himself, by whom all things were made."

5. Again, in the eighth book of *On the Trinity,* chapter three: "When the mind so pleases us that we prefer it to every corporeal light, . . . it does not please us in itself, but in the art by which it was made. For, having been made, it is approved because of that source in which it is seen to have been when it was still to be made; now this is the truth and the simple good."

6. Again, in the ninth book of *On the Trinity,* chapter six: "It is proved that we either accept . . . or reject, when we rightly approve or reject anything, by other rules which remain altogether unchangeable above our mind."

7. Again, in the same book, chapter seven: "In that eternal truth, from which all temporal things are made, we behold by the sight of the mind the form according to which we exist, and in accordance with which we do anything by true and right reason, either in ourselves or in corporeal things."

8. Again, in the fourteenth book of *On the Trinity,* chapter fifteen: "When the ungodly see the rules according to which they ought to live, where do they see them? Not in their own nature, since it is agreed that their minds are mutable, but these rules are unchangeable; nor in the character of their own mind, since these are rules of justice. Where does

he discern that what he does not have is to be had? Where, then, are they written, unless it is in the book of that light which is called truth, from which every just law is copied?" . . . If you say that he retracted this, see, on the contrary, Augustine, *Retractations*, book one: "It is credible, that even those who are unskilled in certain disciplines may give true answers, when they can receive the eternal light of reason, where they perceive these immutable truths—not because they first knew them and then forgot them, as it seemed to Plato." . . . Again: "The intellectual nature is linked not only to intelligible but even to immutable things, having been made in this order so that, when it moves to the things to which it is linked, or even to itself, it may give true answers concerning them, in so far as it sees them."

From these "authorities" of Augustine it is manifestly clear that all things are known in the eternal reasons.

9. Again, Ambrose: "By myself I see nothing save the empty, the fleeting, the perishable." Therefore, if I see something with certitude, I see it through something which is above me.

10. Again, Gregory, on the text of John, ch. 14, "He will teach you all things," says: "Unless the same Spirit is present to the heart of the hearer, the speech of the teacher is useless. Let no one, therefore, ascribe to the man who teaches what he understands from the teacher's mouth, because unless there is within us one who teaches, the tongue of the teacher labors outwardly for nothing."

11. Again, the same in the same place: "Behold, you all alike hear one voice of the speaker, but still you do not perceive alike the sense of the voice you hear. Since, therefore, the voice is not different, why is the understanding of the voice in your heart different, unless it is that, while the speaker's voice admonished all together, there is an inward master who teaches some in particular concerning the understanding of the voice?" But if our intellect were self-sufficient for understanding through the light of created truth, it would not need a teacher from above. Since, therefore, it does need one, it is evident, etc.

12. Again, Anselm, in the *Address*, chapter fourteen: "How great is that light, from which shines every truth that gives light to the rational mind! How full is that truth in which is to be found everything that is true, and outside which there is only nothingness and falsehood!" Therefore, if what is true is not seen, save where it is, nothing true is seen except in the eternal truth.

13. Again, Origen: "Even if human nature had not sinned, it could not shine by its own powers." But understanding is a kind of shining, so that even if it had not sinned, it could not understand by its own powers. Therefore it needs a higher agent.

14. Again, the *Glossa* [*Ordinaria*], on the verse of the psalm, "Thy

hands have made me and formed me; give me understanding": "God alone gives understanding; for it is through himself, who is light, that God enlightens pious minds."

15. Again, Isaac [Stella] says, in dealing with the text of the psalm "In thy light we shall see light": "As that by which the sun can be seen goes out from the sun, and nevertheless that which displays the sun does not desert the sun, so with God light, which goes out from God, irradiates the mind, so that it may first see the very shining, apart from which it would not see at all, and may see other things in it." According to this, therefore, all things are seen in the divine light.

16. Again, the philosopher, in the sixth book of the *Ethics,* chapter three, according to the new translation: "We all suppose that what we know cannot happen otherwise, but when things that may happen otherwise are outside our range of observation, whether they exist or not is hidden from us. Of necessity, then, the object of knowledge is eternal, for all absolutely necessary beings are eternal, and things that are eternal are ungenerated and incorruptible." Therefore, there cannot be knowledge with any kind of certitude, where the nature of eternal truth is not to be found. But this is only to be found in the eternal reasons; therefore, and so on.

Again, the same thing is proved by reasoning, and first by reasons taken from the words of Augustine. . . . For Augustine in the second book of *On Free Will,* in *On the True Religion* and *On the Teacher,* in *On Music,* VI, and *On the Trinity,* VIII, suggests reasons of this sort.

17. Everything unchangeable is higher than the changeable; but that by which it is known with certitude is unchangeable, because it is necessary truth. But our mind is changeable; therefore, that by which we know is above our minds. Now there is nothing above our minds save God and eternal truth; therefore divine truth and eternal reason is that by which knowledge exists.

18. Again, everything that is not subject to judgment is higher than that which is subject to judgment. But the norm by which we judge is not subject to judgment; therefore, that by which we know and judge is above our mind. But this can only be eternal truth and reason; therefore, and so on.

19. Again, everything infallible is higher than the fallible. But the light and truth, by which we know with certitude, is infallible; therefore, since our mind is fallible, that light and truth is above our mind. But this is the eternal light and truth; therefore, and so on.

20. Again, every light that ensures certitude is illimitable, since it shows itself to all and displays the knowable to them with the same certitude. But illimitable light cannot be created light, but can only be uncreated, since every created thing is limited and finite and is multi-

plied in different things; therefore, this light must necessarily be uncreated. But it is by this light that we know with certitude; therefore, and so on.

21. Again, everything necessary is endless, since it cannot be otherwise, now or in the future, but that by which we know with certitude is necessary truth, and is, therefore, endless. But every such thing is above every created thing, since every creature must have proceeded from nonbeing to being, and, as far as lies in it, it can be turned again to nonbeing. Since, then, that by which we know excels every created truth, it is uncreated truth.

22. Again, every created thing is, in itself, comprehensible, but according to the philosopher the laws of numbers, figures, and demonstrations, when they are increased to infinity, are incomprehensible to the human intellect. Therefore, when laws of this sort are seen by human intellect, they must necessarily be seen in something which exceeds everything created. But nothing of this sort can be found save God and eternal reason; therefore, and so on.

23. Again, when a wicked man knows justice, he knows it either by its presence or by a likeness received from without, or by something which is above. But not by its presence since it is not present to him; or through a species received from without, since it has no likeness that can be abstracted through sense; therefore it is necessary for him to know it through something else, which is above his intellect. (The same reasoning holds for all the other spiritual things that he knows.) If, then, the wicked knows in the eternal reasons, this applies a fortiori to others. . . . If you say that he knows it through its effects, it can be objected against this that, if something is not known in any way, what is effected by it is not known. For instance, if I do not know what man is, I never know what is done by man. If, therefore, we do not have knowledge of justice first of all, we shall never know that this or that is done by it. It remains, therefore, that it must be known in the eternal reason. The same argument can be used concerning any intelligible substantial form whatever, and thus to all knowledge with certitude.

24. Again, as God is the cause of being, so he is principle of knowing and order of living. But God is the cause of being in such a way that nothing can be effected by any cause, unless he himself moves that which acts, by himself and his own eternal power. Therefore, nothing can be understood, unless he himself by his eternal truth immediately enlightens him who understands.

25. Again, no being that is defective, so far as lies in it, is known except through a perfect being. But every created truth, as far as lies in its own power, is darkness and defect; therefore nothing enters the understanding save through that highest truth.

26. Again, nothing is known rightly and with certitude unless it is

referred to the rule that cannot in any way be bent. Now this rule is nothing but that which is essentially rectitude itself, and this is nothing save eternal truth and reason. Nothing, therefore, is known with certitude, unless it is referred to the eternal rule.

27. Again, in the twofold division of the soul into "higher" and "lower," lower reason takes its rise from the higher, and not conversely. But reason is called higher in so far as it is turned toward the eternal laws, and lower in so far as it is concerned with temporal things, and therefore, primarily and naturally, the knowledge of eternal things is in the soul before that of temporal things. It is impossible, then, for anything to be known by it with certitude, unless it is aided by those eternal reasons.

All the reasons that I have just presented are drawn out of the words of Augustine in different volumes.

Moreover, other reasoning makes the same thing evident.

28. Knowledge of the same sensible thing cannot be possessed by different people together and at once, except through something common, and similar reasoning applies to the knowledge of the same intelligible object. But some one truth, though in no way multiplied, can be understood by different people, just as it can be stated in a proposition; therefore, it is necessary that it should be understood through some one thing that is not multiplied in any way. But the one reality which is in no way multiplied in different things can only be God; therefore the principle of our knowledge of any given thing is the truth itself, which is God.

29. Again, intellect is related to the truth, as affectivity to the good, and everything true comes from the highest truth, as every good comes from the highest goodness. But it is impossible for our affection to be drawn directly to a good, unless in some way it attains the highest goodness. Therefore, our intellect cannot have certain knowledge of something true, unless in some way it attains to the highest truth.

30. Again, the true is only known through truth, and only by known truth, at that—and especially through the truth that is best known. Now this latter truth is that which cannot be thought of as nonexistent, and this is not created but uncreated truth. Therefore, whatever is known with certitude is known in the eternal truth and reason.

31. Again, by nature the soul is turned toward the intelligible outside it, and toward the intelligible inside it, and toward the intelligible above it. Now turning toward the intelligible outside it is the least simple matter, while turning to the intelligible within it is simpler, and turning to the intelligible above it is the simplest of all, because the latter is closer to the soul than the soul is to itself. But the simpler something is, the greater priority it has; therefore, the turning of the soul toward the truth itself that is closest to it is naturally prior to its turning toward itself or toward eternal truths. It is impossible, therefore, for it to know anything, unless it knows that highest truth first of all.

32. Again, every being in potentiality is reduced to act by means of something existing in act in that genus. But our intellect is in potentiality, as intellect is in a boy; therefore, if it is to become intelligent in act, this can only come about through him who knows all things in actuality. But this describes the eternal wisdom alone; therefore, etc. . . . If you say that this is the active intellect, then I raise this problem: either the active intellect already understood what it learns, or it did not; if not then nothing could be made intelligent in act through it; but if it did, then either that which learns understands and is ignorant of the same thing at the same time, or else the active intellect is not something that belongs to the soul, but is above the soul. But God alone is above the soul; therefore, etc. . . . If you say, that the active intellect is called "active," not because it understands in actuality, but because it causes understanding, I say, on the contrary, that every intelligent thing is higher and better than the nonintelligent. If, then, the active intellect is not intelligent, it will never make itself or another intelligent in act, since it cannot produce something better and higher than itself; therefore, if it is made intelligent in act, this must be done through something above it. But this can only mean the eternal reason and truth; therefore, etc.

33. Again, suppose that all creatures are destroyed, and the rational spirit alone remains; there will remain with it the knowledge of disciplines, namely, of numbers and figures. But this cannot be on account of any true being they have in the spirit or in the universe; therefore, it must necessarily be on account of the being they have with the supreme Artificer.

34. Again, according to all the "saints," God is said to be the teacher of all knowledge, for one of these reasons: Either he co-operates in a general way with every intellect, as he does with other creatures also, or he infuses a gift of grace, or in knowing that the intellect attains to him. If it is because he co-operates in a general way, then it would follow that he teaches the senses as he does the intellect, but this is absurd. If it is because he infuses a gift of grace, then every cognition will be gratuitous or infused, and thus none will be acquired or innate, but this is most absurd. It remains, then, that God is to be called our teacher because our intellect attains to him as to the light or our minds and the principle by which we know every truth.

But objections are brought against this, both from authority and from reason. The arguments from authority are as follows.

1. In the last chapter of First Timothy it is said of God: "Who only hath immortality, and inhabiteth light inaccessible, whom no man hath seen, nor can see." But everything through or in which we know is accessible to the knower; therefore, that through or in which we know cannot be the light of eternal reason or truth.

2. Again, Augustine, *On the Trinity*, I, 52: "The sight of the human

mind is too weak to be focused on so excellent a light, unless it is cleansed by the righteousness of faith." If, then, the light of eternal truth were the principle of our knowing all truths, only the cleansed and holy soul would know the truth. But this is false; therefore the premise on which it depends is false also.

3. Again, *On the Trinity,* XII, 54: "One should believe that the nature of the intellectual mind was so made that in the order of nature, according to the Creator's design, it sees everything related to intelligible things by means of a certain incorporeal light of its own genus, just as the eye of the flesh sees the things that surround it in the corporeal light." It seems, therefore, that if the created light of corporeal nature is adequate for the knowledge of the objects of sense, the created spiritual light is also sufficient (along with the cognitive power) for the knowledge of intelligible objects of the same genus.

5. Again, Gregory in the *Morals:* "When the mind is hung aloft in . . . contemplation, whatever it . . . perfectly sees is not God." But the principle of our knowing is perfectly perceived in knowledge with certitude; therefore, a principle of this sort is not God or something in God. Therefore, and so on.

6. Again, Dionysius, in the *Epistle to Gaius:* "If anyone, seeing God, understands what he sees, he does not see God himself, but some one of those beings and objects of knowledge that exist, while God himself remains above understanding and substance." When we know, therefore, in the present life, our mind does not attain to uncreated truth.

7. Again, the philosopher says, in *On the Soul,* III, that "our intellect is exercised in connection with the continuous and with time." But those eternal reasons are wholly beyond time; when we understand, therefore, our intellect does not attain to those reasons in any way.

8. Again, he says in the same place: "Just as in every nature there is a factor by which it is productive of all things, and another factor by which it may become all things, so we must understand, with respect to the intellect, that there is an active intellect and a potential intellect." But these are sufficient for perfect cognition; therefore, there is no need for the assistance of an eternal reason.

9. Again, experience teaches that "out of many sense-perceptions is produced one memory, out of many memories one experience, out of many experiences one universal, which is the foundation of art and science," since, when we lose one of our senses, we lose the knowledge of the things that are related to that sense. Therefore in the wayfaring state, knowledge with certitude comes from below, while knowledge in the eternal reasons come from above. As long, then, as we are in the state of wayfarers, knowledge by the light of the eternal reasons is not appropriate for us.

10. Again, imaginative knowledge does not need a higher light;

rather, the force of the imaginative power alone is sufficient for knowing something with certitude, apart from any higher light.

11. Again, the senses can enjoy certain knowledge without any certitude that comes from an eternal reason. If the intellect, therefore, is more powerful than sense, it will be even more fully able to know and understand with certitude, apart from any such light.

12. Again, nothing more is required for complete knowledge than the knower and the abstract object of knowledge, together with the turning of the former toward the latter. But all this can come about through the power of our intellect without the eternal reason; therefore, and so on.

13. Again, no power needs external assistance for anything that it can do freely. Now "we understand when we wish"; therefore, in order to know something with certitude, we do not need the light of the eternal reasons.

14. Again, the principles of being and of knowing are the same. Thus, if the proper and intrinsic principles of being of creatures themselves are only created, whatever is known is known through created reasons—and not, therefore, through eternal reasons and lights.

15. Again, to each knowable object there corresponds its proper principle of knowledge, in order that it may be known with certitude. But those principles of knowledge are not distinctly perceived by any wayfarer's intellect; nothing, therefore, has to be known properly and separately in them.

16. Again, suppose that whatever is known with certitude is known in an eternal reason. Since "that by reason of which something is known is itself better known," it will follow that those eternal reasons are better known to us. But this is obviously false, since they are more fully concealed from us than anything else.

17. Again, it is impossible to see anything in a mirror, unless we see the mirror itself. Therefore, if everything that is known with certitude is seen in those eternal reasons, it is necessary that the first light and the eternal reasons should be seen. But this is false and absurd, and therefore the premise is also false and absurd.

18. Again, if everything that is known with certitude is known in those eternal reasons, while those reasons are equally certain with respect to contingent and to necessary things, as well as with respect to future and to present things, then we should have certain knowledge of contingents as well as of necessary things, and of future as well as of present things. But this is false, and consequently the premise is false also.

19. Again, suppose that we know in the eternal reasons. Now the eternal reasons are the highest causes, while wisdom is the knowledge of the highest causes; therefore, everyone who knows something with certitude is wise. But this is false; therefore, and so on.

20. Again, if heavenly knowledge is knowledge through the eternal

reasons, in which the blessed see whatever they see, then, if all certain knowledge came through those eternal reasons, all those who knew with certitude would be blessed, and only the blessed would know with certitude. But this is false.

21. Again, if everything that is known is seen in the eternal reasons, then, since the mirror of the eternal reasons is an expression of will, and whatever is known in such a mirror is known by revelation, it follows that whatever is known in this way is known in a prophetic manner or by revelation.

22. Again, if everything that is known is known in the eternal reasons, it is known either through a veil or without a veil. If it is known through a veil, then nothing is clearly known; if it is known without a veil, then all see God and the eternal exemplar without any obscurity. But this is false, as far as the wayfaring state is concerned; therefore, and so on.

23. If every immutable truth is above the soul, and is, therefore, eternal and God, then, since the truth of every demonstrative principle is immutable, every such truth will be God. Nothing, therefore, would be known except God.

24. Again, suppose that every immutable truth is the truth of the eternal art, while the latter is one and one only. Then all immutable truth will be one and one only. Now it is possible to obtain some immutable truth about any being whatsoever—as is obvious, since this is an immutable truth: If Socrates is running, Socrates is moving. According to this, therefore, all beings will be one.

25. Again, if everything that is God is to be adored with divine worship, and the truth of every immutable principle is God, then every such truth should be adored. Therefore, the truth of the proposition, two and three are five, is to be adored.

26. Again, if every immutable truth is God, then everyone who clearly sees some immutable truth clearly sees God. But the demons and the damned clearly see some immutable truths; therefore, they clearly see God. Since this is to be blessed, the damned are blessed. But nothing could be more absurd than this; therefore, it is most absurd to say that everything that is known, if it is known with certitude, is known in the eternal reasons.

II
Conclusion

I reply. In order to understand the foregoing, we must note that, when it is said that everything that is known with certitude is known in the light of the eternal reasons, this can be interpreted in three ways.

(a) The first interpretation states that the evidence of the eternal light accompanies knowledge with certitude as the whole and sole principle of knowledge. This interpretation is inaccurate, inasmuch as it allows for no knowledge of things except in the Word. But in that case knowledge on earth would not differ from knowledge in heaven, or knowledge in the Word from knowledge in the proper genus, or scientific knowledge from sapiental knowledge, or knowledge of nature from knowledge of grace, or knowledge by reason from knowledge by revelation. Now since all these things are false, this interpretation certainly must not be maintained. For this is the opinion put forward by some—such as those of the first Academy—to the effect that nothing is known with certitude save in the archetypal and intelligible world. But it was from this opinion, as Augustine says in *Against the Academics,* Book II, that the error of those of the new Academy was born, namely, that nothing whatever can really be known, since the intelligible world is concealed from human minds. And therefore, wishing to hold the first opinion together with their own position, they fell into manifest error, since "a little error in the beginning is a great one in the end."

(b) The second interpretation states that the influence of the eternal reason necessarily accompanies knowledge with certitude, so that, in knowing, the knower does not attain to the eternal reason itself, but only to its influence. But this manner of speaking is certainly inadequate, according to the words of blessed Augustine, who showed by express statements and reasoning that in knowledge with certitude the mind has to be directed by immutable and eternal reasons—not as by a habit of its own mind, but as by those things which are above it in the eternal truth. And, therefore, to say that our mind, in knowing, does not reach beyond the influence of uncreated light is to say that Augustine was deceived, since it is not easy in expounding him to make the "authorities" taken from him say this. But this is a highly absurd statement to make about such a great father and a most authoritative doctor among all the expositors of Holy Scripture.

Moreover, that influence of light is either God's general influence upon all creatures or God's special influence by grace. But if it is his general influence, then we should no more call God the giver of wisdom than the giver of fertility to the earth, and it means no more to say that knowledge comes from him than that wealth does. On the other hand, if it is his special influence (of the same sort as grace), then on this assumption all knowledge is infused, and none is acquired or innate. But all these notions are absurd.

(c) This leaves us with the third interpretation, as a kind of mean between two extremes. Thus we shall say that, for knowledge with certitude, an eternal reason is necessarily required as regulative and motive principle—not, indeed, as the sole principle, or in its own complete clarity, but acting with the created reason, and seen by us "in part," in accordance with our wayfaring condition.

And this is what Augustine suggests in *On the Trinity,* XIV, chapter

15: "Even the ungodly think of eternity, and rightly blamed and rightly praise many things in the conduct of men." He says in addition that they do this by rules which are written "in the book of that light which is called truth." Moreover, the nobility of knowledge and the dignity of the knower necessarily require that our mind, when it knows with certitude, should in some way attain to those rules and immutable reasons.

I say that the nobility of knowledge requires this, because certain knowledge cannot exist unless there is immutability on the part of the object of knowledge, and infallibility on the part of the knower. Now created truth is not immutable absolutely, but from its relation to what is above it; similarly, the light of the creature is not altogether infallible by its own power—since each was created and passed from nonbeing into being. If then, for full knowledge recourse is had to a wholly immutable and stable truth and to a wholly infallible light, in knowledge of this kind it is necessary to have recourse to the heavenly art, as to light and truth—light, I say, giving infallibility to the knower, and truth giving immutability to the object of knowledge. Therefore, since things have being in the mind, and in their proper genus, and in the eternal art, the truth of things is not sufficient for the soul itself to have certain knowledge—in so far as they have being in it or in their proper genus—because there is mutability on both sides. For certain knowledge, the soul must in some way attain to them as they are in the eternal art.

The same requirement is imposed by the dignity of the knower. The rational spirit has a reason divided into higher and lower; therefore, just as the lower part without the higher is not sufficient for the full deliberative judgment of reason in matters of action, so it is inadequate for the full judgment of reason in speculative matters. But this higher part is that in which the image of God is to be found; it both cleaves to the eternal reasons and, by them, judges and defines with certitude whatever it defines—in both cases, because it is the image of God.

For the creature is related to God under the Aspects of a vestige, an image, and a likeness. In so far as it is a vestige, it is related to God as its object; but in principle, in so far as it is an image, it is related to God as its object; but in so far as it is a likeness, it is related to God as to a gift infused into it. And, therefore, every creature which proceeds from God is a vestige; every creature which knows God is an image; every creature (and that alone) in which God dwells is a likeness. And according to these three degrees of relationship there are three degrees of the divine co-operation.

In the activity which proceeds from the creature in so far as it is a vestige, God co-operates as the creative principle. In the activity which proceeds from the creature in so far as it is a likeness—such as a meritorious work, pleasing to God—God co-operates in the manner of an infused gift. But in the activity which proceeds from the creature in so far as it is an image, God co-operates as a moving principle, and certain knowledge, which does not come from the lower reason apart from the higher, is an example of this kind of activity.

Since, then, certain knowledge belongs to the rational spirit, in so far as it is the image of God, it follows that in this knowledge the spirit attains to the eternal reasons. But since, as long as it is in the wayfaring state, it is not fully deiform, it does not attain to them clearly and fully and distinctly. Still, in so far as it approximates more or less closely to deiformity, it attains to them more or less closely, but it always does attain to them in some way, since the nature of the image can never be detached from the rational spirit. Therefore, in the state of innocence, because it was the image unmarred by sin, even if it did not possess the full deiformity of glory, it attained to them "in part," but not "in a dark manner." But in the state of fallen nature it lacks deiformity and suffers from deformity, and thus it attains to the eternal reasons both "in part" and "in a dark manner." But in the state of glory it lacks all deformity and possesses full deiformity, and thus it attains to them full and clearly.

Again, since the soul is not an image with respect to its whole self, it attains the likeness of things, abstracted from a phantasm, as proper and distinct principles of knowledge, apart from which it is insufficient in itself to know the light of eternal reason, as long as it is in the wayfaring state—unless perhaps it may transcend this state in some special way, as is the case with those who are enraptured, and with the revelations of certain prophets.

It is to be granted, then, as reasoning shows and as the authoritative statements of Augustine expressly assert, that in all certain knowledge those principles of knowledge are attained by the knower. They are reached in one way, however, by the wayfarer, and in another by him who enjoys the vision of God; in one way when we possess science, and in another when we possess wisdom; in one way by the prophet, and in another by the man who understands in the ordinary way. All this has already been made plain, and will be evident in the solutions offered for the objections.

III

Answers to the Objections

1. To the first objection, then, that God dwells in light inaccessible, we should reply that the text refers to access to that light in the fullness and splendor of its brightness. In this sense it is not approached by the creature's power, but only through the deiformity of glory.

2. To the objection that "the sight of the human mind is too weak to be focused on so excellent a light, etc.," we should reply that in order to know through the eternal reasons the mind does not need to be focused on them, except in so far as it may know in a sapiential way. For the man of wisdom attains to those reasons in one way, and the man of science in

another; the man of science attains to them as things that move him, while the man of wisdom finds rest in them—and to this wisdom no one comes unless he first is "cleansed by the righteousness of faith."

3. In answer to the objection that the mind has knowledge by itself of incorporeal things, it should be said that, just as in the creature's works the Creator's co-operation must not be overlooked, so an uncreated principle of knowledge is not excluded from a created principle of knowledge, but on the contrary is included in the latter.

4. To the objection that the mind sees in a light of its own genus, it can be answered that, in a broad sense, every incorporeal light (created or uncreated) is called a light of its own genus. But even if we interpret this as a reference to a created light, this does not exclude the uncreated light, nor does it follow that we do not know in the eternal truth, but simply that we know in the light of created truth as well as in the eternal truth. Now this is indeed true, yet it does not contradict my opinion as stated.

5, 6. To the objections drawn from Gregory and Dionysius, we should reply that neither of them denies that "the true light, which enlighteneth every man that cometh into this world," is reached by our minds. They merely assert that in this life it is not yet fully seen.

7–9. In reply to the objections drawn from the philosopher, to the effect that we understand in relation to the continuous and to time, and that we have a potential and an active intellect, as well as the objection which has to do with the experience of human knowledge, it is to be said that all this presupposed that the light and reason of created truth concurs with our intelligence. Nevertheless, as was said above, the light and reason of created truth are not excluded, because it is possible for the soul, in its lower part, to attain to the things that are below, while nevertheless the higher part attains to the things that are above.

10. To the objection concerning imaginative cognition, it is to be replied that the cases are not similar, because this cognition does not possess certitude, and therefore does not have recourse to the immutable.

11. In answer to the objection drawn from sense-perception, it should be said that the certitude of sense is not the same as that of understanding. For the certitude of sense stems from the binding of a power which functions by way of nature and has to do with a determinate object. Since, however, the intellect is a power that is free to understand all things, its certitude cannot come from such a source, and thus it is necessary for it to come from something that is not bound, but is free, without any possible defect of mutability or fallibility. Now the light and reason of eternal truth is like this; the intellect, therefore, has recourse to the latter as the fount of all certitude.

12. To the objection that nothing more is required for knowledge than the knower and the knowable, together with the turning of the former toward the latter, it is to be answered that this turning includes a

judgment. Certain judgment, however, is realized only through a law that is itself certain and above judgment—according to Augustine's statement, in the book *On the True Religion* and the book *On Free Will,* to the effect that "no one judges of the truth, and without the truth no one judges rightly." Thus the eternal reason and truth is included in these conditions of knowledge.

13. In reply to the objection that we understand when we will, and in consequence need no external assistance, it is to be said that there are two kinds of external assistance: one which is always present, and another which is absent and distant. It is evident that this objection is conclusive with respect to the second kind of assistance, but not to the first, since, if corporeal light were always present in the eye, as spiritual light is always present in the mind, we should see when we will, just as we understand when we will.

14. To the objection that the principles of being and of knowing are the same, we should reply that the intrinsic principles of being are not sufficient for full knowledge any more than they are for being, apart from that first extrinsic principle, which is God. Therefore, although those principles are in some way a principle of knowledge, they do not on that account exclude the primary ground of knowing from our knowledge, any more than they exclude creation in the case of the act of being.

15. To the objection that to each and every knowable object there corresponds its proper principle of knowledge, it is to be replied, that those reasons are not the whole ground of our knowing, because we do not see them with full distinctness in themselves, but along with them we require a created light of principles, and likenesses of known objects, from which, with respect to each and every thing that is known, we derive the proper principle of our knowledge of it.

16. In reply to the objection that "that by reason of which something is known is itself better known," it is to be said that, as is already evident, it is in conjunction with the truth of principles, and not by itself alone, that the eternal reason moves us to knowledge. (While this condition does not hold for the eternal reason specifically in itself, it applies generally in the wayfaring state.) Thus it does not follow that it is known to us in itself; rather, it is known to us as it shines forth in its principles and in its generality, and so, in a particular way, it is most certain to us, because our intellect simply cannot think that it does not exist, and this assuredly cannot be said of any created truth.

17. As far as the objection drawn from a mirror is concerned, this applies to the mirror whose nature it is to represent something properly and distinctly and, in addition to this, to constitute the term of our vision. This is evident in a material mirror, which represents a visible species distinctly and properly, and is the term of our vision. Now these conditions do apply to the eternal mirror as far as those who have the vision of God are concerned—as is evident from what was said before.

18. In reply to the objection that these reasons are equally certain with respect to contingent and to necessary things, it is to be said that this reasoning would be quite conclusive if these reasons were the total ground of our knowledge, and if an object were seen entirely in them. This is not the case, however, in the circumstances of our present condition, because along with the eternal reasons we need proper likenesses and principles of things, separately received, and we do not come across these in contingent things, but only in necessary things.

19. To the objection that, if we have knowledge in these reasons, everyone who knows anything is wise, we should reply that this does not follow, because attaining to these reasons does not make anyone wise, unless he reposes in them and knows that he attains to them. (The latter, indeed, is characteristic of the wise man.) For the intellects of those who simply know attain to reasons of this sort as motive principles, while the intellects of the wise attain to them as principles which lead them to their repose. And since there are few who attain to them in this way, there are few wise men, even though there are many who have knowledge; indeed, there are few who know that they attain to these reasons. What is more, there are few who want to believe this, because an intellect not yet raised to the contemplation of eternal things finds it difficult to grasp the truth that God is thus present and near to it, despite what Paul says in Acts, ch. 17, that he is "not far from every one of us."

20. The reply to the objection drawn from heavenly knowledge is already obvious—namely, that there is a great difference between knowledge "in part" and "in a dark manner," on the one hand, and perfect and distinct knowledge, on the other. This point was touched on above.

21. To the objection that the mirror of the eternal reasons is an expression of will, etc., we should reply that, as the apostle says in Rom., ch. 1, "That which is known of God is manifest in them." Although God is simple and one in form, nevertheless that eternal light and that exemplar represent certain things as it were outwardly and openly, and other things more deeply and hiddenly. The former are those things that are done according to the necessary rule of the divine art, while the latter are the things that are done according to the disposition of God's hidden will. Now what is called a "voluntary" mirror is so-called with respect to things that have their exemplar in God in the second way, rather than in the first. In the eternal reasons, therefore, natural things are known by reason's natural power of judgment, but supernatural and future things are known only by the gift of revelation from on high; thus this argument does not really affect the position previously stated.

22. To the objection drawn from the fact that whatever we know in them is known either through a veil or without a veil, it should be answered that the reason for our inability in the wayfaring state to know anything in the eternal reasons without a veil and without obscurity lies in the obscuring of the divine image. It does not follow, however, that

nothing is known with certitude or clarity, since the created principles, which in some sense are media of knowledge (though not apart from those reasons), can be seen by our mind clearly and without a veil. (Nevertheless, if it were said that nothing is fully known in this life, this would involve no great incongruity.)

23–26. To the objections against Augustine's reasoning, to the effect that, if the immutable truth is God, then the truth of a demonstrative principle would be God, and that all truths would be one, and that they would be objects of worship, and that the demons would see God—to all these we should reply that the immutable truth is spoken of in two ways: absolutely, and in relation to something higher. Now when it is said that immutable truth is above the mind, and is God, this refers to the absolutely changeless truth. But when it is said that the truth of a demonstrative principle, which refers to something created, is immutable, it is evident that it is immutable, not absolutely, but in relation to something above it, since every creature comes from nonbeing and can return to nonbeing. And if it is objected that this truth is absolutely certain to the soul itself by itself, it must be said that, although a demonstrative principle, in so far as it expresses something complex, is created, nevertheless the truth signified by it can be signified in one of three ways: with respect to what it is in matter, or what it is in the soul, or what it is in the divine art—or, for that matter, in all these ways together. For truth in the external sign is the sign of truth in the soul, because "spoken words are symbols of experiences which are in the soul"; but the soul in its own highest aspect is concerned with higher things, just as in its lower aspect it is concerned with these lower things, since it is a mean between created things and God, and thus truth in the soul is related to that twofold truth, as a mean to two extremes, so that from the lower it receives relative certitude, while it receives absolute certitude from the higher. And thus, as Augustine's reasoning shows, if truth of this kind is absolutely immutable, it is above the soul. But the contrary reasoning is related to the truth—with which demonstration is properly concerned—which is immutable in relation to something above it. Now this truth is multiplied in diverse things; it is not adorable; it is perceptible by the demons and the damned. But the truth which is absolutely immutable can be clearly seen by those alone who can enter into the innermost silence of the mind, and to this no sinner attains, but he who is a supreme lover of eternity, and he alone.

b. St. Thomas Aquinas

The biography of St. Thomas is too complicated for brief treatment here. Suffice it to say that he was an Italian, a Dominican, a disciple of Albertus Magnus, a teacher all his life and the chief representative of the Christian Aristotelian position in theology.

The translation is from *Thomas Aquinas on Nature and Grace*, Vol. XI. LCC. Ed. by A. M. Fairweather. Published 1954, The Westminster Press. Used by permission.

Question Two

THE EXISTENCE OF GOD

Three questions are asked concerning the existence of God. 1. Whether it is self-evident that God exists. 2. Whether the existence of God can be demonstrated. 3. Whether God exists.

Article One

WHETHER IT IS SELF-EVIDENT THAT GOD EXISTS

We proceed to the first article thus:

1. It seems to be self-evident that God exists. Things are said to be self-evident when the knowledge of them is naturally in us, as is obviously the case with first principles. Now the Damascene says that "the knowledge that God exists is naturally inborn in all men" (I *De Fid. Orth.* I, 3). It is therefore self-evident that God exists.

2. Again, as the philosopher says of the first principles of demonstration, whatever is known as soon as the terms are known is self-evident (I *Post. An.*, ch. 2). Thus we know that any whole is greater than its part as soon as we know what a whole is, and what a part is. Now when it is understood what the term "God" signifies, it is at once understood that God exists. For the term "God" means that than which nothing greater can be signified, and that which exists in reality is greater than that which exists only in the intellect. Hence since "God" exists in the intellect as soon as the term is understoood, it follows that God exists also in reality. It is therefore self-evident that God exists.

3. Again, it is self-evident that truth exists. For truth exists if anything at all is true, and if anyone denies that truth exists, he concedes that it is true that it does not exist, since if truth does not exist it is then

true that it does not exist. Now God is truth itself, according to John 14:6: "I am the way, and the truth, and the life." It is therefore self-evident that God exists.

On the other hand: no one can conceive the opposite of what is self-evident, as the philosopher explains in dealing with the first principles of demonstration (4 *Metaph.*, text 9; I *Post. An.*, texts 5 and *ult.*). Now the opposite of "God exists" can be conceived, according to Ps. 53:1: "The fool hath said in his heart, There is no God." It follows that it is not self-evident that God exists.

I answer: there are two ways in which a thing may be self-evident. It may be self-evident in itself, but not self-evident to us. It may also be self-evident both in itself and to us. A proposition is self-evident when its predicate is contained in the meaning of its subject. For example, the proposition "man is an animal" is self-evident, because "animal" is contained in the meaning of "man." Hence if the predicate and the subject are known to everyone, the proposition will be self-evident to everyone. This is obviously the case with regard to the first principles of demonstration, whose terms are universals known to everyone, such as being and not-being, whole, part, and the like. But when there are some to whom the predicate and the subject are unknown, the proposition will not be self-evident to them, however self-evident it may be in itself. Thus Boethius says (*Lib. de Hebd.*—Whether all Existence is Good): "it happens that some universal concepts of mind are self-evident only to the wise, e.g., that the incorporeal is not in space." I say, then, that this proposition "God exists" is self-evident in itself, since its predicate is the same with its subject. For God is his existence, as we shall show in Q. 3, Art. 4. But since we do not know what God is, it is not self-evident to us, but must be proved by means of what is better known to us though less well known to nature, i.e., by means of the effects of God.

On the first point: the knowledge that God exists is inborn in us in a general and somewhat confused manner. For God is the final beatitude of man, and a man desires beatitude naturally, and is also naturally aware of what he desires. But this is not absolute knowledge that God exists, any more than to know that someone is coming is to know that Peter is coming, even though it should actually be Peter who comes. Many indeed think that riches are man's perfect good, and constitute his beatitude. Others think that pleasures are his perfect good, and others again something else.

On the second point: he who hears the term "God" may not understand it to mean that than which nothing greater can be conceived, since some have believed that God is a body. But given that one understands the term to mean this, it does not follow that he understands that that which the term signifies exists in the nature of things, but only that it exists in the intellect. Neither can it be argued that God exists in reality, unless it is granted that that than which nothing greater can be conceived exists in reality, which is not granted by those who suppose that God does not exist.

On the third point: it is self-evident that truth in general exists. But it is not self-evident to us that the first truth exists.

Article Two

WHETHER GOD'S EXISTENCE CAN BE DEMONSTRATED

We proceed to the second article thus:

1. It seems that God's existence cannot be demonstrated. God's existence is an article of faith. But matters of faith cannot be demonstrated, since demonstration makes a thing to be known, whereas the apostle makes it clear that faith is of things not seen (Heb., ch. 11). It follows that God's existence cannot be demonstrated.

2. Again, the medium of demonstration is the essence. But as the Damascene says (I *De. Fid. Orth.* 4), we cannot know what God is, but only what he is not. It follows that we cannot demonstrate that God exists.

3. Again, God's existence could be demonstrated only from his effects. But his effects are not proportionate to God himself, since God is infinite while they are finite, and the finite is not proportionate to the infinite. Now a cause cannot be demonstrated from an effect which is not proportionate to itself. It follows that God's existence cannot be demonstrated.

On the other hand: the apostle says in Rom. I:20: "the invisible things of him . . . are clearly seen, being understood by the things that are made." Now this is possible only if God's existence can be demonstrated from the things that are made. For the first thing that is understood about anything is its existence.

I answer: there are two kinds of demonstration. There is demonstration through the cause, or, as we say, "from grounds," which argues from what comes first in nature. There is also demonstration by means of effects, or "proof by means of appearances," which argues from what comes first for ourselves. Now when an effect is more apparent to us than its cause, we reach a knowledge of the cause through its effect. Even though the effect should be better known to us, we can demonstrate from any effect that its cause exists, because effects always depend on some cause, and a cause must exist if its effect exists. We can demonstrate God's existence in this way, from his effects which are known to us, even though we do not know his essence.

On the first point: the existence of God, and similar things which can be known by natural reason as Rom., ch. I, affirms, are not articles of faith, but preambles to the articles. Faith presupposes natural knowledge as grace presupposes nature, and as perfection presupposes what can be perfected. There is no reason, however, why what is in itself demonstrable and knowable should not be accepted in faith by one who cannot understand the demonstration of it.

On the second point: when a cause is demonstrated by means of its effect, we are bound to use the effect in place of a definition of the cause in proving the existence of the cause. This is especially the case with regard to God. For in proving that something exists, we are bound to accept the meaning of the name as the medium of demonstration, instead of the essence, since the question of what a thing is must follow the question of its existence. Since the names applied to God are derived from his effects, as we shall show in Q. 13, Art. 1, we may use the name "God" as the medium in demonstrating God's existence from his effect.

On the third point: effects which are not proportionate to their cause do not give us perfect knowledge of their cause. Nevertheless, it can be clearly demonstrated from any effect whatever that its cause exists, as we have said. In this way we can prove God's existence from his effects, even though we cannot know his essence perfectly by means of them.

Article Three

WHETHER GOD EXISTS

We proceed to the third article thus:

1. It seems that God does not exist. If one of two contraries were to be infinite, the other would be wholly excluded. Now the name "God" means that he is infinite good. There would therefore be no evil if God were to exist. But there is evil in the world. It follows that God does not exist.

2. Again, what can be explained by comparatively few principles is not the consequence of a greater number of principles. Now if we suppose that God does not exist, it appears that we can still account for all that we see in the world by other principles, attributing all natural things to nature as their principle, and all that is purposive to human reason or will. There is therefore no need to suppose that God exists.

On the other hand: in Ex. 3:14 God says in person: "I AM THAT I AM."

I answer: God's existence can be proved in five ways. The first and clearest proof is the argument from motion. It is certain, and in accordance with sense experience, that some things in this world are moved. Now everything that is moved is moved by something else, since nothing is moved unless it is potentially that to which it is moved, whereas that which moves is actual. To move is nothing other than to bring something from potentiality to actuality, and a thing can be brought from potentiality to actuality only by something which is actual. Thus a fire, which is actually hot, makes wood, which is potentially hot, to be actually hot, so moving and altering it. Now it is impossible for the same thing to be both actual and potential in the same respect, although it may be so in different respects. What is actually hot cannot at the same time be potentially hot, although it is potentially cold. It is therefore impossible that, in the same respect and in the same way, anything should be both mover and moved, or that it should move itself. Whatever is moved must therefore be moved by something else. If, then, that by which it is moved is itself moved, this also must be moved by something else, and this in turn by something else again. But this cannot go on for ever, since there would then be no first mover, and consequently no other mover, because secondary movers cannot move unless moved by a first mover, as a staff cannot move unless it is moved by the hand. We are therefore bound to arrive at a first mover which is not moved by anything, and all men understand that this is God.

The second way is from the nature of an efficient cause. We find that there is a sequence of efficient causes in sensible things. But we do not find that anything is the efficient cause of itself. Nor is this possible, for the thing would then be prior to itself, which is impossible. But neither can the sequence of efficient causes be infinite, for in every sequence the first efficient cause is the cause of an intermediate cause, and an intermediate cause is the cause of the ultimate cause, whether the intermediate causes be many, or only one. Now if a cause is removed, its effect is removed. Hence if there were no first efficient cause, there would be no ultimate cause, and no intermediate cause. But if the regress of efficient causes were infinite, there would be no first efficient cause. There would consequently be no ultimate effect, and no intermediate causes. But this is plainly false. We are therefore bound to suppose that there is a first efficient cause. And all men call this God.

The third way is from the nature of possibility and necessity. There are some things which may either exist or not exist, since some things come to be and pass away, and may therefore be or not be. Now it is impossible that all of these should exist at all times, because there is at least some time when that which may possibly not exist does not exist. Hence if all things were such that they might not exist, at some time or other there would be nothing. But if this were true there would be nothing existing now, since what does not exist cannot begin to exist, unless through something which does exist. If there had been nothing existing, it would have been impossible for anything to begin to exist, and there would now be nothing at all. But this is plainly false, and hence not all existence is merely possible. Something in things must be necessary. Now everything which is necessary either derives its necessity from elsewhere, or does not. But we cannot go on to infinity with necessary things which have a cause of their necessity, any more than with efficient causes, as we proved. We are therefore bound to suppose something necessary in itself, which does not owe its necessity to anything else, but which is the cause of the necessity of other things. And all men call this God.

The fourth way is from the degrees that occur in things, which are found to be more and less good, true, noble, and so on. Things are said to be more and less because they approximate in different degrees to that which is greatest. A thing is the more hot the more it approximates to that which is hottest. There is therefore something which is the truest, the best, and the noblest, and which is consequently the greatest in being, since that which has the greatest truth is also greatest in being, as is said in 2 *Metaph.*, text 4. Now that which most thoroughly possesses the nature of any genus is the cause of all that the genus contains. Thus fire, which is most perfectly hot, is the cause of all hot things, as is said in the same passage. There is therefore something which is the cause of the being of all things that are, as well as of their goodness and their every perfection. This we call God.

The fifth way is from the governance of things. We see how some things, like natural bodies, work for an end even though they have no knowledge. The fact that they nearly always operate in the same way, and so as to achieve the maximum good, makes this obvious, and shows that they attain their end by design, not by chance. Now things which have no knowledge tend towards an end only through the agency of something which knows and also understands, as an arrow through an archer. There is therefore an intelligent being by whom all natural things are directed to their end. This we call God.

On the first point: as Augustine says (*Enchirid.* II): "since God is supremely good, he would not allow any evil thing to exist in his works, were he not able by his omnipotence and goodness to bring good out of evil." God's infinite goodness is such that he permits evil things to exist, and brings good out of them.

On the second point: everything that can be attributed to nature must depend on God as its first cause, since nature works for a predetermined end through the direction of a higher agent. Similarly, whatever is due to purpose must depend on a cause higher than the reason or will of man, since these are subject to change and defect. Anything which is changeable and subject to defect must depend on some first principle which is immovable and necessary in itself, as we have shown.

Question Three

OF THE SIMPLE NATURE OF GOD

When we know that something exists, it still remains to inquire into the manner of its existence, in order to know what it is. But we cannot inquire into the manner in which God exists. We can inquire only into the manner in which he does not exist, since we cannot know of God what he is, but only what he is not. We must therefore consider how God does not exist, how we know him, and how we name him. The manner in which God does not exist can be shown by excluding what is incompatible with God, such as composition, movement, and the like. We shall therefore inquire into the simple nature of God which repels composition. We shall also inquire into the divine perfection, since the simple natures of corporeal things are imperfect, having parts.

Eight questions are asked concerning the simple nature of God. 1. Whether God is a body. 2. Whether there is composition of form and matter in God. 3. Whether there is composition of the quiddity, essence, or nature of God, and God as subject. 4. Whether there is composition of essence and existence in God. 5. Or of genus and difference. 6. Or of substance and attribute. 7. Whether God is composite in any way, or altogether simple. 8. Whether God enters into composition with other things.

Article One

WHETHER GOD IS A BODY

We proceed to the first article thus:

1. It seems that God is a body. For what has three dimensions is a body, and sacred Scripture attributes three dimensions to God, as in Job 11:8–9: "It is as high as heaven; what canst thou do? deeper than hell; what canst thou know? The measure thereof is longer than the earth, and broader than the sea." God is therefore a body.

2. Again, everything that has figure is a body, since figure is a mode of quantity. Now it seems that God has figure, since it is said in Gen. 1:26: "Let us make man in our image, after our likeness," and image means figure, according to Heb. 1:3: "Who being the brightness of his glory, and the express image of his person. . . ." God is therefore a body.

4. Again, there cannot be position without a body, and scriptural sayings about God imply position. It is said in Isa. 6:1: "I saw also the Lord sitting upon a throne," and in Isa. 3:13: "The Lord standeth to judge the people." God is therefore a body.

5. Again, only a body or something which has a body can be a local *terminus a quo* or *ad quem*, and Scripture speaks of God as a *terminus ad quem* in Ps. 34:5: "They looked unto him, and were lightened," and as a *terminus a quo* in Jer. 17:13: "they that depart from me shall be written in the earth." God is therefore a body.

On the other hand: it is said in John 4:24: "God is a spirit."

I answer: God is certainly not a body. This can be proved in three ways. First, particular examples make it plain that no body moves unless it is moved. But it was shown in Q. 2, Art. 3, that God is the unmoved first mover. This proves that God is not a body. Secondly, the first being must be actual, and in no sense potential. Potentiality precedes actuality within any one thing which passes from potentiality to actuality, but actuality is prior to potentiality absolutely, since the potential can become actual only through something which is actual. Now it was shown in Q. 2, Art. 3, that God is the first being. It is therefore impossible that there should be anything potential in him. But every body is potential, since it is continuous, and consequently infinitely divisible. It is therefore impossible that God should be a body. Thirdly, it is clear from Q. 2, Art. 3, that God is the noblest being. Now a body cannot possibly be the noblest being, since it can be either alive or lifeless. A live body is obviously nobler than a lifeless one. But a live body is not alive because it is a body, otherwise all bodies would be alive. It therefore owes its life to something else, as our own bodies owe their life to the soul, and that which gives life to the body is nobler than the body. It is therefore impossible that God should be a body.

On the first point: as was said in Q. 1, Art. 9, sacred Scripture records spiritual and divine things for us in the similitude of corporeal things. The ascription of three dimensions to God denotes the extent of his power, by the simile of physical quantity. His power to know hidden things is denoted by depth, the surpassing excellence of his power by height, his everlasting being by length, and the love which he bears to all things by breadth. Or as Dionysius says: "The depth of God means his incomprehensible essence, the length the power which permeates all things, the breadth the extension of God over all things, in the sense that all things are under his protection" (9 *Div. Nom.*, lect. 3).

On the second point: it is not in respect of the body that man is said to be the image of God, but because he excels the other animals. Thus after saying: "let us make man in our image, after our likeness," Gen. 1:26 adds: "and let them have dominion over the fish of the sea." For man excels all animals in reason and understanding, and is made in the image of God in respect of them. But these are incorporeal.

On the third point: Scripture attributes bodily parts to God metaphorically, in respect of his actions. The function of the eye being to see, the mention of the eye of God denotes his power to see intellectually, not sensibly. Similarly with the other parts mentioned.

On the fourth point: anything attributed to God which implies position is purely metaphorical. Sitting denotes his unchangeableness and his authority. Standing denotes his power to overcome whatever opposes him.

On the fifth point: since God is everywhere, we do not approach him by physical steps, but by the feelings of the mind. We also depart from him in this way. Approach and departure denote spiritual feelings by the metaphor of movement in space.

Article Two

WHETHER THERE IS COMPOSITION OF FORM AND MATTER IN GOD

We proceed to the second article thus:

1. It appears that there is composition of form and matter in God. Anything which has a soul is composed of matter and form, since soul is the form of body. Scripture attributes a soul to God, saying in the person of God: "Now the just shall live by faith: but if any man draw back, my soul shall have no pleasure in him" (Heb. 10:38). Hence God is composed of matter and form.

2. Again, according to 1 *De Anima*, texts 12, 14, 15, anger, joy, and the like are passions of the composite. Scripture ascribes such passions to God in Ps. 106:40: "Therefore was the wrath of God kindled against his people." Hence God is composed of matter and form.

3. Again, matter is the principle of individuation. Now God must be an individual, since he is not predicated of many. Hence God is composed of matter and form.

On the other hand: anything composed of matter and form is a body, since the primary quality of matter is quantitative extension. But it was shown in the preceding article that God is not a body. It follows that God is not composed of matter and form.

I answer: there cannot possibly be matter in God. In the first place, matter is characterized by potentiality, and it has been shown that God is pure act, without any potentiality (Q. 2, Art. 3). It is therefore impossible that God should be composed of matter and form. Secondly, anything composed of matter and form owes its goodness to its form. It must therefore be good through participation, its matter participating in its form. But the first and best good, which is God, is not good by participation, since good which belongs essentially is better than good which is participated. It is therefore impossible that God should be composed of matter and form. Thirdly, every agent acts by means of its form, and the manner in which a thing is an agent depends on how it is related to its form. Therefore that which is first, and an agent in its own right, must be a form primarily and by means of itself. Now God is the first agent, since he is the first efficient cause, as was shown in Q. 2, Art. 3. God is therefore his own form through his essence, and not a composition of form and matter.

On the first point: a soul is attributed to God metaphorically, in order to denote action, since it is by the soul that we will. What is pleasing to God's will is thus said to be pleasing to his soul.

On the second point: such things as anger are attributed to God metaphorically, in order to denote his effects, since an angry man punishes. Anger metaphorically signifies divine punishment.

On the third point: forms which can be received by matter are made individual by the matter of a primary underlying subject, which cannot be in another subject, although the form itself may be in many subjects unless some obstacle intervenes. But a form which cannot be received by matter, and which subsists by itself, is individual for the very reason that it cannot be received by anything else. God is such a form. It does not then follow that there is matter in God.

Article Three

WHETHER GOD IS THE SAME AS HIS ESSENCE, OR NATURE

We proceed to the third article thus:

1. It seems that God is not the same as his essence, or nature. Nothing can be in itself. But the essence or nature of God, which is his divinity, is said to be in God. God cannot then be the same as his essence or nature.

2. Again, an effect is similar to its cause, since every agent acts to produce its own likeness. Now with creatures, a subject is not the same as its essence. A man, for example, is not the same as his humanity. Neither then is God the same as his Divinity.

On the other hand: in John 14:6 it is clearly said that God is not merely living, but life: "I am the way, and the truth, and the life." Thus Divinity is to God as is life to one who lives. God is therefore Divinity itself.

I answer: God is the same as his essence, or nature. In order to understand this, we must realize that the essence or nature is bound to be different from the underlying subject where things are composed of matter and form, because their essence or nature comprises only what is included in their definition. Thus humanity comprises what is included in the definition of man, or that by which a man is a man, and means that by which a man is a man. But the particular matter of the subject, and all the accidents which it possesses as an individual, are not included in the definition of the species. This flesh, these bones, whether the subject be white or black, and such things, are not included in the definition of man. Hence this flesh, these bones, and the accidents which distinguish this matter as individual are not included in the humanity, even though they are included in the man. The subject which is a man, therefore, included something which humanity does not include, so that a man is not precisely the same as his humanity. Humanity denotes the formal part of a man, since the defining principles are related to the individuating matter as its form. But where things are not composed of matter and form, and where individuation is not due to individual matter, that is, to this particular matter, but where forms individualize themselves, the forms are bound to be identical with the subsisting subjects, so that there is no difference between a subject and its nature. Now it was shown in the preceding article that God is not composed of matter and form. It follows that God must be his Divinity, and whatever else is predicated of him.

On the first point: we cannot speak of simple things except in terms of the composites by means of which we know anything. When we speak of God, therefore, we use concrete names to denote his substance, because only composite things subsist around us, and use abstract names to denote his simple nature. Hence when we say that Divinity, or life, or anything of this kind is in God, the compositeness belongs to the way in which our intellect understands, and not at all to that of which we speak.

On the second point: God's effects do not resemble him perfectly, but only in so far as they are able. Their likeness to God is deficient in that they can reflect what is simple and single only by what is many. They have the compositeness which necessitates the difference between a subject and its nature.

Article Four

WHETHER ESSENCE AND EXISTENCE ARE THE SAME IN GOD

We proceed to the fourth article thus:

1. It seems that essence and existence are not the same in God. If they were the same, nothing would be added to God's existence. Now the existence to which nothing is added is the universal existence which is predicable of all things. Hence God would be the universal existence which is predicable of all things. But this is false, according to Wisdom 4:21: "they gave the incommunicable name to stones and wood." It follows that God's essence is not his existence.

2. Again, it was said in Q. 2, Arts. 2 and 3, that we can know that God exists. But we cannot know what God is. Hence God's existence is not the same as what he is, or his quiddity, or nature.

On the other hand: Hilary says: "Existence is not an accident in God, but subsisting truth" (*De Trin.* 7).

I answer: God not only is his essence, as was shown in Art. 3, but also is his existence. This can be shown in many ways. First, whatever a thing possesses in addition to its essence must either be caused by the principles of its essence, as is a property which is consequential to a species, such as laughing, which is consequential to "man" and caused by the essential principles of his species; or it must be caused by something external, as heat in water is caused by a fire. Hence when a thing's existence is different from its essence, its existence must either be caused by the principles of its essence, or be caused by something external. Now a thing's existence cannot possibly be caused by the principles of its own essence alone, since nothing can be the sufficient cause of its own existence, if its existence is caused. Hence anything whose existence is different from its essence must be caused by something other than itself. But we cannot say this of God, who is defined as the first efficient cause. It is therefore impossible that God's existence should be different from his essence.

Secondly, existence is the actuality of every form, or nature. That is, we do not say that goodness or humanity, for example, are actual, unless we mean that they exist. Hence where essence and existence are different, existence must be related to essence as the actual to the potential. But it was shown in Q. 2, Art. 3, that there is nothing potential in God. It follows that essence and existence are not different in God. God's essence, therefore, is his existence.

Thirdly, anything which has existence without being existence exists through participation, just as anything which is alight but is not itself fire is alight through participation.

Now we proved in Art. 3 that God is his essence. It follows that, if God were not his own existence, he would exist not through his essence but through participation. But God would not then be the first being, which is an absurd thing to say. God is therefore his own existence, as well as his own essence.

On the first point: "that to which nothing is added" may mean two things. It may mean that a thing's nature precludes the addition of something. The nature of an irrational animal, for example, excludes reason. But it may also mean that a nature does not necessitate the addition of something. Thus the common nature of animal does not have reason added to it, because it does not necessitate the addition of reason, though neither does it exclude reason. It is in the first sense that nothing is added to God's existence, and in the second sense that nothing is added to universal existence.

On the second point: "is" may signify two things. It may signify the act of existing, or it may signify the synthesis by which the mind joins a subject to a predicate in a proposition. Now we cannot know the divine act of existing, any more than we can know the divine essence. But we do know that God "is" in the second sense, for we know that the proposition which we put together when we say "God exists" is true. We know this from his effects, as we said in Q. 2, Art. 2.

Article Five

WHETHER GOD BELONGS TO A GENUS

We proceed to the fifth article thus:

1. It seems that God does belong to a genus. For "substance" means self-subsistent being, and this is pre-eminently applicable to God. God therefore belongs to the genus "substance."

2. Again, each thing is measured by what belongs to its own genus. Thus lengths are measured by length, and numbers by number. Now the commentator on 10 *Metaph.* says that God is the measure of all substances. God therefore belongs to the genus "substance."

On the other hand: we think of a genus as prior to what it contains. But there is nothing prior to God, whether in reality or in the understanding. Therefore God does not belong to any genus.

I answer: a thing may belong to a genus in two ways. It may belong to it absolutely and properly, as does a species which the genus contains. Or it may be reducible to a genus, as are principles and privations. Point and unity, for example, are reducible to the genus "quantity" as principles of it, while blindness, and all privation, are reducible to the genus of their habits. But God does not belong to a genus in either of these ways.

There are three proofs that God cannot be a species of any genus. First, a species is made up of a genus and a difference. Now that from which the difference which constitutes a species is derived is always related to that from which the genus is derived as the actual to the potential. Thus "animal" is concretely derived from "sensitive nature," a thing being called animal because it has a sensitive nature, while "the rational" is derived from "intellectual nature," since the rational is that which has an intellectual nature. The intellectual is then related to the sensitive as the actual to the potential. This is likewise clear in other things. It is therefore impossible that God should belong to a genus as a species of it, since in God there is no adjunction of the potential with the actual.

Secondly, it was proved in the preceding article that God's existence is his essence. Hence if God belonged to any genus, this genus would have to be "being," since a genus indicates the essence of a thing, and is predicated because of what the thing is. But the philosopher proves that "being" cannot be the genus of anything (3 *Metaph.*, text 10), since every genus includes differences which are external to its essence, and there are no differences external to being, since "not-being" cannot be a difference. It follows from this that God cannot belong to a genus.

Thirdly, all things which belong to one genus agree in their "what," or the essence of their genus, which is predicated of them because of what they are. But they differ in point of existence, since the existence of a man is not the same as that of a horse, nor the existence of one man the same as that of another. Existence and essence are thus bound to be different in anything which belongs to a genus. But they are not different in God, as we proved in the preceding article. This makes it plain that God does not belong to a genus as a species.

It is clear from the foregoing that God has neither genus nor differences, and that there is no definition of God, nor any way of demonstrating him except through his effects. For definition is by means of genus and difference, and definition is the means of demonstration.

That God does not belong to a genus as a principle reducible to it is obvious from the fact that principle which is reducible to a genus does not extend beyond that genus. The point, for example, is the principle of continuous quantity only, and the unit of discrete quantity only. But God is the ground of all existence, as we shall prove in Q. 44, Art. 1. Consequently, he is not contained in any genus as a principle.

On the first point: the term "substance" signifies more than self-subsistent being, for we have shown above that "being" cannot by itself be a genus. It signifies an essence which has the ability to exist, i.e., which can exist through itself, but whose existence is not identical with its essence. This makes it plain that God does not belong to the genus "substance."

On the second point: this objection argues from the measure of proportion. God is not in this way the measure of anything. He is said to be the measure of all things because all things have existence in so far as they are like him.

Article Six

WHETHER THERE IS ANY ACCIDENT IN GOD

We proceed to the sixth article thus:

1. It appears that there are some accidents in God. It is said in 1 *Physics*, texts 27, 30, that a substance can never be an accident. This means that what occurs as accident in one thing cannot be the substance of another, and is used to prove that heat is not the formal substance of fire, since heat occurs as an accident of other things. Now wisdom, virtue, and the like occur as accidents in ourselves, and are also ascribed to God. They must therefore be in God as accidents.

2. Again, in every genus there is something which is first, and there are many genera of accidents. Hence if the principles of these genera are not in God, there will be many things which are first, and which are not in God. But this is impossible.

On the other hand: every accident is in a subject. But God cannot be a subject, since "an absolute form cannot be a subject," as Boethius says (*De Trin.*). There cannot then be any accident in God.

I answer: what we have already said makes it quite clear that there cannot be any accident in God. In the first place, a subject is related to its accident as the potential to the actual, and is actualized through its accident in a particular way. But potentiality is altogether alien to God, as we explained in Q. 2, Art. 3. In the second place, God is his existence. But as Boethius says (*Lib. de Hebd.*), existence itself cannot be augmented by the addition of anything else, although that which is something may have something else added to it. A thing which is hot may have something other than heat added to it, such as whiteness, but heat itself cannot contain anything other than heat. In the third place, what exists through itself is prior to what exists accidentally. But God is altogether primary being, and therefore nothing in him can exist accidentally. Nor can there be in God any inherent accident, such as the accident of laughing in man. Accidents of this kind are caused by the principles of the subject, whereas nothing in God is caused, since God is the first cause. There is therefore no accident in God.

On the first point: virtue and wisdom are not predicated of God and of ourselves univocally, as will be shown (Q. 13, Art. 5). It does not then follow that they are accidents in God as they are in us.

On the second point: principles of accidents are reducible to prior principles of substance because substances are prior to their accidents. God is not the primary content of the genus "substance." He is nevertheless first in relation to all being, and outside every genus.

Article Seven

WHETHER GOD IS ALTOGETHER SIMPLE

We proceed to the seventh article thus:

1. It seems that God is not altogether simple. God's creatures resemble him. Thus all things have being from God the first being, and all things are good since he is the first good. Now nothing that God creates is altogether simple. Therefore God is not altogether simple.

2. Again, whatever is better must be ascribed to God. Now in things around us, what is composite is better than what is simple. Composite bodies, for example, are better than their elements, and animals are better than their parts. Hence we should not say that God is altogether simple.

On the other hand, August says: "God is absolutely and altogether simple" (4 *De Trin.* 6, 7).

I answer: it can be shown in many ways that God is altogether simple. In the first place, this can be proved from what we have already said. There is no combination of quantitative parts in God, since he is not a body. Neither is there in God any composition of form and matter. Neither is there any difference between God's nature and God as subject, nor between his essence and his existence. Neither is there in God any composition of genus and difference. It is thus clear that God is in no way composite, but altogether simple. Secondly, everything that is composite is consequential to its elements, and dependent on them. But God is the first being, as we proved in Q. 2, Art. 3. Thirdly, everything that is composite has a cause, since elements which are naturally separate cannot be combined into one unless some cause unites them. But we proved in the same article that God has no cause, since he is the first efficient cause. Fourthly, everything that is composite must contain both potentiality and actuality. Either one part is the actuality of another, or at least all parts are as it were the potentiality of the whole. But this is not true of God. Fifthly, everything that is composite is more than any of its parts. This is obvious when the parts are dissimilar. No part of a man is a man, and no part of a foot is a foot. But even when the parts are similar, although something can be affirmed equally of the whole and of every part of it, since a part of air is air, and a part of water is water, we can still say something about the whole which cannot be said of any part. For if the whole water measures two cubits, no part of it does so. In this way, there is something other than itself in everything that is composite. We may also say that there is something other than itself in everything that has a form. A thing that is white, for example, may contain something that is not white. But a form itself cannot contain anything other than itself. Now God is pure form, or rather, pure being. He cannot then be composite in any way. Hilary argues in somewhat the same fashion when he says: "God, who is power, is not compounded from what is weak, nor is he who is light composed of things of darkness" (*De Trin.* 7).

On the first point: God's creatures resemble him as effects resemble their first cause. But an effect is naturally composite in some way, since its existence is at least different from its essence, as we shall show in Q. 4, Art. 3.

On the second point: composite things around us are better than simple things because the perfection of creaturely good is to be found not in one simple thing, but in many. The perfection of divine goodness, on the other hand, is to be found in what is single and simple, as we shall prove in Q. 4, Art. 1, and in Q. 6, Art. 2.

Article Eight

WHETHER GOD ENTERS INTO THE COMPOSITION OF OTHER THINGS

We proceed to the eighth article thus:

1. It seems that God enters into the composition of other things. For Dionysius says (4 *Coel. Hier.*): "the being of all things, which transcends existence, is Divinity." The being of all things enters into the composition of all things. Hence God enters into the composition of other things.

2. Again, God is a form. For Augustine says: "The word of God, which is God, is a form not formed" (*De Verb. Dom., Sermo* 33). Now a form is part of a composite. Therefore God is part of a composite.

3. Again, all things which exist, and which are in no wise different, are identical. Now God and primary matter exist, and are in no wise different. They are therefore fundamentally identical. But primary matter enters into the composition of things. Hence God also enters into their composition. The minor premise is proved as follows. Whatever things differ, differ by reason of certain differences, and must accordingly be composite. But God and primary matter are not composite in any way. Hence they do not differ in any way.

On the other hand: Dionysius says: "there is neither contact nor communion with God in the intermingling of parts" (2 *Div. Nom.*, lect. 3). It is also said in the Book on Causes (*Interpretation of Aristotle*, prop. 6): "the first cause rules all things without mingling with them."

I answer: there have been three errors on this question. Augustine writes of some who said that God is a world-soul (7 *De Civ. Dei.* 6), and it is due to this that others have thought God to be the soul of the first heaven. Others again have thought that God is the formal principle of all things, as the Almaricians are said to have believed. The third error was that of David of Dinant, who very foolishly supposed that God was primary matter. But it is obvious that all these notions are false, and that God cannot possibly enter into the composition of other things in any way, either as their formal or as their material principle. In the first place, God is the first efficient cause, as we proved in Q. 2, Art. 3. Now an efficient cause is not numerically one with the thing made, but one with it in kind only. One man begets another man. The matter is neither numerically one with the efficient cause nor similar to it in kind, since it is potential, while the efficient cause is actual. Secondly, God is the first efficient cause, and therefore acts primarily and through himself. Now that which enters into the composition of something does not act primarily and through itself. Rather does the thing composed do so. Thus it is not the hand that acts, but the man who acts by means of it, and it is the fire that heats by means of heat. It follows that God cannot be a part of any composite thing. Thirdly, no part of any composite thing can be the first of all beings, not even its matter or its form, which are the fundamental parts of composite things. Matter is potential, and what is potential is subsequent to what is absolute and actual, as we explained in the first article. The form which is part of a composite thing is a participated form, and this is no less subsequent to what exists through its essence than is the thing which participates. Fire in that which is ignited, for example, is subsequent to what exists through its essence. Now we have proved in Q. 2, Art. 3 that God is the absolute first being.

On the first point: Divinity is said to be the being of all things as their efficient cause and example, not as their essence.

On the second point: the word of God is the exemplary form of a composite thing, not the form which is a part of it.

On the third point: simple things do not differ from each other by reason of differences, which is the way in which composite things differ. A man and a horse, for example, differ by reason of the difference between the rational and the irrational. But these differences do not themselves differ by reason of further differences. Properly speaking, we ought to say that differences are contrary, rather than different. As the philosophers says (10 *Metaph.*, texts 24–25): "Contrariety is predicated absolutely, whereas things which differ differ in some way." But they are contrary to each other. It does not then follow that they are identical.

1336 Schoolcraft